FORMS OF RESPONSIBILITY IN INTERNATIONAL CRIMINAL LAW

MW01224824

Volume I of the International Criminal Law Practitioner Library series focuses on the law of individual criminal responsibility applied in international criminal law, providing a thorough review of the forms of criminal responsibility. The authors present a critical analysis of the elements of individual criminal responsibility as set out in the statutory instruments of the international and hybrid criminal courts and tribunals and their jurisprudence. All elements are discussed, demystifying and untangling some of the confusion in the jurisprudence and literature on the forms of responsibility. The jurisprudence of the ICTY and the ICTR is the main focus of the book. Every trial and appeal judgement, as well as relevant interlocutory jurisprudence, up to 1 December 2006, has been surveyed, as has the relevant jurisprudence of other tribunals and the provisions in the legal instruments of the ICC, making this a highly relevant and timely work.

GIDEON BOAS, a former Senior Legal Officer at the ICTY, is a Senior Lecturer in Law at Monash University Law Faculty and an international law consultant.

JAMES L. BISCHOFF, a former Associate Legal Officer at the ICTY, is a Law Clerk in the Chambers of the Honourable Juan R. Torruella of the United States Court of Appeals for the First Circuit.

NATALIE L. REID, a former Associate Legal Officer at the ICTY, is an Associate with Debevoise & Plimpton LLP, New York.

FORMS OF RESPONSIBILITY IN INTERNATIONAL CRIMINAL LAW

International Criminal Law Practitioner Library Series

Volume I

GIDEON BOAS

JAMES L. BISCHOFF

NATALIE L. REID

The views expressed in this book are those of the authors alone and do not necessarily reflect the views of the International Criminal Tribunal for the former Yugoslavia or the United Nations in general.

CAMBRIDGE
UNIVERSITY PRESS

CAMBRIDGE UNIVERSITY PRESS

Cambridge, New York, Melbourne, Madrid, Cape Town, Singapore, São Paulo, Delhi

Cambridge University Press
The Edinburgh Building, Cambridge CB2 8RU, UK

Published in the United States of America by Cambridge University Press, New York

www.cambridge.org
Information on this title: www.cambridge.org/9780521878319

First published 2007

Printed in the United Kingdom at the University Press, Cambridge

A catalogue record for this publication is available from the British Library

ISBN 978-0-521-87831-9

Contents

Foreword

International criminal law is a new branch of law, with one foot in international law and the other in criminal law. Until the Nuremberg trial, international criminal law was largely 'horizontal' in its operation – that is, it consisted mainly of co-operation between states in the suppression of national crime. Extradition was therefore the central feature of international criminal law. Of course there were international crimes, crimes that threatened the international order, such as piracy and slave trading, but with no international court to prosecute such crimes, they inevitably played an insignificant part in international criminal law. In 1937 came the first attempt to create an international criminal court, for terrorism, but the treaty adopted for this purpose never came into force. The Nuremberg and Tokyo trials mark the commencement of modern international criminal law – that is, the prosecution of individuals for crimes against the international order before international courts. The Nuremberg and Tokyo tribunals have been criticised for providing victors' justice, but they did succeed in developing a jurisprudence for the prosecution of international crimes that courts still invoke today. The Cold War brought this development to an end. Attempts to create a permanent international criminal court failed and it was left to academics to debate and dream about the creation of such a court for the next forty years.

All this changed with the end of the Cold War and the creation of *ad hoc* tribunals for the former Yugoslavia and Rwanda. At last the international community had two genuine international tribunals to dispense justice. 'Vertical' international criminal law – that is, the prosecution of individuals for international crimes before international courts – became a reality. However, no sooner had the International Criminal Tribunal for the Former Yugoslavia (ICTY) and the International Criminal Tribunal for Rwanda (ICTR) started to function than attention was diverted to the creation of a permanent international criminal court to try crimes throughout the world and not just in Yugoslavia and Rwanda. International lawyers applauded the proposal for such a court put forward by the International Law Commission and scrambled to participate in the Rome Conference of 1998 for the creation of an international criminal court. Attention remained focused on the International Criminal Court as the number of states ratifying the Rome Statute grew and the International Criminal Court finally became a reality in 2002. At this time there was a burst of writing and many books and journal articles appeared on the structure, jurisdiction, procedure and substantive law of the International Criminal Court.

In recent times, in part as a result of disillusionment following the slow start of the International Criminal Court, the pendulum of international criminal law has been swung back once more to where it should probably have been all the time – the *ad hoc* tribunals. Throughout the period of excitement and expectation over the creation of the International Criminal Court, the ICTY and ICTR quietly proceeded with the prosecution of international criminals for the most serious crimes known to mankind – genocide, crimes against humanity and war crimes. The trial of Slobodan Milošević received much media attention but little attention was paid to the daily work of the ICTY and ICTR. Lengthy, carefully researched and thoroughly reasoned judgments have been handed down by judges from different backgrounds and with different judicial experience. These judgments have created a new, truly international or transnational international criminal law that draws on the experience of Nuremberg and Tokyo and national criminal courts, and successfully integrates national and international criminal law, humanitarian law and human rights law. At the same time the ICTY and ICTR have created vibrant institutions that attract judges and lawyers from many countries, united in their commitment to international justice. Over 1,000 lawyers and para-legals are today employed in some capacity before international tribunals – and most are with the ICTY or ICTR.

Publications have not kept pace with developments before the ICTY and ICTR. Writings on these courts, particularly in comparison with writings on the International Criminal Court, are few. Moreover, much of the writing on the ICTY and ICTR focuses on the structure of the tribunals and their procedures, rather than on the substantive law applied. *International Criminal Law Practitioner Library Series*, with one volume devoted to forms of responsibility and the other to elements of crime, therefore makes a timely appearance. Written by three young international criminal lawyers who have all worked in the ICTY and been directly involved in the evolution of the law before the tribunal, the study examines the substantive law of the tribunals primarily from the perspective of the international criminal law practitioner, with the needs of the practitioner in mind. However, as one would expect from authors with such distinguished academic credentials, the study has an equal appeal to the legal academic and student.

Inevitably, as the ICTY and ICTR provide the richest source of substantive criminal law, the study focuses on the jurisprudence of these tribunals. The jurisprudence of other tribunals is not, however, ignored. The law of Nuremberg and Tokyo features prominently, and the law and structures of the other international or internationalised tribunals – the Special Court for Sierre Leone (SCSL), the Special Panels for Serious Crimes in East Timor (SPSC), the Supreme Iraqi Criminal Tribunal (SICT), the Extraordinary Chambers of the Courts of Cambodia (ECCC) and, of course, the International Criminal Court – are also examined. The law of the International Criminal Court, contained in its primary instruments dealing with crimes and elements of crimes, receives particular attention.

Volume I deals with the law of individual criminal responsibility in international criminal law. This law seeks to capture all the methods and means by which an individual may contribute to the commission of a crime and be held responsible under the law. It aims to ensure that not only the perpetrator but also the high- or mid-level person – both civil and military – frequently removed from the actual perpetration of the crime, may be held responsible. Consequently this volume focuses on the various forms of participation in international crimes – joint criminal enterprise, superior responsibility, aiding and abetting and planning and instigating international crimes.

Volume II will cover the elements of the core international crimes of genocide, crimes against humanity and war crimes, as seen from the perspective of law of both the *ad hoc* international tribunals and other tribunals.

The authors are not content with a mere portrayal or description of the law. The approaches of different tribunals, and the approaches of different judges within the same tribunal, are compared and contrasted; and decisions are carefully analysed and criticised. Moreover, the views of scholars are considered and integrated into the text.

International Criminal Law Practitioner Library Series will primarily, and in the first instance, assist the international criminal law practitioner, whatever his or her court. But it will also be of assistance to the growing body of national lawyers engaged in the practice of international criminal law before domestic courts. As the Rome Statute of the International Criminal Court gives jurisdiction over international crimes in the first instance to domestic courts, in accordance with the principle of complementarity, it can be expected that this body of lawyers will grow.

Gideon Boas, James Bischoff and Natalie Reid are to be congratulated on a work that concentrates on the jurisprudence of the main source of contemporary international criminal law – the law of the *ad hoc* tribunals – but which at the same time takes account of all the other sources of this rapidly expanding branch of law. Practitioners, academics and students will learn much from this excellent study.

John Dugard
The Hague

Table of authorities

International treaties

National cases and legislation

Other international and United Nations materials

Other international cases

United States v. *von Leeb, Sperrle, von Küchler, Blaskowitz, Hoth, Reinhardt, von Salmuth, Hollidt, Schniewind, von Roques, Reinecke, Warlimont, Wöhlerand Lehmann*, in Trials of War Criminals Before the Nuremberg Military Tribunals Under Control Council Law No. 10 (1950) vol. I 154, 163–4, 173

Selected secondary sources

Akhavan, Payam 'The Crime of Genocide in the ICTR Jurisprudence', (2005) 3 *Journal of International Criminal Justice* 989 281, 300

Ambos, Kai 'Superior Responsibility', in Antonio Cassese, Paola Gaeta, and John R. W. D. Jones (eds.), *The Rome Statute of the International Criminal Court: A Commentary* (2001), vol. I 164

Crespi, Alberto, Giuseppe Zuccalà, and Frederico Stella, *Commentario breve al Codice penale* (1986) 350

Danner, Allison Marston and Jenny S. Martinez, 'Guilty Associations: Joint Criminal Enterprise, Command Responsibility, and the Development of International Criminal Law', (2005) 93 *California Law Review* 75, 124 159

Eboe-Osuji, Chile '"Complicity in Genocide" versus "Aiding and Abetting Genocide": Construing the Difference in the ICTR and ICTY Statutes', (2005) 3 *Journal of International Criminal Justice* 56 299

Grotius, Hugo *De jure belli ac pacis: libri tres* (1625) 145

Gustafson, Katrina 'The Requirement of an "Express Agreement" for Joint Criminal Enterprise Liability: A Critique of *Brđanin*', (2005) 3 *Journal of International Criminal Justice* 10 85, 88–9

Henckaerts, Jean-Marie and Louise Doswald-Beck (eds.), *Customary International Humanitarian Law* (2005) 143–4, 150

Le Gunehec, Francis 'Elément moral de l'infraction', in Marie-Françoise Homassel (ed.), 1 *Juris-Classeur Pénal Code* (2002) 350

Levine, Eugenia 'Command Responsibility: The *Mens Rea* Requirement', available at www.globalpolicy.org/intljustice/general/2005/command.htm 164, 168

Lieber, Francis, Instructions for the Government of Armies of the United States in the Field 146

McCormack, Timothy L. H. 'From Sun Tzu to the Sixth Committee', in Timothy L. H. McCormack and Gerry J. Simpson (eds.), *The Law of War Crimes* (1997) 147

Meron, Theodor, 'Editorial Comment: Revival of Customary Humanitarian Law' (2005) 99 *American Journal of International Law* 817 418

Mundis, Daryl A. 'Crimes of the Commander: Superior Responsibility Under Article 7(3) of the ICTY Statute', in Gideon Boas and William A. Schabas

Special Court for Sierra Leone (SCSL) cases

Special Panels for Serious Crimes (SPSC, East Timor) cases

1

Introduction

1.1 Forms of responsibility in international criminal law

When the United Nations Security Council decided to establish the International Criminal Tribunal for the former Yugoslavia (ICTY), the first international criminal tribunal since the immediate post-war period, it tasked the Secretary-General with the preparation of the legal design of the new tribunal. The latter, in turn, instructed lawyers in the Secretariat of the international organisation, who drew on the relevant fundamental principles of customary international law and drafted the statute of the tribunal in accordance with those tenets.[1] The result was a relatively spare document, which delimited the extent of the tribunal's personal, temporal, geographic and subject-matter jurisdiction in its first eight articles. After reaffirming that contemporary international criminal law was concerned with the penal responsibility of individuals,[2] and articulating the core crimes which were to be the concern of the tribunal,[3] the Statute of the International Criminal Tribunal for the Prosecution of Persons Responsible for Serious Violations of International Humanitarian Law Committed in the Territory of the former Yugoslavia since

[1] See Security Council Resolution 808, 22 February 1993, UN Doc. S/RES/808 (1993), p. 2, para. 2 (requesting the Secretary-General to prepare a report on the creation of the tribunal, and to include specific proposals where appropriate); Report of the Secretary-General Pursuant to Paragraph 2 of Security Council Resolution 808 (1993), UN Doc. S/25704, 3 May 1993 ('Secretary-General's Report'), para. 17 (responding to that request by developing and presenting specific language for the draft statute, invoking, *inter alia*, existing international instruments and texts prepared by the International Law Commission).
[2] Statute of the International Criminal Tribunal for the Prosecution of Persons Responsible for Serious Violations of International Humanitarian Law Committed in the Territory of the former Yugoslavia since 1991, 32 ILM 1159 (1993), as amended by Security Council Resolution 1660 of 28 February 2006 ('ICTY Statute'), Arts. 1, 6.
[3] *Ibid.*, Arts. 2–5.

1991 ('ICTY Statute') set forth a list of the ways in which an individual could be said to participate in, or be responsible for, those crimes:

A person who planned, instigated, ordered, committed or otherwise aided and abetted in the planning, preparation or execution of a crime referred to in articles 2 to 5 of the present Statute shall be individually responsible for the crime.
[. . .]
The fact that any of the acts referred to in articles 2 to 5 of the present Statute was committed by a subordinate does not relieve his superior of criminal responsibility if he knew or had reason to know that the subordinate was about to commit such acts or had done so and the superior failed to take the necessary and reasonable measures to prevent such acts or to punish the perpetrators thereof.[4]

As the report accompanying the draft statute explained:

The Secretary-General believes that all persons who participate in the planning, preparation or execution of serious violations of international humanitarian law in the former Yugoslavia contribute to the commission of the violation and are, therefore, individually responsible.[5]

In fact, all the international or hybrid courts and tribunals that have come after the ICTY have similar provisions in their statutes or constitutive instruments, which set forth the forms of responsibility under their jurisdiction, and which cover similar substantive ground.[6]

Such, then, is the purpose of forms of responsibility in international criminal law: to capture all of the methods and means by which an individual may contribute to the commission of a crime, or be held responsible for a crime under international law.[7] To a limited extent, therefore, the forms of responsibility resonate with that area of substantive or general criminal law in domestic jurisdictions that describes the parties to a crime and ascribes liability according to their personal conduct and mental states with regard to the crime.[8] Certain of the forms, such as aiding and abetting or instigating,

---

[4] *Ibid.*, Art. 7(1), 7(3).   [5] Secretary-General's Report, *supra* note 1, para. 54.
[6] See Chapters 2–5 for specific citations to the relevant provisions of those instruments.
[7] See *Prosecutor* v. *Muvunyi*, Case No. ICTR-00-55A-T, Judgement, 11 September 2006 ('*Muvunyi* Trial Judgement'), paras. 459–460; *Prosecutor* v. *Gacumbitsi*, Case No. ICTR-2001-64-T, Judgement, 14 June 2004, para. 267; *Prosecutor* v. *Semanza*, Case No. ICTR-97-20-T, Judgement and Sentence, 15 May 2003, para. 377; *Prosecutor* v. *Kayishema and Ruzindana*, Case No. ICTR 95-1-T, Judgement, 21 May 1999, paras. 195–196; *Prosecutor* v. *Delalić, Mucić, Delić, and Landžo*, Case No. IT-96-21-T, Judgement, 16 November 1998, paras. 321, 331; *Prosecutor* v. *Akayesu*, Case No. ICTR-96-4-T, Judgement, 2 September 1998 ('*Akayesu* Trial Judgement'), para. 473; *Prosecutor* v. *Tadić*, Case No. IT-94-1-T, Judgement, 14 July 1997, paras. 661–662.
[8] See, e.g., Wayne R. LaFave, *Principles of Criminal Law* (2003), pp. 509–534, 551–557 (describing the common law classification scheme for attribution of responsibility to 'several persons or groups which play distinct roles before, during and after the offense', as well as statutory modifications) (quotation at p. 509); Jean Pradel, *Droit pénal comparé* (2nd edn 2002), pp. 312–325 (reviewing the jurisprudence and codifications of the law on identifying the participants in a crime in several jurisdictions).

which are discussed in Chapters 4 and 5, respectively, are readily identifiable as what has been termed accomplice or accessory liability in certain domestic jurisdictions;[9] that is, either primary or secondary participation in the commission of a crime by a person who is not the physical perpetrator.[10] Others, however, reflect particularities of international criminal law, and its justifiable preoccupation with ensuring that mid- or high-level accused persons or defendants, who are frequently removed to varying degrees from the actual perpetration of the crime, do not escape liability for their own roles in the atrocities that constitute international crimes. The species of commission called 'joint criminal enterprise' is one such form of responsibility, and is the subject of Chapter 2; superior responsibility, the subject of Chapter 3, is another quintessentially and uniquely international form of responsibility that has no true parallel in domestic criminal law.[11] Indeed, as domestic and international avenues for international criminal adjudication proliferate, and regional and international politics become more conducive to supporting such proceedings, cases before international tribunals have increasingly focused on those

---

[9] See *Black's Law Dictionary* (8th edn 2004), pp. 15, 17 (defining 'accessory' and 'accomplice'). For judicial exposition of these terms in the context of forms of responsibility in international law, see *Prosecutor v. Tadić*, Case No. IT-94-1-A, Judgement, 15 July 1999, paras. 220, 223; *Muvunyi* Trial Judgement, *supra* note 7, para. 460; *Prosecutor v. Mpambara*, Case No. ICTR-01-65-T, Judgement, 11 September 2006, para. 37; *Prosecutor v. Orić*, Case No. IT-03-68-T, Judgement, 30 June 2006, para. 292; *Prosecutor v. Blagojević and Jokić*, Case No. IT-02-60-T, Judgement, 17 January 2005 ('*Blagojević and Jokić* Trial Judgement'), para. 776; *Prosecutor v. Brđanin*, Case No. IT-99-36-T, Judgement, 1 September 2004 ('*Brđanin* Trial Judgement'), para. 727; *Prosecutor v. Ndindabahizi*, Case No. ICTR-2001-71-I, Judgement and Sentence, 15 July 2004, para. 456; *Prosecutor v. Kordić and Čerkez*, Case No. IT-95-14/2-T, Judgement, 26 February 2001, para. 373; *Prosecutor v. Furundžija*, Case No. IT-95-17/1-T, Judgement, 10 December 1998, para. 257; *Akayesu* Trial Judgement, *supra* note 7, paras. 468, 532. Unfortunately, there appears to be no consensus on the meaning of the terms, and certain chambers have employed them in a manner that is inconsistent with either their common meaning or the law pertaining to individual criminal responsibility. For the purposes of the analysis in this book, and unless otherwise indicated, 'accomplice liability' should be understood to encompass joint criminal enterprise, planning, instigating and ordering, and 'accessory liability' as limited to aiding and abetting. See Chapter 4, text accompanying note 1. As the doctrine of superior responsibility is unique to international law, it does not lend itself to categorisation by labels derived from domestic criminal practice.

[10] See *infra*, text accompanying notes 18–22, for an explanation of the term 'physical perpetrator', as well as other terms of art used in this book.

[11] Superior responsibility is not different from individual criminal responsibility; it is a part of it. Despite the propensity of the drafters of international criminal statutes to place superior responsibility in a different provision from the other forms of responsibility under the court's jurisdiction, see generally Chapter 3, and contrary to the language of certain *ad hoc* chambers, see, e.g., *Prosecutor v. Aleksovski*, Case No. IT-95-14/1-A, Judgement, 24 March 2000, para. 170; *Prosecutor v. Krnojelac*, Case No. IT-97-25-PT, Decision on the Defence Preliminary Motion on the Form of the Indictment, 24 February 1999, paras. 3, 9, it is clear that superior responsibility is an integral part of the law of individual criminal responsibility in international criminal law. See *Prosecutor v. Blaškić*, Case No. IT-95-14-T, Judgement, 3 March 2000, para. 261 (noting that it is a part of individual criminal responsibility); Draft Code of Crimes Against the Peace and Security of Mankind, in Report of the International Law Commission on the Work of Its Forty-eighth Session, UN Doc. A/51/10 (1996), Art. 2(3)(c) (including it in the same provision with the other forms, with a cross-reference to the article laying out its elements in greater precision). Although superior responsibility is, in many key respects, different from any other form of responsibility, it is at its core a method for the imposition of penal liability on individuals for their own illegal conduct. See Chapter 4, note 327.

believed to be most responsible – civilian and military leaders – and on the forms of responsibility that have developed to reflect the liability of the reputed masterminds or architects of the entire range of alleged criminal conduct.

1.2 Scope of this book and terminology used

This book focuses on the law of individual criminal responsibility as applied in international criminal law, and will provide a thorough review of the forms of criminal responsibility. First and foremost, it presents a critical analysis of the elements of individual criminal responsibility as set out in the statutory instruments of the international and hybrid criminal courts and tribunals and their jurisprudence. As such, although this book is primarily intended for the practitioner of international criminal law, the analysis will also be relevant and useful for academics and students of this subject, because it surveys the available subject-matter law in a detailed and comprehensive manner.

Although 'commission' is always one of the forms of responsibility listed in an international or hybrid court's provision on individual criminal responsibility, this book will limit its discussion of commission to joint criminal enterprise, a form of responsibility the jurisprudence has also classified under the rubric of commission. This choice stems from a simple fact that is rarely explicitly acknowledged in the jurisprudence: unlike the forms of responsibility discussed in this book, which are independent of the crimes to which they may be applied, and are typically designed to apply to all the crimes under the jurisdiction of the court in question, the elements of physical commission vary widely, because they are the elements of the crime itself – the *actus reus* (physical conduct and causation) and *mens rea* (culpable mental state).[12] As such, those elements are worthy of an entirely separate discussion that draws on the wealth of scholarship and jurisprudence articulating and applying the core international crimes, and are beyond the scope of the present volume.[13] For similar reasons, this book will not echo the error of most judgements and decisions in referring to the physical and mental elements of the forms of responsibility as *actus reus* and *mens rea*, because they are not in themselves criminal, but only serve to attribute criminality to

---

[12] See *Muvunyi* Trial Judgement, *supra* note 7, para. 461; *Prosecutor* v. *Kvočka, Kos, Radić, Žigić and Prcać*, Case No. IT-98-30/1-T, Judgement, 2 November 2001 ('*Kvočka et al.* Trial Judgement'), para. 250. See also *Black's Law Dictionary*, *supra* note 9, p. 39 ('The wrongful deed that comprises the physical components of a crime and that generally must be coupled with *mens rea* to establish criminal liability'); *ibid.*, p. 1006 ('The state of mind that the prosecution ... must prove that the defendant had when committing a crime[;] ... the second of two essential elements of every crime at common law').
[13] The elements of the core crimes under international law will be discussed in the second book in this series.

the accused when combined with the criminal conduct and mental state of the physical perpetrator.

There are two other key terms of art in the book that are used to describe concepts fundamental to this area of the law; both have been chosen for their aptness, and for the sake of clarity and consistency.[14] First, while the jurisprudence alternatively refers to the means by which an accused is held responsible for a crime as 'forms',[15] 'heads',[16] or 'modes'[17] of responsibility or liability, this book has adopted and employed the single term 'forms of responsibility'. Second, although the jurisprudence alternatively deems the person who physically perpetrates a crime the 'principal perpetrator',[18] the 'principal offender',[19] the 'immediate perpetrator',[20] or the 'physical perpetrator',[21] this book will use only the term 'physical perpetrator'.[22]

The richest source of the law of individual criminal responsibility comes from the ICTY and the International Criminal Tribunal for Rwanda (ICTR) (collectively, 'Tribunals' or '*ad hoc* Tribunals'), so the jurisprudence of these Tribunals will be the main focus of the book. However, for completeness of analysis, and in recognition that these Tribunals are nearing the end of their mandates, most chapters also include a section that reviews the instruments and the practice to date of five other international or hybrid criminal courts or tribunals with regard to individual criminal responsibility: the International Criminal Court (ICC), the Special Court for Sierra Leone (SCSL), the Special Panels for Serious Crimes in East Timor (SPSC), the Extraordinary

---

[14] Cf. William R. Anson, *Principles of the Law of Contract* (3rd Am. edn 1919), p. 9 ('Accurate legal thinking is difficult when the fundamental terms have shifting senses.').

[15] See, e.g., *Prosecutor* v. *Krstić*, Case No. IT-98-33-A, Judgement, 19 April 2004, para. 268; *Prosecutor* v. *Strugar*, Case No. IT-01-42-T, Judgement, 31 January 2005, para. 331; *Brđanin* Trial Judgement, *supra* note 9, para. 257 n. 683.

[16] See, e.g., *Prosecutor* v. *Blaškić*, Case No. IT-95-14-A, Judgement, 29 July 2004 ('*Blaškić* Appeal Judgement'), para. 91; *Prosecutor* v. *Bagilishema*, Case No. ICTR-95-1A-A, Judgement, 3 July 2002, para. 34; *Blagojević and Jokić* Trial Judgement, *supra* note 9, para. 679.

[17] See, e.g., *Prosecutor* v. *Kordić and Čerkez*, Case No. IT-95-14/2-A, Judgement, 17 December 2004, para. 25; *Prosecutor* v. *Halilović*, Case No. IT-01-48-T, Judgement, 16 November 2005, para. 94 n. 215.

[18] See, e.g., *Prosecutor* v. *Kvočka, Radić, Žigić, and Prcać*, Case No. IT-98-30/1-A, Judgement, 28 February 2005 ('*Kvočka et al.* Appeal Judgement'), para. 90; *Blaškić* Appeal Judgement, *supra* note 1616, para. 48; *Prosecutor* v. *Krnojelac*, Case No. IT-97-25-A, Judgement, 17 September 2003 ('*Krnojelac* Appeal Judgement'), para. 84.

[19] *Kvočka et al.* Appeal Judgement, *supra* note 18, para. 251; *Krnojelac* Appeal Judgement, *supra* note 18, para. 75; *Blagojević and Jokić* Trial Judgement, *supra* note 9, para. 702.

[20] See, e.g., *Prosecutor* v. *Ademi and Norac*, Case No. IT-04-78-PT, Decision for Referral to the Authorities of the Republic of Croatia Pursuant to Rule 11*bis*, 14 September 2205, para. 36; *Prosecutor* v. *Martić*, Case No. IT-95-11-PT, Decision on Preliminary Motion Against the Amended Indictment, 2 June 2003, para. 29.

[21] See *Brđanin* Trial Judgement, *supra* note 9, para. 334 n. 881; *Kvočka et al.* Trial Judgement, *supra* note 12, para. 261; *Prosecutor* v. *Karemera, Ngirumpatse, and Nzirorera*, Case No. ICTR-98-44-AR72.6, Decision on Jurisdictional Appeals: Joint Criminal Enterprise, 12 April 2006, para. 2.

[22] These choices will not affect quotations from judgements, which will retain the original terminology used by the chamber.

Chambers in the Courts of Cambodia (ECCC), and the Supreme Iraqi Criminal Tribunal (SICT).[23]

Notwithstanding – or perhaps because of – the completion strategies at the two *ad hoc* Tribunals,[24] their chambers remain extremely active, releasing interlocutory decisions and judgements relevant to the forms of responsibility at least once a month. In addition, the newer courts and tribunals have begun to, or will soon, produce relevant jurisprudence, or are nearing the stage where the first judgements will be issued. As a consequence, readers should note that this analysis is current as of 1 December 2006. Since that date, the following relevant decisions and judgements have been issued, or can be expected in the first half of 2007:

- *Prosecutor* v. *Ndindabahizi*, ICTR-01-71-A, ICTR Appeal Judgement
- *Prosecutor* v. *Brđanin*, Case No. IT-99-36-A, ICTY Appeal Judgement
- *Prosecutor* v. *Nahimana, Barayagwiza and Ngeze*, Case No. ICTR-96-11-A, ICTR Appeal Judgement
- *Prosecutor* v. *Muhimana*, Case No. ICTR-95-1B-A, ICTR Appeal Judgement
- *Prosecutor* v. *Seromba*, Case No. ICTR-2001-66-T, ICTR Trial Judgement
- *Prosecutor* v. *Karera*, ICTR-01-74-T, ICTR Trial Judgement
- *Prosecutor* v. *Norman, Fofana and Kondewa*, Case No. SCSL-2004-14, SCSL Trial Judgement
- *Prosecutor* v. *Brima, Kamara and Kanu*, Case No. SCSL-04-16-T, SCSL Trial Judgement
- *Prosecutor* v. *Martić*, Case No. IT-95-11-T, ICTY Trial Judgement
- *Prosecutor* v. *Mrksić, Radić, and Šljivančanin*, Case No. IT-95-13/1-T, ICTY Trial Judgement.

---

[23] Formerly known as the Iraqi Special Tribunal (IST). Although the SICT is not, strictly speaking, a hybrid or internationalised tribunal, it is included in these comparative analyses because the portion of its Statute on individual criminal responsibility is clearly modelled on the Rome Statute of the International Criminal Court, and the crimes within its jurisdiction include the core crimes under international law. See Chapter 2, note 783 and accompanying text. Though its practice and jurisprudence are limited, and its proceedings criticised and often chaotic, discussion of the manner in which the law on individual responsibility has been applied by the SICT is nevertheless useful for illustrating the difficulties of adapting international practice and jurisprudence to a particular kind of domestic context.

[24] See Chapter 2, note 798 and accompanying text.

2

Joint criminal enterprise

CONTENTS

7

Article 7(1) of the ICTY Statute, which has served as the model for the statutes of three other courts applying international criminal law,[1] sets forth a seemingly exhaustive list of the forms of responsibility within the jurisdiction of the Tribunal:

A person who planned, instigated, ordered, committed or otherwise aided and abetted in the planning, preparation or execution of a crime referred to in articles 2 to 5 of the present Statute shall be individually responsible for the crime.[2]

'Committed', in this context, would appear to refer only to physical perpetration by the accused of the crime with which he is charged. Beginning in 1999,[3] however, the ICTY Appeals Chamber has consistently held that 'committing' implicitly encompasses participation in a joint criminal enterprise (JCE), even though that term does not expressly appear anywhere in the Statute. As it has been developed in the jurisprudence of the *ad hoc* Tribunals, JCE is a theory of

---

[1] Article 6(1) of the ICTR Statute and Article 6(1) of the Statute of the Special Court for Sierra Leone are essentially identical to Article 7(1) of the ICTY Statute; Article 29 of the Law on the Establishment of the Extraordinary Chambers in the Courts of Cambodia for the Prosecution of Crimes Committed during the Period of Democratic Kampuchea mirrors Article 7(1)'s list of forms of responsibility, but does not reproduce it exactly. See *infra* notes 735–738, 774–782, and accompanying text (full discussion of the statutes and practice of the Sierra Leone and Cambodia examples).

[2] Statute of the International Criminal Tribunal for the Prosecution of Persons Responsible for Serious Violations of International Humanitarian Law Committed in the Territory of the former Yugoslavia since 1991, 32 ILM 1159 (1993), as amended by Security Council Resolution 1660 of 28 February 2006 ('ICTY Statute'), Article 7(1).

[3] *See Prosecutor* v. *Tadić*, Case No. IT-94-1-A, Judgement, 15 July 1999 ('*Tadić* Appeal Judgement'), para. 188. Although the *Furundžija* Trial Judgement was the first time either *ad hoc* Tribunal recognised the existence of common-purpose liability, the *Tadić* Appeal Judgement is the first time any Chamber held that JCE was included within the term 'committed' in the article on forms of responsibility and the first time that JCE was used to impose criminal liability on any accused before the *ad hoc* Tribunals.

common-purpose liability:[4] it permits the imposition of individual criminal responsibility on an accused for his knowing and voluntary participation in a group acting with a common criminal purpose or plan.

The doctrine of JCE has its critics, both within and outside the Tribunals.[5] It is certain, however, that JCE is now firmly established in modern international criminal law as a form of responsibility that responds to the concern of how to characterise the role of individual offenders in contemporary armed conflicts, in which collective and organised criminality is notoriously present. Although international courts are bound to comply with the fundamental principle of criminal law that an individual may only be held liable for his conduct,[6] the advantage of JCE lies in its utility in describing and attributing responsibility to those who engage in criminal behaviour through oppressive criminal structures or organisations, in which different perpetrators participate in different ways at different times to accomplish criminal conduct on a massive scale. Indeed, although it took some years to evolve, JCE has become the principal methodology used by international prosecutors to describe the liability of accused in such circumstances.[7]

---

[4] The ICTY has alternatively referred to joint criminal enterprise with the terms 'common criminal plan', 'common criminal purpose', 'common design or purpose', 'common criminal design', 'common purpose', 'common design', and 'common concerted design'. See *Prosecutor* v. *Brđanin and Talić*, Case No. IT-99-36-PT, Decision on Form of Further Amended Indictment and Prosecution Application to Amend, 26 June 2001 ('*Brđanin and Talić* June 2001 Pre-Trial Decision'), para. 24; *Prosecutor* v. *Milutinović, Šainović and Ojdanić*, Case No. IT-99-37-AR72, Decision on Dragoljub Ojdanić's Motion Challenging Jurisdiction – Joint Criminal Enterprise, 21 May 2003 ('*Milutinović et al.* JCE Appeal Decision'), para. 36 ('the phrases "common purpose" . . . and "joint criminal enterprise" . . . refer to one and the same thing').

[5] See *infra* text accompanying notes 455–591 (section discussing the *Brđanin* Trial Judgement's attempt to restrain JCE); text accompanying notes 600–603 (discussing the *Stakić* Trial Judgement's disapproval of JCE because of its overtones of group criminality, or the impression that liability is imposed for mere membership in a criminal organisation); *Prosecutor* v. *Simić, Tadić and Zarić*, Case No. IT-95-9-T, Judgement, 17 October 2003 ('*Simić et al.* Trial Judgement'), Separate and Partially Dissenting Opinion of Judge Per-Johan Lindholm, para. 2 ('I dissociate myself from the concept or doctrine of joint criminal enterprise in this case as well as generally.'). See also Shane Darcy, 'An Effective Measure of Bringing Justice?: The Joint Criminal Enterprise Doctrine of the International Criminal Tribunal for the Former Yugoslavia', (2004–2005) 20 *American University International Law Review* 153; Allison Marston Danner and Jenny S. Martinez, 'Guilty Associations: Joint Criminal Enterprise, Command Responsibility, and the Development of International Criminal Law', (2005) 93 *California Law Review* 75; William A. Schabas, '*Mens rea* and the International Tribunal for the Former Yugoslavia', (2001) 37 *New England Law Review*, 1025, 1032–1034 (arguing that the JCE doctrine has been used to achieve 'discounted convictions'); Mohamed Elewa Badar, '"Just Convict Everyone!" – Joint Perpetration: From *Tadić* to *Stakić* and Back Again', (2006) 6 *International Criminal Law Review* 293, 301 (criticising the third category of JCE).

[6] This tenet of criminal law is also termed the 'culpability principle'. See Nicola Pasani, 'The Mental Element in International Crime', in Flavia Lattanzi and William A. Schabas (eds.), 1 *Essays on the Rome Statute of the International Criminal Court* ('*Essays*') (1999), pp. 121–125 (discussing the principle of culpability, or *nullum crimen sine culpa*, in national and international law); Mirjan Damaska, 'The Shadow Side of Command Responsibility', (2001) 49 *American Journal of Comparative Law* 455 (discussing the culpability principle in the context of superior responsibility).

[7] See Daryl A. Mundis and Fergal Gaynor, 'Current Developments at the *ad hoc* International Criminal Tribunals', (2005) 3 *Journal of International Criminal Justice* 268; Nicola Piacente, 'Importance of the Joint Criminal Enterprise Doctrine for the ICTY Prosecutorial Policy', (2004) 2 *Journal of International Criminal Justice* 446.

This chapter begins with a discussion of the origins and evolution of JCE in the *ad hoc* Tribunals, and continues with an analysis of the elements of the three categories of JCE established by *Tadić*. Separate sections discuss the most contentious issues in this area of the law: two different attempts by trial chambers to limit JCE or revise the Tribunals' approach to common-purpose liability, the reasons for their occurrence, and the manner in which those attempts have been dealt with in subsequent jurisprudence. The chapter then examines, from a comparative perspective, liability for participation in a common design or purpose in the legal instruments, indictments, and jurisprudence of the other international courts and tribunals, including the ICC, the Special Court for Sierra Leone, the Special Panels for Serious Crimes in East Timor, the Extraordinary Chambers in the Courts of Cambodia, and the Supreme Iraqi Criminal Tribunal.

2.1 Origins and development of Joint Criminal Enterprise in the jurisprudence of the *ad hoc* Tribunals

Contrary to widely held belief, the first judicial pronouncement from the *ad hoc* Tribunals as to the definition and scope of JCE was not the *Tadić* Appeal Judgement, but the *Furundžija* Trial Judgement, rendered in December 1998 by a bench composed of Judges Florence Mumba, Antonio Cassese and Richard May.[8] The indictment alleged that Anto Furundžija, a commander of the Bosnian Croat anti-terrorist police unit known as the Jokers, interrogated two victims – referred to by the pseudonyms Witness A and Witness D – while Miroslav Bralo, another member of the Jokers, beat them with a baton and forced Witness A to have sex with him.[9] For this incident, Furundžija was

---

[8] *Prosecutor* v. *Furundžija*, Case No. IT-95-17/1-T, Judgement, 10 December 1998 ('*Furundžija* Trial Judgement'). The first explicit reference from a chamber of the ICTY to the so-called 'common-purpose' doctrine in the law of individual criminal responsibility occurred in the *Čelebići* Trial Judgement, rendered a few weeks prior to *Furundžija*, in the following terms:

[W]here a [pre-existing plan to engage in criminal conduct] exists, or where there otherwise is evidence that members of a group are acting with a common criminal purpose, all those who knowingly participate in, and directly and substantially contribute to, the realisation of this purpose may be held criminally responsible under Article 7(1) for the resulting criminal conduct.

Prosecutor v. *Delalić, Mucić, Delić and Landžo*, Case No. IT-96-21-T, Judgement, 16 November 1998 ('*Čelebići* Trial Judgement'), para. 328. *Čelebići* did not opine further on the elements or applicability of this doctrine. See also *Prosecutor* v. *Kayishema and Ruzindana*, Case No. ICTR 95-1-T, Judgement, 21 May 1999 ('*Kayishema and Ruzindana* Trial Judgement'), para. 203 (quoting and endorsing this passage in *Čelebići*). The JCE-related findings of the *Kayishema and Ruzindana* Trial Chamber are discussed in detail below. See *infra* text accompanying notes 114–124.

[9] *Prosecutor* v. *Furundžija*, Case No. IT-95-17-I, Indictment, 2 November 1995 ('*Furundžija* Indictment'), para. 26 (redacted version). In this indictment, all references to Bralo are redacted, and the indictment as it pertained to Bralo – a revised version of which was issued on 21 December 1998 – remained under seal

charged with torture and rape as an outrage upon personal dignity, both as violations of the laws or customs of war under Article 3 of the ICTY Statute.[10]

The Trial Chamber found that Furundžija had interrogated Witness A while Bralo subjected her to 'rape, sexual assaults, and cruel, inhuman and degrading treatment' before an audience of soldiers,[11] and that, during the same episode, the accused interrogated Witness D while Bralo inflicted 'serious physical assaults' on him.[12] The Chamber found that 'the acts by [Bralo] were performed in pursuance of the accused's interrogation'.[13] It described the division of responsibilities between Furundžija and Bralo in the following manner: 'There is no doubt that the accused and [Bralo], as commanders, divided the process of interrogation by performing different functions. The role of the accused was to question, while [Bralo's] role was to assault and threaten in order to elicit the required information from Witness A and Witness D.'[14] The Chamber then held that, as the prosecution had pleaded Article 7(1) liability in relation to all the crimes charged without specifying the precise form of responsibility through which Furundžija should be found guilty, the Chamber was 'empowered and obliged ... to convict the accused under the appropriate head of criminal responsibility'.[15]

To assist in ascertaining the elements of aiding and abetting in customary international law, the Trial Chamber engaged in a detailed analysis of a number of post-Second World War cases adjudicated pursuant to Control Council Law No. 10 and the British Royal Warrant of 1945.[16] After examining several judgements purportedly imposing liability for aiding and abetting, the Chamber opined that '[m]ention should also be made of several cases which enable us to distinguish aiding and abetting from the case of co-perpetration involving a group of persons pursuing a common design to commit crimes.'[17] The *Furundžija* Chamber then cited two examples of such cases: the *Dachau*

---

until October 2004. On 19 July 2005, Bralo pleaded guilty to all eight counts of an amended indictment issued on the previous day, and on 7 December 2005, the Trial Chamber sentenced him to 20 years' imprisonment. See *Prosecutor v. Bralo*, Case No. IT-95-17-S, Sentencing Judgement, 7 December 2005 ('*Bralo* Sentencing Judgement'), paras. 1–4, 97; *Prosecutor v. Bralo*, Case No. IT-95-17-PT, Amended Indictment, 18 July 2005, paras. 28–31. As the fact that he had been indicted by the ICTY Prosecutor was still confidential at the time *Furundžija* was rendered, the Trial Chamber refers to Bralo throughout the Judgement by the pseudonym 'Accused B'. See *Furundžija* Trial Judgement, *supra* note 8, para. 74 ('Witness D claims that the accused, a soldier identified hereafter as "Accused B" and another person picked him up by car as he was walking back home.').

[10] *Furundžija* Indictment, *supra* note 9, paras. 25–26. The indictment characterised the accused's individual criminal responsibility in the following terms: 'Each of the accused is individually responsible for the crimes alleged against him in this indictment pursuant to Article 7(1) of the Tribunal Statute. Individual criminal responsibility includes committing, planning, instigating, ordering or otherwise aiding and abetting in the planning, preparation or execution of any crimes referred to in Articles 2 to 5 of the Tribunal Statute.' *Ibid.*, para. 16; see also *ibid.*, para. 17 (re-alleging and incorporating paragraph 16 into each of the counts charging substantive crimes).

[11] *Furundžija* Trial Judgement, *supra* note 8, para. 127. [12] *Ibid.* [13] *Ibid.*, para. 128.
[14] *Ibid.*, para. 130. [15] *Ibid.*, para. 189. [16] *Ibid.*, para. 191. [17] *Ibid.*, para. 210.

Concentration Camp case and the *Auschwitz Concentration Camp* case.[18] By
the *Furundžija* Chamber's account, 'the real basis of the charges [in *Dachau*]
was that all the accused had "acted in pursuance of a common design" to kill
and mistreat prisoners';[19] according to the Trial Chamber, even though the
roles of the various accused ranged from camp commanders to guards, since
each accused made a tangible contribution to the commission of crimes in the
camp, each was convicted for his 'participation' in the crimes, and not for
aiding and abetting them.[20] The Chamber then invoked Articles 25(3)(c) and
(d) of the Rome Statute of the ICC, which had been opened for signature just
five months earlier in July 1998, and remarked that these two provisions draw
a distinction between 'participation in a common plan or enterprise, on the one
hand, and aiding and abetting a crime, on the other'.[21]

On the basis of these three sources – that is, Article 25(3) of the Rome
Statute, the *Dachau Concentration Camp* case and the *Auschwitz Concentration
Camp* case – the Trial Chamber concluded in paragraph 216 that 'two separate
categories of liability for criminal participation appear to have crystallised in
international law – co-perpetrators who participate in a joint criminal enterprise, on the one hand, and aiders and abettors, on the other'.[22] After setting
forth the physical and mental elements of aiding and abetting to be applied by
the ICTY, the Chamber held that 'aiding and abetting is to be distinguished
from the notion of common design, where the *actus reus* consists of participation in a joint criminal enterprise and the *mens rea* required is intent to
participate'.[23] No authority was cited to support the Chamber's articulation
of these specific elements.

The Trial Chamber then explained how to determine 'whether an individual
is a perpetrator or co-perpetrator of torture or must instead be regarded as an
aider and abettor'.[24] It held, based on a teleological construction of the rules

[18] *Ibid.*, paras. 211, 214 (citing *Trial of Martin Gottfried Weiss and Thirty-Nine Others*, 16 *Law Reports of Trials of War Criminals* (1949), p. 5 ('*Dachau Concentration Camp* case'); *Massenvernichtungsverbrechen und NS-Gewaltverbrechen in Lagern; Kriegsverbrechen. KZ Auschwitz, 1941–1945*, reported in 21 *Justiz und NS-Verbrechen* (1979), pp. 361–887 ('*Auschwitz Concentration Camp* case'). The *Furundžija* Trial Chamber cites three elements applied by the Military Tribunal as 'necessary to establish guilt in each case': 'the existence of a system to ill-treat the prisoners and commit the various crime alleged; ... the accused's knowledge of the nature of this system; and ... that the accused encouraged, aided and abetted or participated in enforcing the system'. *Furundžija* Trial Judgement, *supra* note 8, para. 212 (quotation marks removed). These elements are substantially similar to those of the second category of JCE as defined by the *Tadić* Appeals Chamber after reviewing, among other cases, the *Dachau Concentration Camp* case. See *Tadić* Appeal Judgement, *supra* note 3, paras. 202–203.
[19] *Furundžija* Trial Judgement, *supra* note 8, para. 211 (citing no authority).
[20] *Ibid.*, paras. 212–213.
[21] *Ibid.*, para. 216 (citing Rome Statute of the International Criminal Court, entered into force 1 July 2002, UN Doc. A/CONF. 183/9 (1998) ('Rome Statute'), Art. 25(3)(c)–(d)).
[22] *Ibid.* This instance was the first time the term 'joint criminal enterprise' was used in the jurisprudence of the *ad hoc* Tribunals.
[23] *Ibid.*, para. 249.   [24] *Ibid.*, para. 252.

governing torture in international law, that an accused may be convicted as a perpetrator or co-perpetrator of torture if he 'participate[s] in an integral part of the torture and partake[s] of the purpose behind the torture, that is the intent to obtain information or a confession, to punish or intimidate, coerce or discriminate against the victim or a third person'.[25] To be guilty of torture as a mere aider and abettor, on the other hand, 'the accused must assist in some way which has a substantial effect on the perpetration of the crime and with knowledge that torture is taking place'.[26] The Chamber pointed to the following consequence of such a distinction:

256. It follows ... that if an official interrogates a detainee while another person is inflicting severe pain or suffering, the interrogator is guilty of torture as the person causing the severe pain or suffering, even if he does not in any way physically participate in such infliction. Here the criminal law maxim *quis per alium facit per se ipsum facere videtur* (he who acts through others is regarded as acting himself) fully applies.[27]

Having thus set the stage, the Trial Chamber proceeded to find Furundžija guilty of torture as a 'co-perpetrator'.[28] In respect of the count of rape, by contrast, the Chamber found that '[Furundžija] did not personally rape Witness A, nor can he be considered, under the circumstances of this case, to be a co-perpetrator.'[29] Although it did not explain its reasoning further, the Chamber appears to have relegated the accused to aiding and abetting liability for rape because it could not find, on the evidence, that he participated in an 'integral part' of the rape.[30] It sentenced Furundžija to ten years' imprisonment for the torture conviction, and eight years' imprisonment for the rape conviction, to be served concurrently.[31]

Although its reasoning is far from clear, and notwithstanding its reference to 'co-perpetrators who participate in a joint criminal enterprise', the *Furundžija* Chamber appears to have expounded these two concepts as distinct theories of liability separate and apart from aiding and abetting. The first theory is 'joint

---

[25] *Ibid.*, para. 257.   [26] *Ibid.*   [27] *Ibid.*, para. 256.

[28] *Ibid.*, para. 268. See also *ibid.*, para. 269 ('The Trial Chamber ... finds the accused, as a co-perpetrator, guilty of a Violation of the Laws or Customs of War (torture) on Count 13.'). In a subsequent decision, the Appeals Chamber interpreted *Furundžija* as having convicted the accused on 'joint criminal enterprise charges'. See *Milutinović et al.* JCE Appeal Decision, *supra* note 4, para. 17.

[29] *Furundžija* Trial Judgement, *supra* note 8, para. 273.

[30] Cf. *ibid.*, para. 257 (holding that that an accused may be held liable as a perpetrator or co-perpetrator of torture if he 'participate[s] in an integral part of the torture and partake[s] of the purpose behind the torture').

[31] *Ibid.*, p. 112. Furundžija was granted early release on 17 August 2004. International Criminal Tribunal for the former Yugoslavia, 'Indictees Booklet: Individuals Publicly Indicted since the Inception of ICTY', 13 December 2005, p. 16 (on file with authors). Bralo, for his part, pleaded guilty on 19 July 2005 to these and six other counts against him, and was sentenced to twenty years' imprisonment on 7 December 2005. *Bralo* Sentencing Judgement, *supra* note 9, paras. 5, 97.

criminal enterprise' or 'common design', the elements of which were held to be participation by the accused in a joint criminal enterprise and the intent to participate therein.[32] Notwithstanding its holding that this form of responsibility existed under customary international law, *Furundžija* is silent on whether this form could be applied by a chamber of the ICTY or, if so, under which provision of the Tribunal's Statute it would fall.

For liability to arise under the second theory – 'co-perpetration' – the accused must participate in an integral part of the crime and partake of the purpose behind the crime.[33] It is evident that Furundžija's torture conviction was based on this form of responsibility, presumably as a species of 'commission' under Article 7(1) of the ICTY Statute. While he did not physically administer the beatings and sexual assaults that constituted the *actus reus* of the torture,[34] he participated in an integral part of the torture through his interrogation of the victims, and he partook in its purpose by intending to obtain information he believed would benefit the Bosnian Croat army.[35] In spite of the statement in paragraph 256 that 'he who acts through others is regarded as acting himself',[36] the accused's conviction, in respect of the same incident, as an aider and abettor of rape suggests that the Chamber may have wished to avoid reliance on a theory that would impose 'commission' liability on the accused for conduct indirectly perpetrated.[37]

Some eight months after *Furundžija*, the Appeals Chamber, composed of a bench featuring two of the *Furundžija* trial judges – Judges Cassese and Mumba – took on the task of developing in much greater detail the form of responsibility labelled 'joint criminal enterprise' and 'common design' in *Furundžija*.[38] This endeavour resulted in the three-category JCE framework that has become a central component of the practice and jurisprudence of the

---

[32] *Furundžija* Trial Judgement, *supra* note 8, para. 249. See also *ibid.*, para. 216.
[33] See *ibid.*, para. 257.
[34] See *ibid.*, para. 162 (setting out *mens rea* and *actus reus* of torture for purposes of the ICTY).
[35] See *ibid.*, para. 265. The Appeals Chamber upheld the Trial Chamber's findings on Furundžija's individual criminal responsibility for torture and rape, but re-characterised them as having been made on the basis of the common-purpose doctrine. *Prosecutor* v. *Furundžija*, Case No. IT-95–17/1-A, Judgement, 21 July 2000 ('*Furundžija* Appeal Judgement'), para. 120 ('The way the events in this case developed precludes any reasonable doubt that [Furundžija] and [Bralo] knew what they were doing to Witness A and for what purpose they were treating her in that manner; that they had a common purpose may be readily inferred from all the circumstances[.]'). See also *ibid.*, para. 121 ('For these reasons, this element of [Furundžija's] ground [of appeal] must fail.').
[36] *Furundžija* Trial Judgement, *supra* note 8, para. 256.
[37] Cf. Rome Statute, *supra* note 21, Art. 25(3)(a) (setting forth 'co-perpetration' and 'indirect perpetration'); *ibid.*, Art. 25(3)(d) (setting forth something akin to joint criminal enterprise or common design). For a detailed discussion of these provisions of the Rome Statute, see *infra*, text accompanying notes 723–734.
[38] See generally *Tadić* Appeal Judgement, *supra* note 3, paras. 185–229. Curiously, *Tadić* does not rely on the JCE discussion in *Furundžija* or acknowledge the existence of that discussion in any way, and only cites *Furundžija* as having employed the proper approach in determining the persuasive value of the Rome Statute. *Ibid.*, para. 223.

ad hoc Tribunals, as well as that of the Special Court for Sierra Leone.[39] Duško Tadić was charged with responsibility via Article 7(1) of the ICTY Statute for, among other crimes, the murder of five Bosnian Muslim men who were found dead in the village of Jaskići following an attack on the village by an armed group which included Tadić.[40] Although the Trial Chamber convicted him of several other counts of violations of the laws or customs of war and crimes against humanity, and despite its finding that Tadić had been a member of the armed group, the Chamber concluded that it could not, 'on the evidence before it, be satisfied beyond reasonable doubt that the accused had any part in the killing of the five men' at Jaskići.[41]

On appeal, the prosecution argued that Tadić should have been convicted of the killings pursuant to the 'common purpose' doctrine, as the only reasonable inference that could be drawn from the evidence was that the killings were a natural and probable consequence of the attack on Jaskići, and occurred pursuant to a broader policy to rid the region of non-Serbs.[42] The Appeals Chamber found that, while there was no proof that Tadić killed any of the five men, the evidence did establish that the group to which he belonged physically perpetrated the killings.[43] The Chamber then determined that 'it must be ascertained whether criminal responsibility for participating in a common purpose falls within the ambit of Article 7(1) of the Statute',[44] and held that, while Article 7(1) 'covers first and foremost the physical perpetration of a crime by the offender himself', 'the commission of one of the crimes envisaged in Articles 2, 3, 4 or 5 of the Statute might also occur through participation in the realisation of a common design or purpose'.[45] Subsequent jurisprudence has clarified that JCE finds its precise statutory basis within the rubric of 'commission' in Article 7(1) of the ICTY Statute and Article 6(1) of the ICTR Statute ('Article 7/6(1)').[46]

---

[39] The JCE analogue in the Special Court for Sierra Leone is discussed in a later section of this chapter. See *infra* text accompanying notes 735–759.

[40] *Prosecutor* v. *Tadić*, Case No. IT-94-1-I, Second Amended Indictment, 14 December 1995, para. 12.

[41] *Prosecutor* v. *Tadić*, Case No. IT-94-1-T, Judgement, 14 July 1997 ('*Tadić* Trial Judgement'), para. 373. See also *ibid.* ('[I]t is … a distinct possibility that [the murders] may have been the act of a quite distinct group of armed men, or the unauthorized and unforeseen act of one of the force that entered Sivci, for which the accused cannot be held responsible, that caused [the Muslim men's] death.').

[42] *Tadić* Appeal Judgement, *supra* note 3, para. 175.

[43] *Ibid.*, para. 183.   [44] *Ibid.*, para. 187.   [45] *Ibid.*, para. 188.

[46] See *Prosecutor* v. *Gacumbitsi*, Case No. ICTR-2001-64-A, Judgement, 7 July 2006 ('*Gacumbitsi* Appeal Judgement'), para. 158; *Prosecutor* v. *Kvočka, Radić, Žigić and Prcać*, Case No. IT-98-30/1-A, Judgement, 28 February 2005 ('*Kvočka et al.* Appeal Judgement'), para. 79; *Prosecutor* v. *Ntakirutimana and Ntakirutimana*, Case Nos. ICTR-96-10-A and ICTR-96-17-A, Judgement, 13 December 2004 ('*Ntakirutimana and Ntakirutimana* Appeal Judgement'), para. 468; *Prosecutor* v. *Vasiljević*, Case No. IT-98-32-A, Judgement, 25 February 2004 ('*Vasiljević* Appeal Judgement'), para. 95; *Prosecutor* v. *Krnojelac*, Case No. IT-97-25-A, Judgement, 17 September 2003 ('*Krnojelac* Appeal Judgement'), para. 73 (overruling the Trial Chamber's holding that JCE is not a form of commission under Article 7(1), but

The Appeals Chamber reasoned that, as the object and purpose of the ICTY Statute extends the Tribunal's jurisdiction to all those responsible for serious violations of international humanitarian law committed in the former Yugoslavia,[47] the Statute 'does not exclude those modes of participating in the commission of crimes which occur where several persons having a common purpose embark on criminal activity that is then carried out either jointly or by some members of this plurality of persons'.[48] The Chamber invoked the unique nature of international crimes as justification for the imposition of liability on such a basis:

> Most of the time these crimes do not result from the criminal propensity of single individuals but constitute manifestations of collective criminality: the crimes are often carried out by groups of individuals acting in pursuance of a common criminal design. Although only some members of the group may physically perpetrate the criminal act (murder, extermination, wanton destruction of cities, towns or villages, etc.), the participation and contribution of the other members of the group is often vital in facilitating the commission of the offence in question. It follows that the moral gravity of such participation is often no less – or indeed no different – from that of those actually carrying out the acts in question.[49]

The Chamber held that this interpretation, 'based on the Statute and the inherent characteristics of many crimes perpetrated in wartime', warrants the conclusion that international criminal law embraces the common-purpose doctrine.[50] As the ICTY Statute does not specify the physical and mental elements of such a form of responsibility, however, 'one must turn to customary international law' to ascertain such elements.[51]

In its search for these elements in customary international law, the *Tadić* Chamber looked primarily – indeed, almost exclusively – at a handful of judgements rendered by military tribunals in the wake of the Second World War; from these judgements it deduced that 'broadly speaking, the notion of common purpose encompasses three distinct categories of collective criminality'.[52] In the first category, all the participants act pursuant to a common purpose and possess the same intent to commit a crime, and one or more of them actually

finding that the Trial Chamber's error was not so egregious as to render its Judgement invalid); *Milutinović et al.* JCE Appeal Decision, *supra* note 4, para. 20; *Prosecutor* v. *Mpambara*, Case No. ICTR-01-65-T, Judgement, 11 September 2006 ('*Mpambara* Trial Judgement'), para. 12 n. 17; *Prosecutor* v. *Blagojević and Jokić*, Case No. IT-02-60-T, Judgement, 17 January 2005 ('*Blagojević and Jokić* Trial Judgement'), para. 696; *Prosecutor* v. *Brđanin*, Case No. IT-99-36-T, Judgement, 1 September 2004 ('*Brđanin* Trial Judgement'), para. 258; *Prosecutor* v. *Krstić*, Case No. IT-98-33-T, Judgement, 2 August 2001 ('*Krstić* Trial Judgement'), para. 601.
[47] *Tadić* Appeal Judgement, *supra* note 3, para. 189.   [48] *Ibid.*, para. 190.
[49] *Ibid.*, para. 191. This passage has been quoted in a number of subsequent judgements. See, e.g., *Kvočka et al.* Appeal Judgement, *supra* note 46, para. 80; *Krnojelac* Appeal Judgement, *supra* note 46, para. 29; *Blagojević and Jokić* Trial Judgement, *supra* note 46, para. 695.
[50] *Tadić* Appeal Judgement, *supra* note 3, para. 194.   [51] *Ibid.*   [52] *Ibid.*, para. 195.

perpetrates the crime.[53] In the second category, which the Appeals Chamber described as 'really a variant of the first category', an organised criminal system exists in which detainees are systematically mistreated.[54] The third category 'concerns cases involving a common design to pursue one course of conduct where one of the perpetrators commits an act which, while outside the common design, was nevertheless a natural and foreseeable consequence of the effecting of that common purpose'.[55] As an example of this category, the *Tadić* Chamber posited a hypothetical scenario with facts curiously similar to those in the actual case before it: where a group of persons formulates a common plan to remove forcibly members of a particular ethnic group from a town, and one or more of the victims is shot and killed in the course of such removal, all the participants in the plan are equally responsible for the killing because it was 'foreseeable that the forcible removal of civilians at gunpoint might well result in the deaths of one or more of those civilians'.[56] The precise elements of the three categories of JCE, as they have been developed in the post-*Tadić* jurisprudence, are discussed in detail in Section 2.3 of this chapter.

Tadić's unconventional methodology in discerning the existence and elements of these three categories in customary international law has left the Appeals Chamber open to justifiable criticism.[57] One problematic aspect is that, as in *Furundžija*, there is a persistent confusion between the potentially very different notions of liability for participation in a common purpose or design, on the one hand, and liability for co-perpetration, on the other. For example, *Tadić* discusses, as support for the existence of the first category, the British Military Court case of *Sandrock and others*. According to the Appeals

---

[53] *Ibid.*, paras. 197, 220. Accord *Kvočka et al.* Appeal Judgement, *supra* note 46, para. 82; *Ntakirutimana and Ntakirutimana* Appeal Judgement, *supra* note 46, para. 463; *Prosecutor* v. *Vasiljević*, Case No. IT-98-32-T, Judgement, 29 November 2002 ('*Vasiljević* Trial Judgement'), para. 97.

[54] *Tadić* Appeal Judgement, *supra* note 3, paras. 202–203, 220. Accord *Kvočka et al.* Appeal Judgement, *supra* note 46, para. 82; *Ntakirutimana and Ntakirutimana* Appeal Judgement, *supra* note 46, para. 464; *Krnojelac* Appeal Judgement, *supra* note 46, para. 89; *Vasiljević* Trial Judgement, *supra* note 53, para. 98.

[55] *Tadić* Appeal Judgement, *supra* note 3, para. 204. Accord *Kvočka et al.* Appeal Judgement, *supra* note 46, para. 83; *Vasiljević* Appeal Judgement, *supra* note 46, para. 99; *Ntakirutimana and Ntakirutimana* Appeal Judgement, *supra* note 46, para. 465.

[56] *Tadić* Appeal Judgement, *supra* note 3, para. 204.

[57] See, e.g., Danner and Martinez, *supra* note 5, p. 110 (arguing, *inter alia*, that the post-Second World War cases cited by *Tadić* 'do not support the sprawling form of JCE, particularly the extended form of this kind of liability'); Marco Sassòli and Laura M. Olson, 'The Judgement of the ICTY Appeals Chamber on the Merits in the *Tadic* Case', (2000) 82 *International Review of the Red Cross* 733, 749 (asserting, *inter alia*, that *Tadić*'s 'definition of the third category is not very clear and varies throughout the discussion of the Chamber', and criticising the Appeals Chamber for relying on two treaties – the Terrorist Bombings Convention and the Rome Statute – not yet in force at the time); Steven Powles, 'Joint Criminal Enterprise: Criminal Liability by Prosecutorial Ingenuity and Judicial Creativity?', (2004) 2 *Journal of International Criminal Justice* 606, 615 (arguing that 'a closer inspection of the authorities and practice cited in *Tadić* as giving rise to a customary norm of international law in relation to the third category of joint criminal enterprise, the extended form, reveals that the acceptance of such liability was limited' and that the Appeals Chamber 'appear[s] to have cited only one case [– *D'Ottavio et al.* of the Terrano Assise Court –] that unequivocally sets out the third category of joint criminal enterprise').

Chamber, that court found three Germans who had killed a British prisoner of war guilty pursuant to the doctrine of 'common enterprise'; although each of them played a different role in the killing – one fired the fatal shot, one gave the order to shoot, and the other stood guard – they all had the intent to kill the prisoner.[58] In the Appeals Chamber's words, '[t]hey therefore were all co-perpetrators of the crime of murder'.[59] The Chamber went on to describe '[a]nother instance of co-perpetratorship of this nature' in the British case of *Jespen and others*, as ostensibly evidenced by the court's failure to rebut the prosecution when it submitted that '[i]f Jespen was joining in this voluntary slaughter of eighty or so people, helping the others by doing his share of killing, the whole eighty odd deaths can be laid at his door and at the door of any single man who was in any way assisting that act'.[60]

In each of the cases recounted by the Appeals Chamber as support for the first category of JCE, the accused appear to have been very closely involved in the perpetration of the *actus reus* of the crime, playing roles similar to that of Furundžija in the commission of torture. As such, the cases would indeed seem to constitute examples of co-perpetration in the sense of joint commission, similar to that set out in Article 25(3)(a) of the Rome Statute. Yet in a subsequent paragraph, the *Tadić* Chamber refers to these cases as evidence of customary international law manifesting the existence of liability for participation in a common purpose or design, and contrasts them with Italian and German cases that applied the notion of co-perpetration:

> It should be noted that in many post-Second World War trials held in other countries, courts took the same approach to instances of crimes in which two or more persons participated with a different degree of involvement. However, they did not rely upon the notion of common purpose or common design, preferring to refer instead to the notion of co-perpetration. This applies in particular to Italian and German cases.[61]

The Chamber confused the matter further in its re-articulation of the elements of the first category several paragraphs later:

> [T]he case law shows that this notion [of common design] has been applied to three distinct categories of cases. First, in cases of co-perpetration, where all participants in the common design possess the same criminal intent to commit a crime (and one or more of them actually perpetrate the crime, with intent).[62]

On the clearest reading of *Tadić*, the use of the term 'co-perpetration' in the discussion of the first category and the cases relied upon would suggest that,

---

[58] *Tadić* Appeal Judgement, *supra* note 3, para. 197 n. 234.   [59] *Ibid.*, para. 197.
[60] *Ibid.*, para. 198 (citing *Trial of Gustav Alfred Jepsen and others*, 15 *Law Reports of Trials of War Criminals* (1949), p. 172.).
[61] *Ibid.*, para. 201 (footnotes omitted).   [62] *Ibid.*, para. 220.

for the first category, the Appeals Chamber envisioned factual scenarios such
as that in *Furundžija*, where the accused, even if he did not physically perpetrate part of the *actus reus* of the crime himself, was at least present at the scene
and provided active assistance.[63] Subsequent ICTY judgements have not,
however, tended to interpret *Tadić* in this way. Liability has been imposed
pursuant to the first category of JCE for crimes that fell within the object of an
enterprise to which the accused adhered, but which were physically perpetrated by forces on the ground relatively far removed from the accused.[64] In
such cases the accused, who may not even have been present at the time of the
crimes' commission, cannot be said to have 'co-perpetrated' them in the sense
that co-perpetration occurred in *Furundžija* and in the post-Second World
War cases cited by *Tadić*. Furthermore, a number of subsequent chambers
appear to have taken the term 'co-perpetrator' as a synonym for 'participant'
or 'member' of a JCE, using it interchangeably with these two terms when
describing liability on the basis not only of the first category, but the second
and third categories as well.[65]

---

[63] In a separate and partially dissenting opinion to the October 2003 *Simić* Trial Judgement, Judge
Lindholm expressed the same view:

> I dissociate myself from the concept or doctrine of joint criminal enterprise in this case as well as generally. The so-called
> basic form of joint criminal enterprise does not, in my opinion, have any substance of its own. It is nothing more than a
> new label affixed to a since long well-known concept or doctrine in most jurisdictions as well as in international criminal
> law, named co-perpetration.

Simić et al. Trial Judgement, *supra* note 5, Separate and Partially Dissenting Opinion of Judge Per-Johan
Lindholm, para. 2.

[64] See, e.g., *ibid.*, paras. 983–984 (finding that the accused Simić, as president of the Bosanski Šamac Crisis
Staff, was a participant in a first-category JCE to commit persecution as a crime against humanity, where
the physical perpetrators of the underlying offences of persecution were soldiers in the Yugoslav army
and paramilitaries); *Krstić* Trial Judgement, *supra* note 46, paras. 619–645 (finding the accused guilty of
genocide for his participation in a JCE to kill the military-aged Bosnian Muslim men of Srebrenica,
despite the fact that he 'did not conceive the plan to kill the men, nor . . . kill them personally') (quotation
at para. 644). Cf. *Prosecutor v. Krstić*, Case No. IT-98-33-A, Judgement, 19 April 2004 ('*Krstić* Appeal
Judgement'), paras. 134–144 (overturning the Trial Chamber's conviction of the accused for genocide,
not on the basis of his tenuous proximity to the killings, but instead because he lacked the requisite
genocidal intent, and substituting a conviction for aiding and abetting genocide).

[65] See, e.g., *Krnojelac* Appeal Judgement, *supra* note 46, para. 70 (contrasting aiding and abetting from JCE,
and using the term 'co-perpetration' to describe JCE without distinction as to category); *Vasiljević* Trial
Judgement, *supra* note 53, para. 67 n. 131 ('The Trial Chamber understands the term "co-perpetrator" as
referring to a participant in a joint criminal enterprise who was not the principal offender.'); *Prosecutor v.
Krajišnik*, Case No. IT-00-39-T, Judgement, 27 September 2006 ('*Krajišnik* Trial Judgement'), para. 881
(holding that '[t]he third form of JCE is characterized by a common criminal design to pursue a course of
conduct where one or more of the co-perpetrators commits an act which . . . is a natural and foreseeable
consequence of the implementation of that design'); *Simić et al.* Trial Judgement, *supra* note 5, para. 138
(holding, without specification as to category, that 'participation in a joint criminal enterprise is a form of
co-perpetration'); *Prosecutor v. Kordić and Čerkez*, Case No. IT-95-14/2-T, Judgement, 26 February 2001
('*Kordić and Čerkez* Trial Judgement'), para. 831. In a seminal decision reaffirming the jurisdiction of the
ICTY to apply JCE as a form of responsibility, the Appeals Chamber called into question the appropriateness of using the term 'co-perpetrator' to describe a participant in a JCE, but did not expressly
disapprove of the terms' interchangeability:

> The Prosecution pointed out in its indictment against Ojdanić that its use of the word 'committed' was not intended to
> suggest that any of the accused physically perpetrated any of the crimes charged, personally. 'Committing', the

A more troublesome difficulty with the *Tadić* analysis is that, notwithstanding the Appeals Chamber's proclamations to the contrary, many or most of the
judgements it relied upon did not clearly impose liability on the basis of some
version of the common-purpose doctrine.[66] A particularly salient example
is the *Borkum Island* case, in which a United States military court convicted
the mayor of Borkum and several German military officers and soldiers for the
assault and killing of seven American airmen who had crash-landed on the
North Sea island during the war. The *Tadić* Chamber placed great emphasis on
arguments by the prosecution at trial to the effect that the accused were 'cogs
in the wheel of common design, all equally important, each cog doing the part
assigned to it'[67] and that 'it is proved beyon[d] a reasonable doubt that each one
of these accused played his part in mob violence which led to the unlawful
killing[s]' and '[t]herefore, under the law each and everyone of the accused is
guilty of murder'.[68] After deliberating in closed session, the *Borkum Island* judges
rendered an oral verdict in which they convicted a number of the accused,
including the mayor and several officers, of both killing and assault; no reasons
were stated for the verdict, and no written decision was rendered. Nevertheless,
as some of the accused were convicted of assault and killing while others were
convicted only of assault, the *Tadić* Chamber concluded as follows:

> It may be inferred from this case that all the accused found guilty were held responsible
> for pursuing a criminal common design, the intent being to assault the prisoners of
> war. However, some of them were also found guilty of murder, even where there was
> no evidence that they had actually killed the prisoners. Presumably, this was on the
> basis that the accused, whether by virtue of their status, role or conduct, were in a
> position to have predicted that the assault would lead to the killing of the victims by
> some of those participating in the assault.[69]

Notwithstanding *Tadić*'s proclamations to the contrary, it is not at all clear
that the military court imposed liability on the basis of a theory of common
purpose or design, and much less that the convictions were entered pursuant to

---

Prosecution wrote, 'refers to participation in a joint criminal enterprise as a co-perpetrator'. *Leaving aside the appro-*
priateness of the use of the expression 'co-perpetration' in such a context, it would seem therefore that the Prosecution
charges co-perpetration in a joint criminal enterprise as a form of 'commission'[.]

Milutinović et al. JCE Appeal Decision, *supra* note 4, para. 20 (emphasis added).

[66] Moreover, as Professors Danner and Martinez rightly point out, not all of the judgements cited by *Tadić*
are widely available, and some are available only as summaries prepared by the UN War Crimes
Commission in the years after the judgements were rendered. Danner and Martinez, *supra* note 5,
p. 110 n. 141. In addition, the relevant citations in *Tadić* itself concede that at least two of the post-
Second World War cases relied upon therein were unpublished handwritten judgements, which were
made available to the ICTY and placed on record in its library. See *infra* note 77.

[67] *United States* v. *Goebell, Krolikovsky, Wentzel, Weber, Seiler, Schmitz, Pointer, Albrecht, Geyer, Witzke,*
Akkermann, Meyer-Gerhards, Rommel, Garrels, Mammenga, Haksema, Hanken, Heinemann, Wittmaack,
Langer, Haesiker, Schierlau and Rimbach, US Military Government Court, US Forces, European
Theatre, Verdict of 22 March 1946, p. 1188.

[68] *Ibid.*, p. 1190. See also *Tadić* Appeal Judgement, *supra* note 3, para. 210.   [69] *Ibid.*, para. 213.

something akin to the third category of JCE. The court may, for example, have chosen to impose liability for the killings on those accused who held positions of authority because they failed to use that authority to stop the attack on the airmen. Moreover, even if the court did rely on the common-purpose doctrine, it may have convicted the various accused pursuant to one or both of two distinct common designs, one to assault the airmen and another to kill them, where those convicted on both counts adhered to both designs. An examination of the trial transcripts, moreover, does not reveal that anyone who was convicted on both counts possessed the intent to assault but lacked the intent to kill, but was nonetheless found guilty of the killings because of his subjective ability to predict their occurrence.

Perhaps the most worrying characteristic of the *Tadić* analysis is the methodology it used to divine rules of customary international law, and the consequent precedent it set for future chambers of the *ad hoc* Tribunals to employ the same methodology.[70] Traditional public international law posits that two elements are required to manifest the existence of a rule in customary international law: an established, consistent, and widespread state practice in the international realm, and *opinio juris* – that is, a conviction on the part of these states that they are bound to behave in such a way by an already existing rule.[71] While the decisions of domestic courts in relation to a purported international rule – such as one derived from a treaty whose provisions have been implemented in national legislation – can demonstrate state practice,[72] it is doubtful whether international judicial decisions amount to state practice, even where the court rendering the decision is administered by one state and

---

[70] See, e.g., *Prosecutor* v. *Rwamakuma*, Case No. ICTR-98-44-AR72.4, Decision on Interlocutory Appeal Regarding Application of Joint Criminal Enterprise to the Crime of Genocide, 22 October 2004 ('*Rwamakuma* JCE Appeal Decision'), paras. 14–26 (Appeals Chamber holding that '[n]orms of customary international law are characterized by the two familiar components of state practice and *opinio juris*', and proceeding to rely almost exclusively on the Control Council Law No. 10 *Justice* case to support its conclusion that 'customary international law criminalized intentional participation in a common plan to commit genocide prior to 1992') (quotation at para. 14). See *infra* text accompanying notes 101–105 for a discussion of *Rwamakuba*, and note 105 for a full citation to the *Justice* case.

[71] North Sea Continental Shelf (*Federal Republic of Germany* v. *Denmark; Federal Republic of Germany* v. *the Netherlands*), Merits, Judgement of 20 February 1969, [1969] ICJ Rep. 3, para. 77. Accord *Prosecutor* v. *Hadžihasanović, Alagić and Kubura*, Case No. IT-01-47-AR72, Decision on the Interlocutory Appeal Challenging Jurisdiction in Relation to Command Responsibility, 16 July 2003, para. 11; *Rwamakuba* JCE Appeal Decision, *supra* note 70, para. 14.

[72] See *Prosecutor* v. *Kupreškić, Kupreškić, Kupreškić, Josipović, Papić and Šantić*, Case No. IT-95-16-T, Judgement, 14 January 2000 ('*Kupreškić et al.* Trial Judgement'), para. 541, opining as follows:

> In many instances no less value may be given to decisions on international crimes delivered by national courts operating pursuant to the 1948 Genocide Convention, or the 1949 Geneva Conventions or the 1977 Protocols or similar international treaties. In these instances the international framework on the basis of which the national court operates and the fact that in essence the court applies international substantive law, may lend great weight to rulings of such courts.

functions pursuant to a statute, such as Control Council Law No. 10, agreed to among several states.[73] Thus, even if the international judgements discussed in *Tadić* unambiguously expounded the elements of common-purpose liability and were consistent among themselves, they would still not constitute customary international law.[74] It is questionable, moreover, whether the remaining sources relied upon – including Article 2(3)(c) of the Terrorist Bombings Convention,[75] Article 25(3)(d) of the Rome Statute,[76] and a handful of Italian national cases adjudicated after the Second World War[77] – provide sufficient evidence of state practice and *opinio juris* to support the existence of *Tadić*'s very specific list of elements.

In the end the Appeals Chamber did hold Tadić responsible for the murder of the five men at Jaskići pursuant to the third category of the common-purpose doctrine. Basing itself on the Trial Chamber's conclusion that Tadić had actively taken part in the attack on Jaskići,[78] the Appeals Chamber surmised that 'the only possible inference to be drawn is that the Appellant had the intention to further the criminal purpose to rid the Prijedor region of the non-Serb population, by committing inhumane acts against them'.[79] After finding that it was foreseeable that non-Serbs might be killed in the execution of the common plan and that Tadić had been aware that the actions of his associates were likely to lead to such killings,[80] the Appeals Chamber

---

[73] See Jens David Ohlin, 'Applying the Death Penalty to Crimes of Genocide', (2005) 99 *AJIL* 747, 755 ('Although the international tribunals are staffed by prosecutors and judges from members states … [s]ince they make determinations collectively – not individually as state agents – their decisions cannot be regarded as evidence of state practice.'). But see *Kupreškić et al.* Trial Judgement, *supra* note 72, para. 541, providing as follows:

It cannot be gainsaid that great value ought to be attached to decisions of such international criminal courts as the international tribunals of Nuremberg or Tokyo, or to national courts operating by virtue, and on the strength, of Control Council Law no. 10, a legislative act jointly passed in 1945 by the four Occupying Powers and thus reflecting international agreement among the Great Powers on the law applicable to international crimes and the jurisdiction of the courts called upon to rule on those crimes. These courts operated under international instruments laying down provisions that were either declaratory of existing law or which had been gradually transformed into customary international law.

The *Kupreškić* Chamber was, like the *Furundžija* Trial Chamber and the *Tadić* Appeals Chamber, composed in part of Judges Cassese and Mumba.

[74] Nevertheless, while decisions of international courts do not constitute custom, as a recognised subsidiary source of public international law used to determine existence and scope of norms of customary international law, they may provide evidence of custom. See Statute of the International Court of Justice, 26 June 1945, 59 Stat. 1031, Art. 38(1)(d).

[75] International Convention for the Suppression of Terrorist Bombing, entered into force 23 May 2001, GA Res. 52/164, Annex (1997), Art. 2(3)(c). This Convention had not yet entered into force at the time *Tadić* was rendered.

[76] Rome Statute, *supra* note 21, Art. 25(3)(d). The Rome Statute had not yet entered into force at the time *Tadić* was rendered.

[77] See *Tadić* Appeal Judgement, *supra* note 3, paras. 214–219 (citing the Italian cases of *D'Ottavio et al.*, *Aratano et al.*, *Tossani*, *Ferrida*, *Bonati et al.* and *Manelli*). Full citations, where possible, are provided in the judgement's footnotes.

[78] See *Tadić* Trial Judgement, *supra* note 41, para. 370.

[79] *Tadić* Appeal Judgement, *supra* note 3, para. 232.   [80] *Ibid.*

convicted Tadić of wilful killing as a grave breach, murder as a violation of the laws or customs of war, and murder as a crime against humanity.[81]

Despite these methodologically questionable origins, the existence of the common-purpose doctrine – now consistently referred to by the term 'joint criminal enterprise'[82] – and the permissibility of imposing liability pursuant to it under the Statutes of the *ad hoc* Tribunals, have been reaffirmed on many occasions, and the physical and mental elements set forth in *Tadić* have been substantially refined and expanded upon.[83] The crucial reassertion of JCE's existence in customary international law and in the ICTY Statute occurred in May 2003, when the Appeals Chamber rejected Dragoljub Ojdanić's challenge to the jurisdiction of the Tribunal to apply JCE.[84] The indictment operative at the time charged Ojdanić and his two co-accused in the *Milutinović* case with 'commission' under Article 7(1) of the Statute specifically through participation in a JCE:

Each of the accused is individually responsible for the crimes alleged against him in this indictment under Articles 3, 5 and 7(1) of the Statute of the Tribunal. The accused planned, instigated, ordered, committed, or otherwise aided and abetted in the planning, preparation, or execution of these crimes. By using the word 'committed' in this indictment, the Prosecutor does not intend to suggest that any of the accused physically perpetrated any of the crimes charged, personally. 'Committing' in this indictment refers to participation in a joint criminal enterprise as a co-perpetrator.[85]

[81] *Ibid.*, paras. 235–237.
[82] In May 2003 the Appeals Chamber held that, while the phrases 'common-purpose doctrine' and 'joint criminal enterprise' had been used interchangeably in the practice and jurisprudence of the ICTY, 'the later term – joint criminal enterprise – is preferred'. *Milutinović et al.* JCE Appeal Decision, *supra* note 4, para. 36. See also *Brđanin and Talić* June 2001 Pre-Trial Decision, *supra* note 4, para. 24, in which a Trial Chamber remarked that

[t]he Appeals Chamber labelled this concept variously, and apparently interchangeably, as a common criminal plan, a common criminal purpose, a common design or purpose, a common criminal design, a common purpose, a common design, and a common concerted design. The common purpose is also described, more generally, as being part of a criminal enterprise, a common enterprise, and a joint criminal enterprise ... [T]he Trial Chamber prefers the last of these labels, a 'joint criminal enterprise', to describe the common purpose case.

[83] See, e.g., *Gacumbitsi* Appeal Judgement, *supra* note 46, para. 158; *Prosecutor* v. *Stakić*, Case No. IT-97-24-A, Judgement, 22 March 2006 ('*Stakić* Appeal Judgement'), paras. 64–65; *Kvočka et al.* Appeal Judgement, *supra* note 46, paras. 82–86, 97–99, 101, 103, 104, 106, 110, 112, 117–118 (discussing and elaborating upon the elements of the second category); *Ntakirutimana and Ntakirutimana* Appeal Judgement, *supra* note 46, paras. 461–468 (affirming the applicability of JCE to ICTR proceedings); *Prosecutor* v. *Blaškić*, Case No. IT-95-14-A, Judgement, 29 July 2004 ('*Blaškić* Appeal Judgement'), para. 33 (refining the definition of the mental element for the third category); *Vasiljević* Appeal Judgement, *supra* note 46, paras. 96–101, 105, 109, 119; *Krnojelac* Appeal Judgement, *supra* note 46, paras. 73, 81, 84, 89–90, 94, 96–97, 100, 116–117, 121–123 (discussing and elaborating upon the elements of the second category); *Prosecutor* v. *Delalić, Mucić, Delić and Landžo*, Case No. IT-96-21-A, Judgement, 20 February 2001, paras. 345, 366; *Furundžija* Appeal Judgement, *supra* note 35, para. 119.
[84] *Milutinović et al.* JCE Appeal Decision, *supra* note 4.
[85] *Prosecutor* v. *Milutinović, Šainović and Ojdanić*, Case No. IT-99-37-I, Third Amended Indictment, 5 September 2002, para. 16.

Relying on *Tadić* and subsequent Appeal Judgements holding that JCE falls within the jurisdiction of the Tribunal, the Trial Chamber rather summarily denied Ojdanić's motion.[86] On interlocutory appeal, Ojdanić contended, *inter alia*, that the application of JCE to him and his co-accused would infringe the principle of *nullum crimen sine lege* and that, had the drafters of the ICTY intended to include this form of responsibility in the jurisdiction of the Tribunal, they would have done so expressly, as was done in Article 25(3)(d) of the Rome Statute of the ICC.[87]

In reiterating that JCE is implicitly included in Article 7(1) of the ICTY Statute as a form of 'commission', the Appeals Chamber opined that reference to a crime or a form of responsibility need not be explicit in the Statute in order to come within its purview; unlike the Rome Statute, the ICTY Statute 'is not and does not purport to be . . . a meticulously detailed code providing explicitly for every possible scenario and every solution thereto'.[88] Following the lead of the Trial Chamber, the Appeals Chamber then proceeded to invoke *Tadić* for the proposition that customary international law recognised the imposition of JCE liability at the time of the events alleged in Ojdanić's indictment, and it declined to undertake a new analysis of the sources of custom:

21. The Defence suggests that the *Tadić* interpretation of Article 7(1) means that all modes of liability not specifically excluded by the Statute are included therein. It is not necessary to deal with so wide an argument. The Appeals Chamber was satisfied then, and is still satisfied now, that the Statute provides, albeit not explicitly, for joint criminal enterprise as a form of criminal liability and that its elements are based on customary law.[89]

[. . .]

29. . . . The Appeals Chamber does not propose to revisit its finding in *Tadić* concerning the customary status of this form of liability. It is satisfied that the state practice and *opinio juris* reviewed in that decision was sufficient to permit the conclusion that such a norm existed under customary international law in 1992 when Tadić committed the crimes for which he had been charged and for which he was eventually convicted.[90]

---

[86] *Prosecutor v. Milutinović, Šainović and Ojdanić*, Case No. IT-99-37-PT, Decision on Dragoljub Ojdanić's Preliminary Motion to Dismiss for Lack of Jurisdiction – Joint Criminal Enterprise, 13 February 2003, p. 6 ('Considering that the Appeals Chamber has determined that participation in a joint criminal enterprise is a mode of liability in respect of any of the crimes within the jurisdiction of the Tribunal under Article 7(1) of the Statute, and defined its elements and applications in its Judgements in *Tadic, Furundžija* and *Celebici*.') (footnote omitted).

[87] *Milutinović et al.* JCE Appeal Decision, *supra* note 4, paras. 8, 13.

[88] *Ibid.*, para. 18. See also *ibid.*, para. 20 ('The Appeals Chamber . . . regards joint criminal enterprise as a form of "commission" pursuant to Article 7(1) of the Statute.').

[89] *Ibid.*, para. 21.

[90] *Ibid.*, para. 29. Accord *Prosecutor v. Karemera, Ngirumpatse and Nzirorera*, Case Nos. ICTR-98-44-AR72.5, ICTR-98-44-AR72.6, Decision on Jurisdictional Appeals: Joint Criminal Enterprise, 12 April 2006 ('*Karemera et al.* JCE Appeal Decision'), para. 16 (reaffirming that 'it is clear that there is a basis in customary international law for . . . JCE liability').

The Appeals Chamber accordingly upheld the Trial Chamber's dismissal of Ojdanić's jurisdictional challenge.[91]

Steven Powles has criticised this aspect of the May 2003 *Milutinović* decision, deeming the Appeals Chamber's refusal to revisit *Tadić* a 'great pity' because in *Milutinović*, unlike in *Tadić*, the defence challenged the existence of JCE under custom and the Chamber therefore had the benefit of arguments from both parties on this point.[92] The *Milutinović* Appeals Chamber's very evident reluctance to re-examine *Tadić*'s purported sources of custom is certainly unfortunate. It suggests that even the Appeals Chamber as it was composed at the time, some four years subsequent to *Tadić*, was unwilling to undertake a custom analysis to independently conclude whether there was sufficient state practice and *opinio juris* to support JCE's existence at the time of the events alleged in the indictment. It may well be that the Chamber took a pragmatic decision not to embark on a course of action that might risk upsetting the findings of JCE liability in *Tadić* and the various Trial and Appeal Judgements that had been rendered in the interim.[93]

Although neither *Tadić* nor *Milutinović* appears to have restricted the applicability of any of the categories of JCE to any crime in the Statute, the ICTY and ICTR Appeals Chambers addressed the possible existence of such a restriction in two subsequent interlocutory decisions, in *Brđanin* and

---

[91] *Milutinović et al.* JCE Appeal Decision, *supra* note 4, para. 45. In the same decision, the Appeals Chamber held that '[j]oint criminal enterprise and 'conspiracy' are two different forms of liability', *ibid.*, para. 23, and that '[j]oint criminal enterprise is different from membership in a criminal enterprise which was criminalised as a separate criminal offence in Nuremberg and in subsequent trials held under Control Council Law No. 10'. *Ibid.*, para. 25. See also *ibid.*, para. 26 ('Criminal liability pursuant to a joint criminal enterprise is not a liability for mere membership or for conspiring to commit crimes, but a form of liability concerned with the participation in the commission of a crime as part of a joint criminal enterprise, a different matter.'). The Chamber dismissed Ojdanić's argument that the imposition of JCE liability violates the principle of *nullum crimen sine lege* because the criminal law of the former Yugoslavia, the 'extensive state practice noted in *Tadić*', and the 'egregious nature' of the crimes charged 'would have provided notice to anyone that the acts committed by the accused in 1999 would have engaged criminal responsibility on the basis of participation in a joint criminal enterprise'. *Ibid.*, para. 43.

[92] Powles, *supra* note 57, p. 615.

[93] See, e.g., *Tadić* Appeal Judgement, *supra* note 3, paras. 230–233 (finding the accused guilty of murder for his participation in a common plan to attack the village of Jaskići where the killing of five men was the foreseeable consequence of such attack); *Furundžija* Appeal Judgement, *supra* note 35, paras. 115–121 (upholding the Trial Chamber's conviction of the accused as a co-perpetrator of torture, apparently under the rubric of the first category of JCE); *Vasiljević* Trial Judgement, *supra* note 53, paras. 206–211 (finding the accused guilty pursuant to JCE for the murder of five Muslim men); 238–240 (finding the accused guilty of inhumane acts pursuant to JCE); 254–261 (finding the accused guilty of murder and inhumane acts as forms of persecution pursuant to JCE); *Kordić and Čerkez* Trial Judgement, *supra* note 65, paras. 829–831 (finding both accused liable for persecution as part of a common plan or design); *Krstić* Trial Judgement, *supra* note 46, paras. 615–618 (finding the accused guilty of inhumane acts and persecution by virtue of his involvement in a JCE to forcibly transfer Bosnian Muslim women, children and elderly from Potočari and to create a humanitarian crisis); *Prosecutor v. Kvočka, Kos, Radić, Žigić and Prcać*, Case No. IT-98-30/1-T, Judgement, 2 November 2001, paras. 504, 578 (finding two of the accused guilty pursuant to the second category of JCE for crimes including persecution, murder and torture).

Rwamakuba.[94] Together with *Tadić* and *Milutinović*, these decisions comprise the core appellate jurisprudence establishing and setting the parameters of JCE as a form of responsibility in the *ad hoc* Tribunals. In November 2003, the Trial Chamber in *Brđanin* issued a decision acquitting the accused of genocide pursuant to the third category of JCE on the ground that genocide, because of its specific-intent requirement, 'cannot be reconciled with the *mens rea* required for a conviction pursuant to the third category of JCE'.[95] In a brief decision dated 19 March 2004, the Appeals Chamber reversed this holding and reinstated the genocide charge,[96] accepting the prosecution's contention that

[94] The decisions of the respective Appeals Chambers of the ICTY and the ICTR have generally been treated as authoritative by the Trial Chambers of both Tribunals, and the two Appeals Chambers have often been referred to as a single entity. See, e.g., *Prosecutor v. Popović, Beara, Nikolić, Borovčanin, Miletić, Gvero and Pandurević*, Case No. IT-05-88-T, Decision on Prosecution Motion for Judicial Notice of Adjudicated Facts, 26 September 2006, paras. 5–21 (ICTY Trial Chamber relying heavily on a recent decision of the ICTR Appeals Chamber for the requirements for taking judicial notice of adjudicated facts, and referring generically to 'the Appeals Chamber' when discussing rulings of either the ICTY Appeals Chamber or the ICTR Appeals Chamber); *Prosecutor v. Muvunyi*, Case No. ICTR-00-55A-T, Decision on Muvunyi's Additional Objections to the Deposition Testimony of Witness QX pursuant to Article 20 of the Statute and Rules 44, 44 *bis*, and 73(F) of the Rules of Procedure and Evidence, 31 May 2006, para. 10 (ICTR Trial Chamber noting that '[t]he Appeals Chamber has developed considerable jurisprudence at both the ICTR and the ICTY on the issue of effective counsel'); *Prosecutor v. Blagojević, Obrenović, Jokić and Nikolić*, Case No. IT-02-60, Decision on Blagojević's Application pursuant to Rule 15(B), 19 March 2003, para. 13 (ICTY Bureau holding, with respect to the law on actual bias, that 'what both the ICTY and ICTR Appeals Chambers have said with respect to a claim of appearance of bias applies with equal force'); *Prosecutor v. Nahimana, Barayagwiza and Ngeze*, Case No. ICTR-99-52-T, Reasons for Oral Decision of 17 September 2002 on the Motions for Acquittal, 25 September 2002, para. 16 (ICTR Trial Chamber holding that, as the operative words of Rule 98 *bis* are the same in the Rules of Procedure and Evidence of both *ad hoc* Tribunals, 'the Appeals Chamber's formulation of the law of Rule 98 *bis* of the ICTY Rules binds the present Chamber in its interpretation and application of the corresponding ICTR rule'). Moreover, each Appeals Chamber has tended to treat the decisions of the other as highly persuasive. See, e.g., *Prosecutor v. Bagaragaza*, Case No. ICTR-05-86-AR11 *bis*, Decision on Rule 11*bis* Appeal, 30 August 2006, para. 9 (ICTR Appeals Chamber holding that the ICTY Appeals Chamber's case law on referral of cases to national jurisdictions 'is largely applicable in the context of this Tribunal as well'); *Prosecutor v. Naletilić and Martinović*, Case No. IT-98-34-A, Decision on Naletilic's Amended Second Rule 115 Motion and Third Rule 115 Motion to Present Additional Evidence, 7 July 2005, para. 20 (ICTY Appeals Chamber 'endors[ing] the position of the ICTR Appeals Chamber that "the Appeals Chamber ordinarily treats its prior interlocutory decisions as binding in continued proceedings"'); *Blaškić* Appeal Judgement, *supra* note 83, para. 63 (ICTY Appeals Chamber recalling that 'the ICTR Appeals Chamber has on a previous occasion rejected criminal negligence in the context of command responsibility', and stating that '[t]he Appeals Chamber expressly endorses this view'). See also *Prosecutor v. Aleksovski*, Case No. IT-95-14/1-A, Judgement, 24 March 2000 ('*Aleksovski* Appeal Judgement'), para. 113 (establishing the principle that the *ratio decidendi* of ICTY Appeals Chamber decisions are binding on ICTY Trial Chambers); Statute of the International Criminal Tribunal for Rwanda, (1994) 33 ILM 1602, as amended by Security Council Resolution 1534 of 26 March 2004 ('ICTR Statute'), Art. 13(4) ('The members of the Appeals Chamber of the International Tribunal for the Former Yugoslavia shall also serve as the members of the Appeals Chamber of the International Tribunal for Rwanda.').

[95] *Prosecutor v. Brđanin*, Case No. IT-99-36-T, Decision on Motion for Acquittal Pursuant to Rule 98 *bis*, 28 November 2003 ('*Brđanin* Rule 98 *bis* Trial Decision'), para. 57 (holding that liability for genocide pursuant to the third category of JCE 'consists of the Accused's awareness of the risk that genocide would be committed by other members of the JCE', and that '[t]his is a different *mens rea* and falls short of the threshold needed to satisfy the specific intent required for a conviction for genocide under Article 4(3)(a)').

[96] *Prosecutor v. Brđanin*, Case No. IT-99-36-A, Decision on Interlocutory Appeal, 19 March 2004 ('*Brđanin* JCE Appeal Decision'), para. 12.

the Trial Chamber had improperly conflated the *mens rea* of genocide with the mental element required of the form of responsibility through which the accused was charged.[97] The Appeals Chamber affirmed that an accused may be convicted of any crime pursuant to the third category notwithstanding his lack of intent that such crime be committed, provided the prosecution establishes his 'awareness that the commission of th[e] agreed upon crime made it reasonably foreseeable to him that the crime charged would be committed by other members of the joint criminal enterprise'.[98] Where the crime charged is genocide, 'the Prosecution will be required to establish that it was reasonably foreseeable to the accused that an act specified in Article 4(2) [the ICTY Statute's genocide provision] would be committed and that it would be committed with genocidal intent'.[99] This holding could only be based on an implicit conclusion that customary international law permitted the imposition of JCE liability for genocide at the time of the events alleged in Brđanin's indictment.[100]

Nevertheless, and in spite of the *Tadić* Appeals Chamber's comment that 'the commission of one of the crimes envisaged in Articles 2, 3, 4 or 5 of the Statute might ... occur through participation in the realisation of a common design or purpose',[101] shortly after *Brđanin*, André Rwamakuba, the former Rwandan Minister of Education, challenged the jurisdiction of the ICTR to try him for genocide pursuant to JCE. When the Trial Chamber dismissed his motion, Rwamakuba filed an interlocutory appeal, arguing that customary international law did not recognise JCE liability for genocide at the time of the events alleged in his indictment.[102] In an October 2004 decision, the Appeals Chamber, after determining that *Brđanin* had not addressed the precise point raised by Rwamakuba,[103] asserted that it would follow the lead of previous ICTY judgements – including *Furundžija* and *Tadić* – in relying on judgements from international proceedings following the Second World War 'as indicative of principles of customary international law at that time'.[104] On the basis of one Control Council Law No. 10 case purportedly convicting the accused of crimes against humanity for their participation in a common plan to commit genocidal acts, along with certain statements in the *travaux préparatoires* of the 1948 Genocide Convention, the Appeals Chamber concluded that 'customary

---

[97] *Ibid.*, para. 4.   [98] *Ibid.*, para. 5.   [99] *Ibid.*, para. 6.

[100] See *Milutinović et al.* JCE Appeal Decision, *supra* note 4, para. 21 (holding that, in order to come within the ICTY's jurisdiction, any form of responsibility must, *inter alia*, 'be provided for in the Statute, explicitly or implicitly' and 'have existed under customary international law at the relevant time').

[101] *Tadić* Appeal Judgement, *supra* note 3, para. 188.

[102] *Rwamakuba* JCE Appeal Decision, *supra* note 70, para. 3.

[103] *Rwamakuba* JCE Appeal Decision, *supra* note 70, para. 9 (holding that 'the reasoning in *Brđanin* does not indicate that the Appeals Chamber dealt with the problem whether international customary law [*sic*] supports the application of joint criminal enterprise to the crime of genocide').

[104] *Ibid.*, para. 14. See also *ibid.*, para. 14 n. 29.

international law criminalised intentional participation in a common plan to commit genocide prior to 1992'.[105] The combined effect of *Brđanin* and *Rwamakuba* has been to establish, in no uncertain terms, that in the opinion of the Appeals Chambers, JCE existed in customary international law at the time of the events in the former Yugoslavia and Rwanda, and responsibility for any of the three categories may extend to any crime in the Statute of either *ad hoc* Tribunal.

2.2 Limited application of JCE in the ICTR

Although JCE has been recognised in the appellate jurisprudence of the *ad hoc* Tribunals since *Tadić* in 1999, the Prosecutor of the ICTR has been slow to incorporate clear charges of JCE participation into the indictments of accused before that Tribunal.[106] As a consequence, relatively few ICTR chambers have even pronounced on the doctrine's applicability.

In its December 2004 *Ntakirutimana and Ntakirutimana* Judgement, the Appeals Chamber addressed at some length the possibility of convicting an accused pursuant to JCE in the ICTR.[107] The Chamber noted that, 'while joint criminal enterprise liability is firmly established in the jurisprudence of the ICTY[,] this is only the second ICTR case in which the Appeals Chamber has been called upon to address this issue'.[108] The Chamber cited the October 2004 *Rwamakuba* decision, discussed in the previous section of this chapter,[109] as

---

[105] *Ibid.*, paras. 14, 16, 19–22, 31–32 (quotation at para. 14) (invoking the judgement in *United States* v. *Altstoetter, Von Ammon, Barnickel, Cuhorst, Engert, Joel, Klemm, Lautz, Mettgenbert, Nebelung, Oeschey, Petersen, Rothaug, Rothenberger, Schlegelberger and Westphal, 3 Trials of War Criminals before the Nuernberg Military Tribunals under Control Council Law No. 10* (1953) ('*Justice* case'), pp. 1093, 1143).

[106] For example, the accused Rwamakuba was only charged with JCE liability in an amended indictment in 2004. See *Prosecutor* v. *Karemera, Ngirumpatse, Nzirorera and Rwamakuba*, Case No. ICTR-98-44-I, Amended Indictment, 18 February 2004, paras. 27–28, 35–36, 38, 47, 54, 66. It is interesting to note that the separate indictment filed against Rwamakuba after the Appeal Chamber's decision does not include JCE as a basis for liability. See *Prosecutor* v. *Rwamakuba*, Case No. ICTR-98-44C-I, Indictment, 23 February 2005; *Prosecutor* v. *Rwamakuba*, Case No. ICTR-98-44C-T, Decision on Severance of André Rwamakuba and Amendments of the Indictment, 7 December 2004, para. 6 (noting the prosecution's submissions, including the assertion that '[t]he proposed amended version of the Indictment against Rwamakuba would be more narrow and concise, reducing also the proof at trial. *Any reference to joint criminal enterprise as a form of commission would be deleted* as well as four charges against Rwamakuba.') (emphasis added). The Trial Chamber in its judgement subsequently affirmed the absence of JCE charges against Rwamakuba. See *Prosecutor* v. *Rwamakuba*, Case No. ICTR-98-44C-T, Judgement, 20 September 2006, paras. 18–28.

[107] *Ntakirutimana and Ntakirutimana* Appeal Judgement, *supra* note 46, paras. 461–484.

[108] *Ibid.*, para. 468 (footnote removed). Article 6(1) of the ICTR Statute and Article 7(1) of the ICTY Statute – setting forth the forms of responsibility of planning, ordering, instigating, committing, and aiding and abetting – are virtually identical. Compare ICTR Statute, *supra* note 94, Art. 6(1) with ICTY Statute, *supra* note 2, Art. 7(1).

[109] See *supra* text accompanying notes 102–105.

the first case.[110] While *Rwamakuba* had established that JCE liability for genocide existed in customary international law prior to 1992,[111] it had not opined directly on whether the ICTR Statute was broad enough to encompass JCE as a form of responsibility. The *Ntakirutimana and Ntakirutimana* Chamber examined the elements of JCE in terms almost completely identical to those set forth in the *Vasiljević* Appeal Judgement of February 2004,[112] and concluded as follows:

Given the fact that both the ICTY and the ICTR have mirror articles identifying the modes of liability by which an individual can incur criminal responsibility, the Appeals Chamber is satisfied that the jurisprudence of the ICTY should be applied to the interpretation of Article 6(1) of the ICTR Statute.[113]

The *Ntakirutimana and Ntakirutimana* Appeals Chamber's statement that it had dealt with the applicability of JCE to ICTR cases for the first time only in October 2004 is curious, as nowhere in this discussion did the Chamber acknowledge its treatment of JCE in the June 2001 *Kayishema and Ruzindana* Appeal Judgement. There, the Appeals Chamber rejected the claim of the appellant Obed Ruzindana that the Trial Chamber had erred in convicting him of genocide pursuant to the common-purpose doctrine.[114] In its exposition of the general principles of individual criminal responsibility, the Trial Chamber had quoted a passage of the *Čelebići* Trial Judgement stating that where 'a plan exists, or where there otherwise is evidence that members of a group are acting with a common criminal purpose, all those who knowingly participate in, and directly and substantially contribute to, the realisation of this purpose may be held criminally responsible'.[115] At a later point in the judgement, the *Kayishema and Ruzindana* Trial Chamber determined that 'the perpetrators of the culpable acts that occurred within Kibuye *Prefecture* ... were acting with a common intent and purpose ... to destroy the Tutsi ethnic group within Kibuye', and that '[b]oth Kayishema and Ruzindana played pivotal roles in carrying out this common plan'.[116]

Notwithstanding these statements, there appears to be no explicit analysis of Ruzindana's liability pursuant to the common-purpose doctrine in the

---

[110] *Ntakirutimana and Ntakirutimana* Appeal Judgement, *supra* note 46, para. 468.
[111] *Rwamakuba* JCE Appeal Decision, *supra* note 70, para. 31.
[112] Compare *Ntakirutimana and Ntakirutimana* Appeal Judgement, *supra* note 46, paras. 461–467 with *Vasiljević* Appeal Judgement, *supra* note 46, paras. 94–101.
[113] *Ntakirutimana and Ntakirutimana* Appeal Judgement, *supra* note 46, para. 468.
[114] *Prosecutor* v. *Kayishema and Ruzindana*, Case No. ICTR-95-1-A, Judgement (Reasons), 1 June 2001 ('*Kayishema and Ruzindana* Appeal Judgement'), para. 194.
[115] *Kayishema and Ruzindana* Trial Judgement, *supra* note 8, para. 203 (quoting *Čelebići* Trial Judgement, *supra* note 8, para. 328). Beyond making this statement, *Čelebići* did not opine on the elements or applicability of the common-purpose doctrine. See also *supra* note 8 and accompanying text.
[116] *Ibid.*, para. 545.

Kayishema and Ruzindana Trial Judgement.[117] Indeed, as acknowledged by the Appeals Chamber,[118] the Trial Chamber did not specify precisely under which form of responsibility Ruzindana incurred liability for his actions, which included heading a convoy of assailants, transporting attackers, distributing weapons, personally mutilating and murdering certain individuals, and offering to reward attackers with cash and beer.[119] Instead, the Trial Chamber simply concluded that, through his actions, Ruzindana had 'instigated, ordered, committed and otherwise aided and abetted in the preparation and execution of the massacre that resulted in thousands of murders with the intent to destroy the Tutsi ethnic group'.[120] The Appeals Chamber concluded, however, that the Trial Chamber had found that Ruzindana participated in a JCE to destroy the Tutsi ethnic group in Kibuye through these activities, and had convicted him of genocide at least in part on that basis.[121] In upholding Ruzindana's conviction,[122] the Appeals Chamber quoted the *Tadić* Appeal Judgement's enumeration of the physical elements of JCE;[123] it affirmed that, for JCE liability to ensue, 'there is no requirement that the plan or purpose must be previously arranged or formulated'.[124]

In spite of the apparent precedent set by the *Kayishema and Ruzindana* Trial Chamber in convicting at least one of the two accused before it pursuant to JCE, few ICTR chambers have followed suit. Several chambers have disregarded or dismissed JCE as a possible form of responsibility because the prosecution had not pleaded JCE clearly enough to put the accused adequately on notice of the charges against him, and these dismissals have been uniformly upheld by the Appeals Chamber. The first of these was the *Ntakirutimana and Ntakirutimana* Trial Chamber, which made no mention of JCE at all in its February 2003 judgement.[125] On appeal, the prosecution claimed the Trial Chamber had erred in failing to consider the accused's JCE liability, which the prosecution had not argued at trial but had pleaded in certain paragraphs of

---

[117] See *ibid.*, paras. 570–571.   [118] *Kayishema and Ruzindana* Appeal Judgement, *supra* note 114, para. 191.
[119] *Kayishema and Ruzindana* Trial Judgement, *supra* note 8, paras. 543–544, 570–571.
[120] *Ibid.*, para. 571.
[121] *Kayishema and Ruzindana* Appeal Judgement, *supra* note 114, para. 193 ('[T]he Trial Chamber . . . found that at the sites where he was found to have participated, Ruzindana had not only been involved in the commission of crimes but his actions also assisted in and contributed to the execution of the joint criminal enterprise in various ways.'). Nowhere in its judgement did the Trial Chamber use the term 'joint criminal enterprise'.
[122] *Ibid.*, para. 194.
[123] *Tadić* Appeal Judgement, *supra* note 3, para. 227. It is interesting to note that the *Kayishema and Ruzindana* Trial Judgement was rendered on 21 May 1999, slightly less than two months prior to the *Tadić* Appeal Judgement.
[124] *Kayishema and Ruzindana* Appeal Judgement, *supra* note 114, para. 193. See also *infra* text accompanying notes 175–181 (discussing the elaboration of this proposition in the *ad hoc* jurisprudence).
[125] See *Prosecutor v. Ntakirutimana and Ntakirutimana*, Case Nos. ICTR-96-10 and ICTR-96-17-T, Judgement and Sentence, 21 February 2003 ('*Ntakirutimana and Ntakirutimana* Trial Judgement').

its pre-trial brief and closing trial brief.[126] The Appeals Chamber determined that the language used in the indictment, containing general allegations of responsibility pursuant to Article 6(1) of the ICTR Statute and not specifically charging participation in a JCE or a common purpose, did not obviously allege JCE liability.[127] It concluded that the prosecution had not put the accused or the Trial Chamber on adequate notice, and dismissed the ground of appeal.[128]

In respect of an allegation in the indictment that the accused, 'acting in concert with others, participated in the preparation, planning, or execution of a common scheme, strategy or plan to exterminate the Tutsi',[129] the Trial Chamber in *Gacumbitsi* remarked that the prosecution 'seem[ed] to allege that the Accused participated in a joint criminal enterprise'.[130] The Chamber concluded, however, that it could not make findings on whether the accused's JCE liability had been established 'because it was not pleaded clearly enough to allow the Accused to defend himself adequately'.[131] A majority of the Appeals Chamber upheld this refusal to consider JCE, affirming that the indictment had indeed failed to plead JCE in a sufficiently clear manner, and the prosecution had failed to cure this defect in subsequent written and oral submissions at trial.[132] The Trial Chamber in *Ntagerura* held in a similar vein that, where the prosecution intends to rely on a theory of JCE, the category and purpose of the JCE, the identity of the participants, and the accused's role in the enterprise must be pleaded unambiguously in the indictment; as the prosecution had failed to comply with these requirements in the case at hand, the Chamber held that it would 'not consider the Prosecution's arguments, which were advanced for the first time during the presentation of closing arguments, to hold the accused criminally responsible based on th[e] theory'

---

[126] See *Ntakirutimana and Ntakirutimana* Appeal Judgement, *supra* note 46, paras. 448, 479.

[127] *Ibid.*, paras. 481–482.   [128] *Ibid.*, paras. 482, 484.

[129] *Prosecutor* v. *Gacumbitsi*, Case No. ICTR-2001-64-I, Indictment, 20 June 2001, para. 25.

[130] *Prosecutor* v. *Gacumbitsi*, Case No. ICTR-2001-64-T, Judgement, 14 June 2004 ('*Gacumbitsi* Trial Judgement'), para. 289.

[131] *Ibid.* But see *Prosecutor* v. *Gatete*, Case No. ICTR-00-61-I, Decision on the Prosecution's Request for Leave to File an Amended Indictment, 21 April 2005 ('*Gatete* Amendment Decision'), para. 5 (holding that the amendment of that indictment to include specific mention of JCE did not amount to the inclusion of a new charge, because the initial indictment had included language identical to that quoted above in *Gacumbitsi*, which appears in many ICTR indictments).

[132] *Gacumbitsi* Appeal Judgement, *supra* note 46, paras. 164–179. Judges Shahabuddeen and Schomburg dissented from this holding. See *ibid.*, Separate Opinion of Judge Shahabuddeen, paras. 38–39 (opining that Gacumbitsi could have been convicted pursuant to JCE); *ibid.*, Separate Opinion of Judge Schomburg on the Criminal Responsibility of the Appellant for Committing Genocide, para. 10. See also *infra* text accompanying notes 662–702 (discussing these separate opinions in the context of the purported form of responsibility known as 'indirect co-perpetration').

of JCE.[133] Again, the Appeals Chamber upheld the Trial Chamber's refusal to consider JCE on these grounds.[134]

The Trial Judgement in *Ntakirutimana and Ntakirutimana* was rendered in 2003, and those in *Ntagerura* and *Gacumbitsi* were rendered in 2004. In more recent indictments, the ICTR Prosecutor has pleaded JCE explicitly and has described the alleged common purpose in great detail.[135] For example, in an amended indictment dated 10 May 2004, the Prosecutor charged Aloys Simba, a retired Lieutenant Colonel of the Rwandan Armed Forces, with genocide and extermination as a crime against humanity 'by virtue of his affirmative acts in planning, instigating, ordering, committing or otherwise aiding and abetting in the planning, preparation or execution of the crime charged, in concert with others as part of a joint criminal enterprise'.[136] In its judgement the *Simba* Trial Chamber held that, unlike in *Ntagerura*, *Gacumbitsi* and *Ntakirutimana and Ntakirutimana*, the prosecution had given sufficient notice of the purpose and nature of the alleged JCE and the accused's role in it.[137] The Chamber then made findings as to whether the prosecution had established the requisite physical and mental elements,[138] ultimately finding that Simba incurred JCE liability – presumably pursuant to the first category – for genocide and extermination.[139] It declined to make any findings whatsoever in relation to any of the other Article 6(1) forms of responsibility charged in the indictment.[140]

Similarly, in an amended indictment of 7 March 2005, the Prosecutor charged Jean Mpambara, a Rwandan *bourgmestre*, with genocide, complicity in genocide, and extermination as a crime against humanity on the basis of his wilful and knowing participation in a JCE 'whose object, purpose and foreseeable outcome was the destruction of the Tutsi racial or ethnic group throughout Rwanda'.[141] After discussing the elements of JCE in some detail,[142] the

[133] *Prosecutor v. Ntagerura, Bagambiki and Imanishimwe*, Case No. ICTR-99-46-T, Judgement and Sentence, 25 February 2004 ('*Ntagerura et al.* Trial Judgement'), para. 34.
[134] *Prosecutor v. Ntagerura, Bagambiki and Imanishimwe*, Case No. ICTR-99-46-A, Judgement, 7 July 2006, paras. 33–45, 362.
[135] See, e.g., *Prosecutor v. Karemera, Ngirumpatse and Nzirorera*, Case No. ICTR-98-44-I, Amended Indictment, 23 February 2005 ('*Karemera et al.* Amended Indictment'), paras. 4–8, 14–16, 30, 65–66, 69, 72, 76. *Prosecutor v. Mpambara*, Case No. ICTR-01-65-I, Amended Indictment, 7 March 2005 ('*Mpambara* Amended Indictment'), paras. 6–7, 21. See also *infra* note 801 and sources cited therein.
[136] *Prosecutor v. Simba*, Case No. ICTR-2001-76-I, Amended Indictment, 10 May 2004 ('*Simba* Amended Indictment'), pp. 2, 11. See also *ibid.*, para. 14 (listing the other participants in the alleged JCE to commit genocide). The 10 May 2004 Amended Indictment also charged Simba with complicity in genocide and murder as a crime against humanity, but the prosecution withdrew these charges before the end of trial. *Prosecutor v. Simba*, Case No. ICTR-01-76-T, Judgement and Sentence, 13 December 2005 ('*Simba* Trial Judgement'), para. 4.
[137] *Ibid.*, para. 396.   [138] *Ibid.*, paras. 397–419.   [139] *Ibid.*, paras. 419, 426, 427.
[140] Although the 10 May 2004 Amended Indictment also charged Simba with superior responsibility pursuant to Article 6(3) of the ICTR Statute, the Prosecutor withdrew the Article 6(3) charges before the end of trial. *Ibid.*, para. 4.
[141] *Mpambara* Amended Indictment, *supra* note 135, para. 6.
[142] *Mpambara* Trial Judgement, *supra* note 46, paras. 13–15, 24.

Mpambara Trial Chamber found that, as in *Simba*, the prosecution had given sufficient notice that Mpambara was charged with participation in a JCE.[143] The Chamber proceeded to acquit the accused on all counts,[144] however, finding in each instance that the evidence had failed to establish beyond a reasonable doubt all the requisite elements of any of the crimes and all of the forms of responsibility charged in respect of each alleged incident.[145]

The section that follows details the case law setting forth the elements of JCE as a form of responsibility applicable in the *ad hoc* Tribunals. While almost all of the relevant jurisprudence comes from cases before the ICTY, the Trial Judgements in *Simba* and *Mpambara*, along with the Prosecutor's recent practice of expressly alleging JCE liability in new or amended indictments,[146] suggest that future ICTR judgements will constitute more significant sources for the ascertainment of the elements of JCE.

2.3 Elements of Joint Criminal Enterprise

Paradoxically, the most complex and analytically challenging form of responsibility recognised in the jurisprudence of the *ad hoc* Tribunals is the only one not explicitly listed in the Tribunals' respective Statutes. Nevertheless, chambers of both Tribunals have repeatedly held that JCE is implicitly encompassed within the form of responsibility labelled 'commission' in Article 7/6(1) of the *ad hoc* Statutes.[147] As discussed in the previous section, criminal liability through participation in a JCE can arise in relation to any of the crimes within the Tribunal's jurisdiction,[148] including to crimes requiring specific intent, such as genocide and persecution as a crime against humanity.[149]

---

[143] *Ibid.*, para. 40.   [144] *Ibid.*, para. 175.

[145] See *ibid.*, paras. 76, 105, 112–113, 155, 162–164; *ibid.*, para. 163 (finding that 'the evidence of the Accused's involvement in a joint criminal enterprise or other criminal conduct is weak, disconnected, and uncorroborated').

[146] See *infra* note 801 (listing ICTR indictments alleging JCE).

[147] See *Kvočka et al.* Appeal Judgement, *supra* note 46, para. 79; *Ntakirutimana and Ntakirutimana* Appeal Judgement, *supra* note 46, para. 468; *Vasiljević* Appeal Judgement, *supra* note 46, para. 95; *Krnojelac* Appeal Judgement, *supra* note 46, para. 73; *Milutinović et al.* JCE Appeal Decision, *supra* note 4, para. 20 ('The Appeals Chamber . . . regards joint criminal enterprise as a form of "commission" pursuant to Article 7(1) of the Statute.'); *Tadić* Appeal Judgement, *supra* note 3, para. 188; *Simba* Trial Judgement, *supra* note 136, para. 385; *Blagojević and Jokić* Trial Judgement, *supra* note 46, para. 696; *Brđanin* Trial Judgement, *supra* note 46, para. 258; *Krstić* Trial Judgement, *supra* note 46, para. 601. See also *supra* note 46 and sources cited therein.

[148] *Tadić* Appeal Judgement, *supra* note 3, para. 188 ('[T]he commission of one of the crimes envisaged in Articles 2, 3, 4 or 5 of the Statute might . . . occur through participation in the realisation of a common design or purpose').

[149] *Rwamakuba* JCE Appeal Decision, *supra* note 70, paras. 14, 32 (genocide); *Brđanin* JCE Appeal Decision, *supra* note 96, para. 5; *Krnojelac* Appeal Judgement, *supra* note 46, paras. 111–112 (upholding the Trial Chamber's conviction of Krnojelac for persecution pursuant to the second category of JCE).

The chambers have uniformly adhered to the three-category JCE frame-work established by the July 1999 *Tadić* Appeal Judgement.[150] In the first or 'basic' category, all participants, acting pursuant to a common purpose, possess the same intent to commit an offence, and one or more of them actually perpetrates the offence.[151] The second category, 'systemic' JCE, is charac-terised by the existence of an organised criminal system, as in the case of detention camps in which prisoners are mistreated pursuant to a common purpose.[152] The third category, 'extended' JCE, involves cases in which the co-participants have a common purpose to commit an offence and one or more of them engages in criminal conduct which, while outside the common purpose, is nonetheless a natural and foreseeable – or, by the standard of one Appeal Judgement, a 'possible'[153] – consequence of the common purpose.[154]

2.3.1 Physical elements

Trial and Appeals Chambers of both *ad hoc* Tribunals have followed *Tadić's* lead in articulating three broad physical elements common to all categories of JCE:

(i) a plurality of persons

(ii) the existence of a common plan, design, or purpose which amounts to or involves the commission of a crime provided for in the Statute

(iii) the participation of the accused in the common plan, design, or purpose involving the perpetration of one of the crimes provided for in the Statute.[155]

---

[150] See generally *Tadić* Appeal Judgement, *supra* note 3, paras. 195–226 (establishing the three-category framework). See also *supra*, text accompanying notes 43–56 (discussing such establishment).

[151] *Gacumbitsi* Appeal Judgement, *supra* note 46, para. 158; *Kvočka et al.* Appeal Judgement, *supra* note 46, para. 82; *Ntakirutimana and Ntakirutimana* Appeal Judgement, *supra* note 46, para. 463; *Tadić* Appeal Judgement, *supra* note 3, paras. 197, 220; *Krajišnik* Trial Judgement, *supra* note 65, para. 879; *Vasiljević* Trial Judgement, *supra* note 53, para. 97.

[152] *Kvočka et al.* Appeal Judgement, *supra* note 46, para. 82; *Ntakirutimana and Ntakirutimana* Appeal Judgement, *supra* note 46, para. 464; *Krnojelac* Appeal Judgement, *supra* note 46, para. 89; *Tadić* Appeal Judgement, *supra* note 3, paras. 202–203, 220; *Krajišnik* Trial Judgement, *supra* note 65, para. 880.

[153] *Blaškić* Appeal Judgement, *supra* note 83, para. 33.

[154] *Gacumbitsi* Appeal Judgement, *supra* note 46, para. 158; *Stakić* Appeal Judgement, *supra* note 83, para. 65; *Kvočka et al.* Appeal Judgement, *supra* note 46, para. 83; *Krajišnik* Trial Judgement, *supra* note 65, para. 881; *Vasiljević* Appeal Judgement, *supra* note 46, para. 99.

[155] *Stakić* Appeal Judgement, *supra* note 83, para. 64; *Ntakirutimana and Ntakirutimana* Appeal Judgement, *supra* note 46, para. 466; *Vasiljević* Appeal Judgement, *supra* note 46, para. 100; *Tadić* Appeal Judgement, *supra* note 3, para. 227; *Krajišnik* Trial Judgement, *supra* note 65, para. 883; *Simba* Trial Judgement, *supra* note 136, para. 387; *Prosecutor v. Limaj, Bala and Musliu*, Case No. IT-03-66-T, Judgement, 30 November 2005 ('*Limaj et al.* Trial Judgement'), para. 511; *Blagojević and Jokić* Trial Judgement, *supra* note 46, para. 698; *Simić et al.* Trial Judgement, *supra* note 5, para. 156; *Prosecutor v. Stakić*, Case No. IT-97-24-T, Judgement, 29 October 2003 ('*Stakić* Trial Judgement'), paras. 423, 434; *Prosecutor v. Kvočka, Kos, Radić, Žigić and Prcać*, Case No. IT-98-30/1-T, Judgement, 2 November 2001 ('*Kvočka et al.* Trial Judgement'), para. 266; *Krstić* Trial Judgement, *supra* note 46, para. 611; *Kordić and Čerkez* Trial Judgement, *supra* note 65, para. 397; *Kupreškić et al.* Trial Judgement, *supra* note 72, para. 772.

Each of these elements has a variety of nuances which are addressed in the following subsections.

2.3.1.1 The JCE consisted of a plurality of persons: first physical element

Almost all ICTY judgements that have examined the physical elements of JCE, as well as the *Simba* Trial Judgement of the ICTR, have held that JCE liability cannot ensue absent a 'plurality of persons'.[156] The *Ntakirutimana and Ntakirutimana* Appeals Chamber formulated this element slightly differently: 'For joint criminal enterprise liability to arise an accused must act with a number of other persons.'[157] While *Ntakirutimana and Ntakirutimana*'s reference to 'a number of other persons' may give the impression that the requisite 'plurality' must consist of many people, several trial judgements have made it clear that two persons are sufficient to form a JCE; as stated by the *Kvočka* Trial Chamber, '[a] joint criminal enterprise can exist whenever two or more people participate in a common criminal endeavor'.[158] Notwithstanding the probability that many or most JCEs alleged in cases before the *ad hoc* Tribunals have some sort of political or military composition,[159] the plurality of persons that makes up the JCE need not be organised into any sort of military, political or administrative structure.[160]

---

[156] See *Stakić* Appeal Judgement, *supra* note 83, para. 64; *Kvočka et al.* Appeal Judgement, *supra* note 46, para. 81; *Vasiljević* Appeal Judgement, *supra* note 46, para. 100; *Krnojelac* Appeal Judgement, *supra* note 46, para. 31; *Kayishema and Ruzindana* Appeal Judgement, *supra* note 114, para. 193; *Tadić* Appeal Judgement, *supra* note 3, para. 227; *Krajišnik* Trial Judgement, *supra* note 65, para. 154; *Simba* Trial Judgement, *supra* note 136, para. 387; *Blagojević and Jokić* Trial Judgement, *supra* note 46, para. 698; see also *ibid.*, paras. 708–709 (finding that the requisite plurality of persons existed in respect of the accused Blagojević, where Blagojević participated in a JCE along with numerous officers of the Bosnian Serb army and the Serbian Interior Ministry); *Brđanin* Trial Judgement, *supra* note 46, para. 260; *Simić et al.* Trial Judgement, *supra* note 5, para. 156; *Kvočka et al.* Trial Judgement, *supra* note 155, para. 266; *Krstić* Trial Judgement, *supra* note 46, para. 611; *Kordić and Čerkez* Trial Judgement, *supra* note 65, para. 397.

[157] *Ntakirutimana and Ntakirutimana* Appeal Judgement, *supra* note 46, para. 466.

[158] *Kvočka et al.* Trial Judgement, *supra* note 155, para. 307. Accord *Mpambara* Trial Judgement, *supra* note 46, para. 13 ('A joint criminal enterprise arises when two or more persons join in a common and shared purpose to commit a crime under the Statute.'); *Brđanin* Trial Judgement, *supra* note 46, para. 262 ('A common plan amounting to or involving an understanding or an agreement between two or more persons that they will commit a crime must be proved.').

[159] See, e.g., *Prosecutor v. Milošević, Milutinović, Šainović, Ojdanić and Stojiljković*, Case No. Case No. IT-99-37-PT, Motion for Leave to File a Second Amended Indictment, Attachment A, 16 October 2001 ('*Milošević* Kosovo Second Amended Indictment'), para. 17 (alleging a JCE made up of political and military leaders Slobodan Milošević, Milan Milutinović, Nikola Šainović, Dragoljub Ojdanić, Vlajko Stojiljković, and 'others known and unknown'); *Simba* Indictment, *supra* note 136, para. 14 (alleging that Simba, a former military officer and Minister of Defence, 'acted in concert' with several named political and military leaders, including former *gendarmerie* captain Faustin Sebuhura, former *préfet* Laurent Bucyiaruta, and former *bourgmestre* Charles Munyaneza).

[160] *Stakić* Appeal Judgement, *supra* note 83, para. 64; *Ntakirutimana and Ntakirutimana* Appeal Judgement, *supra* note 46, para. 466; *Vasiljević* Appeal Judgement, *supra* note 46, para. 100; *Krnojelac* Appeal Judgement, *supra* note 46, para. 31; *Tadić* Appeal Judgement, *supra* note 3, para. 227; *Krajišnik* Trial Judgement, *supra* note 65, para. 883; *Mpambara* Trial Judgement, *supra* note 46, para. 13; *Simba* Trial Judgement, *supra* note 136, para. 387; *Brđanin* Trial Judgement, *supra* note 46, para. 261; *Simić et al.* Trial Judgement, *supra* note 5, para. 156.

Although no judgement, in its discussion of this physical element, expressly requires the prosecution to identify the individuals that make up the plurality, several form-of-indictment decisions and the *Simić*, *Brđanin* and *Simba* Trial Judgements indicate that the prosecution must have pleaded the identities of such persons in the indictment with sufficient particularity to have put the accused on notice of the composition of the alleged JCE. A chamber will likely refuse to consider allegations of an enterprise between an accused and individuals labelled in the indictment as 'other known and unknown participants' or 'others', and will only evaluate JCE liability as between the accused and identified persons or, for those whose identities were not known at the time the indictment was issued, persons for whom the category to which they belonged was specified in the indictment.[161] Accordingly, the *Brđanin* Trial Chamber in its Judgement declined to consider JCE liability as between the accused and several persons that the prosecution at trial had argued made up the 'others' alleged in the indictment – including members of the Serb police, Serb armed civilians, and unidentified individuals – because the indictment failed to plead the identities of such persons or the group to which they belonged.[162] Nevertheless, if the prosecution demonstrates that, despite such a defect in the indictment, the defendant's ability to prepare his defence was not materially impaired – because, for example, the prosecution's pre-trial brief adequately identified the members of the JCE – a chamber would probably still permit the conviction of an accused for his participation in a JCE with those persons.[163]

[161] *Simba* Trial Judgement, *supra* note 136, para. 389 ('If the Prosecution intends to rely on the theory of joint criminal enterprise to hold an accused criminally responsible ... [it must] plead the purpose of the enterprise, the identity of the co-participants, and the nature of the accused's participation in the enterprise.'); *Brđanin* Trial Judgement, *supra* note 46, para. 346; *Simić et al.* Trial Judgement, *supra* note 5, para. 145; *Prosecutor v. Milutinović, Šainović, Ojdanić, Pavković, Lazarević, Đorđević and Lukić*, Case No. IT-05-87-PT, Decision on Nebojša Pavković's Preliminary Motion on Form of Indictment, 22 July 2005, p. 2; *Prosecutor v. Pavkovic, Lazarević, Đorđević and Lukić*, Case No. IT-03-70-PT, Decision on Vladimir Lazarević's Preliminary Motion on Form of Indictment, 8 July 2005, para. 26; *Prosecutor v. Brđanin and Talić*, Case No. IT-99-36-PT, Decision on Objections by Momir Talić to the Form of the Amended Indictment, 20 February 2001, para. 21; *Prosecutor v. Krnojelac*, Case No. IT-97-25, Decision on Form of Second Amended Indictment, 11 May 2000, para. 16.
[162] *Brđanin* Trial Judgement, *supra* note 46, para. 346. The Trial Chamber did, however, evaluate the possibility of a JCE between the Accused and members of the army and Serb paramilitary forces, persons whose individual identities were unknown but whose group had been pleaded in the indictment. *Ibid.*, paras. 347–356.
[163] See *Kvočka et al.* Appeal Judgement, *supra* note 46, paras. 42–43; *Simić et al.* Trial Judgement, *supra* note 5, para. 146. See also *Krnojelac* Appeal Judgement, *supra* note 46, para. 132 (holding that, in some cases, a defective indictment might be cured if the prosecution provides the accused with timely, clear, and consistent information detailing the factual basis underpinning the charges against him).

2.3.1.2 *Common plan, design, or purpose: second physical element*

A common plan, design, or purpose existed which amounted to or involved the commission of a crime provided for in the Statute

The *Tadić* Appeal Judgement set out the second physical element of JCE as follows: the prosecution must prove '[t]he existence of a *common plan, design or purpose* which amounts to or involves the commission of a crime provided for in the Statute'.[164] Subsequent judgements have restated this requirement using one or more of these three seemingly interchangeable terms.[165]

The *Blagojević and Jokić, Simić, Stakić, Vasiljević* and *Krnojelac* Trial Judgements specified that the common plan, design, or purpose must take the form of '[a]n arrangement or understanding amounting to an agreement between two or more persons that a particular crime will be committed'.[166] The *Brđanin* Trial Judgement conveyed this requirement in a somewhat different manner, holding that a 'common plan amounting to or involving an understanding or an agreement between two or more persons that they will commit a crime must be proved'.[167] Perhaps a clearer way to express this idea while remaining faithful to the jurisprudence would be the following: the prosecution must prove that the accused and at least one other person came to an express or implied agreement that a crime would be committed.[168]

Importantly, however, appellate jurisprudence has clarified that this particular aspect of the agreement requirement for JCE applies only to the first and third categories of JCE. The *Krnojelac* and *Kvočka* Appeal Judgements, which

---

[164] *Tadić* Appeal Judgement, *supra* note 3, para. 227 (emphasis added). Accord *Stakić* Appeal Judgement, *supra* note 83, para. 64 ('[T]he existence of a common plan which amounts to or involves the commission of a crime provided for in the Statute is required.'); *Kvočka et al.* Appeal Judgement, *supra* note 46, para. 81; *Kayishema and Ruzindana* Appeal Judgement, *supra* note 114, para. 193.

[165] See, e.g., *Vasiljević* Appeal Judgement, *supra* note 46, para. 100 ('common purpose'); *Blagojević and Jokić* Trial Judgement, *supra* note 46, para. 698 ('common plan, design or purpose'); *Brđanin* Trial Judgement, *supra* note 46, para. 260 ('common plan, design or purpose'); *Simić et al.* Trial Judgement, *supra* note 5, para. 156 ('common plan, design or purpose'); *Krstić* Trial Judgement, *supra* note 46, para. 611 ('common plan').

[166] *Simić et al.* Trial Judgement, *supra* note 5, para. 158. Accord *Blagojević and Jokić* Trial Judgement, *supra* note 46, para. 699; *Stakić* Trial Judgement, *supra* note 155, para. 435; *Vasiljević* Trial Judgement, *supra* note 53, para. 66; *Prosecutor v. Krnojelac*, Case No. IT-97-25-T, Judgement, 15 March 2002 ('*Krnojelac* Trial Judgement'), para. 80.

[167] *Brđanin* Trial Judgement, *supra* note 46, para. 262. The *Brđanin* Chamber went on later in the judgement to emphasise that the relevant agreement or understanding for purposes of analysing JCE liability is that which is alleged to have existed between the accused and the physical perpetrator of the offence that is the object of the JCE. *Ibid.*, para. 352. This proposition and its important implications are discussed in detail in a later section of this chapter. See *infra* text accompanying notes 455–591.

[168] Cf. *Krajišnik* Trial Judgement, *supra* note 65, para. 883 (holding that this physical element of JCE 'does not presume preparatory planning or explicit agreement among JCE participants'); *Prosecutor v. Popović, Beara, Nikolić, Borovčanin, Tolimir, Miletić, Gvero, Pandurević and Trbić*, Case No. IT-05-88-PT, Decision on Motions Challenging the Indictment pursuant to Rule 72 of the Rules, 31 May 2006 ('*Popović et al.* Pre-Trial Indictment Decision'), para. 20 (holding that 'JCE, at least in the first and third categories, requires some form of agreement, *express or implied*, among the participants in the JCE') (emphasis added).

elaborated substantially on *Tadić*'s definition of the second category of JCE, established that the second category does not require a formal or informal agreement among the participants to commit a crime.[169] Instead, the system of ill-treatment is itself the common plan, design, or purpose. Accordingly the *Kvočka* Trial Chamber found, and the Appeals Chamber upheld, that the Omarska concentration camp was a joint criminal enterprise whose purpose was to persecute and subjugate non-Serb detainees.[170] In this vein the *Krnojelac* Appeals Chamber held that, as long as the prosecution proves that the accused was 'involved' in the system of ill-treatment and fulfilled the requisite mental elements for the second category,[171] it is 'less important to prove' that he had an agreement or understanding with the other participants.[172] The Appeals Chamber accordingly determined that the Trial Chamber had erred in requiring proof of an agreement between Krnojelac and the guards and soldiers at his prison in order to hold him liable for their crimes by virtue of his participation in a JCE to persecute non-Serb detainees.[173] In the words of the Appeals Chamber,

the Trial Chamber should have examined whether or not Krnojelac knew of the system and agreed to it, without it being necessary to establish that he had entered into an agreement with the guards and soldiers – the principal perpetrators of the crimes committed under the system – to commit those crimes.[174]

Referring to all three categories, *Tadić* held that '[t]here is no necessity for this plan, design or purpose to have been previously arranged or formulated. The common plan or purpose may materialise extemporaneously and be inferred from the fact that a plurality of persons acts in unison to put into effect a joint criminal enterprise.'[175] This passage, which several judgements have quoted or otherwise endorsed,[176] sets forth two distinct propositions. First, the JCE may 'materialise extemporaneously', which ostensibly means

---

[169] *Kvočka et al.* Appeal Judgement, *supra* note 46, paras. 118–119; *Krnojelac* Appeal Judgement, *supra* note 46, para. 97.

[170] *Kvočka et al.* Trial Judgement, *supra* note 155, para. 320, affirmed by *Kvočka et al.* Appeal Judgement, *supra* note 46, para. 183.

[171] See *infra*, text accompanying notes 294–372, for a detailed discussion of the mental elements of the second category of JCE.

[172] *Krnojelac* Appeal Judgement, *supra* note 46, para. 96. Accord *Kvočka et al.* Appeal Judgement, *supra* note 46, para. 209; *Simić et al.* Trial Judgement, *supra* note 5, para. 158; *Brđanin* Trial Judgement, *supra* note 46, p. 112 n. 691 (holding that formal agreement between the participants in the second category of JCE is not required 'as long as their involvement in a system of ill treatment has been established').

[173] *Krnojelac* Appeal Judgement, *supra* note 46, para. 97. Accord *Krnojelac* Trial Judgement, *supra* note 166, paras. 170, 487; *Kvočka et al.* Appeal Judgement, *supra* note 46, para. 209 (finding that the Trial Chamber 'did not err in law by not requiring evidence of a formal agreement between the co-perpetrators in order to advance the joint criminal enterprise').

[174] *Krnojelac* Appeal Judgement, *supra* note 46, para. 97.

[175] *Tadić* Appeal Judgement, *supra* note 3, para. 227.

[176] See *Stakić* Appeal Judgement, *supra* note 83, para. 64; *Kvočka et al.* Appeal Judgement, *supra* note 46, para. 116; *Ntakirutimana and Ntakirutimana* Appeal Judgement, *supra* note 46, para. 466; *Vasiljević* Appeal Judgement, *supra* note 46, paras. 100, 109; *Kayishema and Ruzindana* Appeal Judgement, *supra*

that the participants may formulate the enterprise at the scene of the crime, either just before one or more of them begins to physically perform the conduct envisioned, or perhaps even after such performance has begun. The language of the *Krnojelac* Trial Judgement supports the notion that JCE liability may ensue where the JCE anticipates the continued commission of a crime already in progress: the agreement to carry out the common plan 'need not have been reached at any time before the crime is committed'.[177]

Second, a chamber may infer the existence of a 'common plan or purpose . . . from the fact that a plurality of persons acts in unison to put into effect a joint criminal enterprise'.[178] The frequent repetition in the jurisprudence of this tautological phrase, first set forth in paragraph 227 of *Tadić*, is unfortunate.[179] Perhaps a clearer formulation would be that, in determining whether two or more persons acted pursuant to a JCE in the realisation of a particular offence, a chamber may look to the way in which the crime was committed and the circumstances surrounding such commission. This proposed formulation finds support in the simpler terminology of the *Vasiljević*, *Ntakirutimana and Ntakirutimana* and *Stakić* Appeal Judgements, which held that the common plan or purpose 'may . . . be inferred *from the facts*'.[180] It is also consistent with the *Blagojević and Jokić* and *Krnojelac* Trial Judgements, which restated the holding in paragraph 227 of *Tadić* as follows: 'The existence of an agreement or understanding for the common plan, design or purpose need not be express, but may be inferred *from all the circumstances*.'[181]

---

note 114, para. 193; *Furundžija* Appeal Judgement, *supra* note 35, para. 119; *Krajišnik* Trial Judgement, *supra* note 65, para. 883; *Mpambara* Trial Judgement, *supra* note 46, para. 13; *Simba* Trial Judgement, *supra* note 136, para. 387; *Blagojević and Jokić* Trial Judgement, *supra* note 46, para. 699; *Brđanin* Trial Judgement, *supra* note 46, para. 262; *Simić et al.* Trial Judgement, *supra* note 5, para. 158; *Krnojelac* Trial Judgement, *supra* note 166, para. 80; *Krstić* Trial Judgement, *supra* note 46, para. 611.

[177] *Krnojelac* Trial Judgement, *supra* note 166, para. 80. However, it could also be that the Trial Chamber mistakenly excluded the word 'particular' from this phrase: the agreement to carry out the plan 'need not have been reached at any [*particular*] time before the crime is committed'. Such a formulation would imply that, while the agreement need not be reached well in advance of the commission of the crime, it must nonetheless be reached – at the latest – in the moments before commencement of such commission.

[178] *Tadić* Appeal Judgement, *supra* note 3, para. 227.

[179] See, e.g., *Vasiljević* Appeal Judgement, *supra* note 46, para. 109 (quoting para. 227 of *Tadić*); *Furundžija* Appeal Judgement, *supra* note 35, para. 119 (quoting para. 227 of *Tadić*); *Blagojević and Jokić* Trial Judgement, *supra* note 46, para. 699 ('[T]he common plan or purpose may materialise extemporaneously and be inferred from the fact that a plurality of persons acts in unison to put into effect a joint criminal enterprise.'); *Brđanin* Trial Judgement, *supra* note 46, para. 262 ('[The common plan] need not have been previously arranged but may materialise extemporaneously and be inferred from the fact that a plurality of persons acts in unison to put the plan into effect.'); *Simić et al.* Trial Judgement, *supra* note 5, para. 158 ('[T]he plan may materialise extemporaneously and be inferred from the fact that a plurality of persons acts in unison to put into effect the plan[.]'); *Krstić* Trial Judgement, *supra* note 46, para. 611 (quoting para. 227 of *Tadić*).

[180] *Stakić* Appeal Judgement, *supra* note 83, para. 64. Accord *Ntakirutimana and Ntakirutimana* Appeal Judgement, *supra* note 46, para. 466; *Vasiljević* Appeal Judgement, *supra* note 46, para. 100; *Simba* Trial Judgement, *supra* note 136, para. 387.

[181] *Blagojević and Jokić* Trial Judgement, *supra* note 46, para. 699 (emphasis added). Accord *Krnojelac* Trial Judgement, *supra* note 166, para. 80 ('The understanding or arrangement need not be express, and its existence may be inferred from all the circumstances.').

Greater orchestration in the realisation of a crime is more likely to lead to a finding that those who carried it out did so pursuant to a JCE, as evidenced by the *Furundžija* Appeals Chamber's discussion of the infamous rape and interrogation of Witness A:

> There was no need for evidence proving the existence of a prior agreement between [Furundžija] and [Bralo] to divide the interrogation into the questioning by [Furundžija] and physical abuse by [Bralo]. The way the events in this case developed precludes any reasonable doubt that [Furundžija] and [Bralo] knew what they were doing to Witness A and for what purpose they were treating her in that manner; that they had a common purpose may be readily inferred from all the circumstances[.][182]

Since the conduct of one accused contributed to the purpose of the other, and as both acted simultaneously in the same place and in full view of each other over a considerable period of time, the defence contention that no common purpose existed was, in the Appeals Chamber's estimation, 'plainly unsustainable'.[183] Similarly, the *Blagojević and Jokić* Trial Chamber inferred the existence of a JCE to commit murder, extermination and persecutions at Srebrenica from the fact that over 7,000 Bosnian Muslim men and boys were captured, detained, murdered and buried over the course of just five days; according to the Chamber, 'this would not have been possible unless there was a plan and co-ordination between the members of the joint criminal enterprise'.[184]

These judgements suggest that, although a common plan or purpose may be formulated at the scene of the crime and need not be express, mere action in unison in the commission of an offence is insufficient, by itself, to support an inference that such commission occurred pursuant to a JCE. In this regard, the formulation of the *Krnojelac* and *Simić* Trial Chambers in the first paragraph below is preferable to the alternate formulation by other chambers in the second paragraph:

> The *circumstances in which two or more persons are participating together* in the commission of a particular crime may themselves establish an unspoken understanding or arrangement amounting to an agreement formed between them then and there to commit that crime.[185]

---

[182] *Furundžija* Appeal Judgement, *supra* note 35, para. 120.
[183] *Ibid.* The Chamber accordingly upheld the Trial Chamber's conviction of Furundžija for the rape as a form of torture. *Ibid.*, para. 121. For a more detailed discussion of the Trial Chamber's findings in respect of this incident, see *supra*, text accompanying notes 11–15.
[184] *Blagojević and Jokić* Trial Judgement, *supra* note 46, para. 721. The Trial Chambers in *Simić* and *Brđanin* have cautioned that any inference drawn must be the only reasonable one available on the basis of the evidence. *Brđanin* Trial Judgement, *supra* note 46, para. 353; *Simić et al.* Trial Judgement, *supra* note 5, para. 158 n. 288.
[185] *Krnojelac* Trial Judgement, *supra* note 166, para. 80 (emphasis added). Accord *Simić et al.* Trial Judgement, *supra* note 5, para. 158 (same language).

The *participation of two or more persons* in the commission of a particular crime may itself establish an unspoken understanding or arrangement amounting to an agreement formed between them then and there to commit that particular criminal act.[186]

The *Krajišnik* Trial Chamber expressly addressed whether mere action in unison is sufficient to give rise to JCE liability, and concluded that it is not. Instead, '[t]he persons in a criminal enterprise must be shown to act together, or in concert with each other, *in the implementation of a common objective*, if they are to share responsibility for the crimes committed through the JCE'.[187] In a later part of its judgement, the *Krajišnik* Chamber endorsed a non-exhaustive set of indicia or 'links forged in pursuant of a common objective', proposed by the prosecution upon the Chamber's request, 'concerning connections or relationships among persons working together in the implementation of a common objective' that may be considered when determining whether a given crime was committed pursuant to a JCE: whether the physical perpetrator was a member of, or associated with, organised bodies connected to the JCE; whether his act advanced the objective of the JCE; whether he acted at the same time as JCE participants or persons who were tools or instruments of the JCE; whether he advanced the objective of the JCE; whether his conduct was ratified implicitly or explicitly by JCE participants; whether he acted in co-operation or conjunction with JCE participants; whether any meaningful effort was made by JCE participants to punish his conduct; whether similar acts were punished by JCE participants; whether JCE participants or tools of the JCE continued to affiliate with him after his conduct; and whether the conduct was realised in the context of a systematic attack.[188]

The *Brđanin* Trial Chamber, obviously concerned with the propriety of imposing liability on an accused where the link between him and the physical perpetrator of the crime for which he is charged is too attenuated,[189] went further by imposing a requirement that 'between the person physically committing a crime and the Accused, there was an understanding or an agreement to commit that particular crime'.[190] Under the *Brđanin* Chamber's more

---

[186] *Blagojević and Jokić* Trial Judgement, *supra* note 46, para. 699 (emphasis added). See also *Stakić* Trial Judgement, *supra* note 155, para. 435 (same language); *Vasiljević* Trial Judgement, *supra* note 53, para. 66 ('The fact that two or more persons are participating together in the commission of a particular crime may itself establish an unspoken understanding or arrangement amounting to an agreement formed between them then and there to commit that particular criminal act.').

[187] *Krajišnik* Trial Judgement, *supra* note 65, para. 884 (emphasis added).

[188] *Ibid.*, paras. 1081–1082 (quotations at para. 1082).

[189] See *Prosecutor* v. *Milutinović, Šainović, Ojdanić, Pavković, Lazarević, Đorđević and Lukić*, Case No. IT-05-87-PT, Decision on Ojdanić's Motion Challenging Jurisdiction: Indirect Co-Perpetration, 22 March 2006 ('*Milutinović et al.* ICP Pre-Trial Decision'), Separate Opinion of Judge Iain Bonomy, para. 10 ('The Chamber appears to have been – in my opinion quite rightly – concerned that it would be inappropriate to impose liability on an [a]ccused where the link between him and those who physically perpetrated the crimes with which he is charged is too attenuated.').

[190] *Brđanin* Trial Judgement, *supra* note 46, para. 344.

restrictive conception of JCE, mere simultaneous or group commission on the one hand, or approval by the accused of someone else's crime on the other, will not suffice to engage the accused's JCE liability.[191] The implications of this controversial proposition – particularly for cases alleging a very large JCE where the accused is far removed from the physical perpetration of a crime – as well as the reaction to it in subsequent jurisprudence,[192] are discussed in detail in the following section of this chapter.[193]

Most of the relevant judgements have endorsed the *Tadić* Appeals Chamber's assertion that the common plan, design, or purpose must 'amount ... to or involve ... the commission of a crime provided for in the Statute,'[194] although a few judgements omit reference to such an obligation in their discussion of the physical elements of JCE.[195] Further statements in several judgements, to the effect that the participants must enter into an agreement that 'they will commit a crime'[196] or that 'a *particular* crime will be committed',[197] reinforce the proposition that the reason for the JCE's existence must be the realisation of conduct that constitutes a specific crime in the ICTY or ICTR Statute.

Bearing in mind the nature of the conflict in the former Yugoslavia, it is not surprising that the ICTY Prosecutor alleges deportation and forcible

---

[191] See *ibid.*, para. 352 ('An agreement between two persons to commit a crime requires a *mutual* understanding or arrangement with each other to commit a crime.') (emphasis in original); *ibid.* para. 355 (concluding that, given the 'extraordinarily broad nature' of the case and the structural remoteness of the Accused from the commission of the crimes, 'JCE is not an appropriate mode of liability to describe the individual criminal responsibility of the Accused'); *ibid.* para. 356 (dismissing JCE as a possible mode of responsibility to describe Brđanin's individual criminal responsibility). See also *Brđanin and Talić* June 2001 Pre-Trial Decision, *supra* note 4, para. 44.

[192] The *Krajišnik* Trial Chamber, which rendered its judgement some two years after that in *Brđanin*, acknowledged the *Brđanin* Chamber's restriction and opted not to endorse it. See *Krajišnik* Trial Judgement, *supra* note 65, para. 883. This judgement is examined in greater depth in the following section. See *infra* text accompanying notes 483–485, 568–589.

[193] See *infra* text accompanying notes 455–591.

[194] *Tadić* Appeal Judgement, *supra* note 3, para. 227. Accord *Stakić* Appeal Judgement, *supra* note 83, para. 64; *Kvočka et al.* Appeal Judgement, *supra* note 46, para. 81; *Vasiljević* Appeal Judgement, *supra* note 46, para. 100; *Simba* Trial Judgement, *supra* note 136, para. 387; *Blagojević and Jokić* Trial Judgement, *supra* note 46, para. 698; *Brđanin* Trial Judgement, *supra* note 46, para. 260; *Simić et al.* Trial Judgement, *supra* note 5, para. 156; *Stakić* Trial Judgement, *supra* note 155, paras. 423, 434; *Kordić and Čerkez* Trial Judgement, *supra* note 65, para. 397; *Krnojelac* Trial Judgement, *supra* note 166, para. 80; *Krstić* Trial Judgement, *supra* note 46, para. 611; *Kvočka et al.* Trial Judgement, *supra* note 155, para. 266; *Kupreškić et al.* Trial Judgement, *supra* note 72, para. 772. See also *Krajišnik* Trial Judgement, *supra* note 65, para. 883:

> The first form of JCE exists where the common objective amounts to, or involves the commission of a crime provided for in the Statute ... The third form ... depends on whether it is natural and foreseeable that the execution of the JCE in its first form will lead to the commission of one or more other statutory crimes.

[195] See *Ntakirutimana and Ntakirutimana* Appeal Judgement, *supra* note 46, para. 466; *Furundžija* Appeal Judgement, *supra* note 35, para. 119; *Vasiljević* Trial Judgement, *supra* note 53, paras. 65–66.

[196] *Simić et al.* Trial Judgement, *supra* note 5, para. 158. Accord *Brđanin* Trial Judgement, *supra* note 46, para. 262.

[197] *Blagojević and Jokić* Trial Judgement, *supra* note 46, para. 699 (emphasis added). Accord *Stakić* Trial Judgement, *supra* note 155, para. 435; *Vasiljević* Trial Judgement, *supra* note 53, para. 66; *Krnojelac* Trial Judgement, *supra* note 166, para. 80.

transfer[198] as the objective of the JCEs of many accused. Such has been the case with the indictments of Slobodan Milošević,[199] Vidoje Blagojević (whom the Trial Chamber found to have taken part in an agreement to forcibly transfer Bosnian Muslim women and children out of Srebrenica)[200] and Duško Tadić (whom the Appeals Chamber found had participated in a JCE whose purpose was to rid Bosnia's Prijedor region of its non-Serb population by committing inhumane acts against non-Serbs).[201] Another commonly alleged object of the JCEs of ICTY accused is persecution as a crime against humanity. One example of its application is *Kvočka*, in which the Trial Chamber found that the entire Omarska detention camp had functioned as a JCE and had the criminal objective of persecuting non-Serb detainees through offences such as murder, torture and rape.[202] Another, grander example, is the indictment against Milan Milutinović and his co-accused, who are alleged to have participated in a JCE to modify the ethnic balance of Kosovo through the commission of deportation, murder, forcible transfer and persecution.[203]

The *Krajišnik* Trial Chamber expressed the view that the common plan, design, or purpose at the core of a JCE is 'fluid in its criminal means'.[204] As such, JCE liability may ensue for crimes that were not originally contemplated by the JCE participants through the 'expansion of the criminal means of the objective' of the enterprise 'when leading members of the JCE are informed of

[198] The former as a crime against humanity and the latter, as interpreted in the jurisprudence, as an inhumane act as a crime against humanity and a violation of the laws or customs of war. See, e.g., *Simić et al.* Trial Judgement, *supra* note 5, para. 75; *Vasiljević* Trial Judgement, *supra* note 53, para. 235; *Krnojelac* Trial Judgement, *supra* note 166, para. 131.

[199] *Prosecutor v. Milošević*, Case No. IT-02-54-T, Amended Indictment, 21 April 2004, para. 6 (Bosnia indictment alleging that the purpose of the JCE was the 'forcible and permanent removal of the majority of non-Serbs ... from large areas of the Republic of Bosnia and Herzegovina through the commission of crimes in violation of Articles 2, 3, 4, and 5'); *ibid.*, para. 8 (all counts charged as within the object of the JCE, but counts 16 through 18 – charging deportation and forcible transfer – uniquely not charged alternatively as natural and foreseeable consequences of the execution of the object of the JCE); *Milošević* Kosovo Second Amended Indictment, *supra* note 159, para. 16 (alleging that the purpose of the JCE was the 'expulsion of a substantial portion of the Kosovo Albanian population from the territory of the province of Kosovo in an effort to ensure continued Serbian control over the province'); *ibid.*, para. 18 (all counts charged as within the object of the JCE, but counts 1 and 2 – charging deportation and forcible transfer – uniquely not charged alternatively as natural and foreseeable consequences of the execution of the object of the JCE).

[200] *Blagojević and Jokić* Trial Judgement, *supra* note 46, paras. 705–706, 710.

[201] *Tadić* Appeal Judgement, *supra* note 3, para. 232.

[202] *Kvočka et al.* Trial Judgement, *supra* note 155, paras. 319–320.

[203] *Prosecutor v. Milutinović, Šainović, Ojdanić, Pavković, Lazarević, Đorđević and Lukić*, Case No. IT-05-87-PT, Amended Joinder Indictment, 16 August 2005, para. 19; see also *ibid.*, para. 73 (charging deportation as a crime against humanity); *ibid.*, para. 74 (charging forcible transfer as an inhumane act as a crime against humanity); *ibid.*, para. 76 (charging murder as a crime against humanity and as a violation of the laws or customs of war); *ibid.*, para. 78 (charging persecution as a crime against humanity).

[204] *Krajišnik* Trial Judgement, *supra* note 65, para. 1098. See also Heikelina Verrijn Stuart, 'The Idea behind the Krajisnik Judgement', *International Justice Tribune*, 9 October 2006, p. 4 (discussing the notion of 'fluidity' in the *Krajišnik* Trial Judgement's discussion of JCE).

new types of crime committed pursuant to the implementation of the common objective, take no effective measures to prevent recurrence of such crimes, and persist in the implementation of the common objective of the JCE'.[205] According to the *Krajišnik* Chamber, where such requirements are fulfilled, the accused may bear liability pursuant to the first category of JCE, instead of the third.[206] Relying on the principle thus established, the Chamber proceeded to convict the accused Krajišnik under the first category for a number of crimes not initially part of the enterprise's common objective – which originally consisted only of deportation and forcible transfer[207] – because Krajišnik later learned of such crimes and accepted them as an expansion of the means to implement the enterprise.[208] These crimes included unlawful detention,[209] inhumane treatment,[210] killings,[211] sexual violence,[212] appropriation of property[213] and destruction of cultural monuments.[214]

2.3.1.3 *The accused participated in the JCE: third physical element*

The third physical element of JCE, as set forth in the *Tadić* Appeal Judgement and repeated many times since, is the '[p]articipation of the accused in the common design involving the perpetration of one of the crimes provided for in the Statute'.[215] The *Kvočka* Appeals Chamber held that the prosecution must plead the nature of such participation in any indictment that relies upon a theory of JCE.[216]

---

[205] *Ibid.* (citing no authority).
[206] This distinction is presumably significant because the *ad hoc* chambers have tended to impose higher sentences on accused convicted pursuant to the first category of JCE than those convicted pursuant to the third category.
[207] *Ibid.*, para. 1097.
[208] *Ibid.*, paras. 1098, 1126, 1182. See also *ibid.*, para. 1118 ('These crimes came to redefine the criminal means of the JCE's common objective during the course of the indictment period . . . [A]cceptance of this greater range of criminal means, coupled with persistence in implementation, signalled an intention to pursue the common objective through those means.').
[209] *Ibid.*, para. 1100.   [210] *Ibid.*, para. 1101.   [211] *Ibid.*, paras. 1104, 1108.
[212] *Ibid.*, para. 1105.   [213] *Ibid.*, para. 1113.   [214] *Ibid.*, para. 1114.
[215] *Tadić* Appeal Judgement, *supra* note 3, para. 227 (emphasis removed). Accord *Stakić* Appeal Judgement, *supra* note 83, para. 64; *Vasiljević* Appeal Judgement, *supra* note 46, para. 100; *Kayishema and Ruzindana* Appeal Judgement, *supra* note 114, para. 193; *Krajišnik* Trial Judgement, *supra* note 65, para. 884; *Simba* Trial Judgement, *supra* note 136, para. 387; *Blagojević and Jokić* Trial Judgement, *supra* note 46, para. 698; *Brđanin* Trial Judgement, *supra* note 46, para. 260; *Simić et al.* Trial Judgement, *supra* note 5, para. 156; *Stakić* Trial Judgement, *supra* note 155, para. 435; *Vasiljević* Trial Judgement, *supra* note 53, para. 65; *Krnojelac* Trial Judgement, *supra* note 166, para. 79; *Krstić* Trial Judgement, *supra* note 46, para. 611; *Kordić and Čerkez* Trial Judgement, *supra* note 65, para. 397; *Kupreškić et al.* Trial Judgement, *supra* note 72, para. 772.
[216] *Kvočka et al.* Appeal Judgement, *supra* note 46, para. 28 ('If the Prosecution relies on a theory of joint criminal enterprise, then the Prosecutor must plead . . . the nature of the accused's participation in the enterprise.'). Accord *Simba* Trial Judgement, *supra* note 136, para. 389 ('If the Prosecution intends to rely on the theory of joint criminal enterprise . . . [it must plead] the nature of the accused's participation in the enterprise.'); *Simić et al.* Trial Judgement, *supra* note 5, para. 145 ('In the case of a joint criminal enterprise, the following elements need to be pleaded: . . . the nature of the participation of the accused in the enterprise.').

In order to fulfil this element, the accused need not have physically committed the crime that is the object of the JCE, or any other crime for that matter;[217] he need simply have assisted in, or otherwise contributed to, the execution of the common plan, design, or purpose.[218] Indeed, as acknowledged by the Trial Chamber in *Brđanin*, the term 'participation' has been defined quite expansively in the jurisprudence.[219] Unlike aiding and abetting, which requires that the accused perform acts specifically directed to assist, encourage, or lend moral support to another in the perpetration of a specific crime,[220] a JCE participant need merely 'perform acts that in some way are directed to the furtherance of the common plan or purpose'.[221] The *Kvočka* Appeals Chamber and at least three Trial Chambers have sanctioned an even broader definition of participation: '[I]t is sufficient for the accused to have committed an act *or an omission* which contributes to the common criminal purpose.'[222] An accused need not even be

[217] *Stakić* Appeal Judgement, *supra* note 83, para. 64 ('This participation need not involve the commission of a specific crime under one of the provisions (for example, murder, extermination, torture or rape), but may take the form of assistance in, or contribution to, the execution of the common purpose.'); *Kvočka et al.* Appeal Judgement, *supra* note 46, para. 99 ('A participant in a joint criminal enterprise need not physically participate in any element of any crime, so long as the requirements of joint criminal enterprise responsibility are met.'); *Mpambara* Trial Judgement, *supra* note 46, para. 13 (holding that 'the act [of the accused] need not independently be a crime').

[218] *Stakić* Appeal Judgement, *supra* note 83, para. 64; *Vasiljević* Appeal Judgement, *supra* note 46, para. 100; *Ntakirutimana and Ntakirutimana* Appeal Judgement, *supra* note 46, para. 466; *Tadić* Appeal Judgement, *supra* note 3, para. 227; *Mpambara* Trial Judgement, *supra* note 46, para. 13 (holding that '[a]ny act or omission which assists or contributes to the criminal purpose may attract liability'); *Simba* Trial Judgement, *supra* note 136, para. 387; *Brđanin* Trial Judgement, *supra* note 46, para. 263. See also *Krajišnik* Trial Judgement, *supra* note 65, para. 883:

This is achieved by the accused's commission of a crime forming part of the common objective (and provided for in the Statute). Alternatively, instead of committing the intended crime as a principal perpetrator, the accused's conduct may satisfy this element if it involved procuring or giving assistance to the execution of a crime forming part of the common objective.

[219] *Brđanin* Trial Judgement, *supra* note 46, para. 263.

[220] *Kvočka et al.* Appeal Judgement, *supra* note 46, para. 33; *Blaškić* Appeal Judgement, *supra* note 83, paras. 45, 50 (holding that an aider and abettor must have known that his own acts or omissions assisted in the commission of the specific crime for which he is charged via Article 7(1)); *Vasiljević* Appeal Judgement, *supra* note 46, para. 102 (holding that an aider and abettor must lend practical assistance, encouragement, or moral support).

[221] *Tadić* Appeal Judgement, *supra* note 3, para. 229. Accord *Vasiljević* Appeal Judgement, *supra* note 46, para. 102 ('The aider and abettor carries out acts specifically directed to assist, encourage or lend moral support to the perpetration of a certain specific crime[.] By contrast, it is sufficient for a participant in a joint criminal enterprise to perform acts that in some way are directed to the furtherance of the common design.'); *Mpambara* Trial Judgement, *supra* note 46, para. 14 (holding that 'the *actus reus* may be satisfied by any participation, no matter how insignificant'); *Kupreškić et al.* Trial Judgement, *supra* note 72, para. 772.

[222] *Kvočka et al.* Appeal Judgement, *supra* note 46, para. 187 (emphasis added). Accord *Krajišnik* Trial Judgement, *supra* note 65, para. 885; *Mpambara* Trial Judgement, *supra* note 46, para. 24 ('Involvement in a joint criminal enterprise may also be proven by evidence characterized as an omission.'); *Prosecutor v. Popović, Beara, Nikolić, Borovčanin, Tolimir, Miletić, Gvero and Pandurević*, Case No. IT-05-88-PT, Decision on Further Amendments and Challenges to the Indictment, 13 July 2006, para. 28 (quoting this passage from *Kvočka* and remarking that, 'under the Tribunal's jurisprudence on the elements of JCE, in order to fulfil the element that the accused "participate" in the JCE, the accused need not have physically committed any part of the *actus reus* of any crime, and he need not even have performed an overt physical act').

present at the time and place of the physical perpetration of the offence to be found guilty of committing that offence pursuant to a JCE.[223]

On interlocutory appeal from a decision denying his request to dismiss JCE as a form of liability in the indictment against him, Dragoljub Ojdanić argued that 'joint criminal enterprise is akin to a form of criminal liability for membership', and that the Security Council had eschewed such liability when adopting the ICTY Statute.[224] Addressing this claim, the Appeals Chamber opined that '[j]oint criminal enterprise is different from membership of a criminal enterprise',[225] and that such membership would not alone suffice to engage an accused's JCE liability; instead, the accused must have 'participat[ed] in the commission of a crime as part of a joint criminal enterprise, a different matter'.[226] The Trial Chamber in *Stakić* propounded a rationale for this requirement: the imposition of criminal liability for mere membership in an organisation, without more, would amount to a 'flagrant infringement' of the principle of *nullum crimen sine lege* because it would 'constitute a new crime not foreseen under the Statute'.[227] Yet in contrast to certain post-Second World War judgements that required membership in the SS, an accused JCE participant before the *ad hoc* Tribunals need not have been a member of any group to incur responsibility.[228]

In an 11 May 2000 decision on the form of the indictment, the Trial Chamber in *Brđanin and Talić* listed three ways in which a person may participate in a JCE,[229]

---

[223] *Krnojelac* Appeal Judgement, *supra* note 46, para. 81. Accord *Simić et al.* Trial Judgement, *supra* note 5, para. 158 ('[P]resence at the time of the crime is not necessary. A person can still be held liable for criminal acts carried out by others without being present – all that is necessary is that the person forms an agreement with others that a crime will be carried out.'); *Krnojelac* Trial Judgement, *supra* note 166, para. 81 n. 236 ('A person can still be liable for criminal acts carried out by others without being present – all that is necessary is that the person forms an agreement with others that a crime will be carried out.').

[224] *Prosecutor* v. *Milutinović, Šainović and Ojdanić*, Case No. IT-99-37-AR72, General Ojdanić's Appeal from Denial of Preliminary Motion to Dismiss for Lack of Jurisdiction: Joint Criminal Enterprise, 28 February 2003, para. 65. Although Ojdanić did not cite it for this proposition, the *Krstić* Trial Judgement's statement that JCE is 'otherwise formulated as the accused's "membership" in a particular joint criminal enterprise' would appear to provide some support for Ojdanić's claim. *Krstić* Trial Judgement, *supra* note 46, para. 611.

[225] *Milutinović et al.* JCE Appeal Decision, *supra* note 4, para. 25.

[226] *Ibid.*, para. 26. Accord *Brđanin* Trial Judgement, *supra* note 46, para. 263 ('Individual criminal responsibility for participation in a JCE does not arise as a result of mere membership in a criminal enterprise. In order to incur criminal liability, the accused is required to take action in contribution of the implementation of the common plan.'); *Simić et al.* Trial Judgement, *supra* note 5, para. 158.

[227] *Stakić* Trial Judgement, *supra* note 155, para. 433.

[228] *Kvočka et al.* Appeal Judgement, *supra* note 46, para. 103 ('[I]t is clear that there is no requirement of "membership" in a group, beyond playing a role in a camp, in order to incur joint criminal enterprise responsibility.'). See also *Krnojelac* Appeal Judgement, *supra* note 46, para. 89 ('Although the perpetrators of acts tried in the concentration camp cases were mostly members of criminal organisations, the *Tadić* case did not require an individual to belong to such an organisation in order to be considered a participant in the joint criminal enterprise.').

[229] *Prosecutor* v. *Brđanin and Talić*, Case No. IT-99-36-PT, Decision on Form of the Second Indictment, 11 May 2000, para. 15.

and this list has since been endorsed by several judgements.[230] The most recent formulation appeared in the *Blagojević and Jokić* Trial Judgement as follows:

There are various ways in which a person may participate in a joint criminal enterprise: (i) by personally committing the agreed crime as a principal offender; (ii) by assisting the principal offender in the commission of the agreed crime as a co-perpetrator, i.e. facilitating the commission of the crime with the intent to carry out the enterprise; or (iii) by acting in furtherance of a particular system in which the crime is committed by reason of the accused's position of authority or function and with knowledge of the nature of that system and intent to further that system.[231]

The *Vasiljević* Trial Chamber found that the accused had participated in a JCE to commit murder, apparently through the second method enumerated in the quoted passage above: he prevented seven Muslim men fleeing by pointing a gun at them, he escorted them to the bank of the Drina River, and he stood behind them holding his gun in the moments before several of his fellow JCE participants shot them.[232]

The *Kvočka* Trial Chamber held that the accused's participation in a JCE must be 'significant' before liability can ensue.[233] This determination was partially overruled by the Appeals Chamber: 'Contrary to the holding of the Trial Chamber, the Tribunal's case-law does not require participation as a co-perpetrator in a joint criminal enterprise to have been significant, unless otherwise stated.'[234] The Appeals Chamber noted that there may be specific cases which require, 'as an exception to the general rule', proof of a substantial contribution by the accused in order to find that he participated in a JCE.[235] The Chamber gave the example of 'opportunistic visitors' – persons who are not members of a detention camp's regular staff – who enter the camp and commit crimes. While a person need not belong to the camp personnel to be held responsible as a participant in a JCE to mistreat detainees, an opportunistic visitor will only incur JCE liability if he makes a 'substantial contribution to the overall effect of the camp'.[236] Accordingly, the Appeals Chamber

[230] See *Blagojević and Jokić* Trial Judgement, *supra* note 46, para. 702; *Stakić* Trial Judgement, *supra* note 155, para. 435; *Vasiljević* Trial Judgement, *supra* note 53, para. 67; *Krnojelac* Trial Judgement, *supra* note 166, para. 81.

[231] *Blagojević and Jokić* Trial Judgement, *supra* note 46, para. 702.

[232] *Vasiljević* Trial Judgement, *supra* note 53, paras. 67, 208–209.

[233] *Kvočka et al.* Trial Judgement, *supra* note 155, para. 311. Although the *Kvočka* Trial Chamber restricted most of its JCE analysis to the second category, the requirement of a 'significant' level of participation was subsequently endorsed by the Trial Chamber in *Simić*, which evinced no intent to restrict the requirement's scope to the second category of JCE. See *Simić et al.* Trial Judgement, *supra* note 5, para. 159.

[234] *Kvočka et al.* Appeal Judgement, *supra* note 46, para. 187. See also *ibid.*, para. 97 ('[I]n general, there is no specific legal requirement that the accused make a substantial contribution to the joint criminal enterprise.'); *ibid.*, para. 104 ('Joint criminal enterprise responsibility does not require ... proof of a substantial or significant contribution.').

[235] *Ibid.*, para. 97.   [236] *Ibid*, para. 599.

reversed the Trial Chamber's conviction of the accused Žigić 'for the crimes committed in the Omarska camp generally', including persecution, murder and torture.[237] Although it concurred with the Trial Chamber that there was sufficient evidence to prove that Žigić had visited the Omarska camp on several occasions and had engaged in acts of brutality against detainees, the Appeals Chamber found that 'no reasonable trier of fact could conclude from the evidence before the Trial Chamber that Žigić participated in a significant way in the functioning of Omarska camp'.[238]

The *Kvočka* Appeals Chamber also stated that the significance and scope of the accused's material participation in a JCE may be relevant, in addition to evaluating liability in cases such as that of the opportunistic visitor, for determining whether the accused fulfilled the requisite mental elements of JCE.[239] As the significance of the accused's participation continues to be relevant in certain circumstances, it is worth examining the *Kvočka* Trial Chamber's definition of 'significant participation'. The Trial Chamber explained that by 'significant', it meant an act or omission 'that makes an enterprise efficient or effective', such as 'a participation that enables the system to run more smoothly or without disruption'.[240] Physical or direct perpetration of a crime, while not required for JCE liability, would constitute a significant contribution if it advanced the goal of the enterprise.[241] An accused's leadership status militates in favour of a chamber finding that his participation was significant,[242] and although low- or mid-level actors, such as drivers or ordinary soldiers made to stand guard while others perform an execution, may incur JCE liability, 'in most situations, the ... co-perpetrator would not be someone readily replaceable'.[243] Considering that '[i]n situations of armed conflict or mass violence, it is all too easy for individuals to get caught up in the violence or hatred',[244] the Chamber held that the threshold required to impute criminal responsibility to a low- or mid-level participant in a JCE 'normally requires a more substantial level of participation than simply following orders to perform some low-level function in the criminal endeavor on a single occasion'.[245]

The Trial Chamber went on to identify several factors that a chamber may take into account when evaluating whether the level of participation of a given accused was sufficiently significant, including the size of the criminal

---

[237] *Ibid.* (overruling *Kvočka et al.* Trial Judgement, *supra* note 155, para. 691).
[238] *Ibid.* 599.   [239] *Ibid.*, paras. 97, 188.
[240] *Kvočka et al.* Trial Judgement, *supra* note 155, para. 309.   [241] *Ibid.*
[242] *Ibid.*, para. 292 (citing with approval *Krstić* Trial Judgement, *supra* note 46, para. 642, which found Krstić guilty pursuant to JCE because his 'participation [was] of an extremely significant nature and at the leadership level').
[243] *Ibid.*, para. 309.   [244] *Ibid.*, para. 310.   [245] *Ibid.*, para. 311.

enterprise; the functions performed by the accused; the position held by the accused; the amount of time spent participating after acquiring knowledge of the criminality of the system; efforts made to prevent criminal activity or to impede the efficient functioning of the system; the seriousness and scope of the crimes committed; the efficiency, zealousness, or gratuitous cruelty exhibited in performing the actor's function; repeated, continuous, or extensive participation in the system; verbal expressions; and actual physical perpetration of a crime.[246] As an example of an accused who plays a significant role in the commission of a crime, the Chamber gave the example of the lowly guard who pulls the switch to release poisonous gas into a room, killing hundreds of victims; the participation of such a guard in the criminal system is likely more 'significant' than that of a supervising guard posted at the perimeter of the camp who shoots an escaping prisoner.[247] With these considerations in mind, the Trial Chamber ultimately convicted the accused Kvočka for his participation in the Omarska camp JCE

[d]ue to the high position Kvočka held in the camp, the authority and influence he had over the guard service in the camp, and his very limited attempts to prevent crimes or alleviate the suffering of detainees, as well as the considerable role he played in maintaining the functioning of the camp despite knowledge that it was a criminal endeavour.[248]

Notwithstanding the possibility of JCE responsibility for low-level actors at detention camps, the *Kvočka* Trial Chamber underscored the greater likelihood that persons in positions of authority will provide enough of a contribution to the enterprise to incur JCE liability, going so far as to state that even the approving silence of such persons may be sufficient.[249] While the *Kvočka* Appeals Chamber held that participation can take the form of 'an act or an omission which contributes to the common criminal purpose',[250] it did not opine directly on whether a superior's failure to complain about or protest atrocities in his camp automatically fulfils the requirement of participation in the JCE. The Chamber did, however, caution that an accused's position of authority, while relevant for establishing his awareness of the system and his participation in perpetuating the system's criminal purpose,[251] is only one factor that a chamber should take into account when determining whether the accused participated in the common purpose.[252]

[246] *Ibid.* [247] *Ibid.*
[248] *Ibid.*, para. 414. In upholding this finding of guilt, the Appeals Chamber stated as follows: 'It is clear that, through his work in the camp, Kvočka contributed to the daily operation and maintenance of the camp and, in doing so, allowed the system of ill-treatment to perpetuate itself.' *Kvočka et al.* Appeal Judgement, *supra* note 46, para. 196.
[249] *Kvočka et al.* Trial Judgement, *supra* note 155, para. 309.
[250] *Kvočka et al.* Appeal Judgement, *supra* note 46, para. 187. [251] *Ibid.*, para. 192. [252] *Ibid.*, para. 101.

The *Blagojević and Jokić* and *Brđanin* Trial Chambers, likewise evincing a desire to define some minimum threshold of participation that the prosecution must prove before a chamber can hold an accused responsible as a JCE participant, held that the accused's involvement in the criminal conduct envisioned by the enterprise 'must form a link in the chain of causation'.[253] Both Chambers stressed, however, that the accused's contribution need not have been the 'but-for' cause of the commission of the crime.[254] This position was subsequently endorsed by the *Kvočka* Appeals Chamber,[255] which dismissed the argument of the appellant Kvočka that, because the Omarska commanders found it unnecessary to replace him after he had left the camp, his contribution to the JCE should be considered less significant. In spite of the Trial Chamber's comment that 'in most situations, the ... co-perpetrator would not be someone readily replaceable',[256] the Appeals Chamber found the question of whether the criminal purpose could have been achieved without the participation of Kvočka of 'little relevance'.[257]

As JCE is a form of 'commission' under Article 7/6(1),[258] an accused convicted for his participation in a JCE is guilty of the crime committed, regardless of the role he played in the enterprise.[259] As suggested by the *Blagojević and Jokić* Trial Judgement, a chamber may take into account the relative significance of a particular accused's role in the JCE in the sentence it imposes on him if it finds him guilty.[260] Nonetheless, as the *Babić* Appeals

---

[253] *Blagojević and Jokić* Trial Judgement, *supra* note 46, para. 702; *Brđanin* Trial Judgement, *supra* note 46, para. 263.

[254] *Blagojević and Jokić* Trial Judgement, *supra* note 46, para. 702; *Brđanin* Trial Judgement, *supra* note 46, para. 263. Accord *Krajišnik* Trial Judgement, *supra* note 65, para. 883 ('A contribution of the accused to the JCE need not have been, as a matter of law, either substantial or necessary to the achievement of the JCE's objective.') (footnotes omitted).

[255] *Kvočka et al.* Appeal Judgement, *supra* note 46, para. 98 ('The Appeals Chamber agrees that the Prosecutor need not demonstrate that the accused's participation is a *sine qua non*, without which the crimes could or would not have been committed.').

[256] *Kvočka et al.* Trial Judgement, *supra* note 155, para. 309.

[257] *Kvočka et al.* Appeal Judgement, *supra* note 46, para. 193.

[258] *Vasiljević* Appeal Judgement, *supra* note 46, para. 111; *Ntakirutimana and Ntakirutimana* Appeal Judgement, *supra* note 46, para. 468.

[259] *Vasiljević* Appeal Judgement, *supra* note 46, para. 111; *Blagojević and Jokić* Trial Judgement, *supra* note 46, para. 702; *Stakić* Trial Judgement, *supra* note 155, para. 435; *Vasiljević* Trial Judgement, *supra* note 53, para. 67; *Krnojelac* Trial Judgement, *supra* note 166, para. 82. By contrast, an accused convicted as a superior pursuant to Article 7(3) of the ICTY Statute and Article 6(3) of the ICTR Statute is not guilty of the substantive crime committed, but rather for his failure to prevent or punish such crime. See Chapter 3.

[260] See *Blagojević and Jokić* Trial Judgement, *supra* note 46, para. 702 n. 2160. See also *Kvočka et al.* Trial Judgement, *supra* note 155, para. 282 (approving of the differentiation made by the US Military Tribunal in *United States* v. *Otto Ohlendorf et al.*, 4 *Trials of War Criminals Before the Nuremberg Military Tribunals Under Control Council Law No. 10* (1950), p. 411 ('*Einsatzgruppen* case'), between significant and insignificant contributors to the JCE through the imposition of harsher sentences on those with greater moral culpability). Cf. ICTY Statute, *supra* note 2, Art. 24(2) ('In imposing the sentences, the Trial Chambers should take into account such factors as the gravity of the offence and the individual circumstances of the convicted person.').

Chamber emphasised, while a finding of secondary or indirect forms of participation in a JCE relative to others may result in the imposition of a lower sentence, a chamber is not required to impose a lesser sentence.[261]

2.3.2 Mental elements

Subject to a few exceptions and caveats that have been highlighted in the previous section,[262] the three categories of JCE have the same physical elements. Hence, the major differences among the three categories lie in their divergent mental elements,[263] which will now be discussed.

2.3.2.1 Mental elements of the first category of JCE

2.3.2.1.1 Voluntary participation

In their discussion of the requirement that an accused charged pursuant to the first category of JCE must participate in the enterprise,[264] several judgements articulate the mental element that corresponds to such participation. The *Vasiljević* and *Tadić* Appeal Judgements formulate this element as a requirement that 'the accused ... *voluntarily* participate in one aspect of the common design',[265] while the *Brđanin* Trial Judgement frames it as a requirement that 'the accused ... *voluntarily* participate ... in one of the aspects of the common plan'.[266] It would appear that no chamber has expressly stated whether, if the accused does ultimately participate in more than one aspect of the common plan, each act of participation must be voluntary. However, the *Blagojević and Jokić* Trial Chamber's more general formulation would appear to support such a proposition: 'It is necessary to establish that the accused voluntarily participated in the enterprise and intended the criminal result.'[267]

---

[261] *Prosecutor v. Babić*, Case No. IT-03-72-A, Judgement on Sentencing Appeal, 18 July 2005, para. 40 (holding that, while a finding of secondary or indirect forms of participation in a JCE relative to others may result in the imposition of a lower sentence, a chamber is not required to impose a lesser sentence). The jurisprudence on forms of responsibility and sentencing is discussed in greater detail in Chapter 6 of this book.

[262] See especially *supra* text accompanying notes 169–174 (discussing the jurisprudence establishing that the second category, unlike the first and third categories, does not require a formal or informal agreement among the participants to commit a crime, although it does require voluntary participation in the system).

[263] See *Ntakirutimana and Ntakirutimana* Appeal Judgement, *supra* note 46, para. 467; *Vasiljević* Appeal Judgement, *supra* note 46, para. 101; *Tadić* Appeal Judgement, *supra* note 3, para. 228 ('[T]he *mens rea* element differs according to the category of common design under consideration.'); *Blagojević and Jokić* Trial Judgement, *supra* note 46, para. 703; *Brđanin* Trial Judgement, *supra* note 46, para. 264; *Kvočka et al.* Trial Judgement, *supra* note 155, para. 267.

[264] See *supra*, text accompanying notes 215–261, for a discussion of this physical element of JCE.

[265] *Vasiljević* Appeal Judgement, *supra* note 46, para. 119 (discussing the first category) (emphasis added). Accord *Tadić* Appeal Judgement, *supra* note 3, para. 196 (discussing the first category and holding that 'the accused must *voluntarily* participate in one aspect of the common design') (emphasis added).

[266] *Brđanin* Trial Judgement, *supra* note 46, para. 264 (discussing the first category) (emphasis added).

[267] *Blagojević and Jokić* Trial Judgement, *supra* note 46, para. 703.

2.3.2.1.2 Shared intent

The jurisprudence of the *ad hoc* Tribunals habitually identifies the first category of JCE by reference to the participants' shared intent: all participants in a first-category JCE possess the same intent to commit the specific crime that is the object of the JCE.[268] The *Krnojelac* Appeals Chamber clarified this assertion by pointing out that the JCE participants other than the physical perpetrator must share the perpetrator's criminal intent.[269] Nonetheless, although this formulation appears at first glance to be setting forth a discrete mental element that the prosecution must prove, it is likely that a chamber would examine possible shared intent mainly to determine that an alleged JCE should appropriately be considered under the first category of JCE as opposed to the third category, in which the physical perpetrator may have an intent that diverges from or goes beyond that required of the crime that is the object of the JCE.[270] Accordingly the *Simić* Trial Chamber, after finding that Simić and the other members of the Bosanski Šamac Crisis Staff acted with the shared intent to pursue their common goal of persecution, found that the first category of JCE was applicable.[271] Just as the *Simić* Trial Chamber did not engage in an analysis of the mental states of the JCE participants other than the co-accused,[272] and notwithstanding statements such as that of the *Stakić* Appeals Chamber that 'it must be shown that the accused and the other participants in the joint criminal enterprise intended that the crime at issue

---

[268] *Stakić* Appeal Judgement, *supra* note 83, para. 65; *Kvočka et al.* Appeal Judgement, *supra* note 46, para. 82 ('In the first form of joint criminal enterprise, all of the co-perpetrators possess the same intent to effect the common purpose.'); *Ntakirutimana and Ntakirutimana* Appeal Judgement, *supra* note 46, para. 467; *Vasiljević* Appeal Judgement, *supra* note 46, para. 101; *Krnojelac* Appeal Judgement, *supra* note 46, para. 84; *Tadić* Appeal Judgement, *supra* note 3, para. 196; *Krajišnik* Trial Judgement, *supra* note 65, para. 883; *Simba* Trial Judgement, *supra* note 136, para. 388 ('The basic form of joint criminal enterprise requires the intent to perpetrate a certain crime, this intent being shared by all co-perpetrators.'); *Limaj et al.* Trial Judgement, *supra* note 155, para. 511; *Blagojević and Jokić* Trial Judgement, *supra* note 46, para. 703; *Brđanin* Trial Judgement, *supra* note 46, para. 264; *Simić et al.* Trial Judgement, *supra* note 5, paras. 156, 157, 160; *Vasiljević* Trial Judgement, *supra* note 53, para. 64.

[269] *Krnojelac* Appeal Judgement, *supra* note 46, para. 84 ('The Appeals Chamber finds that, apart from the specific case of the extended form of joint criminal enterprise, the very concept of joint criminal enterprise presupposes that its participants, other than the principal perpetrator(s) of the crimes committed, share the perpetrators' joint criminal intent.') (footnote removed).

[270] See *infra*, text accompanying notes 448–452.

[271] *Simić et al.* Trial Judgement, *supra* note 5, para. 992. On appeal, the Appeals Chamber found that JCE had not been pleaded adequately in the indictment against Simić, that this defect was not subsequently cured by the prosecution, and that the trial was consequently rendered unfair in this regard. It accordingly overturned Simić's conviction for persecution as a crime against humanity by virtue of his participation in a JCE. *Prosecutor v. Simić*, Case No. IT-95-9-A, Judgement, 28 November 2006 ('*Simić* Appeal Judgement'), paras. 46, 62, 73–74.

[272] See *Simić et al.* Trial Judgement, *supra* note 5, paras. 995–997, 1009–1011, 1017–1019.

be committed',[273] a chamber will almost certainly not inquire into the intent of every single person alleged in the indictment to have been a member of the JCE, but instead will only require that the prosecution prove the particular state of mind of the accused on the one hand, and the physical perpetrator or perpetrators on the other.[274]

Several judgements seem to have endorsed this reading of the jurisprudence,[275] which finds its most direct support in the language of the *Krnojelac* and *Simić* Trial Judgements:

> To prove the basic form of joint criminal enterprise, the Prosecution must demonstrate that *each of the persons charged* and (if not one of those charged) *the principal offender or offenders* had a common state of mind, that which is required for that crime [that is, the crime that is the object of the JCE].[276]

Support can also be found in the *Kvočka* Appeal Judgement, the relevant discussion of which begins with the general proposition that all participants in a JCE must share the intent of the physical perpetrator, but immediately narrows the required analysis when detailing exactly what the prosecution must prove: 'The Appeals Chamber affirms the Trial Chamber's conclusion that participants in a basic or systemic form of joint criminal enterprise must be shown to share the required intent of the principal perpetrators.'[277] This requirement of shared intent is one of the major factors differentiating the first category of JCE from aiding and abetting; because aiding and abetting demands merely that the accused be aware of the state of mind of the physical perpetrator, it is possible that an accused acquitted of 'committing' a crime due to the prosecution's failure to prove that he shared the intent of the physical perpetrators may still be convicted of aiding and abetting that crime.[278]

---

[273] See, e.g., *Stakić* Appeal Judgement, *supra* note 83, para. 65. See also *Kvočka et al.* Appeal Judgement, *supra* note 46, para. 110 ('The Appeals Chamber affirms the Trial Chamber's conclusion that participants in a basic or systemic form of joint criminal enterprise must be shown to share the required intent of the principal perpetrators.').

[274] See *Brđanin and Talić* June 2001 Pre-Trial Decision, *supra* note 4, at para. 31 ('If the crime charged fell *within* the object of the joint criminal enterprise, the prosecution must establish that the accused shared with the person who personally perpetrated the crime the state of mind required for that crime.') (emphasis in original).

[275] See, e.g., *Krstić* Trial Judgement, *supra* note 46, para. 613 ('[T]he prosecution must establish that the accused shared with the person who personally perpetrated the crime the state of mind required for that crime.'); *Vasiljević* Trial Judgement, *supra* note 53, para. 68 ('The Prosecution must ... establish that the person charged shared a common state of mind with the person who personally perpetrated the crime charged (the "principal offender") that the crime charged should be carried out, the state of mind required for that crime.').

[276] *Simić et al.* Trial Judgement, *supra* note 5, para. 160 (emphases added). Accord *Krnojelac* Trial Judgement, *supra* note 166, para. 83 (same language).

[277] *Kvočka et al.* Appeal Judgement, *supra* note 46, para. 110 (footnote omitted).

[278] See *Blaškić* Appeal Judgement, *supra* note 83, para. 49, *Vasiljević* Appeal Judgement, *supra* note 46, para. 102. *Simić et al.* Trial Judgement, *supra* note 5, para. 160; *Krnojelac* Trial Judgement, *supra* note 166, para. 69.

The *Stakić* Trial Chamber's formulation of this mental element is perhaps the clearest and most precise yet expounded: 'The basic category of joint criminal enterprise requires proof that the accused shared the intent specifically necessary for the concrete offence.'[279] This language seems preferable to that of judgements such as the *Vasiljević* Appeal Judgement, which held that 'the accused, even if not personally effecting the crime, [must] nevertheless [have] *intended this result*'.[280] That the accused shared such intent may be inferred from the circumstances.[281] The *Kvočka* Trial Chamber has held, for example, that 'a knowing and continued participation in [a JCE to kill members of a particular ethnic group] could evince an intent to persecute members of the targeted ethnic group'.[282]

The notion that an accused charged with participation in a first-category JCE must share the intent of the physical perpetrator to commit the crime should be distinguished from the proposition that the physical perpetrator must himself be a JCE participant, or have taken any part whatsoever in establishing the enterprise or helping to formulate its objectives. While a person charged with first-category liability must voluntarily participate in the enterprise and possess the intent to commit the crime that is the JCE's object, and although the physical perpetrator must possess the intent to commit this crime as well, the jurisprudence is unclear as to whether the physical perpetrator must also participate in the JCE, or whether he may, for example, merely be acting on the orders of one of the JCE participants in committing the crime that is the object of the JCE. This important question, which was explored but not definitively decided upon in an ICTY trial decision in March 2006, is examined in detail later in this chapter.[283]

---

[279] *Stakić* Trial Judgement, *supra* note 155, para. 436.

[280] *Vasiljević* Appeal Judgement, *supra* note 46, para. 119 (emphasis added). See also *Tadić* Appeal Judgement, *supra* note 3, para. 196 (holding that 'the accused, even if not personally effecting the killing, must nevertheless intend this result'); *Blagojević and Jokić* Trial Judgement, *supra* note 46, para. 703 ('It is necessary to establish that the accused . . . intended the criminal result.'); *Brđanin* Trial Judgement, *supra* note 46, para. 264 ('To establish responsibility under the first category of JCE, it needs to be shown that the accused . . . intended the criminal result, even if not physically perpetrating the crime.'); *Simić et al.* Trial Judgement, *supra* note 5, paras. 156, 158.

[281] *Vasiljević* Appeal Judgement, *supra* note 46, para. 120; *Vasiljević* Trial Judgement, *supra* note 53, para. 68; *Krnojelac* Trial Judgement, *supra* note 166, para. 83.

[282] *Kvočka et al.* Trial Judgement, *supra* note 155, para. 288. A number of chambers have held, however, that any inference of the accused's intent must be the only reasonable one available on the basis of the evidence. See *Vasiljević* Appeal Judgement, *supra* note 46, para. 120; *Vasiljević* Trial Judgement, *supra* note 53, para. 68; *Krnojelac* Trial Judgement, *supra* note 166, para. 83. Hence, the *Vasiljević* Appeals Chamber overturned the Trial Chamber's finding that the Accused shared the intent of his alleged JCE co-participants to kill seven Muslim men, which the Trial Chamber had based on an inference drawn from the Accused's actions in brandishing a gun and preventing the victims from fleeing the Drina River killing site, *Vasiljević* Trial Judgement, *supra* note 53, para. 118, because the Appeals Chamber found that the Accused's actions supported other reasonable inferences. *Vasiljević* Appeal Judgement, *supra* note 46, para. 131.

[283] See *Milutinović et al.* ICP Pre-Trial Decision, *supra* note 189, paras. 22–24. See also *infra*, text accompanying notes 592–721.

As regards a first-category JCE whose criminal object consists of a crime requiring specific intent, the jurisprudence of the *ad hoc* Tribunals suggests that the prosecution must prove not only that the accused shared the general intent required of the crime – for example, the intent to kill for 'murder' as a form of persecution as a crime against humanity, or 'killing members of the group' as an underlying offence of genocide – but also that he shared with the physical perpetrator the specific intent required. As expressed by the *Kvočka* Trial Chamber, in its discussion differentiating JCE from aiding and abetting,

> [w]here the crime [charged pursuant to JCE] requires special intent, such as the crime of persecution . . . the accused must also satisfy the *additional* requirements imposed by the crime, such as the intent to discriminate on political, racial, or religious grounds if he is a co-perpetrator.[284]

The Chamber's use of the word 'additional' lends support to the proposition that all the 'ordinary' requirements must also be fulfilled in respect of specific-intent crimes, and one such ordinary requirement is general intent.

Affirming the *Kvočka* Trial Chamber's stance with reference to an accused charged with participation in a first- or second-category JCE whose criminal object is a form of persecution, the Appeals Chamber held that 'the Prosecution must demonstrate that the accused shared the common discriminatory intent of the joint criminal enterprise'.[285] The findings of the *Krnojelac* and *Simić* Trial Chambers are consistent with this holding. The *Krnojelac* Chamber found that the prosecution had not adequately established Krnojelac's 'conscious intention to discriminate', and it found that 'the Accused did not share the intent to commit any of the underlying crimes charged as persecution pursuant to any joint criminal enterprise'.[286] 'Accordingly,' the Trial Chamber concluded, 'the crime of persecution cannot be established on the basis of any of these underlying crimes as part of a joint criminal enterprise in which the Accused was involved.'[287] The *Simić* Chamber, for its part, found Simić guilty of persecution after concluding that he 'shared the intention of other participants in the joint criminal enterprise to arrest and detain non-Serb civilians' in Bosanski Šamac, Brčko and Bijeljina, and after drawing an inference that he 'could not have

---

[284] *Kvočka et al.* Trial Judgement, *supra* note 155, para. 288 (emphasis added). See also *Simić et al.* Trial Judgement, *supra* note 5, para. 156 (holding that a first-category JCE accused charged with persecutions must have had discriminatory intent).

[285] *Kvočka et al.* Appeal Judgement, *supra* note 46, para. 110. Accord *Krnojelac* Appeal Judgement, *supra* note 46, para. 111.

[286] *Krnojelac* Trial Judgement, *supra* note 166, para. 487.   [287] *Ibid.*

accepted the continued arrest and detention of non-Serb civilians ... without exercising discriminatory intent'.[288]

The *Krstić* Trial Chamber applied the same principles to arrive at the conclusion that Krstić was guilty of genocide pursuant to the first category of JCE.[289] The Chamber first found that Krstić's involvement in the killings of the Muslim men of Srebrenica – in the form of the provision of Drina Corps assets to the campaign – amounted to 'participation' in a JCE to kill these men;[290] killing was therefore the criminal object of the JCE in which Krstić participated. The Chamber then found that, because he knew of the fatal impact the killing of the men would have on Srebrenica's Muslim community, Krstić himself had 'the genocidal intent to destroy a part of the group',[291] and entered a conviction for genocide.[292] The *Krstić* Trial Chamber did not, however, make an explicit finding that Krstić possessed the general intent to kill the victims in addition to genocidal intent. In similar fashion, a trial chamber of the ICTR found the accused Simba guilty of genocide pursuant to the first category of JCE for the slaughter of thousands of Tutsis at the Murambi Technical School and Kaduha Parish in Gikongoro prefecture:

Given the scale of the killings and their context, the only reasonable conclusion is that the assailants who physically perpetrated the killings possessed the intent to destroy in whole or in part a substantial part of the Tutsi group. This genocidal intent was shared by all participants in the joint criminal enterprise, including Simba.[293]

---

[288] *Simić et al.* Trial Judgement, *supra* note 5, para. 997.

[289] See *Krstić* Trial Judgement, *supra* note 46, paras. 631–645. Also along the lines of *Kvočka, Krnojelac* and *Simić* in respect of persecution, the *Stakić* Trial Chamber remarked as follows in respect of genocide and JCE:

> The Prosecution confuses modes of liability and the crimes themselves. Conflating the third variant of joint criminal enterprise and the crime of genocide would result in the *dolus specialis* being so watered down that it is extinguished. Thus, the Trial Chamber finds that in order to 'commit' genocide, the elements of that crime, including the *dolus specialis* must be met.

Stakić Trial Judgement, *supra* note 155, para. 530.

[290] *Krstić* Trial Judgement, *supra* note 46, paras. 631–633.

[291] *Ibid.*, para. 634.

[292] *Ibid.*, para. 645. The *Krstić* Trial Chamber did not make an explicit finding that Krstić possessed, in addition to genocidal intent, the general intent to kill the victims. As Judge Bonomy pointed out in a separate opinion,

> Although the Appeals Chamber ultimately overturned Krstić's genocide conviction, it did so on the basis of its reading of the Trial Chamber's factual findings which, in the Appeals Chamber's estimation, did not suffice to establish that Krstić himself had genocidal intent. The Appeals Chamber expressed no disapproval of the Trial Chamber's understanding or application of the mental elements of JCE.

Milutinović et al. ICP Pre-Trial Decision, *supra* note 189, Separate Opinion of Judge Iain Bonomy, para. 11 n. 20.

[293] *Simba* Trial Judgement, *supra* note 136, para. 416. See also *ibid.*, para. 419 (finding Simba guilty 'based on his participation in a joint criminal enterprise' to kill these Tutsi civilians, and therefore 'guilty on Count 1 of the Indictment for genocide').

2.3.2.2 *Mental elements of the second category of JCE*

2.3.2.2.1 *Personal knowledge*

Tadić articulated two mental elements for the second category of JCE: 'With regard to the second category ... (1) personal knowledge of the system of ill-treatment is required ... as well as (2) the intent to further this common concerted system of ill-treatment.'[294] While most relevant post-*Tadić* judgements set forth this first element in terms nearly identical to those of *Tadić*,[295] the February 2005 *Kvočka* Appeal Judgement – which, together with the September 2003 *Krnojelac* Appeal Judgement, contain the most thorough interpretation and application of the elements of the second category by either Appeals Chamber – reformulated the element in more restrictive terms: '[T]he systemic form of joint criminal enterprise requires that the accused had personal knowledge of the *criminal nature* of the system.'[296] The requirement of knowledge of the system's criminal nature seemingly requires more than mere awareness on the part of the accused that crimes occurred in the course of the functioning of the system. Instead, it appears to demand that, pursuant to this mental element, the prosecution must prove that the accused knew that the commission of crimes – or of the particular crime that was the object of the alleged JCE – was the reason for the system's existence.[297] This interpretation of the first mental element resonates with the second mental element of second-category JCEs as expressed in more recent appellate jurisprudence. Earlier judgements such as the *Krnojelac* Appeal Judgement track the *Tadić* language closely: 'For the second category ... the accused must have personal knowledge of the system of ill-treatment ... as well as the intent to further this

---

[294] *Tadić* Appeal Judgement, *supra* note 3, para. 228. See also *ibid.*, para. 203 (same).

[295] See *Ntakirutimana and Ntakirutimana* Appeal Judgement, *supra* note 46, para. 467 ('The systemic form ... requires personal knowledge of the system of ill-treatment[.]'); *Vasiljević* Appeal Judgement, *supra* note 46, para. 101 ('With regard to the systemic form of joint criminal enterprise ... personal knowledge of the system of ill-treatment is required[.]'); *Krnojelac* Appeal Judgement, *supra* note 46, para. 32 ('For the second category ... the accused must have personal knowledge of the system of ill-treatment[.]'); *ibid.*, para. 89 ('For there to be the requisite intent, the accused must have had personal knowledge of the system in question[.]'); *Simić et al.* Trial Judgement, *supra* note 5, para. 157 ('Pursuant to the second category, the Prosecution needs to demonstrate that the accused ... personally knew of the system to ill-treat the detainees[.]'); *Kvočka et al.* Trial Judgement, *supra* note 155, para. 272 (quoting *Tadić* Appeal Judgement, *supra* note 3, para. 203).

[296] *Kvočka et al.* Appeal Judgement, *supra* note 46, para. 198 (emphases added). See also *ibid.*, paras. 82, 237, 271; *Limaj et al.* Trial Judgement, *supra* note 155, para. 511 ('In the second type ... the accused has knowledge of the nature of a system of repression, in the enforcement of which he participates, and the intent to further the common concerted design to ill-treat the inmates of a concentration camp.').

[297] See *ibid.*, para. 203 (finding, on the basis of his knowledge that harsh conditions were imposed and crimes were committed, that Kvočka must have been aware of the criminal nature of the system in place at Omarska and thus satisfied the requisite mental element).

concerted system of ill-treatment.'[298] The more recent *Kvočka* and *Stakić*
Appeal Judgements, however, stated that the accused in a second-category
JCE must have the 'intent to further the *criminal purpose* of the system'.[299] It is
difficult to imagine a scenario in which an accused has the intent to further the
criminal purpose of the system when he does not know what that purpose is.

The *Kvočka* Appeals Chamber appears ultimately to have taken the position
that it is sufficient to prove that the accused was aware that crimes occurred, as
long as his knowledge of the system's criminal nature can be inferred from such
awareness.[300] As the *Kvočka* Trial Chamber held and the Appeals Chamber
endorsed, a chamber may draw such an inference from the circumstances
surrounding the accused's participation in the system:

Knowledge of the joint criminal enterprise can be inferred from such indicia as the
position held by the accused, the amount of time spent in the camp, the function he
performs, his movement throughout the camp, and any contact he has with detainees,
staff personnel, or outsiders visiting the camp. Knowledge of the abuses could also be
gained through ordinary senses. Even if the accused were not eyewitnesses to crimes
committed in Omarska camp, evidence of abuses could been [*sic*] *seen* by observing the
bloodied, bruised and injured bodies of detainees, by observing heaps of dead bodies
lying in piles around the camp, and noticing the emaciated and poor condition of
detainees, as well as by observing the cramped facilities or the bloodstained walls.
Evidence of abuses could be *heard* from the screams of pain and cries of suffering,
from the sounds of the detainees begging for food and water and beseeching their
tormentors not to beat or kill them, and from the gunshots heard everywhere in the
camp. Evidence of the abusive conditions in the camp could also be *smelled* as a result
of the deteriorating corpses, the urine and feces soiling the detainees' clothes, the
broken and overflowing toilets, the dysentery afflicting the detainees, and the inability
of detainees to wash or bathe for weeks or months.[301]

---

[298] *Krnojelac* Appeal Judgement, *supra* note 46, para. 32. See also *ibid.*, para. 89 ('For there to be the
requisite intent, the accused must have had … the intent to further the concerted system.'); *Vasiljević*
Appeal Judgement, *supra* note 46, para. 101 ('With regard to the systemic form of joint criminal
enterprise … personal knowledge of the system of ill-treatment is required … as well as the intent to
further this system of ill-treatment.'); *Ntakirutimana and Ntakirutimana* Appeal Judgement, *supra*
note 46, para. 467 ('The systemic form … requires … the intent to further this system of ill-treatment.').

[299] *Stakić* Appeal Judgement, *supra* note 83, para. 65 (emphasis added). Accord *Kvočka et al.* Appeal
Judgement, *supra* note 46, para. 82 ('This form of joint criminal enterprise requires personal knowledge
of the organized system and intent to further the criminal purpose of that system.'); *ibid.*, para. 198 ('On
several occasions, the Appeals Chamber stated that the systemic form of joint criminal enterprise
requires that the accused had personal knowledge of the criminal nature of the system.').

[300] See *Kvočka et al.* Appeal Judgement, *supra* note 46, para. 203:

The Appeals Chamber considers that, even though Kvočka may have participated in the joint criminal enterprise,
without being aware at the outset of its criminal nature, the facts of the case prove that he could not have failed to
become aware of it later on. The harsh detention conditions, the continuous nature of the beatings of non-Serb
detainees and the widespread nature of the system of ill-treatment could not go unnoticed by someone working in the
camp for more than a few hours, and in particular by someone in a position of authority such as that held by Kvočka.
Kvočka's submission that he was not aware of the criminal nature of the system in place at the camp is bound to fail.

[301] *Kvočka et al.* Trial Judgement, *supra* note 155, para. 324 (emphases in original). See also *Kvočka et al.*
Appeal Judgement, *supra* note 46, para. 201.

From this passage it would seem that, for an inference to be drawn that the accused had personal knowledge of the system's criminal nature, he need not even have witnessed crimes being committed; awareness that crimes were committed can itself be inferred, *inter alia*, from the fact that the accused observed the effects of such crimes, or that others told him of such crimes.[302] As support for its conclusion that Kvočka had knowledge of the nature of the system of ill-treatment at the Omarska camp,[303] the *Kvočka* Trial Chamber considered that Kvočka had personally witnessed several crimes being committed, such as guards shooting and otherwise abusing detainees; Kvočka had heard about other crimes, for example, that people had come in from outside the camp at night and abused detainees; and Kvočka had seen the evidence of recent crimes, including bruised, bloody and dead bodies.[304]

In the passage quoted above, the *Kvočka* Trial Chamber also mentioned that knowledge of the criminal nature of the system of ill-treatment can be inferred from 'the position held by the accused'.[305] This assertion was first put forth in the *Tadić* Appeal Judgement[306] and has been echoed in several judgements, including the Appeals Judgements in *Krnojelac*, *Vasiljević* and *Ntakirutimana and Ntakirutimana*, which stated in identical terms that knowledge may be 'proved by express testimony or [may be] a matter of reasonable inference from the accused's position of authority'.[307] Kvočka's *de facto* position of authority at Omarska was a factor considered by both the Trial and Appeals Chambers in their respective determinations that he was indeed aware of the criminal purpose of the camp.[308]

2.3.2.2.2 Intent to further criminal purpose

The overall approach to the mental elements of the second category taken by the Appeals Chamber in *Krnojelac* and *Kvočka* makes it clear that, to incur liability, the accused need not have the general intent to commit the crime with which he is charged; rather, he need merely have the intent to further the

---

[302] See *Kvočka et al.* Trial Judgement, *supra* note 155, para. 384.
[303] *Ibid.*, para. 385.   [304] *Ibid.*, paras. 379–382.   [305] *Ibid.*, para. 324. See also *ibid.*, para. 272.
[306] *Tadić* Appeal Judgement, *supra* note 3, para. 228 (holding that personal knowledge of the system of ill-treatment may be 'proved by express testimony or [as] a matter of reasonable inference from the accused's position of authority').
[307] *Ntakirutimana and Ntakirutimana* Appeal Judgement, *supra* note 46, para. 467; *Vasiljević* Appeal Judgement, *supra* note 46, para. 101; *Krnojelac* Appeal Judgement, *supra* note 46, para. 89. Accord *Stakić* Appeal Judgement, *supra* note 83, para. 65 ('[T]he personal knowledge may be proven by direct evidence or by reasonable inference from the accused's position of authority.'); *Limaj et al.* Trial Judgement, *supra* note 155, para. 511; *Simić et al.* Trial Judgement, *supra* note 5, para. 157 n. 287 ('The co-perpetrator's knowledge of the system may be deduced from his powers.').
[308] *Kvočka et al.* Appeal Judgement, *supra* note 46, paras. 174, 202; *Kvočka et al.* Trial Judgement, *supra* note 155, para. 372.

criminal purpose of the system of ill-treatment and, if charged with a specific-intent crime such as genocide or persecution as a crime against humanity, he must share with the physical perpetrator the specific intent required of the crime. In order to explain fully these propositions, a detailed examination of the respective stances of the *Krnojelac* Trial and Appeal Judgements is necessary.

In a June 2001 decision on the form of the indictment, the Trial Chamber in *Brđanin and Talić* made the following, rather sweeping conclusions concerning the second category of JCE:

> As the Appeals Chamber has suggested, the second category is not substantially different to [*sic*] the first. The position of the accused in the second category is exactly the same as the accused in the first category. Both carry out a role within the joint criminal enterprise to effect the object of that enterprise which is different to [*sic*] the role played by the person who personally perpetrates the crime charged. The role of the accused in the second category is enforcing the plan by aiding and abetting the perpetrator. *Both of them must intend that the crime charged is to take place.* The Trial Chamber accordingly proposes to deal with the first and second categories together as the *basic* form of joint criminal enterprise, and with the third category as the *extended* form of joint criminal enterprise.[309]

Although the Trial Chamber cited the *Tadić* Appeal Judgement as support for this proposition, and notwithstanding *Tadić*'s comment that the second category of JCE 'is really a variant of the first category',[310] nowhere in *Tadić* is it stated that a person accused of responsibility through the second category must intend that the crime *charged* take place. On the contrary, that Judgement holds in paragraph 203, and again in paragraph 228, that such an accused must have 'the intent to further the common concerted design to ill-treat inmates',[311] a potentially very different standard.

Nevertheless, the March 2002 *Krnojelac* Trial Judgement, citing the passage of the *Brđanin and Talić* decision quoted above, reiterated the notion that 'the only basis for the distinction between these two categories made by the *Tadić* Appeals Chamber is the subject matter with which those cases dealt, namely concentration camps during the Second World War.'[312] Accordingly, the Trial Chamber determined that the post-Second World War cases cited by *Tadić* 'may not provide a firm basis for concentration or prison camp cases *as a*

---

[309] *Brđanin and Talić* June 2001 Pre-Trial Decision, *supra* note 4, para. 27 (citing *Tadić* Appeal Judgement, *supra* note 3, para. 202) (footnotes omitted) (first emphasis added; second and third emphases in original).

[310] *Tadić* Appeal Judgement, *supra* note 3, para. 203.

[311] *Ibid.* See also *ibid.*, para. 208 (holding that the accused must have 'the intent to further th[e] common concerted system of ill-treatment').

[312] *Krnojelac* Trial Judgement, *supra* note 166, para. 78.

separate category', and held, just as *Brđanin and Talić* had done, that 'both the first and second categories discussed by the *Tadić* Appeals Chamber require proof that the accused shared the intent of the crime committed by the joint criminal enterprise'.[313] The Chamber continued: 'It is appropriate to treat both as basic forms of the joint criminal enterprise.'[314]

The Trial Chamber went on to consider Krnojelac's liability, as warden of the notorious KP Dom prison in Foča, Bosnia and Herzegovina, for atrocities committed there that were charged or otherwise put forth by the prosecution as part of a 'common plan' to persecute and mistreat non-Serb detainees.[315] Without expressly identifying whether it made each discrete analysis of Krnojelac's individual criminal responsibility for the different counts in the indictment pursuant to the first or second category of JCE – or both together as completely overlapping – the Chamber repeatedly found that Krnojelac was not liable as a participant in a JCE because (1) he did not enter into an agreement with others to mistreat the detainees, and (2) he lacked the intent to commit the particular crime charged.[316] Accordingly, the Trial Chamber relegated Krnojelac to aiding-and-abetting liability for three crimes – inhumane acts as a crime against humanity, cruel treatment as a violation of the laws or customs of war, and persecution as a crime against humanity[317] – and it found him responsible as a superior under Article 7(3) for certain acts of his subordinates charged under the counts alleging inhumane acts and cruel treatment.[318]

The prosecution appealed the *Krnojelac* Judgement, partially on the ground that the Trial Chamber had erroneously conflated the first and second categories of JCE.[319] The Appeals Chamber at first appeared to adopt the same position as the Trial Chamber, stating that, 'apart from the specific case of the extended form of joint criminal enterprise, the very concept of joint criminal enterprise presupposes that its participants, other than the principal perpetrator(s) of the crimes committed, *share the perpetrators' joint*

---

[313] *Ibid.* (emphasis added).

[314] *Ibid.* The subsequent *Vasiljević* Trial Judgement, in setting out the elements of the second category, reiterated the *Krnojelac* formulation that the first and second categories are both 'basic' forms and that both require proof that the accused shared the intent of the physical perpetrators of the crime, but it made no findings in respect of the second category. *Vasiljević* Trial Judgement, *supra* note 53, para. 64.

[315] See *Krnojelac* Trial Judgement, *supra* note 166, paras. 170, 487. See also *Prosecutor* v. *Krnojelac*, Case No. IT-97-25-I, Third Amended Indictment, 25 June 2001, para. 5.2; *Krnojelac* Appeal Judgement, *supra* note 46, paras. 91, 109.

[316] See *Krnojelac* Trial Judgement, *supra* note 166, paras. 127, 170, 313–314, 346, 487. See also *Krnojelac* Appeal Judgement, *supra* note 46, para. 94. Notwithstanding the *Krnojelac* Trial Chamber's position, the Appeals Chamber has held that the second category of JCE does not require that the accused have entered into any agreement. See *supra* text accompanying notes 169–174.

[317] See *Krnojelac* Trial Judgement, *supra* note 166, paras. 170, 171, 316, 487, 489–490.

[318] *Ibid.*, paras. 172, 318.   [319] *Krnojelac* Appeal Judgement, *supra* note 46, paras. 83, 105.

criminal intent.[320] A few paragraphs further on, however, the Appeals
Chamber resuscitated the *Tadić* standard that a second-category accused
must merely have 'the intent to further the concerted system',[321] and this is
the standard that it employed to assess whether the Trial Chamber should have
held Krnojelac responsible as a JCE participant. Although, as mentioned
above, the Trial Chamber had not specified that it was applying the elements
of the first category of JCE to the exclusion of those of the second category, the
Appeals Chamber observed that the Trial Chamber's consistent practice of
inquiring, with respect to each relevant count, whether Krnojelac shared the
intent of the principal offenders demonstrated that it had only considered his
liability under the first category.[322]

Substituting the mental standard of the second category for the first-category
mental standard ostensibly employed by the Trial Chamber,[323] the Appeals
Chamber proceeded to overturn several of the Trial Chamber's findings and
convicted Krnojelac of persecution and cruel treatment pursuant to the second
category of JCE.[324] The Appeals Chamber agreed with the Trial Chamber that
Krnojelac had known that the non-Serb detainees were being unlawfully
detained, beaten and tortured because they were non-Serbs; this finding
appears to have supported an inference that the first mental element
of second-category JCE – knowledge of the criminal nature of the system of
ill-treatment – had been fulfilled.[325] The Appeals Chamber also endorsed the
findings of fact that had led the Trial Chamber to convict Krnojelac as an aider
and abettor, including that Krnojelac knew that, by not taking action to stop
the beatings and acts of torture at his prison, he encouraged his guards to
commit such acts,[326] and that he was aware of the guards' intent.[327] In light of
these findings, the Appeals Chamber determined that the second mental

---

[320] *Ibid.*, para. 84 (emphasis added).
[321] *Ibid.*, paras. 89, 96. At least one trial judgement rendered subsequent to *Krnojelac* has repeated the now
seemingly erroneous proposition that JCE liability requires, in all instances, shared intent between the
accused and the physical perpetrator. See *Mpambara* Trial Judgement, *supra* note 46, para. 14 (holding
that '[t]he *mens rea* [for JCE] is ... no different than if the accused committed the crime alone'); *ibid.*,
para. 38 ('The *mens rea* which must be possessed by a [JCE] co-perpetrator is no different from the *mens
rea* which must be possessed by a person committing a crime on his or her own.'). The *Mpambara* Trial
Chamber did not draw a distinction among the mental elements of the three categories of JCE, nor did it
acknowledge the *Krnojelac* Appeals Chamber's holding in respect of the mental elements of the second
category.
[322] *Krnojelac* Appeal Judgement, *supra* note 46, para. 94:

The Appeals Chamber notes that the Trial Chamber clearly followed the approach taken in the Indictment since, for
each aspect of the common purpose pleaded by the Prosecution, it sought to determine whether Krnojelac shared the
intent of the principal offenders. The Appeals Chamber finds that such an approach corresponds more closely to the
first category of joint criminal enterprise than to the second.

[323] See *ibid.*, paras. 105–114.   [324] *Ibid.*, paras. 112–113.   [325] See *ibid.*, paras. 110–112.
[326] *Ibid.*, para. 108.   [327] *Ibid.*, para. 110.

element of second-category JCE – formulated in *Krnojelac* as 'the intent to further th[e] concerted system of ill-treatment'[328] – had been fulfilled:

> The Appeals Chamber holds that, with regard to Krnojelac's duties, his knowledge of the system in place, the crimes committed as part of that system and their discriminatory nature, a trier of fact could reasonably have inferred from the above findings that he was part of the system and thereby *intended to further it*.[329]

Subsequent appellate jurisprudence has reaffirmed that the second mental element of the second category of JCE is indeed that the accused had 'the intent to further th[e] system of ill-treatment',[330] or 'the intent to further the *criminal purpose* of the system'.[331] The non-inclusion in these judgements of a requirement that the accused share with the physical perpetrator the general intent to commit the crime charged would appear to mark a significant difference between the first category – which requires such intent – and the second. Nevertheless, in all these judgements and as recently as April 2006, the Appeals Chambers have continued to repeat *Tadić* in referring to the second category as 'a variant of the first category'.[332]

As the passage quoted above makes clear, the *Krnojelac* Appeals Chamber took into account several facts surrounding Krnojelac's position, duties, knowledge of the activities at the KP Dom, and knowledge of the intent of the physical perpetrators to infer that he had the intent to further the system of ill-treatment. In the same vein, the *Kvočka* Trial Judgement – rendered in November 2001, almost two years before the *Krnojelac* Appeal Judgement – held expressly that an inference of 'an intent to advance the goal of the enterprise' is indeed permissible, listing two key factors from which such intent may be inferred: knowledge of the plan and participation in its

---

[328] *Ibid.*, para. 32. See also *ibid.*, para. 89 ('For there to be the requisite intent, the accused must have had … the intent to further the concerted system.').

[329] *Ibid.*, para. 111 (emphasis added).

[330] *Ntakirutimana and Ntakirutimana* Appeal Judgement, *supra* note 46, para. 467. Accord *Vasiljević* Appeal Judgement, *supra* note 46, para. 101 ('With regard to the systemic form of joint criminal enterprise … personal knowledge of the system of ill-treatment is required … as well as the intent to further this system of ill-treatment.');

[331] *Stakić* Appeal Judgement, *supra* note 83, para. 65 (emphasis added). Accord *Kvočka et al.* Appeal Judgement, *supra* note 46, para. 82 ('This form of joint criminal enterprise requires personal knowledge of the organized system and intent to further the criminal purpose of that system.').

[332] *Karemera et al.* JCE Appeal Decision, *supra* note 90, para. 12. *See also Ntakirutimana and Ntakirutimana* Appeal Judgement, *supra* note 46, para. 464 ('The second category is … a variant of the basic form[.]'); *ibid.*, para. 467 ('The systemic form … is a variant of the first[.]'); *Vasiljević* Appeal Judgement, *supra* note 46, para. 98 ('The second category … is a variant of the basic form[.]'); *Kvočka et al.* Appeal Judgement, *supra* note 46, para. 82 ('The second form … [is] a variant of the first form[.]'); *Tadić* Appeal Judgement, *supra* note 3, para. 203 ('This category of cases … is really a variant of the first category, considered above.'); *ibid.*, para. 228 (reiterating that the second category 'is really a variant of the first'). See also *Krajišnik* Trial Judgement, *supra* note 65, para. 880 (referring to the second category of JCE 'as a special case of the first form').

advancement.[333] The Trial Chamber then evaluated the circumstances of the case in light of these two factors in order to determine whether an inference could be drawn that Kvočka had the intent to further the goal of the Omarska system, the purpose of which was alleged to be the persecution and subjugation of the camp's non-Serb detainees.[334] The Chamber found that the living conditions in Omarska were harsh, and that discriminatory beatings were regularly meted out to non-Serb detainees.[335] It found additionally that Kvočka worked willingly at the camp and was amply informed of the abusive treatment of non-Serb detainees;[336] participated in the operation of the camp and had some authority over the guards;[337] held a high position at Omarska;[338] wielded considerable authority and influence over the guard service in the camp;[339] was in a position to prevent crimes but did so only on a few occasions;[340] was aware of the discriminatory common criminal purpose of the camp;[341] played a considerable role in maintaining the functioning of the camp despite his knowledge that it was a criminal endeavour;[342] and his participation substantially allowed the criminal system to continue.[343] Ostensibly relying on these facts to draw the inference that Kvočka knew that the purpose of Omarska was to persecute and subjugate non-Serbs, and that he intended to further the system's advancement,[344] the Trial Chamber found that he had indeed participated in the JCE of Omarska camp[345] and entered the convictions for persecution, murder and torture as crimes against humanity.[346]

The February 2005 *Kvočka* Appeal Judgement affirmed the two factors invoked by the Trial Judgement – knowledge of the plan and participation in its advancement – as being the proper criteria for determining whether the accused had the 'intent to further the efforts of the joint criminal enterprise so as to rise to the level of co-perpetration',[347] and it upheld the Trial Chamber's inference of Kvočka's intent.[348] It bears repeating that, while the first mental element of the second category of JCE – 'personal knowledge of the criminal nature of the system'[349] – would appear to be part of the inquiry into whether an inference of intent to further the system's purpose may be drawn, such knowledge must be coupled with actual participation in the plan by the

---

[333] *Kvočka et al.* Trial Judgement, *supra* note 155, para. 271.

[334] See *ibid.*, para. 320. See also *Kvočka et al.* Appeal Judgement, *supra* note 46, para. 183.

[335] *Kvočka et al.* Trial Judgement, *supra* note 155, paras. 116–117.   [336] *Ibid.*, paras. 356, 399–400.

[337] *Ibid.*, paras. 358–372.   [338] *Ibid.*, para. 414.   [339] *Ibid.*   [340] *Ibid.*, paras. 386–396.

[341] *Ibid.*, paras. 408, 413.   [342] *Ibid.*, para. 414.   [343] *Ibid.*, paras. 407–408, 413.

[344] See *ibid.*, paras. 404, 413.   [345] *Ibid.*, para. 414.   [346] *Ibid.*, para. 752.

[347] *Kvočka et al.* Appeal Judgement, *supra* note 46, para. 243.

[348] *Ibid.*, para. 245. See also *ibid.*, para. 213 ('Settled case-law provides that an accused's conduct is a relevant factor in establishing the intentional element of an offence.').

[349] *Ibid.*, para. 198.

accused. Accordingly, both the *Krnojelac* Appeals Chamber and the *Kvočka* Trial Chamber took into account a wide variety of circumstances – including not only the respective accused's knowledge of the system's criminal nature but also such factors as their positions of authority and their failure to intervene – in order to draw the inference that they intended to further the system.[350]

The intent to further the criminal purpose of the system does not imply that the accused has exhibited any enthusiasm or initiative, nor that he has gained personal satisfaction from his participation.[351] Hence, the Appeals Chamber dismissed Kvočka's claim that, in participating in the Omarska system, he had merely been 'carrying out his duties in accordance with the police requirements'.[352]

The *Krnojelac* Appeals Chamber apparently understood the far-reaching effects of its holding that an accused in a second-category JCE need not have the general intent to commit the crime for which he is charged, but need merely have knowledge of the system of ill-treatment and intent to further it. The chambers of the *ad hoc* Tribunals have evinced a policy of imposing lesser sentences for convictions for aiding and abetting than for participation in a JCE because '[a]iding and abetting generally involves a lesser degree of individual criminal responsibility than co-perpetration in a joint criminal enterprise'.[353] The rationale behind this assertion was explained by the *Krnojelac* Trial Chamber and subsequently endorsed by the Appeals Chamber in both *Krnojelac* and *Vasiljević*:

> The seriousness of what is done by a participant in a joint criminal enterprise who was not the principal offender is significantly greater than what is done by one who merely aids and abets the principal offender. That is because a person who merely aids and abets the principal offender *need only be aware of the intent with which the crime was committed by the principal offender*, whereas the participant in a joint criminal enterprise with the principal offender must share that intent.[354]

Under the *Krnojelac-Kvočka* formulation, however, an accused found guilty of having participated in a second-category JCE may ostensibly be sentenced just

---

[350] See *Kvočka et al.* Appeal Judgement, *supra* note 46, paras. 108–111, 213, 243, 245.

[351] *Ibid.*, paras. 106, 242; *Krnojelac* Appeal Judgement, *supra* note 46, para. 100.

[352] *Kvočka et al.* Appeal Judgement, *supra* note 46, para. 242.

[353] *Vasiljević* Appeal Judgement, *supra* note 46, para. 102. See also *Krstić* Appeal Judgement, *supra* note 64, para. 268; *Krnojelac* Appeal Judgement, *supra* note 46, para. 75; *Prosecutor* v. *Semanza*, Case No. ICTR-97-20-A, Judgement, 20 May 2005, para. 388; *Vasiljević* Trial Judgement, *supra* note 53, para. 71; *Krnojelac* Trial Judgement, *supra* note 166, para. 75; *Kvočka et al.* Trial Judgement, *supra* note 155, para. 287; *Krstić* Trial Judgement, *supra* note 46, para. 642. See also Chapter 4, text accompanying notes 139–302 (discussing the elements of aiding and abetting).

[354] *Krnojelac* Trial Judgement, *supra* note 166, para. 75 (emphasis added). Accord *Vasiljević* Appeal Judgement, *supra* note 46, para. 102; *Krnojelac* Appeal Judgement, *supra* note 46, para. 75. See also *Furundžija* Appeal Judgement, *supra* note 35, para. 118; *Tadić* Appeal Judgement, *supra* note 3, para. 229; *Kupreškić et al.* Trial Judgement, *supra* note 72, para. 772.

as severely as any of his fellow JCE participants, despite the fact that he, like a mere aider and abettor,[355] may not share the intent to commit the crime charged. Indeed, the *Krnojelac* Appeals Chamber, which overturned several aiding-and-abetting convictions in favour of convictions pursuant to the second category of JCE, increased Krnojelac's sentence from seven-and-a-half years to fifteen years.[356] This is an area in which the development and application of JCE liability in the *ad hoc* Tribunals can have legally inconsistent and possibly unfair consequences.

In a seeming effort to counter these potentially unfair consequences, the *Krnojelac* Appeals Chamber appears to have introduced two caveats into its discussion of the mental elements of second-category JCE. First, as regards specific-intent crimes charged in the indictment pursuant to the second category, the accused must himself have the requisite specific intent.[357] The authors consider this requirement below as a separate mental element.[358] Second, the Chamber stressed that, when alleging second-category liability, the prosecution must limit its definition of the common purpose to the crimes which were committed strictly pursuant to the system and 'could be considered as common to all the offenders beyond all reasonable doubt'.[359] The crimes which fit into this so-called 'common denominator' may appropriately be charged under the second category, but any crimes which 'go beyond the system's common purpose' must be charged under the first or third category of JCE.[360]

Accordingly, the Chamber held that the Prosecutor should have defined the common purpose of the KP Dom 'as limited only to the acts which sought to further the unlawful imprisonment ... of the mainly Muslim, non-Serb civilians on discriminatory grounds ... and to subject them to inhumane living conditions and ill-treatment'.[361] Any crimes committed outside this common

---

[355] See *Aleksovski* Appeal Judgement, *supra* note 94, para. 162; *Blagojević and Jokić* Trial Judgement, *supra* note 46, para. 727; *Simić et al.* Trial Judgement, *supra* note 5, para. 163; *Vasiljević* Trial Judgement, *supra* note 53, para. 71; *Krnojelac* Trial Judgement, *supra* note 166, para. 90; *Kvočka et al.* Trial Judgement, *supra* note 155, para. 556; *Prosecutor* v. *Kunarac, Kovač and Vuković*, Case No. IT-96-23-T & IT-96-23/1-T, Judgement, 22 February 2001 ('*Kunarac et al.* Trial Judgement'), para. 392; *Furundžija* Trial Judgement, *supra* note 8, para. 245.

[356] See *Krnojelac* Appeal Judgement, *supra* note 46, p. 115; *Krnojelac* Trial Judgement, *supra* note 166, para. 536. See also Chapter 6, text accompanying notes 128–176 (discussing the Appeals Chamber's increase of Krnojelac's sentence in greater detail, together with other issues relating to the forms of responsibility and sentencing).

[357] *Krnojelac* Appeal Judgement, *supra* note 46, para. 111.

[358] See *infra* text accompanying notes 365–372.

[359] *Krnojelac* Appeal Judgement, *supra* note 46, para. 120.

[360] See *ibid.*, paras. 121–122. In order to be an appropriate invocation of the first category, of course, the crime falling outside of the second-category JCE would have to be the object of a different common plan, design, or purpose, that is, a JCE to commit crimes different from those that were the object of the second-category JCE.

[361] *Ibid.*, para. 118.

purpose should have been charged under the first or third category 'without reference to the concept of system'.[362] Thus, for the count charging forced labour, the Appeals Chamber opined that the prosecution should have alleged a separate JCE whose common purpose was to commit forced labour, and any conviction would have depended on whether Krnojelac 'shared the common intent of the principal offenders'.[363] If he did not share such intent, but merely had knowledge of the perpetrators' intent and lent them support which had a significant effect on the perpetration of forced labour, he could only have been convicted as an aider and abettor.[364]

2.3.2.2.3 Shared intent for specific-intent crimes

While it held that the Trial Chamber had, on the whole, applied the wrong standard for the second mental element of the second category of JCE,[365] the *Krnojelac* Appeals Chamber appears to have concluded that the Trial Chamber correctly articulated the intent requirement in one respect: as regards persecution, the prosecution must prove that the accused shared the discriminatory intent of the physical perpetrator.[366] The *Krnojelac* Appeals Chamber's position is consistent with the following statement of the *Kvočka* Trial Judgement from two years earlier:

Where the crime [charged pursuant to JCE] requires special intent, such as the crime of persecution . . ., the accused must also satisfy the *additional* requirements imposed by the crime, such as the intent to discriminate on political, racial, or religious grounds if he is a co-perpetrator [that is, charged with JCE liability].[367]

This assertion was likewise endorsed by the February 2005 *Kvočka* Appeal Judgement.[368] It ostensibly goes beyond the mental standard established by the *Tadić* Appeal Judgement, as it requires that the accused possess in part the intent required for the commission of the charged crime, and not merely the intent to further the system of ill-treatment.[369] It also goes beyond what was held in the *Krnojelac* Appeal Judgement, as it presumably extends the

---

[362] *Ibid.*, para. 122. See also *ibid.*, para. 121.   [363] *Ibid.*, para. 122.   [364] *Ibid.*

[365] See *ibid.*, para. 94.

[366] *Ibid.*, para. 111 (holding that Krnojelac's shared discriminatory intent with the physical perpetrators 'must be established for Krnojelac to incur criminal liability on the count of persecution on this basis' – that is, on the basis of the second category of JCE).

[367] *Kvočka et al.* Trial Judgement, *supra* note 155, para. 288 (emphasis added).

[368] *Kvočka et al.* Appeal Judgement, *supra* note 46, para. 110 (citing *Krnojelac* Appeal Judgement, *supra* note 46, para. 111 and holding that, 'for crimes of persecution, the Prosecution must demonstrate that the accused shared the common discriminatory intent of the joint criminal enterprise'.).

[369] See *Tadić* Appeal Judgement, *supra* note 3, para. 228.

requirement that the accused have specific intent to specific-intent crimes other than persecution, such as genocide.[370]

A finding that the accused possessed the specific intent to commit a specific-intent crime charged pursuant to the second category likely supports an inference that the accused also possessed the intent to further the criminal system – that is, that he fulfilled the second mental element of second-category JCE. Accordingly, the *Kvočka* Appeals Chamber held that, because the purpose of the Omarska camp system was discriminatory ill-treatment, 'Kvočka's discriminatory intent encompasses the intent to further the joint criminal enterprise,'[371] and that the Trial Chamber had not erred in inferring Kvočka's intent to further the system from his discriminatory intent.[372]

2.3.2.3 *Mental elements of the third category of JCE*

2.3.2.3.1 *Intent to participate and further criminal purpose*

The first mental element of the third category concerns the mental state of the accused in respect of the crime or crimes that are the object of the alleged JCE. The *Tadić* Appeals Chamber held in paragraph 220 that, for liability to ensue pursuant to the third category, the accused must possess 'the intention to take part in a joint criminal enterprise and to further – individually and jointly – the criminal purposes of that enterprise'.[373] The Chamber repeated this element in paragraph 228 using different language: 'With regard to the third category, what is required is the *intention* to participate in and further the criminal activity or the criminal purpose of a group and to contribute to the joint criminal enterprise or in any event to the commission of a crime by the group.'[374] A number of judgements have quoted or otherwise endorsed this from paragraph 228 of *Tadić*, including the Appeal Judgements in *Ntakirutimana and Ntakirutimana*,[375] *Vasiljević*[376] and *Krnojelac*,[377] and the Trial Judgement in *Kordić and Čerkez*.[378]

---

[370] See *Krnojelac* Appeal Judgement, *supra* note 46, para. 111.

[371] *Kvočka et al.* Appeal Judgement, *supra* note 46, para. 240.   [372] See *ibid.*, paras. 240–245.

[373] *Tadić* Appeal Judgement, *supra* note 3, para. 220.   [374] *Ibid.*, para. 228 (emphasis in original).

[375] *Ntakirutimana and Ntakirutimana* Appeal Judgement, *supra* note 46, para. 467 ('[T]he extended form of joint criminal enterprise, requires the intention to participate in and further the common criminal purpose of a group and to contribute to the joint criminal enterprise or, in any event, to the commission of a crime by the group.').

[376] *Vasiljević* Appeal Judgement, *supra* note 46, para. 101 ('With regard to the extended form of joint criminal enterprise, what is required is the *intention* to participate in and further the common criminal purpose of a group and to contribute to the joint criminal enterprise or in any event to the commission of a crime by the group.') (emphasis in original).

[377] *Krnojelac* Appeal Judgement, *supra* note 46, para. 32 ('The third category requires the *intent* to participate in and further the criminal activity or the criminal purpose of a group and to contribute to the joint criminal enterprise or, in any event, to the commission of a crime by the group.').

[378] *Kordić and Čerkez* Trial Judgement, *supra* note 65, para. 398 (quoting *Tadić* Appeal Judgement, *supra* note 3, para. 228).

The formulation in paragraph 228 seems at first glance to be somewhat broader than that of paragraph 220. While both formulations require that the accused intend to take part in and further the criminal activity or criminal purpose of the enterprise, paragraph 228 demands in addition that the accused intend to contribute to the enterprise or to the commission of a crime by the enterprise. Yet, on a closer reading, paragraph 228 would appear to add nothing of substance to what is said in paragraph 220. It is difficult to imagine a scenario in which an accused who intends to further the criminal activity or the criminal purpose of an enterprise does not also intend to contribute to it. Furthermore, because the final alternative in paragraph 228 is precisely that – an alternative – the prosecution need not satisfy it in order to establish this mental element. More recent appellate jurisprudence, including the February 2005 *Kvočka* Appeal Judgement[379] and the March 2006 *Stakić* Appeal Judgement,[380] has opted for simpler language akin to that of paragraph 220.

Under paragraph 220's formulation, there are two sub-elements: the accused must have intended to participate in the JCE and he must have intended to further the JCE's criminal purpose. The requirement of intent to participate would appear to be analogous, if not identical in practical terms, to the requirement of 'voluntary' participation in a first-category JCE.[381] Similarly, the requirement of intent to further the JCE's criminal purpose is identical to the second mental element of the second category of JCE, which provides that the accused need not have had the general intent to commit the crime with which he is charged, but need merely have had the intent to further the criminal purpose of the enterprise.[382] The more extensive jurisprudence on the second category in this respect can therefore likely be relied upon when determining whether an accused charged pursuant to the third category had the intent to further the criminal purpose of the enterprise,

[379] *Kvočka et al.* Appeal Judgement, *supra* note 46, para. 83 ('[T]he accused must have the intention to participate in and contribute to the common criminal purpose.'). Accord *Limaj et al.* Trial Judgement, *supra* note 155, para. 511 (holding that 'the accused must have the intention to take part in and contribute to the common criminal purpose.'); *Blagojević and Jokić* Trial Judgement, *supra* note 46, para. 703 (holding that the accused must have had 'the intent to participate in and further a common criminal design or enterprise').

[380] *Stakić* Appeal Judgement, *supra* note 83, para. 65 ('The accused can be found to have third category joint criminal enterprise liability if he or she intended to further the common purpose of the joint criminal enterprise and the crime was a natural and foreseeable consequence of that common purpose.').

[381] See *Vasiljević* Appeal Judgement, *supra* note 46, para. 119 (discussing the first category and holding that the accused 'must *voluntarily* participate in one aspect of the common design') (emphasis added); *Tadić* Appeal Judgement, *supra* note 3, para. 196 (same). See also *supra*, text accompanying notes 264–267, for a discussion of this mental element of the first category.

[382] *Krnojelac* Appeal Judgement, *supra* note 46, para. 94; *ibid.*, paras. 108–111 (inferring Krnojelac's intent to further the JCE of the KP Dom prison from a number of circumstances, including his position of authority as warden, his knowledge that discriminatory abuses were occurring in the prison, and his knowledge that his failure to intervene encouraged further abuses). See also *supra*, text accompanying notes 321–332.

including the two factors set forth in the *Kvočka* Trial and Appeal Judgements from which an intent to further the JCE may be inferred: knowledge of the common plan and participation in its advancement.[383]

In contrast to the second category, however, liability pursuant to the third category may be imposed not only in respect of an accused who lacked general intent to commit the crime with which he is charged, but who also lacked specific intent if charged with a specific-intent crime such as genocide or persecution as a crime against humanity. As the Appeals Chamber held in a March 2004 decision on interlocutory appeal in *Brđanin*: '[T]he third category of joint criminal enterprise is no different from other forms of criminal liability which do not require proof of intent to commit a crime on the part of an accused before criminal liability can attach [for the deviatory crime].'[384] Five years before *Brđanin*, the Appeals Chamber in *Tadić* appears to have taken the same stance, albeit implicitly. The Chamber found that Tadić had participated in a JCE to rid Bosnia's Prijedor region of non-Serbs by committing inhumane acts against them,[385] that he had actively taken part in an attack on the village of Jaskići in which five men were killed, and that he had intended to further the criminal purpose of the enterprise.[386] Since it was foreseeable that non-Serbs might be killed in the execution of the common plan, and because Tadić had been aware that the actions of his confederates were likely to lead to such killings,[387] the Appeals Chamber convicted him of the Jaskići murders.[388] In this inquiry, the Chamber did not make discrete findings as to whether Tadić had the intent to commit murder or any other crime.

2.3.2.3.2 Accused's anticipation of natural and foreseeable commission of charged crime

In order to fully understand the second mental element of the third category of JCE, it is necessary to trace its complicated and convoluted evolution in the

---

[383] *Kvočka et al.* Appeal Judgement, *supra* note 46, para. 243; *Kvočka et al.* Trial Judgement, *supra* note 155, para. 271. See also *supra*, text accompanying notes 333–352, for a discussion of the Trial and Appeals Chambers' applications of these two factors.

[384] *Brđanin* JCE Appeal Decision, *supra* note 96, para. 7. See also *infra*, text accompanying notes 96–100, for a more extensive discussion of the *Brđanin* decision on interlocutory appeal and its contribution to the development of JCE in the jurisprudence of the *ad hoc* Tribunals. At least one trial judgement rendered subsequent to the 2004 *Brđanin* decision on interlocutory appeal has held – apparently erroneously – that JCE liability requires shared intent between the accused and the physical perpetrator, without distinguishing among the three categories. See *Mpambara* Trial Judgement, *supra* note 46, para. 14 (holding that '[t]he *mens rea* [for JCE] is . . . no different than if the accused committed the crime alone'); *ibid.*, para. 38 ('The *mens rea* which must be possessed by a [JCE] co-perpetrator is no different from the *mens rea* which must be possessed by a person committing a crime on his or her own.'). The *Mpambara* Trial Chamber did not acknowledge the *Brđanin* Appeals Chamber's holding that a participant in a third-category JCE need not share with the physical perpetrator the intent to commit the crime with which he is charged.

[385] *Tadić* Appeal Judgement, *supra* note 3, paras. 231–232.   [386] *Ibid.*, para. 232 (emphasis added).
[387] *Ibid.*   [388] *Ibid.*, paras. 233–237.

jurisprudence. *Tadić* itself set forth a number of definitions of this element that are partially inconsistent with one another. In paragraph 220, it expounded two 'requirements concerning *mens rea*':

> With regard to the third category of cases, it is appropriate to apply the notion of 'common purpose' only where the following requirements concerning *mens rea* are fulfilled: (i) the intention to take part in a joint criminal enterprise and to further – individually and jointly – the criminal purposes of that enterprise; and (ii) the foreseeability of the possible commission by other members of the group of offences that do not constitute the object of the common criminal purpose.[389]

The Appeals Chamber went on in the same paragraph to articulate what seem to be two additional requirements:

> Hence, the participants must have had in mind the intent, for instance, to ill-treat prisoners of war (even if such a plan arose extemporaneously) and one or some members of the group must have actually killed them. *In order for responsibility for the deaths to be imputable to the others, however, everyone in the group must have been able to predict this result.* It should be noted that more than negligence is required. *What is required is a state of mind in which a person, although he did not intend to bring about a certain result, was aware that the actions of the group were most likely to lead to that result but nevertheless willingly took that risk.* In other words, the so-called *dolus eventualis* is required (also called 'advertent recklessness' in some national legal systems).[390]

And in paragraph 228 the Chamber set out three '*mens rea* elements' unique to the third category:

> With regard to the third category, what is required is the *intention* to participate in and further the criminal activity or the criminal purpose of a group and to contribute to the joint criminal enterprise or in any event to the commission of a crime by the group. In addition, responsibility for a crime other than the one agreed upon in the common plan arises only if, under the circumstances of the case, (i) it was *foreseeable* that such a crime might be perpetrated by one or other members of the group, and (ii) the accused *willingly took that risk*.[391]

The element concerning the accused's 'intention to take part in a joint criminal enterprise and to further – individually and jointly – the criminal purposes of that enterprise'[392] has already been discussed in this chapter.[393]

---

[389] *Ibid.*, para. 220.   [390] *Ibid.* (emphases added).   [391] *Ibid.*, para. 228 (emphases in original).
[392] *Ibid*, para. 220. See also *ibid.*, para. 228 ('[W]hat is required is the *intention* to participate in and further the criminal activity or the criminal purpose of a group and to contribute to the joint criminal enterprise or in any event to the commission of a crime by the group.').
[393] See *supra* text accompanying notes 373–388.

Taking paragraphs 220 and 228 together, *Tadić* would appear to put forward three additional elements that must be established in order to attribute third-category JCE liability to an accused: (1) it was foreseeable that a crime other than the one agreed upon in the common plan (the 'deviatory crime') might be perpetrated by one or more of the JCE participants; (2) the accused and everyone else in the group must have been able to predict that the deviatory crime would 'most likely' be perpetrated by one or more of the JCE participants; and (3) the accused nevertheless willingly took the risk and participated in the JCE. The first and second elements imply both objective and subjective foreseeability. Not only must the accused have been able to predict the deviatory crime's commission, but each of his fellow participants must also have been able to predict it. In addition, the deviatory crime must have been objectively foreseeable – or, as paragraph 204 of *Tadić* put it, 'a natural and foreseeable consequence of the effecting of th[e] common purpose'[394] – presumably such that a reasonable person in the position of the accused would have been able to foresee its possible commission.

The ostensible requirement that not only the accused, but all the JCE participants, must have been able to predict the deviatory crime's likely commission can almost certainly be discounted at the outset as not forming part of current appellate jurisprudence. No post-*Tadić* judgement or decision has repeated such a requirement. Indeed, it was articulated in *Tadić* only once,[395] not repeated in paragraph 228's restatement of the elements of the third category, and not applied in the Appeals Chamber's analysis of Tadić's responsibility. In other words, the Chamber did not examine whether any of the other participants in Tadić's JCE was in fact able to predict the commission of the murders in Jaskići for which Tadić was convicted.[396] The Chamber does, however, appear to have found that the Jaskići killings were both objectively and subjectively foreseeable:

> Accordingly, the only possible inference to be drawn is that [Tadić] had the intention to further the criminal purpose to rid the Prijedor region of the non-Serb population, by committing inhumane acts against them. That non-Serbs might be killed in the effecting of this common aim *was*, in the circumstances of the present case, *foreseeable*. *[Tadić] was aware* that the actions of the group of which he was a member were likely to lead to such killings, but he nevertheless willingly took the risk.[397]

Furthermore, the requirement that the accused, despite the (objective or subjective) foreseeability of the deviatory crime's commission, nevertheless 'willingly

---

[394] *Tadić* Appeal Judgement, *supra* note 3, para. 204.
[395] *Tadić* Appeal Judgement, *supra* note 3, para. 220.   [396] See *ibid.*, paras. 230–232.
[397] *Ibid.*, para. 232 (emphases added).

took th[e] risk'[398] and participated in the JCE would seem to add nothing in practical terms to what the prosecution must prove to secure a conviction under the third category. One of the physical elements common to all three categories is participation in the JCE: any person charged with a crime pursuant to JCE – whether in the first, second, or third category – must have 'perform[ed] acts that in some way are directed to the furtherance of the common plan or purpose'.[399] Moreover, as discussed above,[400] *Tadić* and its progeny establish that an accused charged under the third category must have had the 'intention to participate in and contribute to the common criminal purpose' of the JCE.[401] 'Intentional' participation and 'willing' participation can probably be regarded as synonymous.

There are thus two key questions that remain to be resolved in an examination of post-*Tadić* jurisprudence on the third category. First, must the commission of the deviatory crime have been objectively foreseeable, or must the accused have been able subjectively to foresee such commission, or both? Paragraphs 220 and 228 of *Tadić*, along with its factual findings on the responsibility of Tadić, would suggest that both types of foreseeability are required.[402] Second, must the deviatory crime's commission have been foreseen to be likely, or merely possible? *Tadić* suggests different answers to this question, depending on the type of foreseeability under analysis. For subjective foreseeability, the deviatory crime's commission must have been foreseen to be likely, as indicated by paragraph 220's pronouncement on the law – '[w]hat is required is a state of mind in which a person, although he did not intend to bring about a certain result, was aware that the actions of the group *were most likely* to lead to that result'[403] – and the finding in paragraph 232: '[T]adić was aware that the actions of the group … *were likely* to lead to such killings.'[404] For objective foreseeability,

---

[398] *Ibid.*, para. 228.

[399] *Ibid.*, para. 229. Accord *Vasiljević* Appeal Judgement, *supra* note 46, para. 102 ('The aider and abettor carries out acts specifically directed to assist, encourage or lend moral support to the perpetration of a certain specific crime[.] By contrast, it is sufficient for a participant in a joint criminal enterprise to perform acts that in some way are directed to the furtherance of the common design.'). See *supra*, text accompanying notes 215–261, for a discussion of the physical element of participation in the JCE.

[400] See *supra* text accompanying notes 373–388.

[401] *Kvočka et al.* Appeal Judgement, *supra* note 46, para. 83. Accord *Stakić* Appeal Judgement, *supra* note 83, para. 65; *Tadić* Appeal Judgement, *supra* note 3, para. 220; *Limaj et al.* Trial Judgement, *supra* note 155, para. 511; *Blagojević and Jokić* Trial Judgement, *supra* note 46, para. 703.

[402] *Tadić* Appeal Judgement, *supra* note 3, paras. 220, 228, 232. But see Danner and Martinez, *supra* note 5, p. 106 (opining that '[t]he Appeals Chamber did not clearly specify whether the foreseeability component of this category should be assessed objectively or subjectively, although, given the difficulty of proving subjective foreseeability, the distinction arguably has little practical importance') (footnotes removed). Danner and Martinez did not elaborate on why they feel that proving subjective foreseeability presents more of a challenge than proving any other subjective mental state – such as the *mens rea* – on the part of an alleged criminal, although they did cite a 1959 article ostensibly 'making the [same] point in the context of liability for conspiracy'. *Ibid.*, p. 106 n. 123 (citing 'Note: Developments in the Law: Criminal Conspiracy', (1959) 72 *Harvard Law Review* 922, 996).

[403] *Tadić* Appeal Judgement, *supra* note 3, para. 220 (emphasis added).

[404] *Ibid.*, para. 232 (emphasis added).

the crime's commission need only have been foreseen to be possible, as indicated by paragraph 228's legal pronouncement – 'it was foreseeable that such a crime *might* be perpetrated by one or other members of the group'[405] – and paragraph 232's finding: 'That non-Serbs *might* be killed in the effecting of this common aim was, in the circumstances of the present case, foreseeable.'[406] Lamentably, subsequent jurisprudence, which tends not to appreciate the level of nuance presented by the *Tadić* formulation, has served more to obfuscate the answer to these two questions rather than to clarify it.

The first extensive post-*Tadić* discussion of the elements of the third category of JCE took place in the influential *Brđanin and Talić* decision on the form of the indictment of June 2001.[407] The Trial Chamber interpreted *Tadić* as containing requirements of both objective and subjective foreseeability:

[I]n the case of a participant in the joint criminal enterprise who is charged with a crime committed by another participant which goes beyond the agreed object of that enterprise, the Trial Chamber interprets the *Tadić* Conviction Appeal Judgement as requiring the prosecution to establish:

(i) that the crime was a natural and foreseeable consequence of the execution of that enterprise, and
(ii) that the accused was aware that such a crime was a possible consequence of the execution of that enterprise, and that, with that awareness, he participated in that enterprise.

The first is an *objective* element of the crime, and does not depend upon the state of mind on the part of the accused. The second is the *subjective* state of mind on the part of the accused which the prosecution must establish.[408]

Yet in the very next paragraph, the Chamber proceeded to present its formulation of the element in question in what seem to be subjective terms:

If the crime charged fell within the object of the joint criminal enterprise, the prosecution must establish that the accused shared with the person who personally perpetrated the crime the state of mind required for that crime. If the crime charged went beyond the object of the joint criminal enterprise, the prosecution needs to establish only that the accused was aware that the further crime was a possible consequence in the execution of that enterprise and that, with that awareness, he participated in that enterprise.[409]

[405] *Ibid.*, para. 228 (original emphasis removed; new emphasis added).
[406] *Ibid.*, para. 232 (emphasis added).
[407] See *Brđanin and Talić* June 2001 Pre-Trial Decision, *supra* note 4, paras. 24–49. While the February 2001 *Kordić and Čerkez* Trial Judgement makes mention of the third category of JCE, it does so merely in a quotation of paragraph 228 of *Tadić*, and does not discuss the third category in detail or make factual findings in relation to it. See *Kordić and Čerkez* Trial Judgement, *supra* note 65, para. 398.
[408] *Brđanin and Talić* June 2001 Pre-Trial Decision, *supra* note 4, para. 30 (emphases in original). Accord *Brđanin* Trial Judgement, *supra* note 46, para. 265 (same language).
[409] *Brđanin and Talić* June 2001 Pre-Trial Decision, *supra* note 4, para. 31 (emphases removed).

The Trial Chamber also relaxed *Tadić*'s ostensible level of probability for subjective foreseeability: the accused need only be aware that the deviatory crime's commission was a possible consequence of the execution of the JCE, not that it was 'most likely' to occur.[410]

The next relevant judicial pronouncement occurred in the August 2001 *Krstić* Trial Judgement, which quoted *Brđanin and Talić* for the propositions that the deviatory crime must have been 'a natural and foreseeable consequence of th[e] enterprise',[411] and that 'the prosecution needs to establish only that the accused was aware that the further crime was a possible consequence in the execution of that enterprise and that, with that awareness, he participated in that enterprise'.[412] In its factual findings the Trial Chamber, like the Appeals Chamber in *Tadić*, appears to have applied both the objective and the subjective foreseeability tests. After finding that Krstić had the intent to further the object of the alleged JCE – the forcible transfer of Muslim civilians out of Srebrenica[413] – the Trial Chamber opined that the murders, rapes, beatings and abuses committed against the refugees at Potočari, while not an agreed-upon objective of the JCE, 'were natural and foreseeable consequences of the ethnic cleansing campaign'.[414] It then determined that Krstić could subjectively foresee the 'inevitable' commission of these deviatory crimes:

> [G]iven the circumstances at the time the plan was formed, General Krstić must have been aware that an outbreak of these crimes would be inevitable given the lack of shelter, the density of the crowds, the vulnerable condition of the refugees, the presence of many regular and irregular military and paramilitary units in the area and the sheer lack of sufficient numbers of UN soldiers to provide protection.[415]

Satisfied that the deviatory crimes in question were both objectively and subjectively foreseeable, the Chamber proceeded to find Krstić liable for the 'incidental' murders, rapes, beatings and abuses that occurred in the course of the forcible transfer,[416] and the Appeals Chamber affirmed this finding as having resulted from a correct application of the law on the third category to

---

[410] As the purpose of this decision was merely to address the accused's contentions that the form of the indictment was defective, the Chamber did not make factual findings on the responsibility of Brđanin or Talić pursuant to the third category. On this relaxation of the *Tadić* standard, see Darcy, *supra* note 5, p. 187 (remarking that *Brđanin and Talić* 'moves the posts considerably by demanding that the accused be aware that the crime in question is *possible*, as opposed to *predictable*, per *Tadić*') (emphases in original).

[411] *Krstić* Trial Judgement, *supra* note 46, para. 613 (quoting *Brđanin and Talić* June 2001 Pre-Trial Decision, *supra* note 4, para. 31).

[412] *Ibid.* (same source) (emphases removed).

[413] *Ibid.*, para. 615. [414] *Ibid.*, para. 616. [415] *Ibid.* [416] *Ibid.*, para. 617.

the facts of the case.[417] It is unclear whether the Trial Chamber would have held Krstić responsible had he, instead of being aware that the deviatory crimes were 'inevitable', merely been aware that they were possible, although the Chamber's invocation of *Brđanin and Talić* suggests that the relaxed standard would have been sufficient. Moreover, while *Krstić* required objective as well as subjective foreseeability, the wording employed by the Trial Chamber – that the deviatory crime '*was* a natural and foreseeable consequence'[418] – does not reveal how likely the commission of such crimes must have been foreseen to be before the fact.

The November 2002 *Vasiljević* Trial Judgement, which made no findings on the third category of JCE because the prosecution had not pleaded it in the indictment,[419] also drew on *Brđanin and Talić* to come up with the following formulation:

[In] the extended form of joint criminal enterprise, . . . a member of that enterprise who did not physically perpetrate the crimes charged himself is nevertheless criminally responsible for a crime which went beyond the agreed object of that enterprise, if (i) the crime was a natural and foreseeable consequence of the execution of that enterprise, and (ii) the accused was aware that such a crime was a possible consequence of the execution of that enterprise, and, with that awareness, he participated in that enterprise.[420]

At least two subsequent Appeal Judgements – *Vasiljević* in November 2002[421] and *Ntakirutimana and Ntakirutimana* in December 2004[422] – and three Trial Judgements – *Stakić* in July 2003,[423] *Brđanin* in September 2004,[424] and *Blagojević and Jokić* in January 2005[425] – adopted this standard (the '*Brđanin and Talić*-*Vasiljević* formulation') verbatim or nearly verbatim. Like that expounded by *Brđanin and Talić* and applied in *Krstić*, the *Brđanin and Talić-Vasiljević* formulation contains a requirement of objective foreseeability that does not indicate how probable the commission of the deviatory

---

[417] *Krstić* Appeal Judgement, *supra* note 64, para. 149. *Krstić* is one of a small handful of cases in which a chamber of the *ad hoc* Tribunals has made findings of guilt in respect of the third category of JCE. Other cases include the *Tadić* Appeal Judgement, in which Tadić was found guilty of murder pursuant to the third category, *Tadić* Appeal Judgement, *supra* note 3, para. 233, and the *Stakić* Appeal Judgement, in which Stakić was found guilty of murder and extermination pursuant to the third category. *Stakić* Appeal Judgement, *supra* note 83, para. 98.

[418] *Krstić* Trial Judgement, *supra* note 46, para. 613 (quoting *Brđanin and Talić* June 2001 Pre-Trial Decision, *supra* note 4, para. 31) (emphasis added).

[419] See *Vasiljević* Trial Judgement, *supra* note 53, paras. 63, 260.

[420] *Ibid.*, para. 63 (citing *Brđanin and Talić* June 2001 Pre-Trial Decision, *supra* note 4, para. 30).

[421] *Vasiljević* Appeal Judgement, *supra* note 46, para. 101.

[422] *Ntakirutimana and Ntakirutimana* Appeal Judgement, *supra* note 46, para. 467.

[423] *Stakić* Trial Judgement, *supra* note 155, para. 436.

[424] *Brđanin* Trial Judgement, *supra* note 46, para. 265.

[425] *Blagojević and Jokić* Trial Judgement, *supra* note 46, para. 703.

crime must have been foreseen to be, as well as a requirement of subjective foreseeability in which the accused must have been aware that the deviatory crime's commission was merely a possible consequence – and not a likely or probable consequence – of the execution of the enterprise.

The March 2004 *Brđanin* decision on interlocutory appeal set forth yet another formulation, in which it coined the bizarre term 'reasonably foreseeable to him':

[I]t is sufficient that the accused entered into a joint criminal enterprise to commit a different crime with the awareness that the commission of that agreed upon crime made it reasonably foreseeable to him that the crime charged would be committed by other members of the joint criminal enterprise, and it was committed . . . For example, an accused who enters into a joint criminal enterprise to commit the crime of forcible transfer shares the intent of the direct perpetrators to commit that crime. However, if the prosecution can establish that the direct perpetrator in fact committed a different crime, and that the accused was aware that the different crime was a natural and foreseeable consequence of the agreement to forcibly transfer, then the accused can be convicted of that different offence.[426]

Under this standard, the accused must ostensibly have been aware not that the deviatory crime was a possible or probable consequence of the execution of the enterprise, but that it was a natural and foreseeable consequence. In other words, the March 2004 *Brđanin* decision appears to require not only that the crime be objectively foreseeable, but that the accused be aware of such objective foreseeability. After invoking the *Brđanin and Talić-Vasiljević* formulation – 'that the crime charged was a natural and foreseeable consequence of the execution of that enterprise and . . . that the Accused was aware that such crime was a possible consequence of the execution'[427] – the *Milošević* Trial Chamber in its June 2004 decision on motion for judgement of acquittal appears also to have endorsed the language of the March 2004 *Brđanin* decision:

The essence of this category of joint criminal enterprise is that an accused person who enters into such an enterprise to commit a particular crime is liable for the commission of another crime outside the object of the joint criminal enterprise, if it was *reasonably foreseeable to him* that as a consequence of the commission of that particular crime the other crime would be committed by other participants in the joint criminal enterprise.[428]

---

[426] *Brđanin* JCE Appeal Decision, *supra* note 96, paras. 5–6.
[427] *Prosecutor v. Milošević*, Case No. IT-02-54-T, Decision on Motion for Judgement of Acquittal, 16 June 2004 ('*Milošević* Rule 98 *bis* Trial Decision'), para. 290 (citing *Tadić* Appeal Judgement, *supra* note 3, para. 204; *Brđanin and Talić* June 2001 Pre-Trial Decision, *supra* note 4, para. 30).
[428] *Milošević* Rule 98 *bis* Trial Decision, *supra* note 427, para. 290 (emphasis added).

In April 2004, one month subsequent to its *Brđanin* decision, the Appeals Chamber rendered the *Krstić* Judgement, in which it once again changed the formulation:

> For an accused to incur criminal responsibility for acts that are natural and foreseeable consequences of a joint criminal enterprise, it is not necessary to establish that he was aware in fact that those other acts would have occurred. It is sufficient to show that he was aware that those acts outside the agreed enterprise were a natural and foreseeable consequence of the agreed joint criminal enterprise, and that the accused participated in that enterprise aware of the probability that other crimes may result.[429]

This standard appears to combine the *Brđanin and Talić-Vasiljević* formulation with that of the March 2004 *Brđanin* decision on interlocutory appeal: the deviatory crime must have been objectively foreseeable, the accused must have been aware of such objective foreseeability, and the deviatory crime must have been subjectively foreseeable. The Appeals Chamber proceeded to find that the Trial Chamber had not erred in not requiring the prosecution to prove that Krstić was actually aware that the deviatory crimes for which he was convicted were being committed; 'it was sufficient that their occurrence was foreseeable to him and that those other crimes did in fact occur'.[430]

Krstić may also be read as going beyond the *Brđanin and Talić-Vasiljević* formulation in articulating something akin to the *Tadić* Appeal Judgement's requirement that the accused be aware that the commission of the deviatory crime was 'most likely' to occur:[431] the accused must have participated in the JCE 'aware of the *probability* that other crimes may result'.[432] In the July 2004 *Blaškić* Judgement, however, the Appeals Chamber seems to have dismissed any prospect that the *Krstić* Appeal Judgement formulation served to resurrect the *Tadić* notion of 'most likely' occurrence:

> [T]he extended form of joint criminal enterprise is a situation where the actor already possesses the intent to participate and further the common criminal purpose of a group. Hence, criminal responsibility may be imposed upon an actor for a crime falling outside the originally contemplated enterprise, even where he only knew that the perpetration of such a crime was merely a *possible* consequence, rather than substantially likely to occur, and nevertheless participated in the enterprise.[433]

Blaškić did not indicate whether objective foreseeability is also required; indeed, beyond this short statement, the *Blaškić* Appeals Chamber did not opine on the elements or application of JCE at all.

---

[429] *Krstić* Appeal Judgement, *supra* note 64, para. 150.   [430] *Ibid.*
[431] *Tadić* Appeal Judgement, *supra* note 3, para. 220.
[432] *Krstić* Appeal Judgement, *supra* note 64, para. 150 (emphasis added).
[433] *Blaškić* Appeal Judgement, *supra* note 83, para 33 (emphasis added).

The February 2005 *Kvočka* Appeal Judgement, which also made no factual findings in respect of the third category, nevertheless held as follows:

The requisite *mens rea* for the extended form is twofold. First, the accused must have the intention to participate in and contribute to the common criminal purpose. Second, in order to be held responsible for crimes which were not part of the common criminal purpose, but which were nevertheless a natural and foreseeable consequence of it, the accused must *also* know that such a crime *might* be perpetrated by a member of the group, and willingly take the risk that the crime might occur by joining or continuing to participate in the enterprise.[434]

This formulation is substantially in line with the *Brđanin and Talić-Vasiljević* formulation: the deviatory crime must have been objectively foreseeable, and the accused must have subjectively foreseen the possible commission of the deviatory crime.[435] Citing *Kvočka*, the November 2005 *Limaj* Trial Judgement articulated a very similar standard.[436]

In its general discussion of the law on JCE, the March 2006 *Stakić* Appeal Judgement quoted the formulation of paragraph 228 of *Tadić*, which omits any perceptible notion of subjective foreseeability. But it added to that formulation a curious sentence derived from paragraph 220 of *Tadić* that would seem to require subjective foreseeability, thereby conforming the formulation to the generally consistent standards of the *Vasiljević, Blaškić, Ntakirutimana and Ntakirutimana* and *Kvočka* Appeal Judgements:

In other words, liability attaches 'if, under the circumstances of the case, (i) it was *foreseeable* that such a crime might be perpetrated by one or other members of the group and (ii) the accused *willingly took that risk*'. [*Tadić* Appeal Judgement, para. 228.] The crime must be shown to have been foreseeable to the accused in particular. [*Tadić* Appeal Judgement, para. 220.][437]

The Appeals Chamber restated this standard just before applying it to the facts of the case before it:

As noted above, for application of third-category joint criminal enterprise liability, it is necessary that: (a) crimes outside the Common Purpose have occurred; (b) these

---

[434] *Kvočka et al.* Appeal Judgement, *supra* note 46, para. 83 (emphases added).

[435] It could be argued, however, that, by including the word 'also' in the quoted passage, the Appeals Chamber intended to maintain the formulation of the March 2004 *Brđanin* decision on interlocutory appeal: not only must the accused have known that the deviatory crime might be committed, but he must also know that such crime was a natural and foreseeable consequence of the execution of the JCE.

[436] *Limaj et al.* Trial Judgement, *supra* note 155, para. 511:

In order to be held responsible for crimes which were not part of the common criminal purpose, but which were nevertheless a natural and foreseeable consequence of it, the accused must also know that such a crime might be perpetrated by a member of the group, and willingly takes the risk that the crime might occur by joining or continuing to participate in the enterprise.

[437] *Stakić* Appeal Judgement, *supra* note 83, para. 65 (quoting *Tadić* Appeal Judgement, *supra* note 3, para. 228; citing *ibid.*, para. 220; citing *Kvočka et al.* Appeal Judgement, *supra* note 46, para. 83).

crimes were a natural and foreseeable consequence of effecting the Common Purpose; and (c) the participant in the joint criminal enterprise was aware that crimes were a possible consequence of the execution of the Common Purpose, and in that awareness, he nevertheless acted in furtherance of the Common Purpose.[438]

The Appeals Chamber determined, on the basis of the Trial Chamber's findings in respect of a different form of responsibility that the Trial Chamber had deemed 'co-perpetratorship', that crimes outside the common purpose had indeed been committed, specifically murder as a violation of the laws or customs of war, murder as a crime against humanity, and extermination as a crime against humanity.[439] It then found that 'the commission of these crimes was a natural and foreseeable consequence of the implementation of the Common Purpose', and endorsed the Trial Chamber's conclusion that Stakić 'and his co-perpetrators acted in the awareness that crimes would occur as a direct consequence of their pursuit of the common goal'.[440] Accordingly, while the Appeals Chamber invalidated the Trial Judgement insofar as it imposed guilt on Stakić under the rubric of 'co-perpetratorship'[441] – which the Appeals Chamber found not to exist in customary international law[442] – it re-classified Stakić's responsibility for these three crimes as pertaining to the third category of JCE and upheld the Trial Chamber's convictions.[443]

While the divergent language in the various holdings of the Appeals Chambers makes it quite difficult to deduce a single, clear and authoritative definition of what the third category of JCE requires under the law of the *ad hoc* Tribunals, something along the lines of the second *Stakić* Appeal Judgement formulation would appear to represent most faithfully the consensus of the majority of recent appeal judgements and decisions. The *Krajišnik* Trial Chamber coherently restated this formulation in its September 2006 judgement:

---

[438] *Stakić* Appeal Judgement, *supra* note 83, para. 87.   [439] *Ibid.*, para. 90.
[440] *Ibid.*, para. 92 (quoting *Stakić* Trial Judgement, *supra* note 155, para. 496).
[441] *Ibid.*, para. 62 ('[I]t appears that the Trial Chamber erred in employing a mode of liability which is not valid law within the jurisdiction of this Tribunal. This invalidates the decision of the Trial Chamber as to the mode of liability it employed in the Trial Judgement.'). See also *ibid.*, para. 63:

For these reasons, the Appeals Chamber finds that the relevant part of the Trial Judgement must be set aside. In order to remedy this error, the Appeals Chamber will apply the correct legal framework to the factual conclusions of the Trial Chamber to determine whether they support joint criminal enterprise liability for the crimes charged.
[442] *Ibid.*, para. 62 ('Upon a careful and thorough review of the relevant sections of the Trial Judgement, the Appeals Chamber finds that the Trial Chamber erred in conducting its analysis of the responsibility of [Stakić] within the framework of "co-perpetratorship"'.). See also *infra*, text accompanying notes 596–622, 647–658, for a more detailed discussion of the Trial Chamber's conception of 'co-perpetratorship' and the Appeals Chamber's disapproval of it.
[443] *Stakić* Appeal Judgement, *supra* note 83, paras. 98, 104.

There are two requirements in this context, one objective and the other subjective. The objective element does not depend upon the accused's state of mind. This is the requirement that the resulting crime was a natural and foreseeable consequence of the JCE's execution. It is to be distinguished from the subjective state of mind, namely that the accused was aware that the resulting crime was a possible consequence of the execution of the JCE, and participated with that awareness.[444]

In accordance with this standard, there are two separate sub-elements contained within the second mental element of the third category. First, the deviatory crime must have been a natural and foreseeable consequence of the execution of the JCE – that is, presumably, that a reasonable person in the accused's position would have been able to foresee the crime's commission.[445] Underlying this 'natural and foreseeable' requirement there seems to be a desire on the part of the chambers to allow third-category liability to be imposed only for those crimes that, while they deviate from the common plan, do not deviate too far from it. Although *Stakić*'s invocation of paragraph 228 of *Tadić* could be read to resurrect a less stringent standard – for example, that a reasonable person in the accused's position *might have been able* to foresee the deviatory crime's commission – none of the other recent appellate jurisprudence has allowed for such a prospect. As noted in the June 2001 *Brđanin and Talić* decision,[446] this sub-element is objective, and for that reason it is not entirely appropriate to classify it under the rubric of the mental elements of the third category.

Second, the accused must be aware that the deviatory crime was a possible consequence of the execution of the JCE. Accordingly, that the deviatory crime was objectively natural and foreseeable will not suffice on its own to engage an accused's liability under the third category of JCE. This conclusion finds additional support in the following observations, made by the *Kvočka* Appeals Chamber, concerning in what circumstances a participant in a prison-camp JCE may be held liable for crimes which deviate from the common purpose of the system of ill-treatment:

---

[444] *Krajišnik* Trial Judgement, *supra* note 65, para. 882.

[445] Accord *Karemera et al.* JCE Appeal Decision, *supra* note 90, para. 13 ('Crucially, under the third – or "extended" – category of JCE liability, the accused can be held responsible for crimes physically committed by other participants in the JCE when these crimes are foreseeable consequences of the JCE, even if the accused did not agree with other participants that these crimes would be committed.') (footnote omitted). Under this standard, even if the accused could subjectively foresee the deviatory crime's possible commission, if such commission were not also objectively foreseeable, then the accused could not be convicted of it. Such might be the case where an accused has unique knowledge that a particular JCE co-participant has a tendency towards an exceptional type of brutality – for example, dismemberment of victims – and a reasonable person in similar circumstances would not have foreseen that someone in the JCE would possibly commit such a crime.

[446] *Brđanin and Talić* June 2001 Pre-Trial Decision, *supra* note 4, at para. 30. Accord *Brđanin* Trial Judgement, *supra* note 46, para. 265. See also *supra* text accompanying note 408.

[T]he Appeals Chamber wishes to affirm that an accused may be responsible for crimes committed beyond the common purpose of the systemic joint criminal enterprise, if they were a natural and foreseeable consequence thereof. However, it is to be emphasised that this question must be assessed in relation to the knowledge of a particular accused. This is particularly important in relation to the systemic form of joint criminal enterprise, which may involve a large number of participants performing distant and distinct roles. *What is natural and foreseeable to one person participating in a systemic joint criminal enterprise, might not be natural and foreseeable to another, depending on the information available to them.* Thus, participation in a systemic joint criminal enterprise does not necessarily entail criminal responsibility for all crimes which, though not within the common purpose of the enterprise, were a natural or foreseeable consequence of the enterprise. A participant may be responsible for such crimes only if the Prosecution proves that the accused had sufficient knowledge such that the additional crimes were a natural and foreseeable consequence *to him.*[447]

Contrary to the formulations of the March 2004 *Brđanin* decision on interlocutory appeal and the June 2004 *Milošević* decision on motion for judgement of acquittal, current appellate jurisprudence almost certainly does not require that the accused have been aware that the commission of the deviatory crime was a natural and foreseeable consequence of the execution of the JCE, but merely that such commission was possible.

Pre-2004 jurisprudence suggested that specific-intent crimes are incompatible with the third category of JCE or, at least, that the accused himself must have had specific intent to commit the deviatory crime, even if the physical perpetrator's general intent to commit that crime may be imputed to the accused. The *Stakić* Trial Judgement held unequivocally that a chamber cannot convict an accused of genocide charged via the third category, providing the following rationale:

Conflating the third variant of joint criminal enterprise and the crime of genocide would result in the *dolus specialis* being so watered down that it is extinguished. Thus, the Trial Chamber finds that in order to 'commit' genocide, the elements of that crime, including the *dolus specialis* must be met. The notions of 'escalation' to genocide, or genocide as a 'natural and foreseeable consequence' of an enterprise not aimed specifically at genocide are not compatible with the definition of genocide under Article 4(3)(a).[448]

In its November 2003 decision on motion for judgement of acquittal, the *Brđanin* Trial Chamber held in the same vein that a chamber cannot convict an accused of genocide where he lacks specific intent; as a consequence, it is

---

[447] *Kvočka et al.* Appeal Judgement, *supra* note 46, para. 86 (original emphasis removed; new emphasis added).
[448] *Stakić* Trial Judgement, *supra* note 155, para. 530.

improper to hold an accused liable for genocide pursuant to JCE where the object of the JCE was a crime other than genocide.[449]

The March 2004 *Brđanin* decision on interlocutory appeal reversed the holdings of the *Stakić* and *Brđanin* Trial Chambers, at least in respect of genocide.[450] The Appeals Chamber held that the prosecution may indeed charge an accused with genocide pursuant to the third category and that the accused himself need not possess the specific intent required of genocide; on the contrary, the prosecution need merely establish 'that it was reasonably foreseeable to the accused that an act specified in Article 4(2) [of the ICTY Statute] would be committed *and that it would be committed with genocidal intent*'.[451] The Appeals Chamber accordingly concluded that the Trial Chamber had 'erred by conflating the *mens rea* requirement of the crime of genocide with the mental requirement of the mode of liability by which criminal responsibility is alleged to attach to the accused', and reversed Brđanin's acquittal for genocide charged via the third category.[452]

To conclude, two final points concerning the third category of JCE warrant mention. First, while several deviatory crimes may have been committed in the execution of a JCE, and while such crimes may all have been natural and foreseeable consequences and the accused may have been aware of their possible commission, the only deviatory crime which a chamber must examine with a view towards pronouncing on guilt or innocence is, of course, that with which the accused is charged.[453] Second, as held by the Appeals Chamber in both the March 2004 *Brđanin* decision on interlocutory appeal and the *Krstić* Judgement, the deviatory crime with which the accused is charged pursuant to the third category must in fact have been committed.[454] Liability under the third category can therefore not be inchoate: an accused cannot be held responsible, even if the crime with which he is charged was a natural and foreseeable consequence of the JCE's execution and he was aware of the crime's possible commission, if that crime was not ultimately committed.

---

[449] *Brđanin* Rule 98 *bis* Trial Decision, *supra* note 95, paras. 30, 57. Accordingly, the Chamber dismissed the charge of genocide against Brđanin via the third category of JCE. *Ibid.*, paras. 32, 57.

[450] See *supra*, text accompanying notes 95–100, for a discussion of this aspect of the Rule 98 *bis* decision and the corresponding decision on interlocutory appeal, and their impact on the development of JCE in the jurisprudence of the *ad hoc* Tribunals.

[451] *Brđanin* JCE Appeal Decision, *supra* note 96, *supra* note 384, para. 6 (emphasis added).

[452] *Ibid.*, para. 10.   [453] See *Brđanin* Trial Judgement, *supra* note 46, para. 265.

[454] *Krstić* Appeal Judgement, *supra* note 64, para. 150; *Brđanin* JCE Appeal Decision, *supra* note 96, *supra* note 384, para. 5.

2.4 The *Brđanin* Trial Judgement: reining in the expansion of JCE?

It is clear from the discussion in this chapter that the *ad hoc* jurisprudence since *Tadić* represents a generally expansive approach to JCE liability. In September 2004, however, Trial Chamber II issued the *Brđanin* Judgement, which marked something of a turning point: for the first time, a trial chamber attempted to limit the circumstances in which JCE liability may apply. The *Brđanin* Trial Chamber expressed concern at the far-reaching application of JCE, holding that it is insufficient merely for the accused and the physical perpetrator each to adhere independently to a common plan formulated among various JCE participants.[455] Instead, it held that there must be a 'mutual understanding' between the accused and the physical perpetrator that the physical perpetrator will commit a concrete crime (and that the physical perpetrator either committed that crime or a crime that was a natural and foreseeable consequence of the mutual understanding).[456] A logical consequence of this approach, and one which was to be considered in subsequent cases before both *ad hoc* Tribunals,[457] was that the accused cannot be held responsible for commission under the JCE doctrine where the physical perpetrator of a crime is outside the JCE. The position taken by the *Brđanin* Trial Chamber appears to have been motivated by the view that JCE is not an appropriate mechanism for holding an accused liable in situations where that accused is far removed from the physical perpetration of the crimes charged.

An essential element of JCE liability is the requirement that a link be established between the accused and the physical perpetrator of the crime. This issue takes on increasing importance when placed in the context of the development of modern international criminal law, in which more senior-level accused are being tried before the international tribunals. Questions arise as to these accused in determining the appropriate manner in which to characterise and establish their responsibility, and, in particular, as to the nature of the link between them and the physical perpetration of a crime. The exact requirements of the JCE doctrine in respect of the nature of this link remain uncertain, and it was precisely this issue that the Trial Chamber in *Brđanin* attempted to clarify. A starting point for this discussion is to set in context the *Brđanin* case itself.

---

[455] See *Brđanin* Trial Judgement, *supra* note 46, para. 351 (holding that mere 'espousal' by the accused and the physical perpetrators of a common plan does not suffice to engage the accused's liability for the perpetrators' crimes committed pursuant to the JCE).

[456] *Ibid.*, para. 344.

[457] See *Karemera et al.* JCE Appeal Decision, *supra* note 90, para. 6 n. 14; *Krajišnik* Trial Judgement, *supra* note 65, paras. 871–884; *Popović et al.* Pre-Trial Indictment Decision, *supra* note 168, paras. 6–22; *Karemera et al.* JCE Pre-Trial Decision, *supra* note 332, paras. 4–6; *Milutinović et al.* ICP Pre-Trial Decision, *supra* note 189, paras. 18–24. See also *infra* text accompanying notes 542–589 (discussing this post-*Brđanin* jurisprudence).

2.4.1 The Brđanin *Trial Judgement*

Radoslav Brđanin was a prominent member of the Serbian Democratic Party (SDS), and played a leading role in the Autonomous Region of Krajina (ARK), an area within the planned Bosnian Serb state.[458] The prosecution alleged that Brđanin was a participant in a joint criminal enterprise, the purpose of which was the 'permanent forcible removal of Bosnian Muslim and Bosnian Croat inhabitants from the territory of this planned Bosnian Serb state'.[459] It was alleged that the members of the JCE included other members of the ARK Crisis Staff, the leadership of the Serbian Republic and the SDS, the army of the Republika Srpska, Serb paramilitary forces, 'and others'.[460] As noted by Katrina Gustafson, this alleged JCE 'covered an extremely broad range of crimes committed over a significant period of time and included a large number of individuals of greatly differing positions within the military and political hierarchies'.[461]

The Trial Chamber stated that in respect of both the first and third categories of JCE, pursuant to which Brđanin had been charged, 'the Prosecution must, *inter alia*, prove the existence of a common plan that amounts to, or involves, an understanding or an agreement to commit a crime provided for in the Statute'.[462] The Trial Chamber found that the evidence did not establish that any of the crimes alleged in the indictment had been physically perpetrated by Brđanin or his alleged co-participants in leadership positions, and it consequently declined to examine the existence of any common plan, agreement, or understanding between Brđanin on the one hand, and these individuals in leadership positions on the other – individuals who included not only the members of the ARK Crisis Staff and Bosnian Serb and SDS leaders,[463] but also 'persons in charge or in control of a military or paramilitary unit committing a crime'.[464] The Chamber also refused to entertain the possibility of a JCE between Brđanin and several persons that the prosecution at trial had argued were included in the category of 'others' referred to in the indictment. The Chamber noted that the prosecution's use of this general term 'others' could not be used to avoid the requirement of specificity in pleading its case. Therefore, the Trial Chamber held that a JCE between Brđanin and members

---

[458] *Brđanin* Trial Judgement, *supra* note 46, paras. 2–9.   [459] *Ibid.*, para. 10.   [460] *Ibid.*
[461] Katrina Gustafson, 'The Requirement of an "Express Agreement" for Joint Criminal Enterprise Liability: A Critique of *Brđanin*', (2005) 3 *Journal of International Criminal Justice* 10, available at http://jicj.oxfordjournals.org/cgi/rapidpdf/mqi085v1?maxtoshow = &HITS = 10&hits = 10&RESULT FORMAT = 1&author1 = gustafson&andorexacttitle = and&andorexacttitleabs = and&andorexactfull text = and&searchid = 1&FIRSTINDEX = 0&sortspec = relevance&resourcetype = HWCIT.
[462] *Brđanin* Trial Judgement, *supra* note 46, para. 341.   [463] *Ibid.*, para. 345.   [464] *Ibid.*, para. 347.

of the Serb police, Serb armed civilians, and other unidentified individuals had not been pleaded and could not be established.[465]

The Trial Chamber discussed the difference between 'espousal' by the accused and the physical perpetrators of a common plan on the one hand, and an arrangement made between them 'to commit a concrete crime' on the other.[466] It found that the Bosnian Serb leadership had elaborated a 'Strategic Plan' in 1991 to permanently remove non-Serbs from the envisioned Serb state 'by the use of force and fear' and 'by the commission of crimes',[467] and that Brđanin and many of the physical perpetrators had 'espoused' this Plan and had acted in advancement of its implementation.[468] The Chamber stressed, however, that the touchstone for JCE liability is that the accused and the physical perpetrators have an understanding between each other, or enter into an agreement, to commit a concrete crime; mere espousal by each of a common plan does not suffice to establish the accused's liability for the perpetrators' crimes pursuant to the JCE.[469] While a JCE may have a number of different criminal objects, the focus of the relevant inquiry is whether, as between the physical perpetrator and the accused, there was a common plan to commit a particular crime.[470] The prosecution need not establish that every participant in the JCE agreed to every one of the crimes committed.[471] Furthermore, the simple fact that the accused's actions facilitated or contributed to the physical perpetrators' commission of the crimes cannot by itself engage his JCE liability.[472] The Trial Chamber explained its reasoning as follows:

> [T]he Accused and the Relevant Physical Perpetrators could espouse the Strategic Plan and form a criminal intent to commit crimes with the aim of implementing the Strategic Plan *independently from each other* and without having an understanding or entering into any agreement between them to commit a crime.[473]

The crucial principle articulated by the Chamber is that an agreement between two persons to commit a crime 'requires a *mutual* understanding or arrangement with each other to commit a crime'.[474] The Trial Chamber supported this principle by reference to submissions elicited from the parties during trial. Both the prosecution and the defence agreed with the proposition that '[i]t is necessary to show that there was an understanding or arrangement amounting to an agreement between two or more persons that they will

---

[465] *Ibid.*, para. 346.   [466] *Ibid.*, para. 351.   [467] *Ibid.*, para. 349.
[468] *Ibid.*, para. 350.   [469] *Ibid.*, para. 351.
[470] For the first category of JCE, this crime would be the one with which the accused is charged. For the third category, the accused would be charged with a crime that is a natural and foreseeable consequence of the execution of an enterprise to commit this crime. See *supra*, text accompanying notes 389–447, for a discussion of this element in the third category.
[471] *Brđanin* Trial Judgement, *supra* note 46, paras. 264–265.   [472] *Ibid.*, para. 352.
[473] *Ibid.*, para. 351 (emphasis in original).   [474] *Ibid.*, para. 352 (emphasis in original).

commit a crime', although the prosecution did not support a differentiation between the 'espousal' of a plan and a 'mutual' understanding or arrangement.[475]

The Trial Chamber found that the prosecution had not led sufficient direct evidence to establish that the requisite understanding or agreement existed between Brđanin and the physical perpetrators,[476] and that it could not infer the existence of an understanding or an agreement from the evidence led, because other reasonable inferences could also be drawn from that evidence, including the possibility that the physical perpetrators committed their crimes in execution of orders and instructions given to them by their military or paramilitary superiors, and that the physical perpetrators did not have any sort of agreement or understanding with Brđanin himself.[477] The Chamber stated:

> [G]iven the physical and structural remoteness between the Accused and the Relevant Physical Perpetrators and the fact that the Relevant Physical Perpetrators in most cases have not even been personally identified, the Trial Chamber is not satisfied that the only reasonable conclusion that may be drawn from the Accused's and the Relevant Physical Perpetrators' respective actions aimed towards the implementation of the Common Plan is that the Accused entered into an agreement with the Relevant Physical Perpetrators to commit a crime.[478]

The Chamber concluded that, considering the 'extraordinarily broad nature' of the case and the structural remoteness of Brđanin from the commission of the crimes, 'JCE is not an appropriate mode of liability to describe the individual criminal responsibility of the Accused',[479] and accordingly dismissed JCE as a possible mode of liability to describe Brđanin's individual criminal responsibility.[480]

It is clear that the Trial Chamber had grave concerns about the remoteness of Brđanin from the physical perpetration of the crime, evincing a determination to prevent JCE becoming a doctrine with a broad or limitless application.[481] The Trial Chamber noted that in the circumstances of this particular

---

[475] *Ibid.*, para. 347 n. 885. See also *Prosecutor v. Brđanin*, Case No. IT-99-36-T, Prosecution's Submission of Public Redacted Version of the 'Prosecution's Final Trial Brief', 17 August 2004, Appendix A, para. 2.
[476] *Brđanin* Trial Judgement, *supra* note 46, para. 353. [477] *Ibid.*, para. 354. [478] *Ibid.*
[479] *Ibid.*, para. 355. While acknowledging the potential applicability of JCE to cases involving ethnic cleansing, the Trial Chamber asserted that the *Tadić* Appeals Chamber apparently 'had in mind a somewhat smaller enterprise than the one that is invoked in the present case.' *Ibid.*
[480] *Ibid.*, para. 356.
[481] JCE has been referred to colloquially as the doctrine of 'just convict everyone'. See, e.g., Badar, *supra* note 5, p. 302 (stating that the term 'just convict everyone' was used by Professor William Schabas in a 2005 course at Galway University to refer to the third category of JCE); *Prosecutor v. Popović, Beara, Nikolić, Borovčanin, Miletić, Gvero and Pandurević*, Case No. IT-05-88-T, T. 596 (23 August 2006) (defence counsel remarking in his opening statement that '[n]ot surprisingly, in Prosecution circles, the joint criminal enterprise liability concept is referred to as the just-convict-everyone liability concept').

case there was both a 'physical and structural' remoteness between Brđanin and the physical perpetrators.[482] It was this inherent weakness in, or tenuousness of, the link between Brđanin and those committing the crimes that caused the Trial Chamber to conclude as it did.

The requirement of a mutual understanding or arrangement was the Trial Chamber's way of ensuring that there would be a close enough connection between Brđanin and the physical perpetrators, and that liability would not be imposed on Brđanin for crimes committed independently by other alleged JCE participants that happened simultaneously to further the objectives of the purported JCE. In its judgement rendered two years subsequently in September 2006, the *Krajišnik* Trial Chamber expressly declined to follow *Brđanin*'s approach,[483] and instead placed emphasis on the requirement of joint action as a way to ensure that liability is not imposed for crimes committed independently:

> It is evident ... that a common objective alone is not always sufficient to determine a group, as different and independent groups may happen to share identical objectives. Rather, it is the interaction or cooperation among persons – their joint action – in addition to their common objective, that makes those persons a group. The persons in a criminal enterprise must be shown to act together, or in concert with each other, in the implementation of a common objective, if they are to share responsibility for the crimes committed through the JCE.[484]

The *Krajišnik* Trial Chamber's discussion of the law on JCE, as well as its conviction of Momčilo Krajišnik for a number of crimes pursuant to JCE even though many (or most) of the physical perpetrators were not expressly found to be JCE participants, is considered in detail below.[485]

Gustafson also suggests that an agreement or understanding between the accused and the physical perpetrators may not be the only way to guard against the risk that the crimes were committed independently:[486] instead, two interlinked JCEs could be used to describe the culpability of an accused. In the scenario described, an accused in Brđanin's position would enter into an agreement with a military or paramilitary commander to commit a crime, and that commander would in turn enter into an agreement with a physical perpetrator to commit the crime charged. These two separate JCEs would then be linked up to create JCE liability for the senior-level accused. Gustafson suggests that such an approach would answer any concern that the senior-level accused 'could be

---

[482] *Ibid.*, para. 354.
[483] *Krajišnik* Trial Judgement, *supra* note 65, para. 883 (holding that 'a JCE may exist even if none or only some of the principal perpetrators are part of it, because, for example, they are not aware of the JCE or its objective and are procured by members of the JCE to commit crimes which further that objective').
[484] *Ibid.*, para. 884.   [485] See *infra* text accompanying notes 568–589.
[486] Gustafson, *supra* note 461, p. 1.

found guilty for crimes for which he has no individual criminal responsibility'.[487] The difficulty with this analysis is that it does nothing to answer the more nuanced concern embodied in the *Brđanin* approach. The Trial Chamber was not concerned with whether Brđanin was guilty of the alleged crimes so much as how his liability was to be properly attributed. The judgement deals with what appears to be a growing obsession in the *ad hoc* Tribunal jurisprudence with finding senior-level accused responsible for *committing* crimes, instead of describing their responsibility as a superior, orderer, planner, instigator, or aider and abettor. The proposal to create two interlinked JCEs to inculpate an accused as a committer of a crime simply emphasises *Brđanin*'s concern. If it is necessary to employ a clearly specious construct to describe a senior-level accused as being responsible for committing a crime, perhaps his responsibility is simply better captured in a different form.

2.4.2 *Warning signs before the* Brđanin *Trial Judgement*

The *Brđanin* Trial Chamber's expressed concern in relation to remoteness was not a wholly surprising appearance in its judgement. An examination of some pre-trial and interlocutory decisions by the Trial Chamber indicates that similar concerns had been voiced early on about the scope of the JCE alleged in the indictment and the nature of the link between Brđanin and the physical perpetrators that arose on the facts of this case.

In June 2001 the Trial Chamber, which was composed of different judges at the time, had rendered a decision on the form of the indictment and an application by the prosecution to amend.[488] In its decision, the Chamber hinted at the difficulties stemming from the very general nature of the case pleaded by the prosecution,[489] and noted that the 'extraordinarily wide nature of the case' brought by the prosecution meant that it would be difficult to prove Brđanin and the persons who committed the crimes charged were participants in a JCE and had agreed to a criminal object.[490] The Trial Chamber accepted that:

where there could be a number of different criminal objects of a joint criminal enterprise, it is not necessary for the prosecution to prove that *every* participant agreed to every one of those crimes being committed. But it *is* necessary for the prosecution to prove that, between the person who personally perpetrated the further crime charged and the person charged with that crime, there was an agreement (or common purpose) to commit at least *a* particular crime, so that it can then be determined whether the further crime charged was a natural and foreseeable consequence of executing *that* agreed crime.[491]

[487] *Ibid.*, p. 14. [488] See *Brđanin and Talić* June 2001 Pre-Trial Decision, *supra* note 4.
[489] See *ibid.*, para. 11. [490] *Ibid.*, para. 44. [491] *Ibid.* (emphasis in original; footnotes omitted).

As in the judgement, the Trial Chamber in this pre-trial decision referred to the *Tadić* Appeal Judgement. In particular, it noted that it was 'obvious' that the Appeals Chamber in *Tadić* 'had in mind a somewhat smaller enterprise than that which is invoked in the present case'.[492] To support this proposition, the Trial Chamber referred to paragraph 204 of *Tadić*, which gave the example of a common, shared intention on the part of a group to forcibly remove members of one ethnicity from their village or region, with the consequence that one or more of the victims was shot and killed.[493] The Trial Chamber also discussed a hypothetical example of a commander directing a small group of soldiers to collect all the inhabitants of a particular ethnicity within a particular town and to remove them forcibly, and contrasted this with the facts of the case before it:

It is only when the prosecution seeks to include within that joint criminal enterprise persons as remote from the commission of the crimes charged as are the two accused in the present case that a difficulty arises in identifying the agreed object of that enterprise.[494]

The Chamber went on to comment that this difficulty was 'of the prosecution's own making', 'necessarily arising' out of the case it sought to establish.[495] The Chamber also suggested that this difficulty might mean that JCE was an inappropriate form of liability for the type of factual scenario presented in that case.[496] In November 2003, the Trial Chamber delivered its decision on the defence's motion for acquittal pursuant to Rule 98 *bis* of the ICTY Rules of Procedure and Evidence;[497] in the decision, the Chamber considered in part the nature of JCE responsibility pleaded in the indictment.[498] The defence had argued in its motion that one of the requirements for establishing a first-category JCE was proof of active participation on the part of the accused, which it termed a 'hands-on' role.[499] The Trial Chamber rejected this submission, noting that participants in a JCE may contribute to the common plan in a variety of ways,

---

[492] *Ibid.*, para. 45.   [493] *Ibid.* See also *Tadić* Appeal Judgement, *supra* note 3, para. 204.

[494] *Brđanin and Talić* June 2001 Pre-Trial Decision, *supra* note 4, para. 45.   [495] *Ibid.*

[496] *Ibid.* ('That very difficulty *may*, of course, indicate that a case based upon a joint criminal enterprise is inappropriate in the circumstances of the present prosecution. That is a matter that will have to be determined at the trial.') (emphasis in original).

[497] Rule 98 *bis* of the ICTY Rules of Procedure and Evidence provides for a chamber to 'enter a judgement of acquittal on any count if there is no evidence capable of supporting a conviction.' Rules of Procedure and Evidence for the International Criminal Tribunal for the Former Yugoslavia, UN Doc. IT/32/Rev.37 (6 April 2006), Rule 98 *bis*. The Appeals Chamber has stated the test for determining an application with respect to any charge in the indictment in the judgement of acquittal as follows: the evidence is sufficient to sustain a conviction if,

there is evidence (if accepted) upon which a tribunal of fact *could* be satisfied beyond reasonable doubt of the guilt of the accused on the particular charge in question[.] [T]hus the test is not whether the trier of fact would in fact arrive at a conviction beyond reasonable doubt on the Prosecution evidence if accepted, but whether it could.

Prosecutor v. *Jelisic*, Case No. IT-95-10-A, Judgement, 5 July 2001, para. 37 (footnotes and internal quotation marks omitted).

[498] See *Brđanin* Rule 98 *bis* Trial Decision, *supra* note 95, paras. 23–32.   [499] *Ibid.*, para. 22.

and that 'participation' could be both direct and indirect.[500] Nevertheless, the Trial Chamber did hold, in terms very similar to those used in the pre-trial indictment decision discussed above,[501] that there must be an agreement to commit at least the particular crime charged:

The Trial Chamber accepts that, while a JCE may have a number of different criminal objects, it is not necessary for the Prosecution to prove that every participant agreed to every one of the crimes being committed. However, it is necessary for the Prosecution to prove that, between the member of the JCE responsible for committing the material crime charged and the person held responsible under the JCE for that crime, there was an agreement to commit at least that particular crime.[502]

The Chamber concluded that, for the purposes of the Rule 98 *bis* decision, there was sufficient evidence for a reasonable finder of fact to find that Brđanin and all other members of the JCE identified in the indictment shared a common plan.[503] The Trial Chamber's rejection of the requirement that an accused have an active or 'hands-on' role indicates that, while concerned with the question of remoteness, the Chamber did not – contrary to the suggestion of one commentator[504] – seek to remove the utility of JCE entirely nor to require an elevation in the required participation of the accused. In its decision, the Chamber stated:

An Accused's involvement in the criminal act must form a link in the chain of causation, but it is not necessary that the participation be a *conditio sine qua non*, or that the offence would not have occurred but for the participation.[505]

An examination of the reasoning of the Trial Chamber, in both its Trial Judgement and pre-trial decisions, indicates that its concerns for remoteness stemmed from the particular factual matrix of the case before it. It took care to distinguish the facts in *Brđanin* from other ICTY jurisprudence on the basis of the scope of the alleged JCE, and the Chamber's principal concern appears to have been with the nature of the link between Brđanin and the physical perpetrator within the JCE in this particular case. While the scope of the JCE will have a bearing on this link – a large JCE making it difficult to prove a close connection – size alone does not seem to be decisive. The Chamber did not express general concerns that the reach of JCE had extended

---

[500] *Ibid.*, para. 23. [501] See *supra* text accompanying note 491.
[502] *Ibid.*, para. 27 (footnotes omitted). [503] *Ibid.*, paras. 28, 30, 31.
[504] See Allen O'Rourke, 'Joint Criminal Enterprise and Brđanin: Misguided Overcorrection', (2006) 47 *Harvard International Law Journal* 307, 324.
[505] *Brđanin* Rule 98 *bis* Trial Decision, *supra* note 95, para. 26.

too far in other ICTY cases, although it was clearly concerned about reducing the risk that JCE could be applied too expansively.[506]

Another issue dealt with by the *Brđanin* Trial Chamber in its Rule 98 *bis* decision also evinces its concern over the expansion and applicability of JCE liability.[507] The prosecution pleaded in its indictment that Brđanin was guilty of the commission of genocide pursuant to the third category of JCE. The Trial Chamber held that the specific intent required for a conviction of genocide was incompatible with the lower standard for the mental element of a third-category joint criminal enterprise. The Chamber explained that a third-category joint criminal enterprise requires the prosecution to prove only awareness on the part of the accused that genocide was a foreseeable consequence of the commission of a separately agreed-upon crime. Because mere awareness of the likelihood of genocide is nowhere near as strict a requirement as the possession of genocidal intent, the Chamber concluded that the mental element required to prove responsibility under the third category of JCE fell short of the threshold that must be satisfied for a conviction of genocide under Article 4(3)(a) of the ICTY Statute. To hold otherwise would be to conclude, through the theory of JCE, that an accused could 'commit' genocide without himself having genocidal intent. The Trial Chamber therefore held that there was no case to answer with respect to the commission of genocide in the context of the third category of JCE, and dismissed all charges of genocide in the indictment.[508]

The Appeals Chamber overturned the Trial Chamber's decision on the basis that the Trial Chamber 'erred by conflating the *mens rea* requirement of the crime of genocide with the mental requirement of the mode of liability by which criminal responsibility is alleged to attach to the accused'.[509] The

---

[506] This issue of the vastness of the JCE subsequently arose in the ICTR in the *Karemera* case. The accused Nzirorera had relied on *Brđanin* for the proposition that the ICTR lacks jurisdiction to convict an accused pursuant to the third category of JCE for crimes committed by fellow participants in the JCE of a 'vast scope'. See *Karemera et al.* JCE Pre-Trial Decision, *supra* note 332, para. 4. The Trial Chamber rejected this argument, holding that 'the scale of a joint criminal enterprise has [no] impact on such form of liability'. *Ibid.*, para. 7. The Appeals Chamber upheld this ruling, first stating (by a negative proposition) that it had never held that JCE liability can only arise in enterprises of limited size and geographic scope and, second, referring to *Tadić*'s reference to the plan to forcibly remove non-Serbs from the non-Serbs' 'region' as evidence that 'region-wide' JCEs had been expressly contemplated by the Appeals Chamber. *Karemera et al.* JCE Appeal Decision, *supra* note 90, para. 16 (citing *Tadić* Appeal Judgement, *supra* note 3, para. 204). Regrettably, as in the *Stakić* Appeal Judgement rendered some three weeks previously, the Appeals Chamber declined to deal with or consider in any reasoned way the important issue of principle raised in the *Brđanin* Trial Judgement. See *Stakić* Appeal Judgement, *supra* note 83, para. 59; *infra* text accompanying notes 596–658 (discussing *Stakić* in detail).

[507] See *supra*, text accompanying notes 95–100, for a discussion of this aspect of the Rule 98 *bis* decision and the corresponding decision on interlocutory appeal, and their impact on the development of JCE in the jurisprudence of the *ad hoc* Tribunals.

[508] *Brđanin* Rule 98 *bis* Trial Decision, *supra* note 95, paras. 55–57.

[509] *Brđanin* JCE Appeal Decision, *supra* note 96, para. 10.

Appeals Chamber provided no indication of how the discrepancy in intent requirements which motivated the Trial Chamber's ruling would be accommodated in a finding of guilt for the commission of genocide under the third category of JCE, although Judge Shahabuddeen, in a separate concurring opinion, offered some explanation.[510] He opined that the use of the concept of 'awareness' in the *Tadić* Appeal Judgement shows that the Appeals Chamber was there referring not merely to awareness, but to 'prediction' that a further crime, other than the agreed crime, would be committed as the natural and foreseeable consequence of the activities of the JCE to which the accused was a willing party. In this way, the accused is said to have formed the specific intent to commit genocide or, as Judge Shahabuddeen put it, 'his intent to commit the original crime included the specific intent to commit genocide also *if and when genocide should be committed*'.[511] While there is force in the Appeals Chamber's holding that forms of responsibility must not be conflated with the elements of crimes, these mental gymnastics engaged in by Judge Shahabuddeen do not allay the concern which appears to have motivated the *Brđanin* Trial Chamber's impugned ruling. The outcome of these decisions highlights the danger involved in the expansive character of the third category of JCE, particularly as it has been interpreted and applied since *Tadić*.

The concern embodied in the *Brđanin* approach, both in the Trial Chamber's pre-judgement rulings and in its judgement, will have significant consequences for cases involving high-level accused, particularly senior political officials. *Brđanin* was the first case in the *ad hoc* Tribunals pleading JCE as a form of liability against a relatively high-level accused for a substantial number of crimes and with a broad temporal and geographical scope. The application of this form of liability to more senior accused, such as Milan Milutinović and his co-accused, Jadranko Prlić and his co-accused, Vojislav Šešelj, and others, will pose questions as to the nature, scope and interpretation of the JCE doctrine in international criminal law.

2.4.3 *Precedent considered in the* Brđanin *Trial Judgement*

The *Brđanin* Trial Chamber engaged in little detailed analysis of the authorities on JCE that preceded it.[512] This approach is certainly surprising, given the significant modifications and restrictions to JCE introduced by the Chamber. It derived support for the proposition that '[a] common plan amounting to or involving an understanding or agreement between two or more persons that

---

[510] See generally *ibid.*, Separate Opinion of Judge Shahabuddeen, paras. 1–8.
[511] *Ibid.*, para. 7 (emphasis added).
[512] See generally *Brđanin* Trial Judgement, *supra* note 46, para. 262 n. 691.

they will commit a crime must be proved' by citing the *Vasiljević* Trial[513] and Appeal Judgements,[514] the *Krnojelac* Trial[515] and Appeal Judgements,[516] the *Simić* Trial Judgement,[517] and the *Tadić* Appeal Judgement.[518]

Even more remarkable, however, is that no authority whatsoever is cited for the Trial Chamber's key holding that a '*mutual* understanding or arrangement with each other to commit a crime' is required.[519] Those authorities that are discussed provide support for the proposition that there must be *some* arrangement or understanding, but *Brđanin* goes further by explicitly identifying the *nature* of the agreement and the accused's involvement in this agreement. Even if *Brđanin* were overturned in this respect on appeal, it will have instigated a significant step forward in the clarification of the confusing jurisprudence on this form of responsibility. The seminal ICTY Appeals Chamber judgement on JCE, *Tadić*, is referred to by the Trial Chamber in both its judgement and one of its decisions on the form of the indictment.[520] The Trial Chamber follows the categorisation of JCE adopted by *Tadić*, but refines the nature of the agreement that must be reached.[521] The key distinctions between the factual scenarios in *Tadić* and *Brđanin* are important: the size, scope and nature of the alleged criminal enterprise. The *Brđanin* Chamber argues that JCE is more suitable for smaller-scale enterprises, citing the trial judgements in *Krstić*, *Simić*, *Vasiljević* and *Krnojelac*.[522] The JCEs in those cases are described as being limited to a specific military operation and only to members of the armed forces (*Krstić*); a restricted geographical area (*Simić*); a small group of armed men acting jointly (*Tadić* and *Vasiljević*); or to a single detention camp (*Krnojelac*).[523] In this way, these cases are distinguished from the factual

---

[513] *Vasiljević* Trial Judgement, *supra* note 53, para. 66 ('The Prosecution must establish the existence of an arrangement or understanding amounting to an agreement between two or more persons that a particular crime will be committed.'). The *Vasiljević* Trial Chamber noted that the arrangement or understanding need not be express, but may be inferred: 'The fact that two or more persons are participating together in the commission of a particular crime may itself establish an unspoken understanding or arrangement amounting to an agreement formed between them then and there to commit that particular criminal act.' *Ibid.*

[514] *Vasiljević* Appeal Judgement, *supra* note 46, paras. 97, 99 (holding that in a first-category JCE all participants, acting pursuant to a common purpose, possess the same criminal intention, while in a third-category JCE one of the participants commits an act which, while outside the common purpose, is nevertheless a natural and foreseeable consequence of the effecting of that common purpose).

[515] *Krnojelac* Trial Judgement, *supra* note 166, para. 82 n. 236.

[516] *Krnojelac* Appeal Judgement, *supra* note 46, paras. 96–97.

[517] *Simić et al.* Trial Judgement, *supra* note 5, para. 158.

[518] *Tadić* Appeal Judgement, *supra* note 3, paras. 196, 204.

[519] *Brđanin* Trial Judgement, *supra* note 46, para. 352 (emphasis in original). See also *Krajišnik* Trial Judgement, *supra* note 65, para. 875 (referring to this criticism of *Brđanin* made by the prosecution in *Krajišnik*).

[520] *Brđanin* Trial Judgement, *supra* note 46, para. 355; *Brđanin and Talić* June 2001 Pre-Trial Decision, *supra* note 4, paras. 24–30, 45.

[521] *Brđanin* Trial Judgement, *supra* note 46, paras. 258–264, 347, 352.

[522] *Ibid.*, para. 355 n. 890.   [523] See *ibid.*

scenario in issue in *Brđanin*, and they are cited as examples of an appropriate use of JCE, where it was properly contained to enterprises of a smaller scale.[524]

The Trial Chamber's reading of *Tadić* has been criticised in the prosecution's brief on appeal. The prosecution contends that there is nothing in *Tadić* which indicates that the JCE doctrine should only be applicable to small cases.[525] The prosecution notes that while the Trial Chamber refers to paragraph 204 of *Tadić* to support its conclusion, that paragraph 'foresees the possibility ... that a JCE could include "a common, shared intention on the part of a group to forcibly remove members of one ethnicity from their ... region"', and argues that 'such a JCE cannot be considered small'.[526] It contends that the *Brđanin* Trial Chamber misinterpreted *Tadić*, and asserts that the Appeals Chamber could not have intended to limit JCE to small criminal structures.[527] In contrast, the defence supports the Trial Chamber's reasoning, submitting that the clear difference between *Tadić* and *Brđanin* was that in *Tadić* (as well as in the post-Second World War cases invoked by *Tadić* as support for the existence of JCE in customary international law) there was a 'hands-on' participation by the accused, which was a very different situation to that involving Brđanin.[528]

In its appeal brief, the prosecution also disputes the Trial Chamber's interpretation of *Krstić* and *Simić*.[529] It argues that in *Krstić*, the Trial Chamber found that Krstić exercised effective control over the Drina Corps troops and assets and that 'from that time onwards, General Krstić participated in the full scope of the criminal plan to kill the Bosnian Muslim men' displaced from the Srebrenica enclave.[530] Such a plan, according to the prosecution, could not be characterised as 'small' in nature.[531] In *Simić*, the prosecution has submitted that, although the Trial Chamber found the evidence did not support the

---

[524] See *ibid.*
[525] *Prosecutor* v. *Brđanin*, Case No. IT-99-36-A, Prosecution's Brief on Appeal, 28 January 2005 ('*Brđanin* Prosecution Appeal Brief'), para. 4.6.
[526] *Ibid.*   [527] *Ibid.*, paras. 4.7–4.8.
[528] *Prosecutor* v. *Brđanin*, Case No. IT-99-36-A, Response to Prosecution's Brief on Appeal, 10 May 2005, para. 40. As stated above, the ICTR Appeals Chamber itself referred to the *Tadić* example cited by the prosecution and concluded that conviction pursuant to participation in a JCE of a 'vast scope' is possible. See *Karemera et al.* JCE Appeal Decision, *supra* note 90, para. 16; *supra* note 506. This holding is an indication of the likely outcome on this issue when the Appeals Chamber renders its judgement in the *Brđanin* case.
[529] *Brđanin* Prosecution Appeal Brief, *supra* note 525, paras. 4.11–4.12.   [530] *Ibid.*, para. 4.11.
[531] *Ibid.* This submission by the prosecution does not seem entirely clear. The prosecution describes the nature of the JCE found by the Trial Chamber and endorsed by the Appeals Chamber in *Krstić*. However, it then states that if the Appeals Chamber in the present case finds the prosecution's argument incorrect and concludes that the physical perpetrators have to be members of the JCE, then the JCE in *Krstić* 'must have included' all of the individual perpetrators. The prosecution then states that '[c]learly such a JCE cannot be characterised as a "smaller" one'. It is unclear whether this comment applies to the JCE that *was* found in *Krstić*, or whether it only relates to the second (hypothetical) JCE that the prosecution alleges would result if its arguments are rejected. If this latter position is correct, then the prosecution seems to be reading back into the findings in *Krstić* in a way that is not entirely convincing.

existence of a JCE at the level of the Republika Srpska to forcibly transfer non-Serbs, the Chamber did not exclude such a large JCE as a matter of law.[532]

Despite these arguments mounted by the prosecution on appeal, the *Brđanin* Trial Chamber is undoubtedly correct in expounding a profound distinction between the nature of the JCEs alleged in *Tadić*, *Simić*, *Vasiljević* and *Krnojelac* – and even *Krstić* – and that alleged in *Brđanin*. A point that appears to have been lost in the limited commentary on the *Brđanin* Trial Judgement[533] is that there are existing forms of responsibility which may better encapsulate that responsibility: ordering, planning, instigating and superior responsibility. As mentioned above, this consideration is particularly apposite for senior leadership cases.

2.4.4 *Post-*Brđanin *jurisprudence*

Notwithstanding the significant restrictions that it introduced to the application of the JCE doctrine, the *Brđanin* Trial Judgement has not yet attracted a great deal of discussion in subsequent *ad hoc* jurisprudence. For example, the *Blagojević and Jokić* Trial Judgement, rendered less than five months after *Brđanin*, discusses the elements of JCE and makes findings in respect of this form of responsibility for both accused. Curiously, however, it does not deal with the question of whether the accused and the physical perpetrator must have had a mutual understanding between each other.[534] Perhaps because it found that neither Vidoje Blagojević nor Dragan Jokić had the requisite intent to commit the underlying offences that were the object of the alleged JCEs – forcible transfer in respect of Blagojević,[535] and murder, extermination and persecutions in respect of Jokić[536] – the Trial Chamber summarily enumerates the physical elements of JCE as having been fulfilled in respect of both accused: there was a plurality of persons consisting of officers of the Bosnian Serb army and the Serbian Interior Ministry, including Blagojević and Jokić;[537] these persons had a common plan to forcibly transfer women and children from Srebrenica[538] and kill the military-aged men;[539] and both accused participated in the execution of the common plan.[540] The Trial Chamber did, however, concur with the *Brđanin* Trial Chamber that, while the participation of the accused need not be a *conditio sine qua non* for the commission of the offence, an accused's involvement in the criminal act must form a link in the chain of causation.[541]

---

[532] *Ibid.*, para. 4.12.   [533] See, e.g., Gustafson, *supra* note 461; O'Rourke, *supra* note 504.
[534] *Blagojević and Jokić* Trial Judgement, *supra* note 46, paras. 708–711, 720–722.
[535] *Ibid.*, paras. 712–714.   [536] *Ibid.*, paras. 723–725.   [537] *Ibid.*, paras. 708, 720.
[538] *Ibid.*, paras. 709–710.   [539] *Ibid.*, para. 721.   [540] *Ibid.*, paras. 711, 722.   [541] *Ibid.*, para. 702.

Importantly, however, the limits of JCE responsibility have been discussed by at least three post-*Brđanin* trial chambers in the ICTY and one in the ICTR.[542] The accused Dragoljub Ojdanić, Milorad Trbić, and Joseph Nzirorera each made pre-trial challenges in their respective cases arguing, *inter alia*, that responsibility for participation in a JCE cannot arise in circumstances where the physical perpetrator of the crime is not a participant in the JCE; all three accused supported this contention with specific reference to *Brđanin*.[543] Furthermore, as noted above,[544] the possibility of imposing JCE liability on an accused where the physical perpetrator is outside the enterprise was also addressed in the *Krajišnik* Trial Judgement.[545]

The first of these chambers to opine on the limits of JCE responsibility was *Karemera* in August 2005. Although it was seised of an application directly asserting a requirement that there be an agreement between the accused and the physical perpetrator, the Trial Chamber appeared to ignore entirely this specific argument, and instead dealt with a broader challenge raised by Nzirorera concerning the applicability of the JCE doctrine to an enterprise of 'vast scope'.[546] Nzirorera subsequently interpreted the Trial Chamber's decision as deferring determination of whether the physical perpetrator must be a JCE participant until the final judgement, and he magnanimously opted not to lodge an interlocutory appeal on this issue.[547] The Appeals Chamber took the matter no further on appeal; it focused instead on whether liability could ensue for participation in a JCE of vast scope, concluding that it could.[548] The result is that neither Chamber in *Karemera* has yet determined whether a requirement exists that the physical perpetrator must be a participant in the enterprise.

The *Milutinović* Trial Chamber issued its decision on Ojdanić's challenge in March 2006. Like the Trial Chamber in *Karemera*, however, the majority of the *Milutinović* Chamber did not address the substance of Ojdanić's specific

---

[542] See *Krajišnik* Trial Judgement, *supra* note 65, paras. 871–884; *Popović et al.* Pre-Trial Indictment Decision, *supra* note 168, paras. 6–22; *Karemera et al.* JCE Pre-Trial Decision, *supra* note 332, paras. 4–6; *Milutinović et al.* ICP Pre-Trial Decision, *supra* note 189, paras. 18–24.

[543] *Popović et al.* Pre-Trial Indictment Decision, *supra* note 542, para. 14 (accused Trbić); *Milutinović et al.* ICP Pre-Trial Decision, *supra* note 189, para. 18 (accused Ojdanić); *Karemera et al.* JCE Pre-Trial Decision, *supra* note 332, para. 4 (accused Nzirorera).

[544] See *supra* text accompanying notes 187–188, 483–485.

[545] See *Krajišnik* Trial Judgement, *supra* note 65, paras. 883–884.

[546] See *Karemera et al.* JCE Pre-Trial Decision, *supra* note 332, paras. 1, 6–8 (quoted text at para. 1). The Trial Chamber's views in relation to applicability of the JCE doctrine to enterprises of vast scope, and the Appeals Chamber's upholding of the Trial Chamber's decision, are discussed above. See *supra* note 506.

[547] *Karemera et al.* JCE Appeal Decision, *supra* note 90, para. 6 n. 14.

[548] See *ibid.*, paras. 6, 11–18. See also *supra* note 506 (discussing these *Karemera* pre-trial and appeal decisions).

challenge.[549] It noted that his submissions accepted that JCE had been established by the Tribunal as a form of responsibility, but that the issue in dispute related to the 'contours of JCE responsibility'.[550] Essentially, the Trial Chamber viewed the challenge as a claim that the doctrine of JCE does not extend liability to circumstances in which the commission of a crime is said to have been effected through the hands of others whose *mens rea* is not explored and determined, and who are not shown to be participants in the JCE.[551] The Trial Chamber instead preferred to leave the issue of participation in the enterprise by the physical perpetrator to be addressed at trial, because it viewed challenges concerning the limits of JCE responsibility to be comparable to challenges relating to the contours of a substantive crime; it cited as support two trial judgements ascertaining the 'contours' of rape as a crime against humanity.[552] According to the Trial Chamber, the issue to be proved at trial would be whether Ojdanić and each of his co-accused, all of whom were alleged to be participants in the JCE, 'committed crimes through participation in the JCE'.[553] Essentially, the majority of the Trial Chamber declined to examine the issue at the pre-trial stage in any detail, and allowed it to go to trial, even though one of the alternative bases of JCE liability alleged in the indictment clearly exposed the co-accused to liability on the basis of a tenuous link between them and the physical perpetrators:

Dragoljub Ojdanić [and others] implemented the objectives of the joint criminal enterprise through members of the forces of the FRY and Serbia, whom they controlled, to carry out the crimes charged in this indictment.[554]

In a separate concurring opinion, Judge Bonomy, while expressing his full agreement with the Chamber's decision, addressed whether the physical perpetrator must be a participant in the JCE in more detail.[555] He noted that most judgements determining JCE liability have implicitly assumed that the physical perpetrator is or would be a participant in the JCE;[556] that only *Brđanin* specifically dealt with this issue; and that the Trial Judgement in *Krstić* had made no mention of a requirement of participation of the physical perpetrator in the JCE.[557]

---

[549] See *Milutinović et al.* ICP Pre-Trial Decision, *supra* note 189, paras. 23–24.   [550] *Ibid.*, para. 23.
[551] *Ibid.*
[552] *Ibid.* (citing *Furundžija* Trial Judgement, *supra* note 8, paras. 180–186; *Kunarac et al.* Trial Judgement, *supra* note 355, paras. 436–460).
[553] *Milutinović et al.* ICP Pre-Trial Decision, *supra* note 189, para. 23.
[554] *Prosecutor* v. *Milutinović, Šainović, Ojdanić, Pavković, Lazarević, Đorđević and Lukić*, Case No. IT-05-87-PT, Prosecution's Notice of Filing Amended Joinder Indictment and Motion to Amend the Indictment with Annexes, 16 August 2005 ('*Milutinović et al.* Proposed Amended Joinder Indictment'), para. 20.
[555] *Milutinović et al.* ICP Pre-Trial Decision, *supra* note 189, Separate Opinion of Judge Iain Bonomy, para. 1.
[556] *Ibid.*, para. 5.   [557] *Ibid.*

Addressing the question of the size of the JCE, Judge Bonomy noted that in *Tadić* and many subsequent ICTY decisions the JCEs alleged were relatively small.[558] These authorities, in his opinion, did not offer 'decisive guidance as to whether the Tribunal's jurisprudence requires that the physical perpetrator be a participant in the JCE'.[559] He noted that the factual scenario in *Brđanin* was closer to that pleaded in the *Milutinović* indictment, the JCE in both cases being of considerable scope.[560] Noting the *Brđanin* Judgement's concern with respect to remoteness or attenuation in the link between a high-level accused and the physical perpetrator, the judge wrote:

It seems to me distinctly possible that the Trial Chamber took this line because of the particular circumstances of the case. The Chamber appears to have been – in my opinion quite rightly – concerned that *it would be inappropriate to impose liability on an Accused where the link between him and those who physically perpetrated the crimes with which he is charged is too attenuated.* Indeed, it is not at all clear that, even if the Trial Chamber had taken a different view on the point, they would have found Brđanin guilty of commission through participation in a JCE, on account of the absence of a direct or close connection between him and the physical perpetrators.[561]

Although Judge Bonomy agreed that the link in that particular case was too attenuated, he did not explicitly approve of the legal basis for the Trial Chamber's holding in *Brđanin*. Indeed, he concluded that it might not be necessary for the physical perpetrator to be a participant in the JCE at all:

It is not inconsistent with the jurisprudence of the Tribunal for a participant in a JCE to be found guilty of commission where the crime is perpetrated by a person or persons who simply act as an instrument of the JCE, are who are not shown to be participants of the JCE.[562]

This separate opinion was later relied upon in the *Krajišnik* Trial Judgement, discussed below,[563] as the only source in support of that Chamber's holding

---

[558] *Ibid.*, paras. 7–8. [559] *Ibid.*, para. 8.

[560] *Ibid.*, paras. 9–10. Judge Bonomy noted, however, that the case against Ojdanić and his co-accused was 'quite different on its facts from *Brđanin* and for that reason distinguishable.' *Ibid.*, para. 10.

[561] *Ibid.*, para. 10 (emphasis added).

[562] *Ibid.*, para. 13. The November 2005 *Limaj* Trial Judgement cited the *Tadić* and *Kvočka* Appeal Judgements in a footnote, and commented that:

[i]n its rulings concerning joint criminal enterprise the Appeals Chamber referred to crimes committed 'by one or more [participants in the common design]' and 'other members of the group', thereby making it clear that only crimes committed by one or more participants in such an enterprise may give rise to liability of other participants[.]

Limaj et al. Trial Judgement, *supra* note 155, para. 511, para. 667 n. 2264. Although it was relied upon by Ojdanić to support the proposition that the physical perpetrator must be a member of the JCE, *Limaj* does not in fact directly resolve this question. The Judgement rejected JCE on the ground that there was a lack of evidence by which the JCE could be established, and not because the accused were not participants in the alleged JCE. See *ibid.*, para. 666.

[563] See *infra* text accompanying notes 568–589.

that there is no requirement whatsoever that the physical perpetrator be a participant in the JCE.[564]

The outcome in the *Popović* decision, issued in May 2006, was the same as that in *Milutinović* and *Karemera*. Indeed, the majority of the Trial Chamber expressly relied upon *Milutinović* and deferred to the final judgement the determination of whether 'the physical perpetrator [must have] an agreement with the accused ... and thus whether the physical perpetrator has to be a participant in the JCE himself'.[565] Interestingly, Judge Agius dissented in a footnote, stating tersely that 'the question of whether the physical perpetrator must be a participant in the JCE should be decided at this stage of the proceedings, in order for the Accused to be able to adequately prepare their respective cases'.[566] It may be regrettable that the majority declined to provide a fully reasoned ruling on this issue prior to trial, and that Judge Agius chose not to relate his views more completely in a separate or dissenting opinion, especially considering that Judge Agius was also the presiding judge of the *Brđanin* Trial Chamber, and he may have provided some further insight into that Chamber's position, thereby preparing a path to final resolution of this issue by the *Brđanin* Appeals Chamber.[567]

The September 2006 *Krajišnik* Trial Judgement was the first judgement since *Brđanin* to address whether a requirement exists that the physical perpetrator be a participant in the JCE. At the time of the events charged in the indictment, Momčilo Krajišnik served as President of the Bosnian Serb Assembly; the Trial Chamber found him to be the 'number two' official in the Bosnian Serb government, behind Radovan Karadžić.[568] He was charged with a number of crimes committed pursuant to, or as natural and foreseeable consequences of, a massive JCE the objective of which was 'the permanent removal, by force or other means, of Bosnian Muslim, Bosnian Croat or other non-Serb inhabitants from large areas of Bosnia and Herzegovina through the commission of crimes'.[569] This purported enterprise, which was very similar to that alleged against Brđanin, included a number of named political and military figures, including Krajišnik, Radovan Karadžić, Slobodan Milošević, Biljana Plavšić, Ratko Mladić, Nikola Koljević, Željko Raznatović, Momir Talić, and Radoslav Brđanin himself, as well as 'other members of the Bosnian Serb

---

[564] See *Krajišnik* Trial Judgement, *supra* note 65, para. 883 n. 1737.
[565] *Popović et al.* Pre-Trial Indictment Decision, *supra* note 168, para. 21.   [566] *Ibid.*, para. 21 n. 49.
[567] Since neither Trial Chamber certified the decision for interlocutory appeal, the Appeals Chamber did not have the opportunity to rule on whether the issue was a jurisdictional question that must be settled before trial. See *infra* note 713.
[568] *Krajišnik* Trial Judgement, *supra* note 65, para. 1085.
[569] *Prosecutor* v. *Krajisnik*, Case No. IT-00-39 & 40-PT, Amended Consolidated Indictment, 7 March 2002, para. 3.

leadership at the Republic, regional and municipal levels; members of the [Yugoslav and Republika Srpska armies]; the Bosnian Serb Territorial Defence ...; the Bosnian Serb police ...; and members of Serbian and Bosnian Serb paramilitary forces and volunteer units'.[570]

In his final brief, Krajišnik invoked *Brđanin* to support the assertion that, given the extraordinarily broad nature of his case, JCE was not an appropriate form of responsibility, as the doctrine was never intended to be used to impose liability on a person so structurally remote from the physical commission of the crimes charged.[571] He contended further that 'liability under JCE requires proof that the [a]ccused had entered into an agreement with the individuals who were the principal perpetrators of the underlying crimes'.[572] This latter claim directly addressed the crucial issue raised in *Brđanin* and in the cases discussed above, and which (perhaps unlike the JCE of 'vast scope' considered by the Appeals Chamber in *Karemera*[573]) remains an important and unresolved point. Surprisingly and regrettably, despite their clearly critical nature to *Krajišnik* and to the development of the *ad hoc* jurisprudence on JCE, as well as the growing body of opinion on them, the Trial Chamber gave both of the accused's arguments scant and almost dismissive attention.

The Chamber rejected Krajišnik's first claim out of hand with a single reference to the Appeals Chamber ruling in *Karemera* concerning enterprises of vast scope.[574] It held that, '[f]ar from being inappropriate, JCE is well suited to cases such as the present one, in which numerous persons are all said to be concerned with the commission of a large number of crimes'.[575] Indeed, upon finding that JCE was 'the most appropriate mode of liability' for the case, the Chamber took the bizarre step of dismissing consideration of Krajišnik's guilt in respect of all other charged forms of responsibility without explanation.[576]

The *Krajišnik* Trial Chamber's treatment of the asserted requirement that there be an agreement between the accused and the physical perpetrator was even less satisfactory. Unlike Judge Bonomy in *Milutinović* – who exhaustively reviewed the case law of the ICTY, jurisprudence from post-Second World

---

[570] *Ibid.*, para. 7.   [571] *Krajišnik* Trial Judgement, *supra* note 65, paras. 871–872.

[572] *Ibid.*, para. 873. The Trial Chamber's apparent dislike of the term 'physical perpetrator' caused it to utilise, sometimes confusingly, the phrase 'principal perpetrator'.

[573] See *supra* notes 506, 548.

[574] *Krajišnik* Trial Judgement, *supra* note 65, para. 876 (citing *Karemera et al.* JCE Appeal Decision, *supra* note 90, paras. 15–16 and remarking that 'the Appeals Chamber has never suggested that JCE liability can arise only from participation in enterprises of small size or scope'). See *supra* notes 506, 548, for a discussion of this decision in *Karemera*.

[575] *Ibid.*, para. 876.

[576] *Ibid.*, para. 877 ('On the facts of this case ... the Chamber finds JCE to be the most appropriate mode of liability. Therefore, other forms of liability charged in the indictment will not be further considered in this judgement.'). Chapter 6 discusses in detail how a chamber goes about choosing among the forms of responsibility charged against an accused in the indictment.

War tribunals, and national laws to determine whether customary international law or the general principles of law support the existence of such a requirement[577] – the *Krajišnik* Chamber disposed of the matter in a single sentence, relying solely on Judge Bonomy's separate opinion for support: '[A] JCE may exist even if none or only some of the principal perpetrators are part of it, because, for example, they are not aware of the JCE or its objective and are procured by members of the JCE to commit crimes which further that objective.'[578] While it acknowledged the 'concern expressed by the Trial Chamber in *Brđanin* about the issue of alleged JCE participants acting independently of each other', the *Krajišnik* Chamber determined that this concern 'is sufficiently addressed by the requirement that joint action among members of a criminal enterprise is proven'.[579] However, that 'joint action' is required begs the question: what action and how is it to be characterised?

Later in the judgement, the Trial Chamber attempted to answer this question by endorsing a non-exhaustive list of indicia proposed by the prosecution at the Chamber's own behest.[580] This list, which is set forth above in its entirety,[581] 'concern[s] connections or relationships among persons working together in the implementation of a common objective' that transform them 'into members of a joint criminal enterprise'.[582] According to the *Krajišnik* Chamber, '[t]hese persons rely on each other's contributions, *as well as on acts of persons who are not members of the JCE but who have been procured to commit crimes*, to achieve criminal objectives on a scale which they could not have attained alone'.[583] Nevertheless, and again unlike Judge Bonomy,[584] beyond stating that a non-JCE participant may be 'procured' by a JCE participant to commit crimes, the Chamber did not elaborate on the types of relationship that may exist between the non-participant and the participant in order for liability for the non-participant's crime to flow through the JCE to the accused.

The Trial Chamber concluded that the enterprise alleged against Krajišnik consisted of such a 'large and indefinite group of persons' that it was neither possible, nor 'desirable [or] necessary', 'to specify fully the membership of the

---

[577] *Milutinović et al.* ICP Pre-Trial Decision, *supra* note 189, Separate Opinion of Judge Iain Bonomy, paras. 5–30.
[578] *Krajišnik* Trial Judgement, *supra* note 65, para. 883 (citing generally *Milutinović et al.* ICP Pre-Trial Decision, *supra* note 189, Separate Opinion of Judge Iain Bonomy).
[579] *Ibid.*, para. 884 (footnote omitted).   [580] *Ibid.*, para. 1081.
[581] See *supra* text accompanying note 188.   [582] *Krajišnik* Trial Judgement, *supra* note 65, para. 1082.
[583] *Ibid.* (emphasis added).
[584] See *Milutinović et al.* ICP Pre-Trial Decision, *supra* note 189, Separate Opinion of Judge Iain Bonomy, paras. 3–4 (stating that persons outside the JCE 'may execute the JCE's common purpose in response to orders or some other inducement of the accused or his fellow participants') (quotation at para. 3).

JCE'.[585] Instead, '[w]hat is necessary is to be convinced that the Accused was sufficiently connected and concerned with persons who committed crimes pursuant to the common objective in various capacities, or who procured other persons to do so'.[586] The Chamber went on to find that the JCE participants included Krajišnik, Karadžić, Plavšić, Brđanin, Mladić and other named leaders, as well as 'local politicians, military and police commanders, paramilitary leaders and others'.[587] It convicted Krajišnik for a number of crimes without, at least in most instances, making explicit findings on whether the physical perpetrator was himself a JCE participant, or had merely been 'procured' by a JCE participant to commit the crime in question.[588]

One reading of *Krajišnik*'s treatment of JCE is that it is a kind of 'anti-*Brđanin*', not just accepting but enthusiastically endorsing the view that JCE is an appropriate framework within which to consider massive-scale criminality in which the accused plays a part and where that accused is extremely remote from, and has no apparent direct relationship with, the physical perpetrators of the crime. However, because *Krajišnik* gave so little attention to the legal elements of JCE (even though it dismissed consideration of the accused's guilt in respect of all other forms of responsibility perfunctorily in two short sentences[589]), it is difficult to consider that it might have any relevance to the development of this aspect of individual responsibility in international criminal law.

2.4.5 *Assessing the impact of* Brđanin

The *Brđanin* Trial Judgement stands for a limitation on the expansive application of the JCE doctrine in international criminal law. Because the Appeals Chambers have not yet reviewed the critical aspect of the issue – the nature of the relationship required between the accused and the physical perpetrator – it remains in some respects an unanswered question about the future development of the doctrine. ICTY judges have confirmed many other indictments that allege JCEs on a considerably greater scale than that in *Brđanin*. *Krajišnik* is an example of one Trial Chamber apparently unconcerned with whether the physical perpetrator is or is not a participant in the JCE, even though the accused was charged with liability pursuant to an arguably more sprawling

---

[585] *Krajišnik* Trial Judgement, *supra* note 65, para. 1086.   [586] *Ibid.*
[587] *Ibid.*, paras. 1087–1088 (quotation at para. 1087).
[588] See, e.g., *ibid.*, paras. 784–786, 792–793, 795–801, 807–808, 810–812, 815, 819–821, 829–830, 836–837, 1095. See also *ibid.*, paras. 1126, 1182 (convicting Krajišnik of persecution, extermination, murder, deportation and inhumane acts as crimes against humanity); *ibid.*, para. 1183 (sentencing Krajišnik to twenty-seven years' imprisonment).
[589] *Ibid.*, para. 877.

JCE than that charged against Brđanin. As Daryl Mundis and Fergal Gaynor correctly point out, if *Brđanin* is upheld on appeal, it will require a 'radical reassessment of the correct legal theory to express the liability of political leaders at the apex of a campaign of persecution for crimes committed by perpetrators from whom they are hierarchically (and often geographically) distant'.[590]

Some commentators have argued that the *Brđanin* approach has reduced the value of the JCE doctrine, described as a useful form of responsibility that is suitable for describing the liability of those involved in mass crimes, making it more difficult to find senior-level accused individually responsible for 'committing' crimes.[591] While it is undoubtedly true that international crimes entail different considerations from domestic crimes, and may necessitate different forms of liability, this argument seems to focus more on the *results* that may be possible with JCE, rather than the proper legal application of the doctrine as a defined and coherent theory of liability in international criminal law.

As Judge Bonomy's separate opinion in the March 2006 *Milutinović* decision indicates, there are considerable gaps and ambiguities in the ICTY's jurisprudence relating to JCE. However, a crucial point that must not be forgotten, and which *Brđanin* highlights, is that 'commission' liability is only one of many different forms of responsibility under which an accused may be held responsible in international criminal law. *Brđanin* expresses the concern that JCE is being applied too broadly, in situations where too tenuous a connection between the accused and the physical perpetration of the crimes exists. If a profound stretching of criminal law principles is required to construct and describe an accused's responsibility in a particular way, it is possible that other forms of responsibility, which better encapsulate the nature of the accused's alleged responsibility, should be employed.

2.5 Indirect co-perpetration: a new form of common-purpose liability?

The *Brđanin* Trial Chamber's attempt to halt the expanding scope of JCE, at a time when cases had begun to focus in earnest on the collective criminal activities of high-ranking political and military leaders, appears to have caused some degree of consternation within the ICTY Office of the Prosecutor. In the wake of *Brđanin*, the prosecution proposed amendments to a number of indictments in order to include allegations in respect of a novel form of

---

[590] Mundis and Gaynor, *supra* note 7, p. 280.
[591] See, e.g., Gustafson, *supra* note 461, pp. 2, 25; O'Rourke, *supra* note 504, p. 323 (arguing that *Brđanin* both makes JCE 'indistinguishable from the conspiracy framework', and 'collapses JCE into the aiding and abetting framework').

common-purpose liability as an alternative to JCE.[592] According to the prosecution, this form of responsibility – usually termed 'indirect co-perpetration' –
would allow the imposition of liability upon an accused where the group to
which he belongs implements its criminal objectives through other persons,
such as police or soldiers, who need not form part of the group.[593]

The prosecution claimed jurisprudential support for such a form of responsibility in the *Stakić* Trial Judgement, rendered in July 2003, which eschewed
reliance on JCE in favour of a theory of liability it labelled 'co-perpetratorship'.[594]
In March 2006, however, an ICTY trial chamber and the ICTY Appeals
Chamber simultaneously issued separate decisions independently declaring
that co-perpetratorship as defined in *Stakić* did not exist in the jurisdiction
of the ICTY.[595] Although the long-term impact of these decisions on the law of
forms of responsibility in the *ad hoc* Tribunals is still uncertain, they have
definitively closed off at least one avenue for the imposition of common-
purpose liability in the ICTY and the ICTR. This section discusses the
Stakić Trial Judgement and each of these decisions in turn.

2.5.1 *The* Stakić *Trial Judgement*

The indictment against Milomir Stakić, the former President of the Crisis Staff
of Prijedor municipality in Bosnia, charged him with JCE responsibility in the
following terms:

26. Milomir Stakić participated in the joint criminal enterprise, in his roles as set out in
paragraph 22 above. The purpose of the joint criminal enterprise was the permanent
forcible removal of Bosnian Muslim and Bosnian Croat inhabitants from the territory
of the planned Serbian state, including a campaign of persecutions through the
commission of the crimes alleged in Counts 1 to 8 of the Indictment. The accused
Milomir Stakić, and the other members of the joint criminal enterprise, each shared
the state of mind required for the commission of each of these offences[.][596]
[...]

---

[592] See, e.g., *Prosecutor v. Tolimir, Miletić, Gvero, Pandurević, Beara, Popović, Nikolić, Trbić and
Borovčanin*, Case No. IT-05-88-PT, Consolidated Amended Indictment, 28 June 2005 ('*Popović et al.*
June 2005 Indictment'), para. 88; *Prosecutor v. Prlić, Stojić, Praljak, Petković, Ćorić and Pušić*, Case No.
IT-04-74-PT, Amended Indictment, 16 November 2005, paras. 15–16, 218; *Milutinović et al.* Proposed
Amended Joinder Indictment, *supra* note 554, paras. 20–22, 34. See also *infra* text accompanying
notes 628–634.
[593] See *Prlić et al.* Indictment, *supra* note 592, para. 218; *Milutinović et al.* ICP Pre-Trial Decision, *supra*
note 189, para. 7 (discussing this contention on the part of the prosecution).
[594] *Stakić* Trial Judgement, *supra* note *supra* note 155, para. 438. See also *infra* text accompanying
notes 601–611.
[595] See *Stakić* Appeal Judgement, *supra* note 83, para. 62; *Milutinović et al.* ICP Pre-Trial Decision, *supra*
note 189, paras. 39–40. *See also infra* text accompanying notes 635–658.
[596] *Prosecutor v. Stakić*, Case No. IT-97-24-PT, Fourth Amended Indictment, 10 April 2002, para. 26.

28. Alternatively, the accused is individually responsible for the crimes enumerated in Counts 1 to 8 on the basis that these crimes were natural and foreseeable consequences of the execution of the common purpose of the joint criminal enterprise and Milomir Stakić was aware that these crimes were the possible consequence of the execution of the joint criminal enterprise.[597]

On the basis of these two paragraphs together with the prosecution's submissions at trial, the Trial Chamber determined that '[t]he Prosecution ... ha[d] pleaded all three categories of joint criminal enterprise in relation to all the Counts charged in the Indictment'.[598] The Chamber acknowledged the existence of JCE within the jurisdiction of the ICTY, as pronounced by *Tadić* and reaffirmed in the May 2003 *Milutinović* decision on interlocutory appeal.[599] The Trial Chamber remarked that 'joint criminal enterprise can not be viewed as membership in an organisation because this would constitute a new crime not foreseen under the Statute and therefore amount to a flagrant infringement of the principle *nullum crimen sine lege*'.[600] After discussing the elements of the three categories of JCE, however, the Chamber opined that:

> joint criminal enterprise is only one of several possible interpretations of the term 'commission' under Article 7(1) and ... other definitions of co-perpetration must equally be taken into account. Furthermore, a more direct reference to 'commission' in its traditional sense *should be given priority* before considering responsibility under the judicial term 'joint criminal enterprise'.[601]

In the four paragraphs that followed, the Chamber defined a form of responsibility that it considered to be 'a more direct reference to "commission"' than JCE; it alternately deemed this 'more direct' form of responsibility 'co-perpetration' and 'co-perpetratorship'.

The Trial Chamber stated that it 'prefer[red] to define "committing" as meaning that the accused participated, physically or otherwise directly or indirectly, in the material elements of the crime charged ... whether individually or jointly with others.'[602] The Chamber explained what it meant by 'indirectly' in a footnote: 'Indirect participation in German Law (*mittelbare Täterschaft*) or "the perpetrator behind the perpetrator"; terms normally used

---

[597] *Ibid.*, para. 28.

[598] *Stakić* Trial Judgement, *supra* note 155, para. 427. In its judgement the Appeals Chamber opined, contrary to the Trial Chamber, that the prosecution had only intended to rely on the first and third categories of JCE, and not the second. *Stakić* Appeal Judgement, *supra* note 83, para. 66.

[599] *Stakić* Trial Judgement, *supra* note 155, para. 432:

> The Appeals Chamber in *Tadić* observed that Article 7(1) 'covers first and foremost the physical perpetration of a crime by the offender himself, or the culpable omission of an act that was mandated by a rule of criminal law. However, the commission of one of the crimes envisaged in Articles 2, 3, 4 or 5 of the Statute might also occur through participation in the realisation of a common design or purpose.' In the *Milutinović* Decision, the Appeals Chamber held unequivocally that joint criminal enterprise is to be regarded as a form of 'commission' pursuant to Article 7(1)[.]

[600] *Ibid.*, para. 433.   [601] *Ibid.*, para. 438 (emphasis added).   [602] *Ibid.*, para. 439.

in the context of white collar crime or other forms of organised crime.'[603] It then set out the physical elements of co-perpetratorship, along with what appears to have been intended as the doctrinal support for the existence of such a form of responsibility in international law:

For co-perpetration it suffices that [1] there was an explicit agreement or silent consent to reach [2] a common goal by [3] coordinated co-operation and [4] joint control over the criminal conduct. For this kind of co-perpetration it is typical, but not mandatory, that one perpetrator possesses skills or authority which the other perpetrator does not. These can be described as shared acts which when brought together achieve the shared goal based on the same degree of control over the execution of the common acts. In the words of *Roxin*: 'The co-perpetrator can achieve nothing on his own[.] . . . The plan only "works" if the accomplice works with the other person.' Both perpetrators are thus in the same position. As *Roxin* explains, 'they can only realise their plan insofar as they act together, but each individually can ruin the whole plan if he does not carry out his part. To this extent he is in control of the act.' *Roxin* goes on to say, '[t]his type of "key position" of each co-perpetrator describes precisely the structure of joint control over the act.' Finally, he provides the following very typical example:

If two people govern a country together – are joint rulers in the literal sense of the word – the usual consequence is that the acts of each depend on the co-perpetration of the other. The reverse side of this is, inevitably, the fact that by refusing to participate, each person individually can frustrate the action.[604]

In the next paragraph, the Chamber acknowledged that 'the end result of its definition of co-perpetration approaches that of the aforementioned joint criminal enterprise and even overlaps in part', but asserted that 'this definition is closer to what most legal systems understand as "committing" and avoids the misleading impression that a new crime not foreseen in the Statute of this Tribunal has been introduced through the backdoor'.[605] The text of a footnote following the words 'new crime' contains the text: 'E.g. "membership in a criminal organization".'[606] Thus, notwithstanding the prior assertion that 'joint criminal enterprise cannot be viewed as membership in an organisation because this would constitute a new crime not foreseen under the Statute',[607] and despite the Appeals Chamber's unequivocal affirmation to the same effect two months previously in the *Milutinović* decision,[608] the Trial Chamber

---

[603] *Ibid.*, para. 439 n. 942.
[604] *Ibid.*, para. 440 (footnotes removed; omissions in original; numbers inserted) (citing Claus Roxin, *Täterschaft und Tatherrschaft* (6th edn 1994), pp. 278–279).
[605] *Ibid.*, para. 441 (footnotes omitted).   [606] *Ibid.*, para. 441 n. 950.
[607] *Ibid.*, para. 433.
[608] *Milutinović et al.* JCE Appeal Decision, *supra* note 4, para. 26 ('Criminal liability pursuant to a joint criminal enterprise is not a liability for mere membership or for conspiring to commit crimes, but a form of liability concerned with the participation in the commission of a crime as part of a joint criminal enterprise, a different matter.'). See also *supra* note 91.

appears to have declined to rely on JCE at least in part out of a fear that such reliance had been or might be viewed as impermissibly imposing liability for mere membership of a criminal organisation.

The Trial Chamber defined the mental elements of co-perpetratorship as follows:

> In respect of the *mens rea*, the Trial Chamber re-emphasises that modes of liability cannot change or replace elements of crimes defined in the Statute and that the accused must also [1] have acted in the awareness of the substantial likelihood that punishable conduct would occur as a consequence of coordinated co-operation based on the same degree of control over the execution of common acts. Furthermore, the accused [2] must be aware that his own role is essential for the achievement of the common goal.[609]

While it reserved the prerogative to impose liability on the basis of other forms of responsibility in relation to specific counts in the indictment,[610] the Trial Chamber found that '"co-perpetratorship" best characterises Dr. Stakić's participation in offences committed in Prijedor Municipality in 1992', and held that this form of responsibility would therefore 'serve as a basis for [the Chamber's] findings in relation to each count in the Indictment'.[611] The Chamber then determined that the physical elements of co-perpetratorship had been fulfilled in respect of Stakić: he and a number of other persons had a common goal to establish a Bosnian Serb state through the creation of a coercive environment for Prijedor's non-Serb residents;[612] at meetings in April 1992, all the participants had come to an agreement to effect this goal;[613] the Crisis Staff, the so-called 'War Presidency', the police, and the army had all acted together in 'coordinated co-operation';[614] and the requirement of inter-dependency had been satisfied: 'No participant could achieve the common goal on his own, although each could individually have frustrated the plan by refusing to play his part or by reporting crimes.'[615] The Chamber likewise found that the requisite mental elements had been fulfilled: 'Dr. Stakić and his co-perpetrators acted in the awareness that crimes would occur as a direct consequence of their pursuit of the common goal,'[616] and 'Dr. Stakić knew that his role and authority as the leading politician in Prijedor was essential for the accomplishment of the common goal.'[617]

Having determined that the prosecution had established all the physical and mental elements of co-perpetratorship, and in spite of the complete absence of

---

[609] *Stakić* Trial Judgement, *supra* note 155, para. 442 (citing no authority) (numbers inserted).
[610] *Ibid.*, para. 468 (holding that, although 'co-perpetratorship' best described Stakić's participation in the crimes charged, 'this is in no way restrictive and additional modes of liability will be considered in respect of specific counts').
[611] *Ibid.*   [612] *Ibid.*, para. 470, 475.   [613] *Ibid.*, para. 472.   [614] See *ibid.*, paras. 484, 488.
[615] *Ibid.*, para. 490.   [616] *Ibid.*, para. 496.   [617] *Ibid.*, para. 498.

allegations in the indictment or submissions at trial in relation to this form of responsibility,[618] the Trial Chamber proceeded to convict Stakić of a number of crimes as a 'co-perpetrator', including persecution[619] and extermination[620] as crimes against humanity; and murder as a violation of the laws or customs of war.[621] The Chamber sentenced Stakić to life imprisonment.[622]

2.5.2 *The Prosecutor's response to the* **Brđanin** *and* **Stakić** *Trial Judgements*

The previous section of this chapter discussed the September 2004 *Brđanin* Judgement, in which a trial chamber of the ICTY imposed significant restrictions on the scope of JCE liability.[623] Specifically, the *Brđanin* Chamber held that there must be a 'mutual understanding' between the accused and the physical perpetrator that the physical perpetrator will commit a concrete crime,[624] and that JCE liability cannot ensue where the identities of the accused's fellow participants are not adequately alleged in the indictment.[625] The Trial Chamber ultimately dismissed JCE as an appropriate mechanism for describing the responsibility of Brđanin due to the 'extraordinarily broad nature' of the enterprise in which he was alleged to have participated.[626]

Out of an apparent concern that this restrictive approach to JCE might be adopted by other trial chambers and ultimately endorsed by the Appeals

---

[618] Cf. *Kvočka et al.* Appeal Judgement, *supra* note 46, para. 42 (footnote removed):

The Appeals Chamber ... considers that the Indictment is defective because it fails to make any specific mention of joint criminal enterprise[.] ... [J]oint criminal enterprise responsibility must be specifically pleaded. Although joint criminal enterprise is a means of 'committing', it is insufficient for an indictment to merely make broad reference to Article 7(1) of the Statute. Such reference does not provide sufficient notice to the Defence or to the Trial Chamber that the Prosecution is intending to rely on joint criminal enterprise responsibility. Moreover, in the Indictment the Prosecution has failed to plead the category of joint criminal enterprise or the material facts of the joint criminal enterprise, such as the purpose of the enterprise, the identity of the participants, and the nature of the accused's participation in the enterprise.

Accord *Stakić* Appeal Judgement, *supra* note 83, para. 66. See also *supra* text accompanying notes 161–163.

[619] *Stakić* Trial Judgement, *supra* note 155, para. 632 (finding Stakić guilty of murder as a crime against humanity); *ibid.*, para. 712 (holding, in respect of deportation as a crime against humanity, that 'the Trial Chamber is convinced that [Stakić] intended to deport the non-Serb population from Prijedor municipality and that, based on this intent, he not only committed the crime of deportation as a co-perpetrator, but also planned and ordered this crime'.); *ibid.*, para. 826 ('The Trial Chamber ... finds [Stakić] guilty as a co-perpetrator of the proven acts alleged under persecution, a crime against humanity under Article 5(h) of the Statute.'); *ibid.*, p. 253 ('incorporating' the findings of guilt for murder and deportation as crimes against humanity into the conviction for persecution as a crime against humanity).

[620] *Ibid.*, para. 661, p. 253.   [621] *Ibid.*, para. 616, p. 253.   [622] *Ibid.*, p. 253.
[623] See *supra* text accompanying notes 458–480.
[624] *Brđanin* Trial Judgement, *supra* note 46, para. 344.
[625] See *ibid.*, para. 346 (refusing to entertain the possibility of a JCE between Brđanin and several persons that the prosecution at trial had argued made up the 'others' alleged in the indictment – including members of the Serb police, Serb armed civilians, and unidentified individuals – because the indictment failed to plead the identities of such persons with sufficient specificity to put Brđanin on notice of the membership of the alleged JCE).
[626] *Ibid.*, paras. 355–356. See also *supra*, text accompanying notes 458–480, for a discussion of the *Brđanin* Trial Chamber's holding.

Chamber, the prosecution filed amended indictments in all three of the ICTY's so-called 'mega-trials'[627] alleging additional forms of common-purpose liability. The June 2005 proposed amended indictment in the *Popović* case contained, along with JCE, a form of responsibility labelled 'direct and/or indirect co-perpetration', in which the accused are alleged to have effected the crimes charged 'through or by way of [their] subordinates or other persons'.[628] The November 2005 indictment in the *Prlić* case alleges not only the accused's responsibility pursuant to JCE,[629] but that 'each accused is also charged as a co-perpetrator and/or indirect perpetrator or indirect co-perpetrator'.[630] The indictment elaborates on this allegation as follows:

Each accused is responsible for the acts or omissions which he accomplished, effected or caused through or by means of other persons, such as subordinates or other persons (including persons he controlled or over whom he exercised substantial influence), whether such persons acted knowingly or as an innocent agent or actor. *In addition or in the alternative*, each accused is responsible for the crimes which he committed or caused to be committed, directly or indirectly through other persons, based on the joint control and co-ordination which he possessed and effected with other persons (including the other persons charged in this indictment) over the criminal conduct of Herceg-Bosna/HVO authorities and forces which were used as tools, by or through organised structures of power which they controlled and in which each of them played a key role. Each accused acted with the knowledge and state of mind required for the commission of the crime charged, was aware of the importance of his own role and the control that he exercised over other persons that

---

[627] Trials of six or more accused. Although there have been proceedings with multiple accused throughout the *ad hoc* Tribunals' existence, the introduction of the completion strategy in the last few years has resulted in the increased incidence of such large trials. See *infra* text accompanying note 798 for more on the completion strategy at both Tribunals.

[628] *Popović et al.* June 2005 Indictment, *supra* note 592, para. 88 (underlining in original, emphasis added):

Pursuant to Article 7(1) of the Statute of the Tribunal, Zdravko Tolimir, Radivoje Miletić, Milan Gvero, Vinko Pandurević, Ljubiša Beara, Vujadin Popović, Drago Nikolić, Milorad Trbić and Ljubomir Borovčanin are individually responsible for the crimes charged against them in this Indictment. Each of them committed, planned, instigated, ordered, and otherwise aided and abetted in the planning, preparation, and execution of these charged crimes, as set out in detail in this Indictment. The term 'committed' as it is used herein, includes two forms of Co-perpetration, namely: . . . Joint Criminal Enterprise – as described in this Indictment, includes membership of at least two persons in a criminal enterprise with an agreement to achieve the criminal objective, and . . . Direct and/or Indirect Co-Perpetration – does not require membership in a criminal enterprise or plan, nor an agreement. In Direct/Indirect Co-Perpetration each accused is responsible as a co perpetrator for his participation in the crimes charged, based on his own acts, whether individually or jointly with others, in participating knowingly, with criminal intent, directly and/or indirectly, with or without an agreement, *through or by way of his subordinates or other persons*, in the commission of the crimes charged including *inter alia*, communicating, organizing, co-ordinating, facilitating, or providing supervision or failing to act in furtherance of the crimes charged.

The June 2005 indictment has since been amended and replaced with a version that does not charge direct or indirect co-perpetration. See *infra* notes 704, 714 and accompanying text.

[629] See *Prlić et al.* Indictment, *supra* note 592, para. 15:

From on or before 18 November 1991 to about April 1994 and thereafter, various persons established and participated in a joint criminal enterprise to politically and militarily subjugate, permanently remove and ethnically cleanse Bosnian Muslims and other non-Croats who lived in areas on the territory of the Republic of Bosnia and Herzegovina which were claimed to be part of the Croatian Community . . . of Herceg-Bosna[.]

[630] *Ibid.*, para. 218.

were used to commit the crime, and acted with the mutual awareness of the substantial likelihood that crimes would occur as a direct consequence of the pursuit of
the common goal.[631]

Similarly, the August 2005 proposed amended indictment in the *Milutinović*
case alleged the accused's liability as participants in a JCE[632] and as 'indirect
co-perpetrators':

21. The crimes enumerated in Counts 1 to 5 of this Indictment were within the object
of the joint criminal enterprise and the accused shared the intent with the other
co-perpetrators that these crimes be perpetrated. Alternatively, the crimes enumerated
in Counts 3 to 5 were natural and foreseeable consequences of the joint criminal
enterprise and the accused were aware that such crimes were the possible consequence
of the execution of that enterprise[.][633]

22. *In the alternative*, the accused are also charged as indirect co-perpetrators, based on
their joint control over the criminal conduct of forces of the FRY and Serbia. The accused
had the *mens rea* for the specific crimes charged in this indictment, acted with the mutual
awareness of the substantial likelihood that crimes would occur as a direct consequence of
the pursuit of the common goal, and were aware of the importance of their own roles.[634]

---

[631] *Ibid.* (emphasis added). See also *ibid.*, para. 15:

From on or before 18 November 1991 to about April 1994 and thereafter, various persons established and participated
in a joint criminal enterprise to politically and militarily subjugated, permanently remove and ethnically cleanse
Bosnian Muslims and other non–Croats who lived in areas on the territory of the Republic of Bosnia and
Herzegovina which were claimed to be part of the Croatian Community ... of Herceg-Bosna[.]

See also *ibid.*, para. 16:

A number of persons joined, participated in and contributed to the joint criminal enterprise, including Franjo Tudjman[;]
Gojko Šušak[;] Janko Bobetko[;] Jadranko Prlić; Bruno Stojić; Slobodan Praljak; Milivoj Petković; Valentin Ćorić;
Berislav Pušić; Dario Kordić; Tihomir Blaškić; and Mladen Naletilić[.] Other members included [Herceg-Bosna governmental authorities; leaders and members of the Croatian Democratic Union; officers and members of the Herceg-Bosna
forces; members of the armed forces and police of Croatia; and others known and unknown].

See also *ibid.*, para. 16.1 (emphasis added):

In addition or in the alternative, the members of the joint criminal enterprise ... *implemented the objectives of the joint
criminal enterprise through the following organisations and persons*, who they controlled, directly or indirectly: [Herceg-
Bosna governmental authorities; leaders and members of the Croatian Democratic Union; officers and members of the
Herceg-Bosna forces; members of the armed forces and police of Croatia; and others known and unknown].

[632] *Milutinović et al.* Proposed Amended Joinder Indictment, *supra* note 554, para. 20:

A number of individuals participated in this joint criminal enterprise during the entire duration of its existence, or,
alternatively, at different times during the duration of its existence, including Milan Milutinović, Nikola Šainović,
Dragoljub Ojdanić, Nebojša Pavković, Vladimir Lazarević, Vlastimir Đorđević, Sreten Lukić, Slobodan Milošević
and Vlajko Stojiljković. Other[] members included Radomir Marković, Obrad Stevanović, Dragan Ilić and unidentified persons who were members of command and coordinating bodies and members of the forces of FRY and Serbia
who shared the intent to effect the purpose of the joint criminal enterprise[.]

[633] *Ibid.*, para. 21.

[634] *Ibid.*, para. 22 (emphasis added). See also *ibid.*, para. 34 (emphasis added):

Each of the accused participated in the joint criminal enterprise in the ways set out (for each accused) in the paragraphs
below. *Alternatively*, each of the accused contributed, as a co-perpetrator based on joint control, to the common goal in
the ways set out in those paragraphs[.]

After the pre-trial decision discussed below, *see* text accompanying notes 635–646, the August 2005
indictment in this case was later replaced with a version that did not charge 'co-perpetratorship'. See
Prosecutor v. *Milutinović, Šainović, Ojdanić, Pavković, Lazarević and Lukić*, Case No. IT-05-87-PT,
Redacted Third Amended Consolidated Indictment, 21 June 2006 ('*Milutinović et al.* June 2006
Indictment'). See also *infra*, text accompanying notes 635–646, for a discussion of this pre-trial decision.

In all three indictments, the prosecution first alleged a very large JCE, comparable in scope to that alleged in *Brđanin*, comprised not only of the various accused and other named individuals in leadership positions, but also unnamed political and military leaders, the police, the army and other unidentified persons. The *Popović* and *Prlić* proposed indictments asserted, in addition, that the accused also or alternatively bear responsibility because they effected crimes, in one way or another, through other persons. The *Prlić* indictment goes on to allege, like the *Milutinović* indictment, what seems to be yet another alternative, obviously based on the definition of 'co-perpetratorship' in paragraphs 440 and 442 of the *Stakić* Trial Judgement.

2.5.3 The March 2006 Milutinović *decision*

The first challenge to the introduction of these new forms of responsibility came in the *Milutinović* case. The accused Ojdanić argued that the ICTY lacked jurisdiction to impose liability on him as an 'indirect co-perpetrator', as alleged in paragraph 22 of the August 2005 proposed amended indictment, because no such form of responsibility existed in customary international law or under the Statute of the Tribunal.[635] In response, the prosecution argued that paragraph 22 'describe[s] the form of indirect co-perpetration based on joint control as applied in *Stakić*'[636] and that, under this theory of liability as set forth in paragraph 439 of *Stakić*, an accused can be held liable 'if he has an agreement with others, plays a key role in the agreement and one or more participants used others to carry out crimes'.[637] The prosecution apparently gleaned this interpretation of *Stakić* from the footnote accompanying the words 'the accused perpetrated ... indirectly' in the judgement: 'Indirect participation in German Law ... or "the perpetrator behind the perpetrator".'[638]

In its decision of 22 March 2006, the Trial Chamber held that the proposed amended indictment had indeed alleged, in addition to JCE, 'a form of responsibility distinct from JCE [that] reflects the physical and mental elements ostensibly set out in paragraphs 440 and 442 of the *Stakić* Trial Judgement'.[639] It then recalled the Appeals Chamber's holding, in the May 2003 *Milutinović* decision on interlocutory appeal, that the jurisdiction of the Tribunal only extends to those forms of responsibility that existed under customary international law at the time of the events alleged in the

---

[635] *Milutinović et al.* ICP Pre-Trial Decision, *supra* note 189, para. 2.   [636] *Ibid.*, paras. 7, 30.
[637] *Ibid.*, para. 7.   [638] *Stakić* Trial Judgement, *supra* note 155, para. 439 n. 942.
[639] *Milutinović et al.* ICP Pre-Trial Decision, *supra* note 189, para. 14.

indictment.[640] In laying the groundwork for its analysis of customary international law, the Chamber emphasised that it would not 'perform an exhaustive investigation of all the available sources in order to ascertain what forms of responsibility exist in customary international law that might arguably be given the label "indirect co-perpetration"', and would instead limit its analysis to determining whether a form of responsibility with the specific physical and mental elements alleged in the proposed amended indictment existed in custom.[641] Thus, the Trial Chamber expressly declined to address whether the Tribunal had jurisdiction over any form of responsibility other than that labelled 'co-perpetratorship' and applied to the facts in *Stakić*.

The Trial Chamber rejected the prosecution's contention that co-perpetratorship as defined in *Stakić* permitted the imposition of liability on an accused 'if he has an agreement with others, plays a key role in the agreement and one or more participants used others to carry out crimes'.[642] The Chamber opined that the source cited by the *Stakić* Trial Chamber as evidence of the existence of co-perpetratorship – a treatise by German legal scholar Claus Roxin – did not support *Stakić*'s definition of the physical elements of co-perpetratorship, namely that 'there was an explicit agreement or silent consent to reach a common goal by coordinated co-operation and joint control over the criminal conduct'.[643] The Chamber held further that:

neither Roxin nor paragraph 440 of *Stakić* provide[s] any support whatsoever for the Prosecution's view that '[t]he accused is liable under a theory of indirect co-perpetration if he has an agreement with others, plays a key role in the agreement and one or more of the participants used others to carry out the crimes.' It is particularly noteworthy that neither source makes mention of the use by one of the participants of persons outside the agreement to physically perpetrate crimes.[644]

The Trial Chamber acknowledged 'the possibility that some species of co-perpetration and indirect perpetration can be found in various legal systems throughout the world', but it held that, even if national legal authorities did clearly support *Stakić*'s 'very specific definition of co-perpetration', 'such

---

[640] *Ibid.*, para. 15 (citing *Milutinović et al.* JCE Appeal Decision, *supra* note 4, para. 21). The Trial Chamber also listed a second condition that, under the *Milutinović* decision on interlocutory appeal, must be fulfilled before the Tribunal may exercise jurisdiction in relation to a form of responsibility: the form must be provided for, explicitly or implicitly, in the ICTY Statute. *Ibid.*, para. 15. The Trial Chamber never reached the question of whether co-perpetratorship was provided for in the Statute, however, because it had already found that such a form of responsibility did not exist in customary international law, and both conditions must be fulfilled. *Ibid.*, paras. 25, 40. The ICTR Appeals Chamber subsequently held that the jurisdiction of that Tribunal also extends to those forms of responsibility that 'were proscribed by treaties forming part of the law to which the accused was subject at the time of the alleged actions under consideration'. *Karemera et al.* JCE Appeal Decision, *supra* note 90, para. 12.
[641] *Milutinović et al.* ICP Pre-Trial Decision, *supra* note 189, para. 26.   [642] *Ibid.*, para. 7.
[643] *Stakić* Trial Judgement, *supra* note 155, para. 440.
[644] *Milutinović et al.* ICP Pre-Trial Decision, *supra* note 189, para. 37 (footnote omitted).

evidence would not support a conclusion that there is state practice and *opinio juris* demonstrating the existence of the *Stakić* definition in customary international law'.[645] In the absence of evidence convincingly establishing state practice and *opinio juris* for *Stakić*'s co-perpetration, the Chamber concluded that the form of responsibility alleged in paragraph 22 of the proposed amended indictment did not exist in customary international law, and that paragraph 22 must accordingly be stricken from the indictment.[646]

2.5.4 *The* Stakić *Appeal Judgement*

On the same day that the *Milutinović* Trial Chamber issued its decision on Ojdanić's motion challenging jurisdiction, the Appeals Chamber rendered its judgement in *Stakić*. Although neither party had appealed the *Stakić* Trial Chamber's reliance on co-perpetratorship, the Appeals Chamber nonetheless addressed the question *proprio motu* as 'an issue of general importance warranting the scrutiny of the Appeals Chamber':[647]

The introduction of new modes of liability into the jurisprudence of the Tribunal may generate uncertainty, if not confusion, in the determination of the law by parties to cases before the Tribunal as well as in the application of the law by Trial Chambers. To avoid such uncertainty and ensure respect for the values of consistency and coherence in the application of the law, the Appeals Chamber must intervene to assess whether the mode of liability applied by the Trial Chamber is consistent with the jurisprudence of this Tribunal. If it is not consistent, the Appeals Chamber must then determine whether the Trial Chamber's factual findings support liability under another, established mode of liability, such as joint criminal enterprise.[648]

The Appeals Chamber then determined, completely independently of the analysis of the *Milutinović* Trial Chamber, that co-perpetratorship as defined in the *Stakić* Trial Judgement 'does not have support in customary international law or in the settled jurisprudence of this Tribunal', and that the Trial Chamber 'erred in employing a mode of liability which is not valid law within the jurisdiction of this Tribunal'.[649] Consequently, the Appeals Chamber held that those portions of the Trial Judgement applying co-perpetratorship 'must be set aside'.[650] Regrettably, in contrast to the *Milutinović* Trial Chamber, the *Stakić* Appeals Chamber gave no explanation of the reasoning that led to its conclusion that co-perpetratorship does not exist in customary international law.

---

[645] *Ibid.*, para. 39.   [646] *Ibid.*, paras. 40, 42.   [647] *Stakić* Appeal Judgement, *supra* note 83, para. 59.
[648] *Ibid.*   [649] *Ibid.*, para. 62.   [650] *Ibid.*, para. 63.

Perhaps loath to remand the case to a Trial Chamber that was now constituted of different judges, the Appeals Chamber resolved to remedy the Trial Chamber's error itself by applying the 'correct legal framework' – which it determined to be JCE – to the Trial Chamber's factual findings.[651] The Appeals Chamber held that the prosecution had properly pleaded both the first and the third categories of JCE in the indictment,[652] and that the Trial Chamber's findings established that Stakić had participated in a JCE 'to ethnically cleanse the Municipality of Prijedor by deporting and persecuting Bosnian Muslims and Bosnian Croats in order to establish Serbian control'.[653] After concluding that the Trial Chamber's findings evinced the existence of shared intent among all the JCE participants,[654] that Stakić intended to further the enterprise, and that he intended to commit persecution, deportation and forcible transfer,[655] the Appeals Chamber reclassified Stakić's responsibility for these three crimes as that of a first-category JCE participant.[656] The Appeals Chamber also determined that, although murder as a violation of the laws or customs of war, murder as a crime against humanity, and extermination as a crime against humanity were not objects of the JCE, the commission of these crimes was nevertheless 'a natural and foreseeable consequence of the implementation of the Common Purpose', and that Stakić and his co-perpetrators 'acted in the awareness that crimes would occur as a direct consequence of their pursuit of the common goal'.[657] Accordingly, the Appeals Chamber reclassified Stakić's responsibility for these three crimes as pertaining to the third category of JCE.[658]

---

[651] *Ibid.*   [652] *Ibid.*, para. 66.

[653] *Ibid.*, para. 73. See also *ibid.*, para. 78 ('The Trial Chamber's factual findings ... support the conclusion that [Stakić] participated in a joint criminal enterprise the Common Purpose of which was to persecute, deport, and forcibly transfer the Bosnian Muslim and Bosnian Croat populations of Prijedor.') (footnote removed).

[654] *Ibid.*, para. 80.   [655] *Ibid.*, para. 84.

[656] *Ibid.*, para. 104. Upon finding that the Trial Chamber had 'incorrectly failed to enter a conviction against [Stakić] for Deportation' as a crime against humanity due to an incorrect application of the law on cumulative convictions, the Appeals Chamber entered such a conviction, presumably pursuant to the first category of JCE. *Ibid.*, p. 141. Also because of the Trial Chamber's incorrect application of the law on cumulative convictions, the Appeals Chamber entered a conviction for forcible transfer as an inhumane act as a crime against humanity. *Ibid.*, pp. 141–142. See also *ibid.*, para. 367:

> [A] proper application of the cumulative convictions test in this case allows convictions to be entered for the Article 5 crimes of extermination, deportation, other inhumane acts and persecutions. A conviction cannot be entered for the crime of murder under Article 5 as this crime is impermissibly cumulative with the crime of extermination.

[657] *Ibid.*, para. 92 (quoting *Stakić* Trial Judgement, *supra* note 155, para. 496).

[658] *Ibid.*, paras. 98, 104. The Appeals Chamber accordingly upheld the Trial Chamber's findings of guilt for extermination as a crime against humanity and murder as a violation of the laws or customs of war. *Ibid.*, pp. 141–142. Nevertheless, while the Appeals Chamber determined that the Trial Chamber had incorrectly applied the law on cumulative convictions, in concluding that it could not convict the accused for murder as a crime against humanity where it had also found him responsible for murder as a form of persecution as a crime against humanity, *ibid.*, para. 359, the Appeals Chamber ultimately declined to enter a conviction for murder as a crime against humanity; such a conviction would have been impermissibly cumulative with the conviction for extermination as a crime against humanity. See *ibid.*, para. 366, p. 141. See also *supra* note 656.

2.5.5 The **Gacumbitsi** *Appeal Judgement*

The conspicuous parsimony of the *Stakić* Appeals Chamber's discussion of co-perpetratorship stands in rather sharp contrast to the analogous discussions in the July 2006 *Gacumbitsi* Appeal Judgement and a series of separate opinions appended to that judgement. The ICTR Appeals Chamber found, by majority,[659] that the Trial Chamber had not erred in convicting Sylvestre Gacumbitsi of genocide where the *actus reus* had been fulfilled through his personal killing of an elderly Tutsi teacher named Murefu.[660] Even though this killing had not been expressly pleaded in the indictment, the majority of the Chamber determined that a witness summary disclosed to the defence prior to trial, describing Gacumbitsi's killing of Murefu had cured the defect by providing him with adequate notice 'that he was being charged with committing genocide through the killing of Mr Murefu'.[661]

With Judge Güney rather forcefully dissenting[662] and Judges Schomburg and Shahabuddeen appending separate concurring opinions,[663] a different majority of the Appeals Chamber then took the surprising and thoroughly gratuitous step of finding that, 'even if the killing of Mr Murefu were to be set aside, the Trial Chamber's conclusion that the Appellant "committed" genocide would still be valid'.[664] Even though it upheld the Trial Chamber's dismissal of JCE because it was not pleaded adequately in the indictment,[665] the majority determined that the conduct for which the Trial Chamber convicted Gacumbitsi of ordering and instigating genocide 'should be characterised not just as "ordering" and "instigating" genocide, but also as "committing" genocide':[666]

In the context of genocide … 'direct and physical perpetration' need not mean physical killing; other acts can constitute direct participation in the *actus reus* of the crime. Here, the accused was physically present at the scene of the Nyarabuye Parish massacre, which he 'directed' and 'played a leading role in conducting and, especially, supervising'. It was he who personally directed the Tutsi and Hutu refugees to separate –

---

[659] Judges Liu and Meron dissented from this portion of the Appeal Judgement. See *Gacumbitsi* Appeal Judgement, *supra* note 46, Joint Separate Opinion of Judges Liu and Meron, paras. 1, 9.

[660] See *ibid.*, paras. 46–58 (upholding *Gacumbitsi* Trial Judgement, *supra* note 130, paras. 259, 261, 285).

[661] *Ibid.*, para. 58 (internal quotation marks omitted).

[662] *Ibid.*, Partially Dissenting Opinion of Judge Güney.

[663] See *ibid.*, Separate Opinion of Judge Schomburg on the Criminal Responsibility of the Appellant for Committing Genocide; *ibid.*, Separate Opinion of Judge Shahabuddeen.

[664] *Ibid.*, para. 59.

[665] *Ibid.*, paras. 164–179. Judges Shahabuddeen and Schomburg dissented from this holding. See *ibid.*, Separate Opinion of Judge Shahabuddeen, paras. 38–39 (opining that Gacumbitsi could have been convicted pursuant to JCE); *ibid.*, Separate Opinion of Judge Schomburg on the Criminal Responsibility of the Appellant for Committing Genocide, para. 10. See also *supra* text accompanying note 132.

[666] *Gacumbitsi* Appeal Judgement, *supra* note 46, para. 59.

and that action, which is not adequately described by any other mode of Article 6(1) liability, was as much an integral part of the genocide as were the killings which it enabled.[667] ... The Appeals Chamber is persuaded that in the circumstances of this case, the modes of liability used by the Trial Chamber to categorize this conduct – 'ordering' and 'instigating' – do not, taken alone, fully capture the Appellant's criminal responsibility. The Appellant did not simply 'order' or 'plan' genocide from a distance and leave it to others to ensure that his orders and plans were carried out; nor did he merely 'instigate' the killings. Rather, he was present at the crime scene to supervise and direct the massacre, and participated in it actively by separating the Tutsi refugees so that they could be killed. The Appeals Chamber finds ... that this constitutes 'committing' genocide.[668]

Several aspects of this unfortunate course of action deserve mention. First, the Chamber's expanded notion of what constitutes 'commission' liability under Article 7/6(1), by the very language of the judgement, would seem to be limited to 'the context of genocide',[669] an approach which is inconsistent with the structure of the Statute and extensive practice of the *ad hoc* Tribunals to date. Second, unlike the Appeals Chamber in *Tadić*, which examined at some length post-Second World War jurisprudence and other sources as purported evidence of the existence of JCE in customary international law,[670] the *Gacumbitsi* majority did not discuss or cite a single source in support of the proposition that commission liability may ensue for conduct akin to Gacumbitsi's; instead, as identified by Judge Güney,[671] the majority merely cited the Judgment at Nuremberg and the District Court of Jerusalem's *Eichmann* judgement as recognising that 'the selection of prisoners for extermination played an integral role in the Nazi genocide'.[672]

Third, the Appeals Chamber did not provide much guidance for future chambers as to precisely which 'other acts can constitute direct participation in the *actus reus* of [genocide]',[673] beyond the precise conduct of Gacumbitsi in this instance – that is, being present at the crime scene, supervising and directing the commission of the crime, and participating in it by separating

---

[667] *Ibid.*, para. 60 (footnotes removed) (quoting *Gacumbitsi* Trial Judgement, *supra* note 130, paras. 172, 261).
[668] *Ibid.*, para. 61.   [669] *Ibid.*, para. 60.
[670] See *Tadić* Appeal Judgement, *supra* note 3, paras. 194–226. See also *supra*, text accompanying notes 52–77 (discussing this portion of *Tadić*).
[671] See *Gacumbitsi* Appeal Judgement, *supra* note 46, Partially Dissenting Opinion of Judge Güney, para. 6 n. 9.
[672] *Ibid.*, para. 60 n. 145 (citing *Göring, Bormann, Dönitz, Frank, Frick, Fritzsche, Funk, Hess, Jodl, Kaltenbrunner, Keitel, von Bohlen und Halbach, Ley, von Neurath, von Papen, Raeder, von Ribbentrop, Rosenberg, Sauckel, Schacht, von Schirach, Seyss-Inquart, Speer and Streicher*, International Military Tribunal, Judgment and Sentence, 1 October 1946, in *Trial of the Major War Criminals Before the International Military Tribunal, Nuremberg, 14 November 1945–1 October 1946* (1947), p. 63; *Attorney General of Israel* v. *Eichmann*, (1961) 36 *International Law Reports* 5, 185).
[673] *Ibid.*, para. 60.

the victims from the rest of the crowd so that they could be killed.[674] Judge Güney in dissent remarked that this approach 'is as vague as it is unsatisfactory'.[675]

Fourth, the Chamber affirmed a clear hierarchy – also seen in the sentencing practice of the chambers of the *ad hoc* Tribunals[676] – whereby participation in a crime that can be given the label 'commission' under Article 7/6(1) is regarded as somehow more culpable than conduct amounting to one of the non-commission forms of responsibility. The Appeals Chamber was obviously quite concerned that the two forms of responsibility under which the Trial Chamber had classified Gacumbitsi's conduct – ordering and instigating – did not seem to carry sufficient weight. This aspect of the Appeals Chamber's holding is perhaps the most bizarre because it attempts to place a square peg in a round hole for reasons that appear to be more visceral than rational: the Chamber re-classified as 'commission' conduct with physical elements clearly closer to those of ordering and instigating[677] – and, indeed, very similar to behaviour earlier affirmed by the Appeals Chamber to make up the *actus reus* of aiding and abetting genocide.[678] For their part, both Judge Güney and Judge Shahabuddeen opined that Gacumbitsi's conduct could easily have qualified as participation in a JCE;[679] in the words of Judge Güney, 'this action certainly constitutes a contribution to the commission of acts of genocide by others, in other words participation in a [JCE]'.[680] As it stands, *Gacumbitsi* serves to perpetuate the *ad hoc* Tribunals' preoccupation, alluded to above in the discussion of the *Brđanin* Trial Judgement,[681] with characterising criminal activity as some manifestation of commission whenever possible.

Upon reading the majority's discussion, Judge Güney's dissent, and the separate opinions of Judges Schomburg and Shahabuddeen, one is left with the clear impression that all are, in one way or another, reacting to the analysis

---

[674] See *ibid.*, paras. 60–61.
[675] *Ibid.*, Partially Dissenting Opinion of Judge Güney, para. 6.
[676] See Chapter 6, text accompanying notes 123–176 (discussing the forms of responsibility and sentencing).
[677] See Chapter 5, text accompanying notes 132–176 (discussing the elements of ordering); text accompanying notes 93–131 (discussing the elements of instigating).
[678] See *Ntakirutimana and Ntakirutimana* Appeal Judgement, *supra* note 46, paras. 371–372 (upholding *Ntakirutimana and Ntakirutimana* Trial Judgement, *supra* note 125, paras. 829–831, which found that Elizaphan Ntakirutimana fulfilled the physical elements of aiding and abetting genocide by transporting attackers to the scene of the attacks, instructing them to pursue Tutsi refugees, and pointing out the locations of Tutsi refugees).
[679] *Gacumbitsi* Appeal Judgement, *supra* note 46, Partially Dissenting Opinion of Judge Güney, para. 7; *ibid.*, Separate Opinion of Judge Shahabuddeen, paras. 38–39. In Judge Shahabuddeen's view, the indictment was not, as the majority had held, defective in its pleading of JCE, and Gacumbitsi could alternatively have been convicted for his actions on that basis. *Ibid.* See also *supra* text accompanying note 132, 665 (discussing the majority's upholding of the Trial Chamber's dismissal of JCE).
[680] *Gacumbitsi* Appeal Judgement, *supra* note 46, Partially Dissenting Opinion of Judge Güney, para. 7.
[681] See *supra* text accompanying notes 486–487, 533, 591.

of the *Stakić* Trial Judgement in the March 2006 *Milutinović* decision. The judges of the Appeals Chamber did not have the benefit of *Milutinović* when drafting the *Stakić* Appeal Judgement, as both were issued on the same day. Yet strangely, of the four relevant separate discussions in *Gacumbitsi*, only Judge Güney's makes any mention of *Milutinović*.[682] Indeed, it appears that Judge Schomburg deliberately avoids invoking *Milutinović* and its criticism of the Trial Judgement for which he served as presiding judge, and instead seems to have seized upon the opportunity to provide further justification for the portion of the *Stakić* Trial Judgement that was impugned in *Milutinović* and the *Stakić* Appeal Judgement.[683] He cited a series of national legislative provisions, case law and treatises,[684] along with two scholarly works on international criminal law,[685] as support for his assertion that 'national as well as international criminal law has come to accept … co-perpetratorship and indirect perpetratorship (perpetration by means) as a form of "committing"'.[686]

For his precise definitions of co-perpetration and indirect perpetration, Judge Schomburg, like the *Stakić* Trial Chamber,[687] relied almost exclusively on the German national criminal law scholar Claus Roxin.[688] He also invoked Article 25(3)(a) of the Rome Statute of the ICC, which provides that individual criminal responsibility can ensue where a person commits a crime 'jointly with

---

[682] See *Gacumbitsi* Appeal Judgement, *supra* note 46, Partially Dissenting Opinion of Judge Güney, para. 5 n. 10 (invoking *Milutinović et al.* ICP Pre-Trial Decision, *supra* note 189, Separate Opinion of Judge Iain Bonomy, paras. 28–30, as demonstrating that 'various legal systems may recognize other forms of commission than the two forms identified until now in the Tribunal's jurisprudence') (quotation in main text).

[683] See *ibid.*, Separate Opinion of Judge Schomburg on the Criminal Responsibility of the Appellant for Committing Genocide, paras. 14–28. Judge Schomburg did not sit on the bench of the *Stakić* Appeals Chamber. Judge Schomburg again elaborated his strong views on this subject four months later in the ICTY Appeals Chamber's *Simić* Judgement, the majority opinion of which did not discuss co-perpetration or indirect perpetration at all. See *Simić* Appeal Judgement, *supra* note 271, paras. 9–23.

[684] See *Gacumbitsi* Appeal Judgement, *supra* note 46, Separate Opinion of Judge Schomburg on the Criminal Responsibility of the Appellant for Committing Genocide, paras. 16–20 nn. 29–38 (citing, *inter alia*, the Colombian, Paraguayan and Finnish Penal Codes; the U.S. Model Penal Code; German and Argentine national cases; and Claus Roxin, *Täterschaft und Tatherrschaft* (7th edn 2000), pp. 142–305).

[685] *Ibid.*, paras. 16–17 nn. 30–31 (citing Gerhard Werle, *Principles of International Criminal Law* (2005); Kai Ambos, 'Individual Criminal Responsibility', in Otto Triffterer (ed.), *Commentary on the Rome Statute of the International Criminal Court* (1999)).

[686] *Ibid.*, para. 16.   [687] See *Stakić* Trial Judgement, *supra* note 155, paras. 440–441.

[688] See *Gacumbitsi* Appeal Judgement, *supra* note 46, Separate Opinion of Judge Schomburg on the Criminal Responsibility of the Appellant for Committing Genocide, para. 17 ('Co-perpetrators must pursue a common goal, either through an explicit agreement or silent consent, which they can only achieve by co-ordinated action and shared control over the criminal conduct. Each co-perpetrator must make a contribution essential to the commission of the crime.'); *ibid.*, para. 18 ('Indirect perpetration … requires that the indirect perpetrator uses the direct and physical perpetrator as a mere "instrument" to achieve his goal[.]') (underlining removed). See also *ibid.*, paras. 17–18 nn. 31–33 (citing Roxin, *supra* note 684, pp. 275–305).

another or through another person',[689] as reflecting existing international criminal law permitting conviction on the basis of both co-perpetration and indirect perpetration.[690] Judge Schomburg opined that, '[a]s an international criminal court, it is incumbent upon [the ICTR] not to turn a blind eye to these developments in modern criminal law and to show open-mindedness by accepting internationally recognized legal interpretations and theories such as the notions of co-perpetration and indirect perpetration'.[691] He concluded that Gacumbitsi could have been convicted under either of these theories of liability: 'Taking into account his predominant role in the genocidal campaign, [Gacumbitsi's] conduct is best described as indirect perpetration; in some respect [he] was also acting as a co-perpetrator.'[692]

In his separate opinion, Judge Shahabuddeen emphasised his agreement with the majority that, through his direction and leading role in the attacks in question, Gacumbitsi was 'plainly ... guilty of "committing" genocide'.[693] Like the majority, he opined that '[j]ustice would not be served',[694] that 'it would be a misunderstanding and misapplication of the law',[695] and that it would 'impose[ ] too great a strain on the legal apparatus'[696] if Gacumbitsi were to be convicted merely pursuant to ordering and instigating and not committing.[697] Curiously, however, although he seemed perfectly willing to expand the scope of committing to include the conduct of Gacumbitsi in this instance, Judge Shahabuddeen disagreed with Judge Schomburg that the Appeals Chamber could properly have convicted the accused pursuant to co-perpetration or indirect perpetration. Coming to the same conclusion as the Trial Chamber in *Milutinović*, Judge Shahabuddeen remarked that, 'since several states adhere to one theory while several other states adhere to the other theory, it is possible that the required state practice and *opinio juris* do not exist so as to make either theory part of customary international law'.[698]

---

[689] Rome Statute, *supra* note 21, Art. 25(3)(a).

[690] *Gacumbitsi* Appeal Judgement, *supra* note 46, Separate Opinion of Judge Schomburg on the Criminal Responsibility of the Appellant for Committing Genocide, para. 21.

[691] *Ibid.*, para. 22 (emphasis removed). In urging reliance on the Rome Statute and the recent progressive development of international criminal law, Judge Schomburg did not discuss the requirement that the forms of responsibility applied by the *ad hoc* Tribunals must have existed in customary international law or in 'treaties forming part of the law to which the accused was subject' at the time of the charged crimes' commission. See *Karemera et al.* JCE Appeal Decision, *supra* note 90, para. 12; *supra* note 640 and accompanying text.

[692] *Gacumbitsi* Appeal Judgement, *supra* note 46, Separate Opinion of Judge Schomburg on the Criminal Responsibility of the Appellant for Committing Genocide, para. 28.

[693] *Ibid.*, Separate Opinion of Judge Shahabuddeen, paras. 21–22 (quotation at para. 22).

[694] *Ibid.*, para. 22.   [695] *Ibid.*   [696] *Ibid.*, para. 23.   [697] *Ibid.*, para. 22.

[698] *Ibid.*, para. 51. See also *Milutinović et al.* ICP Pre-Trial Decision, *supra* note 189, para. 39 (acknowledging 'the possibility that some species of co-perpetration and indirect perpetration can be found in various legal systems throughout the world', but concluding that, even if national legal authorities did

Judge Güney, in dissent, expressed the view that playing a leading role in conducting and supervising the attack, along with directing the separation of Tutsi refugees from the crowd, could not have 'constitute[d] the physical perpetration by [Gacumbitsi] of one of the acts listed in Article 2(2) of the [ICTR] Statute'.[699] He criticised the majority for apparently establishing a new form of commission liability, 'very late in the life of the Tribunal',[700] without stating openly that it was doing so, providing cogent reasons, or citing any supporting authority 'to justify the departure from previous jurisprudence'.[701] Judge Güney pointedly recalled that the ICTY Appeals Chamber in *Stakić* – consisting of four of the same five judges in *Gacumbitsi*, that is, Güney, Pocar, Meron and Shahabuddeen – had just three months earlier rejected an attempt to define 'committing' in Article 7/6(1) as something beyond physical commission and JCE.[702]

2.5.6 *Assessing the impact of* Milutinović, Stakić *and* Gacumbitsi

In the wake of the *Stakić* Appeal Judgement, the prosecution in *Popović* moved to amend the indictment to withdraw the allegations of 'Direct and/or Indirect Co-Perpetration', replacing them with two purported species of JCE liability, one requiring the participation of the physical perpetrator in the JCE and one not requiring such participation.[703] Without opining on whether the precise holding in *Stakić* actually compelled the deletion of 'Direct and/or Indirect Co-Perpetration' in the form in which its physical and mental elements had been defined in the *Popović* indictment, the Trial Chamber allowed the prosecution to withdraw its pleading of this ostensible form of responsibility.[704]

It is unfortunate that the ICTY Prosecutor chose to tie the fate of indirect co-perpetration – which may well have support in customary international law – to that of *Stakić*'s co-perpetratorship. As the *Milutinović* Trial Chamber observed,[705] neither the legal nor the factual discussion in *Stakić* provides tremendous support for the claim the prosecution sought to advance – that is,

clearly support *Stakić*'s 'very specific definition of co-perpetration', 'such evidence would not support a conclusion that there is state practice and *opinio juris* demonstrating the existence of the *Stakić* definition in customary international law').

[699] *Gacumbitsi* Appeal Judgement, *supra* note 46, Partially Dissenting Opinion of Judge Güney, para. 5.

[700] *Ibid.*, para. 6.   [701] *Ibid.*

[702] *Ibid.*, para. 4 (referring to the rejection of 'indirect co-perpetratorship' in *Stakić* Appeal Judgement, *supra* note 83, para. 62).

[703] *Prosecutor* v. *Popović, Beara, Nikolić, Borovčanin, Tolimir, Miletić, Gvero, Pandurević and Trbić*, Case No. IT-05-88-PT, Motion to Amend the Indictment relating to the 22 March 2006 Appeals Chamber Judgement in the Case of *Stakić*, 29 March 2006, para. 5; *ibid.*, Annex I, para. 88.2.

[704] *Popović et al.* Pre-Trial Indictment Decision, *supra* note 542, para. 17 (noting that the prosecution itself had sought withdrawal of these allegations and concluding that '[a]ccordingly, the Trial Chamber will not engage in any further examination as to the pleading of "Direct/Indirect Co-Perpetration" in the Indictment').

[705] *Milutinović et al.* ICP Pre-Trial Decision, *supra* note 189, para. 37.

that 'one or more participants [in the accused's criminal group] used others to carry out crimes'.[706] Indeed, apart from the footnote making reference to the German law concept of 'the perpetrator behind the perpetrator', the *Stakić* Trial Judgement never expressly states the proposition that the prosecution in *Milutinović* ascribed to it, that co-perpetratorship focuses on or even allows the imposition of liability for the indirect implementation of crimes through persons who do not form part of the co-perpetrators' group. The judgement itself offers only meagre support for such a broad interpretation of co-perpetratorship: when listing Stakić's co-perpetrators,[707] the Trial Chamber's findings of fact appear to omit reference to the unnamed military and police who were found to have physically perpetrated most of the crimes.[708]

In its search for precedent on indirect co-perpetration in the jurisprudence of the ICTY, a stronger case for the prosecution to invoke would certainly have been the *Furundžija* Trial Judgement, which discussed and endorsed the principle that 'he who acts through others is regarded as acting himself'.[709] The greatest irony in the prosecution's reliance on *Stakić*, however, lies in the fact that the *Stakić* Trial Chamber, not unlike the Trial Chamber in *Brđanin*, avoided JCE in favour of what it considered to be a more narrowly defined and appropriate form of responsibility. In this sense, the *Stakić* Trial Judgement should be placed alongside *Brđanin* as one of a small handful of judicial pronouncements from the *ad hoc* Tribunals restricting, rather than widening, the scope of common-purpose liability.[710]

Nevertheless, other aspects of more recent trial jurisprudence may ultimately serve to allay the concerns of the prosecution. As discussed in the previous section of this chapter,[711] in addition to challenging the jurisdiction of the ICTY to enter a conviction pursuant to co-perpetratorship, the accused Ojdanić in the *Milutinović* case alleged that the Tribunal lacked jurisdiction to impose JCE liability on him where the physical perpetrator was not a

---

[706] *Ibid.*, para. 7.

[707] See, e.g., *ibid.*, para. 469 (listing many of the co-perpetrators by name and stating that the co-perpetrators also included 'prominent members of the military', but omitting any reference to ordinary police and military personnel).

[708] See, e.g., *Stakić* Trial Judgement, *supra* note 155, paras. 482–484 (discussing Stakić's and the Prijedor Crisis Staff's control over the army and police); *ibid.*, para. 255 (finding that soldiers killed a number of people and threw them into the Sana River); *ibid.*, para. 271 (finding that members of the Republika Srpska Special Forces seriously beat various non-Serb men and killed some of them); *ibid.*, para. 699 (describing deportation convoys organised by police and military).

[709] *Furundžija* Trial Judgement, *supra* note 8, para. 256. See also *ibid.*, paras. 268–269 (finding Furundžija guilty as a co-perpetrator of torture). See also *supra* text accompanying notes 24–27 (discussing this portion of *Furundžija*).

[710] For an extensive discussion of the position of various judgements in relation to the scope of JCE, see *Milutinović et al.* ICP Pre-Trial Decision, *supra* note 189, Separate Opinion of Judge Iain Bonomy, paras. 5–13.

[711] See *supra* text accompanying notes 549–554.

participant in the JCE.[712] While it did not decide definitively that a conviction pursuant to JCE was permissible in such circumstances, the Trial Chamber held that this question would be more appropriately dealt with at trial, and dismissed Ojdanić's challenge.[713] The *Popović* Trial Chamber subsequently endorsed this approach and rejected a prosecution request to plead two separate species of JCE liability in the indictment, one requiring the participation of the physical participation in the enterprise and one not requiring such participation.[714] In a lengthy separate opinion in *Milutinović*, moreover, Judge Bonomy evinced a certain degree of sympathy for the prosecution's view,

---

[712] *Milutinović et al.* ICP Pre-Trial Decision, *supra* note 189, paras. 2, 11, 18.

[713] *Ibid.*, paras. 23–24. Though understandable from a pre-trial case management perspective, the decision to delay determination of the issue raised by Ojdanić was unfortunate in two respects. First, as the Appeals Chamber was later to hold in an interlocutory decision in an ICTR case, the question of whether an accused may be held liable in the situation alleged by the prosecution's indictment is purely legal, not fact-dependent, and should be determined before trial begins, so as to enable the accused to know whether he needs to prepare a defence in respect of the related charge or charges. *Karemera et al.* JCE Appeal Decision, *supra* note 90, para. 22 (noting that 'the question that the Appellant faults the Trial Chamber for deferring is a pure question of law concerning the limits of the Tribunal's jurisdiction to employ a mode of liability'); see especially *ibid.*, para. 23:

> The Trial Chamber cannot avoid deciding the Appellant's motion simply because . . . the count at issue alleges that the Appellant can be found guilty pursuant to several modes of liability. As already mentioned, the text of Rule 72(A) makes clear that its time limits [requiring determination before trial begins] apply to all jurisdictional motions – including . . . those challenging one of many modes of liability alleged in connection with an offence. This reflects each accused's right not to be tried on, and not to have to defend against, an allegation that falls outside the Tribunal's jurisdiction.

Second, despite the *Milutinović* Pre-Trial Chamber's conclusions, this legal issue is not merely a question of the 'contours' of an existing form of responsibility. See *Milutinović et al.* ICP Pre-Trial Decision, *supra* note 189, para. 23:

> [Ojdanić's] challenge amounts to no more than a claim that the concept of JCE does not extend to circumstances in which the commission of a crime is said to have been effected through the hands of others whose *mens rea* is not explored and determined, and who are not shown to be participants in the JCE. In the Trial Chamber's view, that question does not raise the issue of the Tribunal's jurisdiction over the activities of a JCE, but instead relates to the contours of JCE responsibility.

The question of whether an accused may be held liable under a proposed scenario is not answered by the prosecution's invocation of the label of an existing form of responsibility. If, as was the case, no chamber of the ICTY or ICTR had yet decided that the doctrine of JCE extended to the facts as alleged by the prosecution, the principle of legality – that no person should be at risk of conviction for conduct that was not prohibited and punishable by criminal sanction at the time of its commission – required an independent examination of the relevant authority to decide whether customary international law permitted the imposition of criminal liability in that situation. See generally Mauro Catenacci, 'The Principle of Legality', in Lattanzi and Schabas (eds.), 2 *Essays* (2004), *supra* note 6, pp. 85–89, 91–93 (defining the principle of legality as the legal tenet that '[c]onduct may be punished under [a court's] Statute (that is, under its substantive principles, within its jurisdiction and in line with its procedural rules . . .) only if a previous law defines it as "crime" and explicitly sanctions it with penalties'). Failure to conduct such an independent inquiry risks compounding the errors in the conception and application of JCE in these tribunals.

[714] *Popović et al.* Pre-Trial Indictment Decision, *supra* note 542, para. 21 ('Whether the physical perpetrator must be a participant in the JCE is . . . an issue to be addressed at trial.'). See also *supra* text accompanying notes 565–566 (discussing this holding in *Popović*). The *Popović* Trial Chamber accordingly held that 'there is no basis in law for a distinct pleading of "JCE with Common Purpose" and "JCE with Agreement"', and ordered the prosecution 'to plead only participation in a JCE, leaving the contours of JCE responsibility to be determined at trial'. *Ibid.*, para. 22. The current indictment in *Popović* does not allege two species of JCE liability. See *Prosecutor* v. *Popović, Beara, Nikolić, Borovčanin, Miletić, Gvero and Pandurević*, Case No. IT-05-88-T, Indictment, 4 August 2006 ('*Popović et al.* August 2006 Indictment'), paras. 88–91.

arguing that appellate jurisprudence, and quite possibly the general principles of law, would not prohibit a trial chamber from entering a conviction in this scenario.[715] And the *Krajišnik* Trial Chamber had no reservations whatsoever about convicting the accused of a number of crimes pursuant to the JCE doctrine – to the express exclusion of all other forms of responsibility[716] – where many (or most) of the physical perpetrators of the crimes in question were not participants in the enterprise.[717]

The judges of the *ad hoc* Appeals Chambers have also shown a tendency towards accepting the expansion of JCE and recognising other manifestations of common-purpose liability. *Gacumbitsi* is the most recent and most obvious example, where in contrast to the ICTY Appeals Chamber's rejection in *Stakić* of 'indirect co-perpetratorship',[718] the ICTR Appeals Chamber broadened the definition of 'commission', at least in the context of genocide, to include being present at the crime scene, supervising and directing the commission of the crime, and participating in it by separating the victims from the rest of the crowd so that they can be killed.[719] Furthermore, in its identification of the participants in Stakić's JCE, the ICTY Appeals Chamber quoted the Trial Chamber's list of co-perpetrators and found that '[t]his group included the leaders of political bodies, the army, and the police who held power in the Municipality of Prijedor'.[720] The Appeals Chamber then proceeded to enter findings of JCE liability for crimes physically perpetrated, on the whole, by low-level military and police forces.[721] Such a course of action could certainly be taken as evidence that the Appeals Chamber implicitly accepts the proposition that the physical perpetrator may be outside the JCE.

2.6 Joint Criminal Enterprise and its analogues in the International Criminal Court and internationalised tribunals

2.6.1 *The International Criminal Court*

As discussed in an earlier section of this chapter, three different forms of collective participation in the commission of a crime have been considered at one time or another in the jurisprudence of the *ad hoc* Tribunals: co-perpetration; indirect perpetration; and joint criminal enterprise. Although the most

---

[715] *Milutinović et al.* ICP Pre-Trial Decision, *supra* note 189, Separate Opinion of Judge Iain Bonomy, paras. 5–13, 30–31.

[716] *Krajišnik* Trial Judgement, *supra* note 65, para. 877.

[717] See *ibid.*, paras. 1086–1088, 1126, 1182. See also *supra* text accompanying notes 568–589 (discussing *Krajišnik*).

[718] *Stakić* Appeal Judgement, *supra* note 83, para. 59.

[719] See *Gacumbitsi* Appeal Judgement, *supra* note 46, paras. 60–61.

[720] *Stakić* Appeal Judgement, *supra* note 83, para. 69.   [721] See *ibid.*, paras. 85, 98, 104.

recent statements from the chambers of the ICTY appear to have rejected co-perpetration in favour of joint criminal enterprise,[722] the approach taken by the drafters of the Rome Statute differed markedly, and all three forms of participation are included in this constitutive document of the ICC.

Article 25 of the Rome Statute, which describes and circumscribes the ICC's personal jurisdiction with specific reference to forms of individual criminal responsibility under international law, provides:

1. The Court shall have jurisdiction over natural persons pursuant to this Statute.
2. A person who commits a crime within the jurisdiction of the Court shall be individually responsible and liable for punishment in accordance with this Statute.
3. In accordance with this Statute, a person shall be criminally responsible and liable for punishment for a crime within the jurisdiction of the Court if that person:

(a) Commits such a crime, whether as an individual, *jointly with another* or *through another person, regardless of whether that other person is criminally responsible;*
(b) Orders, solicits or induces the commission of such a crime which in fact occurs or is attempted;
(c) For the purpose of facilitating the commission of such a crime, aids, abets or otherwise assists in its commission or its attempted commission, including providing the means for its commission;
(d) *In any other way contributes to the commission or attempted commission of such a crime by a group of persons acting with a common purpose.* Such contribution shall be intentional and shall either:
  (i) Be made with the aim of furthering the criminal activity or criminal purpose of the group, where such activity or purpose involves the commission of a crime within the jurisdiction of the Court; or
  (ii) Be made in the knowledge of the intention of the group to commit the crime;
(e) In respect of the crime of genocide, directly and publicly incites others to commit genocide;
(f) Attempts to commit such a crime by taking action that commences its execution by means of a substantial step, but the crime does not occur because of circumstances independent of the person's intentions. However, a person who abandons the effort to commit the crime or otherwise prevents the completion of the crime shall not be liable for punishment under this Statute for the attempt to commit that crime if that person completely and voluntarily gave up the criminal purpose.[723]

The reference in sub-paragraph (3)(a) to the commission of a crime 'jointly with another' corresponds to the *Furundžija* concept of co-perpetration;[724] the reference in the same provision to commission 'through another person,

[722] See *Stakić* Appeal Judgement, *supra* note 83, para. 62; *Milutinović et al.* ICP Pre-Trial Decision, *supra* note 189, paras. 39–40.
[723] Rome Statute, *supra* note 21, Art. 25 (emphases added).
[724] See *supra*, text accompanying notes 33–37, for a discussion of the *Furundžija* concept of co-perpetration. See also *Situation in the Democratic Republic of the Congo in the Case of Prosecutor* v. *Thomas Lubanga Dyilo*, Case No. ICC-01/04-01/06, Decision on the Prosecutor's Application for a Warrant of Arrest,

regardless of whether that other person is criminally responsible' expresses the concept of indirect perpetration embodied in the Latin maxim invoked by the *Furundžija* Trial Chamber and obliquely discussed in the *Milutinović* pre-trial decision on Ojdanić's jurisdictional challenge;[725] and the terms of sub-paragraph (3)(d) clearly refer to a theory of common-purpose liability that is consistent with joint criminal enterprise.

It is important to note, however, that while the form of common-purpose liability embodied in Article 25(3)(d) (the 'ICC model') is similar to joint criminal enterprise in the three-category form that has been developed by the *ad hoc* Tribunals (the '*ad hoc* model'), the two models are not identical.[726]

Like the *ad hoc* model, the ICC model has three objective or physical elements: a plurality of persons; a common purpose that involves the commission of a crime within the jurisdiction of the Court;[727] and the accused's

---

Article 58, 10 February 2006 ('*Lubanga* Decision on Arrest Warrant'), para. 96 (holding that 'the concept of indirect perpetration ... along with that of co-perpetration based on joint control of the crime ... [are] provided for in article 25 (3) (a) of the Statute').

[725] See *Furundžija* Trial Judgement, *supra* note 8, para. 256, holding that:

if an official interrogates a detainee while another person is inflicting severe pain or suffering, the interrogator is as guilty of torture as the person causing the severe pain or suffering, even if he does not in any way physically participate in such infliction. Here the criminal law maxim *quis per alium facit per se ipsum facere videtur* (he who acts through others is regarded as acting himself) fully applies.

See also *Milutinović et al.* ICP Pre-Trial Decision, *supra* note 189, paras. 27–40; *supra* text accompanying notes 642–646 (discussing this aspect of *Milutinović*); *Lubanga* Decision on Arrest Warrant, *supra* note 724, para. 96. It is unclear, based on the final text of the Rome Statute, whether the qualifying phrase 'regardless of whether that other person is criminally responsible' applies only to commission through another person – and therefore includes the concept of an innocent agent that exists in some jurisdictions – or whether it is equally applicable to joint commission or co-perpetration. The draft statute presented to the United Nations Diplomatic Conference of Plenipotentiaries on the Establishment of an International Criminal Court would support the former interpretation, based on the different punctuation employed in the relevant provision. Compare Rome Statute, *supra* note 21, Art. 25(3)(a), with Report of the Preparatory Committee on the Establishment of an International Criminal Court, UN Doc. A/CONF.183/2/Add.1, Part One, Draft Statute for the International Criminal Court, Art. 23(7)(a), p. 49 ('commits such a crime, whether as an individual, jointly with another, or through another person regardless of whether that person is criminally responsible'). The Spanish text could also be read to support the former interpretation. See Estatuto de Roma de la Corte Penal Internacional, UN Doc. A/CONF.183/9, Art. 25(3)(a) ('Cometa ese crimen por sí solo, con otro o por conducto de otro, sea *éste* o no penalmente responsable') (emphasis added).

[726] Indeed, as has been noted elsewhere, the entire body of the Tribunals' jurisprudence on joint criminal enterprise (and other discussions of collective participation in the commission of a crime) postdates the drafting, negotiation and finalisation of the Rome Statute. See Danner and Martinez, *supra* note 5, p. 154; see also *supra* text accompanying notes 21–22 (discussion of *Furundžija*'s reference to Article 25(3)(d)).

[727] Although only sub-paragraph (3)(d)(i) explicitly refers to 'the *criminal* activity or *criminal* purpose of the group, where such activity or purpose involves the commission of a crime within the jurisdiction of the Court' (emphases added), it is clear from the *travaux préparatoires* that the common purpose referred to in the *chapeau* of sub-paragraph (3)(d) must involve the commission of a crime. See, e.g., Kai Ambos, 'General Principles of Criminal Law in the Rome Statute', 10 (1999) *Criminal Law Forum* 12–13 (recounting the earlier approaches to dealing with collective criminality, and confirming that the common purpose must be a crime); Ambos, *supra* note 685, p. 486 (equating the terms 'criminal activity' or 'criminal purpose' with 'the practical acts and ideological objectives of the group'); Andrea Sereni, 'Individual Criminal Responsibility', in Lattanzi and Schabas (eds.), 2 *Essays* (2004), *supra* note 6, pp. 111–112.

contribution to the commission of such a crime.[728] With regard to the third element, although the *ad hoc* model merely requires 'participation' in the common criminal purpose or plan, because of the jurisprudence on what conduct constitutes participation in a JCE,[729] it is unlikely that the application of the ICC model's 'contribution' requirement would lead to significantly different results, particularly since such contribution could occur '[i]n any other way' than aiding, abetting, or otherwise assisting.[730] Finally, the models are similar in that they both have more than one variant, each characterised by the accused's intent with regard to, or knowledge of, the criminal activity or purpose of the group: the *ad hoc* model has the three categories of JCE; while the ICC model has two variants, which are expressed in sub-paragraphs (3)(d)(i) and (ii).

Unlike the first category of the *ad hoc* model, however, no variant of the ICC model requires that an accused share the *mens rea* of the physical perpetrators. In this regard, it is clear that Article 30 of the Rome Statute, which sets forth the mental element required for all crimes within the jurisdiction of the Court and refers to both knowledge and intent,[731] does not affect this conclusion. First, although Article 30 does speak in general terms of a person being 'criminally responsible and liable for punishment for a crime' and therefore must be read in conjunction with Article 25's provisions on individual criminal responsibility, a plain reading of the text reveals that it does not require that the person being held responsible be the physical perpetrator: instead of insisting that this person commit the crime, it provides that liability may be imposed 'only if the material elements *are committed with* intent and knowledge'.[732] Accordingly, this article merely encapsulates the fundamental

---

[728] The authors ignore, for these purposes, the Rome Statute's reference to an accused's contribution to the attempted commission of a crime, which reflects its inclusion of attempt as a category of inchoate crimes, one which is not included in the *ad hoc* Statutes for crimes other than genocide. Compare Rome Statute, *supra* note 21, Art. 25(3)(f) with ICTY Statute, *supra* note 2, Arts. 4(3)(d), 7(1) and ICTR Statute, *supra* note 94, Arts. 2(3)(d), 6(1). See *infra*, Chapter 5 for a discussion of the forms of commission of genocide.

[729] See *supra* text accompanying notes 215–261 (discussing ICTY jurisprudence on the definition of 'participation').

[730] See Rome Statute, *supra* note 21, Art. 25(3)(c), (d).

[731] See *ibid.*, Art. 30:

1. Unless otherwise provided, a person shall be criminally responsible and liable for punishment for a crime within the jurisdiction of the Court only if the material elements are committed with intent and knowledge.
2. For the purposes of this article, a person has intent where:
    (a) In relation to conduct, that person means to engage in the conduct;
    (b) In relation to a consequence, that person means to cause that consequence or is aware that it will occur in the ordinary course of events.
3. For the purposes of this article, 'knowledge' means awareness that a circumstance exists or a consequence will occur in the ordinary course of events. 'Know' and 'knowingly' shall be construed accordingly.

[732] *Ibid.*, Art. 30(1) (emphasis added).

principle that no one may be held criminally liable unless the conduct for which he or she is responsible – through whichever form of responsibility, including but not limited to commission – actually constitutes a crime. Second, even if Article 30's provisions are intended to apply to the forms of responsibility in Article 25,[733] the specificity of Article 25(3)(d)'s discussion of the mental state required for common-purpose liability would seem to bring it within the '[u]nless otherwise provided' exception of Article 30, so that its two variants would stand alone, unmodified by anything in the latter article.

Although it is clear that an accused who fulfils all the requirements of either variant of the ICC model *and* who shares the physical perpetrator's *mens rea* would still be liable under Article 25(3)(d), it is less clear whether these two variants are identical in scope to the second and third categories of JCE in the *ad hoc* model, such that any accused found liable under either JCE category would also be liable under the ICC model. In particular, it remains to be seen whether, in the course of interpreting and applying Article 25, the chambers of the ICC would construe sub-paragraph (3)(d)(i) as including the situation in which a crime, not originally conceived by the group but nevertheless within the jurisdiction of the Court, is committed. It may be some time before this question is resolved; none of the arrest warrants unsealed so far by the ICC alleges that the accused is responsible pursuant to Article 25(3)(d), relying instead on sub-paragraphs (3)(a) and/or (3)(b) to ground the charges.[734]

2.6.2 The Internationalised Tribunals

2.6.2.1 Special Court for Sierra Leone (SCSL)

Article 6 ('Individual Criminal Responsibility') of the Statute of the Special Court for Sierra Leone (SCSL) closely mirrors Article 7 of the ICTY Statute and Article 6 of the ICTR Statute. Article 6(1) states:

---

[733] Because, as will be seen in later chapters, each form has its own physical and mental elements, which are distinct from the physical and mental elements (*actus reus* and *mens rea*) of the underlying offence, which are simply those required for commission.

[734] See *Situation in Uganda*, Case No. ICC-02/04–01/05, Warrant of Arrest for Joseph Kony issued on 8 July 2005 as amended on 27 September 2005, 27 September 2005, p. 12 *et seq.* (holding that 'there are reasonable grounds to believe that Joseph Kony *committed and*, together with other persons whose arrests are sought by the Prosecutor, *ordered or induced the commission* of crimes within the jurisdiction of the Court', but stating that his alleged responsibility arises solely under Article 25(3)(b)); *ibid.*, Warrant of Arrest for Vincent Otti, 8 July 2005, p. 12 *et seq.* (omitting any reference to commission, and relying only on Article 25(3)(b)); *ibid.*, Warrant of Arrest for Raska Lukwiya, 8 July 2005 (same); *ibid.*, Warrant of Arrest for Okot Odhiambo, 8 July 2005, p. 10 *et seq.* (same); *ibid.*, Warrant of Arrest for Dominic Ongwen, 8 July 2005, p. 8 *et seq.* (same); *Lubanga*, Warrant of Arrest, 10 February 2006, p. 4 (holding that 'there are reasonable grounds to believe that Mr Thomas Lubanga Dyilo is criminally responsible under Article 25 (3) (a) of the Statute for' the crimes with which he is charged).

A person who planned, instigated, ordered, committed or otherwise aided and abetted in the planning, preparation or execution of a crime referred to in Articles 2 to 4 of the present Statute shall be individually responsible for the crime.[735]

Unlike the Rome Statute, the Statute of the SCSL does not contain any express reference to JCE or common-purpose liability.[736] The SCSL Statute is clearly modelled on the ICTY and ICTR Statutes, and was drafted one year after the *Tadić* Appeal Judgement, which was the first to hold explicitly that the concept of joint criminal enterprise, as a theory of common-purpose liability, was included within that of commission as a form of responsibility.[737] It is unsurprising, therefore, that the Special Court has adopted the *ad hoc* model of the common-purpose doctrine, as is reflected in the approaches of the Office of the Prosecutor and at least two trial chambers to date.[738]

Relying heavily on the ICTY jurisprudence on joint criminal enterprise, the Prosecutor of the Special Court has either explicitly charged joint criminal enterprise as a form of responsibility or alleged that the accused acted to implement a common purpose, plan or design.

The initial indictment in *Prosecutor* v. *Taylor* accused the Revolutionary United Front (RUF) and the Armed Forces Revolutionary Council (AFRC) of sharing a 'common plan, purpose or design (joint criminal enterprise) which was to take any actions necessary to gain and exercise political power and control over the territory of Sierra Leone, in particular the diamond mining areas'.[739] It alleged that the natural resources of Sierra Leone, particularly the diamonds, were to be distributed to persons outside Sierra Leone in return for

---

[735] Statute of the Special Court for Sierra Leone, 2178 UNTS 138, UN Doc. S/2002/246 (2002), Appendix II, Art. 6(1).

[736] The SCSL Statute – like that for Cambodia, but unlike the Rome Statute – does not include a variety of defences that may relieve a person of individual criminal responsibility. See Bert Swart, 'Internationalized Courts and Substantive Criminal Law', in Cesare P. R. Romano, André Nollkaemper, and Jann K. Kleffner (eds.), *Internationalized Criminal Courts and Tribunals: Sierra Leone, East Timor, Kosovo, and Cambodia*, (2004), p. 306 (observing that this stems from the silence on these matters in the Statutes of the ICTY and ICTR, upon which the statutes of these internationalised tribunals are modelled, which assume that the tribunals themselves will determine the limits of individual criminal responsibility).

[737] See *supra* text accompanying notes 38–81 (discussing *Tadić* in the context of the development of JCE).

[738] For the Office of the Prosecutor, see *infra* text accompanying notes 739–751. For Trial Chambers, see *infra* note 752 and text accompanying notes 753–759.

[739] *Prosecutor* v. *Taylor*, Case No. SCSL-03-1, Indictment, 3 March 2003 ('Initial *Taylor* Indictment'), para. 23. The Initial *Taylor* Indictment also gave explanations of the parties to the Sierra Leone conflict. See *ibid.*, para. 4 ('The organized armed group that became known as the RUF ... was founded about 1988 or 1989 in Libya. The RUF ... began organized armed operations in Sierra Leone in March 1991. During the ensuing armed conflict, the RUF forces were also referred to as "RUF", "rebels" and "People's Army".'); *ibid.*, para. 5 ('The CDF was comprised of Sierra Leonean traditional hunters, including the Kamajors, Gbethis, Kapras, Tamaboros and Donsos. The CDF fought against the RUF and AFRC.'); *ibid.*, para. 7 ('The AFRC was founded by members of the Armed Forces of Sierra Leone who seized power from the elected government of the Republic of Sierra Leone via a coup d'état on 25 May 1997. ... The AFRC forces were also referred to as "Junta", "soldiers", "SLA", and "ex-SLA".').

assistance in carrying out the JCE,[740] and that Charles Taylor participated in this JCE 'as part of his continuing efforts to gain access to the mineral wealth of Sierra Leone and to destabilize the Government of Sierra Leone'.[741] The initial indictment stated that the crimes listed therein, such as unlawful killings, forced labour, and physical or sexual violence, 'were either actions within the joint criminal enterprise or were a reasonably foreseeable consequence of the joint criminal enterprise',[742] thereby charging both the first and third categories of JCE. Although the structure of the *Taylor* indictment has since been altered,[743] the substance of the allegations with regard to joint criminal enterprise remains the same: as an alternative form of responsibility, the amended indictment charges that the crimes alleged therein 'amounted to or were involved within a common plan, design or purpose in which [Taylor] participated, or were a reasonably foreseeable consequence of such common plan, design or purpose';[744] and the case summary accompanying the indictment[745] repeats the allegations in the initial indictment as to the common purpose of the JCE, the means by which it was accomplished, and the accused's particular role therein.[746] The case summary does provide some additional details on the membership of the alleged JCE, albeit at the end of a paragraph describing the allegations with regard to aiding and abetting:

The essential support set out above provided practical assistance, encouragement and/ or moral support to the RUF, AFRC, AFRC/RUF Junta or alliance and Liberian fighters in carrying out the crimes alleged in the Amended Indictment, and had a

---

[740] *Ibid.*   [741] *Ibid.*, para. 25.   [742] *Ibid.*, para. 24.

[743] See *Prosecutor v. Taylor*, Case No. SCSL-03-01-I, Amended Indictment, 16 March 2006 ('Amended *Taylor* Indictment'). For an explanation of the reasons for which the prosecution sought to amend the initial indictment, see *ibid.*, Decision on Prosecution's Application to Amend Indictment and on Approval of Amended Indictment, 16 March 2006, paras. 9–10. This decision was originally filed *ex parte* and confidentially, but was made public by a subsequent decision on motion of the prosecution. *Ibid.*, Decision and Order for Disclosure, 30 March 2006, p. 3.

[744] Amended *Taylor* Indictment, *supra* note 743, para. 33.

[745] The case summary is appended to the indictment proper, and could arguably be read together with the indictment as constituting the accusatory instrument, as it opens with the phrase 'The Prosecution evidence … will prove the following allegations'. But see *Prosecutor v. Norman, Fofana and Kondewa* ('*CDF* Case'), Case No. SCSL-04-14-A(R73), Decision on Amendment of the Consolidated Indictment, 16 May 2005, para. 52:

> The case summary which should accompany the Indictment forms no part of it … It accompanies the Indictment in order to give the Accused better details of the charges against him and to enable the designated judge to decide whether to approve the indictment under Rule 47(E). It does not bind the Prosecutor in the sense that he is obliged to apply to amend it if his evidence changes … [T]he 'Prosecutor's case summary' is not part of the Indictment, which is the formal document which triggers the trial.

> See also *ibid.*, para. 78 ('By "Indictment", we mean the counts stating the charges and the short particulars which should accompany them.'). Nonetheless, the case summary is crucial for an understanding of the prosecution's JCE allegations in the *Taylor* case, because the amended indictment contains no detail on the purpose, scope, or implementation of the alleged JCE, nor on Taylor's involvement therein.

[746] *Prosecutor v. Taylor*, Case No. SCSL-03-01-I, Case Summary Accompanying the Amended Indictment, 16 March 2006, paras. 42–44.

substantial effect on the commission of those crimes, and/or *furthered the common plan, design or purpose in which the participants included the leadership and members of the RUF, AFRC, AFRC/RUF Junta or alliance and Liberian fighters.*[747]

Wording almost identical to the initial *Taylor* indictment appears in the indictments in the cases of *Prosecutor* v. *Brima, Kamara, and Kanu ('AFRC* case');[748] *Prosecutor* v. *Sesay, Kallon, and Gbao ('RUF* case');[749] *Prosecutor* v. *Koroma;*[750] and *Prosecutor* v. *Norman, Fofana and Kondewa ('CDF* case').[751] Although the *CDF* indictment does not specifically use the term 'joint criminal enterprise', it nonetheless alleges a common criminal plan, purpose, or design – similar to that described in the other indictments – and charges the accused with responsibility on that basis for crimes within, or which were a reasonably foreseeable consequence of, that common purpose, plan or design.

To date, the SCSL has issued one reasoned decision that discusses JCE in any detail.[752] In its decision on the accused's motions for judgement of acquittal after the close of the prosecution's case in chief, the Trial Chamber hearing the *AFRC* case considered the prosecution's allegations of – and the accused's challenges to – individual criminal responsibility on the basis of participation in a joint criminal enterprise.[753] The discussion of the applicable law is unremarkable, as it largely repeats the holdings of the ICTY Appeals Chamber with regard to the categories of JCE and the corresponding physical and

---

[747] *Ibid.*, para. 41.

[748] *Prosecutor* v. *Brima, Kamara and Kanu ('AFRC* Case'), Case No. SCSL-2004-16-PT, Further Amended Consolidated Indictment, 18 February 2005 ('Current *AFRC* Indictment'), para. 33 (alleging that the Armed Forces Revolutionary Council, including the three accused, and the Revolutionary United Front, including three other accused before the SCSL, 'shared a common plan, purpose or design (joint criminal enterprise) which was to take any actions necessary to gain and exercise political power and control over the territory of Sierra Leone, in particular the diamond mining areas'); *ibid.*, para. 34 (stating that 'the crimes alleged in this Indictment ... were either actions within the joint criminal enterprise or were a reasonably foreseeable consequence of the joint criminal enterprise').

[749] *Prosecutor* v. *Sesay, Kallon and Gbao*, Case No. SCSL-2004-15-PT, Amended Consolidated Indictment, 13 May 2004, paras. 36–38.

[750] *Prosecutor* v. *Koroma*, Case No. SCSL-2003-03-I, Indictment, 7 March 2003, paras. 24–26.

[751] *CDF* Case, Case No. SCSL-2004-14-PT, Indictment, 5 February 2004, paras. 19–20.

[752] Although another decision acknowledges that JCE is a form of responsibility within the jurisdiction of the Special Court, it does not discuss the definition of the concept or details of the particular JCE alleged in that case. See *CDF* Case, Case No. 04-14-T, Decision on Motions for Judgement of Acquittal pursuant to Rule 98, 21 October 2005, para. 130:

> The Chamber recognizes, as a matter of law, generally, that Article 6(1) of the Statute of the Special Court does not, in its proscriptive reach, limit criminal liability to only those persons who plan, instigate, order, physically commit a crime or otherwise ... aid and abet in its planning, preparation or execution. Its proscriptive ambit extends beyond that to prohibit the commission of offences through a joint criminal enterprise, in pursuit of the common plan to commit crimes punishable under the Statute.

> The Chamber declined, however, to make detailed findings on the issue of the Accused's criminal responsibility, concluding instead that 'for the purposes of the Rule 98 standard, ... the Accused participated in each of the crimes charged', and that it was therefore 'not in a position at this stage to dismiss any of the modes of liability as alleged in the Indictment'. *Ibid.*, para. 131.

[753] See generally *AFRC* Case, Case. No. SCSL-04-16-T, Decision on Motions for Judgement of Acquittal pursuant to Rule 98, 31 March 2006, paras. 308–326.

mental elements. In rejecting the joint defence submissions challenging the prosecution's JCE allegations, the Trial Chamber concluded that it was 'satisfied that a reasonable tribunal of fact could, on the basis of the evidence before it, if believed, find beyond a reasonable doubt that each of the three Accused and other persons identified in the Indictment participated in a *joint criminal enterprise to commit the crimes charged*'.[754]

As certain commentators have pointed out, however,[755] despite the terms in which this finding is couched, the indictment upon which this case went to trial does not actually allege a JCE to commit certain crimes. Instead, it alleges 'a common plan, purpose or design (joint criminal enterprise) ... to take any actions necessary to gain and exercise political power and control over the territory of Sierra Leone, in particular the diamond mining areas';[756] and that the JCE 'included gaining and exercising control over the population of Sierra Leone in order to prevent or minimize resistance to their geographic control, and to use members of the population to provide support to the members of the joint criminal enterprise'.[757] Although the indictment does assert that the crimes alleged therein 'were either actions within the joint criminal enterprise or were a reasonably foreseeable consequence of the joint criminal enterprise', the common plan or purpose ascribed to the enterprise does not appear to be the sort of activity that would attract criminal liability. The point is not necessarily academic. Under the *ad hoc* model,[758] the common plan must itself be criminal, in that the common mental state of JCE participants must be an express or implied agreement that a crime would be committed.[759]

Under this approach, the Special Prosecutor's indictment is flawed; despite its later description of the relationship between the crimes charged and the alleged JCE, it does not properly plead any category of joint criminal enterprise, because even a third-category JCE requires an agreement to commit a

---

[754] See *ibid.*, para. 325 (emphasis added).

[755] See John R. W. D. Jones, Claire Carlton-Hanicles, Haddijatou Kah-Jallow, Sam Scratch, and Ibrahim Yillah, 'The Special Court for Sierra Leone: A Defence Perspective', (2004) 2 *Journal of International Criminal Justice* 211, 225.

[756] Current *AFRC* Indictment, *supra* note 748, para. 33.   [757] *Ibid.*, para. 34.

[758] Arguably, this proposition holds true under the ICC model as well. See *supra* note 727. It is possible, however, that the ICC model is less restrictive in this aspect, since the common purpose need only 'involve' the commission or attempted commission of international crimes, and no judicial gloss has yet been put on the term to bring it into line with the *ad hoc* Tribunals' jurisprudence.

[759] See *supra* text accompanying notes 166–167 (discussing ICTY jurisprudence holding that the common plan, design, or purpose must amount to or involve an express or implied agreement that an offence be committed). See also, e.g., Milošević Kosovo Second Amended Indictment, *supra* note 159, para. 16 (emphasis added):

> The purpose of this joint criminal enterprise was, *inter alia, the expulsion of a substantial portion of the Kosovo Albanian population from the territory of the province of Kosovo* in an effort to ensure continued Serbian control over the province. To fulfil this criminal purpose, each of the accused, acting individually or in concert with each other and with others known and unknown, significantly contributed to the joint criminal enterprise using the *de jure* and *de facto* powers available to him.

crime; it merely extends liability to crimes that were not the object of that agreement, as long as they were natural and foreseeable consequences of the JCE's execution. The same flaw appears in all the SCSL indictments, except for the recently amended *Taylor* indictment, which omits this pleading only to reprise it in the non-binding summary of the case. If these cases proceed to judgement with no clarification of the respective chamber's understanding of the concept of joint criminal enterprise with regard to such pleadings, it could introduce unwelcome confusion into the jurisprudence on this form of responsibility.

2.6.2.2 *East Timor: Special Panels for Serious Crimes (SPSC)*

The constitutive document for East Timor's Special Panels for Serious Crimes, which concluded their work in May 2005 after hearing several cases, explicitly includes the notion of common-purpose liability. Section 14 of Regulation No. 2000/15 on the Establishment of Panels with Exclusive Jurisdiction over Serious Criminal Offences, promulgated by the UN Transitional Administration in East Timor ('UNTAET Regulation'),[760] mirrors Article 25 of the Rome Statute.[761] Despite this explicit adoption of the ICC model of this form of responsibility, parties before the Special Panels nevertheless referred to the jurisprudence of the *ad hoc* Tribunals in their submissions to the court, probably because those judgements and decisions are to date the only reasoned judicial discussion of common-purpose liability in contemporary international criminal law.

For example, the Trial Judgement in *Prosecutor* v. *Joni Marques et al.*, the longest and most closely reasoned judgement from the Special Panels, summarised the parties' arguments on common-purpose liability before going on to review the evidence and make its own findings. It noted that the prosecution had asserted that:

Section 14.3 (a), (c) and (d) have particular relevance to this Trial. All of the offences charged have co-accused. In every case, the prosecution alleges that the accused were acting together or with others who are not present before this court. For that reason

---

[760] United Nations Transitional Administration in East Timor, Regulation No. 2000/15 on the Establishment of Panels with Exclusive Jurisdiction over Serious Criminal Offences, UN Doc. UNTAET/REG/2000/15, 6 June 2000 ('SPSC Regulation').

[761] See *ibid., supra* note 760, Section 14.3(d):

In accordance with the present regulation, a person shall be criminally responsible and liable for punishment for a crime within the jurisdiction of the panels if that person … in any other way contributes to the commission or attempted commission of such a crime by a group of persons acting with a common purpose. Such contribution shall be intentional and shall either:

(i) be made with the aim of furthering the criminal activity or criminal purpose of the group, where such activity or purpose involves the commission of a crime within the jurisdiction of the panels; or

(ii) be made in the knowledge of the intention of the group to commit the crime[.]

the Prosecution ask the panel to pay special attention to the law under those subsections.[762]

The prosecution's submissions also elaborated upon the notion of participation in a common purpose, with particular emphasis placed on the ICTY's *Tadić* Appeal Judgement.[763] In relation to the murder of Evaristo Lopes, the prosecution submitted that by his presence and encouragement Joni Marques was 'responsible jointly with others involved pursuant to section 14.3(a)' or that, alternatively, he must be responsible pursuant to section 14.3(d), as 'his presence and support ... [were] a contribution to the commission of the offence'.[764]

In turn, counsel for Marques referred to the Judgements of the ICTR in *Akayesu* and *Musema* and the ICTY in *Tadić* in its submissions on criminal responsibility under Section 14.[765] Defence counsel submitted that in order to be found guilty of any crime,

an accused's actions must fall within any one of the categories of participation. It must be proved that the accused participated in any one of the prescribed forms. Each form of participation has separate *mens rea* and *actus reus* and this must be established by the Prosecution. It is not sufficient for the Prosecution to simply state that an accused simply participated in the commission of the offence without specifying what exactly he did and that his actions fall within one of the prescribed forms of participation or individual criminal responsibility.[766]

Unfortunately, although the court ultimately convicted all ten accused of murder, torture and deportation or forcible transfer as crimes against humanity,[767] the legal basis for concluding that they were responsible for those crimes is not always clear. The court's conclusions show that it was satisfied that the accused were deeply involved and participated in the crimes charged – by their presence or encouragement, command of others, or actual physical commission – but the discussion of their roles in those crimes betrays a failure to distinguish between the elements of the substantive crime and the elements of

---

[762] *Prosecutor v. Joni Marques, Manuel da Costa, João da Costa, Paulo da Costa, Amélio da Costa, Hilário da Silva, Gonsalo dos Santos, Alarico Fernandes, Mautersa Monis and Gilberto Fernandes*, Case No. 09/2000, Judgment, 11 December 2001, available at http://ist-socrates.berkeley.edu/~warcrime/ET-Docs/CE-SPSC%20Final%20Decisions/2000/09-2000%20part%201%20Joni%20Marques%20et%20al%20Judgment.pdf, p. 38.

[763] *Ibid.*, pp. 25–28.

[764] *Ibid.*, p. 103. Although contributing to the commission of a crime is certainly a valid reference to Section 14.3(a), the prosecution's argument here, with its reference to Marques' presence and support, seems to invoke aiding and abetting rather than common-purpose liability.

[765] *Ibid.*, pp. 57–59.   [766] *Ibid.*, p. 60.

[767] Deportation or forcible transfer were also charged as forms of persecution as a crime against humanity, and four of the accused were also convicted of these crimes. For the court's conclusions on whether the accused's criminal responsibility had been established beyond a reasonable doubt with regard to each count, see *ibid.*, pp. 366–367, 381, 391, 397, 411.

one or more of the forms of responsibility.[768] Such vagueness in judicial findings in an international criminal case is regrettably not uncommon, particularly where the accused are physical perpetrators, and can even be seen in judgements of the ICTY and ICTR. It is possible that, in the context of the extensive discussions concerning the evidence of the accused's physical commission of the crimes, or of his position of command, that occurs elsewhere in the Judgement, the court found it unnecessary to explain which of the elements of the appropriate form of responsibility had been satisfied. Even if such an approach is understandable in cases of low-level accused, it would not be defensible in cases involving more senior defendants. In any event, despite occasional references to the 'common purpose' of a particular operation,[769] the court did not explicitly ground any of the convictions on any theory of common-purpose liability.

In another judgement, this time explicitly invoking Section 14 of the UNTAET Regulation, the court again laid particular emphasis on ICTY case law. In *Prosecutor* v. *José Cardoso Fereira*, the panel concluded that '[t]he Accused ... is responsible for committing the crime of imprisonment or severe deprivation of liberty in violation of fundamental rules of international law under Section 14.3(a) of UNTAET Regulation 2000/15 pursuant to a joint criminal enterprise to effect' these crimes.[770] The remainder of this section of the judgement relies on the *Tadić* Appeal Judgement, the *Krnojelac* Trial Judgement, and the *Vasiljević* Trial Judgement to ground the panel's finding that the accused was liable because he 'actively took part in the joint criminal enterprise/common criminal purpose of [a certain militia] group to arrest and detain those perceived to be supporters of independence'.[771] Apart from a passing reference to 'Section 14[.3](d)' of the UNTAET Regulation[772] – which mirrors Article 25(3)(d) of the Rome Statute – nowhere does the judgement acknowledge that there may be different forms of collective participation in the commission of a crime, or that it is sub-paragraph (d) that fits closest with the *ad hoc* model of common-purpose liability. Even more troubling, the judgement does not explain why the conduct of the accused which it describes should be characterised as participation in a joint criminal enterprise, rather than simple commission, or even co-perpetration.[773] Absent a clear conception

---

[768] See, e.g., *ibid.*, pp. 357–364, 371–381, 384–391.

[769] See, e.g., *ibid.*, p. 406 (holding, in paragraph 957, that '[s]haring a common purpose in this operation and having previously engaged in unlawful conduct, Paulo da Costa once again, as part of a sequence of events, knowingly carried out a part of a widespread and systematic attack on civilians').

[770] *Prosecutor* v. *José Cardoso [Fereira]*, Case No. 04/2001, Judgement, 5 April 2003, para. 367.

[771] *Ibid.*, para. 371. [772] *Ibid.*, para. 369.

[773] See *ibid.*, para. 371 ('The accused ... actively participated in the rounding up of the victims ..., arresting, beating and interrogating the victims who were then detained .... The accused and his co-perpetrators had a list of victims they targeted.').

of the various approaches to common-purpose liability in international criminal law, however, it is perhaps understandable that the court's application of this form of responsibility might be confused or contradictory.

2.6.2.3 *The Extraordinary Chambers in the Courts of Cambodia (ECCC)*

Article 29 of the Law on the Establishment of the Extraordinary Chambers in the Courts of Cambodia for the Prosecution of Crimes Committed during the Period of Democratic Kampuchea sets forth all the forms of responsibility under the jurisdiction of these chambers. Like the parallel article in the SCSL Statute, it is modelled on Article 7 of the ICTY Statute,[774] and so is less elaborate than the analogous provision of the Rome Statute. Article 29 states that:

> Any Suspect who planned, instigated, ordered, aided and abetted, or committed the crimes referred to in article 3 new, 4, 5, 6, 7 and 8 of this law shall be individually responsible for the crime.[775]

It remains to be seen whether the Extraordinary Chambers will follow through on their apparent adoption of the *ad hoc* model, and interpret Article 29 so as to read JCE or any other form of common-purpose liability into the term 'committed'. To date, there is not much available material relating to the functioning of the Extraordinary Chambers, and little academic discussion. The available documentation on the cases in which preparations have begun is sparse.[776] The prosecutors and judges of the Extraordinary Chambers, both Cambodian and international, were only appointed in May 2006,[777] and trials are not expected to begin before 2007.[778] For these reasons, it will not be

---

[774] Ernestine E. Meijer, 'The Extraordinary Chambers in the Courts of Cambodia for Prosecuting Crimes Committed by the Khmer Rouge: Jurisdiction, Organization, and Procedure of an Internationalized National Tribunal', in Romano *et al.*, *supra* note 736, p. 216.

[775] The Law on the Establishment of the Extraordinary Chambers in the Courts of Cambodia for the Prosecution of Crimes Committed during the Period of Democratic Kampuchea, as amended on 27 October 2004, Doc. No. NS/RKM/1004/006, unofficial translation by the Council of Jurists and the Secretariat of the Task Force, revised on 29 September 2005, available at http://www.cambodia.gov.kh/krt/english/law%20on%20establishment.htm, Art. 29.

[776] The only official information that is widely available on the ECCC is posted on the website of the Task Force for Cooperation with Foreign Legal Experts for the Preparation of the Proceedings for the Trial of Senior Khmer Rouge Leaders, which contains very little information on the scant proceedings to date. See http://www.cambodia.gov.kh/krt/english/index.htm.

[777] See Official List of National and International Judges and Prosecutors for the Extraordinary Chambers in the Courts of Cambodia as selected by the Supreme Council of the Magistracy on 4 May 2006 and appointed by Preah Reach Kret (Royal Decree) NS/RKT/0506/214 of His Majesty Norodom Sihamoni, King of Cambodia on 7 May 2006, available at http://www.cambodia.gov.kh/krt/english/judicial_officer.htm (listing the 17 national and 12 international judges and prosecutors appointed to serve on the Extraordinary Chambers, and noting that one additional international position, as a reserve co-investigating judge, remains to be filled).

[778] Office of the Governor-General of New Zealand, Press Release, 'Cartwright appointed Cambodian War Crimes Tribunal trial judge', 9 May 2006, available at http://www.gov-gen.govt.nz/media/news.asp?type=current&ID=164.

possible to understand how this hybrid court will apply this and other forms of responsibility in international criminal law until pre-trial and trial proceedings get under way.

The website for the Khmer Rouge Trial Task Force,[779] which is one of the few official sources for information on the ECCC's proceedings, contains three documents identified as indictments that have been issued against the two accused in custody since 1999.[780] None of these indictments refers to Article 29 or joint criminal enterprise. However, the document identified as the first indictment against Kaing Khek Iev (known as Duch), charges Duch with being 'involved together with Ung Choeun, known as [Ta] Mok, for crimes against domestic security with the intention of serving the policies of the Democratic Kampuchea group, committed in Cambodia, during the period 1975 to 1999'.[781] In July 2006, Ta Mok died of natural causes, leaving Duch as the sole remaining Khmer Rouge leader in custody at the time.[782]

2.6.2.4 *Supreme Iraqi Criminal Tribunal (SICT), formerly known as the Iraqi Special Tribunal (IST)*

When it was adopted in 2003, the Statute of the Iraqi Special Tribunal included Article 15, which was titled 'Individual Criminal Responsibility', and mirrored Article 25 of the Rome Statute in large part. Article 15(b)(4) of the IST Statute dealt with the commission of crimes with a 'common purpose', and was identical to Article 25(3)(d) of the Rome Statute. It provided that a person shall be criminally responsible and liable for punishment if the person:

In any other way contributes to the commission or attempted commission of such a crime by a group of persons acting with a common purpose. Such contribution shall be intentional and shall either:

(i) be made with the aim of furthering the criminal activity or criminal purpose of the group, where such activity or purpose involves the commission of a crime within the jurisdiction of the panels; or

(ii) be made in the knowledge of the intention of the group to commit the crime.[783]

---

[779] See Website of the Task Force for Cooperation with Foreign Legal Experts for the Preparation of the Proceedings for the Trial of Senior Khmer Rouge Leaders, available at http://www.cambodia.gov.kh/krt/.

[780] See Chronology of Developments relating to the KR [Khmer Rouge] Trial, available at http://www.cambodia.gov.kh/krt/english/chrono.htm (noting that 'Khmer Rouge military leader Ta Mok' and 'Duch, former director of S-21 Tuol Sleng prison', were arrested in 1999).

[781] Second Order to Forward Case for Investigation, Military Court No. 029/99, 10 May 1999 (unofficial translation, available at http://www.cambodia.gov.kh/krt/pdfs/Duch%201st%20indictment.pdf).

[782] See Thomas Fuller, 'Khmer Rouge Leader Dies', *International Herald Tribune*, 21 July 2006, available at http://www.iht.com/articles/2006/07/21/news/khmer.php.

[783] Statute of the Iraqi Special Tribunal, Art. 15(b)(4), available at http://www.iraq-ist.org/en/about/sec4.htm.

In October 2005, the Statute was amended and adopted by Iraq's Transitional National Assembly, which changed the name of the Tribunal to the 'Supreme Iraqi Criminal Tribunal' (SICT).[784] Although substantive modifications were made to the Statute, the essence of its provisions on individual criminal responsibility remain unchanged.[785]

It is therefore clear that the SICT has adopted the ICC model of common-purpose liability, and the basic translations of the charging instruments that are publicly available appear to confirm that all three forms of common-purpose liability were charged in the first proceedings ('Dujail case').[786] Several factors, not least of which the sometimes chaotic nature of the proceedings,[787] meant that this tribunal's interpretation of the applicable forms of individual criminal responsibility was not known until the judgement was finally rendered.[788] Even then, however, it is not always possible to ascertain

---

[784] Human Rights Watch, World Report 2006, Iraq, available at http://hrw.org/english/docs/2006/01/18/iraq12215.htm. See Law No. 10 (2005), Law of the Iraqi Higher Criminal Court, available at http://www.law.case.edu/saddamtrial/documents/IST_statute_official_english.pdf. This translated document, which refers to the 'Iraqi Higher Criminal Court', presents a slightly different wording of this provision:

In accordance with this Law, and the provisions of Iraqi criminal law, a person shall be criminally responsible if that person:
    ... Participating by any other way with a group of persons, with a common criminal intention to commit or attempt to commit such a crime, such participation shall be intentional and shall either:

1. Be made for the aim of consolidating the criminal activity or criminal purpose of the group, where such activity or purpose involves the commission of a crime within the jurisdiction of the Court; or
2. Be made with the knowledge of the intention of the group to commit the crime;

It is clear that the article is still modelled on Article 25 of the Rome Statute, so it is possible that the differences in wording may be the result of translation.

[785] See Human Rights Watch, 'The Former Iraqi Government on Trial', 16 October 2005, Part III, available at http://hrw.org/backgrounder/mena/iraq1005/3.htm ('The SICT Statute preserves most of the provisions of the IST Statute, but emphasizes greater use of Iraqi criminal procedure law.') See also *supra* note 784.

[786] See, e.g., *Saddam Hussein*, Case No. 1/1st Criminal/2005, Document, 15 May 2006, available at http://www.law.case.edu/saddamtrial/documents/20060515_indictment_trans_saddam_hussein.pdf, p. 3:

The person is considered responsible according to the stipulations of this code and to the stipulations of the penal code if he commits the following:
a. If the person commits the crime personally, in participation, or via another person regardless if this person is criminally responsible or not
    ...
c. Contributing with a group of people in a collaborative criminal intention to commit a crime or to start committing it, provided that this participation is deliberate

[787] See, e.g., Mike Woolridge, 'Farce and Gravity at Saddam Trial', 5 April 2006, available at http://news.bbc.co.uk/1/hi/world/middle_east/4881614.stm; Nick Meo, 'Hussein on Trial: The Fear Factor; As Former Strongman Returns to Court, Iraqis Brace for More Suicide Bombings', *Globe and Mail*, 5 April 2006, p. A13; 'Hussein Trial Chaos', *New York Times*, 30 January 2006, p. A13.

[788] The charging instruments in the second trial ('Anfal case'), begun in September 2006, were not yet public by the time this book was concluded. Those proceedings seem marred with chaos and procedural confusion similar to that which marked most of the first trial, so it may be equally difficult to determine how the judges approach the application of these forms of responsibility to the crimes charged in respect of that case. See BBC News, 'Iraq troops "buried family alive"', available at http://news.bbc.co.uk/2/hi/middle_east/6033627.stm (last updated 9 October 2006) ('The previous session of the current trial ended

the precise basis or reasoning for the court's conclusion with regard to individual responsibility on a particular point.[789]

Nonetheless, the written judgement of the SICT issued in the Dujail case discusses the role of each accused in the crimes with which each was charged, often invoking and relying on the *ad hoc* jurisprudence on JCE to guide the tribunal's application of the ICC model of common-purpose liability.[790] While certain aspects of the tribunal's discussion of the JCE jurisprudence seem consistent with the manner in which this form of responsibility has been developed in the *ad hoc* Tribunals,[791] others betray a misapprehension of the doctrine that is perhaps understandable, given its complexities.[792] Some of the judgement's missteps, such as failing to state explicitly or distinguish between the various categories of JCE that it appears to be applying, are similarly excusable. Others are more troubling, because they reveal an approach that is inconsistent with the fundamental principle of culpability in contemporary international criminal law, by placing inappropriate emphasis on the transgressions of the regime in general, and the positions of the accused in that regime, rather than their precise and particular conduct with regard to the crimes charged.[793] Ultimately, Hussein and six of his seven co-accused were convicted of almost all the crimes with which they were charged, through

in chaos after Saddam Hussein and co-defendant, Ali Hassan al-Majid, were ejected. . . . The defence team of lawyers was also absent' from the most recent session, partially in protest 'about the replacement of former chief judge, Abdullah al-Amiri, following accusations of bias towards the former president.'); Reuters UK, 'Woman tells court Saddam forces buried family alive', available at http://today.reuters.co.uk/news/CrisesArticle.aspx?storyId = COL938653&WTmodLoc = World-R5-Alertnet-4 (last updated 9 October 2006) ('Legal rights groups have said the dismissal [of that judge] could hurt the trial's credibility. Gunmen killed a brother-in-law of new chief judge Mohammed al-Ureybi on Sept. 29, which the government called a direct attack on the court by Saddam's followers.').

[789] See Michael P. Scharf, 'Observations on the Dujail Trial Opinion', available at http://www.law.case.edu/saddamtrial/ ('The English translation is a bit awkward, the text is redundant, and the prose certainly won't be compared to the opinions of Oliver Wendell Homes or Learned Hand. But even the harshest critics of the Tribunal will have to admit that it did a competent job writing its Opinion[.]').

[790] See, e.g., Case No. 1/9 1st/2005, Judgement, 22 November 2006 ('Dujail Judgement') (English translation issued 4 December 2006), Part III, pp. 23–25 (citing, though misspelling, the *Tadić* and *Krnojelac* Trial Judgements).

[791] See, e.g., *ibid.*, p. 23 (correctly stating that an agreement must be proved in order to establish liability, and noting that it is unnecessary for such an agreement to be explicit).

[792] See, e.g., *ibid.* (stating, confusingly, that 'an individual becomes an accomplice in a collaborative crime' in three ways, none of which matches the scope of the three categories of JCE; and one of which is readily recognisable as more akin to aiding and abetting, though not necessarily inconsistent with the manner in which the ICTY has applied JCE).

[793] *Ibid.* (holding that 'an act in which [the accused] supports a certain regime during which the crime has taken place', or his position in the government, or his position and knowledge of the criminal nature of the regime was sufficient to ground liability, if coupled with intentional support of the regime); see also *ibid.*, p. 31 (discussing Saddam Hussein's liability for forcible displacement as a crime against humanity under the provision on common-purpose liability, and holding that 'silence and negligence by the accused . . . was an expression of an implicit and unpronounced consent . . . [a]nd the voluntary involvement by the accused . . . in reinforcing the criminal activity and the criminal objective of the group . . . was accomplished in that way (by being silent and negligent).').

multiple forms of responsibility, including common-purpose liability.[794] Three of the seven convicted men – Hussein; Barzan Ibrahim Al-Hassan, his half-brother and former head of the Intelligence Service;[795] and Awad Hamad Al-Bandar, former chief judge of the Iraqi Revolutionary Court – were sentenced to death by hanging as punishment for their roles in murder as a crime against humanity; one accused was sentenced to life imprisonment, and the remaining three to fifteen years' imprisonment for their involvement in the same crime.[796] The death sentences were carried out on 30 December 2006 and 15 January 2007.[797]

2.7 Conclusion

As the *ad hoc* Tribunals draw closer to the end of their mandates, and the ICC and internationalised tribunals either begin or continue their work in earnest, joint criminal enterprise will assume even greater importance in international criminal adjudication. Because JCE enables guilt to be attributed to those who are responsible for orchestrating criminal activity, but do not themselves physically commit such crimes, it is a crucial aspect of the prosecutorial policy in leadership cases – the very kind of case that is increasingly the focus of international criminal law. Due in large part to the completion strategies recently implemented at the ICTY and ICTR, the active cases remaining in their dockets concentrate on 'the most senior leaders suspected of being most responsible for crimes within the jurisdiction of the relevant Tribunal'.[798] Of the twenty-one cases that have not yet proceeded to judgement at trial at the ICTY, fifteen allege JCE as one of the bases, if not the primary basis, for the

---

[794] See *ibid.*, Part VI, p. 50 (acquitting Mohammed Azawi Ali, a local Ba'ath party supporter, for lack of evidence).

[795] Also known as Barzan Ibrahim al-Tikriti.

[796] Dujail Judgement, *supra* note 790, p. 51; see also *ibid.*, pp. 51–52 (pronouncing the lesser sentences also imposed for other crimes).

[797] See BBC News, 'Saddam Hussein executed in Iraq', 30 December 2006, available at http://news.bbc. co.uk/2/hi/middle_east/6218485.stm; John F. Burns, 'Two Hussein Allies Are Hanged; One Is Decapitated', *New York Times*, 15 January 2007, available at http://www.nytimes.com/2007/01/15/ world/middleeast/16iraqcnd.html?ex = 1169614800&en = 75fe7d64a9f1ada7&ei = 5070.

[798] See Security Council Resolution 1534, UN Doc. S/RES/1534 (2004), 26 March 2004 ('Resolution 1534'), p. 2, para. 5; Security Council Resolution 1503 UN Doc. S/RES/1503 (2003), 28 August 2003, pp. 1–2. See also Resolution 1534, p. 2, para. 3, in which the Security Council:

Emphasizes the importance of fully implementing the Completion Strategies, as set out in paragraph 7 of resolution 1503 (2003), that calls on the ICTY and ICTR to take all possible measures to complete investigations by the end of 2004, to complete all trial activities at first instance by the end of 2008 and to complete all work in 2010, and urges each Tribunal to plan and act accordingly[.]

For more on the completion strategies of the Tribunals, including the complementary process for referring cases to national jurisdictions under Rule 11 *bis* of both Statutes, see, for example, Michael Bohlander, 'Referring an Indictment from the ICTY and ICTR to Another Court – Rule 11 *bis* and the Consequences for the Law of Extradition', (2006) 55 *International and Comparative Law Quarterly* 219; Daryl A. Mundis and Fergal Gaynor, 'Current Developments at the *ad hoc* International Criminal Tribunals', (2005) 3 *Journal of International Criminal Justice* 1134, 1154–1159.

accused's liability.[799] After the 2004 *Rwamakuba* interlocutory decision clarified that JCE is a permissible form of responsibility for the crime of genocide,[800] at least five ICTR indictments have been amended to include or clarify JCE charges.[801]

As this chapter has shown, the legal and policy considerations related to applying and expanding JCE liability in leadership cases, which involve accused far removed from the physical perpetration of the alleged crimes, raise the pertinent question as to whether 'commission' is the form of responsibility that appropriately describes their alleged criminal conduct. The remainder of this volume will explore the other forms of responsibility that are applied in international criminal law, which – despite their allegedly inferior status to commission as a basis for liability – may more accurately represent the punishable conduct of the accused in such cases.

---

[799] These cases involve the most high-profile accused or incidents within the jurisdiction of the Tribunal. See *Prosecutor* v. *Gotovina, Čermak and Markač*, Case No. IT-06-90-PT, Joinder Indictment, 21 July 2006, paras. 12–21; *Popović et al.* August 2006 Indictment, *supra* note 714, paras. 27–32, 36–37; *Prosecutor* v. *Trbić*, Case No. IT-05-88/1-PT, Indictment, 18 August 2006, paras. 18–21, 27–28; *Prosecutor* v. *Tolimir*, Case No. IT-05-88/2-PT, Indictment, 28 August 2006, paras. 18–21, 27–28; *Prosecutor* v. *Šešelj*, Case No. IT-03-67-PT, Modified Amended Indictment, 15 July 2005, para. 5; *Prosecutor* v. *Stanišić and Simatović*, Case No. IT-03-69-PT, Second Amended Indictment, 20 December 2005, para. 8; *Prosecutor* v. *Prlić, Stojić, Praljak, Petković, Ćorić and Pušić*, Case No. IT-04-74-I, Indictment, 4 March 2004, paras. 15–17; *Prosecutor* v. *Mićo Stanišić*, Case No. IT-04-79-PT, Revised Amended Indictment, 22 September 2005, paras. 5–12; *Prosecutor* v. *Boškoski and Tarčulovski*, Case No. IT-04-82-PT, Amended Indictment, 2 November 2005, paras. 3–8; *Prosecutor* v. *Haradinaj, Balaj and Brahimaj*, Case No. IT-04-84-PT, Amended Indictment, 26 April 2006, paras. 20–29; *Milutinović et al.* June 2006 Indictment, *supra* note 634, paras. 18–33; *Prosecutor* v. *Đorđević*, Case No. IT-05-87/1-I, Third Amended Consolidated Indictment, paras. 18–33; *Prosecutor* v. *Martić*, Case No. IT-95-11-PT, Second Amended Indictment, 9 September 2003, paras. 3–8; *Prosecutor* v. *Mrkšić, Radić and Šljivančanin*, Case No. IT-95-13/1-PT, Third Consolidated Amended Indictment, 15 November 2004, paras. 4–12; *Prosecutor* v. *Mladić*, Case No. IT-95-5-18-I, Amended Indictment, 11 October 2002, paras. 20–26. Curiously, the current indictment against Radovan Karadžić does not allege JCE, although other indictments – including that of his co-accused, Ratko Mladić – list him as a participant in the joint criminal enterprise(s) alleged therein. See *Prosecutor* v. *Karadžić*, Case No. IT-95-5-18-I, Amended Indictment, 31 May 2000. This omission could be explained by the age of the instrument in question, which is the oldest unamended operative indictment in any case before the ICTY; were Karadžić to be apprehended before the Tribunal closes, it is certain that the prosecution will move to amend the indictment to add, *inter alia*, an explicit charge of JCE.

[800] See *supra* text accompanying notes 103–105.

[801] See *Karemera et al.* Amended Indictment, *supra* note 135, paras. 4–16; *Mpambara* Amended Indictment, *supra* note 135, para. 6; *Prosecutor* v. *Zigiranyirazo*, Case No. ICTR-01-73-I, Amended Indictment, 8 March 2005, paras. 16, 24, 27, 33, 41, 45, 47, 50 (alleging that all the accused's actions 'were committed in concert with' named persons or groups of persons 'for the common purpose of killing' Tutsis or moderate Hutus 'for the period of . . . criminal enterprise[s]' of various durations); *Gatete* Amendment Decision, *supra* note 131, paras. 2–5 (noting recent ICTR jurisprudence recognising applicability of JCE to genocide, and the prosecution's subsequent proposed amendment of the indictment to specify JCE as a basis for individual criminal responsibility); *Prosecutor* v. *Serugendo*, Case No. ICTR-2005-84-I, Corrigendum of Indictment, 21 July 2005, paras. 26, 51, 74. See also *Simba* Amended Indictment, *supra* note 136, pp. 2, 11, (charging JCE before the *Rwamakuba* decision); *Prosecutor* v. *Setako*, Case No. ICTR-04-81-I, Indictment, 24 March 2004, paras. 3–6 (same). Other ICTR indictments contain language that invokes the elements of JCE without specifically charging that form of responsibility. See *supra* note 131 and accompanying text.

3

Superior responsibility

CONTENTS

The doctrine of superior responsibility is the means by which superiors may be held criminally responsible in relation to crimes committed by their subordinates. The customary international humanitarian law study of the International Committee for the Red Cross (ICRC) concludes that:

Commanders and other superiors are criminally responsible for war crimes committed by their subordinates if they knew, or had reason to know, that the subordinates were about to commit or were committing such crimes and did not take all necessary and reasonable measures in their power to prevent their commission, or if such crimes had been committed, to punish the persons responsible.[1]

The ICRC study affirms that '[s]tate practice establishes this rule as a norm of customary international law applicable in both international and non-international armed conflicts'.[2] Superior responsibility is a form of omission

---

[1] Jean-Marie Henckaerts and Louise Doswald-Beck (eds.), *Customary International Humanitarian Law* (2005) ('ICRC Study'), Vol. I: Rules, p. 558 (setting forth Rule 153).
[2] *Ibid.*, p. 559.

liability: the superior is responsible for failing to prevent or punish crimes committed by his subordinates, as opposed to crimes he has in fact committed, planned, ordered, instigated, or otherwise aided and abetted. Criminal responsibility for omissions exists where there is a lawful duty to act and the superior fails to do so.[3]

The terms 'command' and 'superior' have sometimes been used interchangeably as labels for this form of responsibility, but have also been employed in different contexts, particularly to distinguish between a military superior, or commander, and a civilian superior.[4] Unless otherwise specified, the authors employ the term 'superior responsibility' to denote responsibility attaching to all superiors.

This chapter begins with a discussion of the origins and development of the doctrine of superior responsibility. The doctrine has deep historical roots and has been applied and developed particularly in post-Second World War jurisprudence and treaty law, and more recently clarified and refined in the jurisprudence of the *ad hoc* Tribunals. It then considers in detail the development of the three essential elements of superior responsibility, as first defined in the Commentary to Additional Protocol I[5] and endorsed by the *Čelebići* Trial Judgement.[6]

Section 3.2 of this chapter reviews the jurisprudence, analyses the three elements of superior responsibility as applied in the *ad hoc* Tribunals and reflected in customary international law, and examines some aspects of the doctrine that have given rise to controversy. Section 3.3 expands on one aspect of the discussion from Section 3.2, providing more detailed reflection on whether a superior may only be held responsible for crimes physically perpetrated by his subordinates – as a literal reading of the term 'committed' in Article 7(3) of the ICTY Statute and in other formulations of the superior responsibility doctrine would suggest – or whether he may also be held responsible for the conduct of a subordinate who did not himself physically perpetrate any crime, but who, for example, ordered it, planned it or instigated it.

Section 3.4 analyses, from a comparative perspective, the application of the doctrine in the legal instruments, indictments and jurisprudence of the International Criminal Court (ICC), the Special Court for Sierra Leone (SCSL),

---

[3] See *Prosecutor* v. *Hadžihasanović, Alagić and Kubura*, Case No. IT-01-47-AR72, Decision on Interlocutory Appeal Challenging Jurisdiction in Relation to Command Responsibility, 16 July 2003 ('*Hadžihasanović et al.* 7(3) Appeal Decision'), para. 14; *Prosecutor* v. *Delalić, Mucić, Delić and Landžo*, Case No. IT-96-21-T, Judgement, 16 November 1998 ('*Čelebići* Trial Judgement'), paras. 333–334. A detailed discussion of these principles is included in Section 3.2 of this chapter. See especially *infra* text accompanying notes 188–190.

[4] See, e.g., Rome Statute of the International Criminal Court, entered into force 1 July 2002, UN Doc. A/CONF. 183/9 (1998) ('Rome Statute'), Art. 28. See also *infra* text accompanying note 201.

[5] See Yves Sandoz, Christophe Swinarski and Bruno Zimmerman (eds.), *Commentary on the Additional Protocols of 8 June 1977 to the Geneva Conventions of 12 August 1949* (1987) ('ICRC Commentary to the Additional Protocols'), para. 3543.

[6] *Čelebići* Trial Judgement, *supra* note 3, para. 346. See also *infra* text accompanying note 206.

the Special Panels for Serious Crimes in East Timor (SPSC), the Extraordinary Chambers in the Courts of Cambodia (ECCC), and the Supreme Iraqi Criminal Tribunal (SICT). The chapter concludes with a discussion and consideration of the major themes and issues raised and discussed throughout the chapter.

3.1 Origins and development of the superior responsibility doctrine

This section reviews the historical evolution of the doctrine of superior responsibility, from its early development and application in international law to a detailed consideration of the development of each of the three essential elements for a legal finding of superior responsibility.

3.1.1 The roots of the superior responsibility doctrine

It has long been considered that positions of superior command entail duties and impose responsibilities. In 500 BC, in what is considered the oldest military treatise in the world, Sun Tzu wrote: 'When troops flee, are insubordinate, distressed, collapse in disorder or are routed, it is the fault of the general. None of these disorders can be attributed to natural causes.'[7] Punishment for a failure in what would eventually come to be called superior responsibility was first applied in an international context in 1474, when Peter Hagenbach, a knight, was brought to trial by the Archduke of Austria before an international tribunal composed of twenty-eight judges from the allied states of the Holy Roman Empire. He was convicted of crimes of murder, which it was held he should have prevented because, as a knight, he had a duty and was in a position to prevent such crimes.[8]

In 1625, Hugo Grotius recorded the concept of state – and individual – responsibility for failures of rulers to prevent crimes: '[A] community, or its rulers, may be held responsible for the crime of a subject if they knew it and do not prevent it when they could and should prevent it.'[9] In the seventeenth and eighteenth centuries, Sweden and the United States imposed upon military commanders the duty and responsibility for control of their subordinates. The Swedish 'Articles of Military Lawwes to be Observed in the Warres' of 1621

---

[7] Sun Tzu, *The Art of War*, p. 125, cited in William H. Parks, 'Command Responsibility for War Crimes', (1973) 62 *Military Law Review* 1, 3; Elies van Sliedregt, *The Criminal Responsibility of Individuals for Violations of International Humanitarian Law* (2003), p. 119 n. 5.

[8] Parks, *supra* note 7, p. 4. This view is shared by Elies van Sliedregt; see van Sliedregt, *supra* note 7, p. 120. See also Leslie Green, 'Superior Orders and Command Responsibility', (1989) 27 *Canadian Yearbook of International Law* 167, 173.

[9] Hugo Grotius, *De jure belli ac pacis: libri tres* (1625), translated in F. W. Kelsey, *The Classics of International Law* (J. B. Scott ed., 1925), p. 523.

focused on responsibility where the superior had ordered the action.[10] Article 46 provided that '[n]o Colonel or Captain shall command his soldiers to do any unlawful thing; which who so does, shall be punished according to the discretion of the judges'.

Article XII of the American Articles of War, first enacted in 1775 and re-enacted in 1776, speaks of an omission by a superior and a duty to punish:

Every officer, commanding in quarters or on a march, shall keep good order, and, to the utmost of his power, redress all such abuses or disorders which may be committed by any officer or soldier under his command: If upon any complaint [being] made to him, of officers or soldiers beating, or otherwise ill-treating any person, or of committing any kind of riot, to the disquieting of the inhabitants of this Continent; he the said commander, who shall refuse or omit to see justice done on the offender or offenders, and reparation made to the party or parties injured, as far as the offender's wages shall enable him or them, shall, upon due proof thereof, be punished as ordered by a general court-martial, in such manner as if he himself had committed the crimes or disorders complained of.[11]

Article 32 of the 1806 re-enactment went further and authorised specific punishment of the offending commander by dismissal. During the American Civil War, President Lincoln promulgated instructions to the Union Forces of the United States, now known as the Lieber Code, on how soldiers should conduct themselves in wartime. Article 71 provided for punishment of any commander ordering or encouraging the intentional wounding or killing of an already 'wholly disabled enemy'.[12] Other historical examples exist for sanctioning commanders for ordering criminal acts by their subordinates. Although this basis of liability has sometimes been described as 'direct' command responsibility, ordering does not form part of the modern doctrine of superior responsibility, constituting now a discrete form of direct responsibility.[13] Nonetheless, these are early examples of the basic proposition that superiors are and should be singled out for special duties and burdens under international law.

The first codification of the concept of responsible command at an international level was the Fourth Hague Convention of 1907,[14] which was ratified by thirty-five nations. Article 1 of the Annex, which contained the Regulations

[10] See Parks, *supra* note 7, p. 4 (citing this provision of the Articles of Military Lawwes to be Observed in the Warres).

[11] American Articles of War, Section IX, 20 September 1776, reprinted in (1906) 5 *Journal of the Continental Congress* 788.

[12] Francis Lieber, *Instructions for the Government of Armies of the United States in the Field*, reprinted in Daniel C. Gilman (ed.), *The Miscellaneous Writings of Francis Lieber* (1881), p. 247. The Lieber Code is alternatively known as the 'Lieber Instructions'.

[13] See Chapter 5, concerning 'ordering' as a form of responsibility along with 'planning' and 'instigating'.

[14] Convention Respecting the Laws and Customs of War on Land of 18 October 1907, entered into force 26 January 1910, 36 Stat. 2277 (1907), T.S. No. 539, reprinted in (1908) 2 *American Journal of International Law* 90.

concerning the Laws and Customs of War on Land, provided that in order to receive the rights of a lawful belligerent, an armed force must be 'commanded by a person responsible for his subordinates'. Article 43 of the Annex required that the commander of a force occupying enemy territory 'take all measures in his power to restore, and ensure, as far as possible, public order and safety, while respecting, unless absolutely prevented, the laws in force in the country'. William Parks emphasises that this Convention codified principles which had previously been accepted in custom among the signatory nations,[15] and Timothy McCormack notes that the timing of the Hague Conventions coincided with an increasing state practice in relation to domestic punishment of violations of the laws of war. This combination of events reflected a growing recognition and acceptance of a principle of individual culpability for violations of the international law of war crimes at the turn of the twentieth century.[16]

Some commentators suggest that the first recognition in an international context of individual criminal responsibility for the failure to prevent or punish subordinate criminal conduct occurred in the aftermath of the First World War.[17] The report of the Allied Powers' Commission on the Responsibility of the Authors of the War and on the Enforcement of Penalties recommended the establishment of an international tribunal to prosecute individuals who 'ordered, or, with knowledge thereof and with power to intervene, abstained from preventing or taking measures to prevent, putting an end to or repressing, violations of the laws or customs of war'.[18] This recommendation has been heralded as a 'revolutionary development', because the Commission explicitly advocated criminal liability for a commander on the basis of an omission if he had specific knowledge of his subordinates' unlawful actions.[19] Although the tribunal itself was never realised, the report was an important step in the early development of a rule criminalising the failure to prevent or punish.

---

[15] Parks, *supra* note 7, p. 11.

[16] Timothy L. H. McCormack, 'From Sun Tzu to the Sixth Committee', in Timothy L. H. McCormack and Gerry J. Simpson (eds.), *The Law of War Crimes* (1997), p. 43.

[17] See, e.g., Stuart Hendin, 'Command Responsibility and Superior Orders in the Twentieth Century – A Century of Evolution', (2003) 10 *Murdoch University Electronic Journal of Law* 1, para. 21; Eugenia Levine, 'Command Responsibility: The Mens Rea Requirement', available at http://www.globalpolicy.org/intljustice/general/2005/command.htm. See also *Čelebići* Trial Judgement, *supra* note 3, para. 335 (holding that this was the first 'explicit expression in an international context' of individual criminal responsibility for failure to take the necessary measures to prevent or to repress breaches of the laws of armed conflict).

[18] Committee on the Responsibility of the Authors of War and on Enforcement of Penalties, Report Presented to the Preliminary Peace Conference, Versailles, 29 March 1919, reprinted in (1920) 14 *American Journal of International Law* 95, 121.

[19] Weston Burnett, 'Command Responsibility and a Case Study of the Criminal Responsibility of Israeli Military Commanders for the Pogrom at Shatila and Sabra', (1985) 107 *Military Law Review* 71, 81; Michael Stryszak, 'Command Responsibility: How Much Should a Commander be Expected to Know?', (2002) 11 *U.S. Air Force Academy Journal of Legal Studies* 27, 33.

The German Supreme Court at Leipzig, which tried some of the alleged war criminals of the First World War under international law,[20] applied principles consistent with the contemporary concept of command responsibility in at least one case. Emil Muller, a captain in the army reserves and the commander of a prison camp, had witnessed a prisoner being maltreated by a soldier. The court held that Muller had 'at least tolerated and approved of this brutal treatment, even if it was not done on his orders'.[21]

3.1.2 Developments subsequent to the Second World War

A number of *ad hoc* military tribunals were established in the aftermath of the Second World War. The International Military Tribunal tried twenty-four of the most notorious Nazi Germany war criminals.[22] The subsequent Allied Military Tribunals, created pursuant to Control Council Law No. 10,[23] tried twelve other alleged war criminals from Nazi Germany ('subsequent Nuremberg trials'). The International Military Tribunal for the Far East ('Tokyo Tribunal') was convened to try the leaders of the Empire of Japan for crimes committed during the Second World War, including incidents such as the Nanjing Massacre. In addition, other prosecutions of Japanese personnel for war crimes, presided over by international judges, were held in many cities throughout Asia and the Pacific. Although the statutes of these tribunals of the immediate post-war period did not expressly provide for the doctrine of superior responsibility, the jurisprudence of the tribunals identified and developed superior responsibility as a form of individual criminal responsibility. The

---

[20] The Treaty of Versailles provided that First World War war criminals should be tried by an international military tribunal. Treaty of Versailles, opened for signature 28 June 1919, Art. 227, 11 *Martens Nouveau Recueil* 323. The German government objected, however, and advised that the Supreme Court of the Reich would conduct these trials at Leipzig in accordance with international law. Of the forty-five persons the Allies submitted should be tried, the German Supreme Court at Leipzig tried twelve and convicted six. See Yves Beigbeder, *Judging War Criminals: The Politics of International Justice* (1999), p. 29; Antonio Cassese, *International Criminal Law* (2003), p. 328; A. P. V. Rogers, 'War Crimes Trial under the Royal Warrant: British Practice 1945–1949', (1990) 39 *International and Comparative Law Quarterly* 780, 784.

[21] Judgement in the Case of Emil Muller, 30 May 1921, reprinted in (1922) 16 *American Journal of International Law* 684, 691.

[22] See *Göring, Bormann, Dönitz, Frank, Frick, Fritzsche, Funk, Hess, Jodl, Kaltenbrunner, Keitel, von Bohlen und Halbach, Ley, von Neurath, von Papen, Raeder, von Ribbentrop, Rosenberg, Sauckel, Schacht, von Schirach, Seyss-Inquart, Speer and Streicher*, International Military Tribunal, Judgement and Sentence, 1 October 1946, in *Trial of the Major War Criminals Before the International Military Tribunal, Nuremberg, 14 November 1945–1 October 1946* (1947).

[23] Control Council Law No. 10, Punishment of Persons Guilty of War Crimes, Crimes Against Peace and Against Humanity, Trials of War Criminals before the Nuernberg Military Tribunals under Control Council Law No. 10, Nuernberg, October 1946–April 1949, Vol. I, pp. xvi–xix. Control Council Law No. 10 was issued by the Allied Control Council on 20 December 1945, and empowered any of the occupying authorities to try suspected war criminals in their respective occupation zones. See also Control Council Law No. 10, in *Official Gazette of the Control Council for Germany*, Vol. 3 (1946).

judgements of these tribunals are reviewed in detail below, in the subsections that discuss the evolution of each of the three elements of superior responsibility.

The Geneva Conventions of 1949[24] were silent on the issue of superior responsibility, the possible limited exception being Article 39 of the Third Geneva Convention, which required prisoner of war camps to be 'under the immediate authority of a responsible commissioned officer belonging to the regular armed forces of the Detaining Power'.[25] From the end of the Second World War through to the 1970s, although no further treaties were concluded relating to rules governing the conduct of hostilities, a number of national military manuals regularly included provisions concerning superior responsibility.[26] In addition, in the immediate aftermath of the Second World War, legislation was enacted in several states to codify the doctrine, although for the most part these laws treated superior responsibility as a form of accomplice liability, in that the superior's failure to prevent or repress amounted to encouragement or assistance of the subordinates in the commission of the crime.[27]

The first explicit codification of superior responsibility was contained in the two Additional Protocols to the 1949 Geneva Conventions, adopted in 1977.[28]

---

[24] The four Geneva Conventions of 12 August 1949, which entered into force on 21 October 1950 ('Geneva Conventions') are: (1) Geneva Convention for the Amelioration of the Condition of the Wounded and Sick in Armed Forces in the Field, 75 U.N. T.S. 31; (2) Geneva Convention for the Amelioration of the Condition of Wounded, Sick and Shipwrecked Members of Armed Forces at Sea, 75 U.N. T.S. 85; (3) Geneva Convention relative to the Treatment of Prisoners of War, 75 U.N. T.S. 135 ('Third Geneva Convention'); (4) Geneva Convention relative to the Protection of Civilian Persons in Time of War, 75 U.N. T.S. 287.

[25] Third Geneva Convention, *supra* note 24, Art. 39.

[26] See Henckaerts and Doswald-Beck, *supra* note 1, Vol. 1, p. 559. See also *Prosecutor v. Hadžihasanović, Alagić and Kubura*, Case No. IT-01-47-PT, Decision on Joint Challenge to Jurisdiction, 12 November 2002 ('*Hadžihasanović et al.* 7(3) Pre-Trial Decision'), paras. 78–81.

[27] See, e.g., Canadian Act Respecting War Crimes, Regulation 10 (1946), in *Law Reports of Trials of War Criminals*, Vol. IV, Selected and Prepared by the United Nations War Crimes Commission (1948) 125, 127–129; British Royal Warrant, 14 June 1945, Regulation 8(ii), *The Law of War on Land: Being Part III of the Manual of Military Law*, War Office London (1958) 347, 349, cited in A. P. V. Rogers, 'War Crimes Trial Under the Royal Warrant: British Practice 1945–1949', (1990) 39 *International and Comparative Law Quarterly* 780, 790; French Ordinance, 28 August 1944, Article 4, in *Law Reports of Trials of War Criminals*, Vol. IV, Selected and Prepared by the United Nations War Crimes Commission, London (1948), 87. See also *Prosecutor v. Halilović*, Case No. IT-01-48-T, Judgement, 16 November 2005 ('*Halilović* Trial Judgement'), para 43; Ilias Bantekas, 'The Contemporary Law of Superior Responsibility', (1999) 93 *American Journal of International Law* 573, 576–577 (setting out the national laws enacted in this period under which national courts prosecuted superiors who tolerated crimes of their subordinates, including Article IX of the Chinese Law of 24 October 1946 Concerning the Trial of War Criminals and Article 3 of the Law of 2 August 1947 of the Duchy of Luxembourg on the Suppression of War Crimes).

[28] The two Additional Protocols of 1977 to the 1949 Geneva Conventions, which entered into force on 7 December 1978, are: (1) Protocol Additional to the Geneva Convention of 12 August 1949, and Relating to the Protection of Victims of International Armed Conflict, 1125 U.N. T.S. 3 ('Additional Protocol I'); and (2) Protocol Additional to the Geneva Conventions of 12 August 1949, and Relating to the Protection of Victims of Non-International Armed Conflicts, 1125 U.N. T.S. 609 ('Additional Protocol II').

Additional Protocol I, applicable to international armed conflicts, provided as follows:

Article 86: Failure to Act

1. The High Contracting Parties and the Parties to the conflict shall repress grave breaches, and take measures necessary to suppress all other breaches, of the Convention or of this Protocol which result from a failure to act when under a duty to do so.
2. The fact that a breach of the Conventions or of this Protocol was committed by a subordinate does not absolve his superiors from penal or disciplinary responsibility, as the case may be, if they knew, or had information which should have enabled them to conclude in the circumstances at the time, that he was committing or was going to commit such a breach and if they did not take all feasible measures within their power to prevent or repress the breach.

Article 87: Duty of Commanders

1. The High Contracting Parties and the Parties to the conflict shall require military commanders, with respect to members of the armed forces under their command and other persons under their control, to prevent and, where necessary, to suppress and report to competent authorities breaches of the Conventions and of this Protocol.
2. In order to prevent and suppress breaches, High Contracting Parties and Parties to the conflict shall require that, commensurate with their level of responsibility, commanders ensure that members of the armed forces under their command are aware of their obligations under the Conventions and this Protocol.
3. The High Contracting Parties and Parties to the conflict shall require any commander who is aware that subordinates or other persons under his control are going to commit or have committed a breach of the Conventions or of his Protocol, to initiate such steps as are necessary to prevent such violations of the Conventions or this Protocol, and, where appropriate, to initiate disciplinary or penal action against violators thereof.

The ICRC Study notes that the principles were not new, but rather declaratory of customary international law.[29] Additional Protocol II, applicable to non-international armed conflicts, does not include a specific provision on superior responsibility, although its introductory language refers to responsible command:

This Protocol shall apply to all armed conflicts which are not covered by ... [Protocol I] ... and which take place in the territory of a High Contracting Party between its armed forces and dissident armed forces or other organised armed groups which, *under responsible command*, exercise such control over a part of its territory as to enable them to carry out sustained and concerted military operations and to implement this Protocol.[30]

---

[29] ICRC Study, *supra* note 1, p. 559.
[30] Additional Protocol II, *supra* note 28, Art. 1(1) (emphasis added).

In the early 1990s, the ICTY and ICTR were established by resolutions of the United Nations Security Council, and the Statutes of both Tribunals expressly provide for superior responsibility as a form of liability. Article 7(3) of the ICTY Statute provides:

The fact that any of the acts referred to in articles 2 to 5 of the present Statute was committed by a subordinate does not relieve his superior of criminal responsibility if he knew or had reason to know that the subordinate was about to commit such acts or had done so and the superior failed to take the necessary and reasonable measures to prevent such acts or to punish the perpetrators thereof.[31]

Virtually identical wording was used in Article 6(3) of the Statute of the ICTR. The *Čelebići* Trial and Appeal Judgements of the ICTY clarified the three essential elements that must be satisfied for a finding of superior responsibility.[32] The subsequent jurisprudence of both Tribunals has refined the doctrine and its elements, which are discussed in Section 3.2 of this chapter.

In 1991, the International Law Commission (ILC) produced a revised version of its 1954 Draft Code of Offences against the Peace and Security of Mankind ('Draft Code of Offences'), Article 12 of which provided:

The fact that a crime against the peace and security of mankind was committed by a subordinate does not relieve his superiors of criminal responsibility, if they *knew or had information enabling them to conclude*, in the circumstances at the time, that the subordinate was committing or was going to commit such a crime and if they did not take all *feasible* measures within their power to prevent or repress the crime.[33]

Subsequently, Article 6 of the 1996 Draft Code of Offences provided:

The fact that a crime against the peace and security of mankind was committed by a subordinate does not relieve his superiors of criminal responsibility, *if they knew or had reason to know*, in the circumstances at the time, that the subordinate was committing or was going to commit such a crime and if they did not take all *necessary* measures within their power to prevent or repress the crime.[34]

---

[31] Statute of the International Criminal Tribunal for the Prosecution of Persons Responsible for Serious Violations of International Humanitarian Law Committed in the Territory of the former Yugoslavia since 1991, (1993) 32 ILM 1159, as amended by Security Council Resolution 1660 of 28 February 2006 ('ICTY Statute'), Art. 7(3); Statute of the International Criminal Tribunal for Rwanda, (1994) 33 ILM 1602, as amended by Security Council Resolution 1534 of 26 March 2004 ('ICTR Statute'), Art. 6(3).

[32] *Čelebići* Trial Judgement, *supra* note 3, para. 346, affirmed by *Prosecutor* v. *Delalić, Mucić, Delić and Landžo*, Case No. IT-96-21-A, Judgement, 20 February 2001 ('*Čelebići* Appeal Judgement').

[33] Draft Code of Crimes Against the Peace and Security of Mankind (1991), Art. 12, in Report of the International Law Commission on the Work of Its Forty-third Session, UN Doc. A/46/10 (1991) (emphases added).

[34] Draft Code of Crimes Against the Peace and Security of Mankind (1996) ('ILC 1996 Draft Code'), Art. 18(d), in Report of the International Law Commission on the Work of Its Forty-eighth Session, UN Doc. A/51/10 (1996) (emphases added).

Most recently, Article 28 of the ICC Statute deals with superior responsibility and contains certain interesting developments, such as the introduction of a distinction between the standards applicable to military superiors (both *de facto* and *de jure*) on the one hand, and civilian superiors on the other.[35] The approach of the ICC to the doctrine of superior responsibility is discussed in detail in Section 3.4 of this chapter.

3.1.3 Historical evolution of the elements of superior responsibility

The ICRC Commentary to Additional Protocol I states:

Under the terms of this provision three conditions must be fulfilled if a superior is to be responsible for an omission relating to an offence committed or about to be committed by a subordinate:

a) the superior concerned must be the superior of that subordinate ('his superiors');
b) he knew, or had information which should have enabled him to conclude that a breach was being committed or was going to be committed;
c) he did not take the measures within his power to prevent it.[36]

Early in the elucidation of the modern doctrine of superior responsibility, the *Čelebići* Trial Chamber held that these three elements were reflected in the Statutes of the *ad hoc* Tribunals, and encapsulated the requirements under customary international law that must be established for a superior to be held criminally responsible.[37] This subsection traces the evolution of the doctrine of superior responsibility by considering the definition and application of these three elements.

3.1.3.1 Historical evolution of the subordinate-superior relationship element

The touchstone of the subordinate-superior relationship is 'effective control', defined consistently in the relevant jurisprudence of the *ad hoc* Tribunals as a material ability to prevent or punish the commission of offences by subordinates.[38] The nature of the authority and the degree of control required in order to satisfy this element have become clearer over the course of the doctrine's evolution, and the current definition of the element has been repeatedly held to constitute customary international law. Much of this evolution can be viewed

---

[35] See William A. Schabas, *An Introduction to the International Criminal Court* (2004), pp. 105–110; Kai Ambos, 'Superior Responsibility', in Antonio Cassese, Paola Gaeta and John R. W. D. Jones (eds.), *The Rome Statute of the International Criminal Court: A Commentary* (2001), Vol. 1, pp. 823–872.
[36] ICRC Commentary to the Additional Protocols, *supra* note 5, para. 3543.
[37] *Čelebići* Trial Judgement, *supra* note 3, para. 346.
[38] See *infra* text accompanying notes 213–216 and sources cited therein.

through the application of the doctrine in various contexts to different types of superiors, both military and civilian.

3.1.3.1.1 Post-Second World War cases

The first case dealing with superior responsibility in the aftermath of the Second World War was *United States* v. *Yamashita*. This case was significant for a number of reasons, not least of which was the recognition by the US War Crimes Commission and the US Supreme Court that the failure of a commander to carry out his duty – an omission – could lead to individual criminal responsibility for crimes committed by his subordinates. General Yamashita was charged with having 'unlawfully disregarded and failed to discharge his duty as commander to control the operations of the members of his command, permitting them to commit brutal atrocities', and thereby violating the laws of war.[39] There have been many different subsequent interpretations of the court's ruling, which set the scene for the future development of and debate concerning the doctrine of superior responsibility.

The *Yamashita* jurisprudence did little to define the level of control a superior must possess to be liable under this form of responsibility.[40] Yamashita argued in his defence that US forces had cut off his chain of command and communication, rendering him incapable of knowing about or acting to prevent the crimes of his subordinates. Justice Murphy's dissent addressed this contention of Yamashita, focusing on the chaotic circumstances prevailing at the time of the events in question.[41] The majority of the Supreme Court did not consider this issue,[42] however, apparently satisfied that Yamashita's *de jure* position of command was a sufficient basis on which to find the existence of a superior-subordinate relationship with the physical perpetrators.

The International Military Tribunal's judgement dealt only with what was described historically as 'direct' superior responsibility. This type of responsibility, for the positive acts of superiors rather than for a failure to act, is now referred to and characterised in modern international criminal law as liability for ordering. By contrast, the subsequent Nuremburg trials considered and

---

[39] *United States* v. *Yamashita*, in *Law Reports of Trials of War Criminals*, Vol. IV, pp. 3–4 ('*Yamashita* First Instance Judgement'). See also M. Cherif Bassiouni, *Crimes Against Humanity in International Criminal Law* (1992), p. 377.

[40] Allison Marston Danner and Jenny S. Martinez, 'Guilty Associations: Joint Criminal Enterprise, Command Responsibility, and the Development of International Criminal Law', (2005) 93 *California Law Review* 75, 124.

[41] In *re Yamashita*, 327 US 1, 31–33 ('*Yamashita* Supreme Court Habeas Decision') (Justice Murphy dissenting).

[42] The majority opinion did note that 'the commission took account of the difficulties' discussed at length in Justice Murphy's dissent; recalling, however, that such factual issues were not presented by a *habeas corpus* petition, these Supreme Court Justices ultimately stated that '[w]e do not weigh the evidence'. *Yamashita* Supreme Court Habeas Decision, *ibid.* p. 17 n. 4.

applied the doctrine of superior responsibility in a form substantially similar to that applied by the international criminal tribunals in the modern day. The tribunals in both the *Hostages* case[43] and the *High Command* case[44] held commanders liable, but applied a more relaxed knowledge requirement compared with that used in *Yamashita*. In the *High Command* case, for example, General von Leeb was acquitted of charges relating to crimes committed by his subordinates: the court looked to whether von Leeb possessed actual powers of control over those subordinates and found that he did not.[45]

In other subsequent Nuremburg trials, superior responsibility was for the first time extended to civilian government leaders.[46] In the *Medical* case,[47] the twenty-three defendants were medical doctors and administrators, who stood accused of involvement in Nazi human experimentation. Brandt was a civilian, being the senior medical officer of the German government during the Second World War. The other defendants were a mix of armed forces, SS officers and civilians. Brandt was charged with and convicted of war crimes and crimes against humanity for his 'special responsibility for, and participation in' numerous experiments on prisoners of war;[48] these charges related to his failure to monitor the experiments in question.[49] The US Military Tribunal found that Brandt had received reports of the experiments and participated in meetings where the results of these experiments were reviewed. In finding him responsible, the tribunal focused on his position of responsibility and his material ability to 'intervene':

In the medical field Karl Brandt held a position of the highest rank directly under Hitler. He was in a position to intervene with authority on all medical matters; indeed it appears such was his positive duty ... Occupying the position he did and being a

---

[43] *United States* v. *List, Von Weichs, Rendulic, Kuntze, Foertsch, Boehme, Felmy, Lanz, Dehner, von Leyser, Speider and von Geitner*, US Military Tribunal, Judgement, 19 February 1948, in *Trials of War Criminals Before the Nuremberg Military Tribunals Under Control Council Law No. 10* (1950) ('*Hostages* case'), Vol. XI, pp. 1230–1319.

[44] *United States* v. *von Leeb, Sperrle, von Küchler, Blaskowitz, Hoth, Reinhardt, von Salmuth, Hollidt, Schniewind, von Roques, Reinecke, Warlimont, Wöhler and Lehmann*, in *Trials of War Criminals Before the Nuremberg Military Tribunals Under Control Council Law No. 10* (1950) ('*High Command* case'), Vol. I, pp. 462–697.

[45] *Ibid.*, vol. XI, 462, 563. See also Andrew D. Mitchell, 'Failure to Halt, Prevent or Punish: The Doctrine of Command Responsibility for War Crimes', (2000) 22 *Sydney Law Review* 381, 392.

[46] Avi Singh has suggested that there was some criticism of the extension of superior responsibility to civilians, but the only support cited is the dissenting judgement of Judge Röling in Hirota. Avi Singh, 'Criminal Responsibility for Non-State Civilian Superiors Lacking De Jure Authority: A Comparative Review of the Doctrine of Superior Responsibility and Parallel Doctrines in National Criminal Laws', (2005) 28 *Hastings International and Comparative Law Review* 267, 277. See also *infra* note 50.

[47] *United States* v. *Karl Brandt, Becker-Freyseng, Beiglböck, Blome, Brack, Rudolf Brandt, Fischer, Gebhardt, Genzken, Handloser, Hoven, Mrugowsky, Oberheuser, Pokorny, Poppendick, Rombert, Rose, Rostick, Ruff, Schäfer, Schröder, Sievers and Weltz*, in *Trials of War Criminals Before the Nuremberg Military Tribunals Under Control Council Law No. 10* (1950) ('*Medical* case'), Vol. II, pp. 193–194.

[48] *Ibid.*, pp. 189–198.   [49] Van Sliedregt, *supra* note 7, p. 127.

physician of ability and experience, the duty rested on him to make some adequate investigation concerning the medical experiments which he knew had been, were being and doubtless continued to be conducted in the concentration camps.[50]

In the *Roechling* case,[51] civilian superiors were held criminally responsible for the ill-treatment of forced labourers employed in German industry. On appeal, the French Superior Military Court held that three defendants were liable, as they possessed sufficient authority to intervene to improve the treatment of the forced labourers. The military tribunal of first instance held that it was Roechling's duty as the head of the company's operation to inquire into the treatment accorded to the foreign workers and to the prisoners of war of whose employment he must have been aware.[52]

Avi Singh has suggested that superior responsibility may have been extended to Roechling because he was a relative of Marshal Goering.[53] In considering this case, the ICTY Trial Chamber in the *Čelebići* Judgement stressed that it had not been suggested in the US Military Tribunal's judgement that the accused had any formal authority to issue orders to the physical perpetrators of the crimes (who were personnel under Gestapo command), and noted that the phrase 'sufficient authority' was used in order to describe Roechling's relationship with the physical perpetrators and the crimes committed.[54] The *Čelebići* Appeals Chamber agreed with the Trial Chamber's characterisation of this case as an example of the imposition of superior responsibility on the basis of possession of *de facto* powers of control, but rejected the notion that the wording 'sufficient authority' had any significance as a potential test.[55]

Superior responsibility was also arguably attributed to non-military superiors in the *Pohl* case,[56] where the tribunal held Mummenthey criminally

---

[50] *Medical* case, *supra* note 47, pp. 193–194. The court did not explain the source of the duties imposed on Brandt, who, as a civilian superior with no *de facto* military command role, was not necessarily subject to the same international legal obligations as those imposed on military superiors. This failure to examine or articulate clearly the source of the obligations imposed on civilian superiors, even as duties apparently identical in scope and content to those recognised for military superiors are explicitly extended to them by international courts, is a weakness of the modern superior responsibility doctrine.

[51] *The Government Commissioner of the General Tribunal of the Military Government for the French Zone of Occupation in Germany* v. *Herman Roechling and Others*, Indictment and Judgement of the General Tribunal of the Military Government of the French Zone of Occupation in Germany, in *Trials of War Criminals Before the Nuremberg Military Tribunals Under Control Council Law No. 10* (1950) ('*Roechling* First Instance Judgement'), Vol. XIV, Appendix B, p. 1061.

[52] *Ibid.*, p. 1136.   [53] Singh, *supra* note 46, p. 278.

[54] *Čelebići* Trial Judgement, *supra* note 3, para. 376.

[55] *Čelebići* Appeal Judgement, *supra* note 32, para. 263.

[56] *United States* v. *Pohl, Frank, Georg Lörner, Fanslau, Hans Lörner, Vogt, Tschentscher, Scheide, Kiefer, Eirenschmalz, Sommer, Pook, Baier, Hohberg, Volk, Mummenthey, Bobermin and Klein*, in *Trials of War Criminals Before the Nuremberg Military Tribunals Under Control Council Law No. 10* (1950) ('*Pohl* case'), Vol. V, p. 958.

responsible for the mistreatment of prisoners by guards over whom the tribunal found he had control:

> Mummenthey was a definite integral and important figure in the whole concentration camp set-up, and, as an SS officer, wielded military power of command. If excesses occurred in the industries under his control he was in a position not only to know about them, but to do something.[57]

Given that the focus of the tribunal was on Mummenthey's involvement with the Waffen SS, his status as a 'non-military' superior[58] is arguable. The tribunal was, however, clearly examining the accused's ability to exercise some degree of control. As with other post-Second World War cases, the degree of control required for a superior to be considered criminally responsible is unfortunately not clear.

In the *Flick* case,[59] six civilian industrialists were accused of war crimes and crimes against humanity for their direct and indirect involvement in enterprises involving the enslavement of civilians from occupied territory; it was alleged that the accused used tens of thousands of slave labourers in the businesses that they owned or controlled. Weiss and Flick were among three accused found guilty by the US Military Tribunal: Weiss for direct participation in the scheme, and Flick – who was Weiss's superior – on the basis of his 'knowledge and approval' of Weiss's actions; this conviction of Weiss has since been interpreted as an application of superior responsibility.[60]

The concept of superior responsibility was also applied by the Tokyo Tribunal, where its application to non-military personnel was further confirmed. In its overall judgement dealing with twenty-five defendants, the Tokyo Tribunal found a number of civilian officers and political superiors liable through superior responsibility, including ministers and cabinet members. The former Japanese Foreign Minister, Kiko Hirota, was held to have failed in his duty to take adequate steps to prevent breaches of the laws of war by Japanese troops.[61] This judgement has been criticised by both the dissenting judge in that case, Judge Röling, and later commentators for emphasising Hirota's function as foreign minister and ignoring his lack of actual control over the relevant subordinates,[62] particularly as the crimes were committed by subordinates of another ministry over which Hirota had no control:

---

[57] *Ibid.*, pp. 1052–1053.   [58] See van Sliedregt, *supra* note 7, pp. 120–121.

[59] *United States v. Flick, Steinbrinck, Weiss, Burkart, Kaletsch and Terberger*, in *Trials of War Criminals Before the Nuremberg Military Tribunals Under Control Council Law No. 10* (1950) ('*Flick* case'), Vol. VI, p. 1187.

[60] See *Čelebići* Trial Judgement, *supra* note 3, para. 360.

[61] B. V. A. Röling and C. F. Rüter (eds.), *The Tokyo Judgement: The International Military Tribunal for the Far East (I.M.T.F.E.) 29 April 1946–12 November 1948* (1977) ('Tokyo Judgement'), p. 448.

[62] See Ambos, *supra* note 35, p. 831; van Sliedregt, *supra* note 7, p. 129.

Evidence ... shows that it was far from easy for a Foreign Minister to deal with the military .... The peculiar structure in Japan, where the armed forces possessed an independent position, made it the more difficult for the government to intervene in Army affairs.[63]

Former Foreign Minister Shigemitsu and Prime Minister Koiso were also held criminally responsible for their failure to prevent or punish the criminal acts of the Japanese troops.[64] Like Hirota, Koiso and Shigemitsu were found guilty of a charge that they 'deliberately and recklessly disregarded their legal duty [by virtue of their respective offices] to take adequate steps to secure the observance [of the laws and customs of war] and prevent breaches thereof, and thereby violated the laws of war'.[65]

The post-Second World War jurisprudence established that the doctrine of superior responsibility applied not only to military commanders, but also to civilian superiors, as long as the relevant criteria were fulfilled. After considering the nature of the superior-subordinate relationship as outlined in some of these cases, the *Čelebići* Trial Chamber opined that they supported the principle that a superior's liability must be predicated on the actual power of the superior to control the acts of his subordinates.[66] Nevertheless, it must be noted that, in reaching findings of responsibility, these tribunals tended to consider less the actual control of the superior, and more his formal role or function in highly organised military, paramilitary and civilian organisations from which control was imputed.

3.1.3.1.2 *Additional protocols*
Article 86(2) of Additional Protocol I, which expressly provides for individual responsibility of superiors, speaks generally of 'superiors' and 'subordinates' without any limitations such as the requirement of *de jure* command. The ICRC Commentary on Article 86(2), in considering the definition of a superior, states that this provision is not only concerned with commanders under whose direct orders the subordinates are placed, but that the concept should be 'broader' and encompass 'the concept of control'.[67]

It is Article 87, however, which articulates in more detail the obligations on superiors and incorporates duties both to prevent and to punish. Criminal

---

[63] Tokyo Judgement, *supra* note 61, p. 1126 (opinion of Justice Röling).
[64] *Ibid.*, p. 453 (verdict of Koiso); *ibid.*, p. 458 (verdict of Shigemitsu). See also *ibid.*, p. 21 (for a paraphrasing of the indictment); *ibid.*, p. 453.
[65] *Ibid.*, p. 21; see also *ibid.*, p. 453; Annex A-6, pp. 59–60 (*see* Count 55 of the indictment).
[66] *Čelebići* Trial Judgement, *supra* note 3, para. 377.
[67] ICRC Commentary to the Additional Protocols, *supra* note 5, para. 3544 (referring to the *Yamashita* and *High Command* cases).

responsibility for omissions ensues only where a legal obligation to act exists, a point recognised in the ICRC Commentary.[68] There is clearly a strong connection between these two provisions. Indeed, the ICRC Commentary itself notes that Articles 86 and 87 should be read together.[69]

Article 87 also uses control as its touchstone, recognising in Article 87(1) the duty of 'military commanders' to prevent, suppress and report breaches[70] with respect to troops under their command and 'other persons under their control'.[71] The ICRC Commentary on this paragraph speaks of this concept of indirect subordination arising particularly in the context of occupied territories,[72] and Article 87(3) recognises similar duties to prevent and punish of 'any commander' who possesses the requisite knowledge.[73]

3.1.3.1.3 Statutes of the ad hoc Tribunals

In providing for superior responsibility, Article 7(3) of the ICTY Statue and Article 6(3) of the ICTR Statute do not qualify the term 'superior' or limit the provision to military superiors. The jurisprudence of these Tribunals, in considering both the position at customary international law and under their statutes, is clear that the existence of a superior-subordinate relationship depends on 'effective control', which is in turn characterised by the material ability to prevent and punish the commission of offences by subordinates.[74] It is well established that a formal designation as a superior is not necessary and that responsibility may be imposed where a superior exercises *de jure* or *de facto* control.[75] These issues are discussed in Section 3.2 of this chapter, which examines the jurisprudence of the *ad hoc* Tribunals, and in Section 3.4, which reviews superior responsibility in the ICC and the internationalised criminal tribunals.

---

[68] *Ibid.*, para. 3524. In commenting upon Article 86 generally, the ICRC Commentary notes that a failure to act consists of a failure in a duty to act. See *ibid.*, para. 3524. Furthermore, in commenting upon Article 86(1), the Commentary notes that responsibility for a breach consisting of a failure to act can only be established if the person failed to act when he had a duty to act. See *ibid.*, para. 3537.

[69] *Ibid.*, para. 3541 (commenting that Article 86(2) should be read 'in conjunction with' Article 87). See also Ambos, *supra* note 35, p. 838 (opining that Article 86(2) 'must be' read in conjunction with Article 87).

[70] 'Breaches' in this context means breaches of the 1949 Geneva Conventions or of Additional Protocol I, as indicated by the title of the section of Additional Protocol I: 'Repression of Breaches of the Conventions and of this Protocol'.

[71] Additional Protocol I, *supra* note 28, Art. 87(1).

[72] ICRC Commentary to the Additional Protocols, *supra* note 5, para. 3555.

[73] *Ibid.*, para. 3553. Article 87(3) refers to a commander 'who is aware that subordinates or other persons under his control are going to commit or have committed a breach of the Conventions or of this Protocol'. Additional Protocol I, *supra* note 28, Art. 87(3).

[74] See *infra* text accompanying notes 213–216 and sources cited therein.

[75] See *infra* text accompanying notes 210–212, 219 and sources cited therein.

3.1.3.2 Historical evolution of the mental element

The requisite mental element for superior responsibility in the Statutes of the *ad hoc* Tribunals is that the superior 'knew or had reason to know that the subordinate was about to commit [the relevant] acts or had done so'.[76] This formulation of the mental element in the ICTY and ICTR Statutes has been confirmed in the jurisprudence of the *ad hoc* Tribunals as having customary law status.[77] The development of this particular language can be traced back to the First World War Allied Powers' Commission recommendation to establish an international tribunal, which would have included culpability for superiors on the basis of an omission by a commander who had specific knowledge of his subordinate's unlawful actions,[78] demonstrating an early view that actual knowledge was a basis for establishing the mental element of superior responsibility.[79]

3.1.3.2.1 Post-Second World War cases

The post-Second World War judgements considered the knowledge requirement for imposing superior responsibility, although interpretation of their meaning has differed.[80] At least two different possible standards of constructive knowledge emerged from these judgements: (1) a requirement that the superior 'should have known' of subordinate misdeeds, which involves a proactive duty to remain informed of the activities of subordinates; and (2) a failure to discover the actions of subordinates from information already available to the superior.

Alison Danner and Jenny Martinez have noted that in many ways the evolution of the superior responsibility doctrine, particularly the mental element of the doctrine, has consisted of reactions and counter-reactions to the *Yamashita* case.[81] General Yamashita was charged with serious war crimes committed by Japanese troops in the Philippines. The prosecutor did not allege that Yamashita had ordered the crimes, but that the atrocities were so widespread and numerous that he either must have known of them or should have

---

[76] ICTY Statute, *supra* note 31, Art. 7(3); ICTR Statute, *supra* note 31, Art. 6(3). For a detailed discussion of the elements of superior responsibility, see Section 3.2 of this chapter.

[77] See *infra* text accompanying notes 178–180 and sources cited therein. See *also* ICRC Study, *supra* note 1, Vol. I: Rules, p. 558 (setting forth Rule 153).

[78] See Burnett, *supra* note 19, p. 81; Levine, *supra* note 17, p. 2.

[79] The jurisprudence of the *ad hoc* Tribunals holds that the mental element can be proved by establishing that the accused knew ('actual knowledge') or that he had reason to know ('constructive knowledge') that the criminal conduct in question was about to be, was being, or had been realised. See *infra* text accompanying notes 352, 363, 374.

[80] See, e.g., Ambos, *supra* note 35, p. 828; van Sliedregt, *supra* note 7, p. 161; Levine, *supra* note 17, p. 3.

[81] See, e.g., Danner and Martinez, *supra* note 40, p. 124. See also Ilias Bantekas and Susan Nash, *International Criminal Law* (2003), p. 327; Greg R. Vetter, 'Command Responsibility of Non-Military Superiors in the International Criminal Court (ICC)', (2000) 25 *Yale Journal of International Law* 89, 106.

known of them, because of his position and duty as commander. Yamashita argued that he had no control over his troops, no involvement in the acts of forces under his command and no knowledge that war crimes were taking place.

In finding Yamashita guilty, the military commission noted the widespread nature of the atrocities committed by Japanese troops, which 'were not sporadic in nature but in many cases methodically supervised by Japanese officers and non-commissioned officers', and thus held that General Yamashita had 'failed to provide effective control of [his] troops as required by the circumstances'.[82] It further held:

> It is absurd, however, to consider a commander a murderer or rapist because one of his soldiers commits a murder or a rape. Nevertheless, where murder and rape and vicious, revengeful actions are widespread offences, and there is no effective attempt by a commander to *discover* and *control* the criminal acts, such a commander may be held responsible, even criminally liable, for the lawless acts of his troops, depending upon their nature and the circumstances surrounding them.[83]

The US Supreme Court denied a *habeas corpus* application by Yamashita, implicitly approving the military commission's judgement,[84] but with vigorous dissents from Justice Murphy and Justice Rutledge. Justice Murphy opined there was no precedent for such a charge where the commander did not participate in, order, condone or have knowledge of the acts.[85] Justice Rutledge (with whom Justice Murphy agreed) did not believe the military commission had subject-matter jurisdiction, and criticised both the commission's prejudice and technical legal flaws identified by him.[86]

There is some disagreement about what mental standard was actually applied by the military commission in this case. Some commentators assert that the standard applied was one of strict liability, as guilt did not depend on proof of actual or constructive knowledge of the commission of the crimes.[87] Others have argued that the case should be read as rejecting Yamashita's claims of ignorance and inferring actual knowledge from the circumstantial

---

[82] *Yamashita* First Instance Judgment, *supra* note 39, p. 35.   [83] *Ibid.*

[84] *Yamashita* Supreme Court Habeas Decision, *supra* note 41, p. 17 n. 4 ('We do not weigh the evidence. We merely hold that the charge sufficiently states a violation against the law of war, and that the commission, upon the facts found, could properly find petitioner guilty of such a violation.').

[85] *Ibid.*, p. 23 (Justice Murphy dissenting).

[86] *Ibid.*, pp. 41–81 (Justice Rutledge dissenting) (pp. 41–47 dealing with prejudice and legal flaws, and pp. 48–56 dealing with jurisdiction).

[87] See, e.g., Richard Leal, *The Yamashita Precedent: War Crimes and Command Responsibility* (1982), p. 141 (referring to the 'strict accountability' of the *Yamashita* precedent); Jackson Nyamuya Maogoto, 'Presiding over the Ex-President: A Look at Superior Responsibility in Light of the Kosovo Indictment', (2002) 8 *Deakin Law Review* 1, 4; Natalie L. Reid, 'Bridging the Conceptual Chasm: Superior Responsibility as the Missing Link between State and Individual Responsibility under International Law', (2005) 18 *Leiden Journal of International Law* 795, 818.

evidence.[88] In support of this latter view, Parks asserts that the evidence showed that Yamashita participated personally in the crimes by ordering, or at least authorising, at least 2,000 summary executions.[89] Yet another view is that the reference to a failure to 'discover' is a reference to a 'should have known' standard, which would impose on a superior a general and positive duty to remain aware of the actions of his subordinates.[90] The ICTY Appeals Chamber in *Čelebići*, for its part, interpreted *Yamashita* as implying that this duty to know only arises in certain circumstances where the superior is on notice of the crimes, and that in *Yamashita* the widespread nature of the crimes effectively put the accused on notice of the atrocities.[91] Considering all these points of view together, *Yamashita* either stands for a poorly expressed and poorly reasoned version of the law regarding knowledge as it currently stands, or the application of a form of strict liability to superiors, which is not part of the contemporary doctrine of superior responsibility.[92]

In general, the judgements of the Tokyo Tribunal were more explicit about imposing a strong, unqualified 'should have known' standard of knowledge on commanders.[93] For example, in the case against Admiral Toyoda, the Tribunal expressly held that the doctrine of superior responsibility applies to those who 'knew or should have known by use of reasonable diligence' of the commission of crimes by subordinates.[94] The Tokyo Tribunal articulated the doctrine, including the requisite mental element, as follows:

---

[88] See, e.g., Parks, *supra* note 7, pp. 30–38; Bruce D. Landrum, 'The Yamashita War Crimes Trial: Command Responsibility Then and Now', (1995) 149 *Military Law Review* 293, 296, 298; Bassiouni, *supra* note 39, pp. 378–379. See also *infra* text accompanying notes 366–367 (discussing the holding of certain chambers of the *ad hoc* Tribunals that knowledge may be inferred); notes 372–373 (discussing findings of the ICTY Trial Chamber in *Aleksovski* inferring the actual knowledge of the accused); note 459 (discussing the difference between drawing an inference of actual knowledge and finding that the accused had constructive knowledge).

[89] Parks, *supra* note 7, pp. 25, 27–28.

[90] Michael L Smidt, 'Yamashita, Medina and Beyond: Command Responsibility in Contemporary Military Operations', (2000) 164 *Military Law Review* 155, 200; Leal, *supra* note 87, p. 141; Christopher N. Crowe, 'Command Responsibility in the Former Yugoslavia: The Chances for Successful Prosecution', (1994) 29 *University of Richmond Law Review* 191, 207–208. After discussing the *High Command* case and the *Hostage* case, Crowe refers to the emergence of a clear 'should have known' standard. *Ibid.*, pp. 219–220.

[91] *Čelebići* Appeal Judgement, *supra* note 32, paras. 228–229. The Appeals Chamber went on to note that the passage quoted above regarding an obligation to 'discover' was qualified by the military commission itself:

Short of maintaining that a Commander has a duty to *discover* the state of discipline prevailing amongst his troops, Courts dealing with cases such as those at present under discussion may in suitable instances have regarded means of knowledge as being the same as knowledge itself.

Ibid. Yamashita First Instance Judgement, *supra* note 39, pp. 94–95, (emphasis in original).

[92] Reid, *supra* note 87, p. 818; Leal, *supra* note 87, p. 141; Maogoto, *supra* note 87, p. 4. For the rejection of a strict-liability standard in the jurisprudence of the *ad hoc* Tribunals, see *infra* text accompanying notes 352–353.

[93] See Levine, *supra* note 17, p. 3.

[94] *United States* v. *Toyoda*, War Crimes Tribunal Courthouse, Tokyo, Japan, 6 September 1949 ('*Toyoda* case'), pp. 4998–5021, 5006.

[I]n the simplest language it may be said that this Tribunal believes the principle of command responsibility to be that if this accused knew, or should by the exercise of ordinary diligence have learned, of the commission by his subordinates, immediate or otherwise, of the atrocities … and, by his failure to take any action to punish the perpetrators, permitted the atrocities to continue, he has failed in his performance of his duty as a commander and must be punished … If he knew, or should have known, by use of reasonable diligence, of the commission by his troops of atrocities and if he did not do everything within his power and capacity under the existing circumstances to prevent their occurrence and punish the offenders, he was derelict in his duties. Only the degree of his guilt would remain.[95]

As one commentator points out, although this 'should have known' standard was articulated by the Tokyo Tribunal, in most cases there was also evidence presented that the accused had actual knowledge of the atrocities committed.[96]

The subsequent Nuremburg trials also considered the mental element required for superior responsibility. A commander of an occupied territory, German General List, was tried by the US Military Tribunal for the killings of hostages by his subordinates.[97] List argued that he had no express knowledge of the crimes and that he was not present at headquarters when relevant reports arrived. The Military Tribunal dismissed this argument and held him responsible for the acts of his subordinates, adopting the following knowledge standard:

A commanding general of occupied territory is charged with the duty of maintaining peace and order, punishing crime, and protecting lives and property within the area of his command. His responsibility is coextensive with his area of command. He is charged with notice of occurrences taking place within that territory. He may require adequate reports of all occurrences that come within the scope of his power and, if such reports are incomplete or otherwise inadequate, he is obliged to require supplementary reports to apprize him of all the pertinent facts. If he fails to require and obtain complete information, the dereliction of duty rests upon him and he is in no position to plead his own dereliction as a defense. Absence from headquarters cannot and does not relieve one from responsibility for acts committed in accordance with a policy he instituted or in which he acquiesced … His failure to terminate these unlawful killings and to take adequate steps to prevent their recurrence constitutes a serious breach of duty and imposes criminal liability.[98]

[95] *Ibid.*, p. 5006.
[96] Van Sliedregt, *supra* note 7, p. 130 (noting that the 'should have known' standard was coupled with a duty to act to secure proper treatment of the prisoners). The test set out in *Toyoda* is one of negligence, a standard that is inapplicable to the modern doctrine of superior responsibility. For the rejection of a 'should have known' standard in the jurisprudence of the *ad hoc* Tribunals, see *infra* text accompanying notes 375–383.
[97] *Hostages* case, *supra* note 43.   [98] *Ibid.*, pp. 1271–1272.

General List was held to have had notice of the relevant crimes because of reports which were made to him,[99] and the Tribunal expressly stated that lack of knowledge of the contents of those reports was no defence.[100] It held that any failure of a commanding general to acquaint himself with the contents of such reports, or a failure to require additional reports where inadequacy appeared on their face, constituted a dereliction of duty, and that he cannot invoke his failure to read such reports as a defence:[101]

An army commander will not ordinarily be permitted to deny knowledge of reports received at his headquarters, they being sent there for his special benefit. Neither will he ordinarily be permitted to deny knowledge of happenings within the area of his command while he is present therein. It would strain the credulity of the Tribunal to believe that a high ranking military commander would permit himself to get out of touch with current happenings in the area of his command during war time. No doubt such occurrences result occasionally because of unexpected contingencies, but they are the unusual.[102]

Some commentators have asserted that this case confirms the existence of a duty on commanders to remain informed about the activities of subordinates.[103] Other commentators, as well as the Appeals Chamber in *Čelebići*, have focused more on the fact that List had in his possession information that should have prompted him to investigate further, and they assert that the duty is limited to this latter scenario.[104] Without stating so explicitly, the Tribunal in effect held that General List *should have known* of the crimes because of the availability of concrete information that put him on notice such that further investigation was required.[105]

In the *High Command* case,[106] fourteen senior German army officers, including Field Marshal Von Leeb, faced war-crimes charges, and von Leeb was acquitted of charges relating to crimes committed by his subordinates. While the case appears to have been determined on the basis that he lacked actual powers of control over the relevant subordinates,[107] there was discussion relevant to the mental element:

Criminal acts committed by those forces [under his command] cannot in themselves be charged to him on the theory of subordination. The same is true of other high

[99] *Ibid.*
[100] *Ibid.*, p. 1271 (holding that reports made to General List put him on notice of the events); *ibid.*, p. 1260 (holding that lack of knowledge of the contents of the reports was no defence).
[101] *Ibid.*, p. 1271. [102] *Ibid.*, p. 1260.
[103] See, e.g., Daryl A. Mundis, 'Crimes of the Commander: Superior Responsibility under Article 7(3) of the ICTY Statute', in Gideon Boas and William A. Schabas (eds.), *International Criminal Law Developments in the Case Law of the ICTY* (2003), p. 239; van Sliedregt, *supra* note 7, p. 161.
[104] See, e.g., Levine, *supra* note 17, p. 3; *Čelebići* Appeal Judgement, *supra* note 32, para. 229.
[105] Ambos, *supra* note 35, p. 830. [106] *High Command* case, *supra* note 44.
[107] Mitchell, *supra* note 45, p. 392.

commanders in the chain of command. Criminality does not attach to every individual in this chain of command from that fact alone. There must be a personal dereliction. That can occur only where the act is directly traceable to him or where his failure to properly supervise his subordinates constitutes criminal negligence on his part. In the latter case it must be a personal neglect amounting to a wanton, immoral disregard of the action of his subordinates amounting to acquiescence.[108]

Again, the language used relating to the requisite standard of knowledge is imprecise, although the Tribunal clearly applies a negligence standard. The reference only to a 'wanton, immoral disregard' reflects some level of constructive knowledge, but is devoid of any clear yardstick by which to measure legal responsibility. Like other post-Second World War judgements, this judgement has been interpreted in varying ways. Daryl Mundis and Kai Ambos have both suggested that it stands for a 'should have known' standard, commensurate with the idea of a superior's general and positive duty to know of the actions of his subordinates.[109] Eugenia Levine, on the other hand, believes the Tribunal's holding reflects a more lenient standard, such that a commander is not required to attempt to discover the misconduct of his subordinates.[110] Consistent with the *Hostages* case and the terms of the ruling, a better interpretation is that the Tribunal applied a 'should have known' standard in this case.

In the *Pohl* case before the US Military Tribunal,[111] the accused Mummenthey was an officer in the SS – a large paramilitary organisation that was a principal component of the Nazi party – and a manager running businesses that used concentration-camp labour. He was held criminally responsible for the maltreatment of prisoners by camp guards, over whom it was held he had control. Mummenthey argued that he did not know what was happening in the labour camps and was ignorant of aspects of the running of his businesses. The Military Tribunal dismissed this argument and imputed actual knowledge to him, clearly applying a 'must have known' standard: 'Mummenthey could not help knowing about concentration camp labor in the DEST enterprises. In Sachsenhausen-Oranienburg the inmate workers daily passed by the very building in which Mummenthey had his office. Their poor physical condition was very obvious.'[112]

Furthermore, after accepting evidence indicating that Mummenthey in fact knew of the treatment of the prisoners, the Tribunal went on to state that 'Mummenthey's assertions that he did not know what was happening in the labour camps and enterprises under his jurisdiction does not exonerate him. It

---

[108] *High Command* case, *supra* note 44, pp. 543–544.
[109] Ambos, *supra* note 35, p. 830; Mundis, *supra* note 103, p. 246.
[110] See Levine, *supra* note 17, p. 4. [111] *Pohl* case, *supra* note 56. [112] *Ibid.*, p. 1053.

was his duty to know.'[113] While the *Čelebići* Trial Judgement refers to this latter statement as evidence of a 'should have known' standard,[114] the ICTY Appeals Chamber viewed the *Pohl* case as relating to the actual knowledge standard, downplaying this reference to a 'duty to know' as a statement in *obiter*.[115] Even so, the *Pohl* case clearly stands for the view that both the 'should have known' and actual knowledge standards of the mental element at the time would attract liability. The reference by the Tribunal to the 'should have known' test, however, embodies a negligence standard that is now clearly not considered as forming part of the modern doctrine of superior responsibility.[116] The relevance of the case, therefore, to the mental element of the modern doctrine is to the actual knowledge of an accused.

In the *Roechling* case, the French Military Tribunal considered the liability of civilian superiors for ill-treatment of forced labourers employed in German industry. The five accused held senior positions within an iron and steel works that used and mistreated forced labourers from occupied countries and prisoners of war. In the appeal judgement of the French Superior Military Court, it was noted that the defendants were accused of having permitted and supported the treatment which occurred and 'not having done their utmost' to stop it.[117] The court also rejected defence arguments of ignorance and held three of the accused liable. With respect to Roechling himself, the military tribunal of first instance held that it 'was his duty as the head to inquire into the treatment accorded to the foreign workers and to the prisoners of war whose employment ... of which ... he must have been aware'.[118]

The Superior Military Court affirmed the tribunal's judgement, noting that '[n]o superior may prefer this defense [lack of knowledge] indefinitely; for it is his duty to know what occurs in his organisation, and lack of knowledge, therefore, can only be the result of criminal negligence'.[119] The Superior Military Court also noted that Roechling had 'repeated opportunities during inspection of his concerns to ascertain the fate meted out to his personnel, since

[113] *Ibid.*, p. 1055.
[114] *Čelebići* Trial Judgement, *supra* note 3, para. 389.
[115] *Čelebići* Appeal Judgement, *supra* note 32, para. 229. Accord *Prosecutor* v. *Blaškić*, Case No. IT-95-14-T, Judgement, 3 March 2000 ('*Blaškić* Trial Judgement'), para. 317 (opining that '[i]t seems ... that the tribunal held that in actual fact the accused [Mummenthey] *must have known*') (emphasis in original).
[116] For the rejection of a 'should have known' standard in the jurisprudence of the *ad hoc* Tribunals, see *infra* text accompanying notes 375–383.
[117] *Roechling* First Instance Judgement, *supra* note 51, p. 1136.   [118] *Ibid.*
[119] *The Government Commissioner of the General Tribunal of the Military Government for the French Zone of Occupation in Germany* v. *Herman Roechling and Others*, Judgement on Appeal to the Superior Military Court of the French Zone of Occupation in Germany, in *Trials of War Criminals Before the Nuremberg Military Tribunals Under Control Council Law No. 10* (1950), Vol. XIV, Appendix B, ('*Roechling* Appeal Judgement'), pp. 1097–1143 (quotation at p. 1106).

he could not fail to notice the prisoner's uniform on those occasions'.[120] This statement suggests that the court found that Roechling had specific information putting him on notice of the crimes committed by his subordinates. However, in the absence of a clear statement by the Superior Court on this issue, the importance it attached to this aspect is unclear. While the interpretation of this case in the *Čelebići* Trial Judgement only focuses on the 'duty to know',[121] the *Čelebići* Appeals Chamber reasoned that this 'duty to know' is only found where the accused was put on notice of the acts of his subordinates.[122]

Despite varying interpretations, the post-Second World War jurisprudence (with the possible exception of *Yamashita*[123]) rejected strict liability as a possible mental-element test for superior responsibility.[124] It also consistently accepted forms of constructive knowledge and rejected assertions of a lack of actual knowledge as a defence – often inferring such knowledge. Apart from the development of the actual-knowledge test, two different possible standards of constructive knowledge emerged from these cases: (1) that the superior may incur liability where he 'should have known', involving a pro-active duty to keep informed of subordinates' activities; and (2) that the superior may incur liability for his failure to discover acts of subordinates from information already available to the him.[125] Less attractive for those searching for clear guidance from this early jurisprudence on superior responsibility, but perhaps closer to the truth, is the conclusion that no clear standard of constructive knowledge emerged from these cases, a conclusion supported by the *Čelebići* Appeals Chamber in its analysis of the post-Second World War jurisprudence.[126]

Following the post-Second World War cases, there were few developments in this field until the adoption of the Additional Protocols in 1977. One notable exception is the 1971 *Medina* case of the US Court of Military Appeal; in this case, the court considered whether Captain Medina, a US company commander, was liable for acts of his subordinates in the Vietnam War in relation

---

[120] *Ibid.*, pp. 1136–1137.   [121] *Čelebići* Trial Judgement, *supra* note 3, para. 389.
[122] *Čelebići* Appeal Judgement, *supra* note 32, para 229.
[123] See *supra* text accompanying note 87 and sources cited therein.   [124] Parks, *supra* note 7, p. 87.
[125] Ambos, *supra* note 35, p. 830; Levine, *supra* note 17, p. 1.
[126] *Čelebići* Appeal Judgement, *supra* note 32, para 229. By contrast, the *Čelebići* Trial Chamber found that the post-Second World War jurisprudence established a 'should have known' knowledge standard, with a duty on superiors to remain informed of the activities of their subordinates. See *Čelebići* Trial Judgement, *supra* note 3, para. 388. The *Blaškić* Trial Chamber, for its part, characterised the mental element as defined in the post-Second World War cases as liability where the superior 'failed to exercise the means available to him to learn of the offence and, under the circumstances, he should have known and such failure to know constitutes a criminal dereliction'. *Blaškić* Trial Judgement, *supra* note 115, para. 322. See also Mitchell, *supra* note 45, p. 385.

to the My Lai massacre.[127] The constructive-knowledge standards developed by the post-Second World War jurisprudence were ignored by Military Judge Colonel Howard, who directed the jury that a commander cannot be responsible for the acts of his subordinates if he lacked actual knowledge. The judge addressed the jury in relation to command responsibility as follows:

[The] legal requirements placed upon a commander require actual knowledge plus a wrongful failure to act. Thus mere presence at the scene without knowledge will not suffice. That is, the commander subordinate relationship alone will not allow an inference of knowledge. While it is not necessary that a commander actually see an atrocity being committed, it is essential that he know that his subordinates are in the process of committing atrocities or are about to commit atrocities.[128]

Captain Medina was acquitted by the jury, and the case was upheld on appeal.[129] This case appears to be an anomaly in US jurisprudence regarding superior responsibility, particularly in light of the then current regulations in the 1956 US Army Field Manual, which provided for the imposition of responsibility on commanders with either actual or constructive knowledge.[130] This incongruous direction and result has been interpreted as an expression of sympathy for American combatants,[131] and should not be considered representative of the mental-element test currently established as part of customary international law, or even the test applicable in the United States at the time.[132]

3.1.3.2.2 *Additional protocols*
Article 86(2) of Additional Protocol I expressly provides for individual responsibility of superiors for failure to 'prevent or repress' crimes of subordinates. The mental element is articulated as being fulfilled where superiors 'knew, or had information which should have enabled them to conclude in the circumstances at the time' that their subordinates were committing or were going to commit a crime.[133] A literal interpretation of this language clearly provides for the criminal responsibility of the superior where he could have learned of the subordinates' unlawful conduct from information available to him at the

---

[127] *United States* v. *Calley*, 46 CMR 1131 (1971), affirmed by 48 CMR 19 (1973).
[128] Leal, *supra* note 87, pp. 130–131 (quoting Judge Howard's jury instruction). See also Bassiouni, *supra* note 39, p. 386.
[129] Leal, *supra* note 87, p. 131.
[130] See U.S. Department of Army, *Law of Land Warfare Field Manual* 27–10 (1956), Section 501:

The commander is also responsible if he has actual knowledge, or should have knowledge, through reports received by him or through other means, that troops or other persons subject to his control are about to commit or have committed a war crime and he fails to take the necessary and reasonable steps to insure compliance with the law of war or to punish violators thereof.

[131] Crowe, *supra* note 90, pp. 223–224. The one officer who was convicted over the incident, Lieutenant William L. Calley, Jr., was subsequently pardoned by President Nixon.
[132] See Ambos, *supra* note 35, p. 832; Mitchell, *supra* note 45, p. 396.
[133] Additional Protocol I, *supra* note 28, Art. 86(2).

relevant time. Both the Trial and Appeals Chambers in *Čelebići* concluded that the operation of this provision requires that information be available to a superior which would put him on notice of the need for additional investigation.[134]

The ICRC Commentary to Additional Protocol I, in referring to the level of knowledge required by Article 86(2), noted that the information available to the superior may include reports addressed to him, the tactical situation, the level of training and instruction of subordinate officers and their troops, and the character traits of such officers and troops; the Commentary cited *Yamashita* as authority for these factors,[135] and these factors have been cited and evaluated in a number of judgements of chambers of the *ad hoc* Tribunals.[136] Nevertheless, the Commentary itself acknowledges the difficulty of establishing the mental element in the case of such an omission.[137]

Eugenia Levine notes that the operation of this provision is such that superior responsibility might not apply where, for example, no reports are in fact available to the superior due to his negligence in establishing reporting procedures, because in such a case there is no information available to him putting him on notice that his subordinates were about to engage, were engaging, or had engaged in criminal conduct ('admonitory information').[138] The ICRC Commentary acknowledges this scenario, however, and notes that in such 'flagrant cases', the post-Second World War tribunals did not accept a superior's attempt to 'wash his hands' of the matter, but rather 'taking into account the circumstances, a knowledge of breaches committed by subordinates could be presumed'.[139]

3.1.3.2.3 *The Kahan Report (Israeli Commission of Inquiry)*

Although not a criminal court, the Israeli Commission of Inquiry that investigated the responsibility of a number of Israeli superiors for atrocities committed in the Shatila and Sabra refugee camps in Beirut in 1982[140] consisted of a number of eminent judges. As such, the final report of the Commission,

---

[134] *Čelebići* Trial Judgement, *supra* note 3, para. 383; *Čelebići* Appeal Judgement, *supra* note 32, para. 226.
[135] ICRC Commentary to the Additional Protocols, *supra* note 5, para. 3545 (citing *Yamashita* First Instance Judgement, *supra* note 39, p. 35 and the *High Command* case, *supra* note 44).
[136] See *infra* text accompanying notes 393–394 and sources cited therein.
[137] ICRC Commentary to the Additional Protocols, *supra* note 5, para. 3541.
[138] Levine, *supra* note 17, p. 4.
[139] ICRC Commentary to the Additional Protocols, *supra* note 5, para. 3546.
[140] Following Israel's invasion of Lebanon on 16 September 1982, the Israeli Defence Force occupying Beirut permitted a force of Lebanese Christian militia under its control (the Phalangists) to enter the Palestinian refugee camps of Sabra and Shatila. Over a period of thirty-eight hours, this force massacred a number of unarmed civilians, with estimates ranging from between 300 to 3,000 persons killed. See Bassiouni, *supra* note 39, p. 389. For further background on this incident, see Mitchell, *supra* note 45, pp. 398 *et seq.*

which was chaired by Yitzhak Kahan, then-President of the Supreme Court,[141] has been considered a relevant contribution to the development of customary law on superior responsibility.[142] The Report found several Israeli superiors, including then Minister of Defence Ariel Sharon, 'indirectly' responsible for the massacres.[143] It stated that those who should have foreseen the risk of the massacre and did nothing to prevent it, as well as those who did not do everything within their power to stop the massacre once they were aware of it, were indirectly responsible:

The absence of a warning from experts cannot serve as an explanation for ignoring the danger of a massacre. The Chief of Staff [of the Israeli Defence Forces] should have known and foreseen – by virtue of common knowledge, as well as the special information at his disposal – that there was a possibility of harm to the population in the camps at the hands of the Phalangists. Even if the experts did not fulfil their obligation, this does not absolve the Chief of Staff of responsibility.[144]

The Commission held that the inaction of the Chief of Staff of the Israeli Defence Forces constituted a 'breach of duty and dereliction of duty'.[145] As the Commission referred to the Chief's knowledge of the strong feelings of hatred present in the situation, as well as specific information at his disposal, the Report could arguably support the conclusion that the Chief of Staff had failed in his duty to make further enquiries where information was available which put him on notice of the risk of breaches by his subordinates.

3.1.3.2.4 The Statutes of the ad hoc Tribunals
The Statutes of both the ICTY and the ICTR have adopted a standard whereby a superior is liable if he 'knew or had reason to know' that his subordinate was about to commit or had committed breaches of the laws of war. This standard is less explicit than the formulation in Article 86(2) of Additional Protocol I, and both Tribunals have grappled with how to interpret the 'had reason to know' limb.[146] A detailed discussion of the mental element of the doctrine of superior responsibility in the law of these Tribunals is set out in Section 3.2 of this chapter.[147]

3.1.3.2.5 ICC Statute
The ICC Statute differentiates between the mental element required of military commanders on the one hand, and civilian superiors on the

---

[141] Final Report of the Commission of Inquiry into the Events at the Refugee Camps in Beirut, 7 February 1983 ('Kahan report') (authorised translation), reprinted in (1983) 22 ILM 473–520.

[142] See *Blaškić* Trial Judgement, *supra* note 115, para. 331.

[143] Bassiouni, *supra* note 39, p. 389. See also Mitchell, *supra* note 45, p. 399.

[144] Kahan report, *supra* note 141, p. 35.   [145] *Ibid.*, p. 37.

[146] See *infra* text accompanying notes 397–435.   [147] See *infra* text accompanying notes 352–459.

other.[148] In contrast to the *ad hoc* Tribunals' imposition of liability where superiors 'knew or ought to have known' of crimes, the ICC Statue imposes liability on military superiors who 'knew, or owing to the circumstances at the time, should have known'[149] that their subordinates were committing or about to commit crimes. The treatment of the mental element of the doctrine of superior responsibility by the ICC, and that of other international criminal courts and tribunals, is discussed in Section 3.4 of this chapter.

3.1.3.3 Historical evolution of the 'necessary and reasonable measures' element

The third essential element that must be satisfied for liability via superior responsibility to be imposed is that the superior failed to take the necessary and reasonable measures to prevent the criminal act or to punish the relevant subordinate.

3.1.3.3.1 Post-Second World War cases: 'necessary and reasonable measures'

The mental element definition applied in the post-Second World War cases discussed above reveals two different possible standards of constructive knowledge: (1) that the superior 'should have known', involving a proactive duty to remain informed of subordinates' activities; and (2) that the superior failed to discover the actions of subordinates from information already available to him. The former interpretation imposes a more onerous obligation upon the superior to prevent breaches of international criminal law by his subordinates than the latter. Some commentators subscribe to this former interpretation.[150]

A majority of the US Supreme Court in *Yamashita* expressly recognised the existence of an 'affirmative duty' on a commander 'to take such measures as [are] within his power and appropriate in the circumstances to protect prisoners of war and the civilian population'.[151] As discussed above, the reference within that judgement to 'no effective attempt by a commander to *discover* and *control* the acts'[152] has been interpreted by some commentators as reflecting a positive duty to investigate acts of subordinates without prior indications of offences.[153] Another interpretation is that this is only the case where the superior has notice of the offences.[154]

---

[148] Rome Statute, *supra* note 4, Art. 28. See also *infra*, text accompanying notes 622–633, for a detailed discussion of Article 28's differentiation between military commanders and civilian superiors.
[149] Rome Statute, *supra* note 4, Art. 28(1)(a).
[150] See, e.g., Crowe, *supra* note 90, p. 207–208; Smidt, *supra* note 90, p. 184, 233.
[151] *Yamashita* Supreme Court Habeas Decision, *supra* note 41, p. 16.
[152] *Yamashita* First Instance Judgement, *supra* note 39, p. 35 (emphasis added).
[153] See Crowe, *supra* note 90, p. 207–208; Smidt, *supra* note 90, p. 233.
[154] See *Čelebići* Appeal Judgement, *supra* note 32, paras. 228–229.

In the *Medical* case, the US Military Tribunal imposed a high standard in relation to the measures which should be taken by the superior to prevent the commission of crimes. The Tribunal found that Brandt, as the senior medical officer of the German government, was under an obligation to investigate into experiments being conducted by his subordinates. It further held that, once Brandt had been made aware of the experiments, he was under an absolute duty to order his subordinates to immediately terminate them; because he failed to issue such an order, he was found criminally responsible pursuant to the doctrine of superior responsibility.[155]

The Tokyo Tribunal also imposed heavy obligations upon superiors in its judgement. Count 55 of the indictment charged nineteen of the accused as superiors for having 'deliberately and recklessly disregarded their legal duty to take *adequate steps* to secure the observance [of the laws and customs of war] and prevent breaches thereof'.[156] The question of what measures constituted 'adequate steps' varied with the facts of the different cases.[157] Upon receiving reports of the atrocities in Nanjing, Japanese Foreign Minister Hirota took the matter up with the Japanese War Ministry and was assured that the crimes would be stopped. However, following these assurances, reports of the atrocities continued for up to one month. In these circumstances, the Tribunal ruled that Hirota was in dereliction of his duty for not insisting that the Cabinet take immediate action, and for being 'content to rely on assurances which he knew were not being implemented'.[158] The Tribunal held that this inaction amounted to criminal negligence (or the 'should have known' standard),[159] a standard now held by the *ad hoc* Tribunal jurisprudence not to form part of customary international law concerning the responsibility of superiors.[160] As discussed above, this judgement has been criticised for not considering Hirota's actual ability to control the situation, the crimes having been committed by personnel from another Ministry over which Hirota did not have control.[161]

The former Japanese Prime Minister, Koiso, was found by the Tokyo Tribunal to have known of war crimes being committed in 'every theatre of war'. Koiso had requested the issuance of a directive to the competent authorities to prohibit the mistreatment of prisoners of war. Nevertheless, the Tokyo Tribunal considered the fact that Koiso remained in office for another six

---

[155] *Medical* case, *supra* note 47, p. 193.
[156] Tokyo Judgement, *supra* note 61, pp. 59–60 (emphasis added).
[157] See *infra*, text accompanying notes 475–477, for a discussion of the jurisprudence of the *ad hoc* Tribunals holding that the determination of what constitutes 'necessary and reasonable' measures varies from case to case.
[158] Tokyo Judgement, *supra* note 61, p. 448.   [159] *Ibid.*
[160] See *infra* text accompanying notes 375–383 and sources cited therein.
[161] See Ambos, *supra* note 35, p. 831; van Sliedregt, *supra* note 7, p. 129; Tokyo Judgement, *supra* note 61, p. 1126 (separate opinion of Justice Röling). See also *supra* text accompanying notes 62–63.

months after the request and that the treatment of the prisoners of war showed no improvement as amounting to a 'deliberate disregard of duty'.[162] Finally, in relation to the responsibility of former Foreign Minister Mamoru Shigemitsu for the inhumane treatment of prisoners of war the Tokyo Tribunal, in finding him guilty, noted that he 'took no adequate steps to have the matter investigated ... [H]e should have pressed the matter, if necessary to the point of resigning, in order to quit himself of a responsibility which he suspected was not being discharged.'[163]

Some further examples of measures which were held to give rise to superior responsibility in the post-Second World War cases included the following: the lack of an attempt to secure additional information after receiving reports that crimes had been committed;[164] failure to issue orders aimed at bringing practices in accordance with international law, in a case where the superior had actual knowledge;[165] failure to protest against, criticise or condemn criminal action;[166] and failure to insist before a superior authority that immediate action be taken.[167]

3.1.3.3.2 Post-Second World War cases: duty to prevent as a separate duty?

In some of the post-Second World War cases, the tribunal in question held the accused responsible for his failure to punish the crimes of his subordinates, but it is unclear whether these cases considered the duty to punish as a separate duty, or whether the duty to punish was linked to the superior's duty to prevent. For example, the Tokyo Tribunal, in convicting former Prime Minister Tojo, stated that 'he took no adequate steps to punish offenders and to prevent the commission of similar offences in the future'.[168] Further, in convicting the accused Kimura, the Tokyo Tribunal stated that 'he took no disciplinary measures or other steps to prevent the commission of atrocities by the troops under his command'.[169]

The ICTY Appeals Chamber has interpreted the *Hostages* case as authority for the proposition that punishment of subordinates is one of several duties of a commander, making reference to the following statement:

---

[162] *Ibid.*, p. 453.   [163] *Ibid.*   [164] See *Hostages* case, *supra* note 43, p. 1290.
[165] See *ibid.*, p. 1311 (concerning the accused Lanz).
[166] See *High Command* case, *supra* note 44, p. 623.
[167] See Tokyo Judgment, *supra* note 61, p. 448. See also *infra*, note 494, for a list of judgements of the *ad hoc* Tribunals repeating this list.
[168] *Ibid.*, p. 462. Note, however, that Tojo was convicted on the basis of what was historically and inaccurately described as 'direct' superior responsibility, rather than superior responsibility, for his failure to act. Count 54 alleged that he 'ordered, authorised, and permitted' the commission of war crimes or crimes against humanity by subordinates.
[169] *Ibid.*

[I]n his capacity as commanding general of occupied territory, he was charged with the duty and responsibility of maintaining order and safety, the protection of the lives and property of the population, and the punishment of crime. This not only implies a control of the inhabitants in the accomplishment of these purposes, but the control and regulation of all other lawless persons or groups ... The primary responsibility for the prevention and punishment of crime lies with the commanding general[.][170]

Concerning those measures considered to be part of the duty to punish, the post-Second World War cases appear to imply that a superior should take measures to undertake an effective investigation as well as active steps to bring the perpetrators to justice.[171] In the *High Command* case, the Military Tribunal assessed the liability of General Hans von Salmuth for war crimes and crimes against humanity in relation to a number of crimes committed by his subordinates.[172] In respect of one incident involving the execution of ninety-eight Jewish civilians, he responded by issuing an order that 'unpleasant excess on the part of the troops be avoided', and imposed a twenty-day confinement sentence against one subordinate.[173] The Military Tribunal considered this measure insufficient, and found von Salmuth guilty as a superior.

Whether a superior has called for a report on an incident, as well as the thoroughness of an investigation, were also relevant factors in this respect. For example, the Tokyo Tribunal held that the accused Tojo was responsible as a superior because he had not taken adequate steps to investigate or punish: 'He did not call for a report of the incident ... He made perfunctory inquiries about the march but took no action. No one was punished.'[174]

3.1.3.3.3 *Additional protocols*
Article 86(2) of Additional Protocol I requires superiors to 'take all feasible measures within their power to prevent or repress the breach'. Notably, this provision makes no express mention of a duty to punish. In this regard, the Commentary of the ILC considers the term 'repress' to include the duty to punish the offender,[175] although such a construction would not appear to accord with the natural meaning of that term. Yet Article 86(3), in articulating the superior's duties, provides that the superior with requisite knowledge must 'initiate such steps as are necessary to prevent such violations ... and, where appropriate, to initiate diplomacy or penal action against violators'.[176]

---

[170] *Prosecutor* v. *Blaškić*, Case No. IT-95-14-A, Judgement, 29 July 2004 ('*Blaškić* Appeal Judgement'), para. 82 (citing *Hostages* case, *supra* note 43, p. 1272).
[171] See *Halilović* Trial Judgement, *supra* note 27, para. 98.
[172] *High Command* case, *supra* note 44, pp. 614–625.   [173] *Ibid.*, p. 623.
[174] Tokyo Judgement, *supra* note 61, p. 462.
[175] ILC 1996 Draft Code, *supra* note 34, Commentary, p. 37.
[176] Additional Protocol I, *supra* note 28, Art. 86(3).

The ICRC Commentary on Article 86(2) notes that the obligation requires both preventive and repressive actions, but that it reasonably restricts the measures to those which are 'feasible', in recognition of the fact that it is not always possible to prevent or punish the perpetrators.[177] The Commentary refers to this limit upon measures expected of a superior to those within his power as 'common sense', and concludes that this element corresponds precisely to that articulated in the judgements in the post-Second World War cases, noting specifically the Judgement of the Tokyo Tribunal.

While the doctrine of superior responsibility has deep historical roots, it has evolved dramatically over the past century, particularly through the jurisprudence following the Second World War and in recent codification, and has been more thoroughly developed and refined in the jurisprudence of the ICTY and the ICTR.

Although the standards and interpretations of the required elements that constitute the doctrine have differed in the post-Second World War cases and in the limited domestic jurisprudence on the subject, and while codifications of the doctrine have raised questions about the nature and scope of its application to different kinds of superiors in different circumstances, a degree of consistency and certainty has emerged which has allowed the solidification of the doctrine into a more clearly defined form of criminal responsibility. The section that follows discusses the application of the three essential elements of superior responsibility in the jurisprudence of the *ad hoc* Tribunals.

3.2 Elements of superior responsibility

For the imposition of liability pursuant to a given form of responsibility, the appellate jurisprudence of the *ad hoc* Tribunals requires that such form of responsibility existed under customary international law or in treaties binding on the accused at the time relevant to the indictment.[178] The chambers of the *ad hoc* Tribunals have consistently followed the *Čelebići* Trial Judgement in acknowledging that, by the time of the events in the former Yugoslavia and

---

[177] ICRC Commentary to the Additional Protocols, *supra* note 5, para. 3548.

[178] *Prosecutor* v. *Karemera, Ngirumpatse and Nzirorera*, Case Nos. ICTR-98-44-AR72.5, ICTR-98-44-AR72.6, Decision on Jurisdictional Appeals: Joint Criminal Enterprise, 12 April 2006 ('*Karemera et al.* JCE Appeal Decision'), para. 12:

> The Tribunal has jurisdiction to consider only . . . modes of liability which . . . existed in customary international law at the time of the alleged actions under consideration or were proscribed by treaties forming part of the law to which the accused was subject at the time of the alleged actions under consideration.

Accord Prosecutor v. *Milutinović, Šainović and Ojdanić*, Case No. IT-99-37-AR72, Decision on Dragoljub Ojdanić's Motion Challenging Jurisdiction – Joint Criminal Enterprise, 21 May 2003 ('*Milutinović et al.* JCE Appeal Decision'), para. 21; *Prosecutor* v. *Milutinović, Šainović, Ojdanić, Pavković, Lazarević, Đorđević and Lukić*, Case No. IT-05-87-PT, Decision on Ojdanić's Motion Challenging Jurisdiction: Indirect Co-Perpetration, 22 March 2006 ('*Milutinović et al.* ICP Pre-Trial Decision'), para. 15.

Rwanda, both customary international law and international treaty law recognised the individual criminal responsibility of superiors who fail to prevent or punish the crimes of their subordinates.[179] The Appeals Chamber in the July 2003 *Hadžihasanović* decision on interlocutory appeal confirmed that, by the early 1990s, customary international law permitted such responsibility for superiors in internal armed conflicts, at least in respect of violations of the laws or customs of war under Article 3 of the ICTY Statute.[180] Moreover, there is support for the conclusion that customary international law anticipates the imposition of superior responsibility not only for violations of the laws or customs of war, but also for any other crime in the *ad hoc* Tribunals' Statutes, whether committed in international or internal armed conflict; indeed, such responsibility is anticipated even where no armed conflict exists at all if the crime at issue is genocide (in either Tribunal) or a crime against humanity (in the ICTR).[181] First, several trial

---

[179] *Čelebići* Trial Judgement, *supra* note 3, para. 333. See also, e.g., *Blaškić* Appeal Judgement, *supra* note 170, para. 85; *Hadžihasanović et al.* 7(3) Appeal Decision, *supra* note 3, para. 11; *Čelebići* Appeal Judgement, *supra* note 32, para. 195 ('The principle that military and other superiors may be held criminally responsible for the acts of their subordinates is well-established in conventional and customary law.'); *Prosecutor v. Muvunyi*, Case No. ICTR-00-55A-T, Judgement and Sentence, 12 September 2006 ('*Muvunyi* Trial Judgement'), para. 473; *Prosecutor v. Orić*, Case No. IT-03-68-T, Judgement, 30 June 2006 ('*Orić* Trial Judgement'), para. 291; *Prosecutor v. Hadžihasanović and Kubura*, Case No. IT-01-47-T, Judgement, 15 March 2006 ('*Hadžihasanović and Kubura* Trial Judgement'), para. 65; *Prosecutor v. Limaj, Bala and Musliu*, Case No. IT-03-66-T, Judgement, 30 November 2005 ('*Limaj et al.* Trial Judgement'), para. 519; *Halilović* Trial Judgement, *supra* note 27, para. 55; *Prosecutor v. Strugar*, Case No. IT-01-42-T, Judgement, 31 January 2005 ('*Strugar* Trial Judgement'), para. 357; *Prosecutor v. Brđanin*, Case No. IT-99-36-T, Judgement, 1 September 2004 ('*Brđanin* Trial Judgement'), paras. 275; *ibid.*, para. 713 n. 744 (holding that superior responsibility 'was recognised in customary international law at the time of the acts charged' – that is, in 1991 and 1992); *Prosecutor v. Bagilishema*, Case No. ICTR-95-1A-T, 7 June 2001 ('*Bagilishema* Trial Judgement'), para. 37 ('Article 6(3) incorporates the customary law doctrine of command responsibility.'); *Blaškić* Trial Judgement, *supra* note 115, para. 789; *Prosecutor v. Kayishema and Ruzindana*, Case No. ICTR-95-1-T, Judgement, 21 May 1999 ('*Kayishema and Ruzindana* Trial Judgement'), para. 209 ('The principle of command responsibility is firmly established in international law, and its position as a principle of customary international law has recently been delineated by the ICTY in the *[Č]elebi[ć]i* Judgement.').

[180] *Hadžihasanović et al.* 7(3) Appeal Decision, *supra* note 3, para. 18 ('Customary international law recognizes that some war crimes can be committed by a member of an organised military force in the course of an internal armed conflict; it therefore also recognizes that there can be command responsibility in respect of such crimes.'). See also *ibid.*, paras. 26, 31; *Strugar* Trial Judgement, *supra* note 179, para. 216 (noting that Article 3 of the ICTY Statute – setting forth violations of the laws or customs of war – is applicable regardless of the nature of the conflict; that both the prosecution and the defence had agreed that the nature of the conflict 'does not constitute an element of any of the crimes with which the Accused is charged'; and deciding to 'forbear from pronouncing on the matter'); *ibid.*, para. 217 (noting that the evidence established the existence of an armed conflict between the Yugoslav army and the Croatian armed forces at the relevant time, but expressly declining to characterise the nature of the conflict); *ibid.*, para. 446 (finding Strugar responsible pursuant to Article 7(3) of the ICTY Statute for failing to prevent and punish violations of the laws or customs of war); *Prosecutor v. Aleksovski*, Case No. IT-95-14/1-T, Judgement, 25 June 1999 ('*Aleksovski* Trial Judgement'), paras. 44, 118, 228 and p. 92 (convicting the accused for failing to prevent or punish violations of the laws or customs of war notwithstanding the apparent finding that the conflict was non-international in nature).

[181] The text of Article 5 of the ICTY Statute, cataloguing crimes against humanity, contains a requirement that the offences be 'committed in armed conflict'. ICTY Statute, *supra* note 31, Art. 5. This jurisdictional requirement is specific to the ICTY, and does not exist either in customary international law or in the ICTR's analogous provision on crimes against humanity. See *Prosecutor v. Kunarac, Kovač and Vuković*, Case Nos. IT-96-23 & IT-96-23/1-A, Judgement, 12 June 2002, para. 83; ICTR Statute, *supra* note 31, Art. 3. Neither of the respective Statutes, nor customary international law, contains a requirement that genocide be committed in armed conflict.

judgements cite the Appeals Chamber's holding in *Hadžihasanović* without repeating its apparent restriction to violations of the laws or customs of war, suggesting its application to a broader category of crimes.[182] Second, at least one trial chamber of the ICTY has convicted an accused for failing to prevent and punish crimes against humanity without pronouncing on the nature of the armed conflict at the relevant time.[183] Third, trial chambers of the ICTR have convicted accused, including civilian superiors, for their failure to prevent or punish genocide and crimes against humanity without finding that an armed conflict existed at all.[184] Finally, no chamber has ever articulated, as one of the elements of superior responsibility, a requirement that an armed conflict existed.[185]

[182] See, e.g., *Orić* Trial Judgement, *supra* note 179, para. 291; *Limaj et al.* Trial Judgement, *supra* note 179, para. 519 (citing *Hadžihasanović et al.* 7(3) Appeal Decision, *supra* note 3, para. 31, and holding that '[t]he principle of individual criminal responsibility of superiors for failure to prevent or to punish crimes committed by subordinates is an established principle of international customary law, applicable to both international and internal armed conflicts') (footnotes omitted); *Halilović* Trial Judgement, *supra* note 27, para. 55 ('Article 7(3) of the Statute is applicable to all acts referred to in Articles 2 to 5 thereof and applies to both international and non–international armed conflicts.'); *Strugar* Trial Judgement, *supra* note 179, para. 357 (identical language to *Limaj*); *Brđanin* Trial Judgement, *supra* note 179, para. 275 (citing *Hadžihasanović et al.* 7(3) Appeal Decision, *supra* note 3, paras. 13 and 31, and holding that the existence of superior responsibility in customary and conventional international law 'applies both in the context of international as well as internal armed conflicts'.). But see *Hadžihasanović and Kubura* Trial Judgement, *supra* note 179, para. 65 ('[C]ommand responsibility was an integral part of customary international law at the time of the events, *to the extent that it applied to war crimes* committed in the context of an internal or international armed conflict.') (emphasis added).
[183] See *Prosecutor* v. *Krnojelac*, Case No. IT-97-25-T, Judgement, 15 March 2002 ('*Krnojelac* Trial Judgement'), paras. 12, 320, 534 (convicting the accused for his failure to prevent and punish inhumane acts as a crime against humanity).
[184] See, e.g., *Prosecutor* v. *Nahimana, Barayagwiza and Ngeze*, Case No. ICTR-99-52-T, Judgement and Sentence, 3 December 2003 ('*Nahimana et al.* Trial Judgement'), paras. 973, 977, 1033–1035, 1064, 1066, 1081–1083 (making findings of guilt pursuant to Article 6(3) of the ICTR Statute for genocide, direct and public incitement to genocide, and extermination and persecution as crimes against humanity, but making no findings as to the existence of an armed conflict); *Prosecutor* v. *Serushago*, Case No. ICTR-98-39-S, Sentence, 5 February 1999, paras. 26–29 (entering findings of guilt pursuant to Article 6(3) for genocide and murder, extermination and torture as crimes against humanity, but making no findings as to the existence of an armed conflict); *Prosecutor* v. *Kambanda*, Case No. ICTR 97-23-S, Judgement and Sentence, 4 September 1998 ('*Kambanda* Trial Judgement'), para. 40 and pp. 27–28 (entering findings of guilt pursuant to Articles 6(1) and 6(3) for genocide, conspiracy to commit genocide, direct and public incitement to genocide, and murder and extermination as crimes against humanity without making findings as to the existence of an armed conflict). Moreover, while other chambers of the ICTR have found that a non-international armed conflict existed, they have done so only in the context of analysing the accused's liability for violations of the laws or customs of war. See, e.g., *Prosecutor* v. *Musema*, Case No. ICTR-96-13-T, Judgement and Sentence, 27 January 2000 ('*Musema* Trial Judgement'), paras. 245, 259–260, 895, 900, 906, 915, 920, 925–926, 936, 951, 970–972, 974 (finding, in the course of discussing the accused's liability for violations of the laws or customs of war, that a non-international armed conflict existed at the relevant time; acquitting the accused on these charges due to the absence of a nexus between the alleged crimes and the armed conflict; but finding the accused liable as a superior pursuant to Article 6(3) for genocide and extermination as a crime against humanity); *Kayishema and Ruzindana* Trial Judgement, *supra* note 179, paras. 555, 559, 563, 569, 597, 621, 623–624 (finding that a non-international armed conflict existed at the relevant time; that the charged violations of the laws or customs of war were not sufficiently connected to the armed conflict; and convicting the accused of genocide for massacres 'committed parallel to, and not as a result of, the armed conflict') (quoted language at para. 621).
[185] Only one chamber appears to have opined directly on the issue of whether an armed conflict is required at all. The Pre-Trial Chamber in *Hadžihasanović*, in the course of holding that superior responsibility may be imposed for crimes alleged to have occurred during internal armed conflict, remarked as follows:

Article 7(3) of the ICTY Statute sets forth the doctrine of superior responsibility as follows:

The fact that any of the acts referred to in Articles 2 to 5 of the present Statute was committed by a subordinate does not relieve his superior of criminal responsibility if he knew or had reason to know that the subordinate was about to commit such acts or had done so and the superior failed to take the necessary and reasonable measures to prevent such acts or to punish the perpetrators thereof.[186]

Article 6(3) of the ICTR Statute enshrines the doctrine in nearly identical terms.[187] For the sake of convenience, where a particular statement applies equally to the respective provisions of both Statutes, the authors refer to them collectively as 'Article 7/6(3)'.

The Trial Chamber in *Halilović* clarified that superior responsibility is a species of omission liability:

The commander is responsible for the failure to perform an act required by international law. This omission is culpable because international law imposes an affirmative duty on superiors to prevent and punish crimes committed by their subordinates. Thus 'for the acts of his subordinates' as generally referred to in the jurisprudence of the Tribunal does not mean that the commander shares the same responsibility as the subordinates who committed the crimes, but rather that because of the crimes committed by his subordinates, the commander should bear responsibility for his failure to act. The imposition of responsibility upon a commander for breach of his duty is to be weighed against the crimes of his subordinates; a commander is responsible not as though he had committed the crime himself, but his responsibility is considered in proportion to the gravity of the offences committed.[188]

For these reasons, superior responsibility is very different from 'vicarious responsibility', a concept that exists in national legal systems. While both doctrines require a superior-subordinate relationship, a superior found vicariously responsible is liable for his subordinate's substantive misdeeds on the

---

There is nothing on the face of the elements that would suggest that command responsibility is limited to a specific type of armed conflict or that it has any jurisdictional pre-requisites. The manner in which these elements have been applied would rather indicate that the nature of the conflict – or even the existence of an armed conflict – *is not a relevant factor.*

Hadžihasanović et al. 7(3) Pre-Trial Decision, *supra* note 26, para. 30 (emphasis added).

[186] ICTY Statute, *supra* note 31, Art. 7(3).
[187] ICTR Statute, *supra* note 31, Art. 6(3). The only difference between the two Statutes' superior-responsibility provisions is the non–applicability of Article 6(3) of the ICTR Statute to grave breaches of the Geneva Conventions of 1949, a crime over which that Tribunal does not have jurisdiction.
[188] *Halilović* Trial Judgement, *supra* note 27, para. 54 (footnote omitted). Accord *Prosecutor* v. *Krnojelac*, Case No. IT-97-25-A, Judgement, 17 September 2003 ('*Krnojelac* Appeal Judgement'), para. 75; *Orić* Trial Judgement, *supra* note 179, para. 293 ('[T]he superior cannot be considered as if he had committed the crime himself, but merely for his neglect of duty with regard to crimes committed by subordinates.'); *Hadžihasanović and Kubura* Trial Judgement, *supra* note 179, para. 75; *Prosecutor* v. *Blagojević and Jokić*, Case No. IT-02-60-T, Judgement, 17 January 2005, ('*Blagojević and Jokić* Trial Judgement'), paras. 683, 791; *Čelebići* Trial Judgement, *supra* note 3, para. 331 (holding that '[t]he type of individual criminal responsibility *for the illegal acts of subordinates* ... is commonly referred to as "command responsibility"') (emphasis added).

basis of his superior status alone.[189] By contrast, an accused convicted pursuant to the doctrine of superior responsibility is not held liable for the substantive crime of his subordinate, but rather for his own wrongdoing in having failed to honour a legal obligation, placed upon him by customary or conventional international law, to take action to promote and ensure law-abiding behaviour among his subordinates.[190] Accordingly, superior responsibility has independent physical and mental elements – including the requirement of knowledge or reason to know of subordinate misconduct on the part of the accused – that vicarious responsibility appears to lack.

By the terms of Article 7/6(3), a superior may be held responsible for his failure to take the necessary and reasonable measures to prevent his subordinate from committing a crime within the jurisdiction of the Tribunal, or for his failure to punish that subordinate upon acquiring knowledge or reason to know that the subordinate committed a crime. Three important caveats in respect of this proposition will be discussed in greater detail below,[191] but deserve brief mention here. First, although Article 7/6(3) and almost all of the relevant statements in the jurisprudence speak in terms of responsibility for failing to prevent or punish the 'commission' of subordinate criminal 'acts', strong legal and policy arguments can be made in favour of imposing superior responsibility on an accused who fails to prevent or punish the culpable

---

[189] Cf., *Bernard* v. *Attorney General of Jamaica*, [2004] UKPC 47, para. 21 ('Vicarious liability is a principle of strict liability. It is a liability for a tort committed by an employee not based on any fault of the employer.'); *Lister* v. *Hesley Hall Ltd*, [2002] 1 AC 215, 223 ('Vicarious liability is legal responsibility imposed on an employer, although he is himself free from blame, for a tort committed by his employee in the course of his employment.'); *Canadian Encyclopedic Digest Corporations* (Ontario), § 41 (citing John G. Fleming, *The Law of Torts* (9th edn 1998), p. 409) ('Vicarious liability arises where the law holds one person accountable for the misconduct of another although the person so held liable is free from personal blameworthiness or fault.'). See also Čelebići Appeal Judgement, *supra* note 32 ('The Appeals Chamber would not describe superior responsibility as a vicarious liability doctrine, insofar as vicarious liability may suggest a form of strict imputed liability.'), para. 239; Reid, *supra* note 87, p. 822 (footnote omitted, emphasis in original):

> Despite the sometimes confusing terminology used by the historical and contemporary tribunals and legal scholars, the doctrine of superior responsibility is not based on a theory of true *respondeat superior*, or vicarious liability. Individual responsibility of superiors is predicated on the fact that they have violated a duty imposed directly *on them*, by customary international law, to prevent or punish the commission of international crimes; it is liability for an omission in the light of an obligation to act.

[190] *Krnojelac* Appeal Judgement, *supra* note 188, para. 171 ('It cannot be overemphasised that, where superior responsibility is concerned, an accused is not charged with the crimes of his subordinates but with his failure to carry out his duty as a superior to exercise control.'); *Prosecutor* v. *Bagilishema*, Case No. ICTR-95-1A-A, Judgement, 3 July 2002 ('*Bagilishema* Appeal Judgement'), para. 35; Čelebići Appeal Judgement, *supra* note 32, para. 239; *Strugar* Trial Judgement, *supra* note 179, para. 359; *Prosecutor* v. *Kordić and Čerkez*, Case No. IT-95-14/2-T, Judgement, 26 February 2001 ('*Kordić and Čerkez* Trial Judgement'), para. 364; Čelebići Trial Judgement, *supra* note 3, para. 334.

[191] See *infra* text accompanying notes 466–473 (discussing the failure to prevent and the failure to punish as two separate forms of responsibility); text accompanying notes 543–620 (discussing the possibility that liability may be imposed for a superior's failure to prevent and/or punish not only a subordinate's physical perpetration of a criminal act, but also his criminal omission; his participation in a joint criminal enterprise; his ordering, planning, or instigation of a crime; or his own failure to prevent and/or punish the crimes of sub-subordinates).

omissions of subordinates; the planning, instigation, ordering, or aiding and abetting of crimes on the part of subordinates; subordinates' complicity in genocide; or subordinates' participation in a joint criminal enterprise (JCE) pursuant to which crimes are perpetrated.[192] Hence, while direct quotations of the jurisprudence in this section tend to speak in terms of a superior's responsibility for his subordinate's 'commission' of a crime, the authors will refer more broadly to superior responsibility for the subordinate's 'criminal conduct'.[193] Section 3.3 of this chapter discusses superior responsibility for subordinate criminal conduct beyond overt physical commission in considerable detail.[194]

Second, while Article 7/6(3) discusses the failure to prevent *or* punish criminal conduct, the jurisprudence has held that the duty to prevent and the duty to punish are distinct and separate responsibilities under international law,[195] and Article 7/6(3) thus encompasses two distinct forms of superior responsibility.[196] One major consequence of this holding is that an accused superior can be convicted on the basis of one omission (for example, the failure to punish) even if the other (in this case, the failure to prevent) is not proved.[197] Another consequence is that an accused superior cannot make up for his failure to prevent criminal conduct simply by punishing the perpetrators afterwards.[198] Notwithstanding the status of the failure to prevent and the failure to punish as separate forms of superior responsibility, however, the majority of the elements

---

[192] On this hypothesis, an accused military commander may incur Article 7/6(3) liability for failing to prevent or punish the acts of a subordinate who, by providing weapons, intelligence, or logistical support, aided and abetted crimes physically perpetrated by members of another unit not subordinated to the accused. See *Orić* Trial Judgement, *supra* note 179, paras. 301–305; *Prosecutor* v. *Boškoski and Tarčulovski*, Case No. IT-04-82-PT, Decision on Prosecution's Motion to Amend the Indictment and Submission of Proposed Second Amended Indictment and Submission of Amended Pre-Trial Brief, 26 May 2006 ('*Boškoski and Tarčulovski* May 2006 Pre-Trial Decision'), para. 46 ('[T]he Trial Chamber finds that "acts" and "commit" in Article 7(3) of the [ICTY] Statute are meant broadly and permit the imposition of superior responsibility where subordinates have perpetrated a crime, whether by act or omission, through the modes of liability provided for under the Statute.').

[193] Cf. *ibid.*, para. 22 (holding that ' "acts" [in Article 7(3) of the ICTY Statute] refers to the conduct of the subordinate, including both acts and omissions of the subordinate[,] and "commit" refers to any *criminal conduct by a subordinate* perpetrated through any of the modes of liability that are provided for under the Statute').

[194] See *infra* text accompanying notes 543–620.

[195] *Blaškić* Appeal Judgement, *supra* note 170, para. 83 ('[T]he failure to punish and failure to prevent involve different crimes committed at different times: the failure to punish concerns past crimes committed by subordinates, whereas the failure to prevent concerns future crimes of subordinates.'). But see *infra* note 469.

[196] *Halilović* Trial Judgement, *supra* note 27, para. 94 ('The duty to punish is a separate form of liability, distinct from the failure to prevent[.]'). See *infra*, text accompanying notes 466–473, for a more complete discussion of this principle.

[197] *Halilović* Pre-Trial Decision on the Form of the Indictment, *supra* note 195, para. 33.

[198] In other words, even if the superior discharges his legal obligation to punish the perpetrators, he may still be convicted in respect of the crimes that they committed because he failed to prevent such commission in the first place. See *Strugar* Trial Judgement, *supra* note 179, para. 373; *Prosecutor* v. *Semanza*, Case No. ICTR-97-20-T, Judgement and Sentence, 15 May 2003 ('*Semanza* Trial Judgement'), para. 407:

If a superior is aware of the impending or on-going commission of a crime, necessary and reasonable measures must be taken to stop or prevent it. A superior with such knowledge and the material ability to prevent the commission of the crime does not discharge his responsibility by opting simply to punish his subordinates in the aftermath.

under both are identical, including the requirement of a superior-subordinate relationship; the requirement that the accused must have known or had reason to know of subordinate criminal conduct; and the requirement that the accused must have failed to take measures that were 'necessary and reasonable'.

Third, although Article 7/6(3) speaks in terms of a duty to 'punish' subordinate perpetrators, the case law holds that, if an accused's actual and legal powers do not allow him to dispense punishment upon the subordinates himself, he may be able to avoid Article 7/6(3) liability by undertaking an investigation, or by forwarding the information in his possession to his own superior or to the appropriate prosecutorial authorities.[199] For convenience, however, this section will refer to this duty as the duty to 'punish' when restating general propositions concerning the elements of superior responsibility.

The Appeals Chambers of both *ad hoc* Tribunals have held that Article 7/6(3) applies to civilian superiors as well as to military commanders,[200] and the chambers have applied essentially the same set of elements to evaluate an accused's responsibility regardless of his civilian or military status. Accordingly, while the jurisprudence has labelled the doctrine enshrined in Article 7/6(3) both 'superior responsibility' and 'command responsibility', often interchangeably in the same judgement,[201] as noted above,[202] the authors prefer the term 'superior responsibility' when referring generally to this doctrine, as 'command responsibility' may erroneously imply its exclusive applicability to military commanders.[203]

---

[199] *Prosecutor* v. *Kvočka, Kos, Radić, Žigić and Prcać*, Case No. IT-98-30/1-T, Judgement, 2 November 2001 ('*Kvočka et al.* Trial Judgement'), para. 314. See also *infra* text accompanying notes 503–522.

[200] *Prosecutor* v. *Kajelijeli*, Case No. ICTR-98-44A-A, Judgement, 23 May 2005 ('*Kajelijeli* Appeal Judgement'), para. 85; *Bagilishema* Appeal Judgement, *supra* note 190, paras. 50–52; *Čelebići* Appeal Judgement, *supra* note 32, paras. 195–197, 240; *Prosecutor* v. *Aleksovski*, Case No. IT-95-14/1-A, Judgement, 24 March 2000 ('*Aleksovski* Appeal Judgement'), para. 76 (finding in respect of Aleksovski that 'it does not matter whether he was a civilian or military superior, if it can be proved that, within the Kaonik prison, he had the powers to prevent or to punish in terms of Article 7(3).'). Accord *Brđanin* Trial Judgement, *supra* note 179, paras. 281–283; *Nahimana et al.* Trial Judgement, *supra* note 184, paras. 976–977; *Kordić and Čerkez* Trial Judgement, *supra* note 190, para. 446; *Kayishema and Ruzindana* Trial Judgement, *supra* note 179, para. 216; *Čelebići* Trial Judgement, *supra* note 3, paras. 356, 363, 387; *Prosecutor* v. *Akayesu*, Case No. ICTR-96-4-T, Judgement, 2 September 1998 ('*Akayesu* Trial Judgement'), para. 491. See also *infra*, text accompanying notes 264–281, for more complete discussions of the jurisprudence on superior responsibility for civilians.

[201] Compare, e.g., *Prosecutor* v. *Kvočka, Radić, Žigić and Prcać*, Case No. IT-98-30/1-A, Judgement, 28 February 2005 ('*Kvočka et al.* Appeal Judgement'), para. 138 with *ibid.*, para. 695; *Blaškić* Appeal Judgement, *supra* note 170, para. 58 with *ibid.*, para. 375; *Blaškić* Trial Judgement, *supra* note 115, para. 261 with *ibid.*, para. 300; *Čelebići* Trial Judgement, *supra* note 3, para. 332 with *ibid.*, para. 363. See also *Kordić and Čerkez* Trial Judgement, *supra* note 190, para. 364 n. 492 ('The terms "command responsibility" and "superior responsibility" are used interchangeably in this Judgement.').

[202] See *supra* text accompanying note 4.

[203] See *Brđanin* Trial Judgement, *supra* note 179, para. 275 n. 732 ('The Trial Chamber uses the term "superior criminal responsibility" instead of "command responsibility" so as to make clear that the doctrine applies to civilian as well as to military superiors.'); *Muvunyi* Trial Judgement, *supra* note 179, para. 473 ('While the principle was initially applied to the responsibility of military commanders for the criminal actions of their subordinates during war (hence the term "command responsibility"), it is now clearly established that both civilian and military superiors may . . . be held responsible for the actions of

3.2.1 *Elements*

Beginning with the *Čelebići* Trial Judgement, the chambers have uniformly set out three 'essential elements'[204] – or, in the words of the *Blagojević and Jokić* and *Krstić* Trial Chambers, a 'three-pronged test'[205] – that must be satisfied in order to engage an accused's liability pursuant to Article 7(3) of the ICTY Statute and Article 6(3) of the ICTR Statute:

(i) the existence of a superior-subordinate relationship;
(ii) the superior knew or had reason to know that the criminal act was about to be or had been committed;
(iii) the superior failed to take the necessary and reasonable measures to prevent the criminal act or punish the perpetrator thereof.[206]

These elements are examined in turn below.

3.2.1.1 *A superior-subordinate relationship existed between the accused and the person for whose criminal conduct he is alleged to be responsible*

The Trial Chamber in *Strugar* stated that 'the superior-subordinate relationship lies in the very heart of the doctrine of a commander's liability for the crimes of his subordinates' because '[i]t is the position of command over the

those under their authority or command.'). See also Rome Statute, *supra* note 4, Art. 28 (entitled 'Responsibility of commanders and other superiors'); Gerhard Werle, *Principles of International Criminal Law* (2005), pp. 128–129 ('Given the extension of this basic idea to non-military contexts as well ... the idea of "superior responsibility" is now preferable to the more narrow concept of "command responsibility".').

[204] *Čelebići* Trial Judgement, *supra* note 3, para. 346.
[205] *Blagojević and Jokić* Trial Judgement, *supra* note 188, para. 275; *Prosecutor v. Krstić*, Case No. IT-98-33-T, Judgement, 2 August 2001 ('*Krstić* Trial Judgement'), para. 647.
[206] *Čelebići* Trial Judgement, *supra* note 3, para. 346. Accord *Prosecutor v. Gacumbitsi*, Case No. ICTR-2001-64-A, Judgement, 7 July 2006 ('*Gacumbitsi* Appeal Judgement'), para. 143; *Prosecutor v. Kordić and Čerkez*, Case No. IT-95-14/2-A, Judgement, 17 December 2004 ('*Kordić and Čerkez* Appeal Judgement'), paras. 827, 839; *Aleksovski* Appeal Judgement, *supra* note 200, para. 72; *Muvunyi* Trial Judgement, *supra* note 179, para. 474; *Hadžihasanović and Kubura* Trial Judgement, *supra* note 179, pp. 27, 32, 41; *Limaj et al.* Trial Judgement, *supra* note 179, para. 520; *Halilović* Trial Judgement, *supra* note 27, para. 56; *Strugar* Trial Judgement, *supra* note 179, para. 358; *Blagojević and Jokić* Trial Judgement, *supra* note 188, paras. 275, 790; *Halilović* Pre-Trial Decision on the Form of the Indictment, *supra* note 195, para. 14; *Brđanin* Trial Judgement, *supra* note 179, para. 275; *Prosecutor v. Ntagerura, Bagambiki and Imanishimwe*, Case No. ICTR-99-46-T, Judgement and Sentence, 25 February 2004 ('*Ntagerura et al.* Trial Judgement'), para. 627; *Prosecutor v. Galić*, Case. No. IT-98-29-T, Judgement and Opinion, 5 December 2003, para. 173; *Prosecutor v. Kajelijeli*, Case No. ICTR-98-44A-T, Judgement and Sentence, 1 December 2003, para. 772; *Prosecutor v. Stakić*, Case No. IT-97-24-T, Judgement, 29 October 2003, para. 457; *Semanza* Trial Judgement, *supra* note 198, para. 400; *Prosecutor v. Naletilić and Martinović*, Case No. IT-98-34-T, Judgement, 31 March 2003 ('*Naletilić and Martinović* Trial Judgement'), para. 65; *Prosecutor v. Kamuhanda*, Case No. ICTR-99-54A-T, Judgement and Sentence, 22 January 2003, para. 603; *Krnojelac* Trial Judgement, *supra* note 183, para. 92; *Kvočka et al.* Trial Judgement, *supra* note 199, para. 314; *Krstić* Trial Judgement, *supra* note 205, para. 604; *Bagilishema* Trial Judgement, *supra* note 179, para. 38; *Kordić and Čerkez* Trial Judgement, *supra* note 190, para. 401; *Prosecutor v. Kunarac, Kovač and Vuković*, Case No. IT-96-23-T & IT-96-23/1-T, Judgement, 22 February 2001 ('*Kunarac et al.* Trial Judgement'), para. 395; *Blaškić* Trial Judgement, *supra* note 115, para. 294; *Aleksovski* Trial Judgement, *supra* note 180, para. 69.

perpetrator which forms the legal basis for the superior's duty to act, and for his corollary liability for a failure to do so'.[207] In accordance with this principle, the prosecution establishes the first of *Čelebići*'s three essential elements for either of the two forms of superior responsibility in Article 7/6(3) – the failure to prevent or the failure to punish – by proving that a superior-subordinate relationship existed between the accused and the person for whose criminal conduct the accused is charged with responsibility.[208]

The relationship between superior and subordinate need not be a formal one; as the *Strugar* Trial Chamber noted, '[i]t appears from the jurisprudence [on superior responsibility] that the concepts of command and subordination are relatively broad'.[209] Indeed, the chambers have consistently followed *Čelebići* in holding that formal designation as commander or superior is not required in order to trigger responsibility under Article 7/6(3); such responsibility can arise by virtue of a superior's *de facto* as well as *de jure* power over the subordinate in question.[210] The Appeals Chamber in *Čelebići* opined that this

[207] *Strugar* Trial Judgement, *supra* note 179, para. 359. Accord *Limaj et al.* Trial Judgement, *supra* note 179, para. 521 (same language); *Halilović* Trial Judgement, *supra* note 27, para. 57 (same language); *Čelebići* Trial Judgement, *supra* note 3, para. 377 ('The doctrine of command responsibility is ultimately predicated upon the power of the superior to control the acts of his subordinates.').

[208] *Kordić and Čerkez* Appeal Judgement, *supra* note 206, para. 839; *Aleksovski* Appeal Judgement, *supra* note 200, para. 72; *Kunarac et al.* Trial Judgement, *supra* note 206, para. 396; *Čelebići* Trial Judgement, *supra* note 3, para. 346.

[209] *Strugar* Trial Judgement, *supra* note 179, para. 362. See also *Čelebići* Appeal Judgement, *supra* note 32, para. 303 (holding that the necessity to establish the existence of a superior-subordinate relationship does not 'import a requirement of … *formal* subordination'.) (emphasis in original); *Strugar* Trial Judgement, *supra* note 179, para. 446.

[210] *Čelebići* Trial Judgement, *supra* note 3, paras. 354, 370. Accord *Gacumbitsi* Appeal Judgement, *supra* note 206, para. 143; *Kajelijeli* Appeal Judgement, *supra* note 200, para. 85; *Bagilishema* Appeal Judgement, *supra* note 190, paras. 50, 61; *Prosecutor v. Kayishema and Ruzindana*, Case No. ICTR-95-1-A, Judgement (Reasons), 1 June 2001 ('*Kayishema and Ruzindana* Appeal Judgement'), para. 294; *Čelebići* Appeal Judgement, *supra* note 32, paras. 191–192; *ibid.*, para. 197 ('[T]he absence of formal appointment is not fatal to a finding of criminal responsibility, provided certain conditions are met.'); *Muvunyi* Trial Judgement, *supra* note 179, para. 475; *Hadžihasanović and Kubura* Trial Judgement, *supra* note 179, para. 79; *Limaj et al.* Trial Judgement, *supra* note 179, para. 522 ('The existence of the position of command may arise from the formal or *de jure* status of a superior, or from the existence of *de facto* powers of control.'); *Halilović* Trial Judgement, *supra* note 27, para. 58; *Strugar* Trial Judgement, *supra* note 179, para. 362; *Blagojević and Jokić* Trial Judgement, *supra* note 188, para. 791; *Brđanin* Trial Judgement, *supra* note 179, para. 276; *Ntagerura et al.* Trial Judgement, *supra* note 206, para. 628; *Prosecutor v. Galić*, Case. No. IT-98-29-T, Judgement and Opinion, 5 December 2003 ('*Galić* Trial Judgement'), para. 173; *Prosecutor v. Kajelijeli*, Case No. ICTR-98-44A-T, Judgement and Sentence, 1 December 2003 ('*Kajelijeli* Trial Judgement'), para. 773; *Prosecutor v. Stakić*, Case No. IT-97-24-T, Judgement, 29 October 2003 ('*Stakić* Trial Judgement'), para. 459; *Prosecutor v. Niyitegeka*, Case No. ICTR 96-14-T, Judgement and Sentence, 16 May 2003, para. 472; *Semanza* Trial Judgement, *supra* note 198, para. 402; *Naletilić and Martinović* Trial Judgement, *supra* note 206, para. 67; *Prosecutor v. Ntakirutimana and Ntakirutimana*, Case Nos. ICTR-96-10 and ICTR-96-17-T, Judgement and Sentence, 21 February 2003 ('*Ntakirutimana and Ntakirutimana* Trial Judgement'), paras. 819–820; *Prosecutor v. Kamuhanda*, Case No. ICTR-99-54A-T, Judgement and Sentence, 22 January 2003 ('*Kamuhanda* Trial Judgement'), paras. 604–605; *Krnojelac* Trial Judgement, *supra* note 183, para. 93; *Kvočka et al.* Trial Judgement, *supra* note 199, para. 315; *Kordić and Čerkez* Trial Judgement, *supra* note 190, paras. 405–406; *Kunarac et al.* Trial Judgement, *supra* note 206, para. 396 ('[F]ormal designation as a commander is not necessary for establishing command responsibility, as such responsibility may be recognised by virtue of a person's *de facto*, as well as *de jure*, position as a commander.'); *Musema*

holding takes account of the realities of modern conflicts such as those in the former Yugoslavia and Rwanda, where 'there may only be *de facto*, self-proclaimed governments and therefore *de facto* armies and paramilitary groups subordinate thereto'.[211] Invoking this principle as applicable in the ICTR, the *Bagilishema* Appeals Chamber concluded that the Trial Chamber had 'wrongly held that both *de facto* and *de jure* authority need to be established before a superior can be found to exercise effective control over his or her subordinates'.[212]

The key to proving the existence of a superior-subordinate relationship is that the superior possessed real powers of control over the conduct of the relevant subordinate:

[A] position of command is indeed a necessary precondition for the imposition of command responsibility. However, this statement must be qualified by the recognition that the existence of such a position cannot be determined by reference to formal status alone. Instead, the factor that determines liability for this type of criminal responsibility is the *actual possession, or non-possession, of powers of control over the actions of subordinates*[213] ... [I]n order for the principle of superior responsibility to be applicable, it is necessary that the superior have *effective control* over the persons committing the underlying violations of international humanitarian law, in the sense of having the *material ability to prevent and punish the commission of these offences.*[214]

It is therefore 'effective control', defined as the material ability to prevent or punish the relevant subordinate's criminal conduct, that constitutes the 'threshold to be reached in establishing a superior-subordinate relationship for the purpose of Article 7(3) of the [ICTY] Statute'.[215] An accused who does not have such ability in respect of a given subordinate in the circumstances 'cannot properly be considered [his] "superior[ ]" within the meaning of Article 7(3)'.[216] Applying this standard, the Trial Chamber in *Limaj* found that, although the accused Musliu was in a position to exercise effective control over certain forces of the Kosovo Liberation Army operating in the village of Llapushnik, the evidence failed to establish that he enjoyed effective control

---

Trial Judgement, *supra* note 184, paras. 148, 866–867; *Blaškić* Trial Judgement, *supra* note 115, paras. 300–301; *Aleksovski* Trial Judgement, *supra* note 180, para. 76; *Kayishema and Ruzindana* Trial Judgement, *supra* note 179, paras. 218–222, 230, 478, 490–507.

[211] *Čelebići* Appeal Judgement, *supra* note 32, para. 193. Accord *Orić* Trial Judgement, *supra* note 179, para. 309.

[212] *Bagilishema* Appeal Judgement, *supra* note 190, para. 61. Accord *Blagojević and Jokić* Trial Judgement, *supra* note 188, para. 791 ('The hierarchical relationship may exist by virtue of a person's *de jure* or *de facto* position of authority.'). See also *Gacumbitsi* Appeal Judgement, *supra* note 206, paras. 143–145 (holding that the Trial Chamber had erred by considering only the accused's *de jure* authority, and not his *de facto* authority, but ultimately finding that the prosecution had failed to prove that the accused had *de facto* authority over the physical perpetrators and dismissing the ground of appeal).

[213] *Čelebići* Trial Judgement, *supra* note 3, para. 370 (emphasis added).

[214] *Ibid.*, para. 378 (emphases added). Accord *Čelebići* Appeal Judgement, *supra* note 32, para. 196.

[215] *Čelebići* Appeal Judgement, *supra* note 32, para. 256.

[216] *Čelebići* Trial Judgement, *supra* note 3, para. 377.

over those forces who committed crimes against detainees in the Llapushnik prison camp:

> It ... is not established, pursuant to Article 7(3) of the Statute, that [Musliu] had the material ability to prevent the detention of prisoners in the camp, their interrogation, their murder or the brutal and inhumane treatment inflicted upon them, or to put an end to such conduct, or to punish those responsible for it.[217]

As such, Musliu could not be considered the superior of the physical perpetrators of such abuses, and the Trial Chamber acquitted him of all crimes charged pursuant to Article 7(3) in relation to the Llapushnik camp.[218]

The chambers of both *ad hoc* Tribunals have consistently endorsed *Čelebići*'s effective control formulation as applicable to both *de jure* and *de facto* superiors.[219] This position carries with it a number of important consequences. First, an accused may be held responsible pursuant to Article 7/6(3) as a *de facto* superior even if he had no *de jure* authority over the alleged subordinate.[220] Accordingly, the *Kajelijeli* Trial Chamber convicted the former

---

[217] *Limaj et al.* Trial Judgement, *supra* note 179, para. 715.   [218] *Ibid.*, para. 716.

[219] See, e.g., *Gacumbitsi* Appeal Judgement, *supra* note 206, para. 143; *Kajelijeli* Appeal Judgement, *supra* note 200, para. 86; *Kordić and Čerkez* Appeal Judgement, *supra* note 206, para. 840; *Blaškić* Appeal Judgement, *supra* note 170, paras. 67, 375; *Bagilishema* Appeal Judgement, *supra* note 190, paras. 51–52, 61; *ibid.*, para. 56 ('[T]he case law of the International Tribunals makes it mandatory to use the effective control test for both *de jure* and *de facto* superiors.'); *Kayishema and Ruzindana* Appeal Judgement, *supra* note 210, para. 294; *Čelebići* Appeal Judgement, *supra* note 32, paras. 196, 256, 378; *Muvunyi* Trial Judgement, *supra* note 179, para. 474; *Orić* Trial Judgement, *supra* note 179, paras. 309, 311; *Hadžihasanović and Kubura* Trial Judgement, *supra* note 179, para. 77 ('Tribunal case law has consistently held that a superior-subordinate relationship exists under Article 7(3) of the Statute when a superior exercises effective control over his subordinates, that is, when he has the material ability to prevent or punish their acts.'); *Limaj et al.* Trial Judgement, *supra* note 179, para. 522; *Halilović* Trial Judgement, *supra* note 27, para. 58; *Strugar* Trial Judgement, *supra* note 179, para. 360; *Blagojević and Jokić* Trial Judgement, *supra* note 188, para. 791; *Brđanin* Trial Judgement, *supra* note 179, para. 276; *Ntagerura et al.* Trial Judgement, *supra* note 206, para. 628; *Kamuhanda* Trial Judgement, *supra* note 210, para. 605; *Galić* Trial Judgement, *supra* note 210, para. 173; *Kajelijeli* Trial Judgement, *supra* note 210, para. 773; *Stakić* Trial Judgement, *supra* note 210, para. 459; *Semanza* Trial Judgement, *supra* note 198, para. 402; *Naletilić and Martinović* Trial Judgement, *supra* note 206, paras. 66–67; *Ntakirutimana and Ntakirutimana* Trial Judgement, *supra* note 210, paras. 819–820; *Krnojelac* Trial Judgement, *supra* note 183, para. 93; *Kvočka et al.* Trial Judgement, *supra* note 199, para. 315; *Krstić* Trial Judgement, *supra* note 205, paras. 631, 648–649; *Bagilishema* Trial Judgement, *supra* note 179, paras. 38, 45, 48; *Kordić and Čerkez* Trial Judgement, *supra* note 190, paras. 405–406, 416; *Kunarac et al.* Trial Judgement, *supra* note 206, para. 396; *Blaškić* Trial Judgement, *supra* note 115, para. 302; *Musema* Trial Judgement, *supra* note 184, paras. 135, 148; *Aleksovski* Trial Judgement, *supra* note 180, para. 76; *Kayishema and Ruzindana* Trial Judgement, *supra* note 179, paras. 217, 491.

[220] *Kajelijeli* Appeal Judgement, *supra* note 200, para. 85; *Bagilishema* Appeal Judgement, *supra* note 190, para. 51; *Kayishema and Ruzindana* Appeal Judgement, *supra* note 210, para. 294 ('Kayishema's argument that without *de jure* authority, there can be no subordinate and hence, no *de facto* authority, is misconceived. This question turns on whether the superior had effective control over the persons committing the alleged crimes.'); *Čelebići* Appeal Judgement, *supra* note 32, para. 197; *Hadžihasanović and Kubura* Trial Judgement, *supra* note 179, para. 78 ('The formal title of commander is neither required nor sufficient to entail superior responsibility.'); *Limaj et al.* Trial Judgement, *supra* note 179, para. 522; *Kunarac et al.* Trial Judgement, *supra* note 206, para. 396 ('[F]ormal designation as a commander is not necessary for establishing command responsibility, as such responsibility may be recognised by virtue of a person's *de facto*, as well as *de jure*, position as a commander.'); *Blaškić* Trial Judgement, *supra* note 115, para. 302 ('Although ... "actual ability" of a commander is a relevant

mayor of Mukingo commune in Rwanda for his failure to prevent and punish extermination as a crime against humanity committed by Interahamwe militiamen of the Mukingo and Nkuli communes.[221] Notwithstanding Kajelijeli's lack of *de jure* authority over these men, the Trial Chamber considered him their superior for purposes of Article 6(3) of the ICTR Statute: he enjoyed effective control over the men through, among other factors, his supervision of them and his orders to them.[222] Similarly, the *Čelebići* Trial Chamber found that the accused Mucić had been the *de facto* commander of the Čelebići prison camp during the time period relevant to the indictment.[223] In drawing this conclusion, the Chamber took into account several items of evidence, including the following: camp detainees and journalists who visited the camp testified that Mucić was the camp commander and presented himself as such;[224] the camp's guards and its deputy commander, Hazim Delić, referred to Mucić as their commander and executed his orders;[225] he 'had all the powers of a commander to discipline camp guards and to take every appropriate measure to ensure the maintenance of order';[226] Mucić himself admitted that he enjoyed extensive disciplinary powers, including the authority to confine guards to barracks and to remove them from duty;[227] when he was in the camp there was far greater discipline than when he was absent;[228] he was in a position to assist those detainees who were mistreated;[229] on one occasion guards stopped mistreating two detainees when they heard that he was coming;[230] and he maintained a list of detainees which he divulged to members of the Military Investigative Commission for purposes of classifying the detainees and determining whether they should continue to be detained or be released.[231] 'Concisely stated,' concluded the Chamber, 'everything about

---

criterion, the commander need not have any legal authority to prevent or punish acts of his subordinates. What counts is his material ability.'); *Aleksovski* Trial Judgement, *supra* note 180, para. 76; *Čelebići* Trial Judgement, *supra* note 3, para. 370.

[221] *Kajelijeli* Trial Judgement, *supra* note 210, para. 906.

[222] *Ibid.*, paras. 403–405, 781. Although the Appeals Chamber vacated this finding of guilt, it did so on the ground that the Trial Chamber's conviction of Kajelijeli pursuant to both Articles 6(1) and 6(3) was impermissible, and that Article 6(1) takes precedence over Article 6(3) where the elements of at least one form of responsibility from each provision has been fulfilled. The Appeals Chamber upheld the Trial Chamber's finding that Kajelijeli enjoyed effective control over the Mukingo and Nkuli Interahamwe – and was therefore their *de facto* superior – and that this superior position could be taken into account when determining the harshness of his sentence. *Kajelijeli* Appeal Judgement, *supra* note 200, paras. 83, 91, 325. Chapter 6, text accompanying notes 49–122, discusses concurrent convictions under Articles 7/6(1) and 7/6(3).

[223] *Čelebići* Trial Judgement, *supra* note 3, para. 737.

[224] *Ibid.*, paras. 738, 749–750. One journalist testified that it was Mucić who gave journalists permission to film the prison camp and to interview certain prisoners. *Ibid.*, para. 749.

[225] *Ibid.*, paras. 739, 750, 765–766. The Trial Chamber found that Mucić's behaviour toward the guards was that of a commander, and that this factor was 'the most significant for purposes of ascribing superior authority'. *Ibid.*, para. 750.

[226] *Ibid.*, para. 767. [227] *Ibid.* [228] *Ibid.*, para. 743. [229] *Ibid.*, paras. 740, 746.

[230] *Ibid.*, para. 747. [231] *Ibid.*, para. 748.

Mr. Mucić contained the indicia and hallmark of a *de facto* exercise of authority.'[232]

Second, mere *de jure* authority would seem to be insufficient, without more, to engage an accused's Article 7/6(3) responsibility. Hence, even an accused vested with the legal authority to prevent or punish subordinate criminal conduct would not incur Article 7/6(3) liability if he did not also enjoy the material ability to prevent or punish such conduct. Both *ad hoc* Appeals Chambers have made statements to this effect on a number of occasions,[233] and the principle was clearly articulated by the *Brđanin* and *Blagojević and Jokić* Trial Chambers:

A commander vested with *de jure* authority who does not, in reality, have effective control over his or her subordinates would not incur criminal responsibility pursuant to the doctrine of command responsibility, while a *de facto* commander who lacks formal letters of appointment, superior rank or commission but does, in reality, have effective control over the perpetrators of offences could incur criminal responsibility under the doctrine of command responsibility.[234]

Several chambers have held, in accordance with *Brđanin* and *Blagojević and Jokić*, that an accused's *de jure* authority is just one indicium among the many to be considered in determining whether he had effective control over the alleged subordinate in question.[235] These indicia are discussed in detail below.[236]

Nevertheless, a few judgements suggest that proof of an accused's *de jure* authority may be sufficient in and of itself to demonstrate effective control. Although the Appeals Chamber in *Čelebići* endorsed the Trial Chamber's effective control standard, by which it 'is necessary to look to effective exercise of power or control and not to formal titles',[237] in the same paragraph it appears to have held that proof of *de jure* authority establishes a rebuttable presumption of effective control: '[A] court may presume that possession of

---

[232] *Ibid.*, para. 750.

[233] See, e.g., *Kajelijeli* Appeal Judgement, *supra* note 200, para. 86 (holding that, under the effective control standard, any accused superior 'must have the *material ability* to prevent or punish criminal conduct') (emphasis in original); *Blaškić* Appeal Judgement, *supra* note 170, para. 485 (holding that the mere authority to issue or even the actual issuance of binding orders cannot by itself establish the accused's effective control); *Čelebići* Appeal Judgement, *supra* note 32, para. 197 (holding that '[i]n determining questions of responsibility it is necessary to look to effective exercise of power or control and not to formal titles').

[234] *Blagojević and Jokić* Trial Judgement, *supra* note 188, para. 791 (citing *Čelebići* Appeal Judgement, *supra* note 32, para. 197). *Accord Brđanin* Trial Judgement, *supra* note 179, para. 276 (identical language).

[235] See, e.g., *Blaškić* Appeal Judgement, *supra* note 170, para. 69; *Hadžihasanović* Trial Judgement, *supra* note 179, para. 78 ('The formal title of commander is neither required nor sufficient to entail superior responsibility.'); *Halilović* Trial Judgement, *supra* note 27, para. 58; *Strugar* Trial Judgement, *supra* note 179, para. 392; *Brđanin* Trial Judgement, *supra* note 179, para. 277.

[236] See *infra* text accompanying notes 284–350.   [237] *Čelebići* Appeal Judgement, *supra* note 32, para. 197.

[*de jure*] power *prima facie* results in effective control unless proof to the contrary is produced.'[238] Although the Chamber did not elaborate on or apply this proposition to the facts before it, and the chambers that have repeated the proposition have generally tended to do so merely in the course of quoting *Čelebići*,[239] there are at least three chambers that have actually taken an approach where proof of *de jure* authority establishes a rebuttable presumption of effective control: the August 2001 *Krstić* Trial Judgement;[240] the March 2006 *Hadžihasanović and Kubura* Trial Judgement;[241] and the June 2006 *Orić* Trial Judgement.[242] In addition, the ICTR Trial Chamber in *Muvunyi*, while apparently not applying this principle to the facts before it, restated it in two separate parts of its September 2006 Judgement.[243]

The *Krstić* Trial Chamber found that, because 'there [was] no evidence to rebut the presumption that[,] as Commander of the Drina Corps, General Krstić's *de jure* powers amounted to his effective control over subordinate troops',[244] Krstić was found to have 'exercised effective control over Drina Corps troops involved in the [Srebrenica] killings'.[245] In a similar manner, the *Hadžihasanović and Kubura* Trial Chamber found that the prosecution had proven Enver Hadžihasanović's *de jure* authority over the Mujahedin detachment of the Third Corps of the Bosnian army, and had thereby established a presumption of effective control;[246] because the defence put forth no evidence

---

[238] *Ibid.*

[239] See *Kayishema and Ruzindana* Appeal Judgement, *supra* note 210, para. 294 (quoting *Čelebići* Appeal Judgement, *supra* note 32, para. 197); *Galić* Trial Judgement, *supra* note 210, para. 173; *Kvočka et al.* Trial Judgement, *supra* note 199, para. 315 n. 520; *Kordić and Čerkez* Trial Judgement, *supra* note 190, para. 405. See also *Blagojević and Jokić* Trial Judgement, *supra* note 188, paras. 794–796 (finding that Blagojević had *de jure* authority over his subordinate officer Momir Nikolić, but not shifting the burden of to the defence to disprove that Blagojević had effective control, and ultimately concluding that he did not have such control in spite of his *de jure* authority because he lacked the material ability to prevent Nikolić's commission of crimes in Potočari).

[240] See *Krstić* Trial Judgement, *supra* note 205, para. 648.

[241] See *Hadžihasanović and Kubura* Trial Judgement, *supra* note 179, para. 79 (quoting *Čelebići* Appeal Judgement, *supra* note 32, para. 197); *ibid.*, para. 86 ('The Chamber recalls that, by virtue of his official position, it is assumed that a commander exercises effective control.'); *ibid.*, paras. 845–846 (quoting *Čelebići* Appeal Judgement, *supra* note 32, para. 197 and remarking that '[w]hat must be established is whether the presumption noted in the Appeal Judgement has been reversed in this case by the evidence'.) (quotation from *Hadžihasanović and Kubura* Trial Judgement at para. 846).

[242] See *Orić* Trial Judgement, *supra* note 179, para. 312.

[243] *Muvunyi* Trial Judgement, *supra* note 179, para. 51 (citing *Čelebići* and holding that '[w]here *de jure* authority is proved, a court may presume the existence of effective control on a *prima facie* basis. Such a presumption can, however, be rebutted by showing that the superior had ceased to possess the necessary powers of control over subordinates who actually committed the crimes.'). See also, *ibid.*, para. 475 (repetition of identical language).

[244] *Krstić* Trial Judgement, *supra* note 205, para. 648 n. 1418 (citing *Čelebići* Appeal Judgement, *supra* note 32, para. 197).

[245] *Krstić* Trial Judgement, *supra* note 205, para. 648.

[246] *Hadžihasanović and Kubura* Trial Judgement, *supra* note 179, paras. 843, 846.

to rebut this presumption,[247] the Chamber concluded that Hadžihasanović was indeed the superior of the Mujahedin fighters for purposes of Article 7(3).[248] The *Orić* Trial Chamber found that Naser Orić, the Bosnian Muslim commander of the Srebrenica Armed Forces Staff in 1992 and 1993, had effective control over two successive chiefs of staff of the Armed Forces Staff – Osman Osmanović and Ramiz Bećirović – in the following terms:

> The relationship between a chief of staff and a commander is such that the former reports to the latter, takes orders from him and implements them. In this way, a commander exercises effective control over the chief of staff. There is no evidence that would indicate that the situation was different in the case of Osman Osmanović and Ramiz Bećirović.[249]

In other words, because the defence had failed to put forth convincing evidence proving that this particular commander did not exercise effective control over these chiefs of staff, the Trial Chamber entered a finding of effective control. While none of these three judgements stated the burden of persuasion that the defence must satisfy in order to rebut the presumption of effective control, jurisprudence on other matters that the defence bears the burden of proving suggests that a chamber following this approach would hold that the presumption may be rebutted by proof on 'the balance of probabilities'.[250]

    Orić did not cite the *Čelebići* Appeal Judgement as support for its finding of effective control based on *de jure* authority, and *Hadžihasanović and*

---

[247] *Ibid.*, para. 851 ('Despite the special position this detachment held within the 3rd Corps, however, there is no evidence that might reverse the presumption of effective control formulated by the Appeals Chamber in the *Čelebići* Appeal Judgement.'). The Trial Chamber held that the defence of Hadžihasanović could not rebut the presumption in favour of effective control merely by showing that he would have to have used force in order to control his Mujahedin subordinates. *Ibid.*, para. 1407. See also *ibid.*, para. 86; *ibid.*, para. 1406 (footnote omitted):

> [T]he Chamber recalls that the presumption of the exercise of effective control associated with the *de jure* authority of a commander is not rebutted automatically by the fact that a commander needs to use force to control his troops ... [I]f a commander has the material ability to use force, he is under a duty to do so as a last resort.

[248] *Ibid.*, para. 853.

[249] *Orić* Trial Judgement, *supra* note 179, para. 312. The Trial Chamber did not provide concrete examples of how Orić could have exerted his control over Osmanović and Bećirović. See *infra*, text accompanying notes 609–612, for a more detailed analysis of the Chamber's discussion of Orić's effective control.

[250] See, e.g., *Blaškić* Appeal Judgement, *supra* note 170, para. 697 (holding that, whereas the burden of persuasion placed upon the prosecution for establishing factors aggravating the sentence of an accused is beyond a reasonable doubt, the burden placed upon the defence for establishing mitigating factors is merely proof on the balance of probabilities); *Prosecutor v. Jokić*, Case No. IT-01-42/1-A, Judgement on Sentencing Appeal, 30 August 2005, para. 47 (same); *Prosecutor v. Galić*, Case No. IT-98-29-A, Decision on Second Defence Request for Provisional Release of Stanislav Galić, 31 October 2005, para. 3 (Appeals Chamber holding that whether an accused satisfies the requisite conditions to be granted provisional release 'is to be determined on a balance of probabilities'); *Prosecutor v. Strugar*, Case No. IT-01-42-T, Decision re the Defence Motion to Terminate Proceedings, 26 May 2004, para. 38 (holding that the burden of proving lack of fitness to stand trial is on the defence, 'and the standard of that burden should be merely "the balance of probabilities", and not a higher standard as is required of the prosecution when proving guilt'); *Čelebići* Trial Judgement, *supra* note 3, para. 603 ('Whereas the Prosecution is bound to prove the allegations against the accused beyond a reasonable doubt, the accused is required to prove any issues which he might raise on the balance of probabilities.').

Kubura – which did cite *Čelebići* – did not acknowledge the precedent of *Krstić*, the only previous judgement to have applied this standard to actual facts and shift the burden of proof to the defence to disprove that the accused had effective control. It is also curious that *Krstić, Hadžihasanović and Kubura* and *Muvunyi* seized so readily upon a single statement made almost in passing in one appeal judgement, and not repeated by either *ad hoc* Appeals Chamber since. In effect, these four chambers have carved out an exception to the established rule that the prosecution must prove every element of every charged form of responsibility beyond a reasonable doubt.[251] Under *Krstić, Hadžihasanović and Kubura, Orić* and *Muvunyi*, as long as the prosecution manages to prove beyond a reasonable doubt that the accused held the official post of superior over the person for whose conduct he is to be held responsible, it is absolved of its duty to prove that he also had the material ability to prevent or punish this conduct.[252] Such an approach would appear to violate one of the most fundamental procedural rights of the accused.[253]

A third consequence of the applicability of the effective control standard to both *de jure* and *de facto* superiors is that an accused's influence over the relevant subordinate, no matter how substantial, will not give rise to Article 7/6(3) liability if he did not also exercise effective control over that subordinate.[254] Hence the *Čelebići* Appeals Chamber did not disturb the Trial

---

[251] See *Blaškić* Appeal Judgement, *supra* note 170, para. 484:

> The Appeals Chamber ... recalls that to establish superior responsibility, three elements of that responsibility must be proved beyond reasonable doubt: the existence of a superior-subordinate relationship; the fact that the superior knew or had reason to know that the criminal act was about to be or had been committed; and the fact that the superior failed to take the necessary and reasonable measures to prevent the criminal act or punish the perpetrator thereof.

See also *Kordić and Čerkez* Appeal Judgement, *supra* note 206, para. 700 (upholding the Trial Chamber's finding that the Prosecution had proved beyond reasonable doubt that the accused 'planned, instigated and ordered' crimes in Ahmići); *Bagilishema* Appeal Judgement, *supra* note 190, para. 52 (superior-subordinate relationship requires that it be found beyond reasonable doubt that the accused was able to exercise effective control over his or her subordinates).

[252] The *Hadžihasanović and Kubura* Trial Chamber also held – this time citing no authority whatsoever – that evidence that the accused had knowledge or reason to know that his subordinates were about to commit crimes, and that the accused took no action to stop the crimes' commission, establishes a rebuttable presumption that a causality link exists between the accused's failure to act and such commission. *Hadžihasanović and Kubura* Trial Judgement, *supra* note 179, para. 193. The *Orić* Trial Chamber disapproved of this holding in *Hadžihasanović and Kubura*, remarking that the establishment of such a presumption would be inappropriate. *Orić* Trial Judgement, *supra* note 179, para. 338 n. 999. See *infra*, text accompanying notes 463–465, for a more complete discussion of causality and superior responsibility.

[253] See *Prosecutor* v. *Milošević*, Case No. IT-02-54-AR73.5, Decision on the Prosecution's Interlocutory Appeal against the Trial Chamber's 10 April 2003 Decision on Prosecution Motion for Judicial Notice of Adjudicated Facts, 28 October 2003, Dissenting Opinion of Judge David Hunt, para. 14:

> [I]t is inappropriate to impose rebuttable presumptions of fact in favour of the prosecution which carries the onus of proof in relation to that fact. A basic right of the accused enshrined in the Tribunal's Statute is that he or she is innocent until proven guilty by the prosecution. Proof by way of presumptions of fact ... offends that basic right.

[254] *Čelebići* Appeal Judgement, *supra* note 32, paras. 258, 266; *Orić* Trial Judgement, *supra* note 179, para. 311; *Hadžihasanović and Kubura* Trial Judgement, *supra* note 179, para. 80 ('The simple exercise of powers of influence over subordinates does not suffice.'); *Halilović* Trial Judgement, *supra* note 27, para.

Chamber's finding that the accused Delalić, while highly influential at the Čelebići prison camp and intimately involved in broader efforts to 'defend' the Bosnian state, could not be considered the 'superior' of any of the relevant physical perpetrators because he lacked the material ability to prevent or punish their criminal conduct.[255]

A fourth consequence is that, under the effective control standard, the relationship between the accused and the alleged subordinate need not be formal, permanent, or fixed.[256] An accused can therefore be held responsible pursuant to Article 7/6(3) for the criminal conduct of a person only temporarily under his command, provided the accused exercised effective control over that subordinate at the time the subordinate engaged in the criminal conduct in question.[257]

Finally, Article 7/6(3) liability may ensue on the basis of both direct and indirect relationships of subordination.[258] Provided the other requirements of Article 7/6(3) are met, every person in the chain of command who exercises effective control over a subordinate is responsible for the criminal conduct of that subordinate, no matter how far down the chain the subordinate happens to be.[259] Consequently, more than one superior occupying different positions in the same chain of command may incur responsibility for the same conduct

59 ('"Substantial influence" over subordinates which does not meet the threshold of effective control is not sufficient under customary international law to serve as a means of exercising command responsibility and, therefore, to impose criminal liability.'); *Blagojević and Jokić* Trial Judgement, *supra* note 188, para. 791; *Brđanin* Trial Judgement, *supra* note 179, para. 276; *Kordić and Čerkez* Trial Judgement, *supra* note 190, para. 412.

255 See *Čelebići* Appeal Judgement, *supra* note 32, paras. 267–268 (upholding *Čelebići* Trial Judgement, *supra* note 3, para. 658). Accord *Halilović* Trial Judgement, *supra* note 27, para. 752 (footnotes omitted):

The Trial Chamber recalls its finding that Sefer Halilović possessed a degree of influence as a high ranking member of the [Army of Bosnia and Herzegovina] and as one of its founders. However, the Trial Chamber considers that Sefer Halilović's influence falls short of the standard required to establish effective control.

256 *Čelebići* Appeal Judgement, *supra* note 32, para. 193; *Orić* Trial Judgement, *supra* note 179, para. 310; *Limaj et al.* Trial Judgement, *supra* note 179, para. 522; *Strugar* Trial Judgement, *supra* note 179, para. 362; *Blagojević and Jokić* Trial Judgement, *supra* note 188, para. 791; *Brđanin* Trial Judgement, *supra* note 179, para. 276; *Kunarac et al.* Trial Judgement, *supra* note 206, para. 399.

257 *Orić* Trial Judgement, *supra* note 179, para. 310 ('[T]he mere *ad hoc* or temporary nature of a military unit or an armed group does not *per se* exclude a relationship of subordination between the member of the unit or group and its commander or leader.'); *Halilović* Trial Judgement, *supra* note 27, para. 61 ('To hold a commander liable for the acts of troops who operated under his command on a temporary basis it must be shown that[,] at the time when the acts charged in the indictment were committed, these troops were under the effective control of that commander.'); *Kunarac et al.* Trial Judgement, *supra* note 206, para. 399. See also *infra*, text accompanying notes 527–532, for a discussion of the jurisprudence holding that an accused cannot bear superior responsibility for conduct engaged in by subordinates before he acquired his status as their superior.

258 *Čelebići* Appeal Judgement, *supra* note 32, para. 303; *Orić* Trial Judgement, *supra* note 179, para. 310; *Limaj et al.* Trial Judgement, *supra* note 179, para. 522.

259 *Blaškić* Appeal Judgement, *supra* note 170, para. 67; *Čelebići* Appeal Judgement, *supra* note 32, para. 252; *Strugar* Trial Judgement, *supra* note 179, paras. 362, 366 ('[T]here is no legal requirement that the superior-subordinate relationship be a direct or immediate one for a superior to be found liable for a crime committed by a subordinate, provided that the former had effective control over the acts of the latter.'); *Blagojević and Jokić* Trial Judgement, *supra* note 188, para. 791; *Brđanin* Trial Judgement, *supra* note 179, para. 276; *Kajelijeli* Trial Judgement, *supra* note 210, para. 771; *Semanza* Trial Judgement, *supra* note 198, para. 440; *Kordić and Čerkez* Trial Judgement, *supra* note 190, para. 416; *Blaškić* Trial Judgement, *supra* note 115, para. 300.

of mutual subordinates, as long as each superior exercised effective control over those subordinates.[260] Moreover, a superior can be held responsible not only for the conduct of his own immediate subordinates, but also for the conduct of subordinates of subordinates, as long as he wields effective control over such persons.[261] Thus, the *Kordić and Čerkez* Appeals Chamber determined that the Trial Chamber did not err in law when it held that, if the facts were to demonstrate that Čerkez had effective control over the relevant subordinates, as Commander of the Viteška Brigade of the Croatian Defence Council he could be held responsible for the crimes of all Brigade members operating in his 'area of responsibility'.[262] In cases involving the superior responsibility of high-level political accused, it is therefore conceivable that liability might attach to individuals at several different levels of the political and military or paramilitary structures for the conduct of subordinates further down the chain of command.

As discussed above,[263] the chambers of the *ad hoc* Tribunals have consistently held that Article 7/6(3) applies both to military commanders and civilian superiors.[264] In the words of the Appeals Chamber in *Bagilishema*, '[t]he

---

[260] *Orić* Trial Judgement, *supra* note 179, para. 313; *Limaj et al.* Trial Judgement, *supra* note 179, para. 522; *Halilović* Trial Judgement, *supra* note 27, para. 62; *Kunarac et al.* Trial Judgement, *supra* note 206, para. 398; *Blaškić* Trial Judgement, *supra* note 115, para. 303; *Aleksovski* Trial Judgement, *supra* note 180, para. 106.

[261] *Halilović* Trial Judgement, *supra* note 27, para. 63 ('What is required is the establishment of the superior's effective control over the subordinate, whether that subordinate is immediately answerable to that superior or more remotely under his command.'); *Strugar* Trial Judgement, *supra* note 179, para. 363 (identical language).

[262] *Kordić and Čerkez* Appeal Judgement, *supra* note 206, paras. 828–829 (upholding *Kordić and Čerkez* Trial Judgement, *supra* note 190, para. 801).

[263] See *supra* text accompanying notes 200–203.

[264] *Kajelijeli* Appeal Judgement, *supra* note 200, para. 85; *Blaškić* Appeal Judgement, *supra* note 170, para. 69; *Bagilishema* Appeal Judgement, *supra* note 190, paras. 50–52; *ibid.*, para. 51 ('[I]t emerges from international case-law that the doctrine of superior responsibility is not limited to military superiors, but also extends to civilian superiors.'); *Čelebići* Appeal Judgement, *supra* note 32, paras. 195–197, 240; *Aleksovski* Appeal Judgement, *supra* note 200, para. 76; *Orić* Trial Judgement, *supra* note 179, para. 308 ('[T]he scope of Article 7(3) of the Statute extends beyond classical "command responsibility" to a truly "superior criminal responsibility", and does not only include military commanders within its scope of liability, but also political leaders and other civilian superiors in possession of authority.'); *Brđanin* Trial Judgement, *supra* note 179, paras. 281–283; *ibid.*, para. 275 (invoking Article 86(2) of Additional Protocol I); *Stakić* Trial Judgement, *supra* note 210, para. 446; *Nahimana et al.* Trial Judgement, *supra* note 184, paras. 976–977; *Krnojelac* Trial Judgement, *supra* note 183, para. 94; *Kvočka et al.* Trial Judgement, *supra* note 199, para. 315; *Bagilishema* Trial Judgement, *supra* note 179, para. 40; *Kordić and Čerkez* Trial Judgement, *supra* note 190, paras. 416, 446; *Blaškić* Trial Judgement, *supra* note 115, para. 300; *Musema* Trial Judgement, *supra* note 184, para. 148; *Aleksovski* Trial Judgement, *supra* note 180, para. 75; *Kayishema and Ruzindana* Trial Judgement, *supra* note 179, para. 216; *Čelebići* Trial Judgement, *supra* note 3, paras. 357–358 (discussing the cases of *Hirota* and *Tojo and Shigemitsu*, in which the Tokyo Tribunal found several civilian accused guilty pursuant to the doctrine of superior responsibility); *ibid.*, paras. 356–360 (discussing the *Flick* case, *supra* note 59, in which a US military tribunal convicted an industrialist pursuant to Control Council Law No. 10, ostensibly via the doctrine of superior responsibility); *ibid.*, para. 363 ('[I]t must be concluded that the applicability of the principle of superior responsibility in Article 7(3) extends not only to military commanders but also to individuals in non-military positions of superior authority.'); *ibid.*, paras. 363, 387; *ibid.*, para. 356:

effective control test applies to all superiors, whether *de jure* or *de facto*, military or civilian'.[265] Therefore, while both the *Kordić and Čerkez* and *Kvočka* Trial Chambers accepted that civilians could bear liability under Article 7(3),[266] neither Chamber convicted its respective civilian accused on that theory because each found that the prosecution had failed to prove that those accused exercised effective control over the relevant subordinates.[267] Trial Chambers of the ICTR convicted several civilian leaders – including Kambanda, the former prime minister of Rwanda,[268] Musema, the director of a tea factory,[269] Kajelijeli, the former mayor of Mukingo commune in Rwanda,[270] and Kayishema, a civilian administrator[271] – under Article 6(3) of the ICTR Statute after finding that they exercised effective control over the respective individuals who committed the crimes for which they were charged.

The control exercised by a civilian superior need not be of the same nature as that exercised by a military commander.[272] Moreover, while a civilian superior's influence in the community and among the subordinates in question may be a relevant factor for a chamber to consider in determining whether the superior exercised effective control, mere influence alone – no matter how substantial – will not suffice to engage the superior's liability under Article 7/6(3).[273] Nonetheless, considering that civilian superiors cannot be expected to possess disciplinary powers equivalent to those of military leaders in

---

[T]he use of the generic term 'superior' in Article 7(3), together with its juxtaposition to the affirmation of the individual criminal responsibility of 'Head[s] of State or Government' or 'responsible Government official[s]' in Article 7(2), clearly indicates that its applicability extends beyond the responsibility of military commanders to also encompass political leaders and other civilian superiors in positions of authority.

[265] *Bagilishema* Appeal Judgement, *supra* note 190, para. 50 (emphasis in original). Accord *Čelebići* Appeal Judgement, *supra* note 32, para. 196 ('[T]he Appeals Chamber does not consider that the rule is controversial that civilian leaders may incur responsibility in relation to acts committed by their subordinates or other persons *under their effective control*.'); *Stakić* Trial Judgement, *supra* note 210, para. 446; *Kordić and Čerkez* Trial Judgement, *supra* note 190, paras. 415, 446 ('Civilian superiors would be under similar obligations [as military superiors regarding the duty to prevent or punish], depending upon the effective powers exercised and whether they include an ability to require the competent authorities to take action.'); *Aleksovski* Trial Judgement, *supra* note 180, para. 76.

[266] See *Kvočka et al.* Trial Judgement, *supra* note 199, para. 315; *Kordić and Čerkez* Trial Judgement, *supra* note 190, para. 416, 446.

[267] See *Kvočka et al.* Trial Judgement, *supra* note 199, paras. 411 (accused Kvočka); *ibid.*, para. 502 (accused Kos); *ibid.*, para. 570 (accused Radić); *Kordić and Čerkez* Trial Judgement, *supra* note 190, paras. 840–841 (accused Kordić).

[268] *Kambanda* Trial Judgement, *supra* note 184, para. 40.

[269] *Musema* Trial Judgement, *supra* note 184, paras. 900, 906, 915, 920, 925.

[270] *Kajelijeli* Trial Judgement, *supra* note 210, paras. 781, 906.

[271] *Kayishema and Ruzindana* Appeal Judgement, *supra* note 210, para. 304 (upholding Trial Chamber's conviction).

[272] *Kajelijeli* Appeal Judgement, *supra* note 200, para. 87; *Bagilishema* Appeal Judgement, *supra* note 190, para. 55 (overruling *Bagilishema* Trial Judgement, *supra* note 179, para. 42, and implicitly overruling *Čelebići* Trial Judgement, *supra* note 3, para. 378, which held that the doctrine of superior responsibility extends to civilians insofar as they 'exercise a degree of control over their subordinates which is similar to that of military commanders').

[273] *Brđanin* Trial Judgement, *supra* note 179, paras. 276, 281; *Stakić* Trial Judgement, *supra* note 210, para. 459; *Kordić and Čerkez* Trial Judgement, *supra* note 190, para. 415. See also *supra* text accompanying notes 254–255, for a discussion of the jurisprudence on substantial influence and effective control.

analogous positions of command, the *Aleksovski* and *Brđanin* Trial Chambers suggested that it may be easier for the prosecution to prove that a civilian superior had effective control where he had 'the duty to report whenever crimes are committed'.[274] While it would certainly seem appropriate not to require that a civilian superior exercised disciplinary powers of the same degree or quality as those of military commanders, however, a finding of effective control based merely on the duty to report crimes may be too expansive, as it may allow a chamber to find the existence of a superior-subordinate relationship between any common policeman or other officer of the law with such a duty on the one hand, and any civilian wrongdoer on the other.

Invoking language from the *Čelebići* Trial Judgement that a *de facto* superior must enjoy the 'trappings of the exercise of *de jure* authority',[275] the *Bagilishema* Trial Chamber held that, for a *de facto* civilian superior to be held responsible under Article 6(3) of the ICTR, his exercise of authority must have been characterised by such trappings.[276] The Chamber then provided an illustrative list: awareness, presumably between the accused superior and the relevant subordinate, of a chain of command; the practice of issuing and obeying orders; and the expectation that insubordination may lead to disciplinary action.[277] 'It is by these trappings,' the Chamber opined, 'that the law distinguishes civilian superiors from mere rabble-rousers or other persons of influence.'[278] Notwithstanding this rationale, no judgement of the ICTY subsequent to the *Čelebići* Trial Judgement makes any mention of 'trappings'; the *Bagilishema* Appeals Chamber overruled the Trial Chamber's holding as 'erroneous in law';[279] and the *Kajelijeli* Appeals Chamber explicitly held that 'there is no requirement of a finding that a *de facto* civilian superior exercised the trappings of *de jure* authority generally'.[280] The *Kajelijeli* Appeals Chamber added, however, that evidence of a *de facto* civilian superior exercising control in a military fashion, or in a form similar to that of *de jure* authorities, militates in favour of a finding that he had effective control over the alleged subordinate in question.[281]

---

[274] *Brđanin* Trial Judgement, *supra* note 179, para. 281. See also *Aleksovski* Trial Judgement, *supra* note 180, para. 78.
[275] *Čelebići* Trial Judgement, *supra* note 3, para. 646.
[276] *Bagilishema* Trial Judgement, *supra* note 179, para. 43.   [277] *Ibid.*   [278] *Ibid.*
[279] *Bagilishema* Appeal Judgement, *supra* note 190, para. 55 (footnote omitted):

The Appeals Chamber holds the view that the Trial Chamber's approach to the notion of 'effective control' in relation to civilian superior was erroneous in law, to the extent that it suggested that the control exercised by a civilian superior must be of the same nature as that exercised by a military commander. As the Appeals Chamber has already stated, this is not the case. It is sufficient that, for one reason or another, the accused exercises the required 'degree' of control over his subordinates, namely, that of effective control.

[280] *Kajelijeli* Appeal Judgement, *supra* note 200, para. 87. *Accord Orić* Trial Judgement, *supra* note 179, para. 312.
[281] *Kajelijeli* Appeal Judgement, *supra* note 200, para. 87.

Relying on ICTY jurisprudence on the form of the indictment and rejecting a defence contention to the contrary, the Trial Chamber in *Orić* held that proof of a superior-subordinate relationship does not require the prosecution to establish the identity of the physical perpetrators of the crime in question, 'particularly not by name', or that the accused had knowledge of the number or identity of 'possible intermediaries', 'provided that it is at least established that the individuals who are responsible for commission of the crimes were within a unit or a group under the control of the superior'.[282] This holding permitted the Chamber to convict the accused of murder and cruel treatment as violations of the laws or customs of war for his failure to prevent the Srebrenica military police – most of the members of which were not identified by the Chamber – from allowing physical perpetrators, whose identity was largely unknown to the accused, to mistreat and kill Bosnian Serb detainees in Srebrenica.[283]

The *Stakić*, *Brđanin* and *Orić* Trial Chambers emphasised that a chamber must take into account the 'cumulative effect' of an accused's various functions when assessing effective control.[284] The analysis of whether an accused exercised effective control over his alleged subordinates depends heavily on the facts of the particular case;[285] as held by the Trial Chamber in *Musema* and endorsed by the Appeals Chamber, 'it is appropriate to assess on a case-by-case basis the power or authority actually devolved on an accused'.[286] Ostensibly for this reason, no chamber has attempted to propound an exhaustive list of factors to be considered when determining whether an accused had the material ability to prevent or punish the criminal conduct of his alleged subordinates, although the *Halilović* Trial Chamber gave some examples of what such factors might include: 'the official position held by the accused, his

---

[282] *Orić* Trial Judgement, *supra* note 179, para. 311 (citing *Prosecutor* v. *Krnojelac*, Case No. IT-97-25-PT, Decision on the Defence Preliminary Motion on the Form of the Indictment, 24 February 1999, para. 46, which held that an indictment need only identify the subordinates of an accused superior by reference to their category or group).

[283] See *Orić* Trial Judgement, *supra* note 179, paras. 480, 481, 532, 578, 782. See also *infra*, text accompanying notes 599–619, for a detailed discussion of this finding of responsibility.

[284] *Orić* Trial Judgement, *supra* note 179, para. 313 (indicating in particular the need to assess the power actually devolved on an accused where he 'has functioned as a member of a collegiate body with authority shared among various members'); *Brđanin* Trial Judgement, *supra* note 179, para. 277; *Stakić* Trial Judgement, *supra* note 210, para. 494.

[285] See *Blaškić* Appeal Judgement, *supra* note 170, para. 69 (holding that '[t]he indicators of effective control are more a matter of evidence than of substantive law'); *Aleksovski* Appeal Judgement, *supra* note 200, paras. 73–74; *Čelebići* Appeal Judgement, *supra* note 32, para. 206; *Halilović* Trial Judgement, *supra* note 27, para. 58; *Strugar* Trial Judgement, *supra* note 179, para. 366 ('As to whether the superior has the requisite level of control, the Chamber considers that this is a matter which must be determined on the basis of the evidence presented in each case.').

[286] *Musema* Trial Judgement, *supra* note 184, para. 135. Accord *Bagilishema* Appeal Judgement, *supra* note 190, para. 51; *Orić* Trial Judgement, *supra* note 179, para. 312; *Halilović* Trial Judgement, *supra* note 27, para. 63 ('As to whether the superior has the requisite level of control, this is a matter which must be determined on the basis of the evidence presented in each case.'); *Brđanin* Trial Judgement, *supra* note 179, para. 277; *Stakić* Trial Judgement, *supra* note 210, para. 494.

capacity to issue orders, whether *de jure* or *de facto*, the procedure for [his] appointment, the position of the accused within the military or political structure and the actual tasks that he performed'.[287]

Furthermore, the factual findings in a number of judgements point to several indicia that may, in the circumstances, reveal the existence of effective control. *De jure* authority to issue legally binding orders is one of the most relevant factors in an effective control analysis,[288] and the absence of such authority is a significant indicator that the accused lacked effective control.[289] The *Kordić and Čerkez* Trial Chamber accordingly found that the accused Čerkez was not responsible under Article 7(3) for the crimes of the Vitezovi, a special-purpose unit of the Croatian Defence Council, because Darko Kraljević – and not Čerkez – had authority to issue orders to the Vitezovi.[290] Moreover, although the ICTY Appeals Chamber has held that the issuance of binding orders cannot by itself establish an accused's effective control,[291] by endorsing and applying the principle that proof of *de jure* authority establishes a rebuttable presumption in favour of effective control, the Trial Chambers in *Krstić* and *Hadžihasanović and Kubura* suggested that such authority may be the most important indicium in an effective control analysis.[292] That the accused's orders were usually followed by his subordinates militates in favour of a finding of effective control.[293]

The promotion in rank of the accused for successfully directing and commanding his subordinates likewise tends to support a finding of effective control.[294] The *Strugar* Trial Chamber found that the accused's 'extraordinary promotion' to lieutenant-general by the Yugoslav Presidency in November 1991 was indicative of his material ability to prevent or punish the criminal conduct of the troops

---

[287] *Halilović* Trial Judgement, *supra* note 27, para. 58. See also *Hadžihasanović and Kubura* Trial Judgement, *supra* note 179, para. 83 (footnotes removed):

Tribunal case law has identified several elements which make it possible to establish whether there is effective control, including: the official position of an accused, even if 'actual authority, however, will not be determined by looking at formal positions only'; the power to give orders and have them executed; the conduct of combat operations involving the forces in question; the authority to apply disciplinary measures; the authority to promote or remove soldiers, and the participation of the Accused in negotiations regarding the troops in question.

[288] See *Blaškić* Appeal Judgement, *supra* note 170, para. 485; *Orić* Trial Judgement, *supra* note 179, para. 309 ('[F]ormal appointment within a hierarchical structure of command may still prove to be the best basis for incurring individual criminal responsibility as a superior[.]'); *Hadžihasanović and Kubura* Trial Judgement, *supra* note 179, para. 83.

[289] See *Kordić and Čerkez* Appeal Judgement, *supra* note 206, paras. 847, 913.

[290] *Kordić and Čerkez* Trial Judgement, *supra* note 190, para. 597. See also *Kordić and Čerkez* Appeal Judgement, *supra* note 206, paras. 847, 913 (upholding Trial Chamber's findings).

[291] See *Blaškić* Appeal Judgement, *supra* note 170, para. 485.

[292] See *Hadžihasanović and Kubura* Trial Judgement, *supra* note 179, paras. 79, 86, 843–846, 851, 853; *Krstić* Trial Judgement, *supra* note 205, para. 648. Accord *Čelebići* Appeal Judgement, *supra* note 32, para. 197. See also *supra* text accompanying notes 237–251, for a discussion of this proposition and the findings in *Hadžihasanović and Kubura* and *Krstić*.

[293] See *Blaškić* Appeal Judgement, *supra* note 170, para. 69.

[294] See *Strugar* Trial Judgement, *supra* note 179, para. 401.

under his command.[295] Frequent changes of command, by contrast, probably
militate against a finding of effective control if the evidence indicates that such
changes 'had [a] significant effect in practice on the effectiveness of the [a]ccused's
command of, and authority over,' the relevant subordinates.[296]

The *Strugar* Trial Chamber found that the accused exercised effective control over his military subordinates because he had the material ability both to
prevent their 6 December 1991 shelling of the Old Town of Dubrovnik and to
punish them afterwards.[297] When determining that the accused had the material ability to prevent the shelling,[298] the Chamber regarded the following facts
as relevant: as commander of the Second Operational Group (2 OG) of the
Yugoslav Army (JNA), he had the *de jure* authority to give direct combat
orders – including ceasefire orders – not only to the units under his immediate
command, but also to units under his command at lower levels; as representative of the JNA in negotiations with the European Community Monitoring
Mission and the Crisis Staff of Dubrovnik, he had the *de jure* authority to
guarantee an absolute ceasefire in respect of all JNA units;[299] and he had in the
past issued ceasefire orders which were generally heeded by his subordinates,
including as recently as November 1991.[300]

When determining that Strugar had the material ability to punish his subordinates for shelling the Old Town,[301] the Trial Chamber took into account
the following facts: as commander of the 2 OG, he had the *de jure* authority to
issue disciplinary orders and instructions to its units, including the unit
responsible for shelling the Old Town;[302] he had the *de jure* authority to
remove subordinate commanders from duty, even during combat operations;[303] he had the *de jure* authority to seek an increase in the number of
military police assigned to the 2 OG for purposes of aiding with the apprehen-
sion and discipline of offenders;[304] he had the obligation to ensure that any
information regarding a criminal offence committed by a subordinate – even a
subordinate several levels down on the chain of command – reached the
military police, so that the military police could inform the prosecuting authorities, and the unavailability of the military court in Split did not exonerate him
from this legal duty;[305] and criminal proceedings had in fact been initiated in
military courts against soldiers from the 2 OG for offences committed before 6
December 1991, including murder, looting and arson.[306]

Despite the rather heavy reliance of these factors on Strugar's *de jure* powers as
opposed to his actual material ability, the Trial Chamber ultimately concluded

[295] See *ibid.*   [296] *Ibid.*   [297] *Ibid.*, para. 414.   [298] *Ibid.*, paras. 405, 414.
[299] *Ibid.*, paras. 395–396, 398.   [300] *Ibid.*, para. 396.   [301] *Ibid.*, paras. 414, 446.   [302] *Ibid.*, para. 406.
[303] *Ibid.*, para. 412.   [304] *Ibid.*, para. 407.   [305] *Ibid.*, paras. 408–409.   [306] *Ibid.*, para. 410.

that the accused 'had effective control over the perpetrators of the unlawful attack on the Old Town' because he had the 'legal authority and material ability' to do the following: (1) to issue orders prohibiting the attack; (2) to take measures to secure compliance with such orders; (3) to immediately terminate an existing attack; (4) to initiate an effective investigation into the events after they had occurred; and (5) to initiate or take administrative and disciplinary action against the officers responsible for the shelling.[307] After finding that the other requirements for superior responsibility under Article 7(3) of the ICTY Statute had been satisfied, the Chamber convicted Strugar for his failure to prevent and punish attacks on civilians and destruction or wilful damage done to historic monuments, both as violations of the laws or customs of war.[308]

In contrast, the *Brđanin* Trial Chamber dismissed superior responsibility in respect of Brđanin because, in the Chamber's estimation, he lacked effective control over any of the persons alleged in the indictment to have committed the crimes for which he was charged.[309] Notwithstanding the 'great influence' he wielded over the army as president of the Crisis Staff of the Autonomous Region of Krajina, the Trial Chamber found that Brđanin did not have effective control over members of the army because he, as a civilian politician, had no material ability to prevent or punish their criminal conduct.[310] Moreover, although the accused had the *de facto* authority to issue some instructions to the police, and in spite of an *ad hoc* authorisation given to him by Bosnian Serb President Radovan Karadžić to dismiss security chief Stojan Župljanin, Brđanin lacked both the *de jure* authority and the material ability to prevent and punish the commission of crimes by common policemen, because he was not an official of the Serbian Ministry of Internal Affairs.[311]

The *Blagojević and Jokić* Trial Chamber likewise dismissed superior responsibility in respect of the accused Blagojević, the colonel in charge of the Bratunac Brigade of the Bosnian Serb army, in part because it found that he did not exercise control over Momir Nikolić, a captain in the Brigade. Although Blagojević enjoyed *de jure* authority over Nikolić in the military hierarchy, he lacked the material ability to prevent Nikolić's commission of offences in Potočari, and 'it is unlikely that he would have had the support of his superiors' – including General Ratko Mladić – if he had attempted to punish Nikolić or other subordinates.[312]

---

[307] *Ibid.*, para. 414. [308] *Ibid.*, para. 478. [309] *Brđanin* Trial Judgement, *supra* note 179, para. 377.
[310] *Ibid.*, para. 372. For the same reason the Trial Chamber found that the accused lacked effective control over members of Serb paramilitary groups alleged to have been his subordinates. *Ibid.*, para. 373.
[311] *Ibid.*, paras. 374–375.
[312] See *Blagojević and Jokić* Trial Judgement, *supra* note 188, para. 795. Cf. *Prosecutor* v. *Krstić*, Case No. IT-98-33-A, Judgement, 19 April 2004, para. 143 n. 250 (approving of the *Krstić* Trial Chamber's decision to enter finding of guilt under Article 7(1) instead of Article 7(3) in part because 'although General Krstić could have tried to punish his subordinates for their participation in facilitating the executions [at Srebrenica], it is unlikely that he would have had the support of his superiors in doing so'.).

In assessing whether the accused Kayishema, the prefect of Kibuye, enjoyed effective control over the *gendarmes* and the Interahamwe militiamen operating in his prefecture, the *Kayishema and Ruzindana* Trial Chamber considered a number of factors: Rwandan legislative provisions gave Kayishema *de jure* authority over the mayors, the communal police and the *gendarmerie* in his prefecture;[313] the accused's own actions showed that the mayors were subordinated to his authority;[314] he was well respected in the community, and the mayors valued his intervention in situations of unrest in their communes;[315] he transported or led many of the Interahamwe and *gendarme* assailants to massacre sites,[316] including most notoriously to the Kibuye Stadium;[317] he instructed and rewarded Interahamwe militiamen for their success on the 'battlefield';[318] he directed many of the Interahamwe's attacks in Kibuye, including the attack on Tutsi refugees in the cave at Bisesero and on Karongi Hill;[319] and he ordered the attack on the crowd gathered at the Kibuye Stadium and this order was carried out.[320]

The *Kajelijeli* Trial Chamber similarly found that Kajelijeli, the mayor of Mukingo commune, exercised effective control over the Interahamwe militiamen whose crimes he had been charged with failing to prevent and punish,[321] taking into consideration facts such as the following: Interahamwe assailants from the Nkuli and Mukingo communes reported back to the accused daily on what they had achieved;[322] the accused procured weapons for the Interahamwe to use during the massacres, including the massacre at the Ruhengeri Court of Appeal;[323] he transported armed Interahamwe assailants to killing sites, including to the Ruhengeri Court of Appeal;[324] he instructed the Interahamwe to kill and exterminate Tutsis;[325] and he bought beers for Interahamwe militiamen and told them he hoped they had not spared anyone.[326] The respective findings of the *Kayishema and Ruzindana* and *Kajelijeli* Trial Chambers, which were subsequently endorsed by the ICTR Appeals Chamber,[327] suggest that *de jure* authority, prestige in the community and especially among the relevant subordinates, and personal involvement in the form of orders and assistance to the physical perpetrators are all important factors in determining whether an accused exercised effective control.

---

[313] *Kayishema and Ruzindana* Trial Judgement, *supra* note 179, paras. 480–483.
[314] *Ibid.*, para. 488. For example, Kayishema once commanded the mayors to disregard a letter from the Minister of the Interior. *Ibid.*
[315] *Ibid.*, para. 499.   [316] *Ibid.*, para. 501.   [317] *Ibid.*, para. 503.   [318] *Ibid.*, para. 501.   [319] *Ibid.*
[320] *Ibid.*, para. 503.   [321] *Kajelijeli* Trial Judgement, *supra* note 210, para. 740.   [322] *Ibid.*, para. 739.
[323] *Ibid.*   [324] *Ibid.*   [325] *Ibid.*   [326] *Ibid.* See also *ibid.*, paras. 531, 559, 597, 625.
[327] See *Kayishema and Ruzindana* Appeal Judgement, *supra* note 210, para. 299; *Kajelijeli* Appeal Judgement, *supra* note 200, paras. 90–91.

The following list summarises the indicia that chambers have taken into account as supporting a finding of effective control:

1. *De jure* authority to issue orders binding on the alleged subordinates.[328]
2. *De jure* authority to guarantee to other parties to the conflict or neutral observers that one's subordinates will respect a ceasefire.[329]
3. *De jure* or *de facto* authority to order that disciplinary or other measures be taken against the alleged subordinates.[330]
4. *De jure* or *de facto* authority to detain the alleged subordinates or to release them from detention.[331]
5. *De jure* authority to remove subordinate commanders from duty, especially if such authority exists even during combat operations.[332]
6. A *de jure* obligation to ensure that investigations are undertaken with a view toward prosecution of those subordinates who have violated the law.[333]
7. Influence or respect in the community, and especially among the alleged subordinates.[334]
8. That the accused's orders were usually followed by the alleged subordinates.[335]
9. That there was far greater discipline among the accused's alleged subordinates when he was present than when he was absent.[336]
10. That the accused's alleged subordinates ceased unlawful activity when they suspected that the accused might soon be in the vicinity.[337]
11. That the accused's alleged subordinates referred to him as their commander.[338]
12. That the accused's behaviour toward his subordinates was that of a commander.[339]
13. That the accused held himself out as the commander of the alleged subordinates.[340]
14. That the alleged subordinates reported back to the accused on a regular basis on what they had achieved.[341]
15. That criminal investigations and/or prosecutions had in fact been initiated against the accused's subordinates in the past.[342]
16. The promotion in rank of the accused for successfully directing and commanding the alleged subordinates.[343]

---

[328] *See* Blaškić Appeal Judgement, *supra* note 170, para. 485; *Orić* Trial Judgement, *supra* note 179, para. 312; *Strugar* Trial Judgement, *supra* note 179, paras. 395–396, 414.
[329] See *Strugar* Trial Judgement, *supra* note 179, paras. 398, 414; *Hadžihasanović and Kubura* Trial Judgement, *supra* note 179, para. 83.
[330] See *Orić* Trial Judgement, *supra* note 179, para. 312; *Strugar* Trial Judgement, *supra* note 179, paras. 408–409, 414; *Čelebići* Trial Judgement, *supra* note 3, para. 767.
[331] *Hadžihasanović and Kubura* Trial Judgement, *supra* note 179, para. 83; *Čelebići* Trial Judgement, *supra* note 3, para. 767.
[332] See *Strugar* Trial Judgement, *supra* note 179, para. 412. [333] *Ibid.*, para. 414. [334] See *ibid.*
[335] See *Blaškić* Appeal Judgement, *supra* note 170, para. 69; *Orić* Trial Judgement, *supra* note 179, para. 312; *Strugar* Trial Judgement, *supra* note 179, para. 396; *Kayishema and Ruzindana* Trial Judgement, *supra* note 179, para. 503; *Čelebići* Trial Judgement, *supra* note 3, para. 739.
[336] *Orić* Trial Judgement, *supra* note 179, para. 312; *Čelebići* Trial Judgement, *supra* note 3, para. 743.
[337] *Čelebići* Trial Judgement, *supra* note 3, para. 747. [338] *Ibid.*, paras. 739, 750, 765–766.
[339] *Ibid.*, para. 750. The *Čelebići* Trial Chamber held that this factor was 'the most significant for purposes of ascribing superior authority'. *Ibid.*
[340] *Ibid.*, paras. 749–750.
[341] *Kajelijeli* Trial Judgement, *supra* note 210, para. 739. Accord *Kajelijeli* Appeal Judgement, *supra* note 200, paras. 90–91.
[342] See *Strugar* Trial Judgement, *supra* note 179, para. 410. [343] See *ibid.*, para. 401.

17. Orders to the alleged subordinates to undertake an unlawful campaign, or instructions on how to do so.[344]
18. Practical assistance to the alleged subordinates in the commission of crimes, including the provision of weapons and transportation.[345]
19. Rewarding the alleged subordinates for their actions in an unlawful campaign.[346]
20. For a *de facto* and/or civilian superior, evidence that he exercised control in a military fashion or in a form similar to that of *de jure* authorities.[347]

Chambers have considered the following factors as militating against a finding of effective control:

1. A lack of *de jure* authority to issue orders binding on the alleged subordinates.[348]
2. The unlikelihood that the superior would have had the support of his own superiors if he had attempted to initiate disciplinary measures against the alleged subordinates.[349]
3. Frequent changes of command.[350]

3.2.1.2 *The accused knew or had reason to know that the criminal conduct in question was about to be, was being, or had been realised by one or more subordinates*

The second of the three essential elements of superior responsibility is the only one dealing with the accused's state of mind.[351] To establish either the failure to prevent or the failure to punish, the prosecution must prove that the accused

---

[344] See *Kajelijeli* Trial Judgement, *supra* note 210, paras. 739–740; *Kayishema and Ruzindana* Trial Judgement, *supra* note 179, paras. 501, 503. The issuance of orders is just one factor to be considered, and liability can, of course, ensue under Article 7/6(3) in the absence of an order by the accused to the alleged subordinate. *Prosecutor* v. *Naletilić and Martinović*, Case No. IT-98-34-A, Judgement, 3 May 2006 ('*Naletilić and Martinović* Appeal Judgement'), para. 331 ('There is no requirement that the superior "order" the commission of the act.').

[345] *Kajelijeli* Trial Judgement, *supra* note 210, paras. 531, 559, 597, 625, 739; *Kayishema and Ruzindana* Trial Judgement, *supra* note 179, para. 501.

[346] See *ibid.*, para. 501.   [347] *Kajelijeli* Appeal Judgement, *supra* note 200, para. 87.

[348] See *Kordić and Čerkez* Appeal Judgement, *supra* note 206, paras. 847, 913; *Brđanin* Trial Judgement, *supra* note 179, paras. 374–375.

[349] See *Blagojević and Jokić* Trial Judgement, *supra* note 188, para. 795. Although this factor was relevant to the Trial Chamber's conclusion that Blagojević did not exercise effective control over one alleged subordinate, it does not appear to have had broader application.

[350] *Strugar* Trial Judgement, *supra* note 179, para. 401.

[351] But see *Orić* Trial Judgement, *supra* note 179, para. 316 (setting forth an additional mental element but citing no authority):

The basic mental requirement for superior criminal responsibility, although neither explicitly set forth in the Statute nor discussed to any significant extent in the case law of the Tribunal, is first of all that a superior be aware of his own position of authority, i.e., that he or she has effective control, under the specific circumstances, over the subordinates who committed or were about to commit the relevant crimes.

See also, *ibid.*, para. 318 ('[A]n accused must have been aware of his position as a superior and of the reason that should have alerted him to the relevant crimes of his subordinates.'). The *Orić* Chamber's attempt to graft an additional mental element onto the test, which has no support in any part of the relevant law on superior responsibility, may have arisen out of a desire to strengthen its eventual finding, on the facts in that case, that the accused was liable under Article 7(3) for the crimes charged. *See infra*, text accompanying notes 599–619, for a detailed discussion of this portion of the judgement.

knew or had reason to know that the criminal conduct for which he is charged with responsibility was about to be, was being, or had been realised by one or more of his subordinates.[352] Hence, as acknowledged by the ICTY Appeals Chamber, superior responsibility in the *ad hoc* Tribunals is not a form of strict liability.[353]

As discussed above,[354] several chambers have recognised that a conviction pursuant to Article 7/6(3) is not punishment for committing the crime in question, but for failing to discharge a duty to act in the face of criminal conduct by a subordinate.[355] Accordingly, an accused may incur superior responsibility even though he does not by his own conduct fulfil any of the elements of the crime, including the *mens rea;* in other words, the accused need not share with the alleged subordinate the intent to commit the crime,[356] even, it would appear, where he is charged with a specific-intent crime such as genocide or persecution as a crime against humanity.[357] Although relatively few chambers have had occasion to address liability for specific-intent crimes under Article 7/6(3), the *Blagojević and Jokić* and *Brđanin* Trial Chambers held

---

[352] See *Gacumbitsi* Appeal Judgement, *supra* note 206, para. 143; *Bagilishema* Appeal Judgement, *supra* note 190, para. 37; *Muvunyi* Trial Judgement, *supra* note 179, para. 474; *Orić* Trial Judgement, *supra* note 179, para. 317; *Hadžihasanović and Kubura* Trial Judgement, *supra* note 179, para. 91; *Limaj et al.* Trial Judgement, *supra* note 179, para. 523; *Halilović* Trial Judgement, *supra* note 27, para. 64; *Strugar* Trial Judgement, *supra* note 179, para. 367; *Kunarac et al.* Trial Judgement, *supra* note 206, para. 395; *Blaškić* Trial Judgement, *supra* note 115, para. 294. *Čelebići* Trial Judgement, *supra* note 3, para. 346.

[353] *Čelebići* Appeal Judgement, *supra* note 32, para. 239. Accord *Orić* Trial Judgement, *supra* note 179, para. 318; *Hadžihasanović and Kubura* Trial Judgement, *supra* note 179, para. 92; *Halilović* Trial Judgement, *supra* note 27, para. 65. See Chapter 2, note 94 and accompanying text (stating that the decisions of the respective Appeals Chambers of the ICTY and the ICTR have generally been treated as authoritative by the Trial Chambers of both Tribunals, that each Appeals Chamber has tended to treat the decisions of the other as highly persuasive, and providing examples from the jurisprudence).

[354] See *supra* text accompanying notes 15–17.

[355] See, e.g., *Krnojelac* Appeal Judgement, *supra* note 15, para. 171 ('It cannot be overemphasised that, where superior responsibility is concerned, an accused is not charged with the crimes of his subordinates but with his failure to carry out his duty as a superior to exercise control.'); *Hadžihasanović and Kubura* Trial Judgement, *supra* note 179, para. 75 (holding that superior responsibility is 'responsibility for an omission to prevent or punish crimes committed by his subordinates'); *Halilović* Trial Judgement, *supra* note 27, para. 54 ('"[F]or the acts of his subordinates" ... does not mean that the commander shares the same responsibility as the subordinates who committed the crimes, but rather that because of the crimes committed by his subordinates, the commander should bear responsibility for his failure to act.'); *Blagojević and Jokić* Trial Judgement, *supra* note 188, para. 683 ('While certain omissions can be punished under Article 7(1), the Trial Chamber finds that the omission under Article 7(3) is particular: it is a failure to meet ones [sic] duty. ... [I]t is a form of liability that has specifically and purposefully evolved over time to serve a particular and defined purpose.').

[356] *Orić* Trial Judgement, *supra* note 179, para. 317 ('Article 7(3) ... sets itself apart by being satisfied with a *mens rea* falling short of the threshold requirement of intent under Article 7(1) of the [ICTY] Statute.').

[357] *Prosecutor v. Brđanin*, Case No. IT-99-36-A, Decision on Interlocutory Appeal, 19 March 2004, para. 7 (holding that, along with the third category of JCE and aiding and abetting, superior responsibility 'is no different from other forms of criminal liability which do not require proof of intent to commit a crime on the part of an accused before criminal liability can attach'.); *ibid.*, para. 10 (warning against the danger of 'conflating the *mens rea* requirement of the crime of genocide with the mental requirement of the mode of liability by which criminal responsibility is alleged to attach to the accused'.); *Brđanin* Trial Judgement, *supra* note 179, para. 720 (citing the March 2004 decision on interlocutory appeal and holding that:

explicitly that an accused charged with superior responsibility for genocide need not possess genocidal intent.[358] The factual findings of the Trial Chamber in *Ntagerura* – which convicted the accused Imanishimwe for failing to prevent and punish the genocidal actions of his subordinates at the Gashirabwoba football field without finding, for this charge, that Imanishimwe himself possessed genocidal intent[359] – also support this proposition. Similarly, in respect of persecution, the *Krnojelac* Trial Chamber adjudged the accused responsible as a superior for inhumane acts as a form of persecution 'found to have been committed with persecutory intent', but did not make a finding on whether Krnojelac himself possessed discriminatory intent in relation to this conduct.[360] Nevertheless, although the accused need not fulfil any of the elements for the commission of the crime himself, the notion that the accused must know or have reason to know of the subordinate criminal conduct in question would seem to dictate that he know or have reason to know that all the elements of that crime – including, where relevant, specific intent – have been, are being, or are about to be fulfilled. The Trial Chambers in *Blagojević and Jokić* and *Brđanin* held in this regard that, for an accused to bear

---

[t]he Appeals Chamber has held that superior criminal responsibility is a form of criminal liability that does not require proof of intent to commit a crime on the part of a superior before criminal liability can attach. It is therefore necessary to distinguish between the *mens rea* required for the crimes perpetrated by the subordinates and that required for the superior.

[358] *Blagojević and Jokić* Trial Judgement, *supra* note 188, para. 686; *Brđanin* Trial Judgement, *supra* note 179, para. 719 ('The Trial Chamber is unable to agree with the *Stakić* Trial Chamber that a superior need possess the specific intent in order to be held liable for genocide pursuant to Article 7(3) of the Statute.'); *ibid.*, para. 721:

The Trial Chamber finds that the *mens rea* required for superiors to be held responsible for genocide pursuant to Article 7(3) is that superiors knew or had reason to know that their subordinates (1) were about to commit or had committed genocide and (2) that the subordinates possessed the requisite specific intent.

But see *Prosecutor v. Stakić*, Case No. IT-97-24-T, Decision on Rule 98 *bis* Motion for Judgement of Acquittal, 31 October 2002, para. 94 ('It follows from Article 4 and the unique nature of genocide that the dolus specialis is required for responsibility under Article 7(3) as well.'). Indeed, as superior responsibility may be imposed on the basis of both direct and indirect relationships of subordination, it would appear unnecessary to prove that the subordinates on a single level in the chain of command fulfilled all the elements of the crime at issue. For example, a chamber would likely convict an accused for failing to prevent or punish genocide where a mid-level superior over whom the accused exercises effective control possesses genocidal intent, and physical perpetrators over whom both the accused and the mid-level superior exercise effective control fulfil all the other elements of genocide. See *supra* text accompanying notes 258–262.

[359] *Ntagerura et al.* Trial Judgement, *supra* note 206, paras. 653–654. The Appeals Chamber ultimately overturned this conviction on the basis that the prosecution had not pleaded superior responsibility clearly enough to put the accused sufficiently on notice that he faced liability for failing to prevent and punish the Gashirabwoba killings. The Chamber did not opine on whether it was permissible to convict the accused as a superior absent a discrete finding of genocidal intent. See *Prosecutor v. Ntagerura, Bagambiki, and Imanishimwe*, Case No. ICTR-99-46-A, Judgement, 7 July 2006, paras. 164–165, p. 163.

[360] *Krnojelac* Trial Judgement, *supra* note 183, para. 497. *Accord Krnojelac* Appeal Judgement, *supra* note 15, paras. 187–188 (finding that the accused incurred superior responsibility for inhumane acts and cruel treatment as forms of persecution after determining that he knew that his subordinates had committed such crimes 'against the non-Serb detainees [of the KP Dom prison] because of their political or religious affiliation', but absent a finding that the accused himself possessed discriminatory intent).

Article 7/6(3) liability for genocide, he must have known or had reason to know that the relevant subordinate possessed genocidal intent.[361]

The chambers of the *ad hoc* Tribunals have defined and applied the mental element of Article 7/6(3) without drawing any distinction between the two forms of superior responsibility enshrined therein (that is, the failure to prevent and the failure to punish), or between military commanders and civilian superiors.[362] Accordingly, the discussion that follows pertains equally to the failure to prevent and the failure to punish, and to military commanders and civilian superiors.

3.2.1.2.1 *Actual knowledge: first alternative mental element*
The accused knew that the criminal conduct in question was about to be, was being, or had been realised by one or more subordinates.

Construing the elements of superior responsibility 'in light of the content of the doctrine under customary international law', the *Čelebići* Trial Chamber held that an accused may fulfil the mental element where 'he had actual knowledge, established through direct or circumstantial evidence, that his subordinates were committing or about to commit crimes referred to under Article 2 to 5 of the [ICTY] Statute'.[363] Because superior responsibility in the jurisprudence of the *ad hoc* Tribunals is not a form of strict liability,[364] an

[361] See *Blagojević and Jokić* Trial Judgement, *supra* note 188, para. 686; *Brđanin* Trial Judgement, *supra* note 179, para. 721.
[362] See, e.g., *Bagilishema* Appeal Judgement, *supra* note 190, para. 35; *Čelebići* Appeal Judgement, *supra* note 32, paras. 222–241; *Brđanin* Trial Judgement, *supra* note 179, para. 282; *Kajelijeli* Trial Judgement, *supra* note 210, paras. 775–778; *Semanza* Trial Judgement, *supra* note 198, paras. 403–405; *Krnojelac* Trial Judgement, *supra* note 183, para. 94; *Kordić and Čerkez* Trial Judgement, *supra* note 190, paras. 424–436; *Bagilishema* Trial Judgement, *supra* note 179, paras. 44–46; *Aleksovski* Trial Judgement, *supra* note 180, paras. 79–80. See also *Orić* Trial Judgement, *supra* note 179, para. 320 (holding that 'the required knowledge is in principle the same for both military and civil superiors'.). But see *Muvunyi* Trial Judgement, *supra* note 179, para. 473; *Kayishema and Ruzindana* Trial Judgement, *supra* note 179, para. 228 (both endorsing the distinction drawn in Article 25 of the Rome Statute of the ICC between the requisite mental element for military commanders and that for civilian superiors, while ignoring the weight of persuasive and binding authority to the contrary). See also *infra* text accompanying notes 634–646 (discussing the Rome Statute's bifurcated mental-element standard).
[363] *Čelebići* Trial Judgement, *supra* note 3, para. 383. Accord *Kordić and Čerkez* Appeal Judgement, *supra* note 206, para. 839; *Blaškić* Appeal Judgement, *supra* note 170, para. 57; *Krnojelac* Appeal Judgement, *supra* note 15, para. 154; *Čelebići* Appeal Judgement, *supra* note 32, para. 241; *Aleksovski* Appeal Judgement, *supra* note 200, para. 72; *Orić* Trial Judgement, *supra* note 179, para. 319; *Strugar* Trial Judgement, *supra* note 179, para. 368; *Blagojević and Jokić* Trial Judgement, *supra* note 188, para. 792; *Brđanin* Trial Judgement, *supra* note 179, para. 278; *Ntagerura et al.* Trial Judgement, *supra* note 206, para. 629; *Galić* Trial Judgement, *supra* note 210, para. 174; *Kajelijeli* Trial Judgement, *supra* note 210, paras. 775, 777–778; *Stakić* Trial Judgement, *supra* note 210, para. 460; *Semanza* Trial Judgement, *supra* note 198, para. 405; *Naletilić and Martinović* Trial Judgement, *supra* note 206, para. 71; *Kamuhanda* Trial Judgement, *supra* note 210, para. 606, 608–609; *Krnojelac* Trial Judgement, *supra* note 183, para. 94; *Kvočka et al.* Trial Judgement, *supra* note 199, para. 317; *Krstić* Trial Judgement, *supra* note 205, para. 648; *Kordić and Čerkez* Trial Judgement, *supra* note 190, para. 427; *Kunarac et al.* Trial Judgement, *supra* note 206, para. 395; *Blaškić* Trial Judgement, *supra* note 115, para. 307; *Bagilishema* Trial Judgement, *supra* note 179, para. 46; *Aleksovski* Trial Judgement, *supra* note 210, para. 80.
[364] See *supra* text accompanying note 353.

accused's actual knowledge that the criminal conduct in question was about to be, was being, or had been realised may not be presumed merely by his position as a superior.[365] Actual knowledge may, however, be inferred from circumstantial evidence,[366] and an accused's superior position is a significant indicium militating in favour of a finding that he possessed actual knowledge.[367] Indeed, a showing of actual knowledge should, in general, be easier to make for *de jure* military commanders than for commanders in *de facto* military structures and civilian superiors, since it is more likely that *de jure* military commanders will be part of an organised structure with established reporting and monitoring systems.[368]

As additional bases for an inference of actual knowledge, in lieu of or in addition to direct evidence thereof, the chambers have consistently endorsed the non-exhaustive list of indicia identified in the Final Report of the Commission of Experts established pursuant to UN Security Council Resolution 780:[369] the number of illegal acts; the type of illegal acts; the

---

[365] *Blaškić* Appeal Judgement, *supra* note 170, para. 57; *Orić* Trial Judgement, *supra* note 179, para. 319; *Hadžihasanović and Kubura* Trial Judgement, *supra* note 179, para. 94; *Limaj et al.* Trial Judgement, *supra* note 179, para. 524; *Halilović* Trial Judgement, *supra* note 27, para. 66; *Strugar* Trial Judgement, *supra* note 179, para. 368; *Naletilić and Martinović* Trial Judgement, *supra* note 206, para. 71; *Blaškić* Trial Judgement, *supra* note 115, para. 307; *Aleksovski* Trial Judgement, *supra* note 210, para. 106; *Čelebići* Trial Judgement, *supra* note 3, para. 386.

[366] *Orić* Trial Judgement, *supra* note 179, para. 319; *Hadžihasanović and Kubura* Trial Judgement, *supra* note 179, para. 94; *Limaj et al.* Trial Judgement, *supra* note 179, para. 524; *Halilović* Trial Judgement, *supra* note 27, para. 66; *Strugar* Trial Judgement, *supra* note 179, para. 368; *Blagojević and Jokić* Trial Judgement, *supra* note 15, para. 792; *Naletilić and Martinović* Trial Judgement, *supra* note 206, para. 71; *Kordić and Čerkez* Trial Judgement, *supra* note 190, para. 427; *Blaškić* Trial Judgement, *supra* note 115, para. 307; *Aleksovski* Trial Judgement, *supra* note 210, para. 106; *Čelebići* Trial Judgement, *supra* note 3, para. 386. See also *Prosecutor v. Galić*, Case No. IT-98-29-A, Judgement, 30 November 2006 ('*Galić* Appeal Judgement'), paras. 178, 182 (holding that the elements of any form of responsibility, including superior responsibility, may be proven by direct or circumstantial evidence); *infra*, text accompanying note 459, for a discussion of the distinction between inferring actual knowledge and finding that the accused had 'reason to know' of subordinate criminal conduct.

[367] *Blaškić* Appeal Judgement, *supra* note 170, para. 57 (holding that 'the position of command [is] not . . . the criterion for, but [can be one of the] indicia of the accused's knowledge'.); *Orić* Trial Judgement, *supra* note 179, para. 319 ('Although . . . the superior's position may *per se* appear to be a significant indication from which knowledge of a subordinate's criminal conduct can be inferred, such status is not to be understood as a conclusive criterion but must be supported by additional factors.') (footnotes omitted); *Blaškić* Trial Judgement, *supra* note 115, para. 308; *Aleksovski* Trial Judgement, *supra* note 210, para. 80 (holding that 'an individual's superior position *per se* is a significant indicium that he had knowledge of the crimes committed by his subordinates').

[368] See *Orić* Trial Judgement, *supra* note 179, para. 320; *Hadžihasanović and Kubura* Trial Judgement, *supra* note 179, para. 94; *Halilović* Trial Judgement, *supra* note 27, para. 66; *Naletilić and Martinović* Trial Judgement, *supra* note 206, para. 66; *Blagojević and Jokić* Trial Judgement, *supra* note 188, para. 792; *Naletilić and Martinović* Trial Judgement, *supra* note 206, para. 72; *Kordić and Čerkez* Trial Judgement, *supra* note 190, para. 428.

[369] The Security Council established this Commission to examine certain evidence presented on the then ongoing war in the former Yugoslavia and present its views as to whether grave breaches of the 1949 Geneva Conventions and other violations of international humanitarian law had occurred. See SC Res. 780, UN Doc. S/RES/780 (1992); Final Report of the Commission of Experts Established pursuant to Security Council Resolution 780 (1992), UN Doc. S/1994/674 (1994). The Commission's conclusions prompted the Council to establish the ICTY to prosecute those most responsible for such violations. See

scope of illegal acts; the time during which the illegal acts occurred; the number and type of troops involved; the logistics involved, if any; the geographical location of the acts; the widespread occurrence of the acts; the tactical tempo of the operations; the *modus operandi* of similar illegal acts; the officers and staff involved; and the location of the superior at the time.[370] This last factor is particularly significant: several Trial Chambers have emphasised that the more physically proximate the superior was to the commission of the crimes, the more likely it is that he had actual knowledge of such commission.[371]

The *Aleksovski* Trial Chamber inferred that the accused, the warden of Kaonik prison in the Lašva Valley of central Bosnia, had actual knowledge that detainees were being repeatedly ill treated, at least during the period when he lived at the prison.[372] In addition to Aleksovski's geographical proximity to the acts of ill-treatment, the Chamber relied on the following factors to infer actual knowledge: Aleksovski remarked to a witness that guards whose brothers had been killed in battle tended to take revenge on the detainees, and several witnesses testified that Aleksovski observed their beatings at first hand.[373]

3.2.1.2.2 Constructive knowledge: second alternative mental element
The accused had reason to know that the criminal conduct in question was about to be, was being, or had been realised by one or more subordinates.

SC Res. 808, UN Doc. S/RES/808 (1993) (noting the Commission's observation that 'a decision to establish an *ad hoc* international tribunal in relation to events in the territory of the former Yugoslavia would be consistent with the direction of its work', and deciding to establish the ICTY).

[370] See *Blaškić* Appeal Judgement, *supra* note 170, para. 57; *Orić* Trial Judgement, *supra* note 179, para. 319; *Hadžihasanović and Kubura* Trial Judgement, *supra* note 179, para. 94; *Limaj et al.* Trial Judgement, *supra* note 179, para. 524; *Halilović* Trial Judgement, *supra* note 27, para. 66; *Strugar* Trial Judgement, *supra* note 179, para. 368; *Blagojević and Jokić* Trial Judgement, *supra* note 188, para. 792; *Naletilić and Martinović* Trial Judgement, *supra* note 206, paras. 70–71; *Kordić and Čerkez* Trial Judgement, *supra* note 190, para. 427; *Blaškić* Trial Judgement, *supra* note 115, para. 307; *Čelebići* Trial Judgement, *supra* note 3, paras. 386, 398. See also Commission of Experts Report, UN Doc. S/1994/674 (1994), para. 58. See also *Galić* Appeal Judgement, *supra* note 366, para. 183 (reaffirming that trial chambers may consider the Commission of Experts indicia 'along with other factors' when determining whether an accused bears superior responsibility).

[371] *Hadžihasanović and Kubura* Trial Judgement, *supra* note 179, para. 94; *Halilović* Trial Judgement, *supra* note 27, para. 66; *Aleksovski* Trial Judgement, *supra* note 210, para. 80; *Naletilić and Martinović* Trial Judgement, *supra* note 206, para. 72:

[T]he more physically distant the superior was from the commission of the crimes, the more additional indicia are necessary to prove that he knew of the crimes. On the other hand, if the crimes were committed next to the superior's duty-station this suffices as an important indicium that the superior had knowledge of the crimes, even more if the crimes were repeatedly committed.

[372] *Aleksovski* Trial Judgement, *supra* note 210, para. 114. See also *infra*, text accompanying note 459, for a discussion of the distinction between inferring actual knowledge and finding that the accused had 'reason to know' of subordinate criminal conduct.

[373] *Ibid.* The Trial Chamber also noted that Aleksovski admitted to having knowledge of the Geneva Conventions; in the context of this discussion, however, that finding appears directed toward the conclusion that he knew the mistreatment of the detainees was criminal, not that he knew it was occurring.

Construing the elements of superior responsibility 'in light of the content of the doctrine under customary international law', the *Čelebići* Trial Chamber held that an accused may fulfil the mental element where:

> he had in his possession information of a nature, which at the least, would put him on notice of the risk of [crimes referred to under Article 2 to 5 of the Statute] by indicating the need for additional investigation in order to ascertain whether such crimes were committed or were about to be committed by his subordinates.[374]

The chambers of the *ad hoc* Tribunals have had some difficulty interpreting and applying this alternative to actual knowledge.

Early in the evolution of superior responsibility in the jurisprudence of the ICTY, a conflict developed between the 'reason to know' standard of the 1998 *Čelebići* Trial Judgement and that of the 2000 *Blaškić* Trial Judgement. The *Čelebići* Trial Chamber elaborated on the language quoted above in the following manner:

> [A] superior can be held criminally responsible only if some specific information was in fact available to him which would provide notice of offences committed by his subordinates. This information need not be such that it by itself was sufficient to compel the conclusion of the existence of such crimes. It is sufficient that the superior was put on further inquiry by the information, or, in other words, that it indicated the need for additional investigation in order to ascertain whether offences were being committed or about to be committed by his subordinates.[375]

Although it acknowledged the *Čelebići* standard, the Trial Chamber in *Blaškić* preferred to give 'its own interpretation of the "had reason to know standard" in accordance with customary international law':

> [I]f a commander has exercised due diligence in the fulfilment of his duties yet lacks knowledge that crimes are about to be or have been committed, such lack of knowledge cannot be held against him. However, taking into account his particular position of command and the circumstances prevailing at the time, such ignorance cannot be a defence *where the absence of knowledge is the result of negligence in the discharge of his duties*: this commander had reason to know within the meaning of the Statute.[376]

---

[374] *Čelebići* Trial Judgement, *supra* note 3, para. 383. Accord *Čelebići* Appeal Judgement, *supra* note 32, para. 241; *Blagojević and Jokić* Trial Judgement, *supra* note 188, para. 792 (nearly identical language); *Brđanin* Trial Judgement, *supra* note 179, para. 278 (nearly identical language); *Krnojelac* Trial Judgement, *supra* note 183, para. 94 (nearly identical language).

[375] *Čelebići* Trial Judgement, *supra* note 3, para. 393. Earlier in the Judgement, the Trial Chamber provided the rationale for this definition: '[A] superior is not permitted to remain wilfully blind to the acts of his subordinates.' *Ibid.*, para. 387. Accord *Orić* Trial Judgement, *supra* note 179, para. 322 ('[A]s soon as the superior has been put on notice of the risk of illegal acts by subordinates, he or she is expected to stay vigilant and to inquire about additional information, rather than doing nothing or remaining "wilfully blind".') (footnotes omitted).

[376] *Blaškić* Trial Judgement, *supra* note 115, para. 332 (emphasis added). Accord *Akayesu* Trial Judgement, *supra* note 200, para. 489.

The key difference between the respective standards lies in the duty that each places on the superior. Under *Čelebići*, the accused must have specific information available to him that puts him on notice that his alleged subordinates were about to engage, were engaging, or had engaged in criminal conduct; the accused's duty to investigate only arises if he is in fact in possession of such admonitory information, but he has no duty to search for this information in the first place. By contrast, under *Blaškić* the accused bears liability if his lack of awareness results from his failure to exercise due diligence in the discharge of his duties, and one such duty is the obligation to seek out admonitory information concerning subordinate criminal conduct. In other words, *Čelebići* would hold an accused superior responsible if he failed in a duty to investigate upon receiving admonitory information, while *Blaškić* would hold him responsible if he failed in a duty to seek out such information in the first place.

In its arguments before the Appeals Chamber, the prosecution in *Čelebići* invoked the *Blaškić* standard as appropriately reflecting customary international law on superior responsibility at the time of the events alleged in the indictment: a superior may be held responsible if, by virtue of his duty of due diligence, he 'should have known' that his subordinates were committing offences.[377] The Appeals Chamber rejected this contention on the ground that such a reading of Article 7(3) would come impermissibly close to 'the imposition of criminal liability on a strict or negligence basis':[378]

Article 7(3) of the Statute is concerned with superior liability arising from failure to act in spite of knowledge. Neglect of a duty to acquire such knowledge, however, does not feature in the provision as a separate offence, and a superior is not therefore liable under the provision for such failures but only for failing to take necessary and reasonable measures to prevent or to punish.[379]

---

[377] See *Čelebići* Appeal Judgement, *supra* note 32, paras. 226, 235.

[378] *Ibid.*, paras. 226, 239.

[379] *Ibid.*, para. 226. The Appeals Chamber in *Bagilishema* endorsed this definition for purposes of the ICTR, holding that the *Bagilishema* Trial Chamber, which had adopted the *Blaškić* standard, had impermissibly created a 'third form of responsibility' by allowing a superior to be held responsible for negligently failing to acquire knowledge that his subordinates had committed or were about to commit crimes. *Bagilishema* Appeal Judgement, *supra* note 190, para. 37 (overruling *Bagilishema* Trial Judgement, *supra* note 179, para. 46). In overruling the Trial Chamber, the Appeals Chamber remarked that '[r]eferences to "negligence" in the context of superior responsibility are likely to lead to confusion of thought'. *Bagilishema* Appeal Judgement, *supra* note 190, para. 35. *Accord Orić* Trial Judgement, *supra* note 179, paras. 322, 324; *Hadžihasanović and Kubura* Trial Judgement, *supra* note 179, para. 96; *Limaj et al.* Trial Judgement, *supra* note 179, 525; *Halilović* Trial Judgement, *supra* note 27, para. 69 (holding that '[a] superior is not liable for failing to acquire information in the first place', but that 'a commander is not permitted to remain "wilfully blind" of the acts of his subordinates'); *ibid.*, para. 71 ('[C]riminal negligence is not a basis of liability in the context of command responsibility.'); *Strugar* Trial Judgement, *supra* note 179, para. 525.

The Appeals Chamber then endorsed the *Čelebići* Trial Chamber's definition as the correct one: '[A] superior will be criminally responsible through the principles of superior responsibility only if information was available to him which would have put him on notice of offences committed by subordinates.'[380] Subsequent chambers of both Tribunals have consistently followed this formulation,[381] and in July 2004 the Appeals Chamber in *Blaškić* finally had the opportunity to overrule the *Blaškić* Trial Chamber's definition,[382] reiterating that 'the authoritative interpretation of the standard of "had reason to know" shall remain the one given in the *Čelebići* Appeal Judgement'.[383]

The *Čelebići* Appeals Chamber cautioned that any assessment of whether an accused had reason to know should be conducted with regard to the circumstances of each case, 'taking into account the specific situation of the superior concerned at the time in question'.[384] This principle is illustrated by two findings of the *Naletilić and Martinović* Appeals Chamber that appear to be at odds with one another. The Trial Chamber convicted the accused Naletilić for his failure to prevent and punish a number of crimes committed against detainees at the Ljubuški prison in Bosnia,[385] finding that Naletilić had acquired reason to know that his subordinates were beating these detainees 'after he had seen for himself how [his subordinates] had severely mistreated some of the same prisoners, as for instance, [W]itness Y, already on the bus

---

[380] *Čelebići* Appeal Judgement, *supra* note 32, para. 241.

[381] See *Galić* Appeal Judgement, *supra* note 366, para. 184; *Blaškić* Appeal Judgement, *supra* note 170, para. 62; *Krnojelac* Appeal Judgement, *supra* note 15, para. 154; *Bagilishema* Appeal Judgement, *supra* note 190, paras. 28, 33, 35, 37, 42; *Orić* Trial Judgement, *supra* note 179, paras. 321–322; *Hadžihasanović and Kubura* Trial Judgement, *supra* note 179, para. 95; *Limaj et al.* Trial Judgement, *supra* note 179, para. 525; *Halilović* Trial Judgement, *supra* note 27, para. 67; *Strugar* Trial Judgement, *supra* note 179, paras. 369, 416; *Blagojević and Jokić* Trial Judgement, *supra* note 188, para. 792; *Brđanin* Trial Judgement, *supra* note 179, para. 278; *Ntagerura et al.* Trial Judgement, *supra* note 206, para. 629; *Kamuhanda* Trial Judgement, *supra* note 210, para. 609; *Galić* Trial Judgement, *supra* note 210, para. 175; *Kajelijeli* Trial Judgement, *supra* note 210, para. 778; *Stakić* Trial Judgement, *supra* note 210, para. 460; *Semanza* Trial Judgement, *supra* note 198, para. 405; *Naletilić and Martinović* Trial Judgement, *supra* note 206, para. 75; *Krnojelac* Trial Judgement, *supra* note 183, para. 94; *Kvočka et al.* Trial Judgement, *supra* note 199, para. 317 ('Action is required on the part of the superior from the point at which he "knew or had reason to know" of the crimes committed or about to be committed by his subordinates ... Article 7(3) does not impose a duty upon a superior to go out of his way to obtain information about crimes committed by subordinates, unless he is in some way put on notice that criminal activity is afoot.'); *ibid.*, para. 318; *Kordić and Čerkez* Trial Judgement, *supra* note 190, para. 437.

[382] See *Blaškić* Appeal Judgement, *supra* note 170, para. 62 ('The Trial Judgement's interpretation of the standard is not consistent with the jurisprudence of the Appeals Chamber ... and must be corrected accordingly.'); *ibid.*, para. 63 ('expressly endors[ing]' the *Bagilishema* Appeals Chamber view that '[r]eferences to "negligence" in the context of superior responsibility are likely to lead to confusion of thought'); *ibid.*, para. 406. See also *infra* note 379.

[383] *Ibid.*, para. 64.

[384] *Čelebići* Appeal Judgement, *supra* note 32, para. 239. Accord *Krnojelac* Appeal Judgement, *supra* note 15, para. 156; *Hadžihasanović and Kubura* Trial Judgement, *supra* note 179, para. 101 ('In particular, ... that evaluation must distinguish between the time the information was available to the superior and the time the breach was committed.'); *Halilović* Trial Judgement, *supra* note 27, para. 70.

[385] *Naletilić and Martinović* Trial Judgement, *supra* note 206, paras. 453, 682.

ride on their way to the Ljubuški prison'.[386] In overturning these Ljubuški-related convictions, the Appeals Chamber accepted Naletilić's contention on appeal that he could not have had reason to know about his subordinates' mistreatment of the detainees on the basis of this one incident: 'The Appeals Chamber is of the view that no reasonable trier of fact could have found beyond reasonable doubt, on the sole basis of [the Witness Y] incident, that Naletilić had reason to know that his subordinates would commit such crimes in Ljubuški prison.'[387] Later in its Judgement, however, the Appeals Chamber upheld another of the Trial Chamber's 'reason to know' findings, even though this finding was also ostensibly based on Naletilić having witnessed a single incident of relevant subordinate misconduct. The Trial Chamber convicted Naletilić for his failure to prevent and punish plunder as a violation of the laws or customs of war committed by his subordinates at Mostar;[388] Naletilić challenged this finding as having 'made too much' of the testimony of one witness that Naletilić was present on one occasion when soldiers under his authority loaded looted goods into their cars.[389] The Appeals Chamber affirmed Naletilić's conviction:[390]

[E]ven if Naletilić is correct in arguing that the Trial Chamber was unreasonable because it 'ma[de] too much of [the witness's] actual testimony' when it found that Naletilić 'was present in *some instances* of plunder' carried out by soldiers under his authority, the Appeal[s] Chamber is of the view that he has not shown that this error led to a miscarriage of justice. Under the circumstances, Naletilić's personal observation of even one instance of his subordinates' looting was sufficient to put him on notice and obligate him to take action to punish the perpetrators and prevent further plunder.[391]

The admonitory information triggering an accused superior's duty to investigate could have become available to him by way of a written or oral report, and it need not have come via an official or authorised monitoring system.[392] A number of chambers have cited the four factors listed in the ICRC Commentary to Article 86(2) of Additional Protocol I as examples of the

---

[386] *Ibid.*, para. 428.

[387] *Naletilić and Martinović* Appeal Judgement, *supra* note 344, para. 305. As the mental element required for superior responsibility was now absent, the Appeals Chamber set aside Naletilić's convictions for failing to prevent and punish cruel treatment as a violation of the laws or customs of war, wilfully causing great suffering as a grave breach of the 1949 Geneva Conventions, and persecution as a crime against humanity in respect of the Ljubuški detainees. *Ibid.*, para. 306.

[388] *Naletilić and Martinović* Trial Judgement, *supra* note 206, para. 631.

[389] *Naletilić and Martinović* Appeal Judgement, *supra* note 344, para. 387.   [390] *Ibid.*, para. 388.

[391] *Ibid.*, para. 387 (emphasis in original, footnotes removed).

[392] See *Galić* Appeal Judgement, *supra* note 366, para. 184; *Čelebići* Appeal Judgement, *supra* note 32, para. 238; *Orić* Trial Judgement, *supra* note 179, para. 323.

type of information that could give rise to a duty to investigate: reports addressed to the accused drawing attention to the behaviour of his alleged subordinates; the tactical situation; the level of training and instruction of the alleged subordinates; and the subordinates' character traits.[393] The *Čelebići* Appeals Chamber provided an example of this last factor: '[A] military commander who has received information that some of the soldiers under his command have a violent or unstable character, or have been drinking prior to being sent on a mission, may be considered as having the required knowledge.'[394]

Perhaps most importantly, the jurisprudence has been fairly consistent in holding that the admonitory information need not provide specific details about unlawful subordinate conduct,[395] and that it need not be sufficient in and of itself to compel the conclusion that such conduct had occurred, was occurring, or would occur.[396] Yet while several judgements contain statements indicating how suggestive of subordinate criminal conduct the admonitory information must be, these statements are often inconsistent with one another. For example, the *Čelebići*, *Krnojelac*, *Blagojević and Jokić* and *Orić* Trial Chambers held that the admonitory information must provide 'notice of the *risk* of [criminal conduct] by indicating the need for additional investigation'.[397] The Appeals Chambers in both *Čelebići* and *Bagilishema* opined that information putting the accused 'on notice of *possible* unlawful acts by

---

[393] *Hadžihasanović and Kubura* Trial Judgement, *supra* note 179, para. 99; *Halilović* Trial Judgement, *supra* note 27, para. 68; *Kordić and Čerkez* Trial Judgement, *supra* note 190, paras. 436–437 (also invoking the list of indicia compiled by the UN Commission of Experts, cited in note 370 *supra* as useful in determining whether the accused was on notice of his alleged subordinates' criminal conduct).

[394] *Čelebići* Appeal Judgement, *supra* note 32, para. 238. Accord *Orić* Trial Judgement, *supra* note 179, para. 323; *Hadžihasanović and Kubura* Trial Judgement, *supra* note 179, para. 100; *Halilović* Trial Judgement, *supra* note 27, para. 68 ('[A] commander's knowledge of ... the criminal reputation of his subordinates may be sufficient to meet the *mens rea* standard required by Article 7(3) of the [ICTY] Statute if it amounted to information which would put him on notice of the present and real risk of offences[.]').

[395] See *Krnojelac* Appeal Judgement, *supra* note 15, paras. 154–155; *Bagilishema* Appeal Judgement, *supra* note 190, para. 42; *Čelebići* Appeal Judgement, *supra* note 32, para. 238; *Orić* Trial Judgement, *supra* note 179, para. 322 (also holding, however, that the information 'must be sufficiently specific to demand further clarification'); *Hadžihasanović and Kubura* Trial Judgement, *supra* note 179, para. 97; *Halilović* Trial Judgement, *supra* note 27, para. 68; *Kordić and Čerkez* Trial Judgement, *supra* note 190, para. 436.

[396] See *Čelebići* Appeal Judgement, *supra* note 32, para. 236; *Orić* Trial Judgement, *supra* note 179, para. 322; *Hadžihasanović and Kubura* Trial Judgement, *supra* note 179, para. 97; *Limaj et al.* Trial Judgement, *supra* note 179, para. 525; *Halilović* Trial Judgement, *supra* note 27, para. 68; *Kordić and Čerkez* Trial Judgement, *supra* note 190, para. 434; *Čelebići* Trial Judgement, *supra* note 3, para. 393. See also *Strugar* Trial Judgement, *supra* note 179, para. 369:

[A]n accused cannot avoid the intended reach of the provision by doing nothing, on the basis that what he knows does not make it entirely certain that his forces were actually about to commit offences, when the information he possesses gives rise to a clear prospect that his forces were about to commit an offence. In such circumstances he must at least investigate[.]

[397] *Čelebići* Trial Judgement, *supra* note 3, para. 383 (emphasis added). Accord *Orić* Trial Judgement, *supra* note 179, para. 322; *Blagojević and Jokić* Trial Judgement, *supra* note 188, para. 792; *Krnojelac* Trial Judgement, *supra* note 183, para. 94.

his subordinates would be sufficient to prove that he had "reason to know"'.[398] By contrast, the Trial Chambers in *Kordić and Čerkez*, *Limaj* and *Halilović* appear to have articulated a standard making it more difficult for the prosecution to prove reason to know: the admonitory information must provide 'notice of the *likelihood* of subordinate illegal acts' so as to justify further inquiry.[399] The *Strugar* Trial Chamber stated similarly that an accused military commander cannot avoid liability 'when the information he possesses gives rise to a *clear prospect* that his forces were about to commit an offence',[400] and the *Brđanin* Trial Chamber held that 'the superior [must have] had in his or her possession information that would at least put him or her on notice of the *present and real risk* of such offences'.[401]

It would appear that these latter three formulations come very close to contradicting the holding of these same chambers that the information in the accused's possession need not compel the conclusion that his subordinates were about to engage, were engaging, or had engaged in criminal conduct.[402] Indeed, the findings of the Trial Chamber in *Strugar* intimate that an accused cannot be deemed to have 'reason to know' if the admonitory information only puts him on notice of the mere possibility or risk of subordinate criminal conduct, and that the information must instead alert him that the conduct *would* occur. Strugar, a general in the JNA, was charged with several counts of violations of the laws or customs of war for failing to prevent or punish the shelling of the Old Town of Dubrovnik by his troops on the morning of

---

[398] *Čelebići* Appeal Judgement, *supra* note 32, para. 241 (emphasis added). Accord *Bagilishema* Appeal Judgement, *supra* note 190, para. 42.

[399] *Kordić and Čerkez* Trial Judgement, *supra* note 190, para. 437 (emphasis added). Accord *Limaj et al.* Trial Judgement, *supra* note 179, para. 525; *Halilović* Trial Judgement, *supra* note 27, para. 68. In the same paragraph, the *Halilović* Trial Chamber appears to have endorsed the *Brđanin* formulation whereby an accused superior only has 'reason to know' if the admonitory information put him 'on notice of the "*present and real risk*" of offences'. *Ibid.* (emphasis added).

[400] *Strugar* Trial Judgement, *supra* note 179, para. 416.

[401] *Brđanin* Trial Judgement, *supra* note 179, para. 278 (emphasis added). Accord *Halilović* Trial Judgement, *supra* note 27, para. 68.

[402] See *Limaj et al.* Trial Judgement, *supra* note 179, para. 525; *Halilović* Trial Judgement, *supra* note 27, para. 68; *Strugar* Trial Judgement, *supra* note 179, para. 369; *Kordić and Čerkez* Trial Judgement, *supra* note 190, para. 434. By contrast, the *Brđanin* Trial Chamber did not restate the proposition that the admonitory information need not be conclusive. See *Brđanin* Trial Judgement, *supra* note 179, para. 278. See also *Orić* Trial Judgement, *supra* note 179, para. 322 n. 921 (noting the different terms used to describe how suggestive of criminal conduct the admonitory information must be, but attempting to resolve the conflict by holding that 'this language, rather than requiring a higher standard, seems merely to express that with such a degree of likelihood the risk test is definitely satisfied'). This interpretation appears to ignore, however, the terms in which other trial chambers couched their statements: clear, if contradictory, conclusions about the law, not hypothetical statements about whether a lower standard would be satisfied by such proof. As discussed below, adoption of the lower standard was crucial to the *Orić* Chamber's findings on the accused's criminal responsibility. See *infra*, text accompanying notes 428–429. Reading other trial judgments so as to exclude any potential conflict in standards would therefore have provided stronger support for the eventual disposition in *Orić*.

6 December 1991.[403] After finding that the accused had effective control over his troops,[404] the Trial Chamber examined whether he had reason to know, prior to or at the commencement of the attack on Croatian defensive positions on Mount Srđ, that his troops would shell the Old Town as well. The Chamber found that Strugar knew of similar unlawful shelling incidents perpetrated by these same forces in October and November 1991, and that he knew that no disciplinary or other action had been taken in relation to these attacks.[405] Nonetheless, while the Chamber found that this information gave the accused 'reason to know that criminal acts such as those *might* be committed by his forces',[406] it did not provide him with reason to know that such acts 'would' or 'were about to' occur:

> In the Chamber's assessment of what was known to the Accused at or before the commencement of the attack on Srđ, there has been shown to be a real and obvious prospect, a clear possibility, that in the heat and emotion of the attack on Srđ, the artillery under his command *might well* get out of hand once again and commit offences of the type charged. It has not been established, however, that the Accused had reason to know that this *would* occur. This is not shown to be a case, for example, where the Accused had information that before the attack his forces planned or intended to shell the Old Town unlawfully, or the like. It is not apparent that additional investigation before the attack could have put the Accused in any better position. Hence, the factual circumstances known to the Accused at the time are such that the issue of 'reason to know' calls for a finely balanced assessment by the Chamber. In the final analysis, and giving due weight to the standard of proof required, the Chamber is not persuaded that it has been established that the Accused had reasonable grounds to suspect, before the attack on Srđ, that his forces were about to commit offences such as those charged. Rather, he knew only of a risk of them getting out of hand and offending in this way, a risk that was not slight or remote, but nevertheless, in the Chamber's assessment, is not shown to have been so strong as to give rise, in the circumstances, to knowledge that his forces were about to commit an offence, as that notion is understood in the jurisprudence. It has not been established, therefore, that, before the commencement of the attack on Srđ, the Accused knew or had reason to know that during the attack his forces would shell the Old Town in a manner constituting an offence.[407]

Thus, in spite of the Trial Chamber's earlier holding that the admonitory information need not be conclusive and need merely have 'indicated the need for additional investigation',[408] it found that Strugar's knowledge of the 'not slight or remote' risk that his forces might shell the Old Town did not trigger his duty to investigate or give rise to the consequent 'reason to know'.

---

[403] *Strugar* Trial Judgement, *supra* note 179, para. 2.   [404] *Ibid.*, para. 414.   [405] *Ibid.*, para. 415.
[406] *Ibid.*, para. 416 (emphasis in original).   [407] *Ibid.*, para. 417 (emphases in original).
[408] *Ibid.*, para. 369. See also *supra* text accompanying notes 381, 396, 402.

The Trial Chamber did, however, find that Strugar had reason to know, once the attack on the Croatian defensive positions had begun, that his troops were in the process of shelling the Old Town.[409] At around 7.00 am, Strugar was informed that the European Community Monitoring Mission was protesting the then ongoing shelling of Dubrovnik. As this protest was made in Belgrade, 'effectively at the highest level', and the troops were already shelling the city of Dubrovnik itself well before sunrise, the Chamber determined that the accused had by that time been put 'on notice of the clear and strong risk' that shelling beyond what he had ordered was occurring:

In the Chamber's assessment the risk that [unlawful shelling] was occurring was so real, and the implications were so serious, that the [Monitoring Mission protest] ought to have sounded alarm bells to the Accused, such that at the least he saw the urgent need for reliable additional information, i.e. for investigation, to better assess the situation to determine whether the JNA artillery were in fact shelling Dubrovnik, especially the Old Town, and doing so without justification, i.e. so as to constitute criminal conduct.[410]

The Trial Chamber concluded that Strugar had reason to know of the unlawful shelling.[411] After finding that he had also failed to take the necessary and reasonable measures to prevent further shelling or punish the troops afterwards,[412] the Chamber convicted Strugar of attacks on civilians and destruction of or wilful damage to historic monuments, both violations of the laws or customs of war under Article 3 of the ICTY Statute.[413]

The key to the Trial Chamber's different conclusions appears to lie in its determination that a pre-dawn investigation would not have turned up enlightening information. In other words, because the Trial Chamber found that, even had the accused carried out an investigation, 'it [was] not apparent' that he would have been 'in any better position', the Chamber had to examine whether the information of which he was in fact aware was by itself sufficient to have given him reason to know that his subordinates were about to shell the Old Town. After making this 'finely balanced assessment', the Chamber concluded that the risk of which Strugar was aware, while real, was nevertheless 'not so strong as to give rise ... to knowledge that his forces were about to commit an offence'.[414] It is apparent that, in making this finding, the Chamber sought to bring some common sense to the jurisprudence by reaffirming that effective control is the touchstone for superior responsibility, and thereby give true effect to the oft-repeated caveat in the jurisprudence that a superior is 'not

---

[409] *Strugar* Trial Judgement, *supra* note 179, para. 418.   [410] *Ibid.*   [411] *Ibid.*, para. 446.
[412] *Ibid.*, paras. 434, 444.   [413] *Ibid.*, para. 446 and p. 198.
[414] *Ibid.*, para. 417.

obliged to perform the impossible'.[415] In other words, by making its 'reason to know' determination turn on whether the accused's investigation, if carried out, would have been successful, the Chamber sought to link the formalities of the 'reason to know' test to what the accused can realistically have been expected to know and to do.

Although the Trial Chamber's concern is well placed and its efforts to meet it admirable, the limitations it attempts to place on the 'reason to know' test may be both underappreciative of the flexibility afforded by existing jurisprudence, and ultimately unnecessary. First, the Chamber's narrow focus on those parts of the 'had reason to know' jurisprudence that discuss knowledge sufficient to trigger the superior's duty to investigate[416] – that is, whether he was put on 'inquiry notice' – ignores other parts of the jurisprudence which interpret this standard as fulfilled by superiors' knowledge of their subordinates' commission of similar crimes in the past, propensity to criminal conduct, or general lack of discipline.[417] The resulting overemphasis on whether an investigation would have divulged the certainty of Strugar's subordinates' imminent criminal activity effectively turns the 'had reason to know' standard into 'would have known if', thereby incorporating an additional requirement of a successful investigation that is inconsistent with the statutory text, and which no other chamber has recognised as part of the test.

Second, the Trial Chamber's innovative approach appears unnecessary, both on the facts of the case and in light of concerns for the rights of the accused. It would certainly seem as though, in the assessment of whether the accused had constructive knowledge of crimes, a chamber should analyse only the information that was in fact available to the accused at the time the prosecution alleges that he acquired 'reason to know'.[418] The Chamber's concern may have been that, if Strugar was unaware and unable to confirm that an illegal attack was in fact going to occur, it would be inconsistent with principles of individual criminal responsibility to hold him liable for a failure to prevent the attack. Under the doctrine of superior responsibility, however, all three elements must be evaluated in light of the prevailing circumstances,[419]

---

[415] *Krnojelac* Trial Judgement, *supra* note 183, para. 95. See also *infra* note 480.

[416] See *supra* text accompanying notes 405–413.

[417] See *supra* text accompanying notes 393–394.

[418] In this regard, Silva Hinek criticises the Trial Chamber's method of analysis as 'result-oriented', in that it suggests that a chamber may only impute 'reason to know' to an accused who has failed in his duty to investigate where it is convinced that the investigation would have verified the admonitory information previously received. See Silva Hinek, 'The Judgement of the International for the Former Yugoslavia in *Prosecutor* v. *Pavle Strugar*', (2006) 19 *Leiden Journal of International Law* 477, 489.

[419] See *supra* text accompanying notes 213–216, 288–327, 380–381; *infra* text accompanying notes 475–477, 489–491.

so Strugar could only have been found guilty of a failure to take all necessary and reasonable measures to prevent the attack given the information he had at the time. If that information merely apprised him of his subordinates' past crimes, and therefore of the possibility or likelihood that the crimes would be repeated, his duty may well have been fulfilled by reminding those under his command of their obligations under international law and threatening them with discipline if disobeyed – steps the Trial Chamber also faulted him for shirking.[420] If the criminal conduct was nevertheless undertaken, the rest of the Chamber's findings would remain correct: Strugar had reason to know that the crimes were occurring, and was responsible for his failure to take all necessary and reasonable measures to halt the attack. Each of Strugar's actual failures to intervene effectively, before the attack began and while it was ongoing, would therefore have been a fair and sufficient basis for liability for failure to prevent the crimes.

The *Strugar* Trial Chamber's formulation of the 'had reason to know' test, including its articulation of how suggestive of subordinate criminal conduct the admonitory information must be, is the most demanding version of the test that a chamber has yet imposed on the prosecution. The least demanding version of the test yet articulated and applied in the *ad hoc* Tribunals appeared in the *Orić* Trial Judgement, rendered at the end of June 2006. At the core of the *Orić* Chamber's approach to superior responsibility is its interpretation of the 'had reason to know' standard,[421] which is almost diametrically opposed to the *Strugar* Chamber's approach on both the law and its application to the facts. Seemingly unaware of the Appeals Chambers' explicit and repeated rejections of negligence as an appropriate standard,[422] the *Orić* Trial Chamber referred to liability for a superior's failure to exercise due diligence as the defining feature of superior responsibility,[423] and resurrected earlier uses

---

[420] See *Strugar* Trial Judgement, *supra* note 179, paras. 420–422. The Trial Chamber did note that:

the known risk was sufficiently real and the consequences of further undisciplined and illegal shelling were so potentially serious, that a cautious commander may well have thought it desirable to make it explicitly clear that the order to attack Srđ did not include authority to the supporting artillery to shell, at the least, the Old Town.

Ultimately, however, the Chamber reaffirmed its earlier ruling, and held that it was 'not persuaded that a failure to make any such clarification before the attack commenced gives rise to criminal liability of the Accused, pursuant to Article 7(3) of the Statute, for what followed. Any such clarification would have been merely by way of wise precaution.' *Ibid.*, para. 420.

[421] See Tilman Blumenstock and Wayde Pittman, '*Prosecutor* v. *Naser Orić*: The ICTY Judgment of Srebrenica's Muslim Wartime Commander', (2006) 19 *Leiden Journal of International Law* 1077, 1087.

[422] See *supra* text accompanying notes 378–383. But see *Orić* Trial Judgement, *supra* note 179, para. 324 (dismissing a defence argument about negligence by quoting the *Bagilishema* Appeal Judgement's statement that references to negligence are 'likely to lead to confusion of thought').

[423] *Orić* Trial Judgement, *supra* note 179, para. 317 (holding that Article 7(3) 'permit[s] the attribution of criminal responsibility to a superior for what is in actual fact a lack of due diligence in supervising the conduct of his subordinates').

of the term 'negligence' to characterise the doctrine.[424] It is the *Orić* Chamber's case-specific findings on the accused's superior responsibility, however, which most clearly distinguish its judgement from the strict *Strugar* approach. Both trial chambers concluded that the accused in question had actual knowledge of past similar crimes, either committed by the same subordinates,[425] or against the same type of victim.[426] Unlike the *Strugar* Trial Chamber, which refused to conclude that the accused had reason to know of future crimes based solely on his knowledge of past similar crimes by his subordinates, the *Orić* Chamber found that such knowledge was crucial to the accused's responsibility in that case.

Naser Orić was ultimately convicted only for his failure to prevent crimes committed at a building behind the Srebrenica municipal building between December 1992 and March 1993.[427] Recalling its conclusion that Orić knew of the murder and cruel treatment of Serb detainees in September and October 1992, the Chamber stated that '[h]is knowledge about this killing incident, as well as of the cruel treatment of the other detainees, put him on notice that the security and the well-being of all Serbs detained henceforth in Srebrenica was at risk, and that this issue needed to be adequately addressed and monitored'.[428] The Chamber discounted the role Orić played in the replacement of the commander of the Srebrenica military police who had been in charge at the time the earlier offences occurred, and instead laid great weight on the accused's failure, given his awareness of the risk of the crimes' reoccurrence, to take any action regarding Serb detainees after the new commander was appointed.[429] Key to its finding of responsibility was the Chamber's determination that the accused's actual knowledge of the September and October crimes put him on notice for the entire remainder of the period implicated in the indictment,[430] and its belief that such notice obliged a superior to

---

[424] See *ibid.*, para. 318 (holding that 'superior criminal responsibility by no means involves the imposition of "strict liability", for even if it may be described as the "imputed responsibility or criminal negligence"...') (quoting *Bagilishema* Trial Judgement, *supra* note 179, para. 897, and citing *Blaškić* Trial Judgement, *supra* note 179, para. 562). As noted above, however, both the *Bagilishema* and *Blaškić* Trial Chambers' holdings have been explicitly overturned by the ICTR and ICTY Appeals Chambers, in judgements that were themselves cited by the *Orić* Trial Chamber to support its rejection of a defence contention about negligence. See *Orić* Trial Judgement, *supra* note 179, para. 324 n. 932; see *supra* text accompanying notes 378–383.

[425] See *supra* text accompanying note 405 (citing *Strugar* Trial Judgement, *supra* note 179, para. 415).

[426] See *Orić* Trial Judgement, *supra* note 179, paras. 543, 550, 557. As noted elsewhere in this chapter, the *Orić* Trial Judgement's treatment of the relationship between the accused and the physical perpetrators, who were not his subordinates, is troubling. See *supra* text accompanying notes 282–283.

[427] See *Orić* Trial Judgement, *supra* note 179, paras. 5–6, 782.   [428] *Ibid.*, para. 550.

[429] *Ibid.*, paras. 557, 570.

[430] *Ibid.*, paras. 5–6 (summarising the charges in the indictment, including the relevant time period).

continually seek information about detainees from those to whom responsibility for their care is delegated:[431]

> The Trial Chamber is convinced that, had the Accused at least made an effort to ensure that he was kept informed of the fate of the captured prisoners during their detention in Srebrenica, he would have been able to at least redistribute the available resources to provide the required amount and quality of guards, if necessary also from his own fighters . . . Given the circumstances, it was possible for the Accused to address it, and one could reasonably expect him to address it. In the present case, the obligation of the Accused to prevent extended over a considerable period of time, namely from the appointment of Atif Kržić on 22 November 1992 to 20 March 1993, during which time he was not always on the front-line and found time to attend meetings in Srebrenica, at least until the Serb winter offensive started in late January or early February 1993.[432]

Despite its concession that military demands made it impossible for the accused to attend meetings in Srebrenica after January or February 1993, the Chamber nonetheless concluded that he was responsible for failing to prevent all crimes committed up until March 1993, including the murders committed between February and March 1993.[433] Even though it acknowledged the 'desperate situation . . . in which the Accused was operating', the *Orić* Chamber considered that 'the protection of prisoners is of such fundamental importance that it cannot be allowed to become a secondary priority'.[434]

Without expressly endorsing any of the formulations explored above,[435] the *Krnojelac* Appeals Chamber upheld the Trial Chamber's finding that

---

[431] *Ibid.*, para. 559 (holding that it is permissible for a superior to delegate part of his responsibilities with regard to care of prisoners, as long as he inquires about the performance of such responsibilities from time to time).

[432] *Ibid.*, para. 570.

[433] *Ibid.*, paras. 395, 399, 405, 411, 572, 782. But see *ibid.*, para. 559 (holding that the general rule it pronounces, that there is no military consideration of greater importance than the treatment of prisoners in armed conflict, is 'predicated on the assumption that at all times, the [superior] is in a position to fulfil this obligation. It does not, and cannot, apply when . . . there is the impossibility to act, or when it would be utterly unreasonable to expect one to act, as in the case of a life-threatening situation.').

[434] *Ibid.*, para. 570. The difference in the types of crimes at issue could therefore be seen as sufficient to distinguish the holdings in *Strugar* and *Orić*, but the latter trial chamber cited no authority for its conclusions on the relative importance of the protection of prisoners and its consequent finding as to the obligations of superiors in this regard. It may be worth noting as well that the *Orić* Trial Chamber never discussed the *Strugar* Chamber's markedly different approach to superior responsibility at any point in its judgement, and therefore made no attempt to distinguish its own application of the law. In fact, the sole reference to the *Strugar* Trial Judgement's different interpretation of a superior responsibility standard occurs in the *Orić* Chamber's attempt, in a footnote, to explain its adoption of 'risk' instead of 'substantial' or 'clear likelihood' as the appropriate test for how suggestive of criminal conduct the admonitory information must be. See *supra* note 402. This attempt appears misguided at best, since it is precisely the difference between the mere risk of criminal conduct and the near certainty of criminal conduct that proved dispositive for the *Strugar* Chamber. See *supra* text accompanying notes 405–414.

[435] See *supra* text accompanying notes 397–402.

Krnojelac had reason to know, based on complaints expressed to him by detainees, that the guards in his prison – the KP Dom – were beating these and other detainees.[436] Responding to a defence contention that the Trial Chamber could not permissibly regard the detainees' complaints as proof that the accused had learned of the beatings, the Appeals Chamber found that 'the question for the Trial Chamber was not whether what was reported to Krnojelac was in fact true but whether the information he received from the detainees was enough to constitute "alarming information" requiring him, as a superior, to launch an investigation or to make inquiries'.[437] That Krnojelac was not present at the prison at night, when most of the beatings took place, was of no consequence; all that mattered was that he had 'sufficient information to put him on notice that beatings were being given and that the guards of the KP Dom were involved in giving them'.[438] The Appeals Chamber accordingly dismissed the ground of appeal and affirmed Krnojelac's conviction.[439]

Another holding in this Appeal Judgement, rendered in September 2003, appears to have placed a significant restriction on the type of information that can trigger an accused's duty to investigate when such information relates to previous criminal conduct on the part of the accused's subordinates. The *Krnojelac* Appeals Chamber held that, while such information need not point toward the commission of the precise crime for which the accused is charged with responsibility, it must at least suggest the commission of a crime which contains all the elements of the crime for which he is charged.[440] In other words, if the admonitory information merely put the accused on notice that a certain crime had been, was being, or was about to be committed, a chamber cannot consider the accused as having also been put on notice of a second, more serious crime that contains all the elements of the first crime but also some unique elements of its own.[441] The Chamber gave the example of an accused charged with failing to prevent or punish torture. Such an accused may not be deemed to have 'reason to know' if he fails in his duty to investigate upon receiving information admonishing him merely of subordinate commission of 'other inhumane acts' – which, like torture, is a crime against humanity under the Statute of the Tribunal – because torture contains an additional element that beating as an example of 'other inhumane acts' lacks: the

---

[436] *Krnojelac* Appeal Judgement, *supra* note 15, paras. 58–59.
[437] *Ibid.*, para. 59.   [438] *Ibid.*, para. 62.
[439] *Ibid.*   [440] *Ibid.*, para. 155.   [441] *Ibid.*

mistreatment be inflicted for a prohibited purpose, such as to coerce a confession.[442]

Applying this standard, the Appeals Chamber overruled the Trial Chamber in finding that 'sufficiently alarming information was available to Krnojelac to put him on notice of the risk that torture was being or might be being carried out'.[443] The Appeals Chamber considered a number of facts as constituting 'a sufficiently alarming body of information to put [Krnojelac] on notice of the risk of torture': he admitted that he knew that non-Serbs were being detained because they were non-Serbs, and that he knew that none of the procedures in place for legally detained persons was ever followed at the KP Dom; he knew of the detention conditions under which the non-Serb prisoners were being held, in part because he had been told about the conditions by detainees themselves; he knew, from observing their physical condition, that non-Serb detainees were being beaten and generally mistreated;[444] he knew that interrogations of detainees were frequent and that detainees were subjected to beatings during their interrogation;[445] and he witnessed his subordinate, the guard Burilo, beating a detainee named Zeković for the purpose of punishing him for his failed escape.[446] The Chamber appears to have placed a great deal of weight on this last fact. While Krnojelac was not charged with superior responsibility for the torture of Zeković and although his knowledge of Zeković's beating was 'insufficient, in itself, to conclude that Krnojelac *knew* that acts of torture were being inflicted on the [other] detainees', the Chamber found that 'it may nevertheless [have] constitute[d] sufficiently alarming information such as to alert him to the risk of other acts of torture being committed, meaning that Krnojelac *had reason to know* that his subordinates were committing or about to commit acts of torture'.[447] Considering all of these pieces of admonitory information together, the Chamber opined that 'no reasonable trier of fact could fail to conclude that Krnojelac had reason to know that some of the acts had been or could have been committed for one of the purposes prohibited by the law on torture'.[448]

---

[442] See *ibid.*, para. 155:

[U]sing the ... example of the crime of torture, in order to determine whether an accused 'had reason to know' that his subordinates had committed or were about to commit acts of torture, the court must ascertain whether he had sufficiently alarming information (bearing in mind that, as set out above, such information need not be specific) to alert him to the risk of acts of torture being committed, that is of beatings being inflicted not arbitrarily but for one of the prohibited purposes of torture. Thus, it is not enough that an accused has sufficient information about beatings inflicted by his subordinates; he must also have information – albeit general – which alerts him to the risk of beatings being inflicted for one of the purposes provided for in the prohibition against torture.

Accord *Hadžihasanović and Kubura* Trial Judgement, *supra* note 179, para. 113.
[443] *Krnojelac* Appeal Judgement, *supra* note 15, para. 166.   [444] *Ibid.*, paras. 166–167.
[445] *Ibid.*, para. 168.   [446] *Ibid.*, para. 169.   [447] *Ibid.*, para. 170 (emphases in original).
[448] *Ibid.*, para. 171.

Finding that Krnojelac 'must incur responsibility pursuant to Article 7(3)' of the ICTY Statute,[449] the Appeals Chamber concluded that the Trial Chamber had committed an error of fact resulting in a miscarriage of justice. It accordingly found Krnojelac guilty 'pursuant to Article 7(3)' for having failed to punish those acts of torture that occurred prior to the torture of Zeković, and for having failed to prevent those acts of torture that occurred subsequent to the Zeković torture.[450]

This restriction on the type of admonitory information that may give rise to 'reason to know' has not been widely cited in the jurisprudence since *Krnojelac*.[451] Two exceptions are the November 2005 *Halilović* Trial Judgement, which mentioned the *Krnojelac* holding in a footnote without expressly endorsing it,[452] and the March 2006 *Hadžihasanović and Kubura* Trial Judgement, which discussed *Krnojelac* at length[453] and formulated two additional limitations on the basis of the Appeals Chamber's findings. First, for an accused to be deemed to have 'reason to know' of subordinate crimes on the basis that his subordinates committed crimes in the past, the crimes that he is charged with failing to prevent or punish must be of a similar nature to those past crimes.[454] This limitation was endorsed by the *Orić* Trial Chamber as appropriately drawn from the holding of the Appeals Chamber in *Krnojelac*.[455] Second, these crimes must have been committed by the same identifiable group of subordinates and not, for example, by subordinates belonging to some other battalion or brigade also under the accused's effective control.[456] To conclude otherwise, according to the *Hadžihasanović and Kubura* Trial Chamber,[457] would run afoul of the Appeals Chamber's observation in *Čelebići* that 'customary law [does] not impose ... a general duty to

---

[449] *Ibid.*   [450] *Ibid.*, para. 172.

[451] For example, the following post-*Krnojelac* judgements make no mention whatsoever of this restriction in their discussions of the law of superior responsibility: *Kordić and Čerkez* Appeal Judgement, *supra* note 206, paras. 889–891; *Blaškić* Appeal Judgement, *supra* note 170, paras. 58–64; *Kajelijeli* Appeal Judgement, *supra* note 200, paras. 81–97; *Strugar* Trial Judgement, *supra* note 179, paras. 367–371; *Blagojević and Jokić* Trial Judgement, *supra* note 188, paras. 792, 794–796; *Brđanin* Trial Judgement, *supra* note 179, para. 278.

[452] *Halilović* Trial Judgement, *supra* note 27, para. 68 n. 164.

[453] *Hadžihasanović and Kubura* Trial Judgement, *supra* note 179, paras. 108–114.

[454] *Ibid.*, paras. 156, 159, 164.

[455] *Orić* Trial Judgement, *supra* note 179, para. 323 ('[T]he Trial Chamber would find that a "reason to know" existed only if, as appears also to be required by the Appeals Chamber, these indications point to the same type of crimes as the superior was supposed to prevent or punish, as opposed to merely general criminal activity.') (footnotes removed).

[456] *Hadžihasanović and Kubura* Trial Judgement, *supra* note 179, paras. 116, 169. See also *ibid.*, para. 118:

> [T]he Chamber considers that a superior's prior knowledge must be interpreted narrowly in that it derives from a situation of recurrent criminal acts and from circumstances where those acts could not be committed in isolation by a single identifiable group of subordinates.

[457] *Ibid.*, para. 116.

know upon commanders or superiors, breach of which would be sufficient to render him responsible for subordinates' crimes'.[458]

To conclude the discussion of the mental element of superior responsibility, an important distinction between actual and constructive knowledge needs to be emphasised. As discussed above, an accused's actual knowledge of subordinate criminal conduct may not be presumed from his position of authority, but may be inferred from circumstantial evidence.[459] For example, where the evidence indicates that the accused was present at a given crime site, and that detainees were subjected to regular and conspicuous beatings there, a chamber might consider such evidence sufficient to find that the accused must have known of such beatings; in other words, neither the accused nor anyone else in the vicinity of the crime site could have failed to become aware of the beatings, and the accused can therefore be deemed to have had actual knowledge of them. By contrast, a finding that the accused had reason to know is very different, in that liability may be imposed on an accused where it is obvious that he had no actual knowledge whatsoever that subordinate criminal conduct was afoot.

3.2.1.3 *The accused failed to take the necessary and reasonable measures to prevent or punish the subordinate criminal conduct in question*

The last of the three 'essential elements' of superior responsibility is that 'the superior failed to take the necessary and reasonable measures to prevent the criminal act or punish the perpetrator thereof'.[460] The Appeals Chamber has held that an accused cannot incur responsibility under Article 7/6(3) if he assumed his position as superior subsequent to the commission of the crimes

---

[458] *Čelebići* Appeal Judgement, *supra* note 32, para. 230.

[459] *See supra* text accompanying notes 365–368; see also *supra* text accompanying notes 372–373 (discussing the *Aleksovski* Trial Chamber's finding inferring that the accused had actual knowledge of subordinate criminal conduct in the Kaonik prison).

[460] *Čelebići* Trial Judgement, *supra* note 3, para. 346. Accord *Gacumbitsi* Appeal Judgement, *supra* note 206, para. 143; *Kordić and Čerkez* Appeal Judgement, *supra* note 206, para. 839; *Blaškić* Appeal Judgement, *supra* note 170, para. 72; *Krnojelac* Appeal Judgement, *supra* note 15, para. 172; *Kayishema and Ruzindana* Appeal Judgement, *supra* note 210, para. 302; *Muvunyi* Trial Judgement, *supra* note 179, para. 474; *Orić* Trial Judgement, *supra* note 179, para. 325; *Strugar* Trial Judgement, *supra* note 179, para. 372; *Blagojević and Jokić* Trial Judgement, *supra* note 188, para. 793; *Brđanin* Trial Judgement, *supra* note 179, para. 279; *Ntagerura et al.* Trial Judgement, *supra* note 206, para. 630; *Kamuhanda* Trial Judgement, *supra* note 210, para. 610; *Galić* Trial Judgement, *supra* note 210, para. 176; *Kajelijeli* Trial Judgement, *supra* note 210, para. 779; *Stakić* Trial Judgement, *supra* note 210, para. 461; *Semanza* Trial Judgement, *supra* note 198, para. 406; *Naletilić and Martinović* Trial Judgement, *supra* note 206, para. 76; *Krnojelac* Trial Judgement, *supra* note 183, para. 95; *Kvočka et al.* Trial Judgement, *supra* note 199, para. 314; *Krstić* Trial Judgement, *supra* note 205, para. 604; *Kordić and Čerkez* Trial Judgement, *supra* note 190, para. 441; *Kunarac et al.* Trial Judgement, *supra* note 206, para. 395; *Blaškić* Trial Judgement, *supra* note 115, para. 294; *Bagilishema* Trial Judgement, *supra* note 179, para. 47; *Aleksovski* Trial Judgement, *supra* note 210, para. 81.

in question.[461] This important proposition is discussed in further detail below.[462]

The chambers have consistently held that superior responsibility in the *ad hoc* Tribunals contains no requirement of causality: an accused's failure to take the necessary and reasonable measures to prevent the criminal conduct of his subordinate does not have to have caused that conduct.[463] Indeed, as the ICTY Appeals Chamber has emphasised, 'the very existence of the principle of superior responsibility for the failure to punish . . . demonstrates the absence of a requirement of causality as a separate element of the doctrine of superior responsibility'.[464] The *Halilović* Trial Chamber opined that a requirement of causality 'would change the basis of command responsibility for failure to prevent or punish to the extent that it would practically require involvement on the part of the commander in the crime his subordinates committed, thus altering the very nature of the liability imposed under Article 7(3)'.[465]

As mentioned above,[466] Article 7/6(3) encompasses two distinct forms of superior responsibility.[467] The duty to prevent and the duty to punish are separate responsibilities under international law, and an omission to carry out either duty in respect of the same subordinate criminal conduct may give rise to separate charges in an indictment.[468] The Appeals Chamber rejected as 'illogical' Blaškić's contention on appeal that, under Article 87(3) of Additional

---

[461] *Hadžihasanović et al.* 7(3) Appeal Decision, *supra* note 3, paras. 45, 51; see also *Hadžihasanović and Kubura* Trial Judgement, *supra* note 179, paras. 197–198.

[462] See *infra* text accompanying notes 527–534.

[463] *Blaškić* Appeal Judgement, *supra* note 170, para. 77; *Kordić and Čerkez* Appeal Judgement, *supra* note 206, para. 832; *Orić* Trial Judgement, *supra* note 179, para. 338; *Hadžihasanović and Kubura* Trial Judgement, *supra* note 179, paras. 186, 188; *Halilović* Trial Judgement, *supra* note 27, para. 78 (holding that 'the nature of command responsibility itself, as a *sui generis* form of liability, which is distinct from the modes of individual responsibility set out in Article 7(1) [of the ICTY Statute], does not require a causal link'.); *Brđanin* Trial Judgement, *supra* note 179, para. 280; *Kordić and Čerkez* Trial Judgement, *supra* note 190, para. 447; *Čelebići* Trial Judgement, *supra* note 3, para. 398.

[464] *Blaškić* Appeal Judgement, *supra* note 170, para. 76 (citing *Čelebići* Trial Judgement, *supra* note 3, para. 400). Accord *Orić* Trial Judgement, *supra* note 179, para. 338 ('[W]ith regard to the superior's failure to punish, it would make no sense to require a causal link between an offence committed by a subordinate and the subsequent failure of a superior to punish the perpetrator of that same offence.'); *Halilović* Trial Judgement, *supra* note 27, para. 76; *Kordić and Čerkez* Trial Judgement, *supra* note 190, para. 445.

[465] *Halilović* Trial Judgement, *supra* note 27, para. 78. The *Orić* Trial Chamber elaborated on this point, adding that, if the prosecution were obliged to prove causality between the superior's failure to act and the subordinate's criminal conduct, 'then the borderline between Article 7(3) of the Statute and participation according to Article 7(1) would be transgressed and, thus, superior criminal responsibility would become superfluous'. *Orić* Trial Judgement, *supra* note 179, para. 338.

[466] See *supra* text accompanying notes 195–198.

[467] *Halilović* Trial Judgement, *supra* note 27, para. 94 ('The duty to punish is a separate form of liability, distinct from the failure to prevent[.]').

[468] *Halilović* Pre-Trial Decision on the Form of the Indictment, *supra* note 195, para. 31. Accord *Hadžihasanović et al.* 7(3) Appeal Decision, *supra* note 3, para. 55; *Limaj et al.* Trial Judgement, *supra* note 179, para. 527 ('Under Article 7(3), a superior has a duty both to prevent the commission of the offence and punish the perpetrators. These are not alternative obligations.'); *Strugar* Trial Judgement, *supra* note 179, para. 373.

Protocol I, the failure to punish is a subcategory of the failure to prevent and liability only ensues for the failure to prevent if such failure results in the commission of further offences. It held that 'the failure to punish and failure to prevent involve different crimes committed at different times: the failure to punish concerns past crimes committed by subordinates, whereas the failure to prevent concerns future crimes of subordinates'.[469] The Chamber also invoked the Regulations Concerning the Application of International Law to the Armed Forces of the Socialist Federal Republic of Yugoslavia as support for the proposition that the failure to punish is a 'separate head of responsibility' from the failure to prevent.[470]

Elaborating on the stance taken by the *Blaškić* Appeal Judgement, the Pre-Trial Chamber in a December 2004 decision on the prosecution's motion to amend the indictment in *Halilović* held that the bases for the imposition of criminal liability under Article 7(3) are 'two alternative omissions':

> It is well-established in the Tribunal's jurisprudence that the disjunctive 'or' in the last phrase of Article 7(3) – 'the superior failed to take the necessary and reasonable measures to prevent such acts <u>or</u> to punish the perpetrators thereof' – reflects the fact that the duty to prevent crimes and the duty to punish the perpetrators are distinct and separate responsibilities under international law.[471]

As the Pre-Trial Chamber observed, a major consequence of the failure to prevent and the failure to punish as separate forms of superior responsibility is that an accused superior can be convicted on the basis of one omission even if the other is not proved.[472] Moreover, several chambers have highlighted a second major consequence of the disjunctive nature of the bases of superior

---

[469] *Blaškić* Appeal Judgement, *supra* note 170, para. 83. Accord *Orić* Trial Judgement, *supra* note 179, para. 326; *Hadžihasanović and Kubura* Trial Judgement, *supra* note 179, para. 195; *Prosecutor v. Kordić and Čerkez*, Case No. IT-95-14/2-PT, Decision on the Joint Defence Motion to Dismiss for Lack of Jurisdiction Portions of the Amended Indictment Alleging 'Failure to Punish' Liability, 2 March 1999 ('*Kordić and Čerkez* March 1999 Pre-Trial Decision'), paras. 9–16. Nevertheless, while it has been cited as the jurisprudential basis for the holding that the failure to prevent and the failure to punish are two separate forms of responsibility, this statement of the *Blaškić* Appeals Chamber is not entirely accurate. As subsequent jurisprudence has shown and as the very proposition expounded in *Blaškić* implies, the failure to prevent and the failure to punish can indeed involve the same crimes committed at the same time: an accused superior can be held responsible both for his failure to prevent and for his failure to punish the same subordinate criminal activity, and he cannot escape liability for failing to prevent such conduct merely by punishing it after the fact. See *infra* note 473 and accompanying text.

[470] *Blaškić* Appeal Judgement, *supra* note 170, para. 84.

[471] *Halilović* Pre-Trial Decision on the Form of the Indictment, *supra* note 195, para. 31 (emphasis in original). Accord *Prosecutor v. Hadžihasanović Alagić and Kubura*, Case No. IT-01-47-PT, Decision on Form of Indictment, 7 December 2001, para. 23 (holding that there was 'no ambiguity in the use of the disjunctive formulation [of the bases of superior responsibility] – the Prosecution is entitled to plead both versions and the Defence is sufficiently and clearly put on notice that it has to prepare its case to answer both versions'.); *Kordić and Čerkez* March 1999 Pre-Trial Decision, *supra* note 470, paras. 13–14 (concluding that the failure to prevent crimes and the failure to punish crimes are independent bases of criminal liability).

[472] *Halilović* Pre-Trial Decision on the Form of the Indictment, *supra* note 195, para. 33.

responsibility: a superior cannot make up for his failure to prevent crimes simply by punishing the perpetrators afterwards. In other words, even if the accused satisfactorily punishes the perpetrators, he may still be charged with and convicted of the crimes they committed because he failed to prevent such commission in the first place when he had prior or concurrent knowledge of the crimes.[473]

This section will discuss the unique features of the failure to prevent and the failure to punish in two separate subsections, but will begin with an examination of the common sub-element that the accused must have failed to take measures that were 'necessary and reasonable'.

3.2.1.3.1 Common sub-element for the failure to prevent and the failure to punish
The accused failed to take measures that were necessary and reasonable

For responsibility to ensue based either on the failure to prevent or the failure to punish, the prosecution must prove that the accused failed to take 'necessary and reasonable measures to prevent the criminal act or punish the perpetrator thereof'.[474] Determining what measures qualify as necessary and reasonable is, in the words of the *Čelebići* Trial Chamber, 'so inextricably linked to the facts of each particular situation that any attempt to formulate a general standard *in abstracto* would not be meaningful'.[475] The *Blaškić* Appeals Chamber remarked in this vein that '[w]hat constitutes such measures is not a matter of substantive law but of evidence',[476] and several trial chambers have cautioned that a chamber must consider all the circumstances when undertaking its analysis.[477] The *Strugar* Trial Chamber provided a list of the

---

[473] *Orić* Trial Judgement, *supra* note 179, paras. 326, 332; *Hadžihasanović and Kubura* Trial Judgement, *supra* note 179, paras. 125–126; *Limaj et al.* Trial Judgement, *supra* note 179, para. 528; *Halilović* Trial Judgement, *supra* note 27, para. 72; *Strugar* Trial Judgement, *supra* note 179, para. 373 ('[I]f a superior has knowledge or has reason to know that a crime is being or is about to be committed, he has a duty to prevent the crime from happening and is not entitled to wait and punish afterwards.'); *Blagojević and Jokić* Trial Judgement, *supra* note 188, para. 793; *Brđanin* Trial Judgement, *supra* note 179, para. 279; *Semanza* Trial Judgement, *supra* note 198, para. 407; *Stakić* Trial Judgement, *supra* note 210, para. 461; *Kordić and Čerkez* Trial Judgement, *supra* note 190, paras. 444; *Blaškić* Trial Judgement, *supra* note 115, para. 336. In this regard, the *Orić* Trial Chamber characterised the two forms of superior responsibility enshrined in Article 7/6(3) as 'consecutive': '[I]t is [the superior's] primary duty to intervene as soon as he becomes aware of crimes about to be committed, while taking measures to punish may only suffice, as a substitute, if the superior became aware of these crimes only after their commission.' *Orić* Trial Judgement, *supra* note 179, para. 326.

[474] *Čelebići* Trial Judgement, *supra* note 3, para. 346. Accord *Stakić* Trial Judgement, *supra* note 210, para. 461; *Blaškić* Trial Judgement, *supra* note 115, para. 294.

[475] *Čelebići* Trial Judgement, *supra* note 3, para. 394. Accord *Orić* Trial Judgement, *supra* note 179, para. 329; *Kayishema and Ruzindana* Trial Judgement, *supra* note 179, para. 231.

[476] *Blaškić* Appeal Judgement, *supra* note 170, para. 72. Accord *Orić* Trial Judgement, *supra* note 179, para. 329; *Halilović* Trial Judgement, *supra* note 27, para. 74 ('It is well established that these measures may vary from case to case.') (internal quotation marks omitted); *Brđanin* Trial Judgement, *supra* note 179, para. 279.

[477] *Orić* Trial Judgement, *supra* note 179, para. 329; *Hadžihasanović and Kubura* Trial Judgement, *supra* note 179, para. 123; *Kordić and Čerkez* Trial Judgement, *supra* note 190, para. 445; *Bagilishema* Trial Judgement, *supra* note 179, para. 48 ('Such a material ability must not be considered abstractly, but must be evaluated on a

type of circumstances that may be relevant to such an inquiry: whether specific orders prohibiting or stopping the criminal activities were or were not issued; what measures to secure the implementation of these orders were or were not taken; what other measures were taken to ensure that the unlawful acts were interrupted; whether these measures were reasonably sufficient in the specific circumstances; and what steps were taken after the commission of the crime to secure an adequate investigation and to bring the perpetrators to justice.[478]

It is primarily a superior's degree of effective control – that is, his material ability to prevent or punish the criminal conduct of his subordinates – that guides a chamber in determining whether he took measures that were necessary and reasonable in the circumstances.[479] Although a superior is 'not obliged to perform the impossible'[480] and 'may only be held criminally responsible for failing to take such measures that are within his powers',[481] he must take all measures that are within his material ability.[482] Thus, although the

---

[478] case-by-case basis, considering all the circumstances.'); *Aleksovski* Trial Judgement, *supra* note 210, para. 81 (holding that a superior's material possibility to take necessary and reasonable measures 'must not be considered abstractly but must be evaluated on a case by case basis depending on the circumstances').

[478] *Strugar* Trial Judgement, *supra* note 179, para. 378. Accord *Halilović* Trial Judgement, *supra* note 27, para. 74 (repeating the same list).

[479] *Blaškić* Appeal Judgement, *supra* note 170, para. 72 ('necessary and reasonable measures are such that can be taken within the competence of a commander as evidenced by the degree of effective control he wielded over his subordinates'); *Kayishema and Ruzindana* Appeal Judgement, *supra* note 210, para. 302; *Orić* Trial Judgement, *supra* note 179, para. 329; *Halilović* Trial Judgement, *supra* note 27, para. 73; *Strugar* Trial Judgement, *supra* note 179, para. 372; *Blagojević and Jokić* Trial Judgement, *supra* note 188, para. 793; *Brđanin* Trial Judgement, *supra* note 179, para. 279; *Ntagerura et al.* Trial Judgement, *supra* note 206, para. 630; *Kamuhanda* Trial Judgement, *supra* note 210, para. 610; *Galić* Trial Judgement, *supra* note 210, para. 176; *Kajelijeli* Trial Judgement, *supra* note 210, para. 779; *Stakić* Trial Judgement, *supra* note 210, para. 461; *Semanza* Trial Judgement, *supra* note 198, para. 406; *Naletilić and Martinović* Trial Judgement, *supra* note 206, para. 76; *Krnojelac* Trial Judgement, *supra* note 183, para. 95; *Kordić and Čerkez* Trial Judgement, *supra* note 190, para. 445; *Blaškić* Trial Judgement, *supra* note 115, para. 335; *Bagilishema* Trial Judgement, *supra* note 179, para. 48; *Kayishema and Ruzindana* Trial Judgement, *supra* note 179, paras. 81, 228–230; *Aleksovski* Trial Judgement, *supra* note 210, para. 81; *Čelebići* Trial Judgement, *supra* note 3, para. 395.

[480] *Krnojelac* Trial Judgement, *supra* note 183, para. 95. Accord *Blaškić* Appeal Judgement, *supra* note 170, para. 417; *Bagilishema* Appeal Judgement, *supra* note 190, para. 35; *Kayishema and Ruzindana* Appeal Judgement, *supra* note 210, para. 302; *Orić* Trial Judgement, *supra* note 179, para. 329; *Hadžihasanović and Kubura* Trial Judgement, *supra* note 179, para. 122; *Blagojević and Jokić* Trial Judgement, *supra* note 188, para. 793; *Brđanin* Trial Judgement, *supra* note 179, para. 279; *Stakić* Trial Judgement, *supra* note 210, para. 461; *Kayishema and Ruzindana* Trial Judgement, *supra* note 179, para. 511; *Čelebići* Trial Judgement, *supra* note 3, para. 395.

[481] *Blaškić* Appeal Judgement, *supra* note 170, para. 417. Accord *Hadžihasanović and Kubura* Trial Judgement, *supra* note 179, para. 122; *Strugar* Trial Judgement, *supra* note 179, para. 372; *Blagojević and Jokić* Trial Judgement, *supra* note 188, para. 793; *Brđanin* Trial Judgement, *supra* note 179, para. 279; *Stakić* Trial Judgement, *supra* note 210, para. 461.

[482] *Blaškić* Appeal Judgement, *supra* note 170, para. 417; *Orić* Trial Judgement, *supra* note 179, para. 329; *Limaj et al.* Trial Judgement, *supra* note 179, para. 526 ('A superior will be held responsible if he failed to take such measures that are within his material ability.'); *Halilović* Trial Judgement, *supra* note 27, para. 73; *Strugar* Trial Judgement, *supra* note 179, para. 372 ('[W]hether *de jure* or *de facto*, a superior will be held responsible for failing to take such measures that are within his material possibility.'); *Krnojelac* Trial Judgement, *supra* note 183, para. 95 ('The measures required of the superior are limited to those which are feasible in all the circumstances and are "within his power".'); *Kordić and Čerkez* Trial Judgement, *supra* note 190, para. 445 ('[A] superior has discharged his duty to prevent or punish if he uses every means in his powers to do so.'); *Čelebići* Trial Judgement, *supra* note 3, para. 395.

Blaškić Appeals Chamber could not find beyond reasonable doubt that the accused had 'full effective control' over the Vitezovi unit of the Croatian Defence Council due to his inability to discipline its members, he did have the material ability to report their criminal acts to the appropriate authorities who could administer such discipline. The Chamber consequently found that Blaškić had a sufficient degree of effective control to give rise to his duty to punish: 'If reporting criminal acts of subordinates to appropriate authorities is eviden[ce] of the material ability to punish them in the circumstances of a certain case, albeit only to a very limited degree, the Appellant had that limited ability in this case.'[483] The Trial Chamber in *Orić* remarked that the duty of a superior to take all measures within his power carries with it an obligation to be more attentive and to react more quickly where the subordinate criminal conduct is more grievous or more imminent.[484]

As it is a superior's actual material ability that determines which measures are necessary and reasonable under the circumstances,[485] a lack of formal legal competence to take measures to prevent or repress a given offence 'does not necessarily preclude the criminal responsibility of the superior'.[486] As held by the Appeals Chamber in *Kayishema and Ruzindana*, 'in the assessment of whether a superior failed to act, it is necessary to look beyond formal competence to actual capacity to take measures'.[487] The Appeals Chamber accordingly dismissed as irrelevant Kayishema's argument that he, as a mere civilian prefect, had no legal competence to prevent or punish offences committed by the Interahamwe.[488]

---

[483] *Blaškić* Appeal Judgement, *supra* note 170, para. 499. See also *Blaškić* Trial Judgement, *supra* note 115, para. 335 ('[U]nder some circumstances, a commander may discharge his obligation to prevent or punish by reporting the matter to the competent authorities.'); *Brđanin* Trial Judgement, *supra* note 179, para. 279 n. 754 (same).

[484] *Orić* Trial Judgement, *supra* note 179, para. 329.

[485] Indeed, the qualifier 'reasonable' in the term 'necessary and reasonable measures' in Article 7/6(3) is a textual indicator that effective control is the touchstone for superior responsibility. See also Additional Protocol I, *supra* note 28, Art. 86(2) ('if they did not take *all feasible measures within their power* to prevent or repress the breach') (emphasis added).

[486] *Čelebići* Trial Judgement, *supra* note 3, para. 395 (declining to follow ILC 1996 Draft Code, *supra* note 34, Commentary, pp. 38–39, which states that 'for the superior to incur responsibility, he must have had the legal competence to take measures to prevent or repress the crime and the material possibility to take such measures'.).

[487] *Kayishema and Ruzindana* Appeal Judgement, *supra* note 210, para. 302. Accord *Hadžihasanović and Kubura* Trial Judgement, *supra* note 179, para. 122 ('[T]he superior need not possess the formal legal competence to take the necessary measures if it is proved that he has the material ability to act.'); *Limaj et al.* Trial Judgement, *supra* note 179, para. 526; *Halilović* Trial Judgement, *supra* note 27, para. 73; *Strugar* Trial Judgement, *supra* note 179, para. 372 ('[T]he question of whether a superior had explicit legal capacity to take such measures will be immaterial if he had the material ability to act.'); *Blagojević and Jokić* Trial Judgement, *supra* note 188, para. 793; *Brđanin* Trial Judgement, *supra* note 179, para. 279; *Kajelijeli* Trial Judgement, *supra* note 210, para. 779; *Stakić* Trial Judgement, *supra* note 210, para. 461; *Kordić and Čerkez* Trial Judgement, *supra* note 190, para. 443.

[488] *Kayishema and Ruzindana* Appeal Judgement, *supra* note 210, para. 302.

3.2.1.3.2 First form of superior responsibility: the failure to prevent

As examined above in respect of both the failure to prevent and the failure to punish, the actions that an accused superior must take in order to discharge his duty to prevent subordinate criminal conduct depend on his level of effective control,[489] that is, his 'material ability to intervene'.[490] Therefore, in order to establish the first form of responsibility enshrined in Article 7/6(3), in addition to proving the existence of all the common elements discussed up to this point, the prosecution must prove that the accused failed to intervene to prevent or stop his subordinate's imminent or ongoing criminal conduct in spite of a material ability to do so in the circumstances.[491]

Regarding the time at which a superior's duty to prevent arises, the *Kordić and Čerkez* Trial Chamber held that 'the duty to prevent should be understood as resting on a superior at any stage before the commission of a subordinate crime if he acquires knowledge that such a crime is being prepared or planned, or when he has reasonable grounds to suspect subordinate crimes'.[492] The term 'reasonable grounds to suspect' can probably be taken as synonymous with 'reason to know', as suggested by the more straightforward formulation of the

---

[489] See *supra* text accompanying notes 214–218, for a more complete discussion of 'effective control'.

[490] *Limaj et al.* Trial Judgement, *supra* note 179, para. 528. Accord *Orić* Trial Judgement, *supra* note 179, para. 327 ('[B]oth in temporal and functional terms, the superior, as soon and as long as he or she has effective control over subordinates which he or she knows, or has reason to know, are about to commit relevant crimes, must counteract with appropriate measures.'); *Hadžihasanović and Kubura* Trial Judgement, *supra* note 179, para. 152; *Halilović* Trial Judgement, *supra* note 27, para. 89; *Strugar* Trial Judgement, *supra* note 179, para. 374.

[491] See *Hadžihasanović and Kubura* Trial Judgement, *supra* note 179, para. 127 (holding that the duty to prevent includes the duty to stop criminal conduct already in progress); *ibid.*, para. 155 ('[T]he Chamber finds that the necessary and reasonable measures a superior must take to prevent the commission of a crime must be evaluated on a case-by-case basis in view of the particular facts of the case.'). The *Halilović*, *Hadžihasanović and Kubura*, and *Orić* Trial Chambers elaborated that this form of responsibility relates to the accused's failure to carry out his 'specific' obligation to prevent subordinate criminal conduct, as opposed to his 'general' obligation to ensure law-abiding behaviour and maintain order among his subordinates. See *Orić* Trial Judgement, *supra* note 179, para. 330; *Hadžihasanović and Kubura* Trial Judgement, *supra* note 179, paras. 145–155; *Halilović* Trial Judgement, *supra* note 27, paras. 81–90. While an accused's failure to carry out his general obligation may be an element to consider when determining whether he failed in his specific obligation to prevent the precise criminal conduct for which he is charged with superior responsibility, 'no criminal liability may attach to the commander for failure in [the general] duty *per se*'. *Halilović* Trial Judgement, *supra* note 27, para. 88. Accord *Orić* Trial Judgement, *supra* note 179, para. 330; *Hadžihasanović and Kubura* Trial Judgement, *supra* note 179, para. 147. Moreover, the *Hadžihasanović and Kubura* Trial Chamber suggested that whether a given accused fulfilled or did not fulfil this general obligation may be relevant in the determination of his sentence. See *ibid.*, para. 151.

[492] *Kordić and Čerkez* Trial Judgement, *supra* note 190, para. 445. Accord *Orić* Trial Judgement, *supra* note 179, para. 328; *Halilović* Trial Judgement, *supra* note 27, para. 79 ('[T]he duty to prevent should be understood as resting on a superior *at any stage* before the commission of a subordinate crime if he acquires knowledge that such a crime is being prepared or planned, or has reason to know thereof.'); *ibid.*, para. 72; *Strugar* Trial Judgement, *supra* note 179, para. 373 (holding that the duty arises 'from the moment [the superior] acquires knowledge or has reasonable grounds to suspect that a crime is being or is about to be committed'.); *Semanza* Trial Judgement, *supra* note 198, para. 407 ('If a superior is aware of the impending or on-going commission of a crime, necessary and reasonable measures must be taken to stop or prevent it.').

Kvočka Trial Judgement: 'Action is required on the part of the superior from the point at which he "knew or had reason to know" of the crimes committed or about to be committed by subordinates.'[493]

The *Strugar* Trial Chamber invoked several examples of failures to prevent identified in post-Second World War jurisprudence that, depending on the accused's material ability to intervene, may engage his superior responsibility: the failure to secure reports that military actions have been carried out in accordance with international law; the failure to issue orders aimed at bringing the relevant practices into accord with the rules of war; the failure to protest against or to criticise criminal action; the failure to take disciplinary measures to prevent the commission of atrocities by those under the accused's command; and the failure to insist before an authority superior to the accused that immediate action be taken.[494] If the accused's material ability to intervene merely allows that he report imminent or ongoing crimes of which he knows or has reason to know to the competent authorities, then making such a report may be sufficient to carry out his duty to prevent.[495]

If the accused's material ability allows him to issue an order not to engage in unlawful activity, or to cease unlawful activity already begun, the mere issuance of such an order, without more, will probably not suffice to insulate the accused from responsibility. As the *Strugar* Trial Chamber held, any order issued must be 'effective': the accused must take all measures within his material ability and legal authority to ensure that the order is complied with and, in the military context, that all units involved in an operation actually receive the order.[496] Accordingly, the Chamber found that, even if it had been

---

[493] *Kvočka et al.* Trial Judgement, *supra* note 199, para. 317. This proposition also finds support in the *Hadžihasanović and Kubura* and *Limaj* Trial Judgements:

> [A] commander has the duty to prevent his subordinates from committing crimes when he knows or has reason to know that they are about to commit them and also has a duty to punish the perpetrators of crimes when he knows or has reason to know that his subordinates have already committed them.

> *Hadžihasanović and Kubura* Trial Judgement, *supra* note 179, para. 195. Accord *Limaj et al.* Trial Judgement, *supra* note 179, para. 527 ('The duty to prevent arises from the time a superior acquires knowledge, or has reasons to know that a crime is being or is about to be committed[.]').

[494] *Strugar* Trial Judgement, *supra* note 179, para. 374 (citing *Hostages* case, *supra* note 43, pp. 1290, 1311; *High Command* case, *supra* note 44, p. 623; and Tokyo Judgment, *supra* note 63, pp. 448, 452). Accord *Orić* Trial Judgement, *supra* note 179, para. 331; *Hadžihasanović and Kubura* Trial Judgement, *supra* note 179, para. 153 (repeating the *Strugar* list); *Limaj et al.* Trial Judgement, *supra* note 179, para. 528 (repeating the *Strugar* list); *Halilović* Trial Judgement, *supra* note 27, para. 89 (repeating the *Strugar* list). See also *supra* text accompanying notes 164–167, for a discussion of these holdings of the *Hostages* and *High Command* cases and the Tokyo Judgement.

[495] See *Hadžihasanović and Kubura* Trial Judgement, *supra* note 179, para. 154; *Blagojević and Jokić* Trial Judgement, *supra* note 179, para. 793; *Brđanin* Trial Judgement, *supra* note 179, para. 279; *Stakić* Trial Judgement, *supra* note 210, para. 461; *Blaškić* Trial Judgement, *supra* note 115, paras. 302, 335.

[496] See *Strugar* Trial Judgement, *supra* note 179, para. 434. Accord *Hadžihasanović and Kubura* Trial Judgement, *supra* note 179, para. 153; *Halilović* Trial Judgement, *supra* note 27, para. 89 ('The Tokyo Trial held that a superior's duty may not be discharged by the issuance of routine orders and that more active steps may be required.').

satisfied that Strugar issued a timely order that his forces terminate the attack on Mount Srđ and its environs, his complete failure to ensure that all of the units active in the attack received and complied with the order would have been sufficient for him to incur liability for failing to prevent the shelling of Dubrovnik.[497]

The requirement that any order must be effective may also give rise to the accused's need to reinforce the order or to reiterate an order given previously, especially where he has issued a subsequent order to engage in a limited attack that may be misinterpreted as repealing the previous order.[498] The *Strugar* Trial Chamber found in this regard that, even though orders had been issued to Strugar's subordinates sometime prior to October 1991 that they were not to shell the city of Dubrovnik itself, Strugar should have reiterated these orders at the time he gave the 6 December 1991 order to attack Croatian defensive positions on Mount Srđ:[499]

In the absence of [a reiterated order not to target Dubrovnik,] there was a very clear prospect that those planning, commanding and leading the attack would understand the new and specific order to attack Srđ as implying at least that shelling necessary to support the attack on Srđ was authorised, notwithstanding existing orders. The events of 6 December 1991 demonstrate, in the view of the Chamber, that this prospect was realised.[500]

A chamber is more likely to consider an existing order ineffective if the relevant subordinates had contravened it on a previous occasion and the accused took no action to punish them.[501] Thus, because Strugar did not punish those subordinates who shelled Dubrovnik in October and November 1991 despite the standing pre-October order not to attack the city, the Trial Chamber found that the order was not sufficiently effective to constitute a necessary and reasonable measure discharging his duty to stop the 6 December 1991 shelling.[502]

3.2.1.3.3 *Second form of superior responsibility: the failure to punish*
Despite the label typically given to the second form of superior responsibility, if an accused's actual and legal powers do not allow him to dispense

---

[497] *Strugar* Trial Judgement, *supra* note 179, para. 434.   [498] *Ibid.*, para. 421.   [499] See *ibid.*

[500] *Ibid.* It is worth noting that a chamber applying the more common, less stringent standard of 'reason to know', see *supra* text accompanying notes 397–401, would almost certainly have concluded, in light of this finding, that the mental element of superior responsibility was satisfied.

[501] See *Strugar* Trial Judgement, *supra* note 179, para. 421. Accord *Bagilishema* Trial Judgement, *supra* note 179, para. 50.

[502] *Strugar* Trial Judgement, *supra* note 179, paras. 421–422. While the Trial Chamber classified this omission as a failure to prevent, it is clear from the context of its discussion that Strugar was being found responsible for his failure to intervene adequately to ensure that the shelling was stopped. In *ad hoc* jurisprudence, because the Statutes of the ICTY and the ICTR contain just two alternative bases for superior responsibility, such culpable omissions are routinely treated as failures to prevent. See *infra* note 659 (discussing the differences between 'prevention', 'repression' and 'punishment').

punishment on the relevant subordinate himself, he may be able to avoid Article 7/6(3) liability simply by undertaking an investigation, or by forwarding the information in his possession to his own superior or to the prosecutorial authorities.[503] As examined above in respect of both the failure to prevent and the failure to punish, the actions that an accused superior must take in order to discharge his duty to punish subordinate criminal conduct depend on his level of effective control[504] – that is, his material ability to take action in the circumstances.[505] Therefore, in order to establish this form of responsibility, in addition to proving the existence of all the common elements discussed above, the prosecution must prove that the accused failed to take all measures within his power to ensure that the relevant subordinate was brought to justice and that any appropriate punishment was dispensed upon him.[506]

As concerns the time at which the superior's duty to punish arises, the *Blaškić* Appeals Chamber remarked that '[d]isciplinary or penal action can only be initiated *after* a violation is discovered, and a violator is one who has already violated a rule of law'.[507] The *Strugar* Trial Chamber held in a similar vein that '[t]he duty to prevent arises for a superior from the moment he acquires knowledge or has reasonable grounds to suspect that a crime is being or is about to be committed, while the duty to punish arises after the commission of the crime'.[508] Both these formulations are silent as to exactly when after the completed commission of a crime the superior must act. The language of the *Limaj* Trial Judgement is more precise, holding that '[t]he duty to prevent arises from the time a superior acquires knowledge, or has reasons to know that a crime is being or is about to be committed, while the duty to punish arises after the superior acquires knowledge of the commission of the crime'.[509] The *Limaj* Chamber did not expressly allow for the possibility that the superior's duty to punish may be implicated as soon as he acquires reason

---

[503] See *Halilović* Trial Judgement, *supra* note 27, para. 100 ('The superior does not have to be the person who dispenses the punishment, but he must take an important step in the disciplinary process.'); *Hadžihasanović and Kubura* Trial Judgement, *supra* note 179, para. 173 (same); *Kvočka et al.* Trial Judgement, *supra* note 199, para. 316 (same).

[504] See *supra* text accompanying notes 214–218, for a more complete discussion of 'effective control'.

[505] *Hadžihasanović and Kubura* Trial Judgement, *supra* note 179, para. 177 (holding that the appropriateness of the action taken depends on what is necessary and reasonable in light of the facts of each case); *Halilović* Trial Judgement, *supra* note 27, para. 100 (holding that the accused 'has a duty to exercise all measures possible within the circumstances' and that 'lack of formal legal competence on the part of the commander will not necessarily preclude his criminal responsibility').

[506] *Limaj et al.* Trial Judgement, *supra* note 179, para. 529 ('The obligation on the part of the superior is to take active steps to ensure that the perpetrators will be punished.'); *Halilović* Trial Judgement, *supra* note 27, para. 98.

[507] *Blaškić* Appeal Judgement, *supra* note 170, para. 83 (emphasis in original).

[508] *Strugar* Trial Judgement, *supra* note 179, para. 373.

[509] *Limaj et al.* Trial Judgement, *supra* note 179, para. 527.

to know, and not only when he acquires actual knowledge, but this exclusion does not appear to have been deliberate. Nonetheless, because it refers to both alternative mental states for the failure to prevent, the formulation of the *Kvočka* Trial Chamber may be the most accurate: 'Action is required on the part of the superior from the point at which he "knew or had reason to know" of the crimes committed . . . by subordinates.'[510]

Grounding itself on jurisprudence holding that the superior's duty to prevent may arise not only during the crime's commission, but also during its preparation or planning stages,[511] the *Orić* Trial Chamber expressed disapproval of the timing formulations in the judgements cited in the previous paragraph, stating that they 'seem . . . to suggest that only completed crimes may be sanctioned'.[512] The Chamber elaborated its view as follows:

[S]uperior criminal responsibility . . . appears indeed to presuppose that the crime of a subordinate must have been completed in the same way as would be necessary for other modes of participation. On the other hand, this is not to say that only a subordinate who completes a crime should be punished. Since Article 7(3) of the Statute, in referring to Article 7(1) of the Statute, does not restrict the participation in a crime exclusively to acts which complete its execution, but includes those acts which comprise its planning and preparation, it is necessary only to prove that the criminal activities of a subordinate finally leads to a completed principal crime. This means that the superior must also bring to justice those subordinates who contributed to the principal crime merely by participating in the planning and preparation of it. Thus, although it is certainly true that without a violation of the law there is not yet a violator to be punished, such a violator can already be seen in a subordinate participating in the direct crime of others.[513]

As discussed in considerable detail below,[514] the *Orić* Chamber held in another part of its Judgement that an accused superior may bear liability not only for failing to prevent or punish his subordinates' overt physical commission of crimes, but also their culpable omissions and their participation in a crime through any of the other forms of responsibility listed in Article 7(1) of the ICTY Statute, including planning.[515] A careful reading of this passage reveals that, while the Trial Chamber took the view that a superior 'should' punish those subordinates who he later discovers participated in the planning of a crime that was never brought to fruition, it also recognised that criminal responsibility pursuant to Article 7(3) cannot be imposed on a superior for

[510] *Kvočka et al.* Trial Judgement, *supra* note 199, para. 317.
[511] *Halilović* Trial Judgement, *supra* note 27, para. 79 ('[T]he duty to prevent should be understood as resting on a superior *at any stage* before the commission of a subordinate crime if he acquires knowledge that such a crime is being prepared or planned, or has reason to know thereof.'). See also *supra* notes 492–493 and accompanying text.
[512] *Orić* Trial Judgement, *supra* note 179, para. 334.   [513] *Ibid.* (footnotes omitted).
[514] See *infra* text accompanying notes 543–620.   [515] *Orić* Trial Judgement, *supra* note 179, para. 301.

his failure to punish subordinate planning that does not result in the commission of a crime. In other words, the conduct engaged in by the subordinate – whether it be through physical perpetration or some other form of responsibility – must be criminal itself in order to engage the superior responsibility of an accused.[516] As the forms of responsibility are not criminal in and of themselves, but merely serve to attribute criminality to a person when combined with the criminal conduct and mental state of the physical perpetrator, an accused should not incur liability for failing to punish subordinate conduct fulfilling the physical and mental elements of a form of responsibility if that conduct did not contribute to the actual commission of a crime.[517]

Several chambers have pointed to a number of minimum obligations where 'failure to punish' liability may arise if the accused does not discharge such obligations properly: the obligation to investigate or order to be investigated subordinate misconduct;[518] the obligation to establish the facts;[519] the obligation to report the results of any investigation to the competent authorities;[520] and the obligation to take active steps to ensure that the perpetrators of a crime are brought before the appropriate judicial or administrative authorities.[521] A chamber should examine the thoroughness of any investigation ordered in

---

[516] See *Kordić and Čerkez* Appeal Judgement, *supra* note 206, para. 26 (holding that a crime must actually be committed for liability for planning to be triggered); *Aleksovski* Appeal Judgement, *supra* note 200, para. 165 (holding that a crime must actually be committed for liability for aiding and abetting to be triggered).

[517] See *Kordić and Čerkez* Appeal Judgement, *supra* note 206, paras. 26–27 (holding that an accused's planning or instigating of a crime need not have been the 'but for' cause of the crime, but need merely have been a factor 'substantially contributing to ... criminal conduct constituting one or more statutory crimes that are later perpetrated') (quotation at para. 26); *Blaškić* Appeal Judgement, *supra* note 170, para. 48 (making the same observation for aiding and abetting); *Strugar* Trial Judgement, *supra* note 179, para. 332 (making the same observation for ordering). Chapter 4, text accompanying notes 139–302, contains a complete discussion of the elements of aiding and abetting, and Chapter 5 examines the elements of planning, instigating and ordering.

[518] *Hadžihasanović and Kubura* Trial Judgement, *supra* note 179, paras. 174, 176; *Limaj et al.* Trial Judgement, *supra* note 179, para. 529; *Halilović* Trial Judgement, *supra* note 27, paras. 97, 100; *Strugar* Trial Judgement, *supra* note 179, para. 376.

[519] *Hadžihasanović and Kubura* Trial Judgement, *supra* note 179, paras. 174, 176; *Limaj et al.* Trial Judgement, *supra* note 179, para. 529; *Halilović* Trial Judgement, *supra* note 27, paras. 97, 100; *Strugar* Trial Judgement, *supra* note 179, para. 376.

[520] *Hadžihasanović and Kubura* Trial Judgement, *supra* note 179, paras. 173, 174, 176; *Limaj et al.* Trial Judgement, *supra* note 179, para. 529; *Halilović* Trial Judgement, *supra* note 27, paras. 97, 99, 100; *Strugar* Trial Judgement, *supra* note 179, para. 376; *Blagojević and Jokić* Trial Judgement, *supra* note 188, para. 793 ('The obligation to ... punish may, under some circumstances, be satisfied by reporting the matter to the competent authorities.'); *Brđanin* Trial Judgement, *supra* note 179, para. 279; *Stakić* Trial Judgement, *supra* note 210, para. 461; *Kvočka et al.* Trial Judgement, *supra* note 199, para. 316; *Kordić and Čerkez* Trial Judgement, *supra* note 190, para. 446; *Blaškić* Trial Judgement, *supra* note 115, paras. 302, 335; *Aleksovski* Trial Judgement, *supra* note 210, para. 78.

[521] See *Hadžihasanović and Kubura* Trial Judgement, *supra* note 179, paras. 175, 176; *Halilović* Trial Judgement, *supra* note 27, para. 99 (citing ICRC Commentary to the Additional Protocols, *supra* note 5, para. 3562); *Strugar* Trial Judgement, *supra* note 179, para. 376 (citing *High Command* case, *supra* note 44, p. 623).

determining whether the investigation contributed to the discharging of an accused's duty to punish.[522]

After determining that all three essential elements for superior responsibility had been fulfilled in respect of Krstić[523] – including that he had effective control over not only the officers of the Drina Corps of the Bosnian Serb army, but also Drina Corps troops on the ground[524] – the Trial Chamber found the accused responsible for his failure to take any action whatsoever to punish the troops who carried out underlying offences of genocide by killing Muslim men and boys at Srebrenica.[525] The Trial Chamber declined to find Krstić guilty for his failure to punish genocide, however, because it had already entered a conviction under Article 7(1) of the ICTY Statute for the same conduct.[526]

While the *Kordić and Čerkez* Trial Judgement held that '[p]ersons who assume command after the commission [of crimes by subordinates] are under the same duty to punish' as those who were in command at the time of the offences' commission,[527] this position was effectively overruled in the July 2003 *Hadžihasanović* decision on interlocutory appeal. After analysing superior responsibility under customary international law as it stood at the time of the events in the former Yugoslavia, three judges of a five-judge bench of the Appeals Chamber held as follows:

In this particular case, no practice can be found, nor is there any evidence of *opinio juris* that would sustain the proposition that a commander can be held responsible for crimes committed by a subordinate prior to the commander's assumption of command over that subordinate[528] ... Having examined the above authorities, the Appeals Chamber holds that an accused cannot be charged under Article 7(3) of the Statute for crimes committed by a subordinate before the said accused assumed command over that subordinate.[529]

Two subsequent trial judgements discussed at some length their disagreement with the policy implications of the majority's holding, although they

---

[522] See *Strugar* Trial Judgement, *supra* note 179, para. 376 (citing Tokyo Judgement, *supra* note 61, p. 458).

[523] *Krstić* Trial Judgement, *supra* note 205, para. 647.

[524] *Ibid.*, paras. 648–649.

[525] *Ibid.*, para. 650. See also ICTY Statute, *supra* note 31, Art. 4(2)(a) (listing 'killing members of the group' as an underlying offence of genocide).

[526] *Krstić* Trial Judgement, *supra* note 205, para. 652. The relationship between Article 7(1) (Article 6(1) of the ICTR Statute on the one hand, and Article 7/6(3) on the other, is discussed in Chapter 6, text accompanying notes 49–122.

[527] *Kordić and Čerkez* Trial Judgement, *supra* note 190, para. 446.

[528] *Hadžihasanović et al.* 7(3) Appeal Decision, *supra* note 3, para. 45.

[529] *Ibid.*, para. 51. Accord *Prosecutor v. Orić*, Case No. IT-03-68-T, T.8998 (8 June 2005) ('An [a]ccused cannot be found liable under the principle of superior responsibility for crimes committed by a subordinate before the said [a]ccused assumed command over that subordinate.').

234 *Forms of responsibility in international criminal law*

accepted it as binding authority.[530] The Trial Chamber in *Orić* agreed that, since it requires action by the superior prior to or during the commission of the relevant criminal conduct, the duty to prevent 'presupposes his power to control the conduct of his subordinates' and thus requires that he have effective control at the time the criminal conduct took place. The duty to punish, by contrast, becomes relevant only after the occurrence of criminal conduct of which the superior need not have been aware at the time it was occurring:

Since a superior in such circumstances is obliged to take punitive measures notwith-standing his or her inability to prevent the crime due to his or her lack of awareness and control, it seems only logical that such an obligation would also extend to the situation wherein there has been a change of command following the commission of a crime by a subordinate. The new commander in such a case, now exercising power over his or her subordinates and being made aware of their crimes committed prior to the change of command, for the sake of coherent prevention and control, should not let them go unpunished.[531]

In its judgement, the *Hadžihasanović and Kubura* Trial Chamber expressed sympathy for the views of Judge Shahabuddeen, one of the two Appeals Chamber dissenters:

Since the commanders of troops change on a regular basis in times of war, there is a serious risk that a gap in the line of responsibilities will be created as the changes occur. Considering the aforementioned case, if the superior in command at the time a crime is committed is replaced very soon after its commission, it is very likely that the perpetrators of that crime will go unpunished and that no commander will be held criminally responsible under the principles of command responsibility. It must be recognised that in such a case military practice, whose purpose is to establish the internal order and discipline necessary to run the armed forces, and from which the power to punish flows, falls short of achieving its objective.[532]

The holding of the majority of the Appeals Chamber in *Hadžihasanović*, which is still binding law for the trial chambers of the *ad hoc* Tribunals, would certainly seem to be at odds with the assertion of that same majority that '[c]ommand responsibility is the most effective method by which international

---

[530] *Orić* Trial Judgement, *supra* note 179, para. 335; *Hadžihasanović and Kubura* Trial Judgement, *supra* note 179, para. 198.
[531] *Orić* Trial Judgement, *supra* note 179, para. 335.
[532] *Hadžihasanović and Kubura* Trial Judgement, *supra* note 179, para. 199. See also *Hadžihasanović et al.* 7(3) Appeal Decision, *supra* note 3, Partial Dissenting Opinion of Judge Shahabuddeen, para. 14 ('[T]here appears to be force in the argument that the responsibilities of a new commander extend to dealing with crimes committed by subordinates before he assumes command if he knows or has reason to know of the crimes. Otherwise, such crimes could fall between two stools.').

criminal law can enforce responsible command'.[533] It makes no sense not to impose liability on an accused for his failure to punish the past criminal conduct of those over whom he acquires effective control, as long as he also acquires knowledge or reason to know of such conduct. As the Trial Chamber in *Hadžihasanović and Kubura* noted, a contrary rule would allow subordinate wrongdoers to escape reproach by their immediate superiors whenever the person in charge at the time of the misconduct has been replaced by someone else.[534] The *Hadžihasanović* Appeals Chamber majority's position may ostensibly shield from liability those superiors who would otherwise be held responsible under an approach more consistent with the object and purpose of the 'failure to punish' provision in the Statutes of the *ad hoc* Tribunals.

Moreover, as emphasised by both dissenters,[535] it would appear that the majority took an overly rigid and somewhat self-contradictory view of the requirements imposed by customary international law, in situations where it must be determined whether a previously unforeseen factual scenario falls within an existing customary rule. In performing its analysis, the majority looked mainly at a handful of documents it considered to be indicative of the customary status of superior responsibility at the time of the events at issue, including Article 86(2) of Additional Protocol I, Article 28 of the Rome Statute of the ICC, and the Article 6 of the ILC's 1996 Draft Code of Crimes against the Peace and Security of Mankind. Unlike Article 7/6(3), which expressly refers to past crimes as well as future crimes, all these provisions speak of the superior having knowledge or reason to know that his subordinates were committing or were about to commit crimes. In the view of the majority, the emphasis in these instruments 'is on the superior-subordinate relationship existing at the time the subordinate was committing or was going to commit a crime'.[536] The majority apparently afforded this consideration great weight in arriving at its final conclusion that customary international law does not recognise the imposition of liability for a superior's failure to prevent crimes committed before he acquired effective control over the relevant subordinates.

At the very end of its analysis, even after pronouncing its holding, the majority expounded the principle that it apparently applied in arriving at

---

[533] *Hadžihasanović et al.* 7(3) Appeal Decision, *supra* note 3, para. 16. Accord *Hadžihasanović et al.* 7(3) Pre-Trial Decision, *supra* note 26, para. 197 (stating that the object and purpose of the doctrine of superior responsibility is to require superiors to fulfil their duty to ensure subordinates comply with principles of international humanitarian law).

[534] See *Hadžihasanović and Kubura* Trial Judgement, *supra* note 179, para. 198.

[535] *Hadžihasanović et al.* 7(3) Appeal Decision, *supra* note 3, Separate and Partially Dissenting Opinion of Judge David Hunt, para. 10–11; *ibid.*, Partial Dissenting Opinion of Judge Shahabuddeen, paras. 8–13.

[536] *Hadžihasanović et al.* 7(3) Appeal Decision, *supra* note 3, para. 49. See also, *ibid.*, paras. 46–47.

this conclusion: '[T]he Appeals Chamber holds the view that this Tribunal can impose criminal responsibility only if the crime charged was clearly established under customary international law at the time the events in issue occurred.'[537] Yet, as noted by Judge Hunt in his dissent,[538] a rule requiring 'clear' establishment under customary international law varies materially from the rule put forth and applied unanimously by the Appeals Chamber in the first part of the same decision, and which has been applied at least twice since.[539] In the first part of its decision the Chamber stated that, where it can be shown that a given principle exists in customary international law, 'it is not an objection to the application of the principle to a particular situation to say that the situation is new if it *reasonably* falls within the application of the principle'.[540] By holding later that superior responsibility exists in customary international law, and that liability can ensue for the failure to prevent or punish crimes committed in the course of an internal armed conflict,[541] the Chamber implicitly determined that the ascription of criminal sanction reasonably falls within the application of the doctrine as recognised by custom. The Chamber gave no indication of whether such imposition was also 'clearly established' in custom at the time of the events at issue.

Furthermore, if the majority is correct in asserting that the present- and future-focused superior responsibility provisions of Additional Protocol I, the Rome Statute, and the 1996 ILC Draft Code correctly reflect the status of customary international law, then a logical corollary would be that any imposition of liability on an accused for his failure to punish past criminal conduct, even where the accused had effective control at the time such conduct occurred, runs contrary to custom. As such, that portion of Article 7/6(3) which refers to the superior having knowledge or reason to know that his

---

[537] *Ibid.*, para. 51. This reference to 'the crime charged' is not entirely accurate, as the Appeals Chamber's analysis here concerned the customary status of a form of responsibility, not a crime. Cf. *Milutinović et al.* JCE Appeal Decision, *supra* note 178, para. 10 (referring specifically to forms of responsibility and holding that they must have existed in customary international law at the time the alleged criminal conduct occurred in order to come within the ICTY's jurisdiction); *Milutinović et al.* ICP Pre-Trial Decision, *supra* note 178, para. 15 (same).

[538] *Hadžihasanović et al.* 7(3) Appeal Decision, *supra* note 3, Separate and Partially Dissenting Opinion of Judge David Hunt, para. 10.

[539] See *Karemera et al.* JCE Appeal Decision, *supra* note 178, paras. 15–16 (holding that a clear basis exists in customary international law for JCE liability, and that the imposition of liability for participation in enterprises not of limited size or geographical scope reasonably falls within the application of this principle); *Brđanin* Trial Judgement, *supra* note 179, para. 715:

> The Trial Chamber is satisfied that it reasonably falls within the application of the doctrine of superior criminal responsibility for superiors to be held liable if they knew or had reason to know that their subordinates were about to commit genocide or had done so and failed to take the necessary and reasonable measures to prevent the crimes or punish the perpetrators thereof.

[540] *Hadžihasanović et al.* 7(3) Appeal Decision, *supra* note 3, para. 12 (emphasis added).

[541] See *ibid.*, para. 31. See also *supra* text accompanying notes 180–185, for a fuller discussion of this part of the Appeals Chamber's decision.

subordinates 'had done so' – that is, had committed criminal acts listed in Articles 2 to 5 of the ICTY Statute – should be considered *ultra vires* customary international law and should no longer be applicable in the *ad hoc* Tribunals. Perhaps for obvious reasons, the majority did not extend its reasoning this far.[542]

3.3 The scope of the subordinate criminal conduct that may give rise to superior responsibility

As suggested above,[543] a strict textual reading of the words 'committed' and 'commit' in Article 7/6(3) would compel the conclusion that a superior may only be held responsible for his failure to prevent the physical commission of crimes by subordinates, or to punish those subordinate physical perpetrators for having committed such crimes. Article 7(3) of the ICTY Statute provides:

> The fact that any of the *acts* referred to in articles 2 to 5 of the present Statute was *committed* by a subordinate does not relieve his superior of criminal responsibility if he knew or had reason to know that the subordinate was about to *commit* such acts or had done so and the superior failed to take the necessary and reasonable measures to prevent such *acts* or to punish the perpetrators thereof.[544]

Under this interpretation, an accused would only incur superior responsibility where he has effective control over the physical perpetrator of the crime in question, and would escape such responsibility where he only has effective control over an individual who, for example, ordered, instigated, or aided and abetted the physical commission of the crime, but did not himself engage in any part of the *actus reus* of that crime. Moreover, if the phrase 'acts referred to in articles 2 to 5' were construed to include only overt acts, the accused would also avoid superior responsibility where the person over whom he has effective control engages in criminal conduct that constitutes a culpable omission, but does not perform any express criminal acts.

Statements in most of the jurisprudence have tended to follow the language of Article 7/6(3) in referring to the subordinate criminal conduct for which an accused may be held liable as the 'commission' of a crime,[545] and most factual

---

[542] For academic commentary in support of the majority's opinion, see Theodor Meron, 'Revival of Customary Humanitarian Law', (2005) 99 *American Journal of International Law* 817; Christopher Greenwood, 'Command Responsibility and the *Hadžihasanović* Decision', (2004) 2 *Journal of International Criminal Justice* 598.

[543] See *supra* text accompanying notes 192–194.

[544] ICTY Statute, *supra* note 31, Art. 7(3) (emphases added). Article 6(3) of the ICTR Statute enshrines the doctrine in nearly identical terms, also employing the phrase 'committed by a subordinate'. ICTR Statute, *supra* note 31, Art. 6(3).

[545] See, e.g., *Čelebići* Appeal Judgement, *supra* note 32, para. 241 (holding that 'a superior will be criminally responsible through the principles of superior responsibility only if information was available to him

scenarios in which an accused has been convicted pursuant to Article 7/6(3) have involved subordinates found to have physically perpetrated overt criminal acts. Nevertheless, with three possible exceptions, the chambers have not evinced any apparent intention through such language to restrict the subordinate conduct that triggers superior responsibility to overt physical commission.[546] The exceptions appear respectively in the *Brđanin* and *Blagojević and Jokić* Trial Judgements, and in the *Hadžihasanović* pre-trial decision on command responsibility:

In order to hold the Accused criminally responsible pursuant to Article 7(3) of the Statute, the Prosecution must in the first place prove a superior-subordinate relationship between the Accused and the physical perpetrators of the crimes in question.[547]

In relation to the participation of the units in the murder operation, the Trial Chamber is convinced that they rendered practical assistance that furthered the crimes of murder and extermination. However, the Trial Chamber is unable to determine that they 'committed' any of the crimes charged under the counts of murder or extermination.[548]

Article 7(3) is clear in its wording and intent: 'the fact that any of the acts referred to in articles 2 to 5 ... *was committed* by a subordinate does not relieve his superior of criminal responsibility if he knew or had reason to know that the subordinate was *about to commit such acts* or had done so *and* the superior failed to take the necessary and reasonable measures *to prevent such acts* or to punish the perpetrators thereof.' Criminal liability under the Statute cannot attach because subordinates 'were about to plan, prepare' crimes within the jurisdiction of the Statute.[549]

None of the three Chambers went into any further detail on this question. Moreover, even with regard to *Brđanin*, which would appear to contain the

which would have put him on notice of offences *committed* by subordinates') (emphasis added); *Strugar* Trial Judgement, *supra* note 179, para. 367 ('A superior may be held responsible under Article 7(3) of the Statute for crimes *committed* by a subordinate if, *inter alia*, he knew or had reason to know that the subordinate *was about to commit* or *had committed* such crimes.') (emphases added); *Blaškić* Trial Judgement, *supra* note 115, para. 301 (holding that 'a commander may incur criminal responsibility for crimes *committed* by persons who are not formally his (direct) subordinates, insofar as he exercises effective control over them') (emphasis added); *Čelebići* Trial Judgement, *supra* note 3, para. 378 (holding that 'it is necessary that the superior have effective control over the persons *committing* the underlying violations of international humanitarian law') (emphasis added).

[546] See, e.g., *Blaškić* Appeal Judgement, *supra* note 170, para. 67 (noting that both the *Čelebići* Trial Chamber and the *Blaškić* Trial Chamber stated that the accused must have effective control over the person 'committing' the crime in question, and asserting that both these conclusions 'fall within the terms of Article 7(3) of the [ICTY] Statute', but not proceeding to examine what other interpretations may also fall within those terms because the accused Blaškić did not challenge the Trial Chamber's holding in this regard). The Trial Chamber in *Orić* presented its view as to why this question had not been explicitly addressed in the jurisprudence:

Until recently, both the requirement of a principal crime (committed by others than the accused) and its performance in [that is, through] any of the modes of liability provided for in Article 7(1) *appeared so obvious* as to hardly need to be explicitly stated. Since this position, however, has been challenged by the Defence, some clarification is needed.

Orić Trial Judgement, *supra* note 179, para. 295 (emphasis added) (footnote omitted).
[547] *Brđanin* Trial Judgement, *supra* note 179, para. 370.
[548] *Blagojević and Jokić* Trial Judgement, *supra* note 188, para. 794.
[549] *Hadžihasanović et al.* 7(3) Pre-Trial Decision, *supra* note 26, para. 209 (emphases in original).

clearest disapproval of superior responsibility for anything but subordinate physical commission, it is not entirely clear that the Chamber was cognisant of the potential limiting effect of its holding on future jurisprudence.

Prior to mid-2006, no other Chamber of either Tribunal appears to have addressed this question directly. In May and June of that year, however, a bench of Trial Chamber II of the ICTY addressed this question at great length, holding in a *Boškoski and Tarčulovski* pre-trial indictment decision, and then reaffirming in the *Orić* Trial Judgement, that superior responsibility does indeed extend to the failure to prevent or punish subordinate conduct beyond overt physical commission.[550] In *Boškoski and Tarčulovski*, the prosecution proposed amending the indictment to charge Boškoski with superior responsibility in the following terms:

> Ljube Boškoski is charged with superior responsibility for the crimes of regular and reserve police, including special police units, both for the commission of crimes by those police, as well as for the acts or omissions of those police, which aided and abetted prison guards, hospital personnel and civilians to commit those crimes as described in the Second Amended Indictment counts.[551]

Boškoski challenged this amendment on the ground that he could only be held liable under Article 7(3) for the acts of his alleged subordinates, not their omissions.[552] The Trial Chamber determined that it could not properly assess this claim without examining the 'broader issue' of whether an accused may incur superior responsibility for his failure to prevent or punish subordinate criminal conduct effected, 'by act or omission, through any of the modes of liability provided for under Article 7(1) of the [ICTY] Statute'.[553]

In the process of rejecting Boškoski's challenge and allowing the prosecution to amend the indictment as proposed,[554] the Trial Chamber looked first to the meaning of the words 'acts' and 'commission' in various parts of the Statute. The Chamber opined that, while 'committed' in Article 7(1) 'was intended to denote a particular mode of liability' through which the crimes set forth in Articles 2 to 5 can be realised, 'acts' and 'commit' in Article 7(3) should be interpreted much more broadly: '"acts" refers to the conduct of the subordinate, including both acts and omissions of the subordinate[,] and "commit" refers to any criminal conduct by a subordinate perpetrated through

---

[550] *Orić* Trial Judgement, *supra* note 179, para. 301; *Boškoski and Tarčulovski* May 2006 Pre-Trial Decision, *supra* note 192, para. 46. The bench in both *Boškoski and Tarčulovski* and *Orić* consisted of Presiding Judge Carmel Agius, Judge Hans Henrik Brydensholt, and Judge Albin Eser. In *Orić*, the Trial Chamber acknowledged that it had 'already dealt with the[ ] legal aspects [of this question], and gave its position on them, in … *Boškoski and Tarčulovski*', and asserted that it would accordingly 'limit itself to [a number of] reconfirmations and clarifications'. *Orić* Trial Judgement, *supra* note 179, para. 298 (footnote omitted).
[551] *Boškoski and Tarčulovski* May 2006 Pre-Trial Decision, *supra* note 192, para. 16.   [552] *Ibid.*
[553] *Ibid.*, para. 19.   [554] *Ibid.*, paras. 48, 71.

any of the modes of liability that are provided for under the Statute'.[555] In both *Boškoski and Tarčulovski* and *Orić*, the Chamber invoked the use of these two terms in their broader sense in other parts of the Statute. For instance, although Article 2 lists 'acts against persons and property' as a grave breach of the Geneva Conventions and Article 5 refers to 'other inhumane acts' as a crime against humanity, both these crimes can be perpetrated not only through overt action, but also through omission.[556]

The Trial Chamber in both cases similarly pointed to various other provisions of the Statute that speak in terms of 'serious violations of international humanitarian law *committed* in the territory of the former Yugoslavia',[557] as well as Article 29, which refers to 'the investigation and prosecution of persons accused of *committing* violations of international humanitarian law'.[558] According to the Chamber, 'committed' in all these contexts encompasses all forms of responsibility.[559] To interpret 'committed' and 'committing' in these other provisions to include only physical commission 'would have absurd results',[560] as 'the Prosecutor would have no authority to investigate and prosecute any cases where the mode of liability was anything other than "commission" in person'.[561]

The Trial Chamber in both cases then proceeded to examine the object and purpose of Article 7(3) of the ICTY Statute in support of its conclusion that superior responsibility must extend to the failure to prevent or punish

---

[555] *Ibid.*, para. 22.
[556] *Ibid.*, para. 23; *Orić* Trial Judgement, *supra* note 179, para. 302. The *Orić* Chamber opined that the words 'act' and 'committing' are 'legal umbrella-terms for conduct that consists of actively causing a certain result to occur or in failing to prevent its occurrence'. *Ibid.*
[557] *Boškoski and Tarčulovski* May 2006 Pre-Trial Decision, *supra* note 192, para. 24 (emphasis added) (invoking the preamble of the Statute and Articles 1, 9, and 16). Accord *Orić* Trial Judgement, *supra* note 179, para. 299 (invoking Articles 1, 2, 4, 5, 9 and 16).
[558] ICTY Statute, *supra* note 31, Art. 29 (emphasis added).
[559] See *Orić* Trial Judgement, *supra* note 179, para. 296. In *Boškoski and Tarčulovski*, the Trial Chamber invoked Article 25 of the Rome Statute of the ICC as support for the proposition that that Court's Statute also contains a narrow and a broad meaning of the word 'commit', as evidenced by the obviously broad meaning given to it in Article 25(2) and the narrow meaning in Article 25(3). *Boškoski and Tarčulovski* May 2006 Pre-Trial Decision, *supra* note 192, paras. 44–45. Curiously, this discussion does not appear with the related discussion concerning the terms of the Statute of the ICTY, but instead appears at the very end of the decision immediately preceding the Trial Chamber's conclusion.
[560] *Boškoski and Tarčulovski* May 2006 Pre-Trial Decision, *supra* note 192, para. 24. But see *Prosecutor v. Popović, Beara, Nikolić, Borovčanin, Tolimir, Miletić, Gvero, Pandurević and Trbić*, Case No. IT-05-88-PT, Decision on Motions Challenging the Indictment pursuant to Rule 72 of the Rules, 31 May 2006, para. 89 (holding that 'the term "committed" in the settled jurisprudence of the Tribunal refers specifically to the physical perpetration of a crime or participation in a JCE, *and does not encompass the other forms of responsibility with which the Accused are charged*', and accordingly ordering the prosecution to delete the word 'committed' under each count of the indictment and replace it with the words 'are responsible for') (emphasis added).
[561] *Ibid.* The Trial Chamber in *Orić* expressed this view in a more cautious manner, opining merely that the possibility of different meanings of 'committed' across various provisions of the Statute 'can certainly not be excluded'. *Orić* Trial Judgement, *supra* note 179, para. 299.

subordinate criminal conduct beyond overt physical commission. In the words of the Chamber in *Boškoski and Tarčulovski*:

The mode of liability of superior responsibility is the method by which responsible command can be enforced and a commander can be held responsible for the conduct of his subordinates. It imposes a duty on a commander to ensure that those under this command do not commit violations of international humanitarian law and is, there-fore, central to the enforcement of international humanitarian law itself. To view 'commit' in Article 7(3) narrowly as referring to the 'commission' mode of liability would drastically reduce the types of situations in which superior responsibility could be found to the extent that the form of liability would have minimal impact on the enforcement of either responsible command or international humanitarian law.[562]

Although regrettably restricted on its face to military commanders and viola-tions of international humanitarian law – as opposed to violations of inter-national criminal law in general – this observation comports with the Appeals Chamber's acknowledgement that the purpose behind the doctrine of superior responsibility in customary international law is the regulation of military and civilian discipline.[563] The Trial Chamber also invoked the 1993 Report of the UN Secretary-General to the Security Council recommending the establish-ment of the ICTY,[564] in which the Secretary-General stated that a person in position of superior authority 'should ... be held responsible for failure to prevent a crime or to deter the *unlawful behaviour* of his subordinates'.[565]

Finally, the Trial Chamber in *Boškoski and Tarčulovski* examined at con-siderable length discussions in several cases providing jurisprudential support for its holding;[566] in *Orić* the Chamber did not repeat this analysis, noting that it had already done so in *Boškoski and Tarčulovski*, and instead merely cited

---

[562] *Boškoski and Tarčulovski* May 2006 Pre-Trial Decision, *supra* note 192, para. 26 (footnote omitted) (citing *Halilović* Trial Judgement, *supra* note 27, para. 39). The *Orić* Trial Chamber seconded these comments in the following manner:

[D]ecisive weight must be given to the purpose of superior criminal responsibility: it aims at obliging commanders to ensure that subordinates do not violate international humanitarian law, either by harmful acts or by omitting a protective duty. This enforcement of international humanitarian law would be impaired to an inconceivable degree if a superior had to prevent subordinates only from killing or maltreating in person, while he could look the other way if he observed that subordinates 'merely' aided and abetted others in procuring the same evil.

Orić Trial Judgement, *supra* note 179, para. 300.
[563] See *Hadžihasanović et al.* 7(3) Appeal Decision, *supra* note 3, para. 16 (holding that '[c]ommand responsibility is the most effective method by which international criminal law can enforce responsible command').
[564] *Boškoski and Tarčulovski* May 2006 Pre-Trial Decision, *supra* note 192, paras. 27–28; *Orić* Trial Judgement, *supra* note 179, para. 300 n. 851.
[565] Report of the Secretary-General pursuant to Paragraph 2 of Security Council Resolution 808 (1993), UN Doc. S/25704 (1993), para. 56 (emphasis added). In the next sentence, the Secretary-General went on to refer to superior responsibility as 'imputed responsibility or criminal negligence'. *Ibid.* As discussed at length above, the Appeals Chambers have since clarified that superior responsibility in the *ad hoc* Tribunals cannot be engaged on the basis of an accused's negligence in performing his duties as superior. See *supra* text accompanying notes 375–383.
[566] *Boškoski and Tarčulovski* May 2006 Pre-Trial Decision, *supra* note 192, paras. 30–40.

some of the relevant cases in footnotes.[567] In *Boškoski and Tarčulovski*, the Chamber recalled a number of judgements holding that criminal responsibility can ensue where the person in question engages in a culpable omission, either under the rubric of 'commission' in Article 7(1);[568] for JCE where the accused's contribution to the enterprise takes the form of a culpable omission;[569] or for planning, ordering, instigating, or aiding and abetting a crime where the omission of the accused satisfies the requisite physical element of the form of responsibility in question.[570] It also invoked the *Krnojelac* Trial Judgement where, in its view, 'the Trial Chamber expressly found that a superior could be held responsible for the omissions of his subordinates',[571] making particular reference to the following passage:

[567] *Orić* Trial Judgement, *supra* note 179, para. 301 and n. 852; *ibid.* para. 302 nn. 855–857.

[568] *Boškoski and Tarčulovski* May 2006 Pre-Trial Decision, *supra* note 192, para. 32 (citing *Prosecutor* v. *Tadić*, Case No. IT-94-1-A, Judgement, 15 July 1999 ('*Tadić* Appeal Judgement'), para. 188, referring to Article 7(1) as covering 'first and foremost the physical perpetration of a crime by the offender himself, or the culpable omission of an act that was mandated by a rule of criminal law'; *Blagojević and Jokić* Trial Judgement, *supra* note 188, para. 694; *Ntagerura et al.* Trial Judgement, *supra* note 206, para. 659; *Stakić* Trial Judgement, *supra* note 210, para. 439; *Naletilić and Martinović* Trial Judgement, *supra* note 206, para. 62; *Kvočka et al.* Trial Judgement, *supra* note 199, para. 251; *Krstić* Trial Judgement, *supra* note 205, para. 601; *Kordić and Čerkez* Trial Judgement, *supra* note 190, para. 376).

[569] *Boškoski and Tarčulovski* May 2006 Pre-Trial Decision, *supra* note 192, para. 32 (citing *Kvočka et al.* Appeal Judgement, *supra* note 201, para. 187, which held that 'it is sufficient for the accused [charged with participation in a JCE] to have committed an act or an omission which contributes to the common criminal purpose'). Accord *Prosecutor* v. *Popović, Beara, Nikolić, Borovčanin, Tolimir, Miletić, Gvero and Pandurević*, Case No. IT-05-88-PT, Decision on Further Amendments and Challenges to the Indictment, 13 July 2006, para. 28 (observing that, 'under the Tribunal's jurisprudence on the elements of JCE, in order to fulfil the element that the accused "participate" in the JCE, the accused need not have physically committed any part of the *actus reus* of any crime, and he need not even have performed an overt physical act').

[570] *Boškoski and Tarčulovski* May 2006 Pre-Trial Decision, *supra* note 192, para. 32 (citing *Prosecutor* v. *Rutaganira*, Case No. ICTR-95-1C-T, Sentencing Judgement, 14 March 2005, para. 68, finding the accused responsible for extermination as a crime against humanity through aiding and abetting by omission; *Galić* Trial Judgement, *supra* note 210, para. 168, listing the forms of responsibility of planning, instigating, ordering, aiding and abetting, and physical commission, and holding that '[t]hese forms of participation in a crime may be performed through positive acts or through culpable omission'; *Prosecutor* v. *Simić, Tadić and Zarić*, Case No. IT-95-9-T, Judgement, 17 October 2003, paras. 162–163; *Krnojelac* Trial Judgement, *supra* note 183, paras. 88, 90; *Kvočka et al.* Trial Judgement, *supra* note 199, para. 256, holding that aiding and abetting 'may consist of an act or omission of a crime perpetrated by another' where such act or omission has 'a significant effect on the commission of a crime'). Accord *Orić* Trial Judgement, *supra* note 179, para. 303 ('[S]ince commission through culpable omission is not limited to perpetration but, according to the case [law] of this Tribunal, is open to all forms of participation, instigating as well as aiding and abetting can also be carried out by omission.') (footnotes omitted); *ibid.*, para. 305 (holding that all forms of responsibility in Article 7(1) of the ICTY Statute, 'be it perpetration by committing the relevant crime (alone or jointly with others) in person or be it participation, as in the form of instigation or otherwise aiding and abetting ... may be performed by positive action or culpable omission'). But see *Galić* Appeal Judgement, *supra* note 366, paras. 176–177 (holding that 'ordering by omission' does not exist). A discussion of the jurisprudence of the *ad hoc* Tribunals on aiding and abetting by omission appears in Chapter 4, text accompanying notes 192–216; a discussion on instigating by omission appears in Chapter 5, text accompanying notes 115–120, 125–127; and the *Galić* Appeals Chamber's rejection of ordering by omission is discussed in Chapter 5, text accompanying notes 148–150.

[571] *Boškoski and Tarčulovski* May 2006 Pre-Trial Decision, *supra* note 192, para. 30.

The Trial Chamber is also satisfied that the Accused incurred criminal responsibility in his position as warden of the KP Dom for the acts *and omissions* of his subordinates, pursuant to Article 7(3) of the Tribunal's Statute. The Trial Chamber is satisfied that the Accused was aware of the participation of his subordinates in the creation of living conditions at the KP Dom which constituted inhumane acts and cruel treatment, that he omitted to take any action to prevent his subordinates from maintaining these living conditions and that he failed to punish his subordinates for the implementation of these living conditions.[572]

The Trial Chamber also cited several judgements ostensibly holding accused responsible under Article 7(3) 'for acts of subordinates that cannot be categorised as falling under the "commission" mode of liability'.[573] The Chamber again invoked *Krnojelac* as its strongest support, where the accused was found responsible and convicted pursuant to Article 7(3) for 'the actions of the KP Dom guards . . . who permitted individuals from outside the KP Dom to enter the KP Dom in order to participate in the mistreatment of detainees, thereby (at least) aiding and abetting them in that mistreatment'.[574] The *Boškoski and Tarčulovski* Chamber also recalled the *Krstić* Trial Judgement, in which the Trial Chamber found that the accused fulfilled all the elements of superior responsibility by virtue of his failure to prevent and punish the criminal conduct of certain troops of the Bosnian Serb army over whom he had effective control.[575] The *Krstić* Chamber characterised the contribution of these troops to the genocidal campaign as 'render[ing] tangible and substantial assistance and technical support to the detention, killing and burial' of the victims,[576] including through such activities as scouting for appropriate reburial sites and driving the trucks that transported the victims to detention and execution sites.[577]

---

[572] *Krnojelac* Trial Judgement, *supra* note 183, para. 172 (emphasis added). The *Krnojelac* Chamber did not ultimately convict the accused on the basis of his superior responsibility in respect of these incidents, however, because it had already found him liable as an aider and abettor pursuant to Article 7(1), and it would be 'inappropriate to convict under both heads of responsibility for the same count based on the same acts'. *Ibid.*, para. 173. Chapter 6, text accompanying notes 49–122, discusses concurrent convictions under Articles 7/6(1) and 7/6(3).

[573] *Boškoski and Tarčulovski* May 2006 Pre-Trial Decision, *supra* note 192, para. 36.

[574] *Krnojelac* Trial Judgement, *supra* note 183, para. 319. See also *ibid.*, para. 320 (entering finding of guilt). In the view of the *Boškoski and Tarčulovski* Trial Chamber, this holding demonstrates that the *Krnojelac* Trial Chamber 'clearly considered that responsibility can be attributed pursuant to Article 7(3) for crimes perpetrated by subordinates through forms of liability other than "commission"'. *Boškoski and Tarčulovski* May 2006 Pre-Trial Decision, *supra* note 192, para. 37.

[575] *Boškoski and Tarčulovski* May 2006 Pre-Trial Decision, *supra* note 192, para. 38 (citing *Krstić* Trial Judgement, *supra* note 205, paras. 641, 647–648, 650).

[576] *Krstić* Trial Judgement, *supra* note 205, para. 624.

[577] *Ibid.*, para. 623. Here again, however, the Trial Chamber declined to convict Krstić pursuant to Article 7(3), because it determined that he also bore liability for these events as a JCE participant pursuant to Article 7(1). *Ibid.*, paras. 605, 633, 652.

As another example purportedly in support of its holding, the *Boškoski and Tarčulovski* Chamber discussed the conviction of the accused Naletilić and Martinović for failing to prevent and punish plunder as a violation of the laws or customs of war.[578] The *Naletilić and Martinović* Trial Chamber found that the subordinates of the two accused had not only engaged in acts of looting themselves, but had also forced prisoners under their control to engage in such acts.[579] In the interpretation of the *Boškoski and Tarčulovski* Chamber, because the *Naletilić and Martinović* Chamber did not distinguish between the looting performed by the accused's subordinates and the looting performed by the prisoners, 'the Judgement indicates an acceptance of the view that superior responsibility could be attributed to commanders where their subordinates aided and abetted the crime in question'.[580]

While both *Krnojelac* and *Krstić* would appear to be well cited as instances in which a chamber made findings of superior responsibility on the basis of subordinate aiding and abetting, it is less clear that the *Naletilić and Martinović* Trial Chamber can be appropriately said to have done the same, for at least two reasons. First, although the imposition of Article 7(3) liability for subordinate aiding and abetting in *Krnojelac* and *Krstić* seems to have been advertent and deliberate, nowhere did the *Naletilić and Martinović* Chamber characterise the subordinate conduct at issue in its analysis as aiding and abetting, and indeed it is highly questionable whether forcing an innocent agent to engage in criminal conduct qualifies as the 'practical assistance, encouragement, or moral support' that is the requisite physical element of aiding and abetting.[581] Second, even if that Chamber did implicitly consider such conduct to constitute aiding and abetting, it simultaneously found that the relevant subordinates also physically perpetrated many of the criminal acts at issue. As such, it remains uncertain whether the Trial Chamber would have convicted Naletilić and Martinović pursuant to Article 7(3) solely for failing to prevent their subordinates from forcing or inducing these prisoners to engage in plunder.[582]

---

[578] *Boškoski and Tarčulovski* May 2006 Pre-Trial Decision, *supra* note 192, para. 39.

[579] *Naletilić and Martinović* Trial Judgement, *supra* note 206, paras. 619–631.

[580] *Boškoski and Tarčulovski* May 2006 Pre-Trial Decision, *supra* note 192, para. 39.

[581] *Blaškić* Appeal Judgement, *supra* note 170, para. 45. *Accord Tadić* Appeal Judgement, *supra* note 568, para. 229; *Strugar* Trial Judgement, *supra* note 179, para. 349.

[582] Unlike the Rome Statute of the ICC, forcing or inducing the commission of a crime has not been classified in the Statutes of the *ad hoc* Tribunals as a form of responsibility, nor has it yet been held to constitute a form of responsibility in the jurisprudence. See Rome Statute, *supra* note 4, Art. 25(3)(b) ('In accordance with this Statute, a person shall be criminally responsible and liable for punishment for a crime within the jurisdiction of the Court if that person . . . induces the commission of such a crime which in fact occurs or is attempted.').

Before concluding its analysis, the *Boškoski and Tarčulovski* Trial Chamber addressed two of the three passages cited above as examples of jurisprudential disapproval of superior responsibility for subordinate criminal conduct beyond physical commission.[583] The Chamber acknowledged that *Hadžihasanović* suggested the impermissibility of imposing Article 7(3) liability on an accused for subordinate planning of crimes,[584] and that *Blagojević and Jokić* suggested the impermissibility of such liability for subordinate aiding and abetting, and that this latter judgement may accordingly 'be read as supporting a narrow interpretation of Article 7(3) of the Statute'.[585] Although it remarked that '[i]t is not clear whether the *Blagojević and Jokić* Trial Chamber intended such a limited application', however, the *Boškoski and Tarčulovski* Chamber simply asserted that, 'insofar as such interpretation was intended, this Trial Chamber is not in a position to support it'.[586]

In the end, the Trial Chamber in both *Boškoski and Tarčulovski* and *Orić* held that superior responsibility may be engaged for the failure to prevent or punish subordinate criminal conduct beyond overt physical commission,[587] although exactly what such conduct may constitute is not entirely clear. Specifically, the *Boškoski and Tarčulovski* Trial Chamber made a number of contradictory statements, some suggesting that the subordinate criminal conduct may consist of any form of responsibility in the jurisdiction of the ICTY, whether effected by way of an act or an omission, and some suggesting that such conduct may only entail those forms of responsibility contained in Article 7(1) of the ICTY Statute, whether effected by way of an act or an omission. The following three statements are representative of the internal contradiction:

The Trial Chamber is of the view that these two issues cannot be dealt with in isolation of the wider issue, which is whether superior responsibility can be attributed under Article 7(3) of the Statute for crimes committed by a subordinate, by act or omission, through any of the modes of liability provided for under Article 7(1) of the Statute.[588]

---

[583] See *supra* text accompanying notes 547–549.
[584] *Boškoski and Tarčulovski* May 2006 Pre-Trial Decision, *supra* note 192, para. 41.   [585] *Ibid.*, para. 43.
[586] *Ibid.*
[587] *Ibid.*, para. 46; *Orić* Trial Judgement, *supra* note 179, para. 301. The *Boškoski and Tarčulovski* Trial Chamber reaffirmed this holding less than four months later in dismissing a second challenge by Boškoski, this time claiming that the ICTY lacked jurisdiction to impose superior responsibility on him for failing to prevent or punish 'acts committed by third parties which subordinates are alleged to have aided and abetted'. *Prosecutor* v. *Boškoski and Tarčulovski*, Case No. IT-04-82-PT, Decision on Assigned *Pro Bono* Counsel Motion Challenging Jurisdiction, 8 September 2006, para. 8. The Trial Chamber recalled that it had 'already rejected [this argument] in the present proceedings in relation to the same amendment of the Indictment'. *Ibid.*, para. 16. Boškoski appealed this decision, and his appeal was still pending as of 1 December 2006, the date of submission of this book to the publisher. See *Prosecutor* v. *Boškoski and Tarčulovski*, Case No. IT-04-82-AR72.2, Boškoski Defence Appeal on Jurisdiction, 22 September 2006.
[588] *Boškoski and Tarčulovski* May 2006 Pre-Trial Decision, *supra* note 192, para. 19.

This Trial Chamber ... considers that if a subordinate's acts can be categorised as criminal under any of the modes of liability set out in Article 7(1) of the Statute then responsibility under Article 7(3) for failure to prevent and punish these acts may arise.[589]

On the basis of the reasons provided above, the Trial Chamber finds that 'acts' and 'commit' in Article 7(3) of the Statute are meant broadly and permit the imposition of superior responsibility where subordinates have perpetrated a crime, whether by act or omission, through the modes of liability provided for under the Statute.[590]

Discerning exactly what the Trial Chamber intended to hold is particularly difficult in light of its failure to state expressly in its conclusion (the third passage above) that it consciously went beyond the scope both of its characterisation of the accused Boškoski's challenge (the first passage above), and of its ostensible interim holding lodged in the middle of the analysis (the second passage above). The more apt reading of *Boškoski and Tarčulovski*, however, would appear to be that the absence of language in the third passage limiting the subordinate criminal conduct in question to those forms of responsibility in Article 7(1) was inadvertent.

This interpretation finds support in the generally consistent statements of the same Trial Chamber one month later in the *Orić* Judgement, perhaps upon realising that its conclusion in *Boškoski and Tarčulovski* had not been expressed with sufficient precision. After noting with approval the analysis in its earlier decision and reiterating a portion of it,[591] the Trial Chamber held that 'the criminal responsibility of a superior under Article 7(3) of the Statue is not limited to crimes committed by subordinates in person but encompasses any modes of criminal responsibility proscribed in Article 7(1) of the Statute, in particular, instigating as well as otherwise aiding and abetting'.[592] This singling out of subordinate instigating and aiding and abetting 'in particular'

---

[589] *Ibid.*, para. 41.
[590] *Ibid.*, para. 46. See also *ibid.*, para. 22 (commenting that '"acts" refers to the conduct of the subordinate, including both acts and omissions of the subordinate[,] and "commit" refers to any criminal conduct by a subordinate perpetrated through any of the modes of liability that are provided for under the Statute'); *ibid.*, para. 24 ('The Trial Chamber considers that "commit" is ... used in the broad sense throughout the Statute to refer to all modes of liability.'); *ibid.*, para. 28 ('[T]he Trial Chamber notes that ... "commit or had committed" must be intended in the broad sense to encompass all types of unlawful behaviour under the Statute.').
[591] *Orić* Trial Judgement, *supra* note 179, paras. 298–300.
[592] *Ibid.*, para. 301 (footnote omitted). Accord *ibid.*, para. 294 (listing, as an element that must be fulfilled for superior responsibility, 'an act or omission incurring criminal responsibility according to Articles 2 to 5 and 7(1) of the Statute'). The authors refer to the statements on this subject in the *Orić* Trial Judgement as 'generally consistent' because later in the judgement, immediately before discussing its relevant factual findings, the Trial Chamber recalled its holding in paragraph 301 as 'not presuppos[ing] that the direct perpetrators of a crime ... be identical to the subordinates of the superior', and only requiring that 'the relevant subordinates, by their own acts and omissions, be criminally responsible for the acts and omissions of the direct perpetrators'. *Ibid.*, para. 478. Accord, *ibid.*, para. 691 (identical language). The absence of the restriction to Article 7(1) forms of responsibility in this passage would appear to be the result of inadvertence, however, and not a deliberate revision of the Chamber's earlier holding.

as appropriate bases for the imposition of superior responsibility is a curious innovation that did not appear in the analogous discussion in *Boškoski and Tarčulovski.*

In clarifying that its holding extends to forms of responsibility effected by positive action as well as by culpable omission, the Trial Chamber repeated the limitation to those forms in Article 7(1):

> [W]ith regard to the consequences for the superior's responsibility, the Trial Chamber holds that his or her duty to prevent or punish concerns all modes of conduct a subordinate may be criminally responsible for under Article 7(1) of the Statute, be it perpetration by committing the relevant crime (alone or jointly with others) in person or be it participation, as in the form of instigation or otherwise aiding and abetting, and further, that any of these modes of liability may be performed by positive action or culpable omission.[593]

Although *Orić* appears to have remedied the ambiguity in *Boškoski and Tarčulovski,* an examination of the Trial Chamber's respective discussions on this subject raises questions as to whether it fully appreciated the consequences of imposing its textual limitation on subordinate criminal conduct. If, as the Trial Chamber rightly put it, the purpose behind the doctrine of superior responsibility is to ensure discipline and law-abiding behaviour among subordinates,[594] then why should an accused escape superior responsibility where he has failed to prevent or punish subordinate conduct amounting to complicity in genocide, which is contained in Article 4(3) of the ICTY Statute, and not Article 7(1)?[595] A plain reading of Article 7(3), which refers to responsibility for the failure to prevent or punish 'any of the acts referred to in articles 2 to 5' of the Statute,[596] by its very terms encompasses Article 4, and thus complicity in genocide. This proposition also finds support in the *Kambanda* Trial

---

[593] *Ibid.*, para. 305. Accord, *ibid.*, para. 302 ('[A]s regards the nature of the "acts" referred to in Article 7(3) of the Statute, the Trial Chamber holds that a superior's criminal responsibility for crimes of subordinates is not limited to the subordinates' active perpetration or participation, but also comprises their committing by omission.'). The remainder of paragraph 305 foreshadows the Trial Chamber's subsequent factual findings that the accused Orić bore superior responsibility for his failure to prevent the Srebrenica military police from allowing criminal conduct to be perpetrated against Serb detainees:

> The superior's responsibility for omissions of subordinates is of particular relevance in cases where subordinates are under a protective duty to shield certain persons from being injured, as in the case of detainees kept in custody. If, due to a neglect of protection by subordinates, protected persons sustain injuries, it is these subordinates' culpable omissions (in terms of Article 7(1) of the Statute) for which the superior is made responsible under Article 7(3) of the Statute. Consequently, if for instance the maltreatment of prisoners by guards, and/or by outsiders not prevented from entering the location, is made possible because subordinates in charge of the prison fail to ensure the security of the detainees by adequate measures, it does not matter any further by whom else, due to the subordinates' neglect of protection, the protected persons are being injured, nor would it be necessary to establish the identity of the direct perpetrators.

> *Ibid.*, para. 305 (footnote omitted). See also *infra*, text accompanying notes 599–619, for a more detailed discussion of the Trial Chamber's factual findings in relation to this criminal conduct.

[594] See *Orić* Trial Judgement, *supra* note 179, para. 299.
[595] Chapter 4 discusses complicity in genocide in detail.   [596] ICTY Statute, *supra* note 31, Art. 7(3).

Judgement of the ICTR, in which the Trial Chamber accepted the accused's guilty plea for complicity in genocide pursuant not only to Article 6(1) of the ICTR Statute, but also to Article 6(3).[597]

Similarly, why should an accused escape superior responsibility where he has omitted to punish a subordinate for that subordinate's failure to prevent or punish the criminal conduct of his own subordinates? By its terms, the Trial Chamber's formulation in *Orić* appears to shield the accused from liability in situations where he enjoys effective control over a mid-level superior, who in turn enjoys effective control over the physical perpetrators – for example, a group of paramilitaries – but where the accused himself lacks the material ability to prevent or punish the conduct of these perpetrators, either through direct action or by means of orders to the mid-level superior. Although it is admittedly uncertain how often such a scenario would arise in practice, the Trial Chamber's failure to recognise superior responsibility where the subordinate criminal conduct at issue is an omission under Article 7(3) would appear to be at odds with one of the major pronouncements in both *Orić* and *Boškoski and Tarčulovski* – that superiors are responsible for guarding against the criminal omissions of subordinates and not only their acts.[598] Indeed, while the jurisprudence is clear in holding that all the forms of responsibility in Article 7(1) – with the possible exception of ordering and planning – may occasionally be effected by means of an omission, superior responsibility under Article 7(3) is the archetypical form of omission liability and is always effected through omission.

The Trial Chamber applied its expanded view of superior responsibility in convicting Naser Orić, the Bosnian Muslim commander of the Srebrenica Armed Forces Staff in 1992 and 1993, for his failure to prevent certain incidents of murder and cruel treatment as violations of the laws or customs of war perpetrated against Serb detainees.[599] The indictment alleged that a number of Serb individuals detained at and near the Srebrenica police station 'were subjected to physical abuse, serious suffering and serious injury to body and health, and inhumane treatment by the guards and/or by others with the support of the guards'.[600] While the Chamber found that incidents of

[597] *Kambanda* Trial Judgement, *supra* note 184, para. 40. But see *Blagojević and Jokić* Trial Judgement, *supra* note 188, paras. 685, 794–796 (holding that complicity in genocide is a form of responsibility and not a crime, and accordingly declining to address the accused's superior responsibility pursuant to Article 7(3) of the ICTY Statute for failing to prevent or punish his alleged subordinates' complicity in genocide); *Brđanin* Trial Judgement, *supra* note 179, paras. 725 n. 1765, 727 (same).
[598] See *Orić* Trial Judgement, *supra* note 179, paras. 302, 305; *Boškoski and Tarčulovski* May 2006 Pre-Trial Decision, *supra* note 192, para. 32.
[599] *Orić* Trial Judgement, *supra* note 179, paras. 578, 782.
[600] *Prosecutor* v. *Orić*, Case No. IT-03-68-PT, Third Amended Indictment, 30 June 2005, para. 23; *Orić* Trial Judgement, *supra* note 179, paras. 5, 476.

inhumane treatment and killing had occurred, it could not determine, on the evidence before it, whether any of the physical perpetrators were members of the Srebrenica military police; instead the perpetrators consisted of the guards at the detention facility who were under the employ of the police and wore a combination of civilian clothes and military uniforms, as well as unidentified visitors whom the guards had permitted to enter the facility.[601] The Chamber found that the Srebrenica military police were 'the competent authority dealing with Serb detainees' at the facility,[602] and that the police thereby assumed a duty under international law to ensure that the detainees were treated humanely.[603] The Chamber focused specifically on the two successive commanders of the military police during the period – Mirzet Halilović and Atif Krdžić – finding that they failed to provide adequate supervision of the detention facility, that both knew or must have known of the crimes committed there, and that as a consequence 'the Srebrenica military police, through its commanders . . . Mirzet Halilović and Atif Krdžić respectively, are responsible for the acts and omissions by the guards at the [detention facility]'.[604]

Having concluded that the Srebrenica military police were responsible, through an unspecified form of responsibility, for the criminal acts perpetrated against the detainees, the Trial Chamber examined the military structure in place at the relevant time to discern whether Orić had effective control over the military police. It determined that two successive chiefs of staff of the Srebrenica Armed Forces Staff – Osman Osmanović and Ramiz Bećirović – 'were directly involved in the interrogation of, and decision-taking process regarding[,] Serb prisoners',[605] issued orders and decisions directly to the Srebrenica military police,[606] and 'indirectly involved themselves in matters relating to the detention of Serb detainees'.[607] On the basis of these factors, the Chamber concluded that Osmanović and Bećirović exercised effective control over the military police.[608]

The Trial Chamber then found that Orić, as the commander of the Srebrenica Armed Forces Staff and thus of Osmanović and Bećirović, exercised effective control over them.[609] In spite of its earlier assertion that 'the requisite level of control is a matter to be determined on the basis of the evidence presented in each case' and its listing of a number of indicia of effective control set forth in earlier jurisprudence,[610] the Chamber did not provide concrete examples of how Orić could have exerted his control over Osmanović and Bećirović in a way that would have resulted in their taking

---

[601] See *ibid.*, paras. 354, 368, 480–481, 446, 489–490, 530.   [602] *Ibid.*, para. 485.
[603] *Ibid.*, paras. 489–490.   [604] *Ibid.*, para. 496.   [605] *Ibid.*, para. 526.   [606] *Ibid.*
[607] *Ibid.*, para. 527.   [608] *Ibid.*   [609] *Ibid.*, para. 529.   [610] *Ibid.*, para. 312.

action towards the Srebrenica military police, with the ultimate consequence that the crimes in question were either prevented or punished, or both. The Chamber appears instead to have placed great weight on the abstract relationship between a chief of staff and a commander, and on Orić's *de jure* status as commander, to divine the existence of effective control:

> The relationship between a chief of staff and a commander is such that the former reports to the latter, takes orders from him and implements them. In this way, a commander exercises effective control over the chief of staff. There is no evidence that would indicate that the situation was different in the case of Osman Osmanović and Ramiz Bećirović.[611]

Having established a superior-subordinate relationship between Orić and the superiors of the Srebrenica military police, the Trial Chamber rather summarily found that Orić consequently exercised effective control over the military police: 'The chain of superior-subordinate relationship for the purposes of responsibility pursuant to Article 7(3) descends from the Accused to the Srebrenica military police that w[ere] responsible for the safety and proper treatment of the Serb detainees via the chain of command explained above.'[612]

As with its finding that the Srebrenica military police incurred responsibility for the acts and omissions of the guards at the detention facility, the Chamber did not explicitly indicate the form of responsibility under which the conduct of Osmanović and Bećirović fell, and it did not evaluate Orić's superior responsibility for the criminal conduct of these two men. The Chamber evidently preferred to confine the remainder of its analysis to his responsibility exclusively for the criminal conduct of the Srebrenica military police, and Osmanović and Bećirović effectively dropped out of the Chamber's discussion once it was able to create a link through them between Orić and the military police. After determining that Orić had reason to know of a number of the incidents of murder and cruel treatment in question,[613] the Trial Chamber convicted him for his failure to prevent the criminal conduct of the Srebrenica military police, which ostensibly consisted of the police's own failure to prevent the criminal conduct of guards under their effective control.[614] The guards, in turn, both physically perpetrated murder and cruel treatment and omitted to carry out their duty to impede outsiders from doing so.

---

[611] *Ibid*. See *supra*, text accompanying notes 240–253, for a discussion of this finding as an example of proof of *de jure* authority creating a rebuttable presumption of effective control.

[612] *Ibid*., para. 531. Accord, *ibid*., para. 532 ('[T]he Trial Chamber is satisfied beyond reasonable doubt that subsequent to 27 November 1992, a superior-subordinate relationship for the purposes of Article 7(3) of the Statute existed between the Accused and the Srebrenica military police.').

[613] *Ibid*., paras. 542–543, 560.   [614] See *ibid*., paras. 560, 578.

As the Trial Chamber correctly pointed out in an earlier part of its judgement, superior responsibility can ensue on the basis of both direct and indirect relationships of subordination: 'Whether [effective] control is directly exerted upon a subordinate or mediated by other sub-superiors or subordinates is immaterial, as long as the responsible superior would have the means to prevent the relevant crimes from being committed or to take efficient measures for having them sanctioned.'[615] This principle can be illustrated by the following syllogism: if A has effective control over B, and C has effective control over A, then C must also have effective control over B. The proper application of this principle clearly depends on the strength of each link of effective control, and for each link the chamber must determine whether, on the facts of the case, each superior in the chain actually possessed real powers of control over the conduct of the relevant subordinate.[616] Only where such powers exist at every level at the relevant time can the accused be said to exercise effective control over sub-subordinates through, for example, his material ability to issue orders to his immediate subordinates that those subordinates will heed and have the material ability to implement.

Where the accused is found to have effective control over his immediate subordinate, but a link further down the chain is too weak to support a finding that a particular sub-superior enjoyed effective control over his own immediate subordinate, the *Boškoski and Tarčulovski* and *Orić* innovation allows a chamber still to impose superior responsibility on the accused, but not for the criminal conduct of those persons in a position below the broken link. This may have been the key to the Trial Chamber's imposition of superior responsibility on Orić for failing to prevent the criminal conduct of the Srebrenica military police, as opposed to the conduct of the guards and opportunistic visitors who physically perpetrated the crimes in question. While it found – albeit with arguably insufficient reasoning – that Orić had effective control over Osmanović and Bećirović, and that these two men had effective control over the Srebrenica military police, nowhere did it expressly find that the military police exercised effective control over the guards and opportunistic visitors. On the other hand, several statements in the judgement imply that the military police did indeed enjoy real powers of control over the guards that could have been exercised, had a superior of the police issued an order to do so.[617] These statements include, most tellingly, the following: 'The Trial Chamber simply does not see how it could have been impossible for the guards

---

[615] *Ibid.*, para. 311. See also *supra* text accompanying notes 258–262.
[616] See *Kajelijeli* Appeal Judgement, *supra* note 200, para. 86; *Kordić and Čerkez* Appeal Judgement, *supra* note 206. See also *supra* text accompanying notes 213–219.
[617] See *Orić* Trial Judgement, *supra* note 179, paras. 492–495.

and/or the commander of the Srebrenica military police to prevent crimes such as murder and cruel treatment from occurring, had adequate control been exercised.'[618] In this regard, it remains a mystery why the Chamber did not hold Orić responsible as a superior for failing to prevent the criminal conduct of the guards themselves, especially considering its earlier holding that 'proof of the existence of a superior-subordinate relationship does not require the identification of the principal perpetrators . . . nor that the superior had knowledge of the number or identity of possible intermediaries'.[619]

In the final analysis, while both *Boškoski and Tarčulovski* and *Orić* have their flaws, the overall result achieved by the Trial Chamber is promising. Not only does it fill a considerable gap in the jurisprudence, but it also affords the chambers of the *ad hoc* Tribunals a greater degree of flexibility in reaching just results in an era of prosecutorial policy focusing increasingly on 'the most senior leaders suspected of being most responsible for crimes within the jurisdiction of the relevant Tribunal'.[620] It may be advisable for future chambers of the *ad hoc* Tribunals to endorse an interpretation of *Boškoski and Tarčulovski* and *Orić* that does not restrict the Trial Chamber's holding to those forms of responsibility that appear in Article 7(1) of the ICTY Statute and Article 6(1) of the ICTR Statute.

3.4 Superior responsibility in the International Criminal Court and internationalised tribunals

3.4.1 The International Criminal Court

Article 28 of the Rome Statute, entitled 'Responsibility of commanders and other superiors', provides:

In addition to other grounds of criminal responsibility under this Statute for crimes within the jurisdiction of the Court:

(a) A military commander or person effectively acting as a military commander shall be criminally responsible for crimes within the jurisdiction of the Court committed by forces under his or her effective command and control, or effective authority and control as the case may be, as a result of his or her failure to exercise control properly over such forces, where:
  (i) That military commander or person either knew or, owing to the circumstances at the time, should have known that the forces were committing or about to commit such crimes; and
  (ii) That military commander or person failed to take all necessary and reasonable measures within his or her power to prevent or repress their commission

---

[618] *Ibid.*, para. 568.   [619] *Ibid.*, para. 311.
[620] Security Council Resolution 1534, UN Doc. S/RES/1534 (2004), 26 March 2004, p. 2, para. 5.

or to submit the matter to the competent authorities for investigation and prosecution.

(b) With respect to superior and subordinate relationships not described in paragraph (a), a superior shall be criminally responsible for crimes within the jurisdiction of the Court committed by subordinates under his or her effective authority and control, as a result of his or her failure to exercise control properly over such subordinates, where:

(i) The superior either knew, or consciously disregarded information which clearly indicated, that the subordinates were committing or about to commit such crimes;

(ii) The crimes concerned activities that were within the effective responsibility and control of the superior; and

(iii) The superior failed to take all necessary and reasonable measures within his or her power to prevent or repress their commission or to submit the matter to the competent authorities for investigation and prosecution.

It would appear that there has been no actual practice at the ICC on the scope and application of Article 28. As discussed in Chapter 2, the arrest warrants unsealed so far rely on sub-paragraphs (3)(a) and/or (3)(b) of Article 25 to ground the charges against the accused;[621] none to date alleges that the accused is responsible pursuant to Article 28. In addition, no chamber of the ICC has yet opined on Article 28 in a public decision.

Nonetheless, the text of the Article, the relevant *travaux*, and the subsequent commentary already reveal several significant differences between the Rome Statute's approach to superior responsibility and that which has been developed in the jurisprudence of the *ad hoc* Tribunals.

3.4.1.1 A bifurcated standard

The most obvious divergence between the approaches of the *ad hoc* Tribunals and the ICC, and that which has been the primary subject of the scholarship and commentary on Article 28,[622] is that the Rome Statute provides for two

---

[621] See Chapter 2, text accompanying note 734. It is interesting to note, however, that the arrest warrant in the Court's first case refers specifically to the nature of the accused's control over the alleged physical perpetrators, even though he is not charged with superior responsibility. See *Situation in the Democratic Republic of the Congo in the Case of Prosecutor* v. *Thomas Lubanga Dyilo*, Case No. ICC-01/04-01/06, Warrant of Arrest, 10 February 2006, pp. 3–4 (finding that 'there are reasonable grounds to believe that Mr Thomas Lubanga Dyilo ... exercised *de facto* authority which corresponded to his positions as President of the UPC and Commander-in-Chief of the FPLC' and 'had ultimate control over the adoption and implementation of the policies/practices of the UPC/FPLC – a hierarchically organised armed group between July 2002 and December 2003').

[622] See, e.g., Ambos, *supra* note 35; Greg R. Vetter, 'Command Responsibility of Non-Military Superiors in the International Criminal Court (ICC)', (2000) 25 *Yale Journal of International Law* 89; Danner and Martinez, *supra* note 40, p. 120; Mirjan Damaska, 'The Shadow Side of Command Responsibility', (2001) 49 *American Journal of Comparative Law* 455, 470; van Sliedregt, *supra* note 7, pp. 191–192; William J. Fenrick, 'Responsibility of commanders and other superiors', in Otto Triffterer (ed.),

different standards of superior responsibility: sub-paragraph (a) sets one standard, applicable only to a 'military commander or person effectively acting as a military commander'; sub-paragraph (b) establishes another standard, applicable to 'superior and subordinate relationships not described in paragraph (a)', in other words, civilian superiors.[623] As an earlier section of this chapter explained, the jurisprudence of the *ad hoc* Tribunals has established that the same standard applies to both military and civilian superiors, although differences in the nature and degree of control of subordinates are taken into account when determining whether a particular element of the form of responsibility has been proved.[624]

The distinction in Article 28 between military and civilian superiors, and many of the key terms used in its finalised text, are the direct result of the intervention of the United States delegation to the Diplomatic Conference that negotiated and agreed upon the text of the Rome Statute.[625] The draft article on superior responsibility that had been proffered by the Preparatory Committee, at that time numbered Article 25, was similar to Article 7/6(3) in the *ad hoc* Statutes, and provided:

Article 25 Responsibility of [commanders] [superiors] for acts of [forces under their command] [subordinates]

[In addition to other forms of responsibility for crimes under this Statute, a [commander] [superior] is criminally responsible] [A [commander] [superior] is not relieved of responsibility] for crimes under this Statute committed by [forces] [subordinates] under his or her command [or authority] and effective control as a result of the [commander's] [superior's] failure to exercise properly this control where:

(a) the [commander] [superior] either knew, or [owing to the widespread commission of the offences] [owing to the circumstances at the time] should have known, that the [forces] [subordinates] were committing or intending to commit such crimes; and

---

Commentary on the Rome Statute of the International Criminal Court: Observer's Notes, Article by Article (1999), pp. 517, 519–522; Matthias Neuner, 'Superior Responsibility and the ICC Statute', in Gaetano Carlizzi *et al.* (eds.), *La Corte Penale Internazionale Problemi e Prospettive* (2003), pp. 268–272.

[623] The language chosen for subparagraph (b) suggests a broader category than merely civilian superiors, that is, a category defined as every relationship that is not one of *de jure* or *de facto* military command. Although it is possible that cases before the ICC may eventually present factual situations that lead the chambers to adopt such a broader reading of this provision, the *travaux* reviewed below demonstrate that the drafters did indeed focus on civilian superiors when creating the bifurcated standard of Article 28.

[624] See *supra* text accompanying notes 200–203, 263–281; see also Ambos, *supra* note 35, p. 18 n. 77 and accompanying text.

[625] See generally Ambos, *supra* note 35, pp. 16–18; M. Cherif Bassiouni, 'Negotiating the Treaty of Rome on the Establishment of an International Criminal Court', (1999) 32 *Cornell International Law Journal.* 443, 457 (noting that the US delegation had 'secured broad concessions on many points' with regard to the text of the Statute).

(b) the [commander] [superior] failed to take all necessary and reasonable measures within his or her power to prevent or repress their commission [or punish the perpetrators thereof].

[10] Most delegations were in favour of extending the principle of command responsibility to any superior.

[11] One delegation held the view that this principle should be dealt with in connection with the definitions of the crimes.

[12] The alternatives highlight the question whether command responsibility is a form of criminal responsibility in addition to others or whether it is a principle that commanders are not immune for the acts of their subordinates.[626]

On the first day of work by the Committee of the Whole, however, the United States submitted a proposal that radically altered the text of the provision. This proposed text read:

In addition to other forms of responsibility for crimes under this Statute,

(a) A commander is criminally responsible for crimes under this Statute committed by forces under his or her command and effective control as a result of the commander's failure to exercise properly this control where:

   (i) The commander either knew or, owing to the circumstances at the time, should have known, that the forces were committing or intending to commit such crimes; and

   (ii) The commander failed to take all necessary and reasonable measures within his or her power to prevent or repress their commission [or punish the perpetrators thereof];

(b) A civilian superior is criminally responsible for crimes under this Statute committed by subordinates under his or her authority where:

   (i) The superior knew that the subordinates were committing or intending to commit a crime or crimes under this Statute;

   (ii) The crimes concerned activities that were within the official responsibility of the superior;

   (iii) The superior had the ability to prevent or repress the crime or crimes; and

   (iv) The superior failed to take all necessary and reasonable measures within his or her power to prevent or repress their commission.[627]

---

[626] Report of the Preparatory Committee on the Establishment of an International Criminal Court, UN Doc. A/CONF.183/2/Add.1, 14 April 1998, p. 51. The question referred to in the extract's footnote 12 was at issue, in part, because of the slightly vague wording of Article 7/6(3) of the *ad hoc* Statutes. As the jurisprudence of those Tribunals and the finalised title of the ICC's Article clearly show, however, superior responsibility is a two-pronged basis for the imposition of criminal liability, not merely a legal principle.

[627] Proposal Submitted by the United States of America for Article 25, UN Doc. A/CONF.183/C.1/L.2, 16 June 1998.

In introducing the proposal, the United States delegation explained the reasons for its suggested bifurcated standard:

[The United States] delegation had had serious doubts about extending the concept of command responsibility to a civilian supervisor because of the very different rules governing criminal punishment in civilian and military organizations. Recognizing, however, that there was a strong interest in some form of responsibility for civilian supervisors, it was submitting a proposal in an endeavour to facilitate agreement. The main difference between civilian supervisors and military commanders lay in the nature and scope of their authority. The latter's authority rested on the military discipline system, which had a penal dimension, whereas there was no comparable punishment system for civilians in most countries. Another difference was that a military commander was in charge of a lethal force, whereas a civilian supervisor was in charge of what might be termed a bureaucracy. An important feature in military command responsibility and one that was unique in a criminal context was the existence of negligence as a criterion of criminal responsibility. Thus, a military commander was expected to take responsibility if he knew or should have known that the forces under his control were going to commit a criminal act. That appeared to be justified by the fact that he was in charge of an inherently lethal force.

Civilian responsibility as proposed in paragraph (2) of the draft was set forth according to a similar basic structure as for military responsibility, with some differences. One was that the superior must know that subordinates were committing a criminal act. The negligence standard was not appropriate in a civilian context and was basically contrary to the usual principles of criminal law responsibility. In addition, civilian supervisors were responsible for their subordinates and the latter's acts only at work and not for acts they committed outside the workplace in their individual capacity, whereas military commanders were responsible for the forces under their command at all times. Lastly, the provision regarding the ability of the supervisor to prevent or repress the crimes took into account the very different nature of civilian accountability mechanisms and the weak disciplinary and administrative structure of civilian authority as opposed to that of the military. In some Governments with well-developed bureaucracies, it was not even possible to dismiss subordinates, and enforcement might be difficult even if they were suspended.[628]

Almost all the delegations who responded to the suggested revision of Article 25 in this meeting supported the United States' position. Only the Australian delegation noted that the *Karadžić* indictment at the ICTY highlighted an issue that should not be ignored in the drafting, 'namely, a situation in which civilians were effectively part of a command structure that involved military or paramilitary forces. The question did not concern a straightforward civilian bureaucracy, but civilians at a high level who were in fact engaged in the command or

---

[628] Committee of the Whole, Summary Record of the 1st Meeting, held on 16 June 1998, UN Doc. A/CONF.183/C.1/SR.1, 20 November 1998 ('Summary Record'), paras. 67–68.

control of lethal forces.'[629] Given the heightened political sensitivities surrounding the issue of superior responsibility in the statute of a permanent international criminal court, it is unfortunate but unsurprising that this comment, which laid bare a fundamental flaw in the reasoning of the American delegation, had ultimately little effect on the final text of Article 28.[630]

The Rome Statute was finalised a few months before the *Čelebići* Trial Judgement began the line of authority that has given such detail and nuance to the unitary standard of superior responsibility that is applied in every other international or internationalised criminal tribunal,[631] so the plenipotentiaries in Rome that summer could perhaps be forgiven for failing to foresee the manner in which civilian superiors would be treated under such an approach. Nevertheless, it appears that no other delegation publicly challenged the United States' reasoning, or questioned the appropriateness of using an implicit analogy to vicarious liability doctrines in domestic law to justify the creation of a different standard for civilian superiors charged with international crimes, which are frequently committed in situations far removed from the regularly functioning operations of bureaucracies, administrative structures, and accountability mechanisms. Instead, the American proposal was adopted as the new basis for the draft Article, and relatively minor changes to the text were made in response to the comments and 'political guidance'[632] given in this meeting and subsequent discussions in the working group devoted to this part of the Statute.[633]

---

[629] *Ibid.*, para. 82.

[630] It is possible that the Australian delegation's comment is reflected in the references in finalised Article 28(a) to a 'person effectively acting as a military commander', so that the kind of civilian superiors that concerned the delegation would fall under this provision. Given the clear distinction between the standards applicable to different kinds of superiors, however, it is far more likely that an ICC chamber's attention will be focused on developing a test to distinguish between 'regular' civilian superiors and those who are effective, or *de facto*, military commanders, and that at least some high-level accused involved in the command or control of lethal forces would nonetheless be considered civilians, subject only to the standard in subparagraph (b).

[631] See *infra*, text accompanying notes 661–662 (Special Court for Sierra Leone); text accompanying notes 684–685 (Special Panels for Serious Crimes); text accompanying notes 703–705 (Extraordinary Chambers in the Courts of Cambodia); text accompanying notes 709–711 (Supreme Iraqi Criminal Tribunal).

[632] Summary Record, *supra* note 628, para. 20.

[633] See Working Group on General Principles of Criminal Law, Working Paper on Article 25, UN Doc. A/CONF.183/C.1/WGGP/L.7, 22 June 1998; Working Group on General Principles of Criminal Law, Working Paper on Article 25, UN Doc. A/CONF.183/C.1/WGGP/L.7/Rev.1, 25 June 1998; Report of the Working Group on General Principles of Criminal Law, UN Doc. A/CONF.183/C.1/WGGP/L.4/Add.1/Rev.1, 2 July 1998, p. 2 n. 2 ('The Working Group draws the attention of the Drafting Committee to the fact that the text of this article was the subject of extensive negotiations and represents quite delicate compromises.'); Compendium of Draft Articles Referred to the Drafting Committee by the Committee of the Whole as of 9 July 1998, UN Doc. A/CONF.183/C.1/L.58, 9 July 1998, p. 12.

3.4.1.2 *Mental element: a higher standard for civilian superiors*

The core of the bifurcated approach in the Rome Statute is the different mental states that are sufficient to ground liability for military and civilian superiors. Under Article 28(a)(i), assuming all other elements of the test are satisfied, a *de jure* or *de facto* military commander is responsible for subordinates' conduct if he or she 'knew or, *owing to the circumstances at the time, should have known*' that the crimes in question were being committed or about to be committed. Under Article 28(b)(i), on the other hand, a civilian superior is only responsible if he or she 'knew, or *consciously disregarded information which clearly indicated*' that subordinates were committing or about to commit such crimes. The addition of an alternative mental state for civilian superiors, short of actual knowledge, was the only major deviation from the American proposal.

Although much could be (and has been) made of the fact that the phrase 'should have known' suggests a negligence standard for military superiors,[634] the deliberate inclusion of the qualifying phrase 'owing to the circumstances at the time' by the drafters invokes both the terms of Article 86(2) of Additional Protocol I to the Geneva Conventions,[635] and the 'had reason to know' standard of the *ad hoc* Statutes. Accordingly, it is possible that this alternative mental state for military superiors will be construed so as to bring it relatively close to the *ad hoc* jurisprudence relating to the 'had reason to know' standard.[636] Such an interpretation would avoid a direct conflict between eventual ICC jurisprudence and the *ad hoc* Appeals Chambers' explicit rejection of negligence as an appropriate standard for superior responsibility.[637] On the other hand, even the earliest drafts of the eventual Article 28 used the phrase 'should have known' – which had been specifically abandoned by the diplomatic conference negotiating the Additional

---

[634] See *supra* notes 377–379 and accompanying text; see also, e.g., Nicola Pasani, 'The Mental Element in International Law', in Flavia Lattanzi and William A. Schabas (eds.), *Essays on the Rome Statute of the International Criminal Court: Volume II* (2004), p. 135.

[635] This sub-paragraph of Additional Protocol I provides:

> The fact that a breach of the Conventions or of this Protocol was committed by a subordinate does not absolve his superiors from penal or disciplinary responsibility, as the case may be, if they knew, or *had information which should have enabled them to conclude in the circumstances at the time*, that he was committing or was going to commit such a breach and if they did not take all feasible measures within their power to prevent or repress the breach.

> (Emphasis added.)

[636] See *supra* text accompanying notes 378–459.

[637] See *supra* notes 377–379 and accompanying text. See also Vetter, *supra* note 622, p. 122 n. 190 (arguing that the Rome Statute's reference to 'circumstances' and not 'information' could result in the consideration of a broader range of clues to the superior about the crimes in question, and might therefore even extend liability beyond the reach of the *ad hoc* standard).

Protocol[638] – as the alternative mental standard, perhaps indicating the purposeful adoption of a lower standard, similar to negligence, by the plenipotentiaries in Rome.[639]

Turning to the second subparagraph of Article 28, it is apparent that the Rome Statute's drafters intended to create a standard for the civilian superior's alternative mental state that is higher than the corresponding alternative for military superiors, as indicated by the use of the terms 'consciously disregarded' and 'clearly indicated'. Given the direction, however, that *ad hoc* jurisprudence has taken on its 'had reason to know' alternative standard, it is unclear whether a civilian superior before the ICC would be treated any differently than he or she would before the ICTY or ICTR. The Commentaries to the Geneva Conventions and their Protocols have been given considerable weight in the jurisprudence of the *ad hoc* Tribunals, and the Commentary to Article 86(2) of the Additional Protocol states that '[i]t seems to be established that a superior cannot absolve himself from responsibility by pleading ignorance of reports addressed to him', a reading of the law that ostensibly imposes a duty on a superior to be apprised, at least, of information that is made directly available to him.[640] Although both this approach and the Rome Statute's formulation have been interpreted as referring to impermissible wilful blindness on the part of a superior,[641] a duty to remain apprised would demand more of

---

[638] See IRC Commentary to the Protocol Additional to the Geneva Conventions of 12 August 1949, and relating to the Protection of Victims of International Armed Conflicts (Protocol I) ('Additional Protocol Commentary'), p. 1006, para. 3526 & n. 2 (noting that the draft article presented to the conference provided that superiors would not be absolved of penal responsibility 'if they knew or *should have known*' of a subordinate's crime); Vetter, *supra* note 622, pp. 121–122 and n. 190 (noting that in the negotiations on Additional Protocol I, another formulation of the phrase – 'should reasonably have known in the circumstances at the time' – was specifically rejected in favour of the finalised text quoted in note 635 above). Note that the English text of Article 86(2) retains a 'should have' reference, this time to the information itself, which 'should have enabled' the superior to conclude that crimes were going to be or being committed. Any hint of the consequent re-introduction of a negligence standard is probably excluded by the Commentary's direction that the French version '*leur permettant de conclure*' ('enabling them to conclude') best encapsulates the object and purpose of the treaty. Additional Protocol Commentary, p. 1014, para. 3545.

[639] See also Summary Record, *supra* note 628, pp. 10–12 (repeated implicit references to 'should have known' as a negligence standard appropriate for military superiors, but not civilian superiors).

[640] The drafters of the Additional Protocol Commentary relied on the *Hostages* case as authority for this statement. *See* Additional Protocol Commentary, *supra* note 5, p. 1014, para. 3545, nn. 35–36; *supra* text accompanying notes 97–105. See also *Čelebići* Appeal Judgement, *supra* note 32, para. 241 ('[A] superior will be criminally responsible through the principles of superior responsibility only if information was available to him which would have put him on notice of offences committed by subordinates.').

[641] See *supra* note 375 and accompanying text; Vetter, *supra* note 622, p. 124. Note, however, that in explicitly rejecting the *Blaškić* Trial Judgement's negligence standard, the Appeals Chamber held that '[n]eglect of a duty to acquire such knowledge . . . does not feature in the provision [Article 7(3)] . . . and a superior is not therefore liable under the provision for such failures'. *Čelebići* Appeal Judgement, *supra* note 32, para. 226. See also *Blaškić* Appeal Judgement, *supra* note 170, para. 64. Under ICTY jurisprudence, which has been followed in the ICTR, the duty of the superior is not therefore to seek out admonitory information, but rather to be aware of such information available to him; an obligation to investigate possible or probable criminal activity is triggered only after the admonitory information is already available. See *supra* text accompanying notes 375–383.

a superior than that he or she not consciously disregard information clearly indicating criminal activity, because this latter formulation appears to assume that the superior is already aware of that information. As this chapter's survey of the recent *ad hoc* jurisprudence shows, however, the concern of various chambers to avoid enunciating a standard that even implies negligence would seem to mean that mere possession of a report addressed to the superior would be insufficient to ground liability.[642] Moreover, since the *ad hoc* chambers use different terms to describe the requisite nature of the admonitory information and its suggestiveness of subordinate criminal conduct,[643] the Rome Statute's requirement that the information in question 'clearly indicate' (imminent) criminal activity is not necessarily that much stricter.[644]

Most of these questions will only be resolved once the ICC begins to issue judicial statements on the meaning and scope of Article 28. Nonetheless, two conclusions may still be drawn about the future application of these different mental elements. First, in light of the drafting history of the Article, the chambers of the ICC are supposed to apply different alternative mental standards to military and civilian superiors, though there may be some room for judicial discretion in the interpretation of those standards so as to reduce the starkness of the distinction. Second, the alternative mental state in the unitary superior responsibility standard of the *ad hoc* Tribunals turns on inquiry notice; that is, the admonitory information available to the superior need not establish the certainty of subordinate criminal activity, but need only trigger the superior's investigation.[645] The plain text of Article 28(b)(i), however, requires that the information 'clearly indicate . . . that the subordinates were committing or about to commit such crimes', a constraint that is likely to be read as referring to a situation where investigation of the sort discussed in ICTY judgements is unnecessary. Since the *ad hoc* jurisprudence on superior responsibility would hold a superior responsible if he had been in possession of information falling short of 'clear indication' of ongoing or imminent criminal activity,[646] it extends liability to situations ostensibly forbidden to the ICC by the Rome Statute.

3.4.1.3 Causation

Another point of textual divergence between the *ad hoc* Statutes and the Rome Statute is the latter's requirement, applicable equally to military and civilian

---

[642] See *supra* text accompanying notes 377–379. But see *Čelebići* Appeal Judgement, *supra* note 32, para. 239 ('[T]he relevant information only needs to have been provided or available to the superior, or in the Trial Chamber's words, "in the possession of". It is not required that he actually acquainted himself with the information.').

[643] See *supra* text accompanying notes 395–401.

[644] See especially *Strugar* Trial Judgement, *supra* note 179, para. 416; *Brdanin* Trial Judgement, *supra* note 179, para. 278.

[645] See *supra* text accompanying notes 376–380.   [646] See *supra* text accompanying notes 395–398.

superiors, that the 'crimes within the jurisdiction of the Court committed by forces under his or her effective command [or authority] and control' occur '*as a result of* his or her failure to exercise control properly over such forces'. Nothing in the text of Article 7/6(3) explicitly requires such a nexus between the superior's omission and the crime for which he or she is ultimately held responsible, and the settled jurisprudence of the *ad hoc* Tribunals has not included it as part of the test for superior responsibility.[647] A strong argument could be made that the purpose of the effective control test is not just to ensure that the appropriate person is held liable,[648] but also to ensure that if the accused had chosen to intervene, the crime would not have occurred – in effect, assurance that the accused is in fact convicted for a culpable omission. Viewed in this light, there is no substantive difference between Article 7/6(3) and Article 28, because the former has been given a judicial gloss that results in the importation of an implicit causation requirement.[649]

Such an approach would ignore, however, the *ad hoc* Statutes' explicit reference to past crimes, and the fact that the only obligation imposed on a superior with after-the-fact knowledge of such crimes is the duty to punish.[650] If the *ad hoc* effective control test meant that a superior could only be held liable for a failure to punish crimes that occurred because of a prior failure to control his or her subordinates, the range of punishable omissions could be dramatically constrained, a possibility that has not been borne out by the actual practice of those tribunals. Moreover, in the many instances where an accused has been held responsible for a failure to punish, no chamber of either *ad hoc* Tribunal has required that the crimes for which he was convicted have occurred as a result of inadequate prior control. In fact, it is worth remarking that the Rome Statute makes no mention of past crimes at all;[651] the subordinates' conduct for which a superior may be liable is limited to crimes that are either in the course of commission or about to be committed. The next subsection of this chapter examines the possible legal effects of this textual omission.

---

[647] See *supra* text accompanying notes 463–465.
[648] See Reid, *supra* note 87, p. 825.
[649] See *Čelebići* Trial Judgement, *supra* note 3, para. 399. But see *ibid.*, paras. 398, 400 (rejecting the principle of causation as an element of superior responsibility).
[650] See *supra* text accompanying note 31 (quoting Article 7/6(3), which provides that '[t]he fact that any of the acts ... was committed by a subordinate does not relieve his superior of criminal responsibility if he knew or had reason to know that the subordinate was about to commit such acts *or had done so*') (emphasis added). See also *Halilović* Trial Judgement, *supra* note 27, para. 76 (citing the *Čelebići* Trial Judgement for the proposition that 'the very existence of the principle of superior responsibility for failure to punish ... demonstrates the absence of a requirement of causality as a separate element of the doctrine of superior responsibility'); *accord Blaškić* Appeal Judgement, *supra* note 170, para. 77; *Kordić and Čerkez* Trial Judgement, *supra* note 190, para. 445.
[651] If the *Halilović* Trial Chamber is correct in its reasoning, see *supra* note 650, it is this omission of past crimes which may make possible the introduction of a causation requirement.

Several issues of textual interpretation and practical effect are raised by Article 28's causation requirement, including whether 'as a result of' is interpreted to mean but-for causation, or whether the superior's omission need only be one of multiple direct or indirect causes of the subordinates' criminal conduct; and, as cautioned by the *Halilović* Trial Chamber,[652] whether the extent to which the causation requirement affects the required level of a superior's involvement in a crime to such an extent that it alters the nature of the liability imposed. These and other related issues will have to be resolved by the ICC once work is begun on indictments alleging superior responsibility.

3.4.1.4 Past crimes and independent obligations

One of the most important developments in the law of superior responsibility has been the clarification that it involves at least two separate and distinct duties imposed on superiors. As the ICTY Appeals Chamber noted, '[t]he failure to punish and failure to prevent involve different crimes committed at different times: the failure to punish concerns past crimes committed by subordinates, whereas the failure to prevent concerns future crimes of subordinates'.[653] Since, under the *ad hoc* approach, a superior may also be held liable for the failure to punish crimes of which he or she had prior knowledge,[654] liability will be imposed in three types of situations, assuming the existence of a qualifying superior-subordinate relationship: first, where the superior had actual or constructive knowledge of future or current crimes and failed to prevent or stop them;[655] second, where he or she had knowledge of future or current crimes and failed to punish the perpetrators;[656] and

---

[652] See *Halilović* Trial Judgement, *supra* note 27, para. 78.

[653] *Blaškić* Appeal Judgement, *supra* note 170, para. 83. But see *supra* note 469.

[654] See *supra* text accompanying note 473.

[655] See *supra* notes 491, 492, 502 and accompanying text. As conveyed by the use of these alternatives – prevent or stop – the *ad hoc* Tribunals also recognise the imposition of liability for failure to intervene to stop ongoing criminal conduct. Accordingly, there may actually be three separate and distinct duties related to superior responsibility, not two, as the *ad hoc* chambers repeatedly note. See *infra* text accompanying notes 722–725.

[656] In practice, most accused in such a position would be held liable for the failure to prevent, because they must have had the material ability to prevent (in order to satisfy the first *Čelebići* element) and yet have failed to do so, or the crime would not have been committed. In addition, since the ICTY Appeals Chamber has held that a superior who assumes command after the commission of a crime cannot be held liable for a failure to punish, accused in this second situation would also be excluded. See *supra* text accompanying notes 527–534. Nonetheless, the situation may exist where a superior in command at the time of the crime lacked the material ability to prevent its commission – because of a logistical or communications failure, for example – but retained the material ability to punish the perpetrators after the fact. Under the *ad hoc* approach, failure to impose punishment in such circumstances should still result in criminal liability.

third, where he or she had knowledge of past crimes and failed to punish the perpetrators.[657]

Under the Rome Statute, however, the third situation would seem to be excluded.[658] This omission of reference to past crimes gains potentially greater importance when read in context with subparagraphs (a)(ii) and (b)(iii), which refer to three culpable omissions with regard to crimes: failures '[1] to prevent or [2] repress their commission or [3] to submit the matter to the competent authorities for investigation and prosecution'.[659] While the jurisprudence of the *ad hoc* Tribunals interprets the similar structure of Article 7/6(3) as nonetheless recognising two *independent* obligations of superiors, the Rome Statute's apparent exclusion of past crimes gives credence to an interpretation of those subparagraphs as setting forth *alternative* obligations of superiors. That is, instead of holding that a superior's duty to prevent is separate from, and therefore not satisfied by compliance with, his or her duty to punish,[660] an ICC chamber applying Article 28 could hold that a superior's obligation to respond to the criminal conduct of his or her subordinates is satisfied by choosing any of the three options in these sub-paragraphs; for example, an accused could potentially remedy a failure to prevent a given instance of subordinate criminal conduct merely by waiting and punishing those subordinates afterward. This more lenient approach, though beneficial to any accused

---

[657] Since the *ad hoc* Tribunals' practice also recognises the imposition of liability for failure to intervene to stop ongoing criminal conduct, there may actually be three separate and distinct duties related to superior responsibility. See *infra* text accompanying notes 722–725.

[658] In omitting specific reference to past crimes, the Rome Statute's drafters may have been trying to achieve the maximum possible uniformity with the terms of Article 86(2) of Additional Protocol I. Such had also been the preoccupation of the drafters of the ICTY Statute, however, who nonetheless referred to a superior's responsibility to prevent and punish such crimes, and structured the primary instrument accordingly. See Report of the Secretary-General pursuant to Paragraph 2 of Security Council Resolution 808 (1993), UN Doc. S/25704, 3 May 1993 ('Secretary-General's Report'), para. 56; see also *infra* note 659.

[659] It is unclear what the reference to repression of the commission of crimes actually means, and the *travaux préparatoires* are unhelpful. Article 86(2) of Additional Protocol I refers to prevention and repression of the breach of international humanitarian law, though Article 86(1) limits the obligation of repression by States to grave breaches alone, and requires them to 'suppress' all other breaches. The Commentary to Article 86 seems to equate repression with punishment, at least in the context of the duties of superiors. See Additional Protocol Commentary, *supra* note 5, p. 1015, para. 3548 ('Using relatively broad language, the clause requires both *preventive and repressive action*. However, it reasonably restricts the obligation upon superiors to "feasible" measures, since it is not always possible to *prevent a breach or punish the perpetrators*.') (emphases added). There are other indications, however, that 'repression' could mean intervention to stop an ongoing crime. If, as the *travaux* indicate, the last phrase in subparagraphs (a)(ii) and (b)(iii) of Article 28 – 'submit the matter to the competent authorities for investigation and prosecution' – is intended to take the place of references in earlier drafts to 'punishment of the perpetrators', then a separate reference to repression must mean something different than punishment. See also Secretary-General's Report, *supra* note 658, para. 56 (noting that superior responsibility is engaged if the superior had actual or constructive knowledge 'and yet failed to take the necessary and reasonable steps to *prevent or repress the commission of such crimes* or to punish those who had committed them') (emphasis added).

[660] See *supra* text accompanying note 473.

before the ICC, would seem inconsistent with the fundamental principles underpinning the superior responsibility doctrine, because it would remove any requirement or incentive for the superior to act at every appropriate moment to ensure that crimes are not committed, and that criminal conduct is neither condoned nor repeated.

3.4.2 The internationalised tribunals

3.4.2.1 Special Court for Sierra Leone (SCSL)

Article 6(3) of the SCSL Statute is essentially identical to Article 7(3) of the ICTY Statute and Article 6(3) of the ICTR Statute, and provides:

> The fact that any of the acts referred to in articles 2 to 4 of the present Statute was committed by a subordinate does not relieve his or her superior of criminal responsibility if he or she knew or had reason to know that the subordinate was about to commit such acts or had done so and the superior had failed to take the necessary and reasonable measures to prevent such acts or to punish the perpetrators thereof.[661]

As such, and unlike the Rome Statute, it would seem that this court's approach to superior responsibility makes no distinction between military and civilian superiors, and would extend liability to the situation where a superior knew or had reason to know of subordinates' past crimes. To date, however, the pleading practice of the Special Prosecutor and the decisions of the trial chambers have neither taken a clear position on the content or scope of superior responsibility, nor added much to the relevant international jurisprudence.[662]

The work of the SCSL is focused on five indictments;[663] all five allege that the accused charged therein are responsible under Article 6(1) of the SCSL

---

[661] Statute of the Special Court for Sierra Leone, 2178 UNTS 138, UN Doc. S/2002/246 (2002), Appendix II ('SCSL Statute'), Article 6(3). The only alteration to the text of the *ad hoc* Tribunals' Article 7/6(3) is that the SCSL Statute includes both the masculine and feminine pronouns as alternatives, referring to 'his or her superior' and whether 'he or she knew'. It must also be noted that, befitting the SCSL's status as a hybrid court, this provision of the SCSL Statute apparently limits the direct application of the superior responsibility doctrine of international criminal law to the international crimes listed in the Statute. By referring specifically to Articles 2 to 4 of the Statute, Article 6(3) explicitly excludes the crimes under Sierra Leonean law listed in Article 5. Pursuant to Article 6(5) of the Statute, '[i]ndividual criminal responsibility for the[se] crimes . . . shall be determined in accordance with the respective laws of Sierra Leone'.

[662] Thus far, what is clear is that the SCSL will apply the *Čelebići* three-pronged test. See *Prosecutor v. Brima, Kamara and Kanu*, Case No. SCSL-04-16-T ('*AFRC* Case'), Decision on Defence Motions for Judgement of Acquittal Pursuant to Rule 98, 31 March 2006, para. 328 (holding that the three elements of superior responsibility discussed at length earlier in this chapter are the prongs of the test for liability under Article 6(3)).

[663] These indictments are those against Charles Taylor; Brima, Kamara and Kanu ('*AFRC* Case'); Sesay, Kallon and Gbao ('*RUF* Case'); Norman, Fofana and Kondewa ('*CDF* Case'); and Johnny Paul Koroma. The current total of five is the result of the consolidation of several indictments into the joint indictments faced by the three groups of accused in the multi-defendant trials, as well as the withdrawal of indictments against Foday Sankoh and Sam Bockarie after their deaths in 2003. See

Statute, and are additionally or alternatively liable, under Article 6(3), for the specified crimes 'while holding positions of superior responsibility and exercising command and control over [their] subordinates'.[664] None of the indictments specify which form of superior responsibility, be it the failure to prevent or the failure to punish, is implicated with regard to a particular accused or a particular crime, and at least one pre-trial decision has confirmed that the law does not require such specificity. In a decision on challenges to the form of the indictment raised by the accused Sesay, the pre-trial chamber referred to the persuasive authority of the ICTY and ICTR and the requirements of Articles 6(1) and 6(3), and noted that:

depending on the circumstances of the case, it may be required that with respect to an Article 6(1) case against an Accused, the Prosecution is under an obligation to 'indicate in relation to each individual count precisely and expressly the particular nature of the responsibility alleged,' in other words, that the particular head or heads of liability should be indicated.[665]

The Chamber noted that it may be necessary for an indictment to indicate disjunctively whether the accused 'planned, instigated, ordered, committed or otherwise aided and abetted in the planning, preparation, or execution' of the particular crime, as such precision and clarity may be required to enable the accused to adequately and effectively prepare a defence.[666] For Article 6(3), however, the Chamber noted that, although certain minimum material facts must be pleaded,[667] it was permissible to employ a lesser degree of specificity than under Article 6(1); in some situations, it may be sufficient to plead only the legal prerequisites of superior responsibility as the pertinent material

---

Prosecutor v. Sankoh, Case No. SCSL-2003-02-PT, Withdrawal of Indictment, 8 December 2003 (Trial Chamber endorsing Prosecutor's withdrawal of indictment); *Prosecutor v. Bockarie*, Case No. SCSL-2003-04-PT, Withdrawal of Indictment, 8 December 2003 (same). Trials have concluded in two of the three multi-defendant cases – judgements are expected in 2007 – and pre-trial proceedings against Taylor began after his rendition in March 2006; Koroma is still at large.

[664] See *AFRC* Case, Case No. SCSL-2004-16-PT, Further Amended Consolidated Indictment, 18 February 2005 ('Current *AFRC* Indictment'), para. 36; *Prosecutor v. Sesay, Kallon and Gbao*, Case No. SCSL-2004-15-T, Corrected Amended Consolidated Indictment, 2 August 2006 ('Current *RUF* Indictment'), para. 39; *Prosecutor v. Norman, Fofana and Kondewa*, Case No. SCSL-2004-14-PT, Indictment, 5 February 2004 ('*CDF* Indictment'), para. 21; *Prosecutor v. Koroma*, Case No. SCSL-2003-03-I, Indictment, 7 March 2003 ('*Koroma* Indictment'), para. 27; *Prosecutor v. Taylor*, Case No. SCSL-03-01-I, Amended Indictment, 16 March 2006 ('Amended *Taylor* Indictment'), p. 2 (alleging simply that 'the Accused, pursuant to Article 6.1 and, or alternatively, Article 6.3 of the Statute, is individually criminally responsible for the crimes alleged below'); *ibid.*, para. 33 (including language virtually identical to that used in indictments in other cases).

[665] *Prosecutor v. Sesay*, Case No. SCSL-2003-05-PT, Decision and Order on Defence Preliminary Motion for Defects in the Form of the Indictment, 13 October 2003 ('*Sesay* Decision'), para. 12 (footnotes omitted). Sesay is now the lead defendant in the *RUF* Case, and he and his co-accused face an amended consolidated indictment. See *supra* note 664. In all material respects, however, the relevant paragraph of the indictment charging superior responsibility has not changed, as the only alteration has been the addition of the names of all three accused.

[666] *Sesay* Decision, *supra* note 665, para. 12.   [667] See *ibid.*, para. 13.

facts.[668] Indeed, such has been the approach of the Special Prosecutor: although the indictments generally provide an adequate explanation of the relationship between the accused and his alleged subordinates,[669] no precise details are given of the accused's knowledge or his omissions with regard to exercising effective control over those subordinates. Instead, the indictments simply repeat the terms of Article 6(3), alleging that each accused 'is responsible for the criminal acts of his subordinates in that he knew or had reason to know that the subordinate was about to commit such acts or had done so and [the Accused] failed to take the necessary and reasonable measures to prevent such acts or to punish the perpetrators thereof'.[670]

Although it does not appear that any chamber has yet issued a clear judicial statement on whether military and civilian superiors should be subject to the same standards in international criminal law, it would appear that the SCSL will follow the lead of the *ad hoc* Tribunals, as it has in other aspects of its jurisprudence and practice on individual criminal responsibility.[671] As noted above, unlike the Rome Statute, the SCSL Statute does not distinguish between military and civilian superiors with regard to any of the elements of superior responsibility. Moreover, the limited practice to date suggests that no such distinction would be made.

Although most of the accused before the SCSL are charged with crimes committed during their tenure solely as *de jure* or *de facto* military commanders,[672] three accused are alleged to have had both military and civilian authority, or an imprecise mixture of the two, at different times relevant to their respective indictments. In the case involving the leaders of the Civil Defence Forces (CDF), 'an organized armed force comprising various tribally-based traditional hunters',[673] the indictment alleges that the accused Kondewa 'was the High Priest of the CDF'.[674] As such, he 'had supervision

---

[668] *Ibid.*, para. 14.

[669] See *ibid.*, para. 16 (rejecting, after reproducing the relevant paragraphs of the indictment, the defence complaint that the indictment did not adequately describe the relationship between the accused and the alleged perpetrators). See also Current *AFRC* Indictment, *supra* note 664, para. 36; Current *RUF* Indictment, *supra* note 664, para. 39; *CDF* Indictment, *supra* note 664, para. 21; *Koroma* Indictment, *supra* note 664, para. 27; *Taylor*, Case Summary Accompanying the Amended Indictment, 16 March 2006 ('*Taylor* Case Summary'), para. 33.

[670] Current *AFRC* Indictment, *supra* note 664, para. 36; Current *RUF* Indictment, *supra* note 664, para. 39; *CDF* Indictment, *supra* note 664, para. 21; *Koroma* Indictment, *supra* note 664, para. 27; *Taylor* Case Summary, *supra* note 669, para. 33.

[671] See Chapter 2, text accompanying notes 735–738, 742, 753–754; *supra* note 662; Chapter 4, text accompanying notes 343–354; Chapter 5, text accompanying notes 186–192, 198.

[672] See Current *AFRC* Indictment, *supra* note 664, paras. 12, 22–30 (describing the creation of the AFRC and the respective roles of the accused therein); Current *RUF* Indictment, *supra* note 664, paras. 7, 20–33 (describing the creation of the RUF and the respective roles of the accused therein); *CDF* Indictment, *supra* note 664, paras. 6, 13–15, 17 (describing the creation of the RUF and the respective roles of the accused Norman and Fofana therein).

[673] *CDF* Indictment, *supra* note 664, para. 6.   [674] *Ibid.*, para. 14.

and control over all initiators within the CDF and was responsible for all initiations within the CDF' – an allegation relevant to the charges pertaining to child soldiers – and, in addition, 'frequently led or directed operations and had direct command authority over units within the CDF responsible for carrying out special missions'.[675]

Another accused in a different case, Johnny Paul Koroma, was alleged to be the founder of the Armed Forces Revolutionary Council (AFRC), one of the parties to the Sierra Leone conflict, and was alleged to be both the leader of this group and the President of Sierra Leone during part of the period relevant to the indictment.[676] According to the *Koroma* indictment, the accused was at all relevant times the leader of the AFRC, and a senior leader of an alliance between the AFRC and another party to the conflict; by virtue of this double position, he 'exercised authority, command and control' over all members of the AFRC and the alliance.[677] In addition, during the almost nine months that the junta he led was in power in Sierra Leone, Koroma had 'authority, command and control', in his role as President, over the Armed Forces and the police of Sierra Leone.[678]

Finally, the amended indictment against Charles Taylor alleges both that '[f]rom the late 1980's [he] was the Leader or Head of the National Patriotic Front of Liberia (NPFL), an organized armed group',[679] and that between 1997 and 2003, he was the President of Liberia.[680] Although the indictment does not specifically state that he ever held these positions simultaneously, both the open-ended phrasing used to describe his leadership of the NPFL and the indictment's later allegations of direction, control, or subordination of NPFL and ex-NPFL fighters as late as 2002[681] would strongly support such an interpretation.

None of these three indictments asserts or implies that a different standard should be applied to these accused to the extent that the power they wielded was civilian rather than military in nature. Moreover, since the facts giving rise to these cases do not lend themselves to clear distinctions between an accused's role as a military commander and any control exercised by virtue of a nominally civilian position, it is unlikely that an SCSL chamber would devote considerable effort to the legal implications of such a distinction. Given the identity of their statutes and the established SCSL practice of referring to persuasive *ad hoc* jurisprudence, it is more likely that – if the issue arises at all – the Special Court would adopt the position of the *ad hoc* Tribunals and hold

---

[675] *Ibid.*, para. 16. [676] *Koroma* Indictment, *supra* note 664, paras. 19–21.
[677] *Ibid.*, para. 18. [678] *Ibid.*, paras. 20, 21.
[679] Amended *Taylor* Indictment, *supra* note 664, para. 2.
[680] *Ibid.*, para. 3. [681] See *ibid.*, paras. 5, 6, 9, 14, 18, 22, 23, 28, 34.

that any difference between types of superiors should have no effect on the elements of the test to be applied, but rather be taken into account in consideration of the case-specific factors that contribute to the determination of whether a particular element has been established.[682]

3.4.2.2 *East Timor: Special Panels for Serious Crimes (SPSC)*

The primary provision of the constitutive document for the Special Panels with regard to individual criminal responsibility, Section 14 of UNTAET Regulation No. 2000/15, mirrors Article 25 of the Rome Statute.[683] When it came to superior responsibility, however, the SPSC departed from the ICC model, and instead adopted the *ad hoc* approach, and Section 16 provides:[684]

In addition to other grounds of criminal responsibility under the present regulation for serious criminal offences referred to in Sections 4 to 7 of the present regulation, the fact that any of the acts referred to in the said Sections 4 to 7 was committed by a subordinate does not relieve his superior of criminal responsibility if he knew or had reason to know that the subordinate was about to commit such acts or had done so and the superior failed to take the necessary and reasonable measures to prevent such acts or to punish the perpetrators thereof.[685]

Several indictments issued by the Special Panels allege superior responsibility as a basis for liability, and either explicitly incorporate the language of Section 16, or allege all the elements of superior responsibility set forth therein. These indictments include those against Hulman Gultom, the District Police Chief in Dili, the East Timorese capital, during the period in which the alleged crimes were allegedly committed;[686] Ruben Gonsalves, Ruben Tavares, João Oliveira, Joaquim Maia Pereira and João Tavares, who were, respectively, joint commanders of the pro-Indonesia Sako Loro Monu militia, commander and deputy commander of the pro-Indonesia FIRMI militia, and the head of

---

[682] See *supra* text accompanying notes 200–203, 263–281, 624.

[683] See Chapter 2, text accompanying notes 760–761.

[684] See *Prosecutor* v. *Fereira*, Case No. 04-2001, Judgement, 5 April 2003 ('*Fereira* Judgement'), para. 507 ('The concept of command responsibility as stated in the ... UNTAET regulation is not new and follows the examples set in the ICTY and ICTR Statutes[.]'). See also Bert Swart, 'Internationalized Courts and Substantive Criminal Law', in Cesare P. R. Romano, André Nollkaemper, and Jann K. Kleffner (eds.), *Internationalized Criminal Courts and Tribunals: Sierra Leone, East Timor, Kosovo and Cambodia* (2004), p. 306; Allison Marston Danner and Jenny S. Martinez, 'Guilty Associations: Joint Criminal Enterprise, Command Responsibility, and the Development of International Criminal Law', (2005) 93 *California Law Review* 75, 121; Suzannah Linton, 'Cambodia, East Timor and Sierra Leone: Experiments in International Justice', (2001) 12 *Criminal Law Forum* 185, 211.

[685] United Nations Transitional Administration in East Timor, Regulation No. 2000/15 on the Establishment of Panels with Exclusive Jurisdiction over Serious Criminal Offences, UN Doc. UNTAET/REG/2000/15, 6 June 2000 ('SPSC Regulation'), Section 16.

[686] *Deputy General Prosecutor* v. *Gultom*, Case No. 10-2004, Indictment, 9 December 2004, available at http://ist-socrates.berkeley.edu/~warcrime/ET-Docs/MP-SCU%20Indictments/2004/10-2004%20 Hulman%20Gultom%20Indictment.pdf, paras. 16, 83, 84.

all such militias in East Timor during the relevant period;[687] Lieutenant Colonel Muhammad Nur, First Sergeant Melky, Second Sergeant Hilario, Lukas Martins, Jeca Pereira and Cipriano da Costa, all commanders in the Indonesian army or the Darah Merah militia, another pro-Indonesia armed group;[688] and Vasco da Cruz, Domingos Alves, Guilhermino de Araújo, Napoleon dos Santos, Simão Tasion, Lino Barreto and Câncio Lopes de Carvalho, all alleged to have effective command and control over members of the Mahidi militia, one of the pro-Indonesia armed groups.[689] These indictments, which allege various crimes against humanity, including murder and deportation, were never tested at trial, as the Special Panels concluded their work while the accused were still at large.[690]

As far as can be determined, only a handful of SPSC cases involving superior responsibility made it to trial and judgement.[691] To the limited extent that

---

[687] *Deputy General Prosecutor v. Gonsalves, Tavares, Oliveira, Maia Pereira and Tavares*, Case No. 05-2004, Indictment, 30 November 2004, available at http://ist-socrates.berkeley.edu/warcrime/ET-Docs/MP-SCU%20Indictments/2004/05-2004%20Ruben%20Gonsalves%20et%20al%20Indictment.pdf, pp. 2, 11–15.

[688] *Deputy General Prosecutor v. Nur, Melky, Hilario, Martins, Pereira and da Costa*, Indictment, Case No. 12-2004, Indictment, 16 December 2004, available at http://ist-socrates.berkeley.edu/warcrime/ET-Docs/MP-SCU%20Indictments/2004/12-2004%20Muhhamad%20Nur%20et%20al%20Indictment.pdf, paras. 100, 102–103. The accused with no reported military rank were alleged to be the commanders of the militia, which was an East Timorese group that supported integration or autonomy with Indonesia. Despite the positions held by all accused during the relevant period, however, only Lieutenant Nur was charged with superior responsibility; the others were charged with other forms of responsibility for the alleged crimes. See *ibid.*, pp. 18–23.

[689] See *Deputy General Prosecutor v. da Cruz, Alves, de Araújo, dos Santos a.k.a. Alves, Tasion, Barreto and Lopes de Carvalho*, Case No. 04-2004, Indictment, 29 November 2004, available at http://ist-socrates.berkeley.edu/~warcrime/ET-Docs/MP-SCU%20Indictments/2004/04-2004%20Vasco%20Da%20Cruz%20et%20al%20Indictment.pdf, para. 26.

[690] See Judicial System Monitoring Programme, SPSC Case Information 2004, available at http://www.jsmp.minihub.org/Court%20Monitoring/spsccaseinformation2004.htm; República Democrática de Timor-Leste, District Court of Dili, Special Panels for Serious Crimes, Information, Case No. 10-2004, available at http://ist-socrates.berkeley.edu/~warcrime/ET-Docs/CE-SPSC%20Final%20Decisions/2004/10-2004%20Hulman%20Gultom.doc (noting that there were no proceedings and no final decision in this matter); República Democrática de Timor-Leste, District Court of Dili, Special Panels for Serious Crimes, Information, Case No. 05-2004, available at http://ist-socrates.berkeley.edu/~warcrime/ET-Docs/CE-SPSC%20Final%20Decisions/2004/05-2004%20Ruben%20Gonsalves%20et%20al.doc (same); República Democrática de Timor-Leste, District Court of Dili, Special Panels for Serious Crimes, Information, Case No. 12-2004, available at http://ist-socrates.berkeley.edu/~warcrime/ET-Docs/CE-SPSC%20Final%20Decisions/2004/12-2004%20Lt%20Col%20Muhammad%20Nur%20et%20al.doc (same).

[691] In August 2004, *The Economist* reported that:

the Serious Crimes Unit set up by the United Nations ... has indicted some 375 people and secured more than 50 convictions. Most of those convicted are militiamen who say they were acting under the orders of the Indonesian armed forces. About 280 indictees remain at large in Indonesia. They include the Indonesian commander at the time, General Wiranto, for whom the unit has issued an arrest warrant.

... East Timor itself, eager to maintain healthy relations with its vast and powerful neighbour, opposes the idea of an international tribunal. Indeed, the government has refused to forward General Wiranto's arrest warrant to Interpol.

'Indonesia's Security Forces: Above the Law', 12 August 2004 (European edition). See also Human Rights Watch, Indonesia: Justice Denied in East Timor Church Massacre: Acquittal of Five Officials Highlights Need for U.N. Mechanism, Press Release, 11 March 2004, available at http://

this form of responsibility received judicial attention at the SPSC, the results were varied. The accused in one case, the commander of one of the pro-Indonesia militias, pleaded guilty to all the charges in the indictment; in the subsequent judgement, which imposed liability partially on the basis of superior responsibility, the court did not actually analyse whether all the elements of form of responsibility had been established.[692] Instead, the judgement either repeated the text of the regulation and merely concluded that the accused was 'criminally responsible as [a] superior';[693] or explicitly found that only certain of the material facts relevant to superior responsibility had been proved;[694] or, worse yet, confused superior responsibility with other forms of individual criminal responsibility.[695]

The judgement in a different case, against an accused alleged to be the commander of another pro-Indonesia militia, included a significantly longer discussion of superior responsibility, although it focused most of its efforts on tracing the development of the doctrine.[696] While the court referred to Article 28 of the Rome Statute, it relied heavily on the *ad hoc* jurisprudence on superior responsibility, and adopted the three 'essential elements of superior responsibility' as set forth in the *Čelebići* Trial Judgement.[697] The accused was ultimately acquitted of superior responsibility for the relevant crimes, because the court essentially concluded that the prosecution had not established that he had effective control over the perpetrators.[698]

In a case against a village level commander of the Indonesian military, conversely, the court concluded that he was criminally responsible for the

hrw.org/english/docs/2004/03/22/indone8148.htm (noting that '[t]he Indonesian government has vowed not to extradite anyone to the U.N. -backed courts in Dili'); Human Rights Watch, Justice Denied for East Timor: Indonesia's Sham Prosecutions, the Need to Strengthen the Trial Process in East Timor, and the Imperative of U.N. Action, 1 January 2004, available at http://www.hrw.org/backgrounder/ asia/timor/etimor1202bg.htm (lamenting 'a lack of political will in Jakarta to prosecute senior Indonesian civil and military officials responsible for the violence' in East Timor in 1999).

[692] See *Prosecutor* v. *João Franca da Silva a.k.a. Jhoni Franca*, Case No. 04a-2001, Judgement, 5 December 2002.

[693] See *ibid.*, paras. 54, 125; see also *ibid.*, para. 124 ('Moreover Joao Franca Da Silva . . . knew or had reason to know that the TNI and Militia under his direction and control were committing the acts described above, or had done so. Additionally they [*sic*] failed to take necessary and reasonable measures to prevent such acts or to punish the perpetrators thereof.')

[694] See *ibid.*, paras. 94, 110 (holding, '[i]n light of the admissions [*sic*] of all the evidence' that 'Joao Franca Da Silva alias Jhoni Franca as Commander of the KMP militia had authority and control over members of the KMP militia' between early May and early June 1999). The judgement does not discuss whether the control was 'effective', as required by customary international law and *ad hoc* jurisprudence.

[695] See *ibid.*, para. 125:

Joao Franca Da Silva . . . is criminally responsible as a superior for the acts of his subordinates . . . It has been shown that acts incriminated [*sic*] were committed by, or at the instigation of, or with the consent of a person in authority. That person was Joao Franca Da Silva . . . who instigated acts that were subsequently committed by their [*sic*] subordinates.

[696] See *Fereira* Judgement, *supra* note 684, paras. 504–517.   [697] *Ibid.*, paras. 519–521.

[698] See *ibid.*, para. 521(a), (c).

murder of an East Timorese man who had been taken into custody by members of the military, only some of whom were under his command:[699]

> As mentioned above ... the Court is convinced that [the victim] died during the night after the arrest due to the severe wounds inflicted by the Indonesian TNI [*Tentara Nasional Indonesia*, the military or armed forces] and by the Timorese TNI under the command of the accused. Since the amount and the severity of wounds inflicted by the Timorese TNI were a substantial cause for the death, the wounds inflicted by the Indonesian TNI are not in the nature to sever the chain of cause and effect.
>
> Thus the death resulted from an omission by the accused to take measures against his subordinates to prevent them from inflicting severe wounds on the victim. Even if he had reason to assume that the Indonesian TNI were intent on inflicting severe wounds, and if he had reason to respect these soldiers (because they unlike his subordinates were armed), he could have ordered his men to not inflict wounds of such severe nature that they were likely to cause death. He therefore bears command responsibility ... for the acts of his subordinates.[700]

The accused was also held responsible, as both a 'committer' and a superior, for the torture of two other East Timorese detainees.[701] Relying on ICTY jurisprudence and Indonesian statutory law, however, the court held that the accused could not be convicted concurrently for both forms of responsibility, but would be convicted and sentenced only for commission of those crimes.[702]

3.4.2.3 The Extraordinary Chambers in the Courts of Cambodia (ECCC)

As is the case with common-purpose liability,[703] the approach taken by the governing law of the hybrid Cambodia chambers to the question of superior responsibility largely adopts the wording of the *ad hoc* Statutes. In relevant part, Article 29 of the Law on the Establishment of the Extraordinary Chambers in the Courts of Cambodia for the Prosecution of Crimes Committed during the Period of Democratic Kampuchea provides:

> The fact that any of the acts referred to in Articles 3 new, 4, 5, 6, 7 and 8 of this law were committed by a subordinate does not relieve the superior of personal criminal responsibility if the superior had effective command and control or authority and control over the subordinate, and the superior knew or had reason to know that the subordinate was about to commit such acts or had done so and the superior failed to

---

[699] *Prosecutor v. Soares*, Case No. 11-2003, Judgement, 11 December 2003, p. 3.

[700] *Ibid.*, paras. 12–13, p. 8. The court had earlier found that the victim 'was repeatedly beaten by the accused [and] by Timorese soldiers under the command of the accused and in his presence, without him intervening or punishing them afterwards'. *Ibid.*, p. 4. The accused Soares was convicted of both the torture and the death of the victim. *Ibid.*, para. 23.4, p. 12.

[701] *Ibid.*, para. 20, p. 10.

[702] *Ibid.*, para. 23(1)(a), p. 11. See Chapter 6, text accompanying notes 49–122 (discussing the *ad hoc* jurisprudence holding that an accused may not be convicted concurrently pursuant to a form of responsibility under Article 7/6(1) and superior responsibility under Article 7/6(3)).

[703] See Chapter 2, text accompanying note 774.

take the necessary and reasonable measures to prevent such acts or to punish the perpetrators.

The key difference between Article 29's provisions on superior responsibility and those of the *ad hoc* Statutes is the former's specific requirement, similar to that invoked repeatedly in Article 28 of the Rome Statute,[704] that the superior 'had effective command and control or authority and control over the subordinate'. In practical terms, however, this textual divergence should have no discernible effect on the application of superior responsibility in the Extraordinary Chambers, because although Article 7/6(3) in the *ad hoc* Statutes does not mention the degree of command or control required to justify the imposition of liability for subordinates' crimes, the jurisprudence of those Tribunals has created and consistently enforced a definition of superior responsibility that requires a showing of effective control.[705]

The available documentation on the cases in which preparations have begun is sparse.[706] The prosecutors and judges of the Extraordinary Chambers, both Cambodian and international, were only appointed in May 2006,[707] and trials are not expected to begin before 2007.[708] For these reasons, it will not be possible to understand how this hybrid court will apply this and other forms of responsibility in international criminal law until pre-trial and trial proceedings get under way.

3.4.2.4 Supreme Iraqi Criminal Tribunal (SICT)

In contrast to its approach to common-purpose liability, where it adopted the ICC model and mirrored the text of Article 25 of the Rome Statute,[709] the relevant provision of the SICT Statute imposes liability for superior responsibility in terms similar to Article 7/6(3) of the *ad hoc* Statutes. According to the

---

[704] See *supra* text accompanying note 621.

[705] See *supra* text accompanying notes 214–236 (discussing the first element of superior responsibility and the importance of effective control for concluding that a superior-subordinate relationship existed between the accused and the alleged subordinate(s) in question).

[706] The only official information that is widely available on the ECCC is posted on the website of the Task Force for Cooperation with Foreign Legal Experts for the Preparation of the Proceedings for the Trial of Senior Khmer Rouge Leaders, which contains very little information on the scant proceedings to date. See http://www.cambodia.gov.kh/krt/english/index.htm.

[707] See Official List of National and International Judges and Prosecutors for the Extraordinary Chambers in the Courts of Cambodia as selected by the Supreme Council of the Magistracy on 4 May 2006 and appointed by Preah Reach Kret (Royal Decree) NS/RKT/0506/214 of His Majesty Norodom Sihamoni, King of Cambodia on 7 May 2006, available at http://www.cambodia.gov.kh/krt/english/judicial_officer.htm (listing the 17 national and 12 international judges and prosecutors appointed to serve on the Extraordinary Chambers, and noting that one additional international position, as a reserve co-investigating judge, remains to be filled).

[708] Office of the Governor-General of New Zealand, Press Release, 'Cartwright appointed Cambodian War Crimes Tribunal trial judge', 9 May 2006, available at http://www.gov-gen.govt.nz/media/news.asp?type=current&ID=164.

[709] See Chapter 2, text accompanying notes 783–785.

imperfect translation of the SICT Statute that is publicly available, Article 15(4) provides:

The crimes that were committed by a subordinate do not relieve his superior of criminal responsibility if he knew or had reason to know that the subordinate was about to commit such acts or had done so, and the superior failed to take the necessary and appropriate measures to prevent such acts or to submit the matter to the competent authorities for investigation and prosecution.[710]

The terms of this provision are quoted differently, however, in the charging instruments in the first case against Saddam Hussein and his co-accused ('Dujail case'), which were issued in May 2006. These instruments, including those pertaining to accused other than the former President, translate Article 15(4) as follows:

The Supreme President is not exempted from the criminal liability of the crimes committed by his subordinates, if *the President* is aware or has reasons to be aware that his subordinate has committed or is about to commit these acts and *the President* did not take the necessary and suitable measures to prevent these acts or submit the case to the competent authorities for interrogation and trial.[711]

Moreover, in the written judgement finally issued in November 2006, the court referred to the person who is the focus of this provision as the 'commander-in-Chief', the 'supreme leader', and the 'top official'.[712]

Notwithstanding these terms, which suggest that Hussein was the only accused facing superior responsibility charges, it is clear that the SICT followed international practice by applying the doctrine's standards to all accused for whom it was appropriate, not merely the most senior.[713] In general, the tribunal's legal analysis and findings of fact were influenced by existing international jurisprudence, endorsing and applying the three-pronged test for superior responsibility, and stating explicitly that liability imposed on this

---

[710] See Law No. 10 (2005), Law of the Iraqi Higher Criminal Court, available at http://www.law.case.edu/saddamtrial/documents/IST_statute_official_english.pdf, Art. 15(4). Note that, if the drafters' intention was to mirror the *ad hoc* Statutes, the first phrase should read 'That [the] crimes were committed . . . '.

[711] See *Saddam Hussein*, Case No. 1/1st Criminal/2005, Accusation Document, 15 May 2006, available at http://www.law.case.edu/saddamtrial/documents/20060515_indictment_trans_saddam_hussein.pdf ('*Hussein* Charging Instrument'), p. 3 (emphasis added); *Barzan Ibrahim Al-Hasan*, Case No. 1/1st Criminal/2005, Accusation Document, 15 May 2006, available at http://www.law.case.edu/saddam trial/documents/20060515_ indictment_trans_barzan_ibrahim.pdf ('*Al-Hasan* Charging Instrument'), p. 3 (emphasis added); *Taha Yasin Ramadan*, Case No. 1/1st Criminal/2005, Accusation Document, 15 May 2006, available at http://www.law.case.edu/saddamtrial/documents/20060515_indictment_trans_ taha_yasin_ramadan.pdf ('*Ramadan* Charging Instrument'), p. 3 (emphasis added).

[712] See Case No. 1/9 1st/2005, Judgement, 22 November 2006 ('Dujail Judgement') (English translation issued 4 December 2006), Part III, p. 25.

[713] See, e.g., *Al-Hasan* Charging Instrument, *supra* note 711, p. 3; *Ramadan* Charging Instrument *supra* note 711, p. 3; Dujail Judgement, *supra* note 712, Part V, p. 4–5 (convicting Barzan Ibrahim, Hussein's brother-in-law, for five international crimes on several bases, including superior responsibility).

basis is 'an individual accountability that is based on the conduct of ... subordinates ... and the leader's infringement of his legal obligation'.[714] In
particular, the tribunal correctly explained how the doctrine functioned to
attribute liability to two or more superiors in the same chain of command,[715]
a relatively simple yet vitally important aspect of superior responsibility that
few *ad hoc* chambers have articulated clearly. In certain of its findings,
however – especially those relating to Saddam Hussein – the tribunal
appeared content to rely on the alternative mental element, and conclude
that it was satisfied primarily by the accused's position in the regime, rather
than present a clear and independent analysis of the evidence relating to his
knowledge of the criminal conduct of his subordinates.[716]

Ultimately, Hussein and six of his seven co-accused were convicted of
almost all the crimes with which they were charged, through multiple forms
of responsibility, including superior responsibility.[717] Three of the seven convicted men – Hussein; Barzan Ibrahim Al-Hassan, his half-brother and former
head of the Intelligence Service;[718] and Awad Hamad Al-Bandar, former chief
judge of the Iraqi Revolutionary Court – were sentenced to death by hanging
as punishment for their roles in murder as a crime against humanity; one
accused was sentenced to life imprisonment, and the remaining three to fifteen
years' imprisonment for their involvement in the same crime.[719] The death
sentences were carried out on 30 December 2006 and 15 January 2007.[720]

3.5 Conclusion

Superior responsibility can be a difficult concept to understand, in part
because it is different in many key respects from other forms of responsibility
in international and domestic criminal law.[721] Like the forms of accomplice

---

[714] See Dujail Judgment, *supra* note 712, Part III, pp. 25–27 (quotation at p. 27).
[715] *Ibid.*, pp. 25–26.
[716] *Ibid.*, p. 27 (holding that the knowledge of a close subordinate, at least in the case where that subordinate is the accused's relative, constitutes reason to know); *ibid.*, p. 41 (holding that knowledge or constructive knowledge of torture was available to the accused 'as a normal and logical sequence of a regime that was described a totalitarian and brutal and a president described as an authoritarian and known for using the most brutal methods for eliminating his opponents').
[717] See *ibid.*, Part VI, p. 50 (acquitting Mohammed Azawi Ali, a local Ba'ath party supporter, for lack of evidence).
[718] Also known as Barzan Ibrahim al-Tikriti.
[719] Dujail Judgment, *supra* note 712, Part VI, p. 51; see also *ibid.*, pp. 51–52 (pronouncing the lesser sentences also imposed for other crimes).
[720] See BBC News, 'Saddam Hussein executed in Iraq', 30 December 2006, available at http://news.bbc.co.uk/2/hi/middle_east/6218485.stm; John F. Burns, 'Two Hussein Allies Are Hanged; One Is Decapitated', *New York Times*, 15 January 2007, available at http://www.nytimes.com/2007/01/15/world/middleeast/16iraqcnd.html?ex=1169614800&en=75fe7d64a9f1ada7&ei=5070.
[721] Indeed, superior responsibility has no clear parallel in domestic criminal law. See e.g., Damaska, *supra* note 622, p. 457; Reid, *supra* note 87, pp. 822–824.

and accessory liability reviewed in the remaining chapters of this book, the criminal conduct giving rise to superior responsibility is frequently removed in time and space from the physical commission of the crime; unlike most of those other forms of responsibility, superior responsibility is often incorrectly described as responsibility for the crimes of others, not the accused's own punishable conduct.[722] This characterisation undoubtedly has a kernel of truth: neither superior responsibility nor the forms of accomplice liability require that the accused share the *mens rea* of the physical perpetrators,[723] but only superior responsibility permits the imposition of liability on an individual in relation to a crime in which he played no substantial part, and of which he learned only after its commission. Nevertheless, the manner in which superior responsibility has been treated, and the terminology used in those discussions, have often obscured the fundamental principles of the doctrine and complicated its translation into the context of criminal law.

For superior responsibility has also proved to be a difficult concept to apply, as shown by the divergence of judicial opinion on the various elements to be established, and the plethora of conflicting scholarly views interpreting those decisions. Now, however, after the initial efforts of the postwar tribunals, a long hiatus punctuated by occasional domestic prosecutions, and the recent detailed jurisprudence of the *ad hoc* Tribunals, the state of the law is relatively settled. With international criminal proceedings increasingly focusing on higher-level accused in a range of cases, the law on superior responsibility may undergo even more elucidation and refinement, as the jurisprudence and the fundamental principles animating the doctrine are applied to diverse fact patterns.

At the core of the modern doctrine, as it is applied in international criminal law, is the principle that superior responsibility does not impose liability for mere negligence. Instead of being convicted because they have been compared

---

[722] Such imprecision in language is evident even in the dispositions of many judgements of the *ad hoc* Tribunals, which either neglect to mention the form of responsibility or fail to explain that an accused is responsible for, rather than straightforwardly and simply guilty of, a given crime. *Compare Musema* Trial Judgement, *supra* note 184, p. 276 (noting, without qualification, 'that Musema has been found guilty of Genocide . . . Crime against humanity (extermination). . . and Crime against humanity (rape)'), with *Strugar* Trial Judgement, *supra* note 179, para. 478 (finding 'the Accused guilty pursuant to Article 7(3) of the Statute' of two crimes under Article 3 of the Statute), and *Orić* Trial Judgement, *supra* note 179, para. 782 (convicting Orić for '[f]ailure to discharge his duty as a superior to take necessary and reasonable measures to prevent the occurrence of murder [and cruel treatment] from 27 December 1992 to 20 March 1993 pursuant to Articles 3 and 7(3) of the Statute').

[723] See Chapter 4, text accompanying notes 248–250, 283–302 (aiding and abetting); Chapter 5, text accompanying notes 45–61 (planning, instigating and ordering). See also Chapter 2, text accompanying notes 309–350, 382–388 (joint criminal enterprise). For a comparative perspective of the respective intent requirements for all of the forms of responsibility, see the chart 'Comparison of required mental states, with regard to intent, for imposition of liability under each form of responsibility' in the Annex of this book.

to a hypothetical reasonably diligent superior and found wanting, accused are judged by a standard defined by a clear culpable omission in light of equally clear positive obligations to act.[724] In their exclusion of negligence as an appropriate basis for superior responsibility, the *ad hoc* Tribunals have marked their clearest departure from the plain text of the post-war jurisprudence, and have steered the doctrine onto firmer moral and theoretical ground.

Nor, it has long been settled, is superior responsibility a version of strict liability, and three characteristics of the doctrine serve to distinguish it from this automatic assessment of guilt by virtue of position. First, the mental requirement of actual or constructive knowledge prevents the attribution of responsibility to any superior who cannot be shown to have had knowledge or reason to know, within the meaning developed in the jurisprudence, of subordinate criminal conduct. Second, while an accused's position in a military or civilian hierarchy is one of the factors courts consider when determining whether liability for failure to intervene with regard to subordinate criminal conduct should be imposed, it is not the dispositive factor. Last, and most importantly, one of the cornerstones of superior responsibility is the requirement of effective control: without it, an accused cannot be considered a superior, and any attempt to attribute liability on that basis fails; moreover, it is the accused's degree of effective control that guides the judicial determination of what measures he could have taken to fulfil his responsibilities under international law. Indeed, for all its theoretical complexity, the modern doctrine lays significant emphasis on pragmatic considerations of what the law may realistically expect of individuals in positions of authority. Accordingly, it is clear that an accused convicted for international crimes pursuant to superior responsibility is punished for his own conduct, his breach of independent duties imposed on him by international law.

One question that this chapter has raised, but not resolved, is whether there are two or three independent duties contained within the doctrine of superior responsibility. The jurisprudence of the *ad hoc* Tribunals, constrained by the terms of their Statutes, refers to two separate and independent obligations, namely the duty to prevent criminal conduct, and the duty to punish it. Yet it is clear that accused have been held responsible for their failure to intervene to halt criminal conduct while it was ongoing.[725] Given only two choices by Article 7/6(3), chambers have opted to describe that basis for liability as the

---

[724] The concept of reasonableness is incorporated into the test applied for superior responsibility, especially with regard to the third element. As noted below, however, the focus of the inquiry is on the steps that a superior in the position of the accused could reasonably have been expected to take; reasonableness does not form an intrinsic part of the standard against which an accused is judged.

[725] See, e.g., *Strugar* Trial Judgement, *supra* note 179, paras. 422, 425, 427; *Kajelijeli* Trial Judgement, *supra* note 210, para. 779.

failure to prevent the crimes in question, but it is possible that customary international law recognises the failure to intervene as a third independent obligation, particular to a superior, which could give rise to criminal liability. Applying the same logic used to establish the duties to prevent and punish as separate obligations,[726] it would seem that a superior who had no prior knowledge of criminal conduct, but who later acquires knowledge of ongoing crimes, could not avoid liability by waiting to punish the perpetrators after the fact, as long as he had the ability to intervene to stop the crimes at the time of their occurrence. Moreover, although it is unclear whether the ICC will treat these obligations as separate duties, rather than alternative methods of discharging responsibility,[727] the terms and drafting history of the Rome Statute appear to support an interpretation of international law as imposing three distinct duties on superiors,[728] each of which should arguably be an independent basis for criminal responsibility if breached.

Finally, a note on terminology. As the extensive discussions in this chapter demonstrate, the mental element of superior responsibility is frequently the most difficult part of the doctrine to explain succinctly and accurately, and to apply consistently. Academic or judicial attempts to render the law in simple, clear terms frequently run afoul of some requirement of the doctrine or some aspect of the detailed, complicated jurisprudence. For this reason, care should be taken to employ as precise terms as possible, in order to avoid confusion about which standard is being advocated or applied. It may be useful, therefore, to include 'translations' into plain English of some of the different standards that have been applied over the decades of the development of the doctrine, such as negligence or constructive knowledge. These explanations are included in the portion of the Annex that deals with superior responsibility.

---

[726] See *supra* text accompanying notes 195–198. [727] See *supra* text accompanying notes 658–660.
[728] See *supra* note 659.

4

Complicity and aiding and abetting

CONTENTS

The Statutes of the ICTY and ICTR include two provisions that have been interpreted, in the case law of those Tribunals, as reflecting what is termed 'accessory liability' in some domestic jurisdictions – that is, secondary participation in the commission of a crime. In such contexts, accessory liability is generally contrasted with 'accomplice liability', which covers any and all participation in the crime, including that of an individual who is as much (or more) an author of the crime as the physical perpetrator.[1] In international criminal jurisprudence, however, the relationship between these two concepts

---

[1] See, e.g., *Black's Law Dictionary* (8th edn 2004), pp. 15, 17 (but also citing authority which would take a stricter view of accomplices, limiting application of the term to exclude accessories after the fact).

has been complicated – and perhaps unnecessarily confused – by the terms used in the *ad hoc* Statutes, which include 'aiding and abetting' as a form of responsibility in Article 7(1) of the ICTY Statute and Article 6(1) of the ICTR Statute, and 'complicity in genocide' as a 'punishable act' in Article 4(3) of the ICTY Statute and Article 2(3) of the ICTR Statute.

This chapter reviews the practice of the *ad hoc* Tribunals with regard to the interpretation and application of these two sets of provisions, before moving to a comparative analysis of the manner in which other international and internationalised tribunals have approached the issues of aiding and abetting and complicity in genocide. The chapter discusses both aiding and abetting and complicity because the most sustained efforts to explain and clarify the scope and function of these provisions have come in the context of decisions and judgements examining the similarities and distinctions between the two concepts.

Section 4.1 of the chapter focuses on the respective provisions of the ICTY and ICTR Statutes dealing with genocide, and concludes that the phrase 'complicity in genocide' is a package that combines a form or forms of responsibility ('complicity') with the category of offences that constitute genocide. Section 4.2 of the chapter explores the jurisprudence that has attempted to resolve the textual confusion caused by the inclusion of 'complicity in genocide' in a different provision from that which lists the other forms of responsibility, in particular aiding and abetting, which are applied to all crimes within the Tribunals' jurisdiction, including genocide. Sections 4.3 and 4.4 analyse, respectively, the elements of aiding and abetting and complicity in genocide as they have been developed by the judgements and decisions of the *ad hoc* Tribunals. Section 4.5, in discussing the manner in which complicity in genocide and aiding and abetting are treated in other international criminal jurisdictions, provides a perspective on the issues that highlights the possible missteps that have been made by ICTY and ICTR chambers in struggling to give effect to all provisions of their Statutes.

4.1 The modes of participation in genocide: inchoate crimes or forms of responsibility?

There has been considerable uncertainty in the jurisprudence of the *ad hoc* Tribunals regarding the scope of the activities enumerated in Article 4(3) of the ICTY Statute and Article 2(3) of the ICTR Statute ('Article 4/2(3)'), which reproduce *verbatim* Article III of the 1948 Genocide Convention.[2] The chambers have set forth somewhat inconsistent views on whether these activities constitute

---

[2] Convention on the Prevention and Suppression of the Crime of Genocide of 1948, entered into force 12 January 1951, 78 U.N.T.S. 277 ('Genocide Convention'), Art. III. See also *Prosecutor v. Brđanin*, Case No. IT-99-36-T, Judgement, 1 September 2004 ('*Brđanin* Trial Judgement'), para. 725; *Prosecutor*

inchoate crimes or forms of responsibility, and on how they relate to the forms of responsibility in Articles 7(1) and 7(3) of the ICTY Statute and Articles 6(1) and 6(3) of the ICTR Statute ('Article 7/6(1)' and 'Article 7/6(3)', respectively).

Articles 4(3), 7(1) and 7(3) of the ICTY Statute provide as follows:

Article 4: Genocide
[. . .]
3. The following acts shall be punishable:

(a) genocide;
(b) conspiracy to commit genocide;
(c) direct and public incitement to commit genocide;
(d) attempt to commit genocide;
(e) complicity in genocide.[3]

Article 7: Individual criminal responsibility
1. A person who planned, instigated, ordered, committed or otherwise aided and abetted in the planning, preparation or execution of a crime referred to in Articles 2 to 5 of the present Statute, shall be individually responsible for the crime.[4]
[. . .]
3. The fact that any of the acts referred to in Articles 2 to 4 of the present Statute was committed by a subordinate does not relieve his or her superior of criminal responsibility if he or she knew or had reason to know that the subordinate was about to commit such acts or had done so and the superior failed to take the necessary and reasonable measures to prevent such acts or to punish the perpetrators thereof.

At least three chambers of the *ad hoc* Tribunals have referred to all the activities in subparagraphs (b) to (e) of Article 4/2(3) as forms or heads of responsibility. In the words of the Trial Chamber in *Krstić*, 'Article 4(3) provides for a broad range of heads of criminal responsibility, including heads which are not included in Article 7(1), such as "conspiracy to commit genocide" and "attempt to commit genocide"'.[5] The *Semanza* Trial Chamber remarked in the same vein

---

v. *Semanza*, Case No. ICTR-97-20-T, Judgement and Sentence, 15 May 2003 ('*Semanza* Trial Judgement'), para. 391; *Prosecutor* v. *Krstić*, Case No. IT-98-33-T, Judgement, 2 August 2001 ('*Krstić* Trial Judgement'), para. 640.

[3] Statute of the International Criminal Tribunal for the Prosecution of Persons Responsible for Serious Violations of International Humanitarian Law Committed in the Territory of the former Yugoslavia since 1991, (1993) 32 ILM 1159, as amended by Security Council Resolution 1660 of 28 February 2006 ('ICTY Statute'), Art. 4(3). Article 2(3) of the ICTR Statute is identical to Article 4(3) of the ICTY Statute. See Statute of the International Criminal Tribunal for Rwanda, (1994) 33 ILM 1602, as amended by Security Council Resolution 1534 of 26 March 2004 ('ICTR Statute'), Art. 2(3).

[4] ICTY Statute, *supra* note 3, Art. 7(1). Article 6(1) of the ICTR Statute is nearly identical to Article 7(1) of the ICTY Statute. See ICTR Statute, *supra* note 3, Art. 7(1).

[5] *Krstić* Trial Judgement, *supra* note 2, para. 640. See also Steven Powles, 'Joint Criminal Enterprise: Criminal Liability by Prosecutorial Ingenuity and Judicial Creativity', (2004) 2 *Journal of International Criminal Justice* 606, 613 (opining that '[g]enocide is the only crime in the ICTY Statute to include additional modes of criminal liability to those contained in Article 7(1) and 7(3)', and that the two of these 'modes' that most resemble joint criminal enterprise are conspiracy to commit genocide and complicity in genocide).

that 'Article 2(3) lists the forms of criminal responsibility that are applicable to the crime of genocide under the Statute, namely genocide, conspiracy to commit genocide, direct and public incitement to commit genocide, attempt to commit genocide, and complicity in genocide.'[6] In delineating the relationship between Article 7/6(1) and Article 4/2(3), the *Blagojević and Jokić* Trial Chamber opined that 'some heads of responsibility listed under Article 7(1) are necessarily included in those forms of liability listed in Article 4(3), or vice versa'.[7]

Notwithstanding this understandable desire to group all the activities in sub-paragraphs (b) to (e) into the same category of conduct – that is, under the rubric of forms of responsibility – the manner in which the elements of these activities have been defined and applied betrays a more complex relationship among the various sub-paragraphs. Specifically, the case law has tended to treat sub-paragraphs (b), (c) and (d) as inchoate crimes and not forms of responsibility, while sub-paragraph (e) is treated most often[8] – and most authoritatively[9] – as referring to a form or forms of responsibility instead of a crime.

It is relatively uncontroversial that conspiracy to commit genocide, direct and public incitement to commit genocide, and attempt to commit genocide are inchoate crimes and not forms of responsibility. Several chambers of both Tribunals have made explicit statements to this effect,[10] and there appears to

---

[6] *Semanza* Trial Judgement, *supra* note 2, para. 390.
[7] *Prosecutor* v. *Blagojević and Jokić*, Case No. IT-02-60-T, Judgement, 17 January 2005, ('*Blagojević and Jokić* Trial Judgement'), para. 679.
[8] See, e.g., *Prosecutor* v. *Popović, Beara, Nikolić, Borovčanin, Miletić, Gvero and Pandurević*, Case No. IT-05-88-T, Decision on Prosecution Motion for Judicial Notice of Adjudicated Facts, 26 September 2006, para. 13 (referring to 'the forms of responsibility in Articles 7(1), 7(3), and 4(3)(e) of the [ICTY] Statute'); *Prosecutor* v. *Karemera, Ngirumpatse and Nzirorera*, Case No. ICTR-98-44-T, Decision on Defence Motions Challenging the Pleading of a Joint Criminal Enterprise in a Count of Complicity in Genocide in the Amended Indictment, 18 May 2006 ('*Karemera et al.* May 2006 Pre-Trial Decision'), para. 8 ('Whereas genocide is the crime, joint criminal enterprise and complicity in genocide are two modes of liability, two methods by which the crime of genocide can be committed and individuals held responsible for this crime.'); *Blagojević and Jokić* Trial Judgement, *supra* note 7, para. 684 (holding that 'complicity in genocide, as recently reiterated by the *Krstić* Appeal Chamber, is a form of liability of the crime of genocide and not a crime itself'); *Brđanin* Trial Judgement, *supra* note 2, para. 724; *Semanza* Trial Judgement, *supra* note 2, para. 390; *Krstić* Trial Judgement, *supra* note 2, para. 640. But see *Karemera et al.* May 2006 Pre-Trial Decision, *supra*, Separate Opinion of Judge Short on Complicity in Genocide and Joint Criminal Enterprise Theory, para. 8 ('I am ... of the view that the term "complicity in genocide" referred to under Article 2(3)(e) is a crime (genocide) to which a particular mode of criminal responsibility is attached (complicity, or accomplice liability).').
[9] See *Semanza* v. *Prosecutor*, Case No. ICTR-97-20-A, Judgement, 20 May 2005 ('*Semanza* Appeal Judgement'), para. 316; *Prosecutor* v. *Ntakirutimana and Ntakirutimana*, Case Nos. ICTR-96-10-A and ICTR-96-17-A, Judgement, 13 December 2004 ('*Ntakirutimana and Ntakirutimana* Appeal Judgement'), para. 500; *Prosecutor* v. *Krstić*, Case No. IT-98-33-A, Judgement, 19 April 2004 ('*Krstić* Appeal Judgement'), paras. 138–139. But see *Prosecutor* v. *Stakić*, Case No. IT-97-24-A, Judgement, 22 March 2006 ('*Stakić* Appeal Judgement'), para. 88 (stating that 'Counts 1 to 8 [of the indictment against the accused] encompassed the *crimes* of genocide, complicity in genocide, murder ..., extermination, persecutions, deportation and other inhumane acts') (emphasis added). See also *infra* text accompanying notes 93–113.
[10] See, e.g., *Brđanin* Trial Judgement, *supra* note 2, para. 725 ('The *verbatim* incorporation of Article III of the Genocide Convention results in that the inchoate offences relating to genocide (conspiracy, direct and

be considerable support for this proposition in the scholarly literature.[11] Payam Akhavan, for example, has asserted that:

[the] incorporation of Article III(a) and (e) of the Genocide Convention [dealing respectively with genocide and complicity in genocide] into the ICTR Statute may have created some overlap … Article 2(3)(b)–(d), however, enumerates inchoate crimes or *infractions formelles*, giving rise to liability for particular conduct, irrespective of result.[12]

Thus, the primary characteristic that distinguishes the activities in sub-paragraphs (b) to (d) of Article 4/2(3) from those in the other sub-paragraphs is that they are sufficient, in themselves, to ground criminal liability, and do not depend on the completion of some other activity. The chambers are consistent in holding that an accused may be convicted for conspiracy to commit genocide,[13]

---

public incitement and attempt), as well as complicity in genocide, are included in the Statute for the purposes of genocide along with Article 7(1)[.]'); *Prosecutor* v. *Nahimana, Barayagwiza and Ngeze*, Case No. ICTR-99-52-T, Judgement and Sentence, 3 December 2003 ('*Nahimana et al.* Trial Judgement'), para. 1017; *Prosecutor* v. *Kajelijeli*, Case No. ICTR-98-44A-T, Judgement and Sentence, 1 December 2003 ('*Kajelijeli* Trial Judgement'), para. 855 (labelling direct and public incitement to commit genocide an 'inchoate crime'); *Semanza* Trial Judgement, *supra* note 2, para. 378 ('Article 6(1) does not criminalize *inchoate* offences, which are punishable only for the crime of genocide pursuant to Article 2(3)(b), (c), and (d).') (emphasis in original); *Prosecutor* v. *Musema*, Case No. ICTR-96-13-T, Judgement and Sentence, 27 January 2000 ('*Musema* Trial Judgement'), para. 115 (holding that 'attempt is by definition an inchoate crime'); *ibid.*, para. 193 (holding that 'conspiracy is an inchoate offence ("*infraction formelle*")' which is punishable by virtue of the criminal act as such and not as a consequence of the result of that act'); *Prosecutor* v. *Rutaganda*, Case No. ICTR-96-3-T, Judgement and Sentence, 6 December 1999 ('*Rutaganda* Trial Judgement'), para. 34. Accord *Karemera et al.* May 2006 Pre-Trial Decision, *supra* note 8, Separate Opinion of Judge Short on Complicity in Genocide and Joint Criminal Enterprise Theory, para. 5.

[11] See, e.g., William A. Schabas, *The UN International Criminal Tribunals: The Former Yugoslavia, Rwanda and Sierra Leone* (2006), p. 179 ('Three of the acts listed in paragraph (3) [of ICTY Statute Article 4 and ICTR Statute Article 2] are inchoate or incomplete offences, in that they can be committed even if the crime of genocide itself does not take place. This is the case for conspiracy, incitement and attempt.'); John R. W. D. Jones, 'The Inchoate Forms of Genocide: Attempts, Direct and Public Incitement and Conspiracy', in Laurence Burgorgue-Larson (ed.), *La repression internationale du génocide rwandais* (2003), p. 282 ('Attempts, incitements and conspiracy are often referred to as "inchoate offences". That is, they are offences that may be committed notwithstanding that the substantive offence to which they relate is not committed.').

[12] Payam Akhavan, 'The Crime of Genocide in the ICTR Jurisprudence', (2005) 3 *Journal of International Criminal Justice* 989, 992.

[13] See *Kajelijeli* Trial Judgement, *supra* note 10, para. 788 ('With respect to the *actus reus* of the crime of conspiracy to commit genocide it is the agreement which is punishable, whether or not it results in the actual commission of genocide.'). Accord *Prosecutor* v. *Bagosora, Kabiligi, Ntabakuze and Nsengiyumva*, Case No. ICTR-98-41-T, Decision on Motions for Judgement of Acquittal, 2 February 2005 ('*Bagosora et al.* Rule 98 *bis* Trial Decision'), para. 12; *Musema* Trial Judgement, *supra* note 10, paras. 193–194. Although the Appeals Chamber has stated on one occasion that 'joint criminal enterprise and "conspiracy" are two different forms of liability', it appears to have made this statement merely to differentiate conspiracy from JCE in addressing one of the arguments of the accused. See *Prosecutor* v. *Milutinović, Šainović and Ojdanić*, Case No. IT-99-37-AR72, Decision on Dragoljub Ojdanić's Motion Challenging Jurisdiction – Joint Criminal Enterprise, 21 May 2003 ('*Milutinović et al.* JCE Appeal Decision'), para. 23. The majority of the Chamber engaged in no discussion of why conspiracy should not be considered an inchoate crime, and implied that its proper classification is indeed as an inchoate crime by noting that, 'while mere agreement is sufficient in the case of conspiracy, the liability of a member of a joint criminal enterprise will depend on the commission of criminal acts in furtherance of that enterprise'. *Ibid.* In a separate opinion, moreover, Judge Hunt asserted expressly that '[c]onspiracy is not a mode of individual criminal responsibility for the commission of a crime. Conspiracy is itself a crime (of an

direct and public incitement to commit genocide,[14] and attempt to commit genocide[15] regardless of whether someone executed the conspiratorial agreement, acted upon the incitement, or realised the attempted crime.

Forms of responsibility, by contrast, are not punishable in and of themselves, but merely serve to attribute criminality to a person when combined with the criminal conduct and mental state of the physical perpetrator. As a consequence, under the approach of the *ad hoc* Tribunals, an accused cannot incur liability for having engaged in conduct satisfying the elements of one of the forms of responsibility if that conduct either did not contribute to the actual commission of a crime, or, in the case of superior responsibility, a crime was not actually committed.[16] The Trial Chamber in *Kamuhanda* explained this principle in the following manner:

inchoate nature) which is complete once the agreement between the conspirators has been reached.' *Ibid.*, Separate Opinion of Judge David Hunt, para. 23. Criticising Judge Hunt as ranking among those 'international judges [who] fail to acknowledge that conspiracy is not only a substantive crime but also constitutes a liability theory in its own right', Alison Marston Danner and Jenny Martinez have opined that, 'as *Pinkerton* demonstrates, conspiracy (at least as practiced in some U.S. jurisdictions) does play an important role as a liability theory and also functions in ways virtually identical to JCE'. Allison Marston Danner and Jenny S. Martinez, 'Guilty Associations: Joint Criminal Enterprise, Command Responsibility, and the Development of International Criminal Law', (2005) 93 *California Law Review* 75, 119 (referring to *Pinkerton* v. *United States*, 328 US 640 (1946)). Nevertheless, while certain national jurisdictions may regard conspiracy as a form of responsibility or as some analogous mechanism for the attribution of liability to an accused, it is clear that, at least in that body of international criminal law applied by the *ad hoc* Tribunals, conspiracy to commit genocide is an inchoate crime and not a form of responsibility.

[14] See *Kajelijeli* Trial Judgement, *supra* note 10, para. 855 (holding, in respect of direct and public incitement to commit genocide, that 'the communication alone is punishable, irrespective of the accomplishment of the object of the communication'). Accord *Bagosora et al.* Rule 98 *bis* Trial Decision, *supra* note 13, para. 22; *Prosecutor* v. *Ndindabahizi*, Case No. ICTR-2001-71-I, Judgement and Sentence, 15 July 2004 ('*Ndindabahizi* Trial Judgement'), para. 456; *Rutaganda* Trial Judgement, *supra* note 10, para. 38; *Prosecutor* v. *Akayesu*, Case No. ICTR-96-4-T, Judgement, 2 September 1998 ('*Akayesu* Trial Judgement'), para. 562.

[15] *Musema* Trial Judgement, *supra* note 10, para. 115 (holding that 'attempt is by definition an inchoate crime, inherent in the criminal conduct per se, it may be punishable as a separate crime irrespective of whether or not the intended crime is accomplished'). Accord *Rutaganda* Trial Judgement, *supra* note 10, para. 34. The elements of attempt to commit genocide have not been discussed at length in the jurisprudence because no accused before either *ad hoc* Tribunal has ever been charged with attempt.

[16] See *Prosecutor* v. *Kordić and Čerkez*, Case No. IT-95-14/2-A, Judgement, 17 December 2004 ('*Kordić and Čerkez* Appeal Judgement'), paras. 26–27 (holding that an accused's planning or instigating of a crime need not have been the 'but for' cause of the crime, but need merely have been a factor 'substantially contributing to … criminal conduct constituting one or more statutory crimes that are later perpetrated') (quotation at para. 26); *Prosecutor* v. *Blaškić*, Case No. IT-95-14-A, Judgement, 29 July 2004 ('*Blaškić* Appeal Judgement'), para. 48 (making this observation for aiding and abetting); *Prosecutor* v. *Strugar*, Case No. IT-01-42-T, Judgement, 31 January 2005 ('*Strugar* Trial Judgement'), para. 332 (making the same observation for ordering); *Ndindabahizi* Trial Judgement, *supra* note 14, para. 456 ('Unlike the crime of direct and public incitement, instigation does not give rise to liability unless the crime is actually committed by a principal or principals.'). See also Chapter 2, text accompanying notes 149, 151–152, 225, 453 (discussing similar jurisprudence on joint criminal enterprise); *Prosecutor* v. *Gacumbitsi*, Case No. ICTR-2001-64-A, Judgement, 7 July 2006 ('*Gacumbitsi* Appeal Judgement'), para. 143 ('To establish liability under Article 6(3) of the Statute, the following must be shown: … A crime over which the Tribunal has jurisdiction was committed'); Chapter 3, text accompanying notes 188, 354–357, 513–517 (discussing similar jurisprudence on superior responsibility). Section 4.3 of this chapter contains a complete discussion of the elements of aiding and abetting, and Section 4.4 discusses the elements of complicity in genocide. Chapter 5 of this book examines the elements of planning, instigating, and ordering.

Pursuant to Article 6(1) [of the ICTR Statute], an individual's participation in the planning or preparation of an offence within the Tribunal's jurisdiction will give rise to criminal responsibility only if the criminal act is actually committed. Accordingly, crimes which are attempted but not consummated are not punishable, except for the crime of genocide, pursuant to Article 2(3)(b), (c) and (d) of the Statute.[17]

The status of complicity in genocide is somewhat less clear than that of conspiracy to commit genocide, direct and public incitement to commit genocide, and attempt to commit genocide. The enumeration of complicity along with the crime of genocide and these associated inchoate crimes in the sub-paragraphs of Article 4/2(3) has led to some confusion in the jurisprudence,[18] as well as in the scholarly literature,[19] over its proper classification. No doubt fuelling this confusion is the routine practice of the *ad hoc* Tribunals' Prosecutors of charging complicity in genocide as a separate count in the indictment, alleged to have been perpetrated through one or more of the forms of responsibility in Articles 7/6(1) and 7/6(3), as if it were a substantive crime like genocide, grave breaches, violations of the laws or customs of war, or crimes against humanity.[20]

Several chambers have held that complicity in genocide, like the forms of responsibility in Articles 7/6(1) and 7/6(3) and unlike conspiracy, incitement and attempt, cannot bring about the imposition of liability where a crime – in this case, genocide – is not actually perpetrated.[21] Only three chambers, however, appear to have dedicated considered and thoughtful discussions to the

---

[17] *Prosecutor* v. *Kamuhanda*, Case No. ICTR-99-54A-T, Judgement and Sentence, 22 January 2003 ('*Kamuhanda* Trial Judgement'), para. 589.

[18] For example, compare *Blagojević and Jokić* Trial Judgement, *supra* note 7, para. 684 (holding that 'complicity in genocide, as recently reiterated by the *Krstić* Appeal[s] Chamber, is a form of liability of the crime of genocide and not a crime itself') with the sources cited in note 22, *infra*.

[19] Compare, e.g., Jones, *supra* note 11, p. 281 (stating that complicity in genocide 'is not an inchoate offence but a form of responsibility for a completed offence') with Chile Eboe-Osuji, ' "Complicity in Genocide" versus "Aiding and Abetting Genocide": Construing the Difference in the ICTR and ICTY Statutes', (2005) 3 *Journal of International Criminal Justice* 56, 64 (stating that 'Article 2(3) of the [ICTR] Statute contains a list of punishable crimes, including "genocide" and "complicity in genocide"').

[20] See, e.g., *Prosecutor* v. *Karemera, Ngirumpatse and Nzirorera*, Case No. ICTR-98-44-I, Amended Indictment, 23 February 2005 ('*Karemera et al.* Amended Indictment'), p. 13 (Count 3 charging '[g]enocide pursuant to Articles 2, 6(1) and 6(3) of the Statute', and Count 4 charging '[c]omplicity in Genocide pursuant to Articles 2 and 6(1) of the Statute'); *Prosecutor* v. *Milošević*, Case No. IT-02-54-T, Amended [Bosnia] Indictment, 22 November 2002, para. 32 (Count 1 charging '[g]enocide, punishable under Articles 4(3)(a) and 7(1) and 7(3) of the Statute of the Tribunal', and Count 2 charging '[c]omplicity in genocide, punishable under Articles 4(3)(e) and 7(1) and 7(3) of the Statute of the Tribunal'). See also *Karemera et al.* May 2006 Pre-Trial Decision, *supra* note 8, Separate Opinion of Judge Short on Complicity in Genocide and Joint Criminal Enterprise Theory, para. 8 (remarking that complicity in genocide 'is often charged as alternative count to the count of genocide ... and can result in a finding of guilt for "complicity in genocide"').

[21] See, e.g., *Prosecutor* v. *Krajišnik*, Case No. IT-00-39-T, Judgement, 27 September 2006 ('*Krajišnik* Trial Judgement'), para. 864; *Blagojević and Jokić* Trial Judgement, *supra* note 7, para. 638; *Brđanin* Trial Judgement, *supra* note 2, para. 728; *Prosecutor* v. *Stakić*, Case No. IT-97-24-T, Judgement, 29 October 2003 ('*Stakić* Trial Judgement'), para. 534; *Prosecutor* v. *Stakić*, Case No. IT-97-24-T, Decision on Rule 98 *bis* Motion for Judgement of Acquittal, 31 October 2002 ('*Stakić* Rule 98 *bis* Trial Decision'), para. 52;

question of whether complicity in genocide is a crime or a form of responsibility,[22] and all three have come to the conclusion that it is a form of responsibility. These are, in turn, the *Brđanin* Trial Judgement of September 2004,[23] the *Blagojević and Jokić* Trial Judgement of January 2005,[24] and an interlocutory decision of the *Karemera* Trial Chamber in May 2006 granting a motion challenging the Tribunal's jurisdiction.[25]

Radoslav Brđanin was charged with 'complicity in genocide, punishable under Articles 4(3)(e), and 7(1) and 7(3) of the Statute of the Tribunal'.[26] The Trial Chamber held that 'complicity is one of the forms of responsibility recognised by the general principles of criminal law, and in respect of genocide, it is also recognised by customary international law'.[27] It declined to 'endors[e] the view that complicity in genocide is a distinct crime separate from genocide',[28] and instead 'agree[d] with' the ICTR Trial Chamber in *Bagilishema* that '"genocide and complicity in genocide are two different forms of participation in the same offence"'.[29] The Chamber accordingly concluded that it was 'unnecessary to address' whether Brđanin could incur superior responsibility under Article 7(3) for his failure to prevent or punish complicity in genocide.[30] It continued:

Musema Trial Judgement, *supra* note 10, paras. 171, 173; *Akayesu* Trial Judgement, *supra* note 14, paras. 527, 529. Accord Jones, *supra* note 11, p. 281 (stating that complicity in genocide 'is not an inchoate offence but a form of responsibility *for a completed offence*') (emphasis added).

[22] A number of chambers have made statements to the effect that complicity in genocide is a crime, although most of these appear to have been inadvertent and none have been accompanied by a considered discussion of why complicity in genocide should be considered a crime and not a form of responsibility. See, e.g., *Stakić* Appeal Judgement, *supra* note 9, para. 88 (remarking, in the course of an enumeration of the counts charged in an indictment in which the prosecution had placed complicity in genocide in its own count, that 'Counts 1 to 8 encompassed the crimes of genocide, complicity in genocide, murder as both a war crime and a crime against humanity, extermination, persecutions, deportation and other inhumane acts'); *Prosecutor v. Muvunyi*, Case No. ICTR-00-55A-T, Judgement, 11 September 2006 ('*Muvunyi* Trial Judgement'), para. 460 (remarking that 'accomplice liability under Article 6(1) is different from the substantive crime of complicity in genocide under Article 2(3)(e) of the Statute', but later dismissing the count of complicity in genocide without having provided any elaboration as to its scope or elements); *Prosecutor v. Kambanda*, Case No. ICTR-97-23-S, Judgement and Sentence, 4 September 1998 ('*Kambanda* Trial Judgement'), para. 40 (accepting the accused's guilty plea and finding that he 'committed complicity in genocide stipulated in Article 2(3)(e) of the Statute as a crime, and attributed to him by virtue of article 6(1) and 6(3)'); *Akayesu* Trial Judgement, *supra* note 14, para. 700 (holding that 'the crime of genocide and that of complicity in genocide [a]re two distinct crimes, and ... the same person c[an] certainly not be both the principal perpetrator of, and accomplice to, the same offence').

[23] See *Brđanin* Trial Judgement, *supra* note 2, paras. 724–727.

[24] See *Blagojević and Jokić* Trial Judgement, *supra* note 7, paras. 684–685.

[25] See *Karemera et al.* May 2006 Pre-Trial Decision, *supra* note 8.

[26] *Prosecutor v. Brđanin*, Case No. IT-99-36-T, Sixth Amended Indictment, 9 December 2003, para. 44.

[27] *Brđanin* Trial Judgement, *supra* note 2, para. 724 (footnotes omitted).

[28] *Ibid.*, para. 725 n. 1765.

[29] *Ibid.* (quoting *Prosecutor v. Bagilishema*, Case No. ICTR-95-1A-T, Judgement, 7 June 2001 ('*Bagilishema* Trial Judgement'), para. 67). The *Bagilishema* Trial Chamber made this statement in the context of its holding that an accused cannot be convicted of both genocide and complicity in genocide on the basis of the same acts, and did not provide further detail on its conception of the relationship between genocide and complicity in genocide. *Ibid.*

[30] *Brđanin* Trial Judgement, *supra* note 2, para. 725 n. 1765.

The Trial Chamber regards genocide under Article 4(3)(a) as encompassing principal offenders, including but not limited to the physical perpetrators and to those liable pursuant to the theory of JCE. By contrast, an accomplice to genocide under Article 4(3)(e) is someone who associates him or herself in the crime of genocide committed by another.[31]

In its categorisation of genocide and complicity in genocide as 'two different forms of participation in the same offence', the Chamber appears to have regarded complicity in genocide as encompassing all forms of 'accomplice liability' charged in relation to the crime of genocide, but not as a separate and distinct crime itself. Under this approach, forms of responsibility for genocide that do not fall within the purview of 'accomplice liability' are appropriately pleaded in connection with the crime of genocide under sub-paragraph (a) of Article 4/2(3), and not with complicity in genocide under sub-paragraph (e).

In the course of rejecting a prosecution claim that the accused should incur superior responsibility pursuant to Article 7(3) of the ICTY Statute for his failure to prevent or punish complicity in genocide, the Trial Chamber in *Blagojević and Jokić* stated that:

Article 7(3) is a mode of liability that according to the Statute explicitly refers to the crime within the jurisdiction of the Tribunal. Since complicity in genocide, as recently reiterated by the *Krstić* Appeal[s] Chamber, is a form of liability of the crime of genocide and not a crime itself, Article 7(3) cannot but refer to the crime of genocide[32] ... The Trial Chamber therefore finds that command responsibility would be more appropriately pleaded under Article 4(3)(a).[33]

Evincing an understanding of the relationship between genocide and complicity in genocide very similar to that of the *Brđanin* Trial Chamber, the *Blagojević and Jokić* Trial Chamber proceeded to analyse Vidoje Blagojević's superior responsibility for failing to prevent or punish not complicity in genocide under Article 4(3)(e), but the crime of genocide itself under Article 4(3)(a).[34]

The three accused in *Karemera* were charged with complicity in genocide 'pursuant to Articles 2 and 6(1) of the Statute',[35] and the indictment specifically alleged that all references to Article 6(1) included participation in a joint

[31] *Ibid.*, para. 727 (footnotes omitted).
[32] *Blagojević and Jokić* Trial Judgement, *supra* note 7, para. 684.   [33] *Ibid.*, para. 685.
[34] *Ibid.*, paras. 794–796. The Trial Chamber ultimately found that Blagojević could not incur superior responsibility because the evidence failed to establish a superior-subordinate relationship between him and the relevant subordinates. *Ibid.*, paras. 795–796. The *Krstić* Appeal Judgement, cited by the Trial Chamber as support for its conclusion that complicity in genocide is a form of responsibility, did not make an express holding to this effect, although it arguably treated complicity in genocide as a form of responsibility in its comparative analysis between the elements of complicity and those of aiding and abetting. See *Krstić* Appeal Judgement, *supra* note 9, paras. 138–142. This analysis is explored in detail below. See *infra* text accompanying notes 93–113.
[35] *Karemera et al.* Amended Indictment, *supra* note 20, p. 11 (Count 2).

criminal enterprise (JCE).[36] Joseph Nzirorera challenged this allegation, claiming the ICTR lacked jurisdiction to convict him for complicity in genocide effected by means of a JCE. In its initial decision, the Trial Chamber declined to address this question because, as the indictment charged complicity in genocide as an alternative to genocide, there may ultimately be no need to resolve it; such resolution could be made, if necessary, at the time of judgement.[37] In overruling the Trial Chamber, the Appeals Chamber held that the accused's challenge concerned a 'pure question of law concerning the limits of the Tribunal's jurisdiction to employ a mode of liability';[38] as such, the Trial Chamber was obliged to dispose of it immediately to avoid infringing the accused's 'right not to be tried on, and not to have to defend against, an allegation that falls outside the Tribunal's jurisdiction'.[39]

On remand, a majority of the Trial Chamber concluded that the Tribunal lacks jurisdiction to impose liability for complicity in genocide 'through the form of a joint criminal enterprise':[40]

Whereas the [*sic*] genocide is the crime, joint criminal enterprise and complicity in genocide are two modes of liability, two methods by which the crime of genocide can be committed and individuals held responsible for this crime. It is therefore impossible to plead that complicity in genocide has been committed by means of a joint criminal enterprise. Complicity can only be pleaded as a form of liability for the crime of genocide.[41]

The Chamber purported to base this conclusion on the case law of the ICTR and the ICTY[42] although, of the cited judgements, only *Blagojević and Jokić* and *Brđanin* dealt directly with the proper classification of complicity in genocide.[43] A three-judge panel of the Appeals Chamber allowed the prosecution's appeal

---

[36] *Ibid.*, para. 4. *See* Chapter 2, text accompanying notes 46, 147 (JCE falling under 'committing' in Article 7/6(1)).
[37] *Prosecutor v. Karemera, Ngirumpatse and Nzirorera*, Case No. ICTR-98-44-PT, Decision on Defence Motions Challenging the Indictment as Regards the Joint Criminal Enterprise Liability, 14 September 2005, para. 10. *Prosecutor v. Milutinović, Šainović, Ojdanić, Pavković, Lazarević, Đorđević and Lukić*, Case No. IT-05-87-PT, Decision on Ojdanić's Motion Challenging Jurisdiction: Indirect Co-Perpetration, 22 March 2006, para. 23 (Pre-Trial Chamber deferring until the final judgement the question of whether JCE liability can arise where the physical perpetrator is not a JCE participant); *Prosecutor v. Popović, Beara, Nikolić, Borovčanin, Tolimir, Miletić, Gvero, Pandurević and Trbić*, Case No. IT-05-88-PT, Decision on Motions Challenging the Indictment pursuant to Rule 72 of the Rules, 31 May 2006 ('*Popović et al.* May 2006 Pre-Trial Decision'), para. 21 (endorsing the *Milutinović* approach and likewise deferring this question for the ultimate judgement).
[38] *Prosecutor v. Karemera, Ngirumpatse and Nzirorera*, Case No. ICTR-98-44-AR72.6, Decision on Jurisdictional Appeals: Joint Criminal Enterprise, 12 April 2006, para. 22.
[39] *Ibid.*, para. 23.   [40] *Karemera et al.* May 2006 Pre-Trial Decision, *supra* note 8, para. 10.
[41] *Ibid.*, para. 8.   [42] *Ibid.*, para. 7.
[43] See *ibid.*, Separate Opinion of Judge Short on Complicity in Genocide and Joint Criminal Enterprise Theory, para. 7 (correctly making this observation in respect of the *Blagojević and Jokić* Trial Judgement, but omitting to mention the *Brđanin* Trial Judgement).

of the *Karemera* decision to proceed to the full bench,[44] but the Appeals Chamber did not give its views on the substantive issue because the prosecution subsequently withdrew its appeal.[45]

In a separate opinion, Judge Short agreed with the result achieved by the *Karemera* Trial Chamber majority – that the Tribunal lacks jurisdiction to impose liability for complicity in genocide effected by means of a JCE – but disagreed with the majority's reasoning in relation to the status of complicity in genocide.[46] He opined that the confusion associated with complicity in genocide 'arises as a result of the overlap between "complicity" in Article 2(3)(e) of the Statute and forms of accomplice liability in Article 6(1)':[47]

In my view, complicity in genocide has the indicia of a criminal offence, whilst encompassing a particular mode of liability. It is often charged as an alternative count to the count of genocide, as in the Indictment in this case, and can result in a finding of guilt for 'complicity in genocide'. In the case of *Semanza*, for example, the Accused, who was charged with Counts of genocide and complicity in genocide in the alternative, was found not guilty of genocide and convicted of complicity in genocide. It certainly cannot be said that the Accused in that case was convicted of a mode of liability. I am therefore of the view that the term 'complicity in genocide' referred to under Article 2(3)(e) is a crime (genocide) to which a particular mode of criminal responsibility is attached (complicity, or accomplice liability).[48]

Judge Short is correct in noting the prosecution's habitual practice of charging complicity in genocide in its own count in the indictment, although chambers are certainly not bound to regard complicity in genocide as a crime simply based on the way the prosecution chooses to organise its charging instrument.[49] Yet Judge Short's conceptualisation of the relationship between genocide and complicity in genocide contains a simple but insightful observation that had not been made previously in the jurisprudence (nor, apparently, in the scholarly literature), and that could serve to reconcile the persistent confusion over the

---

[44] *Prosecutor v. Karemera, Ngirumpatse and Nzirorera*, Case No. ICTR-98-44-AR72.7, Decision pursuant to Rule 72(E) of the Rules of Procedure and Evidence on Validity of the Prosecution Appeal Regarding the Pleading of Joint Criminal Enterprise in a Count of Complicity in Genocide, 14 July 2006, para. 6.

[45] *Prosecutor v. Karemera, Ngirumpatse and Nzirorera*, Case No. ICTR-98-44-AR72.7, Decision on Prosecution Motion to Withdraw Appeal Regarding the Pleading of Joint Criminal Enterprise in a Count of Complicity in Genocide, 25 August 2006, para. 4.

[46] *Karemera et al.* May 2006 Pre-Trial Decision, *supra* note 8, Separate Opinion of Judge Short on Complicity in Genocide and Joint Criminal Enterprise Theory, paras. 1, 5.

[47] *Ibid.*, para. 5.

[48] *Ibid.*, para. 8 (footnote omitted) (citing *Semanza* Trial Judgement, *supra* note 2, paras. 433, 533).

[49] Cf. *Prosecutor v. Haradinaj, Balaj and Brahimaj*, Case No. IT-04-84-PT, Decision on Motion to Amend the Indictment and on Challenges to the Form of the Amended Indictment, 25 October 2006, para. 13 ('[I]t is each charge that holds the potential of exposing the accused to individual criminal liability. The counts in an indictment, by contrast, merely reflect the way in which the Prosecution chose to organise the charges in relation to the crimes allegedly committed.'); *Prosecutor v. Popović, Beara, Nikolić, Borovčanin, Tolimir, Miletić, Gvero and Pandurević*, Case No. IT-05-88-PT, Decision on Further Amendments and Challenges to the Indictment, 13 July 2006, para. 11 n. 26 (same).

status of complicity in genocide. The term 'complicity in genocide' would actually appear to be something more than just a form of responsibility or a crime. It could be considered an amalgam of the two: 'genocide' is the crime; and 'complicity' is one, or a collection, of the several forms of responsibility through which genocide may be realised. In this sense, the term 'complicity in genocide' is analogous to the terms 'ordering torture as a crime against humanity', 'planning murder as a violation of the laws or customs of war' or, indeed, 'aiding and abetting genocide'. Under this approach, the only conceptual difference between genocide and the other crimes in the ICTY and ICTR Statutes as they relate to forms of responsibility would be that, while the forms of responsibility in Articles 7/6(1) and 7/6(3) apply to all the crimes in the Statutes – including genocide – 'complicity' applies uniquely to genocide.

The methodology used by one of the few chambers of the *ad hoc* Tribunals to have actually entered a conviction for complicity in genocide is consistent with this interpretation.[50] After finding that the elements of genocide had been fulfilled by Interahamwe physical perpetrators with respect to events charged in two counts of the indictment,[51] the *Semanza* Trial Chamber analysed the physical conduct and mental state of the accused to determine whether they satisfied the elements of complicity.[52] In performing this analysis, it applied the legal elements of complicity set forth earlier in the judgement, which it defined in terms identical to those of aiding and abetting under Article 7/6(1).[53] The Chamber concluded that Semanza's physical actions – including gathering Interahamwe to assist in certain killings – combined with his mental state, constituted complicity.[54] He was accordingly convicted of complicity in genocide on these two counts.[55]

Ultimately, the weight of the jurisprudence would seem to point to two logical conclusions. First, of the punishable conduct in Article 4/2(3), conspiracy to commit genocide, direct and public incitement to commit genocide, and attempt to commit genocide are inchoate crimes, not forms of responsibility. The discussion of the elements of these crimes, except to the extent that they relate to the forms of responsibility, is therefore outside the scope of the present volume. Second, 'complicity in genocide' incorporates both the crime of genocide and

---

[50] The other chambers are the *Blagojević and Jokić* Trial Chamber of the ICTY and the *Kambanda* Trial Chamber of the ICTR, which entered its complicity in genocide conviction on the basis of a guilty plea. See *Blagojević and Jokić* Trial Judgement, *supra* note 7, paras. 787, 797, p. 304; *Kambanda* Trial Judgement, *supra* note 22, para. 40.

[51] See *Semanza* Trial Judgement, *supra* note 2, paras. 424–425. Genocide was perpetrated in this instance through the underlying offence of 'killing'. See ICTR Statute, *supra* note 3, Art. 2(2)(a).

[52] See *Semanza* Trial Judgement, *supra* note 2, paras. 425–433.

[53] See *ibid.*, paras. 390–398. See *infra*, text accompanying notes 308–326, for a discussion of these elements.

[54] See *ibid.*, paras. 435–436.

[55] See *ibid.*, para. 553. The Appeals Chamber affirmed the conviction for complicity in genocide on one of the counts, but reversed it on the other and substituted a conviction for ordering genocide pursuant to Article 6(1) of the ICTR Statute. *Semanza* Appeal Judgement, *supra* note 9, para. 364, p. 129.

either a single form of responsibility[56] or a group of forms of responsibility ordinarily labelled 'accomplice liability' in certain domestic jurisdictions.[57]

The following section examines in greater detail the interaction between the inchoate crimes in Article 4/2(3) and complicity in genocide, on the one hand, and the forms of responsibility in Articles 7/6(1) and 7/6(3), on the other.[58] The discussion focuses specifically on another point of considerable disagreement in the jurisprudence: the relationship between 'aiding and abetting genocide' and 'complicity in genocide', and whether or not these two concepts are completely coterminous. The elements of complicity in genocide – to the extent they have been expounded in the *ad hoc* case law – will be set forth in Section 4.4 of this chapter.

4.2 The relationship between 'aiding and abetting genocide' and 'complicity in genocide'

Relatively few chambers of the *ad hoc* Tribunals have had occasion to examine complicity in genocide in detail, including how complicity relates to the other forms of responsibility under the Statutes. In most cases in which judgement has been rendered in respect of an accused charged with a count of complicity in genocide, the Trial Chamber has acquitted the accused of this count without examining whether his conduct fulfilled any of the physical or mental elements of complicity in genocide. These judgements fall into three categories. In the first category, the Trial Chamber found the accused guilty of the crime of genocide through one of the forms of responsibility in Articles 7/6(1) and 7/6(3), and acquitted the accused of complicity in genocide without much further discussion.[59] In the second category, which includes most of the relevant ICTR judgements, the Trial Chamber found the accused guilty of genocide through one of the forms of responsibility in Articles 7/6(1) and 7/6(3), and acquitted the accused of complicity in genocide because the indictment charged him with

---

[56] This form of responsibility may be identical to aiding and abetting, see *infra* text accompanying notes 306–308, but merely have been termed 'complicity' because of the appreciable influence of the Genocide Convention on the drafting of Article 4/2 of the *ad hoc* Statutes.

[57] See, e.g., *Black's Law Dictionary, supra* note 1, p. 17 (defining 'accomplice' as a 'person who is in any way concerned with another in the commission of a crime, whether as a principal . . . or as an accessory'). See *infra* text accompanying notes 101–115 (after appellate holding that complicity encompasses conduct broader than aiding and abetting, two trial judgements conclude that complicity includes all forms of responsibility in Article 7/6(1) except JCE and superior responsibility, that is, all forms of accomplice liability).

[58] See *infra* text accompanying notes 335–342 for a brief discussion of inchoate crimes in the ICC.

[59] See *Prosecutor v. Ntagerura, Bagambiki and Imanishimwe*, Case No. ICTR-99-46-T, Judgement and Sentence, 25 February 2004, para. 695 (accused Imanishimwe pursuant to Article 6(3)); *Nahimana et al.* Trial Judgement, *supra* note 10, paras. 973–974, 977–977A, 1056; *Krstić* Trial Judgement, *supra* note 2, paras. 636, 644–645, 727 (pursuant to Article 7(1) by means of a JCE).

genocide and complicity in genocide in the alternative.[60] In the third category, the Trial Chamber found that the evidence did not establish that genocide had occurred at all, and thus made no findings on whether the accused was liable for complicity in genocide because such liability cannot ensue where genocide is not perpetrated by someone.[61]

As a result, the more detailed discussions in ICTR case law come mainly from just four trial judgements: *Akayesu* in September 1998,[62] *Musema* in January 2000,[63] *Bagilishema* in June 2001[64] and *Semanza* in May 2003.[65] Six ICTY Trial Chambers[66] and both Appeals Chambers[67] have also examined complicity in genocide at some length. It would appear that, once *Akayesu* established that an accused cannot be convicted of both complicity in genocide and genocide (through one of the other forms of responsibility) for the same underlying conduct,[68] the Prosecutor began to charge complicity in genocide as an alternative to genocide.[69]

---

[60] See *Muvunyi* Trial Judgement, *supra* note 22, para. 499; *Prosecutor* v. *Muhimana*, Case No. ICTR-95-1B-T, Judgement and Sentence, 28 April 2005 ('*Muhimana* Trial Judgement'), para. 520; *Prosecutor* v. *Gacumbitsi*, Case No. ICTR-2001-64-T, Judgement, 14 June 2004, para. 295; *Kajelijeli* Trial Judgement, *supra* note 10, para. 847; *Prosecutor* v. *Niyitegeka*, Case No. ICTR 96-14-T, Judgement and Sentence, 16 May 2003 ('*Niyitegeka* Trial Judgement'), para. 421; *Prosecutor* v. *Ntakirutimana and Ntakirutimana*, Case Nos. ICTR-96-10 and ICTR-96-17-T, Judgement and Sentence, 21 February 2003 ('*Ntakirutimana and Ntakirutimana* Trial Judgement'), paras. 796, 837; *Kamuhanda* Trial Judgement, *supra* note 17, para. 654.

[61] See *Krajišnik* Trial Judgement, *supra* note 21, paras. 867–869, 1181; *Brđanin* Trial Judgement, *supra* note 2, paras. 989, 991, 1152; *Stakić* Trial Judgement, *supra* note 21, paras. 534, 559–561; *Prosecutor* v. *Sikirica, Došen and Kolundžija*, Case No. IT-95-8-T, Decision on Defence Motions to Acquit, 1 September 2001, paras. 90, 97, 172 (accused Sikirica acquitted of genocide and complicity in genocide). Final judgement in *Sikirica* was rendered two months later pursuant to a guilty plea. See *Prosecutor* v. *Sikirica, Došen and Kolundžija*, Case No. IT-95-8-T, Sentencing Judgement, 13 November 2001. In at least one case for which judgement has been rendered, the prosecution has voluntarily withdrawn the charge of complicity in genocide. See *Prosecutor* v. *Mpambara*, Case No. ICTR-01-65-T, Judgement, 11 September 2006 ('*Mpambara* Trial Judgement'), para. 6 n. 3. See also *infra* note 129.

[62] *Akayesu* Trial Judgement, *supra* note 14, paras. 525–548.

[63] *Musema* Trial Judgement, *supra* note 10, paras. 168–183.

[64] *Bagilishema* Trial Judgement, *supra* note 29, paras. 66–71.

[65] *Semanza* Trial Judgement, *supra* note 2, paras. 390–398.

[66] *Krajišnik* Trial Judgement, *supra* note 21, paras. 864–865; *Blagojević and Jokić* Trial Judgement, *supra* note 7, paras. 678–680, 776–782; *Brđanin* Trial Judgement, *supra* note 2, paras. 722–730; *Prosecutor* v. *Milošević*, Case No. IT-02-54-T, Decision on Motion for Judgement of Acquittal, 16 June 2004 ('*Milošević* Rule 98 *bis* Trial Decision'), paras. 295–297; *Stakić* Trial Judgement, *supra* note 21, paras. 531–534; *Stakić* Rule 98 *bis* Trial Decision, *supra* note 21, paras. 45–95; *Krstić* Trial Judgement, *supra* note 2, paras. 639–643.

[67] *Semanza* Appeal Judgement, *supra* note 9, paras. 316, 318; *Ntakirutimana and Ntakirutimana* Appeal Judgement, *supra* note 9, para. 371; *Krstić* Appeal Judgement, *supra* note 9, paras. 138–142.

[68] *Akayesu* Trial Judgement, *supra* note 14, para. 532. Accord *Karemera et al.* May 2006 Pre-Trial Decision, *supra* note 8, para. 9; *Semanza* Trial Judgement, *supra* note 2, para. 397; *Nahimana et al.* Trial Judgement, *supra* note 10, para. 1056; *Bagilishema* Trial Judgement, *supra* note 29, para. 67; *Musema* Trial Judgement, *supra* note 10, para. 175. Chapter 6, text accompanying notes 3–122, discusses in detail how a chamber goes about choosing among different forms of responsibility charged in relation to the same conduct.

[69] See, e.g., *Karemera et al.* Amended Indictment, *supra* note 20, p. 13 (Count 3 charging '[g]enocide pursuant to Articles 2, 6(1) and 6(3) of the Statute', and Count 4 alternatively charging complicity in genocide); *Prosecutor* v. *Kamuhanda*, Case No. ICTR-99-54 A, Indictment, 10 November 2000, pp. 66–67 (Count 2 charging genocide pursuant to Articles 2(3)(a), 6(1), and 6(3) of the Statute and Count 3

The co-existence in the *ad hoc* Statutes of the inchoate crimes and complicity in genocide in Article 4/2(3), on the one hand, and the forms of responsibility in Articles 7/6(1) and 7/6(3), on the other, has resulted in what several chambers have termed an 'overlap' between certain provisions.[70] The overlap arises because the forms of responsibility in Articles 7/6(1) and 7/6(3) are, by their terms[71] and as affirmed by the ICTY Appeals Chamber,[72] applicable to all the crimes in the *ad hoc* Statutes, including the crime of genocide.[73] This overlap has presented interpretational challenges, especially for those activities in Article 4/2(3) that have elements akin to those of a particular form of responsibility in Article 7/6(1) when genocide is alleged through that form. Conspiracy to commit genocide under subparagraph (b) of Article 4/2(3), for example, could be said to bear some resemblance to genocide effected by means of a JCE.[74] Likewise, direct and public incitement to commit genocide under subparagraph (c) of Article 4/2(3) and instigating genocide – that is, liability for genocide imposed through the form of responsibility 'instigating' in Article 7/6(1) – involve very similar criminal conduct. Indeed, the *Akayesu* Trial Chamber held that the two activities were largely identical to one another, with the only difference being that instigating genocide cannot trigger liability where genocide is not actually perpetrated.[75] The

---

alternatively charging complicity in genocide). See also *Stakić* Rule 98 *bis* Trial Decision, *supra* note 21, para. 36 ('Dr. Stakić is charged in the alternative with genocide and complicity in genocide since an individual cannot be both the principal perpetrator of genocide and an accomplice thereto.').

[70] See *Krstić* Appeal Judgement, *supra* note 9, para. 138; *Popović et al.* May 2006 Pre-Trial Decision, *supra* note 37, para. 31; *Bagosora et al.* Rule 98 *bis* Trial Decision, *supra* note 13, para. 21; *Blagojević and Jokić* Trial Judgement, *supra* note 7, para. 679; *Brđanin* Trial Judgement, *supra* note 2, para. 726; *Stakić* Trial Judgement, *supra* note 21, para. 531; *Semanza* Trial Judgement, *supra* note 2, para. 391 (noting that 'an overlap exists between "genocide" in Article 2(3)(a) and "committing" in Article 6(1), and between "complicity" in Article 2(3)(e) and forms of accomplice liability in Article 6(1)', and attributing this 'redundancy' to 'the drafters' *verbatim* incorporation into the Statute of Article III of the Genocide Convention'); *Stakić* Rule 98 *bis* Trial Decision, *supra* note 21, para. 47; *Krstić* Trial Judgement, *supra* note 2, para. 640.

[71] See ICTY Statute, *supra* note 3, Art. 7(1) (ascribing criminal responsibility to any person 'who planned, instigated, ordered, committed or otherwise aided and abetted … a crime referred to in articles 2 to 5 of the present Statute'); *ibid.*, Art. 7(3) (ascribing superior responsibility to a superior who failed to prevent or punish 'any of the acts referred to in articles 2 to 5 of the present Statute'). *Accord* ICTR Statute, *supra* note 3, Arts. 7(1), 7(3).

[72] *Krstić* Appeal Judgement, *supra* note 9, para. 138 (noting that 'there is an overlap between Article 4(3) as the general provision enumerating punishable forms of participation in genocide and Article 7(1) as the general provision for criminal liability which applies to all the offences punishable under the Statute, including the offence of genocide'). *Accord Popović et al.* May 2006 Pre-Trial Decision, *supra* note 37, para. 30 (noting that '[t]he *Krstić* Appeals Chamber found that the forms of responsibility enumerated in Article 7(1) should be read into Article 4(3)').

[73] See, e.g., *Nahimana et al.* Trial Judgement, *supra* note 10, paras. 946, 973–974, 977–977A, 1056 (convicting the accused Nahimana pursuant to Article 6(1) for instigating genocide; the accused Ngeze pursuant to Article 6(1) for ordering and aiding and abetting genocide; and the accused Barayagwiza pursuant to Article 6(3) for failing to prevent genocide).

[74] See, e.g., *Hamdan* v. *Rumsfeld*, 126 S. Ct. 2749, 2785 n. 40 (2006) (making reference to the doctrine of JCE in the ICTY in the course of a discussion about conspiracy to commit genocide and conspiracy to wage aggressive war in international criminal law); *Milutinović et al.* JCE Appeal Decision, *supra* note 13, paras. 23, 26 (dismissing the contention of the accused Ojdanić that conspiracy and JCE are synonymous); *ibid.*, Separate Opinion of Judge David Hunt, paras. 22–23 (same).

[75] *Akayesu* Trial Judgement, *supra* note 14, paras. 481–482.

Appeals Chamber overruled this position in part, holding that there is a second difference: instigation, unlike incitement, need be neither direct nor public.[76] Subsequent chambers have followed the Appeals Chamber, and the relationship between incitement and instigation has not caused further uncertainty in the jurisprudence.[77]

The relationship between complicity in genocide and aiding and abetting genocide – that is, participation in the commission of genocide through the form of responsibility 'aiding and abetting' in Article 7/6(1) – has also been the subject of inconsistent jurisprudence. In their attempts to reconcile the two species of criminal conduct, the chambers that have addressed this issue have taken three different approaches. The first is that of the *Akayesu* Trial Chamber, which held that aiding and abetting genocide and complicity in genocide have certain physical and mental elements that are distinct from one another. With respect to the physical element, while complicity requires that the accused engage in an overt act, aiding and abetting 'may consist in failing to act or refraining from action'.[78] As concerns the mental element, the *Akayesu* Chamber held that liability for aiding and abetting genocide can only ensue where an accused himself possesses genocidal intent,[79] whereas complicity in genocide merely requires that the accused knew that his acts or omissions provided assistance to the physical perpetrator in the commission of genocide.[80]

The second approach is that of the *Stakić* and *Semanza* Trial Chambers, which declined to follow *Akayesu* and held instead that complicity in genocide and aiding and abetting genocide are identical to one another. In the words of the *Semanza* Trial Chamber,

> there is no material distinction between complicity in Article 2(3)(e) of the Statute and the broad definition accorded to aiding and abetting in Article 6(1). The Chamber further notes that the *mens rea* requirement for complicity to commit genocide in Article 2(3)(e) mirrors that for aiding and abetting and the other forms of accomplice liability in Article 6(1).[81]

---

[76] *Prosecutor* v. *Akayesu*, Case No. ICTR-96-4-A, Judgement, 1 June 2001 ('*Akayesu* Appeal Judgement'), paras. 482–483. See Chapter 5, text accompanying note 110 (noting that this distinction may not withstand scrutiny, and questioning whether indirect instigation can even exist, given that there is a stronger causality link for that form than for the inchoate crime of incitement).

[77] See *Kajelijeli* Trial Judgement, *supra* note 10, para. 762; *Nahimana et al.* Trial Judgement, *supra* note 10, para. 1030; *Semanza* Trial Judgement, *supra* note 2, para. 381.

[78] *Akayesu* Trial Judgement, *supra* note 14, para. 548.   [79] *Ibid.*, para. 485.

[80] *Ibid.*, para. 538. Accord *Bagilishema* Trial Judgement, *supra* note 29, para. 71; *Musema* Trial Judgement, *supra* note 10, paras. 181, 183.

[81] *Semanza* Trial Judgement, *supra* note 2, para. 394. Accord *Stakić* Trial Judgement, *supra* note 21, para. 531 (endorsing and quoting *Semanza*). See also *Stakić* Rule 98 *bis* Trial Decision, *supra* note 21, para. 60 ('This Trial Chamber is reluctant to endorse the distinctions drawn in *Akayesu*.').

The *Semanza* Chamber held that the mental element of complicity in genocide 'mirrors that for aiding and abetting . . . in Article 6(1)':[82] '[t]he accused must have acted intentionally and with the awareness that he was contributing to the crime of genocide, including all its mental elements'.[83] The Chamber did not take a clear view on whether complicity in genocide requires that the accused also possess genocidal intent, however, finding that Semanza knew of the Interahamwe physical perpetrators' intent to destroy the Tutsi and that he shared such intent.[84] The Chamber set forth physical elements of complicity in genocide identical to those of aiding and abetting: 'all acts of assistance or encouragement that have substantially contributed to, or have had a substantial effect on, the completion of the crime of genocide'.[85] It did not address *Akayesu*'s proposition that complicity may be committed only by means of a positive act and not by an omission.[86]

The *Semanza* Trial Chamber characterised the overlap between complicity in genocide and the forms of responsibility in Article 6(1) of the ICTR Statute as a 'redundancy'.[87] The *Stakić* Trial Chamber opined that this overlap could be interpreted in two different ways that 'would lead to the same result':[88] Article 4/2(3) could either be regarded as *lex specialis* in relation to the *lex generalis* of Article 7/6(1) – seemingly favouring a conviction for complicity in genocide over aiding and abetting genocide for the same conduct – or the forms of responsibility in Article 7/6(1) could be 'read into' Article 4/2(3).[89] The *Semanza* Chamber appears to have opted for the former alternative. The Prosecutor had charged Semanza in Count 1 of the Indictment with 'ordering, instigating, committing or otherwise aiding and abetting' genocide, and in Count 3 with complicity in genocide; the Chamber determined that, if there were to be a conviction under Count 1, it could not be for aiding and abetting, as such conduct would more appropriately be addressed under the rubric of complicity in genocide in Count 3.[90] Ultimately, the Trial Chamber found that the accused's

---

[82] *Ibid.* (internal citations omitted).   [83] *Semanza* Trial Judgement, *supra* note 2, para. 388.

[84] *Ibid.*, paras. 427–428, 433.

[85] *Ibid.*, para. 395. See also *ibid.*, para. 385 ('In the Tribunal's jurisprudence, "aiding and abetting" refers to all acts of assistance that lend encouragement or support to the commission of a crime.') (footnote removed).

[86] See *Akayesu* Trial Judgement, *supra* note 14, para. 548.

[87] *Semanza* Trial Judgement, *supra* note 2, para. 391. See also Akhavan, *supra* note 11, p. 994 ('Unlike inchoate crimes enumerated under Article 2(3)(b)–(d), inclusion of complicity appears to be superfluous given the broad scope of the term "otherwise aided and abetted" as a residual category under Article 6(1).').

[88] *Stakić* Rule 98 *bis* Trial Decision, *supra* note 21, para. 48.

[89] *Stakić* Trial Judgement, *supra* note 21, para. 531. See also *Milošević* Rule 98 *bis* Trial Decision, *supra* note 66, para. 297 (stating that 'because complicity in genocide under Article 4(3)(e) of the Statute is, following the [*Stakić*] Judgement . . . the *lex specialis* in relation to liability under Article 7(1) of the Statute, the proper characterisation of the Accused's liability in this case may be complicity in genocide'.) (footnote omitted).

[90] See *Semanza* Trial Judgement, *supra* note 2, para. 397 ('Where a count seemingly charges both direct and accomplice liability under Article 6(1) and another count specifically alleges complicity for the identical criminal acts, the Chamber will narrow the scope of the broader count so as to eliminate any overlap.').

conduct amounted to complicity in genocide, and it entered a conviction under Article 2(3)(e) of the ICTR Statute.[91] For its part, the *Stakić* Chamber found that the evidence had not established that genocide had occurred at all, and thus made no findings on whether the accused was liable for complicity in genocide because such liability cannot ensue where genocide is not perpetrated by someone.[92]

The third, most recent, and most authoritative approach is that of the *Krstić* Appeals Chamber. The Trial Chamber found that Radislav Krstić had participated in a JCE to commit genocide with the intent to destroy 'a substantial part of the Bosnian Muslim group' at Srebrenica.[93] It accordingly convicted him of genocide under Articles 4(2) and 4(3)(a) of the ICTY Statute to the exclusion of complicity in genocide under Article 4(3)(e), for which he had also been charged.[94] The Appeals Chamber overturned this conviction.[95] In its view, the evidence had failed to establish that Krstić or his corps of the Bosnian Serb Army (VRS) perpetrated any crimes, but the evidence did establish that he allowed corps resources to be used in support of a genocidal plan devised by other VRS leaders with 'knowledge of the genocidal intent' of some of the perpetrators.[96] Noting that Krstić had also been charged with aiding and abetting all the crimes alleged against him in the indictment,[97] the Appeals Chamber concluded that 'Krstić's responsibility is accurately characterized as aiding and abetting genocide under Article 7(1) ... , not as complicity in genocide under Article 4(3)(e)',[98] and entered a conviction on this basis.[99]

In reaching this conclusion, the Appeals Chamber acknowledged the *Stakić* Trial Judgement's two alternative interpretations of the relationship between

---

[91] *Ibid.*, paras. 433, 436, 553, 585. This conduct included taking soldiers, Interahamwe militiamen, and weapons to the Musha church and Mwulire Hill massacre sites; separating Hutu from Tutsi refugees; and firing into the crowd. *Ibid.* paras. 425–435.

[92] *Stakić* Trial Judgement, *supra* note 21, paras. 534, 559–561.

[93] *Krstić* Trial Judgement, *supra* note 2, paras. 634–636 (quotation at para. 634).

[94] *Ibid.*, paras. 644–645, 727.

[95] *Krstić* Appeal Judgement, *supra* note 9, para. 143 ('[T]he Trial Chamber's conviction of Krstić as a participant in a joint criminal enterprise to commit genocide is set aside and a conviction for aiding and abetting genocide is entered instead.'); *ibid.*, p. 87 (disposition).

[96] *Ibid.*, para. 137.

[97] See *Prosecutor v. Krstić*, Case No. IT-98-33-I, Amended Indictment, 27 October 1999, para. 18:

Radislav Krstić is individually responsible for the crimes alleged against him in this indictment, pursuant to Article 7(1) of the Tribunal Statute. Individual criminal responsibility includes committing, planning, instigating, ordering or otherwise aiding and abetting in the planning, preparation or execution of any crimes referred to in Articles 2 to 5 of the Tribunal Statute.

[98] *Krstić* Appeal Judgement, *supra* note 9, paras. 137–138 (quotation at para. 138).

[99] *Ibid.*, paras. 143–144, p. 87. In dissenting from this portion of the judgement, Judge Shahabuddeen opined that a conviction for aiding and abetting genocide was permissible, because 'the reference in [A]rticle 4(3)(e) to "complicity in genocide" can and does include aiding and abetting' and 'the reference to aiding and abetting in [A]rticle 7(1) of the Statute merely reproduces customary international law as contained in the reference to complicity in genocide as mentioned in [A]rticle 4(3)(e) of the Statute'. *Ibid.*, Partial Dissenting Opinion of Judge Shahabuddeen, paras. 63–64. Nevertheless, Judge Shahabuddeen agreed with the Trial Chamber that Krstić's conduct and mental state made him liable for 'committing' genocide through a JCE, and disapproved of the majority's re-characterisation of the accused's liability as that of a mere aider and abettor of genocide. See *ibid.*, paras. 69–75.

complicity in genocide and aiding and abetting genocide, and expressly opted for the latter as 'the correct one in this case'.[100] The Chamber elaborated:

Article 7(1) of the Statute, which allows liability to attach to an aider and abettor, expressly applies that mode of liability to any 'crime referred to in articles 2 to 5 of the present Statute,' including the offence of genocide prohibited by Article 4. Because the Statute must be interpreted with the utmost respect to the language used by the legislator, the Appeals Chamber may not conclude that the consequent overlap between Article 7(1) and 4(3)(e) is a result of an inadvertence on the part of the legislator where another explanation, consonant with the language used by the Statute, is possible. In this case, the two provisions can be reconciled, because the terms 'complicity' and 'accomplice' may encompass conduct broader than that of aiding and abetting. Given the Statute's express statement in Article 7(1) that liability under Article 4 may attach through the mode of aiding and abetting, Radislav Krstić's responsibility is properly characterized as that of aiding and abetting genocide.[101]

Under this formulation, complicity in genocide is not the *lex specialis* and does not necessarily preclude a conviction for aiding and abetting genocide via Article 7/6(1) when both activities are charged in respect of the same conduct. This position is at odds with, and thus implicitly overrules, that of the *Semanza* Trial Chamber.[102]

The *Krstić* Appeals Chamber reaffirmed earlier appellate jurisprudence holding that liability for aiding and abetting a specific-intent crime such as genocide may ensue even where the accused does not share the specific intent of the physical perpetrator, as long as he knows that the perpetrator possesses such intent.[103] In addition, 'there is authority to suggest that complicity in genocide, where it prohibits conduct broader than aiding and abetting, requires proof that the accomplice had the specific intent to destroy a protected group'.[104] In support of this proposition, the Chamber cited just two authorities. First, it invoked the structure of ICTY Statute itself: 'Article 4(2)'s requirement that a perpetrator of genocide possess the requisite "intent to

---

[100] *Krstić* Appeal Judgement, *supra* note 9, para. 139.   [101] *Ibid.*

[102] See *Semanza* Trial Judgement, *supra* note 2, paras. 397–398.

[103] *Krstić* Appeal Judgement, *supra* note 9, para. 140 (citing *Prosecutor* v. *Vasiljević*, Case No. IT-98-32-A, Judgement, 25 February 2004 ('*Vasiljević* Appeal Judgement'), para. 142; *Prosecutor* v. *Krnojelac*, Case No. IT-97-25-A, Judgement, 17 September 2003 ('*Krnojelac* Appeal Judgement'), para. 52; *Prosecutor* v. *Tadić*, Case No. IT-94-1-A, Judgement, 15 July 1999 ('*Tadić* Appeal Judgement'), para. 229). See *infra*, text accompanying notes 283–302, for a more detailed discussion of aiding and abetting and specific-intent crimes.

[104] *Krstić* Appeal Judgement, *supra* note 9, para. 142. While this language on the part of the Appeals Chamber is rather tentative, the *Krajišnik* Trial Chamber apparently regarded it as definitively asserting that the accused must always possess genocidal intent to be convicted of any manifestation of complicity in genocide broader than aiding and abetting: 'For complicity that is "broader", the Prosecution must prove that the accomplice not only *knew* of the principal's specific intent to destroy the protected group in whole or in part, but also shared that intent himself or herself.' *Krajišnik* Trial Judgement, *supra* note 21, para. 865 (emphasis in original).

destroy" a protected group applies to all of the prohibited acts enumerated in Article 4(3), including complicity in genocide.'[105] Second, it referred to a statement made by the UK delegate at the Genocide Convention drafting conference proposing to add the word 'deliberate' before 'complicity', as 'it was important to specify that complicity must be deliberate, because there existed some systems where complicity required intent, and others where it did not'.[106] It is important to note that the Appeals Chamber did not express a clear view on whether an accused without genocidal intent can be convicted of complicity in genocide under Article 4/2(3)(e) – as opposed to aiding and abetting genocide via Article 7/6(1) – for conduct exclusively constituting aiding and abetting.[107] The subsequent *Blagojević and Jokić* Trial Chamber convicted the accused Blagojević of complicity in genocide without making an explicit finding that he possessed genocidal intent.[108]

The Appeals Chamber in *Krstić*, and again in *Ntakirutimana and Ntakirutimana*[109] and *Semanza*,[110] declined to provide guidance on what sorts of activities other than aiding and abetting genocide could come under the umbrella of complicity in genocide, apparently leaving such a determination to future chambers.[111] In following *Krstić*, the Trial Chambers in *Brđanin* and *Blagojević and Jokić* suggested that complicity in genocide may encompass not only aiding and abetting, but also participation in genocide through any of the other forms of accomplice liability in Article 7/6(1),[112] which the *Brđanin* Chamber appears to have defined as including planning, instigating, and ordering, but excluding physical perpetration and participation in a JCE.[113] The *Blagojević and Jokić* Chamber suggested that complicity in genocide could also include those activities listed under the 'complicity' provision of the Rwandan Penal Code,[114] which had been invoked by the pre-*Krstić* ICTR Trial Judgements in *Akayesu*, *Musema*, *Bagilishema* and *Semanza*:

---

[105]   *Ibid.* Article 4(2) of the ICTY Statute defines genocide as any of a number of underlying offences 'committed with the intent to destroy, in whole or in part, a national, ethnical, racial or religious group, as such'. ICTY Statute, *supra* note 3, Art. 4(2).

[106]   *Krstić* Appeal Judgement, *supra* note 9, para. 142.

[107]   See *Milošević* Rule 98 *bis* Trial Decision, *supra* note 66, para. 296:

There is ... no authoritative decision within the Tribunal as to whether there is a difference in *mens rea* for aiding and abetting genocide and complicity in genocide, either when the latter is broader than aiding and abetting, or indeed, when it is of the same scope as aiding and abetting.

[108]   *Blagojević and Jokić* Trial Judgement, *supra* note 7, para. 677 (finding that the physical perpetrators possessed genocidal intent); *ibid.* paras. 783, 786 (finding that Blagojević knew of the physical perpetrators' genocidal intent).

[109]   See *Ntakirutimana and Ntakirutimana* Appeal Judgement, *supra* note 9, paras. 371, 500–501.

[110]   See *Semanza* Appeal Judgement, *supra* note 9, para. 316.

[111]   See *Krstić* Appeal Judgement, *supra* note 9, paras. 138–142.

[112]   See *Brđanin* Trial Judgement, *supra* note 2, para. 727; *Blagojević and Jokić* Trial Judgement, *supra* note 7, paras. 777–778.

[113]   See *Brđanin* Trial Judgement, *supra* note 2, paras. 726–727.

[114]   *Blagojević and Jokić* Trial Judgement, *supra* note 7, para. 777.

- complicity by procuring means, such as weapons, instruments or any other means, used to commit genocide, with the accomplice knowing that such means would be used for such a purpose;
- complicity by knowingly aiding or abetting a perpetrator of a genocide in the planning or enabling acts thereof;
- complicity by instigation, for which a person is liable who, though not directly participating in the crime of genocide crime, gave instructions to commit genocide, through gifts, promises, threats, abuse of authority or power, machinations or culpable artifice, or who directly incited to commit genocide.[115]

Although it did not ultimately convict Brđanin for any genocide-related conduct, because it found the evidence insufficient to prove that genocide had occurred,[116] the *Brđanin* Trial Chamber suggested that a chamber convicting an accused of accomplice liability for genocide should enter that conviction under the count in the indictment charging complicity in genocide, and not the count charging genocide:

The Trial Chamber regards genocide under Article 4(3)(a) as encompassing principal offenders, including but not limited to the physical perpetrators and to those liable pursuant to the theory of JCE. By contrast, an accomplice to genocide under Article 4(3)(e) is someone who associates him or herself in the crime of genocide committed by another.[117]

The *Blagojević and Jokić* Trial Chamber found that genocide had occurred in Srebrenica, and convicted the accused Blagojević under the count charging complicity in genocide pursuant to Article 4(3)(e) for conduct fulfilling all the physical and mental elements of aiding and abetting.[118] The Trial Chamber in *Ntakirutimana and Ntakirutimana* took the opposite approach, entering its conviction of the accused Elizaphan Ntakirutimana for aiding and abetting genocide under the count charging Article 2(3)(a) of the ICTR Statute, and dismissing the alternative count of complicity in genocide under Article 2(3)(e).[119]

Academic opinion is divided with respect to the *Krstić* Appeals Chamber's interpretation of the relationship between Articles 7/6(1) and 4/2(3)(e). Chile

---

[115] *Akayesu* Trial Judgement, *supra* note 14, para. 537 (underlining removed). *Accord Semanza* Trial Judgement, *supra* note 2, para. 393; *Bagilishema* Trial Judgement, *supra* note 29, para. 69; *Musema* Trial Judgement, *supra* note 10, para. 179. The *Semanza* Trial Chamber appears to have treated all three of these activities as manifestations of aiding and abetting. See *Semanza* Trial Judgement, *supra* note 2, para. 393.

[116] See *Brđanin* Trial Judgement, *supra* note 2, paras. 989–991, 1152.

[117] *Ibid.*, para. 727. This phrasing is unfortunate, as it is clear that an accused found liable under any of the forms of responsibility in Article 7/6(1) has also associated himself with the crime.

[118] See *Blagojević and Jokić* Trial Judgement, *supra* note 7, paras. 677, 785–787, p. 304. The *Blagojević and Jokić* Trial Chamber declined to consider what conduct other than aiding and abetting might fall under the umbrella of complicity in genocide, ostensibly because the accused had not been properly put on notice of the potential scope and nature of such conduct. See *ibid.*, para. 780.

[119] *Ntakirutimana and Ntakirutimana* Trial Judgement, *supra* note 60, paras. 831, 837.

Eboe-Osuji approves of the Chamber's adherence to the rule of effective construction,[120] which 'is indeed a well established rule of interpretation in international law'.[121] According to Eboe-Osuji, 'there is a duty on the Tribunals' Judges
to make every interpretative effort at giving those two notions meanings and
effect as if they imported different messages at their respective places in the
Statutes';[122] as such, the judges must 'exhaust ... all reasonable alternative
constructions' before declaring provisions of the Statute overlapping or redundant.[123] On the other hand, William Schabas and Payam Akhavan take the
view that there is an overlap between Article 7/6(1) and 4/2(3)(e), and that it
is, in fact, 'a result of an inadvertence on the part of the legislator'.[124] Schabas
describes the overlap as an 'innocent consequence of the *verbatim* incorporation' of Article III into the Statutes,[125] and one of the effects of the '"cut and
paste" approach to legislative drafting' taken by those who drew up the
ICTY and ICTR Statutes.[126] Akhavan criticises the *Krstić* Appeals
Chamber for bending over backward to distinguish the two provisions in
professed accordance with the rule of effective construction: 'While [the
Krstić Chamber's holding that complicity in genocide prohibits conduct
broader than aiding and abetting] may be a more elegant solution, it still
avoids the conclusion that "complicity in genocide" is redundant in view of
the broadly defined general principles of individual criminal liability under
both the ICTR and ICTY Statutes.'[127]

It is indeed difficult to imagine a scenario in which the criminality of a person
associated in some way with the commission of genocide could not be captured

---

[120] Eboe-Osuji, *supra* note 19, p. 71.
[121] *Ibid.*, p. 60 (citing, *inter alia*, *Chorzów Factory* (Ger. v. Pol.), 1927 PCIJ Ser. A, No. 8, p. 2; *Corfu Channel*
(Merits) (UK v. Alb.), 1949 ICJ Rep. 4). Eboe-Osuji invokes the Latin maxim *ut res magis valeat quam
pereat*, or 'that the matter may have effect rather than fail', as embodying the rule of effective construction. Eboe-Osuji, *supra* note 19, para. 59.
[122] *Ibid.*, p. 59.
[123] *Ibid.*, p. 60 ('The judicial duty is to give all meaning and effect, which is not absurd, to the words of the
Statute which immediately governs the judicial work – in this case, the ICTR or ICTY Statute.'). Eboe-
Osuji purports to avoid all overlap or redundancy by characterising 'complicity in genocide' as a crime of
lesser gravity than genocide, *ibid.*, p. 74, and aiding and abetting as a mere form of responsibility that
'cannot stand on its own' and 'has no basis without Articles 2–4 of the [ICTR] Statute.' *Ibid.*, p. 68. Like
genocide, conspiracy to commit genocide, or direct and public incitement to commit genocide, complicity
in genocide may be realised through any of the forms of responsibility in Article 7/6(1), including aiding
and abetting. *Ibid.*, p. 74. For Eboe-Osuji, a person found responsible for aiding and abetting genocide is
guilty of genocide, and his sentence should reflect the greater opprobriousness of such conduct. *Ibid.*, p. 72.
[124] *Krstić* Appeal Judgement, *supra* note 9, p. 139.   [125] Schabas, *supra* note 11, p. 183.
[126] *Ibid.*, p. 291. Accord Akhavan, *supra* note 11, p. 994 (referring to this discussion in *Krstić* as the Appeals
Chamber's attempt to rationalise this 'normative redundancy' created by the 'strict fidelity' of the *ad hoc*
Statutes' drafters to the construction of Articles II and III of the Genocide Convention). Schabas points to a
second statutory anomaly that results from the 'cut and paste' approach to drafting: the overlap between the
form of responsibility 'ordering' in Article 6(1) of the ICTY Statute and the language of the *chapeau* of
Article 2, which speaks of persons 'committing or *ordering to be committed*' grave breaches of the Geneva
Conventions. Schabas, *supra* note 11, p. 291 (quoting ICTY Statute, *supra* note 3, Art. 2) (emphasis added).
[127] Akhavan, *supra* note 11, p. 995.

through aiding and abetting or one of the other forms of responsibility in Articles 7/6(1) and 7/6(3). As will become evident in the next section of this chapter, the scope of aiding and abetting is exceedingly broad, and the chambers of the *ad hoc* Tribunals have convicted accused pursuant to this form of responsibility for a wide variety of participatory conduct in the perpetration of crimes by others.[128] When the possibility of convicting an accused for planning, instigating, or ordering genocide, participating in a JCE whose object or natural and foreseeable consequence is genocide, or failing to prevent or punish genocide as a superior are also taken into account, the practical need for additional potential bases for liability through complicity in genocide becomes negligible. The Prosecutors of both *ad hoc* Tribunals seem to have become aware of this reality, and in at least two post-*Krstić* cases have voluntarily withdrawn counts in indictments previously charging complicity in genocide under Article 4/2(3)(e).[129]

Considering the interpretive acrobatics that necessarily accompany any attempt to reconcile complicity in genocide with the other provisions of the *ad hoc* Statues governing individual criminal responsibility, chambers may find it preferable simply to avoid complicity in genocide altogether, and limit their analysis to determining whether the accused incurs liability for genocide under Article 4/2(3)(a) through one of the several forms of responsibility in Articles 7/6(1) and 7/6(3).[130] The permissibility of such an approach is evidenced by the *ad hoc* Appeals Chambers' own practice on at least two occasions.[131] First, in

---

[128] See *infra* Section 4.3.1.

[129] These cases are *Popović* in the ICTY and *Mpambara* in the ICTR. The prosecution in *Popović* requested leave to withdraw the charge of complicity in genocide against certain of the co-accused that had existed in their pre-joinder indictments 'in light of the *Krstić* Appeals Judgement ... in order to avoid redundancy in or ambiguity created by the provision on complicity in Article 4(3)(e) and the mode of liability of aiding and abetting in Article 7(1)'. *Popović et al.* May 2006 Pre-Trial Decision, *supra* note 37, para. 29. See also *ibid.*, para. 31 (Trial Chamber allowing such withdrawal). As a consequence, the currently operative indictment in *Popović* does not charge complicity in genocide. See *Prosecutor v. Popović, Beara, Nikolić, Borovčanin, Miletić, Gvero and Pandurević*, Case No. IT-05-88-T, Indictment, 4 August 2006, para. 33 (Count 1 alleging genocide under Article 4(3)(a) through the forms of responsibility in Articles 7(1) and 7(3)); *ibid.*, para. 44 (Count 2 alleging conspiracy to commit genocide under Article 4(3)(b) through the forms of responsibility in Articles 7(1) and 7(3)). As noted in note 61 above, the prosecution in *Mpambara* likewise withdrew the charge of complicity in genocide. 'Given the divergent views on the distinction between [c]omplicity under Art. 2(3)(e) and aiding and abetting [g]enocide under Art (6)(1),' the prosecution concluded that aiding and abetting was a more appropriate description of the conduct of the accused under the circumstances. *Mpambara* Trial Judgement, *supra* note 61, para. 6 n. 3 (quoting prosecution's final brief).

[130] In such cases, if the Trial Chamber ultimately decides on the basis of the evidence that an accused bears accomplice liability for genocide, the conviction will have to be entered under the count charging genocide pursuant to Article 4/2(3)(a), and not complicity in genocide pursuant to Article 4/2(3)(e), as was done in the *Blagojević and Jokić* Trial Judgement and suggested as the appropriate approach by the Trial Chamber in *Brđanin*. See *Blagojević and Jokić* Trial Judgement, *supra* note 7, paras. 677, 785–787, p. 304; *Brđanin* Trial Judgement, *supra* note 2, para. 727.

[131] See Chapter 2, note 94 and accompanying text (decisions of each Appeals Chamber treated as authoritative for each other, and the Trial Chambers of the other Tribunal, thereby treated in general as one body of jurisprudence, albeit with individual judgments having technically different statuses as binding or persuasive).

replacing the accused's conviction for participating in a JCE to commit genocide with a conviction for aiding and abetting genocide, the *Krstić* Appeals Chamber entered the new conviction under Count 1, which charged genocide, not Count 2, which charged complicity in genocide.[132] Second, the post-*Krstić* Appeals Chamber in the *Ntakirutimana and Ntakirutimana* Judgement upheld as proper the Trial Chamber's conviction of the accused Elizaphan Ntakirutimana for aiding and abetting genocide, pursuant to Articles 2(3)(a) and 6(1) of the ICTR Statute, and its consequent dismissal of the alternative count of complicity in genocide under Article 2(3)(e).[133]

A final issue that deserves brief mention is the scarcely discussed relationship between the forms of responsibility in Articles 7/6(1) and 7/6(3) on the one hand, and the genocide-related inchoate crimes in Article 4/2(3)(b) to (d) on the other. Early in the development of the jurisprudence, the *Musema* Trial Chamber stated:

> [T]he Chamber notes from the *Travaux Préparatoires* of the Genocide Convention that the crime of complicity in genocide was recognised only where genocide had actually been committed. The Genocide Convention did not provide the possibility for punishment of complicity in an attempt to commit genocide, complicity in incitement to commit genocide nor complicity in conspiracy to commit genocide, all of which were, in the view of some States, too vague to be punishable under the Convention.[134]

This remark could be taken as implicitly excluding a conviction for conspiracy to commit genocide, direct and public incitement to commit genocide, or attempt to commit genocide through any of the forms of accomplice liability in Article 7/6(1). No subsequent chamber appears to have made such a holding, however. Furthermore, at least two ICTR Trial Chambers appear to have found accused liable for inchoate crimes through forms of responsibility other than 'commission',[135] and the clear intimation of the *Krstić* Appeal Judgement and its progeny is that the forms of responsibility in Article 7/6(1) may be 'read

---

[132] *Krstić* Appeal Judgement, *supra* note 9, para. 139, p. 87.

[133] *Ntakirutimana and Ntakirutimana* Appeal Judgement, *supra* note 9, paras. 371–372. See also *Ntakirutimana and Ntakirutimana* Trial Judgement, *supra* note 60, para. 831 (finding Elizaphan Ntakirutimana guilty of aiding and abetting genocide pursuant to Article 6(1)); *ibid.*, para. 837 (dismissing the alternative count of complicity in genocide against Elizaphan Ntakirutimana).

[134] *Musema* Trial Judgement, *supra* note 10, para. 172. The Trial Chamber did not cite the precise segment of the *travaux* of the Genocide Convention indicating this proposition.

[135] See *Nahimana et al.* Trial Judgement, *supra* note 10, paras. 973, 1034–1035, 1093 (finding the accused Barayagwiza 'guilty of direct and public incitement to genocide under Article 2(3)(c), pursuant to Article 6(3) of [the ICTR] Statute') (quotation at para. 1034); *Prosecutor v. Niyitegeka*, Case No. ICTR-96-14-T, Judgement, 16 May 2003, paras. 427–429 (finding Niyitegeka guilty, 'pursuant to Article 6(1)' of the ICTR Statute, of 'planning, leading and participating in attacks against' Tutsi refugees at Bisesero, and entering a conviction for conspiracy to commit genocide under Article 2(3)(b)) (quotations at para. 429). The *Orić* Trial Chamber of the ICTY, moreover, seems to have implied that one may instigate attempt to commit genocide. See *Prosecutor v. Orić*, Case No. IT-03-68-T, Judgement, 30 June 2006 ('*Orić* Trial Judgement'), para. 269 n. 732 ('Instigation distinguishes itself from "incitement"[.] . . . The former must lead to the "actual" completion (or at least attempt, if this is punishable as in the case of genocide according to Article 4(3)(d) of the Statute) of the principal crime[.]').

into' any of the provisions of Article 4/2(3), including those containing the three inchoate crimes.[136]

Again, however, the added utility of reading the Article 7/6(1) forms of responsibility other than 'commission' into the provisions of Article 4/2(3) governing inchoate crimes would appear to be marginal at best. While there is theoretically no bar to the imposition of accomplice liability for an inchoate crime, there are certain combinations of forms of accomplice liability and inchoate crimes that would lead to absurd results, such as planning a conspiracy or instigating incitement.[137] Furthermore, it may well be that any such combination comes impermissibly close to violating the principle of culpability, because the relationship between the accused and the crime that such a combination describes would be more tenuous and remote than is appropriate for any system of criminal law.[138]

4.3 Elements of aiding and abetting

Since the early *Tadić* and *Furundžija* Trial Judgements, the elements of aiding and abetting have been applied fairly consistently in the jurisprudence of the *ad hoc* Tribunals.[139] Most subsequent case law has differed only by clarifying the

---

[136] See *supra* text accompanying notes 71–73, 100–102.

[137] See Eboe-Osuji, *supra* note 19, p. 74 (remarking that certain combinations of an inchoate crime with a form of responsibility 'may seem a little awkward'). Note that if JCE is considered a form of accomplice liability, see Chapter 1, note 9, the jurisprudence *does* prohibit liability for an inchoate crime on this basis. See, e.g., Chapter 2, text accompanying note 454 *et seq.*

[138] See Nicola Pasani, 'The Mental Element in International Crime', in Flavia Lattanzi and William A. Schabas (eds.), 1 *Essays on the Rome Statute of the International Criminal Court* (1999), pp. 121–125 (discussing the principle of culpability, or *nullum crimen sine culpa*, in national and international law). See also *ibid.*, p. 124:

> The principle of culpability marks an evolution from a 'strict liability' concept of personal responsibility, under which a person is always responsible for the results brought about by his actions ... to a more subject-oriented concept of responsibility ... under which criminal responsibility is imposed for the consequences of a person's conduct only when he or she knew that conduct to be blameworthy or where the lack of knowledge is in itself blameworthy.

[139] See *Prosecutor v. Tadić*, Case No. IT-94-1-T, Opinion and Judgement, 7 May 1997 ('*Tadić* Trial Judgement'), para. 673; *Prosecutor v. Furundžija*, Case No. IT-95-17/1-T, Judgement, 10 December 1998 ('*Furundžija* Trial Judgement'), paras. 190–249. To establish a basis for aiding and abetting as a form of responsibility, as well as to establish its elements in international criminal law, the *Tadić* Trial Chamber examined a range of post-Second World War cases, including *Trial of Werner Rohde and Eight Others*, 5 *Law Reports of Trials of War Criminals* (1948), p. 54; *United States v. von List et al.*, 10 *Trials of War Criminals before the Nuernberg Military Tribunals under Control Council Law No. 10* (1953) ('*Hostages* case'); *United States v. Altstoetter, von Ammon, Barnickel, Cuhorst, Engert, Joel, Klemm, Lautz, Mettgenbert, Nebelung, Oeschey, Petersen, Rothaug, Rothenberger, Schlegelberger and Westphal*, 3 *Trials of War Criminals before the Nuernberg Military Tribunals under Control Council Law No. 10* (1953) ('*Justice* case'); *Trial of Hans Alfuldisch and Six Others*, 11 *Law Reports of Trials of War Criminals* (1949), p. 15 ('*Mauthausen Concentration Camp* case'); *Trial of Franz Schonfeld and Nine Others*, 11 *Law Reports of Trials of War Criminals* (1949), p. 64; *Trial of Karl Adam Golkel and 13 Others*, 5 *Law Reports of Trials of War Criminals* (1948), p. 54; *Trial of Max Wielen and 17 Others*, 11 *Law Reports of Trials of War Criminals* (1949), p. 31; *Trial of Bruno Tesch and Two Others*, 1 *Law Reports of Trials of War Criminals* (1947), p. 93 ('*Zyklon B* case'); *Trial of Otto Sandrock and Three Others*, 1 *Law Reports of Trials of War Criminals* (1947), p. 35 ('*Almelo* case'); *Trial of Martin Gottfried Weiss and Thirty-Nine Others*, 16 *Law Reports of Trials of War Criminals* (1949) p. 5 ('*Dachau Concentration Camp* case'). The *Furundžija* Trial Chamber

wording first used in those two judgements. The formulation of the elements set forth in *Furundžija* are the most often quoted and applied for this form of responsibility.

4.3.1 Physical elements

There are two physical elements that must be established for a finding of guilt for aiding and abetting a crime within the jurisdiction of the *ad hoc* Tribunals. First, the accused must lend practical assistance, encouragement, or moral support to the physical perpetrator or perpetrators in committing a crime.[140] There is some authority to suggest that, alternatively, this element may be satisfied by proof that the accused deliberately omitted to take action. Examples given in the jurisprudence of such culpable omissions are where the accused is present and inactive at the scene of the crime, or where he fails to discharge a duty to intervene, and such omission lent practical assistance, encouragement, or moral support to the physical perpetrator in committing the crime.[141] For reasons discussed in detail below, however, the authors do not consider aiding and abetting by omission to be an established form of responsibility in international criminal law.[142] The second physical element that must be established is that such practical assistance, encouragement, or moral support must have a substantial effect on the commission of a crime by the physical perpetrator or perpetrators.[143]

By the very terms of the *ad hoc* Statutes,[144] and as affirmed in the jurisprudence,[145] the accused may aid and abet at one or more of three possible stages of the crime – planning, preparation, or execution – and the accused's

---

examined a similar range of post-Second World War cases in a more coherent and structured manner, which is most likely why (at least in part) the elements set out in that judgment have been more consistently followed since. In addition to the authorities cited in *Tadić*, *Furundžija* also cited *Strafsenat. Urteil vom 10. August 1948 gegen K. und A.* StS 18/48, I *Entscheidungen*, pp. 53, 56 ('*Synagogue* case'); *Strafsenat. Urteil vom 10. August 1948 gegen L. u. a.* StS 37/48, I *Entscheidungen*, pp. 229, 234 ('*Pig-Cart Parade* case'); *Massenvernichtungsverbrechen und NS-Gewaltverbrechen in Lagern; Kriegsverbrechen. KZ Auschwitz, 1941–1945*, reported in 21 *Justiz und NS-Verbrechen* (1979), pp. 361–887 ('*Auschwitz Concentration Camp* case'); *United States* v. *Otto Ohlendorf et al.*, 4 *Trials of War Criminals Before the Nuremberg Military Tribunals Under Control Council Law No. 10* (1950), p. 411 ('*Einsatzgruppen* case'); and LG Hechingen, 28.6.1947, K ls 23/47 and OLG Tübingen, 20.1.1948, Ss 54/47 (decision on appeal), reported in I *Justiz und NS-Verbrechen*, case 022, p. 469 ('*Hechingen Deportation* case').

[140] *Prosecutor* v. *Simić*, Case No. IT-95-9-A, Judgement, 28 November 2006 ('*Simić* Appeal Judgement'), para. 85; *Blaškić* Appeal Judgement, *supra* note 16, para. 45; *Vasiljević* Appeal Judgement, *supra* note 103, para. 102. See also *infra* text accompanying notes 148–163.

[141] See, e.g., *Mpambara* Trial Judgement, *supra* note 61, para. 22. See also *infra* text accompanying notes 192–193.

[142] See *infra* text accompanying notes 194–216.

[143] *Simić* Appeal Judgement, *supra* note 140, para. 85; *Blaškić* Appeal Judgement, *supra* note 16, para. 46; *Vasiljević* Appeal Judgement, *supra* note 103, para. 102; *Prosecutor* v. *Blaškić*, Case No. IT-95-14-T, Judgement, 3 March 2000 ('*Blaškić* Trial Judgement'), para. 284. See also *infra* text accompanying notes 231–246.

[144] See ICTY Statute, *supra* note 3, Article 7(1); ICTR Statute, *supra* note 3, Article 6(1).

[145] See *Orić* Trial Judgement, *supra* note 135, para. 282; *Prosecutor* v. *Kordić and Čerkez*, Case No. IT-95-14/2-T, Judgement, 26 February 2001 ('*Kordić and Čerkez* Trial Judgement'), para. 371.

contribution can be given before, during, or after the criminal act of the physical perpetrator.[146] The accused need not necessarily be physically present when the physical perpetrator commits the crime.[147]

4.3.1.1 *Practical assistance, encouragement, or moral support: first physical element*

4.3.1.1.1 *The accused lent practical assistance, encouragement, or moral support to the physical perpetrator in committing a crime*

The chambers of the ICTY and the ICTR have had many opportunities to discuss aiding and abetting. The *Tadić* Trial Chamber in 1997, drawing on principles of national criminal law and customary international law, defined the physical element of aiding and abetting very broadly as 'all acts of assistance by words or acts that lend encouragement or support [to the physical perpetrator], as long as the requisite intent is present'.[148] The December 1998 *Furundžija* Trial Judgement reformulated this characterisation as encompassing three possible activities – 'practical assistance, encouragement, or moral support'[149] – and this has been the terminology adopted by most subsequent judgements.[150] Such practical assistance, encouragement, or moral support must have a 'substantial effect on the perpetration of the crime'[151]

---

[146] *Simić* Appeal Judgement, *supra* note 140, para. 85; *Orić* Trial Judgement, *supra* note 135, para. 282; *Prosecutor* v. *Limaj, Bala and Musliu*, Case No. IT-03-66-T, Judgement, 30 November 2005 ('*Limaj et al.* Trial Judgement'), para. 517. See also *infra* text accompanying notes 217–225.

[147] *Simić* Appeal Judgement, *supra* note 140, para. 85; *Muvunyi* Trial Judgement, *supra* note 22, para. 471. See also *infra* text accompanying notes 226–230.

[148] *Tadić* Trial Judgement, *supra* note 139, para. 689. Accord *Prosecutor* v. *Delalić, Mucić, Delić and Landžo*, Case No. IT-96-21-A, Judgement, 20 February 2001 ('*Čelebići* Appeal Judgement'), para. 352; *Kajelijeli* Trial Judgement, *supra* note 10, para. 766; *Semanza* Trial Judgement, *supra* note 2, para. 385; *Prosecutor* v. *Delalić, Mucić, Delić and Landžo*, Case No. IT-96-21-T, Judgement, 16 November 1998, para. 327.

[149] *Furundžija* Trial Judgement, *supra* note 139, paras. 235, 249.

[150] See *Simić* Appeal Judgement, *supra* note 140, para. 85; *Blaškić* Appeal Judgement, *supra* note 16, para. 45; *Vasiljević* Appeal Judgement, *supra* note 103, para. 102; *Tadić* Appeal Judgement, *supra* note 103, para. 229; *Orić* Trial Judgement, *supra* note 135, para. 281 (any contributions making the planning, preparation or execution of the crime possible or at least easier); *Limaj et al.* Trial Judgment, *supra* note 146, para. 517; *Strugar* Trial Judgement, *supra* note 16, para. 349; *Blagojević and Jokić* Trial Judgement, *supra* note 7, para. 726; *Brđanin* Trial Judgement, *supra* note 2, para. 271; *Kamuhanda* Trial Judgement, *supra* note 17, para. 597; *Kajelijeli* Trial Judgement, *supra* note 10, para. 766; *Prosecutor* v. *Simić, Tadić and Zarić*, Case No. IT-95-9-T, Judgement, 17 October 2003 ('*Simić et al.* Trial Judgement'), para. 162; *Prosecutor* v. *Naletilić and Martinović*, Case No. IT-98-34-T, Judgement, 31 March 2003 ('*Naletilić and Martinović* Trial Judgement'), para. 63; *Prosecutor* v. *Vasiljević*, Case No. IT-98-32-T, Judgement, 29 November 2002 ('*Vasiljević* Trial Judgement'), para. 70; *Kordić and Čerkez* Trial Judgment, *supra* note 145, para. 399; *Prosecutor* v. *Kunarac, Kovač and Vuković*, Case No. IT-96-23-T and IT-96-23/1-T, Judgement, 22 February 2001 ('*Kunarac et al.* Trial Judgement'), para. 391; *Blaškić* Trial Judgement, *supra* note 143, para. 283; *Musema* Trial Judgement, *supra* note 10, para. 126 ('physical or moral support'); *Rutaganda* Trial Judgement, *supra* note 10, para. 43 ('physical or moral support').

[151] *Furundžija* Trial Judgement, *supra* note 139, paras. 235, 249. Accord *Simić* Appeal Judgement, *supra* note 140, para. 85; *Gacumbitsi* Appeal Judgement, *supra* note 16, para. 140; *Blaškić* Appeal Judgement, *supra* note 16, para. 46; *Vasiljević* Appeal Judgement, *supra* note 103, para. 102; *Čelebići* Appeal Judgement, *supra* note 148, para. 352; *Tadić* Appeal Judgement, *supra* note 103, para. 229; *Strugar*

(discussed in detail below[152]) but need not be causal to the act of the physical perpetrator.[153]

No evidence of a plan or agreement between the aider and abettor and the physical perpetrator is required,[154] and proof of aiding and abetting can be given by direct or circumstantial evidence.[155] Thus, although the Trial Chamber lacked direct evidence that Duško Tadić was present when Šefik Sivac, a detainee at the Omarska concentration camp, was beaten, it nonetheless found the accused guilty of aiding and abetting the beating (which constituted cruel treatment as a violation of the laws or customs of war and inhumane acts as a crime against humanity) based on testimony that Tadić had thrown the beaten Sivac into his cell with the admonition: '[Y]ou cannot touch a Serb or say anything to a Serb.'[156]

The phrase 'aiding and abetting' actually refers to two discrete activities. 'Aiding', in the words of the *Akayesu* Trial Chamber, 'means giving assistance to someone. Abetting, on the other hand, would involve facilitating the commission of an act by being sympathetic thereto'.[157] Applying *Akayesu*'s definitions to the three activities enumerated in *Furundžija*, aiding seems to correspond to 'practical assistance', and abetting to the less tangible notions of

---

Trial Judgement, *supra* note 16, para. 349; *Blagojević and Jokić* Trial Judgement, *supra* note 7, para. 726; *Ndindabahizi* Trial Judgement, *supra* note 14, para. 457; *Brđanin* Trial Judgement, *supra* note 2, para. 271; *Kajelijeli* Trial Judgement, *supra* note 10, para. 766; *Vasiljević* Trial Judgement, *supra* note 150, para. 70; *Kordić and Čerkez* Trial Judgement, *supra* note 145, para. 399; *Kunarac et al.* Trial Judgement, *supra* note 150, para. 391; *Blaškić* Trial Judgement, *supra* note 143, para. 283; *Prosecutor v. Aleksovski*, Case No. IT-95-14/1-T, Judgement, 25 June 1999 ('*Aleksovski* Trial Judgement'), para. 61; *Tadić* Trial Judgement, *supra* note 139, para. 692.

[152] See *infra* text accompanying notes 231–246.

[153] *Simić* Appeal Judgement, *supra* note 140, para. 85; *Blaškić* Appeal Judgement, *supra* note 16, para. 48; *Orić* Trial Judgement, *supra* note 135, para. 284; *Limaj et al.* Trial Judgment, *supra* note 146, para. 517; *Strugar* Trial Judgement, *supra* note 16, para. 349; *Blagojević and Jokić* Trial Judgement, *supra* note 7, para. 726; *Brđanin* Trial Judgement, *supra* note 2, para. 271; *Kajelijeli* Trial Judgement, *supra* note 10, para. 766; *Simić et al.* Trial Judgement, *supra* note 150, para. 162; *Naletilić and Martinović* Trial Judgement, *supra* note 150, para. 63; *Vasiljević* Trial Judgement, *supra* note 150, para. 70; *Prosecutor v. Krnojelac*, Case No. IT-97-25-T, Judgement, 15 March 2002 ('*Krnojelac* Trial Judgement'), para. 88; *Prosecutor v. Kvočka, Kos, Radić, Žigić and Prcać*, Case No. IT-98-30/1-T, Judgement, 2 November 2001 ('*Kvočka et al.* Trial Judgement'), para. 255; *Kunarac et al.* Trial Judgement, *supra* note 150, para. 391; *Blaškić* Trial Judgement, *supra* note 143, para. 285; *Aleksovski* Trial Judgement, *supra* note 151, para. 61.

[154] *Krnojelac* Appeal Judgement, *supra* note 103, para. 33; *Tadić* Appeal Judgement, *supra* note 103, para. 229; *Simić et al.* Trial Judgement, *supra* note 150, para. 162; *Kvočka et al.* Trial Judgement, *supra* note 153, para. 472. But see *Blagojević and Jokić* Trial Judgement, *supra* note 7, para. 731 ('It is required for *ex post facto* aiding and abetting that at the time of the planning, preparation or execution of the crime, a prior agreement exists between the principal and the person who subsequently aids and abets in the commission of the crime.').

[155] *Prosecutor v. Galić*, Case No. IT-98-29-A, Judgement, 30 November 2006 ('*Galić* Appeal Judgement'), para. 178 (holding that the elements of any form of responsibility may be proven by direct or circumstantial evidence); *Strugar* Trial Judgement, *supra* note 16, para. 331; *Prosecutor v. Galić*, Case No. IT-98-29-T, Judgement and Opinion, 5 December 2003 ('*Galić* Trial Judgement'), para. 171.

[156] *Tadić* Trial Judgement, *supra* note 139, paras. 735, 738.

[157] *Akayesu* Trial Judgement, *supra* note 14, para. 484. Accord *Muvunyi* Trial Judgement, *supra* note 22, para. 471; *Limaj et al.* Trial Judgment, *supra* note 146, para. 516; *Kajelijeli* Trial Judgement, *supra* note 10, para. 765; *Semanza* Trial Judgement, *supra* note 2, para. 384; *Kvočka et al.* Trial Judgement, *supra* note 153, para. 254; *Blaškić* Trial Judgement, *supra* note 143, p. 92 n. 510; Rome Statute of the International Criminal Court, entered into force 1 July 2002, UN Doc. A/CONF. 183/9 (1998) ('Rome Statute'), Art. 25(3)(c), ('aids, abets or otherwise assists in its commission or its attempted commission').

'encouragement' and 'moral support'.[158] While either aiding or abetting alone would suffice to render the accomplice criminally liable,[159] however, the distinction between the two forms of assistance does not seem to have made much of a difference in practice, as the prosecution in both the ICTY and the ICTR has habitually charged them in tandem. Moreover, despite acknowledgement that culpability might flow from one or the other,[160] the chambers have almost invariably dealt with them as a single legal concept.[161] For example, while Jean-Paul Akayesu appears only to have abetted rape through his presence at the Taba *bureau communal* and his words of encouragement to the victims' Interahamwe rapists, the Trial Chamber found him guilty of crimes against humanity for having 'aided and abetted' the rapes.[162] Nevertheless, on a few occasions it appears that chambers have convicted the accused only of abetting in respect of a given count in the indictment.[163]

4.3.1.1.2 The accused may aid and abet by mere presence at the scene of the crime

Several judgements have discussed the possibility of aiding and abetting liability for a person present at the scene who stands idly by while his associates commit a crime. The weight of the jurisprudence supports the proposition that an accused's mere presence at the scene is not conclusive evidence of aiding and abetting unless such presence demonstrates, in the words of the *Furundžija* Trial Chamber, a 'significant legitimising or encouraging effect on the principals',[164] and the accused has the requisite mental state.[165] The *Furundžija* Trial Chamber endorsed this formulation, drawn from post-Second World War German cases and supported by the provisions of the 1996 International Law Commission Draft Code.[166] It disapproved of the formulation set forth by *Tadić* – 'direct and

---

[158] See *Furundžija* Trial Judgement, *supra* note 139, para. 235; *Simić et al.* Trial Judgement, *supra* note 150, para. 162 (holding that '[t]he acts of aiding and abetting need not be tangible, but may consist of moral support or encouragement'); *Aleksovski* Trial Judgement, *supra* note 151, para. 63.

[159] *Muvunyi* Trial Judgement, *supra* note 22, para. 471; *Ntakirutimana and Ntakirutimana* Trial Judgement, *supra* note 60, para. 787 n. 1150; *Musema* Trial Judgement, *supra* note 10, para. 125; *Akayesu* Trial Judgement, *supra* note 14, para. 484.

[160] See *Muvunyi* Trial Judgement, *supra* note 22, para. 470.

[161] See *Ndindabahizi* Trial Judgement, *supra* note 14, para. 457; *Kajelijeli* Trial Judgement, *supra* note 10, para. 765; *Semanza* Trial Judgement, *supra* note 2, para. 384.

[162] *Akayesu* Trial Judgement, *supra* note 14, para. 693.

[163] See, e.g., *Muhimana* Trial Judgement, *supra* note 60, para. 553; *Musema* Trial Judgement, *supra* note 10, para. 908; *Akayesu* Trial Judgement, *supra* note 14, para. 707.

[164] *Furundžija* Trial Judgement, *supra* note 139, para. 232. This standard was endorsed by the Trial Chamber in *Kunarac*. See *Kunarac et al.* Trial Judgement, *supra* note 150, para. 393 ('significant legitimising or encouraging effect').

[165] *Aleksovski* Trial Judgement, *supra* note 151, para. 64.

[166] *Furundžija* Trial Judgement, *supra* note 139, para. 232 (citing Draft Code of Crimes Against the Peace and Security of Mankind (1996), in Report of the International Law Commission on the Work of Its Forty-eighth Session, UN Doc. A/51/10 (1996) ('1996 Draft Code')).

substantial effect'[167] – as misleading; in the *Furundžija* Chamber's view, the word 'direct' erroneously implied that, for a finding of aiding and abetting, the assistance must be tangible or be the cause of the crime committed.[168]

It is unclear whether the *Furundžija* Trial Chamber, whose language was endorsed in *Kunarac*,[169] *Vasiljević*,[170] *Kvočka*,[171] *Krnojelac*,[172] *Simić*,[173] *Ndindabahizi*[174] and *Strugar*,[175] intended for the standard of 'significant legitimising or encouraging effect' to be higher than the 'substantial effect' standard most chambers apply to all ways in which aiding and abetting can occur.[176] It may be that through these words *Furundžija* was simply emphasising that the aider and abettor must be something more than just another spectator.[177] The subsequent *Aleksovski* Trial Judgement states only that the accused's presence must have had a 'significant effect on the commission of the crime by promoting it'.[178] For its part, the *Orić* Trial Judgement formulates the requirement as being 'substantial and efficient enough to make the performance of the crime possible or easier',[179] while many other judgements make no mention whatsoever of a separate 'effect' requirement for presence at the scene.[180]

Presence at the scene is the quintessential example of 'intangible' aiding and abetting – that is, abetting through encouragement or moral support, or both.[181] In *Furundžija*, the Trial Chamber convicted the accused of rape as a violation of the laws or customs of war for continuing his interrogation while the person being interrogated was subjected to sexual violence. In the words of the Chamber, 'the presence of the accused [Furundžija] and the continued interrogation aided and abetted the crimes committed by the Accused B'.[182] The

---

[167] *Tadić* Trial Judgement, *supra* note 139, para. 689.
[168] *Furundžija* Trial Judgement, *supra* note 139, para. 232.
[169] *Kunarac et al.* Trial Judgement, *supra* note 150, para. 393.
[170] *Vasiljević* Trial Judgement, *supra* note 150, para. 70 ('significant encouraging effect').
[171] *Kvočka et al.* Trial Judgement, *supra* note 153, para. 257.
[172] *Krnojelac* Trial Judgement, *supra* note 153, para. 88.
[173] *Simić et al.* Trial Judgement, *supra* note 150, para. 165.
[174] *Ndindabahizi* Trial Judgement, *supra* note 14, para. 457 ('encouraging effect').
[175] *Strugar* Trial Judgement, *supra* note 16, para. 349. See also *Prosecutor* v. *Kayishema and Ruzindana*, Case No. ICTR-95-1-A, Judgement (Reasons), 1 June 2001 ('*Kayishema and Ruzindana* Appeal Judgement'), para. 201 n. 311 (quoting the *Furundžija* standard).
[176] See *infra* text accompanying notes 231–246.
[177] See *Furundžija* Trial Judgement, *supra* note 139, para. 232.
[178] *Aleksovski* Trial Judgement, *supra* note 151, para. 64.
[179] *Orić* Trial Judgement, *supra* note 135, para. 288.
[180] See, e.g., *Blagojević and Jokić* Trial Judgement, *supra* note 7, para. 726; *Brđanin* Trial Judgement, *supra* note 2, para. 272; *Kajelijeli* Trial Judgement, *supra* note 10, para. 769; *Semanza* Trial Judgement, *supra* note 2, para. 386; *Naletilić and Martinović* Trial Judgement, *supra* note 150, para. 63; *Bagilishema* Trial Judgement, *supra* note 29, para. 36.
[181] See *Kayishema and Ruzindana* Appeal Judgement, *supra* note 175, para. 201; *Prosecutor* v. *Kayishema and Ruzindana*, Case No. ICTR 95-1-T, Judgement, 21 May 1999 ('*Kayishema and Ruzindana* Trial Judgement'), para. 200; *Furundžija* Trial Judgement, *supra* note 139, para. 232.
[182] *Furundžija* Trial Judgement, *supra* note 139, para. 274. Accord *Prosecutor* v. *Furundžija*, Case No. IT-95-17/1-A, Judgement, 21 July 2000, para. 125.

Aleksovski Trial Chamber found that the accused's presence, without making any objection, during the systematic mistreatment of detainees at the prison for which he was responsible contributed substantially to the mistreatment; since Aleksovski was aware of his contribution, the Trial Chamber found that he had aided and abetted the mistreatment through his presence.[183] The *Tadić* Trial Chamber pointed to another scenario of aiding and abetting through mere presence: where the accused previously played an active role in similar acts (for example, beatings of detainees) committed by the same group, and stayed with those group members, even though no longer physically participating, as they committed further criminal acts. The Chamber noted that the only ways in which an accused could avoid responsibility in such a circumstance would be to actively withdraw from the group or speak out against its conduct.[184]

In its discussion of aiding and abetting by omission, the *Blaškić* Trial Judgement referred to the position of superior authority of the person who is present at a crime scene as a 'probative indication for determining whether that person encouraged or supported the perpetrators of the crime'.[185] A few ICTR judgements have also endorsed language from *Furundžija* suggesting that the present person's position of authority alone might engage his responsibility for complicity,[186] but these judgements are in the minority.[187] The clear majority has followed the position of the *Aleksovski* Trial Chamber, which appears to be substantively identical to that of the *Blaškić* Chamber and which was articulately restated in *Brđanin*: 'An individual's position of superior authority does not suffice to conclude from his mere presence at the scene of the crime that he encouraged or supported the crime. However, the presence of a superior can be perceived as an important *indicium* of encouragement or support.'[188] Nonetheless, *ad hoc* trial jurisprudence suggests that, even though an accused's position of authority provides strong evidence of aiding and abetting, 'responsibility is not automatic and merits consideration against the background of the

[183] *Aleksovski* Trial Judgement, *supra* note 151, para. 87.
[184] *Tadić* Trial Judgement, *supra* note 139, para. 690.
[185] *Blaškić* Trial Judgement, *supra* note 143, para. 284 (affirmed by *Blaškić* Appeal Judgement, *supra* note 16, para. 47).
[186] *Furundžija* Trial Judgement, *supra* note 139, para. 207.
[187] See *Kayishema and Ruzindana* Appeal Judgement, *supra* note 175, para. 201; *Ndindabahizi Trial Judgement*, *supra* note 14, para. 457; *Bagilishema* Trial Judgement, *supra* note 29, para. 34; *Kayishema and Ruzindana* Trial Judgement, *supra* note 181, para. 200.
[188] *Brđanin* Trial Judgement, *supra* note 2, para. 271 (emphasis in original). Accord *Muvunyi* Trial Judgment, *supra* note 22, para. 472; *Mpambara* Trial Judgment, *supra* note 61, para. 22; *Orić* Trial Judgement, *supra* note 135, para. 283; *Strugar* Trial Judgement, *supra* note 16, para. 349; *Kamuhanda* Trial Judgement, *supra* note 17, para. 600; *Kajelijeli* Trial Judgement, *supra* note 10, para. 769; *Simić et al* Trial Judgement, *supra* note 150, para. 165; *Semanza* Trial Judgement, *supra* note 2, para. 386; *Naletilić and Martinović* Trial Judgement, *supra* note 150, para. 63; *Kvočka et al.* Trial Judgement, *supra* note 153, para. 257; *Blaškić* Trial Judgement, *supra* note 143, para. 284; *Aleksovski* Trial Judgement, *supra* note 151, para. 65.

factual circumstances'.[189] The *Akayesu* Trial Chamber invoked Akayesu's status as *bourgmestre* of Taba commune as evidence that his silence in the face of nearby rapes was a 'clear signal of official tolerance for sexual violence, without which these acts would not have taken place';[190] the sending of this signal of official tolerance was a factor in holding Akayesu guilty as an aider and abettor of rape and other inhumane acts as crimes against humanity.[191]

4.3.1.1.3 Does a form of responsibility known as 'aiding and abetting by omission' exist in international criminal law?

Many chambers have suggested that the aider and abettor's lending of assistance or support may occur not only by means not only of positive action, but also through an omission.[192] As the judgements discussed above show, aiding and abetting through inactive presence at the scene of the crime has been discussed at considerable length in the jurisprudence of the *ad hoc* Tribunals. The *Aleksovski*, *Galić*, *Simić*, *Strugar*, *Kayishema and Ruzindana*, *Rutaganira*, *Muvunyi* and *Mpambara* Trial Chambers have pointed to another scenario in which liability for an omission is said to be possible: where the aider and abettor has a duty to act and fails to do so, irrespective of his presence at or absence from the scene.[193]

---

[189] *Aleksovski* Trial Judgement, *supra* note 151, para. 65. Accord *Mpambara* Trial Judgement, *supra* note 61, para. 22; *Simić et al.* Trial Judgement, *supra* note 150, para. 165; *Semanza* Trial Judgement, *supra* note 2, para. 386; *Kvočka et al.* Trial Judgement, *supra* note 153, para. 257.

[190] *Akayesu* Trial Judgement, *supra* note 14, para. 693.   [191] *Ibid.*

[192] See *Blaškić* Appeal Judgement, *supra* note 16, para. 47; *Muvunyi* Trial Judgement, *supra* note 22, para. 470; *Mpambara* Trial Judgement, *supra* note 61, para. 22; *Orić* Trial Judgement, *supra* note 135, para. 283; *Strugar* Trial Judgement, *supra* note 16, para. 349; *Blagojević and Jokić* Trial Judgement, *supra* note 7, para. 726; *Brđanin* Trial Judgement, *supra* note 2, para. 271; *Galić* Trial Judgement, *supra* note 155, para. 168; *Kajelijeli* Trial Judgement, *supra* note 10, para. 766; *Simić et al.* Trial Judgement, *supra* note 150, para. 162; *Naletilić and Martinović* Trial Judgement, *supra* note 150, para. 63; *Vasiljević* Trial Judgement, *supra* note 150, para. 70; *Krnojelac* Trial Judgement, *supra* note 153, para. 88; *Kunarac et al.* Trial Judgement, *supra* note 150, para. 391; *Blaškić* Trial Judgement, *supra* note 143, para. 284; *Aleksovski* Trial Judgement, *supra* note 151, para. 129. While the *Galić* Appeals Chamber held unequivocally that liability for ordering cannot ensue on the basis of an omission, it left open the possibility that the physical elements of other Article 7/6(1) forms of responsibility may be fulfilled by omission where a superior-subordinate relationship exists between the accused and the physical perpetrator. See *Galić* Appeal Judgement, *supra* note 155, para. 176 ('The failure to act of a person in a position of authority, who is in a superior-subordinate relationship with the physical perpetrator, may give rise to another mode of responsibility under Article 7(1) of the [ICTY] Statute or superior responsibility under Article 7(3)[.]'); see also Chapter 5, text accompanying notes 148–150 (discussing *Galić*'s holding that 'ordering by omission' does not exist).

[193] *Muvunyi* Trial Judgement, *supra* note 22, para. 472; *Mpambara* Trial Judgment, *supra* note 61, para. 22; *Prosecutor v. Rutaganira*, Case No. ICTR-95-1C-T, Judgement and Sentence, 14 March 2005 ('*Rutaganira* Trial Judgement'), para. 64; *Strugar* Trial Judgement, *supra* note 16, para. 249; *Galić* Trial Judgement, *supra* note 155, para. 168; *Simić et al.* Trial Judgement, *supra* note 150, para. 162; *Aleksovski* Trial Judgement, *supra* note 151, para. 88; *Kayishema and Ruzindana* Trial Judgement, *supra* note 181, para. 202. The Prosecution before the *Kordić and Čerkez* Trial Chamber made a similar assertion, which the Chamber appears to have implicitly endorsed in a footnote earlier in the judgement. *Kordić and Čerkez* Trial Judgement, *supra* note 145, para. 375 n. 509 ('In relation to the requisite *actus reus* of "planning, instigating, ordering, committing or otherwise aiding and abetting in the execution of a crime", the Prosecution avers that not only positive acts but also culpable omissions may give rise to individual responsibility. However, an individual will incur criminal liability for an omission only when the individual is under a duty to act.').

These two scenarios have been considered in the jurisprudence as possibly exemplifying a separate but related form of liability: aiding and abetting by omission.

The proposition that aiding and abetting by omission is a form of responsibility in international criminal law is undeveloped and – as will be argued – inaccurate. It has been repeated on several occasions by scholars commenting on the elements of forms of responsibility before the *ad hoc* Tribunals, without discussing or articulating the role of aiding and abetting by omission in international criminal law.[194] The *Blaškić* Trial Judgement was the first in the *ad hoc* jurisprudence to speak explicitly of aiding and abetting by omission, suggesting that for such omission liability to arise it must have had a 'decisive effect' on the commission of the crime.[195] While the *Blaškić* Trial and Appeal Judgements left open the possibility that circumstances beyond inactive presence at the scene could constitute aiding and abetting by omission[196] – a proposition repeated by the ICTR Appeals Chamber in the *Ntagerura* Judgement in respect of a superior who fails to act, but not applied in that case[197] – most judgements subsequent to the *Blaškić* Trial Judgement have simply reiterated that aiding and abetting can occur by omission without going into further detail.[198]

The *Aleksovski* Trial Chamber held the accused, a prison commander, responsible as an aider and abettor to the systematic abuse of two detainees by guards within earshot of his office because he did not intervene, 'as his position required', but instead remained silent.[199] Similarly, the *Rutaganira* Trial Chamber affirmed the responsibility of the accused, the *conseiller* of the Mubuga *secteur*, as an aider and abettor to extermination for having remained inactive while the civilian population under his watch joined armed attackers in massacring the Tutsis taking refuge in the Mubuga church.[200] The Chamber identified the accused's failure to fulfil his obligations under Article 256 of the Rwandan Penal Code, including his duty to stop the inhabitants of his *secteur* from engaging in acts of violence and to report them to the appropriate

---

[194] See, e.g., Schabas, *supra* note 11, p. 304; Elies van Sliedregt, *The Criminal Responsibility of Individuals for Violations of International Humanitarian Law* (2003), p. 67; Gerhard Werle, *Principles of International Criminal Law* (2005), p. 170; Antonio Cassese, *International Criminal Law* (2003), p. 200.

[195] *Blaškić* Trial Judgement, *supra* note 143, para. 284.

[196] *Ibid.*; *Blaškić* Appeal Judgement, *supra* note 16, para. 47.

[197] *Prosecutor* v. *Ntagerura, Bagambiki and Imanishimwe*, Case No. ICTR-99-46-A, Judgement, 7 July 2006, paras. 370, 377.

[198] See *Mpambara* Trial Judgement, *supra* note 61, para. 22; *Blagojević and Jokić* Trial Judgement, *supra* note 7, para. 726; *Brđanin* Trial Judgement, *supra* note 2, para. 271; *Galić* Trial Judgement, *supra* note 155, para. 168; *Kajelijeli* Trial Judgement, *supra* note 10, para. 766; *Simić et al.* Trial Judgement, *supra* note 150, para. 162; *Naletilić and Martinović* Trial Judgement, *supra* note 150, para. 63; *Vasiljević* Trial Judgement, *supra* note 150, para. 70; *Krnojelac* Trial Judgement, *supra* note 153, para. 88; *Kunarac et al.* Trial Judgement, *supra* note 150, para. 391.

[199] *Aleksovski* Trial Judgement, *supra* note 151, para. 88.

[200] *Rutaganira* Trial Judgement, *supra* note 193, paras. 74, 100.

authorities, as the crucial factor which transformed his idleness into culpable aiding and abetting.[201]

The treatment by the *Strugar* Trial Judgement of whether an accused may be found guilty as an aider and abettor for failing to discharge a duty is revealing. In that case, the prosecution alleged that, even though Strugar was not physically present to witness his troops' unlawful shelling of the Old Town of Dubrovnik, he should nevertheless be held responsible as an aider and abettor because he failed to intervene to stop them. While Strugar had issued a ceasefire order, he only did so three hours after he discovered that his troops might be engaging in unlawful shelling, and he took no steps subsequently to launch an adequate investigation into the events.[202] The Trial Chamber acknowledged that the *Blaškić* Appeal Judgement left open the possibility 'that in the circumstances of a given case an omission may constitute the *actus reus* of aiding and abetting', and that trial chambers had held this might be the case, for example, where a military commander is present or failed in an explicit duty to act in prevention of a crime being committed by his subordinates.[203] However, the Trial Chamber found that Strugar could not be held responsible as an aider and abettor;[204] he had, after all, made an effort to stop the firing, and his failure to carry out an investigation occurred so long after the commission of the offences that it could not have had the requisite 'direct and substantial effect' on them.[205] '[I]n the absence of more settled jurisprudence as to whether, and if so in what circumstances, an omission may constitute the *actus reus* of aiding and abetting,' the Chamber determined that Strugar's failure to take more effective measures was more properly regarded in the context of superior responsibility under Article 7(3) of the ICTY Statute.[206]

Therefore, according to the *Strugar* Chamber, a superior should not be held liable as an aider or abettor – at least in the absence of 'more settled jurisprudence' – for prior crimes in such circumstances. This challenge to the proposition that the physical elements of aiding and abetting can be satisfied by an omission raises questions about the proper foundation for such a form of responsibility. The *Strugar* Trial Judgement in fact stands for the inappropriateness of imposing aiding and abetting liability on a superior for failing to intervene to stop the criminal conduct or to carry out a proper investigation, as well as, by logical analogy, for failing to punish those responsible for committing crimes. As will be seen below, this argument extends further into other purported categories of aiding and abetting by omission.

Close examination of the relevant jurisprudence reveals that instances of mere inactive presence at the scene of a crime are not properly characterised as aiding

---

[201] *Ibid.*, paras. 81, 84, 91, 99–100.   [202] *Strugar* Trial Judgement, *supra* note 16, paras. 352–355.
[203] *Ibid.*, para. 349.   [204] *Ibid.*, para. 356.   [205] *Ibid.*, para. 355.   [206] *Ibid.*

and abetting 'by omission'. In most cases in which a chamber would find the requisite 'significant encouraging effect',[207] the aider and abettor intentionally made himself available at the scene, or intentionally stayed on the scene if already there, for the express purpose of showing solidarity with the physical perpetrators or approval of their actions.[208] By intentionally making himself present, it is apparent that the accused is in fact *actively* aiding and abetting the crime, even though he may take no overt action or say anything once at the scene.

If this characterisation is accurate, then the only circumstances in which aiding and abetting by omission might be said to arise is where a superior with a duty to act fails to take action – the scenario envisaged or mentioned by the Trial Chambers in *Galić*, *Simić* and *Rutaganira*. Nevertheless, it would appear that this failure-to-act scenario is precisely the basis for the form of omission liability known as superior responsibility. Superior responsibility, which covers exactly the circumstances discussed in these cases, is a well-developed and clear form of indirect liability under customary international law which arises out of the superior-subordinate relationship, and which is explicitly included within the jurisdiction of all contemporary international criminal tribunals. Unlike aiding and abetting by omission, the foundation, purpose, elements and meaning of superior responsibility have all been expounded and are comprehensible. Contorting the physical elements of aiding and abetting to fit into a scenario already clearly provided for under superior responsibility makes no sense and has some undesirable side-effects. As discussed in Chapter 6 of this book,[209] the *ad hoc* Tribunals' Appeals Chambers require a conviction to be entered for liability under Article 7/6(1) in preference to Article 7/6(3), regardless of the appropriateness of the Article 7/6(1) liability to describe the conduct of an accused.[210] This approach would mean that a failure to act – for example, in the scenario envisaged in the *Blaškić* Trial

---

[207] See *Ndindabahizi* Trial Judgement, *supra* note 14, para. 457; *Strugar* Trial Judgement, *supra* note 16, para. 349; *Simić et al.* Trial Judgement, *supra* note 150, para. 165; *Vasiljević* Trial Judgement, *supra* note 150, para. 70; *Krnojelac* Trial Judgement, *supra* note 153, para. 88; *Kvočka et al.* Trial Judgement, *supra* note 153, para. 257; *Kunarac et al.* Trial Judgement, *supra* note 150, para. 393.

[208] See, e.g., *Strugar* Trial Judgement, *supra* note 16, para. 349.

[209] See Chapter 6, text accompanying notes 49–122.

[210] See *Blaškić* Appeal Judgement, *supra* note 16, paras. 91–92 (overturning the Trial Chamber's concurrent convictions pursuant to forms of responsibility under Article 7(1) and Article 7(3) of the ICTY Statute in respect of the same crime). See also *Prosecutor v. Kvočka, Radić, Žigić and Prcać*, Case No. IT-98-30/1-A, Judgement, 28 February 2005 ('*Kvočka et al.* Appeal Judgement'), para. 104 ('Where the legal requirements of both forms of responsibility are met, a conviction should be entered on the basis of Article 7(1) only, and the superior position should be taken into account as an aggravating factor in sentencing.'); *Kordić and Čerkez* Appeal Judgement, *supra* note 16, paras. 33–35 (following *Blaškić* and overturning the Trial Chamber's concurrent convictions); *Brđanin* Trial Judgement, *supra* note 2, para. 285 (following *Blaškić*); *Stakić* Trial Judgement, *supra* note 21, para. 466; *Krstić* Trial Judgement, *supra* note 2, para. 605 ('The Trial Chamber adheres to the belief that where a commander participates in the commission of a crime through his subordinates, by "planning", "instigating" or "ordering" the commission of the crime, any responsibility under Article 7(3) is subsumed under Article 7(1).').

Judgement[211] – would always require a finding of guilt as an accomplice for aiding and abetting (on the basis that this is a 'direct' form of responsibility, which it clearly is not), rather than the more appropriate and suitable finding of superior responsibility. The inappropriate outcome of applying *Blaškić* may require Trial Chambers to pursue counterintuitive avenues of legal reasoning to determine the applicability of aiding and abetting by omission in circumstances clearly more appropriately characterised as superior responsibility. It also renders confusing sentencing principles that should apply in findings between these two forms of responsibility for ostensibly the same (in)action. This was perhaps in the minds of the judges of the *Strugar* Trial Chamber when determining the applicability of such a form of responsibility in the circumstances before them.

Interestingly, some recent ICTR jurisprudence also exposes the inappropriateness, or practical inapplicability, of omission liability for aiding and abetting. The Trial Chamber in the *Muvunyi* case, while simply stating that liability for aiding and abetting may be incurred by way of omission, was unable to produce an example of where such responsibility might arise beyond the approving-spectator scenario dealt with above.[212] The *Mpambara* Trial Judgement is more interesting. While the Trial Chamber in that case suggested that the physical elements of aiding and abetting might be evidenced by omission, a close reading of the judgement reveals that the Trial Chamber was not itself convinced by the proposition. The Chamber commenced by stating that '[e]vidence which is characterised as an omission can be used to show that an accused aided and abetted a crime'.[213] It then referred to the presence of a person in a position of authority at the scene of a crime as a possible example of aiding and abetting by omission, and stated that '[o]ther examples of aiding and abetting through failure to act are not to be easily found in the annals of the *ad hoc* Tribunals'.[214] The Chamber itself held that an accused, by choosing to be present, is in fact taking a positive step which may contribute to the crime,[215] and then asserted that aiding and abetting liability in such circumstances is established 'from the omission combined with the choice to be present'.[216] Apparently the choice to be present is action while mere presence is omission. The struggle in which the Trial Chamber engages to try to establish the proposition that at least part of the culpable conduct of an accused in such circumstances constitutes omission further demonstrates the farcicality of seeking to establish 'aiding and abetting by omission' as a form of

---

[211] *Blaškić* Trial Judgement, *supra* note 143, para. 337.
[212] See *Muvunyi* Trial Judgement, *supra* note 22, para. 472.
[213] *Mpambara* Trial Judgement, *supra* note 61, para. 22.   [214] *Ibid.*, para. 23.
[215] *Ibid.*, para. 22.   [216] *Ibid.*

responsibility recognised in international criminal law and applicable in the *ad hoc* Tribunals.

For these reasons, and despite flirtatious references to it in the trial and appellate jurisprudence of the *ad hoc* Tribunals, there is no true support for aiding and abetting by omission as a form of responsibility in international criminal law.

4.3.1.1.4 *The accused may aid and abet in the planning, preparation, or execution of a crime, and before, during, or after the crime of the physical perpetrator*

Article 7/6(1) of the *ad hoc* Statutes provides that aiding and abetting can occur in the 'planning, preparation or execution of a crime',[217] and the chambers have universally held that the act of assistance may occur before, during, or after the crime of the physical perpetrator.[218] Such temporally removed assistance includes providing the means to commit the crime or promising to perform certain acts once the crime has been committed.[219] An example of assistance provided before the crime was committed is set out in *Tadić*, where the Trial Chamber cited a case from the French Permanent Military Tribunal holding criminally responsible, for aiding and abetting illegal arrest and deportation, a Nazi who had created lists of dissidents upon which the arresting authorities later relied.[220]

Notwithstanding the consistent application of this proposition, however, the position adopted by the *Strugar* Trial Chamber suggests that acts of assistance occurring too long after the crime of the physical perpetrator quite possibly lack the 'substantial effect' required of aiding and abetting.[221] The prosecution in that case had argued that, because Strugar failed to subsequently punish his troops for shelling the Old Town of Dubrovnik, this omission amounted to aiding and abetting the unlawful shelling. The Chamber rejected this argument, stating that it was not satisfied that 'the conduct of this nature, *well after the offences were committed*, could have a

---

[217] ICTY Statute, *supra* note 3, Art. 7(1); ICTR Statute, *supra* note 3, Art. 6(1).

[218] *Simić* Appeal Judgement, *supra* note 140, para. 85; *Blaškić* Appeal Judgement, *supra* note 16, para. 48; *Orić* Trial Judgement, *supra* note 135, para. 282; *Strugar* Trial Judgement, *supra* note 16, para. 349; *Blagojević and Jokić* Trial Judgement, *supra* note 7, para. 726; *Brđanin* Trial Judgement, *supra* note 2, para. 271; *Kamuhanda* Trial Judgement, *supra* note 17, para. 597; *Kajelijeli* Trial Judgement, *supra* note 10, para. 766; *Simić et al.* Trial Judgement, *supra* note 150, para. 162; *Semanza* Trial Judgement, *supra* note 2, para. 386; *Naletilić and Martinović* Trial Judgement, *supra* note 150, para. 63; *Krnojelac* Trial Judgement, *supra* note 153, para. 88; *Kvočka et al.* Trial Judgement, *supra* note 153, para. 256; *Kunarac et al.* Trial Judgment, *supra* note 150, para. 391; *Vasiljević* Trial Judgement, *supra* note 150, para. 70; *Blaškić* Trial Judgment, para. 285; *Aleksovski* Trial Judgment, *supra* note 151, paras. 62, 129.

[219] *Mpambara* Trial Judgement, *supra* note 61, para. 23; *Orić* Trial Judgement, *supra* note 135, para. 285; *Aleksovski* Trial Judgement, *supra* note 151, para. 62.

[220] *Tadić* Trial Judgement, *supra* note 139, paras. 687–688 (citing *Trial of Gustav Becker, Wilhelm Weber and 18 Others*, 7 *Law Reports of Trials of War Criminals* (1948), pp. 67, 70).

[221] See *infra* text accompanying notes 231–246 (setting forth the jurisprudence holding that the accused's contribution must have a 'substantial effect' on the physical perpetrator's commission of the crime).

direct and substantial effect on the commission of the offences', and refused to convict Strugar as an aider and abettor in this circumstance.[222] Likewise, the *Blagojević and Jokić* Trial Chamber held that Blagojević could not be held responsible for aiding and abetting the mass executions of Srebrenica victims by permitting the use of personnel and resources for the victims' reburial; the Chamber found that there was insufficient evidence to show that the reburial operation was agreed upon or even foreseen at the time of the planning, preparation, or execution of the killings.[223] In contrast, the *Naletilić and Martinović* Trial Chamber found that Martinović rendered a substantial contribution to the murder when it came to the disposal of the corpses: 'He gave direct orders with regard to the burial of the body, thereby initiating and substantially contributing to the covering up of the murder of Nenad Harmandžić.'[224] However, this post-commission conduct was but one aspect of the contribution rendered by the accused which gave rise to his responsibility for aiding and abetting, the other forms of contribution coming at the planning and execution phases of the crime.[225]

4.3.1.1.5 *The accused need not be physically present when the physical perpetrator commits the crime*

While, as discussed in detail above,[226] mere presence may in some cases amount to aiding and abetting, the case law does not generally require that the aider and abettor be physically present when the physical perpetrator commits the crime.[227] The *Tadić* Trial Chamber gave the example of the associate who drives the victim to the woods to be killed, and leaves before the killing takes place.[228] The *Bagilishema* and *Semanza* Trial Chambers pointed to one obvious exception to the proposition that the aider and abettor need not be geographically proximate: the case of the approving

---

[222] *Strugar* Trial Judgement, *supra* note 16, para. 355 (emphasis in original).
[223] *Blagojević and Jokić* Trial Judgement, *supra* note 7, paras. 731, 745.
[224] *Naletilić and Martinović* Trial Judgement, *supra* note 150, para. 507.   [225] *Ibid.*
[226] See *supra* text accompanying notes 181–191, 207–208.
[227] *Simić* Appeal Judgement, *supra* note 140, para. 85; *Blaškić* Appeal Judgement, *supra* note 16, para. 48; *Muvunyi* Trial Judgement, *supra* note 22, para. 471; *Strugar* Trial Judgement, *supra* note 16, para. 349; *Simić et al.* Trial Judgement, *supra* note 150, para. 162; *Kvočka et al.* Trial Judgement, *supra* note 153, para. 256; *Semanza* Trial Judgement, *supra* note 2, para. 385; *Bagilishema* Trial Judgement, *supra* note 29, para. 33; *Rutaganda* Trial Judgement, *supra* note 10, para. 43; *Kayishema and Ruzindana* Trial Judgement, *supra* note 181, para. 200; *Akayesu* Trial Judgement, *supra* note 14, para. 484. See also *Prosecutor* v. *Haradinaj, Balaj and Brahimaj*, Case No. IT-04-84-PT, Decision on Motion to Amend the Indictment and on Challenges to the Form of the Amended Indictment, 25 October 2006, para. 25 (holding, in respect of planning, instigating, ordering, aiding and abetting, and JCE, that '[n]one of these forms of responsibility contains an element requiring that the [a]ccused be present when the crime for which he is charged with responsibility is physically perpetrated').
[228] *Tadić* Trial Judgement, *supra* note 139, para. 691.

spectator.[229] According to these Chambers, the approving spectator must be present during the commission of the crime, or must at least be present in the immediate vicinity of the crime scene, and such presence must be perceived by the physical perpetrator as approval of his conduct.[230]

4.3.1.2 *Substantial effect: second physical element*

4.3.1.2.1 *The practical assistance, encouragement, or moral support had a substantial effect on the commission of the crime by the physical perpetrator*

Most judgements have specified that the aider and abettor's acts of practical assistance, encouragement, or support must have a 'substantial effect' on the perpetration of the crime,[231] although the *Krstić*, *Galić* and *Naletilić and Martinović* Trial Chambers provided a slightly different formulation: '"Aiding and abetting" means rendering a substantial contribution to the commission of a crime.'[232] The *Tadić* Trial Chamber explained that a sub-stantial contribution 'calls for a contribution that in fact has an effect on the commission of the crime.'[233] The *Naletilić and Martinović* Trial Chamber held Martinović responsible as an aider and abettor to murder because he had acted in contribution to the crime at various stages of its planning and execution.[234] There appears in practice to be no substantive difference between having a 'substantial effect' and rendering a 'substantial contribution'.

While the accused's lending of assistance must have some real effect on the crime's commission,[235] the chambers have consistently held that the

---

[229] See *Semanza* Trial Judgement, *supra* note 2, para. 385; *Bagilishema* Trial Judgement, *supra* note 29, para. 36. See also *supra* text accompanying notes 181–191, 207–208 (discussing the *ad hoc* jurisprudence on the approving spectator scenario in detail).

[230] *Semanza* Trial Judgement, *supra* note 2, para. 386; *Bagilishema* Trial Judgement, *supra* note 29, para. 36.

[231] See *Furundžija* Trial Judgement, *supra* note 139, paras. 235, 249; *Simić* Appeal Judgement, *supra* note 140, para. 85; *Kvočka et al.* Appeal Judgement, *supra* note 210, para. 90; *Blaškić* Appeal Judgement, *supra* note 16, para. 46; *Vasiljević* Appeal Judgement, *supra* note 103, para. 102; *Čelebići* Appeal Judgement, *supra* note 148, para. 352; *Tadić* Appeal Judgement, *supra* note 103, para. 229; *Muvunyi* Trial Judgement, *supra* note 22, para. 469; *Mpambara* Trial Judgement, *supra* note 61, para. 17; *Orić* Trial Judgement, *supra* note 135, para. 284; *Limaj et al.* Trial Judgement, *supra* note 146, para. 517; *Strugar* Trial Judgement, *supra* note 16, para. 349; *Brđanin* Trial Judgement, *supra* note 2, para. 271; *Ndindabahizi* Trial Judgement, *supra* note 14, para. 457 ('direct and substantial effect'); *Kajelijeli* Trial Judgement, *supra* note 10, para. 766; *Vasiljević* Trial Judgement, *supra* note 150, para. 70; *Kordić and Čerkez* Trial Judgment, *supra* note 145, para. 399; *Kunarac et al.* Trial Judgment, *supra* note 150, para. 391; *Blaškić* Trial Judgement, *supra* note 143, para. 283; *Aleksovski* Trial Judgement, *supra* note 151, para. 61; *Tadić* Trial Judgement, *supra* note 139, para. 692.

[232] *Krstić* Trial Judgement, *supra* note 2, para. 601. Accord *Galić* Trial Judgement, *supra* note 155, para. 168 (same language); *Naletilić and Martinović* Trial Judgement, *supra* note 150, para. 63 (same language).

[233] *Tadić* Trial Judgement, *supra* note 139, para. 688.

[234] *Naletilić and Martinović* Trial Judgement, *supra* note 150, para. 507.

[235] On its face, this statement would appear to exclude the situation where the accused's aid or support occurred after the crime was committed. To date, few *ad hoc* chambers have attempted to reconcile the substantial effect requirement with the oft-repeated holding that the accused may aid and abet after the crime has been completed. See *supra* text accompanying note 218. But see text accompanying notes 221–225 (trial chambers imposing certain limitations on liability for post-crime aiding and abetting). Given the manner in which aiding and abetting liability is applied by the *ad hoc* Tribunals,

prosecution need not prove that the crime would not have been committed but for the accused's participation.[236] Nevertheless, the position of both *ad hoc* Tribunals seems to be that the anticipated crime must actually have been committed for the aider and abettor to incur liability. As discussed in Section 4.1 above, a number of chambers have stated unequivocally that 'conspiracy to commit genocide', 'direct and public incitement to commit genocide', and 'attempt to commit genocide' – sub-paragraphs (b), (c) and (d) of Article 4/2(3), respectively – are the only inchoate crimes in the *ad hoc* Statutes.[237] Several ICTY chambers have explicitly declared that the criminal conduct of the physical perpetrator for which the aider and abettor is held responsible must be 'established',[238] and both the explicit statements of trial chambers[239] and their use of the phrase 'substantial effect on the *perpetration of the crime*'[240] clarify that liability for aiding and abetting cannot arise if the physical perpetrator does not actually commit the crime in question.

Notwithstanding this requirement that the crime be ultimately committed, the physical perpetrator need not have been tried or even identified[241] – even where the underlying crime requires specific intent[242] – and he need not be

there are moral and theoretical difficulties with holding an accused who only rendered post-crime assistance or support liable as an aider and abettor, because he has not truly participated in the commission of the crime. Certain domestic jurisdictions have resolved this problem by recasting the accused's conduct as a separate crime of obstruction of justice, instead of a form of participation in the principal crime. See, e.g., George P. Fletcher, *Rethinking Criminal Law* (1978), p. 646 n. 34 (citing statutes which replace the category with 'specially legislated offenses of obstructing justice'). As a result of the limited subject-matter jurisdiction of international tribunals, however, that solution would seem unavailable, so chambers must work within the constraints of the principles of legality and culpability to craft holdings that are appropriate for international criminal law.

236 See *Simić* Appeal Judgement, *supra* note 140, para. 85; *Blaškić* Appeal Judgement, *supra* note 16, para. 48; *Orić* Trial Judgement, *supra* note 135, para. 284; *Limaj et al.* Trial Judgment, *supra* note 146, para. 517; *Strugar* Trial Judgement, *supra* note 16, para. 349; *Blagojević and Jokić* Trial Judgement, *supra* note 7, para. 726; *Brđanin* Trial Judgement, *supra* note 2, para. 271; *Kajelijeli* Trial Judgement, *supra* note 10, para. 766; *Simić et al.* Trial Judgement, *supra* note 150, para. 162; *Naletilić and Martinović* Trial Judgement, *supra* note 150, para. 63; *Vasiljević* Trial Judgement, *supra* note 150, para. 70; *Krnojelac* Trial Judgement, *supra* note 153, para. 88; *Kvočka et al.* Trial Judgement, *supra* note 153, para. 255; *Kunarac et al.* Trial Judgement, *supra* note 150, para. 391; *Blaškić* Trial Judgement, *supra* note 143, para. 285; *Aleksovski* Trial Judgement, *supra* note 151, para. 61.

237 See *Brđanin* Trial Judgement, *supra* note 2, para. 725; *Nahimana et al.* Trial Judgement, para. 1017; *Kajelijeli* Trial Judgement, *supra* note 10, para. 855, *Semanza* Trial Judgement, *supra* note 2, para. 378, *Musema* Trial Judgement, *supra* note 10, para. 115 *Rutaganda* Trial Judgement, *supra* note 10, para. 34. Accord *Karemera et al.* May 2006 Pre-Trial Decision, *supra* note 8, Separate Opinion of Judge Short on Complicity in Genocide and Joint Criminal Enterprise Theory, para. 5. See also *supra* text accompanying note 10.

238 *Blagojević and Jokić* Trial Judgement, *supra* note 7, para. 727. Accord *Prosecutor* v. *Aleksovski*, Case No. IT-95-14/1-A Judgement, 24 March 2000 ('*Aleksovski* Appeal Judgement'), para. 165; *Orić* Trial Judgement, *supra* note 135, para. 269; *Brđanin* Trial Judgement, *supra* note 2, para. 271.

239 See *Furundžija* Trial Judgement, *supra* note 139, para. 246; *Orić* Trial Judgement, *supra* note 135, para. 282; *Stakić* Trial Judgement, *supra* note 21, para. 533.

240 *Furundžija* Trial Judgement, *supra* note 139, para. 235 (emphasis added). Accord *Blaškić* Appeal Judgement, *supra* note 16, para. 46.

241 *Brđanin* Trial Judgement, *supra* note 2, para. 273; *Stakić* Trial Judgement, *supra* note 21, para. 534 (stating that 'an individual can be prosecuted for complicity even where the perpetrator has not been tried or even identified').

242 *Krstić* Appeal Judgement, *supra* note 9, para. 140; *Vasiljević* Appeal Judgement, *supra* note 103, para. 142; *Brđanin* Trial Judgement, *supra* note 2, para. 273. See *infra*, text accompanying notes 283–302, for a more detailed discussion of aiding and abetting and specific-intent crimes.

aware of the accused's contribution.[243] The *Naletilić and Martinović* Trial Chamber accordingly found Martinović guilty of aiding and abetting the murder of Nenad Harmandžić – even though there was no evidence that Martinović had been personally involved in the shooting, and the shooter had not been conclusively identified – by encouraging his soldiers to mistreat the victim, preventing the victim from leaving the military base, and instructing the victim's co-detainees not to tell anyone about what they had witnessed.[244] Similarly the *Krstić* Appeals Chamber, after overturning the accused's conviction for participating in a JCE to commit genocide, substituted a conviction for aiding and abetting genocide, in spite of the absence of trial chamber findings individually identifying the principal participants in the genocidal enterprise of the Bosnian Serb Army.[245] The *Vasiljević* Appeals Chamber found Mitar Vasiljević responsible for aiding and abetting persecution without having had the alleged physical perpetrator on trial and without having identified two other alleged physical perpetrators.[246]

4.3.2 Mental elements

4.3.2.1 Intentional action

4.3.2.1.1 The accused acted intentionally with knowledge or awareness that his act would lend assistance, encouragement, or moral support to the physical perpetrator

While a few trial chambers have suggested that the aider and abettor must have intended to assist or facilitate the commission of the crime through his act,[247] the subsequent *Blaškić* Appeal Judgement determined that such a standard varied impermissibly from the correct one applied in several other trial and appeal judgements: an accused charged with aiding and abetting liability need merely have knowledge or awareness that his own acts assist the physical

---

[243] *Tadić* Appeal Judgement, *supra* note 103, para. 229; *Simić et al.* Trial Judgement, *supra* note 150, para. 161.

[244] *Naletilić and Martinović* Trial Judgement, *supra* note 150, paras. 500, 507.

[245] *Krstić* Appeal Judgement, *supra* note 9, para. 143. See also *supra* text accompanying notes 93–106 (discussing this aspect of *Krstić* at greater length). See also *Krnojelac* Trial Judgement, *supra* note 153, paras. 489–490 (finding the accused liable for having aided and abetted the crime of persecution, which requires the specific intent to discriminate on political, racial, or religious grounds, where the principal perpetrators of the crime were not identified).

[246] *Vasiljević* Appeal Judgement, *supra* note 103, para. 143.

[247] See *Kamuhanda* Trial Judgement, *supra* note 17, para. 597 ('acts of assistance that intentionally provide encouragement or support to the commission of a crime'); *Kajelijeli* Trial Judgement, *supra* note 10, para. 766 ('acts of assistance that intentionally provide encouragement or support to the commission of a crime'); *Kvočka et al.* Trial Judgement, *supra* note 153, para. 255; *Bagilishema* Trial Judgement, *supra* note 29, para. 32; *Blaškić* Trial Judgement, *supra* note 143, para. 286.

perpetrator in the commission of the crime.[248] Such awareness need not have
been overtly expressed, but may be inferred from the circumstances.[249]

The aider and abettor's intention to facilitate the crime by acting is distinct
from the intention of the perpetrator committing the crime, a point well illustrated by Judge Shahabuddeen when discussing the application of aiding and
abetting to the specific-intent crime of genocide in his partial dissenting
opinion in *Krstić*:

> Intent must always be proved, but the intent of the perpetrator of genocide is not the
> same as the intent of the aider and abettor. The perpetrator's intent is to commit genocide.
> The intent of the aider and abettor is not to commit genocide; his intent is to provide
> the means by which the perpetrator, if he wishes, can realise his own intent to commit
> genocide.[250]

The *Orić* Trial Chamber speaks of a 'double intent' requirement to establish
aiding and abetting, although it does not clarify the exact meaning of this term.
The language of the judgement seems to suggest a requirement that the aider
and abettor share the criminal intent of the physical perpetrator, but the
Chamber explains in a footnote that its statement does not mean that an
aider and abettor must share the 'special intent' of the perpetrator.[251] The
sources cited by the Trial Chamber suggest that, by 'intent', the Chamber
means cognitive knowledge, as the cases to which it refers merely state that an
individual must be aware that he is assisting in the commission of a crime, and
must be aware of the *mens rea* of the physical perpetrator.[252] These references
appear to suggest that the *Orić* language is simply a confusing re-wording of
settled requirements without actually changing them in any substantive way.

---

[248] *Blaškić* Appeal Judgement, *supra* note 16, para. 49. Accord *Simić* Appeal Judgement, *supra* note 140, para.
86; *Vasiljević* Appeal Judgement, *supra* note 103, para. 102; *Kayishema and Ruzindana* Appeal Judgement,
supra note 175, para. 186; *Aleksovski* Appeal Judgement, *supra* note 238, para. 162; *Tadić* Appeal
Judgement, *supra* note 103, para. 229; *Furundžija* Trial Judgement, *supra* note 139, paras. 245, 249;
Muvunyi Trial Judgement, *supra* note 22, para. 470; *Mpambara* Trial Judgment, *supra* note 61, para. 16;
Limaj et al. Trial Judgment, *supra* note 146, para. 518; *Strugar* Trial Judgement, *supra* note 16, para. 350;
Brđanin Trial Judgement, *supra* note 2, para. 272; *Kajelijeli* Trial Judgement, *supra* note 10, para. 768;
Simić et al. Trial Judgement, *supra* note 150, para. 163; *Naletilić and Martinović* Trial Judgement, *supra*
note 150, para. 63; *Vasiljević* Trial Judgement, *supra* note 150, para. 71; *Krnojelac* Trial Judgement,
supra note 153, para. 90; *Kvočka et al.* Trial Judgement, *supra* note 153, para. 255; *Blaškić* Trial
Judgement, *supra* note 143, para. 283.
[249] *Strugar* Trial Judgement, *supra* note 16, para. 350. See also *Galić* Appeal Judgement, *supra* note 155,
para. 178 (holding that the elements of any form of responsibility may be proven by direct or circumstantial evidence).
[250] *Krstić* Appeal Judgement, *supra* note 9, Partial Dissenting Opinion of Judge Shahabuddeen, para. 66.
[251] *Orić* Trial Judgement, *supra* note 135, para. 288 n. 825.
[252] See *Strugar* Trial Judgement, *supra* note 16, para. 350; *Blagojević and Jokić* Trial Judgement, *supra*
note 7, para. 727; *Brđanin* Trial Judgement, *supra* note 2, para. 273; *Simić et al.* Trial Judgement, *supra*
note 150, para. 163; *Naletilić and Martinović* Trial Judgement, *supra* note 150, para. 63; *Vasiljević* Trial
Judgement, *supra* note 150, para. 71; *Krnojelac* Trial Judgement, *supra* note 153, para. 90; *Furundžija*
Trial Judgement, *supra* note 139, para. 245.

Although the *Orić* Trial Chamber acknowledged the extensive jurisprudence supporting the proposition that the mental element of aiding and abetting is satisfied by mere awareness that one's actions will aid in the commission of a crime, it also considered that such knowledge must be accompanied by an element of volition.[253] It seems that in doing so, the Trial Chamber intended to narrow the scope of the situations which could be classified as aiding and abetting – for example, by eliminating instances of recklessness.[254] Yet it is difficult to imagine that awareness that one's actions aid in the perpetration of a crime could be severed from a volitional element of acceptance. In the jurisprudence of the *ad hoc* Tribunals, Chambers have found that an accused had cognitive awareness by inferring this fact from the circumstances.[255] It is unclear what kind of proof could be required to show volitional acceptance. If one has cognitive awareness of the results of his actions, the fact that he then carried out these actions could be considered indicative of his acceptance of the consequences.

Despite these somewhat confusing interventions from the *Orić* Trial Chamber, the *Kunarac* Trial Chamber's formulation of the accused aider and abettor's own required intent appears to remain the most precise and accurate in this regard: the accused must take 'the conscious decision to act in the knowledge that he thereby supports the commission of the crime'.[256]

4.3.2.2 *Awareness of crime*

4.3.2.2.1 *The accused was aware of the essential elements of the physical perpetrator's crime, including the perpetrator's mental state*

In addition to being aware that his acts or omissions lend assistance or encouragement to the actions of the physical perpetrator, the accused aider and abettor must be aware of the essential elements of the crime ultimately committed by the perpetrator.[257] The *Simić* Trial Chamber identified an apparent conflict in the jurisprudence of the ICTY concerning whether fulfilment of this element requires that the accused also know the precise crime the physical perpetrator will commit, is committing, or has committed with his

---

[253] *Orić* Trial Judgement, *supra* note 135, paras. 286–288.   [254] *Ibid.*

[255] See, e.g., *Naletilić and Martinović* Trial Judgement, *supra* note 150, para. 507; *Limaj et al.* Trial Judgment, *supra* note 146, para. 518.

[256] *Kunarac et al.* Trial Judgement, *supra* note 150, para. 392. See also *Aleksovski* Trial Judgement, *supra* note 151, para. 61; *Tadić* Trial Judgement, *supra* note 139, para. 674.

[257] *Simić* Appeal Judgement, *supra* note 140, para. 86; *Aleksovski* Appeal Judgement, *supra* note 238, para. 162; *Mpambara* Trial Judgement, *supra* note 61, para. 17; *Orić* Trial Judgement, *supra* note 135, para. 288; *Limaj et al.* Trial Judgment, *supra* note 146, para. 518; *Strugar* Trial Judgement, *supra* note 16, para. 349; *Blagojević and Jokić* Trial Judgement, *supra* note 7, para. 727; *Brđanin* Trial Judgement, *supra* note 2, para. 273; *Simić et al.* Trial Judgement, *supra* note 150, para. 163; *Naletilić and Martinović* Trial Judgement, *supra* note 150, para. 63; *Vasiljević* Trial Judgement, *supra* note 150, para. 71; *Krnojelac* Trial Judgement, *supra* note 153, para. 90; *Kvočka et al.* Trial Judgement, *supra* note 153, para. 255; *Kunarac et al.* Trial Judgement, *supra* note 150, para. 392.

assistance or encouragement.[258] One line of cases, beginning with the *Tadić* Appeal Judgement, holds that 'the requisite mental element is knowledge that the acts performed by the aider and abettor assist the commission of a *specific crime* by the principal';[259] this language was repeated in the *Kunarac*,[260] *Krnojelac*[261] and *Blagojević and Jokić*[262] Trial Judgements, and the *Aleksovski*,[263] *Vasiljević*,[264] *Kvočka*[265] and *Simić*[266] Appeal Judgements. The other line of cases, beginning with the *Furundžija* Trial Judgement and endorsed by the *Blaškić*,[267] *Kvočka*,[268] *Naletilić and Martinović*,[269] *Brđanin*[270] and *Strugar*[271] Trial Judgements, provides as follows:

[I]t is not necessary that the aider and abettor should know the precise crime that was intended and which in the event was committed. If he is aware that one of a number of crimes will probably be committed, and one of those crimes is in fact committed, he has intended to facilitate the commission of that crime, and is guilty as an aider and abettor.[272]

The *Simić* Chamber opted to endorse the 'stricter' definition set out in the former group of cases (*Kunarac*, *Krnojelac* and so on), and to reject the proposition in the quoted passage above.[273]

Several of the cases on both sides of the purported divide were rendered subsequent to the *Simić* Trial Judgement, and no post-*Simić* appeal judgement has attempted explicitly to resolve the conflict; indeed, it would appear that no other judgement has even mentioned that a conflict exists. The July 2004 *Blaškić* Appeal Judgement actually endorsed both 'alternatives' without bringing up *Simić* at all. The Appeals Chamber discussed the *Tadić* criterion (that the aider and abettor know that his acts assist in the commission of the specific crime), stating that 'there are no reasons to depart from this

258 *Simić et al.* Trial Judgement, *supra* note 150, para. 163.
259 *Tadić* Appeal Judgement, *supra* note 103, para. 229 (emphasis added).
260 *Kunarac et al.* Trial Judgement, *supra* note 150, para. 392.
261 *Krnojelac* Trial Judgement, *supra* note 153, para. 90.
262 *Blagojević and Jokić* Trial Judgement, *supra* note 7, para. 727.
263 *Aleksovski* Appeal Judgement, *supra* note 238, paras. 162–163.
264 *Vasiljević* Appeal Judgement, *supra* note 103, para. 102.
265 *Kvočka et al.* Appeal Judgement, *supra* note 210, para. 89. See also *Krnojelac* Appeal Judgement, *supra* note 103, para. 33 (quoting with approval *Tadić* Appeal Judgement, *supra* note 103, para. 229); *Kordić and Čerkez* Trial Judgement, *supra* note 145, para. 399 (same).
266 *Simić* Appeal Judgement, *supra* note 140, para. 86.
267 *Blaškić* Trial Judgement, *supra* note 143, para. 287.
268 *Kvočka et al.* Trial Judgement, *supra* note 153, para. 255.
269 *Naletilić and Martinović* Trial Judgement, *supra* note 150, para. 63.
270 *Brđanin* Trial Judgement, *supra* note 2, para. 272.
271 *Strugar* Trial Judgement, *supra* note 16, para. 350.
272 *Furundžija* Trial Judgement, *supra* note 139, para. 246. Although its judgement was rendered subsequent to *Simić* and the appellate jurisprudence discussed below, the *Orić* Trial Chamber also aligned itself with this position. *Orić* Trial Judgement, *supra* note 135, para. 288.
273 *Simić et al.* Trial Judgement, *supra* note 150, para. 163.

definition';[274] the Chamber then turned to the *Furundžija* criterion (that the aider and abettor need only be aware that one of a number of crimes may be committed, and one of those crimes is in fact committed), stating finally that '[t]he Appeals Chamber concurs with this conclusion'.[275]

In the November 2006 *Simić* Appeal Judgement, the Appeals Chamber again endorsed both alternatives without acknowledging the conflict identified by the *Simić* Trial Chamber, and in a manner that is more strikingly inconsistent than that of the *Blaškić* Appeals Chamber. The *Simić* Appeals Chamber held that 'the aider and abettor must be aware of the essential elements of the crime which was ultimately committed', and that, '[i]n relation to the crime of persecutions ... he must ... be aware not only of the crime whose perpetration he is facilitating but also of the discriminatory intent of the perpetrators'.[276] These statements would certainly seem to hold that the accused must know the precise crime the physical perpetrator would commit with his assistance. Yet once again, in the same paragraph the Appeals Chamber repeated that 'it is not necessary that the aider and abettor knows either the precise crime that was intended or the one that was, in the event, committed', as long as he 'is aware that one of a number of crimes will probably be committed, and one of those crimes is in fact committed'.[277]

The Appeals Chamber's bewildering approach to this aspect of the mental element of aiding and abetting suggests two possible interpretations. One interpretation is that the two alternatives are in fact reconcilable, notwith-standing the position of the *Simić* Trial Chamber. If this is indeed what the Appeals Chamber had in mind, the proposition might appropriately be formulated as follows: the accused aider and abettor must have known that his own acts assisted in the commission of the specific crime for which he is charged – which the perpetrator actually carried out and for which the Trial Chamber must determine the accused's guilt or innocence – but this crime may have been one of several crimes in respect of which the accused provided practical assistance or encouragement, and which he knew would probably be committed. The second alternative is to acknowledge that the Appeals Chamber's treatment of this issue does not express a coherent principle and, therefore, leaves unresolved the divergent jurisprudence on this matter.

In the absence of a clear statement by the Appeals Chamber, the most appropriate and safest approach to this issue is that which places a greater burden on the prosecution to establish this element. In other words, the accused must have had the specific crime with which he is charged in mind when he rendered the assistance or encouragement, whether or not he

---

[274] *Blaškić* Appeal Judgement, *supra* note 16, para. 45.   [275] *Ibid.*, para. 50.
[276] *Simić* Appeal Judgement, *supra* note 140, para. 86.   [277] *Ibid.*

simultaneously had other crimes in mind as well. This requirement constitutes a key distinction between aiding and abetting and participation in a joint criminal enterprise. When acting in pursuance of a joint criminal enterprise, an accused need not have known the pool of crimes which his fellow participants would possibly commit, or even that one or more of them would commit the crime with which he is charged; as long as it was foreseeable that that crime might have been perpetrated by one or more members of the group and, despite such foreseeability, the accused took the risk and participated in the common design anyway, he can be found guilty of that crime as if he himself had physically committed it.[278] This interpretation finds support in the *Naletilić and Martinović* Trial Judgement, which opined that the *Tadić* Appeals Chamber's oft-cited statement that the aider and abettor must have known that his acts assisted in the commission of the specific crime of the physical perpetrator 'has to be read only in the context of contrasting aiding and abetting with the participation in a common purpose or design'.[279]

Among the essential elements of the perpetrator's crime of which an accused aider and abettor must be aware is the *mens rea* of the perpetrator; that is, the accused must know the *mens rea* that a physical perpetrator would have to have in order to be convicted of committing the crime. Perhaps most importantly, the accused need not share the physical perpetrator's *mens rea*.[280] This factor makes up another of the main differences between aiding and abetting and participation in a JCE in the first category,[281] and has been invoked as lessening the aider and abettor's level of culpability from what it would have been if he were found to be a participant in a joint criminal enterprise.[282]

4.3.2.3 *The requisite intent of the accused aider and abettor for specific-intent crimes*

The chambers of both *ad hoc* Tribunals are united in holding that the requirement that the accused aider and abettor merely know of the physical

---

[278] *Stakić* Appeal Judgement, *supra* note 9, para. 65; *Kvočka et al.* Appeal Judgement, *supra* note 210, para. 83; *Tadić* Appeal Judgement, *supra* note 103, para. 229. See Chapter 2, text accompanying notes 389–454, for a complete discussion of this element of JCE.

[279] *Naletilić and Martinović* Trial Judgement, *supra* note 150, para. 63 n. 170.

[280] *Aleksovski* Appeal Judgement, *supra* note 238, para. 162; *Blagojević and Jokić* Trial Judgement, *supra* note 7, para. 727; *Brđanin* Trial Judgement, *supra* note 2, para. 273; *Simić et al.* Trial Judgement, *supra* note 150, para. 163; *Naletilić and Martinović* Trial Judgement, *supra* note 150, para. 63; *Vasiljević* Trial Judgement, *supra* note 150, para. 71; *Krnojelac* Trial Judgement, *supra* note 153, para. 90; *Kvočka et al.* Trial Judgement, *supra* note 153, para. 556; *Kunarac et al.* Trial Judgement, *supra* note 150, para. 392; *Aleksovski* Trial Judgement, *supra* note 151, para. 245; *Furundžija* Trial Judgement, *supra* note 139, para. 245.

[281] See Chapter 2, text accompanying notes 268–293.

[282] See *Vasiljević* Trial Judgement, *supra* note 150, para. 71. See also Chapter 6, text accompanying notes 123–176 (discussing the legal holdings and factual findings of trial and appellate jurisprudence supporting this principle in the context of sentencing).

perpetrator's intent – and need not share it – applies equally to specific-intent crimes such as genocide and persecution as a crime against humanity. As expressed by the Appeals Chamber in its April 2004 *Krstić* Judgement: 'The Appeals Chamber has previously explained, on several occasions, that an individual who aids and abets a specific intent offense may be held responsible if he assists the commission of the crime knowing the intent behind the crime.'[283] Among those 'previous occasions' are the *Vasiljević*[284] and *Krnojelac*[285] Appeal Judgements, which both dealt with persecution. In *Krnojelac*, the Appeals Chamber stated that 'the aider and abettor in persecution ... must be aware ... of the discriminatory intent of the perpetrators of that crime ... but need not share [that] intent'.[286] Several trial chambers have expressly applied the Appeals Chamber's position, including *Kvočka*,[287] *Krnojelac*,[288] *Simić*,[289] *Brđanin*[290] and *Blagojević and Jokić*.[291] The *Kvočka* Trial Chamber qualified the general requirement that the accused must be aware of the essential elements of the crime by emphasising that, in respect of persecution, the accused 'must be aware of the broader discriminatory context', but he need not know or intend 'each and every act of discrimination'.[292]

Applying this standard, the *Krnojelac* Trial Chamber found the accused, the warden of a prison at which Muslim civilians were illegally detained, guilty as an aider and abettor not only of illegal imprisonment as a crime against humanity, but also of persecution: in addition to Krnojelac's knowledge that his acts and omissions substantially contributed to the offence of imprisonment, 'it was obvious to the Accused, as it was to anyone who was at [his prison] the KP Dom, that the principal offenders in imprisoning the Muslim and other non-Serb men intended to discriminate against them on religious and political grounds'.[293] Likewise, the *Vasiljević* Appeals Chamber convicted the accused

[283] *Krstić* Appeal Judgement, para. 140. For a comparative perspective of the respective intent requirements for all of the forms of responsibility, see the chart 'Comparison of required mental states, with regard to intent, for imposition of liability under each form of responsibility' in the Annex of this book.
[284] *Vasiljević* Appeal Judgement, *supra* note 103, para. 142.
[285] *Krnojelac* Appeal Judgement, *supra* note 103, para. 52.
[286] *Ibid.* Accord *Simić* Appeal Judgement, *supra* note 140, para. 86 (holding with respect to persecution that the accused 'must ... be aware not only of the crime whose perpetration he is facilitating but also of the discriminatory intent of the perpetrators of that crime', and that '[h]e need not share that intent').
[287] *Kvočka et al.* Trial Judgement, *supra* note 153, para. 262.
[288] *Krnojelac* Trial Judgement, *supra* note 153, para. 489.
[289] *Simić et al.* Trial Judgement, *supra* note 150, para. 164.
[290] *Brđanin* Trial Judgement, *supra* note 2, para. 271.
[291] *Blagojević and Jokić* Trial Judgement, *supra* note 7, para. 753.
[292] *Kvočka et al.* Trial Judgement, *supra* note 153, para. 262. Accord *Simić* Appeal Judgement, *supra* note 140, para. 86 (holding that the accused 'must be aware of the discriminatory context in which the crime is to be committed and know that his support or encouragement has a substantial effect on its perpetration').
[293] *Krnojelac* Trial Judgement, *supra* note 153, para. 489. See also *Krnojelac* Appeal Judgement, *supra* note 103, para. 52 (upholding the Trial Chamber's findings and dismissing Krnojelac's ground of appeal).

of aiding and abetting murder and inhumane acts as forms of persecution as a crime against humanity, because he forcibly prevented the victims from fleeing 'with full awareness that the intent of the [physical perpetrators] was to persecute the local Muslim population ... through the commission of the underlying crimes'.[294] Moreover, since it considered that the evidence presented at trial had conclusively established Krstić's awareness of the physical perpetrators' genocidal intent, the *Krstić* Appeals Chamber found the accused guilty of aiding and abetting genocide.[295]

The position of the ICTY chambers has significant ramifications because it exposes the accused to liability for aiding and abetting persecution and genocide even though he may not have possessed discriminatory or genocidal intent. Perhaps for this reason, two ICTR trial judgements – *Akayesu* and *Ntakirutimana and Ntakirutimana* – held that an aider and abettor to genocide must himself have the specific intent to commit genocide.[296] The *Akayesu* Trial Chamber stated that 'when dealing with a person [a]ccused of having aided and abetted in the planning, preparation and execution of genocide, it must be proven that such a person did have the specific intent to commit genocide'.[297] The Chamber then stated that the major distinction between aiding and abetting genocide and complicity in genocide is that the latter does not require that the accomplice possess specific intent.[298] Ultimately, the December 2004 *Ntakirutimana and Ntakirutimana* Appeal Judgement – the first ICTR appeal judgement to rule directly on this issue – rejected the position of the *Akayesu* and *Ntakirutimana and Ntakirutimana* Trial Chambers and endorsed that of the *Semanza* Trial Chamber[299] and the *Krstić* Appeals Chamber:

> The Appeals Chamber ... finds that a conviction for aiding and abetting genocide upon proof that the defendant knew about the principal perpetrator's genocidal intent is permitted by the Statute and case-law of this Tribunal. Accordingly, the Trial Chamber erred in determining that the *mens rea* for aiding and abetting genocide requires intent to commit genocide.[300]

The Chamber then determined that, because the evidence demonstrated that Elizaphan Ntakirutimana had knowledge of the genocidal intent of the

---

[294] *Vasiljević* Appeal Judgement, *supra* note 103, para. 142 (quoting *Vasiljević* Trial Judgement, *supra* note 150, para. 251).

[295] *Krstić* Appeal Judgement, *supra* note 9, para. 143. See also *supra* text accompanying notes 93–108, for a more detailed discussion of these findings in relation to Krstić.

[296] *Akayesu* Trial Judgement, *supra* note 14, para. 485; *Ntakirutimana and Ntakirutimana* Trial Judgement, para. 787.

[297] *Akayesu* Trial Judgement, *supra* note 14, para. 485.

[298] *Ibid.* See also *supra* text accompanying notes 79–108, for a detailed discussion of this holding and the disapproval of it in subsequent trial judgements.

[299] *Semanza* Trial Judgement, *supra* note 2, para. 388.

[300] *Ntakirutimana and Ntakirutimana* Appeal Judgement, para. 501.

physical perpetrators, he thereby incurred criminal responsibility as an aider and abettor to genocide.[301] This holding and its approval by the May 2005 *Semanza* Appeal Judgement[302] bring ICTR case law into line with that of the ICTY in respect of aiding and abetting specific-intent crimes.

4.4 Elements of complicity in genocide

As discussed in Section 4.2 above, there has been relatively little attention paid in the jurisprudence to complicity in genocide,[303] and only a small handful of trial judgements actually go into detail on its physical and mental elements.[304] Furthermore, if, as the *Krstić* Appeals Chamber suggested may be the case,[305] complicity encompasses conduct broader than aiding and abetting, it is likely impossible to conceive of one set of elements that applies to all of the possible manifestations of it. Indeed, both the *Brđanin* and *Blagojević and Jokić* Trial Judgements, which were rendered subsequent to *Krstić*, seem to acknowledge this impossibility, and confine their respective discussions on the elements of complicity in genocide to that species of complicity consisting of aiding and abetting ('complicity in genocide-aiding and abetting').[306] Moreover, the *Semanza* Trial Judgement, which examined the elements of complicity in genocide in light of its own proposition that aiding and abetting genocide and complicity in genocide are identical,[307] can probably only be taken as authority for the elements of complicity in genocide-aiding and abetting. Unsurprisingly, the elements identified by these chambers are virtually identical to those consistently applied since the *Furundžija* Trial Judgement for aiding and abetting under Article 7/6(1) and discussed in detail in the previous section.[308]

As there has not yet been any *ad hoc* jurisprudence defining a manifestation of complicity in genocide other than complicity in genocide-aiding and abetting, the authors confine the following brief discussion to complicity in genocide-aiding and abetting.

---

[301] *Ibid.*, para. 509. [302] *Semanza* Appeal Judgement, para. 316.
[303] See *supra* text accompanying notes 50, 59–69, and accompanying text.
[304] See *Blagojević and Jokić* Trial Judgement, *supra* note 7, paras. 678–680, 776–782; *Brđanin* Trial Judgement, *supra* note 2, paras. 728–730; *Stakić* Trial Judgement, *supra* note 21, paras. 533–534; *Semanza* Trial Judgement, *supra* note 2, paras. 390–398; *Bagilishema* Trial Judgement, *supra* note 29, paras. 66–71; *Musema* Trial Judgement, *supra* note 10, paras. 168–183; *Akayesu* Trial Judgement, *supra* note 14, paras. 525–548.
[305] *Krstić* Appeal Judgement, *supra* note 9, para. 139.
[306] See *Blagojević and Jokić* Trial Judgement, *supra* note 7, para. 781; *Brđanin* Trial Judgement, *supra* note 2, paras. 729–730.
[307] See *Semanza* Trial Judgement, *supra* note 2, paras. 390–398.
[308] See *Furundžija* Trial Judgement, *supra* note 139, paras. 235, 249.

4.4.1 Practical assistance, encouragement, or moral support: first physical element

4.4.1.1 The accused lent practical assistance, encouragement, or moral support to the physical perpetrator in committing a crime

The *Blagojević and Jokić* Trial Chamber characterised the physical elements of complicity in genocide-aiding and abetting as follows: '[T]he accused carried out an act which consisted of practical assistance, encouragement or moral support to the principal that had a "substantial effect" on the commission of the crime.'[309] This language is a near duplicate of that in the *Brđanin*,[310] *Stakić*[311] and *Semanza*[312] Trial Judgements. Hence, as with all manifestations of aiding and abetting, the contribution of the accused can take any of three forms: assistance, encouragement, or moral support. *Akayesu* specified that complicity in genocide, unlike ordinary aiding and abetting, could not be committed by means of an omission,[313] and the newer judgements do not list omission as a possibility.[314]

4.4.2 Substantial effect: second physical element

4.4.2.1 The practical assistance, encouragement, or moral support had a substantial effect on the commission of the crime by the physical perpetrator

All the relevant judgements hold that the acts that constitute complicity in genocide-aiding and abetting must have 'substantially contributed to, or have had a substantial effect on, the completion of the crime of genocide by the principal offender'.[315] The *Blagojević and Jokić* Trial Chamber found that Blagojević rendered practical assistance in the Bratunac town killings by allowing resources of his brigade of the VRS to be used in the perpetration of the killings, and that such acts of practical assistance had a substantial effect on the commission of genocide.[316] Since, as described above, Blagojević also possessed the requisite mental state for complicity in genocide-aiding and abetting, the Trial Chamber found him guilty of complicity in genocide and entered a conviction 'pursuant to Articles 4(3)(e) and 7(1) of the [ICTY] Statute'.[317] The

---

[309] *Blagojević and Jokić* Trial Judgement, *supra* note 7, para. 782.
[310] *Brđanin* Trial Judgement, *supra* note 2, para. 729.
[311] *Stakić* Trial Judgement, *supra* note 21, para. 533.
[312] *Semanza* Trial Judgement, *supra* note 2, para. 395.
[313] *Akayesu* Trial Judgement, *supra* note 14, para. 536.
[314] See *Semanza* Trial Judgement, *supra* note 2, para. 395; *Blagojević and Jokić* Trial Judgement, *supra* note 7, para. 782; *Brđanin* Trial Judgement, *supra* note 2, para. 729; *Stakić* Trial Judgement, *supra* note 21, para. 533. See *supra* text accompanying notes 192–216 for a discussion of 'aiding and abetting by omission'.
[315] *Brđanin* Trial Judgement, *supra* note 2, para. 729. Accord *Blagojević and Jokić* Trial Judgement, *supra* note 7, para. 782; *Stakić* Trial Judgement, *supra* note 21, para. 533; *Semanza* Trial Judgement, *supra* note 2, para. 395.
[316] *Blagojević and Jokić* Trial Judgement, *supra* note 7, para. 784.   [317] *Ibid.*, paras. 787, 797.

Semanza Trial Chamber similarly found that Semanza's acts of assistance – which included gathering Interahamwe militiamen to assist in the Musha church killings, participating in the separation of Tutsi from Hutu refugees, directing the killings of the Tutsi refugees, and bringing soldiers and Interahamwe militiamen to assist in the Mwulire Hill killings – were substantial enough to qualify as complicity in genocide; since Semanza himself possessed genocidal intent, the Chamber determined that the elements of complicity had been fulfilled and entered a conviction under Article 2(3)(e) of the ICTR Statute.[318]

The chambers are likewise united in holding that the prosecution must establish that the physical perpetrator did indeed commit genocide,[319] but the perpetrator need not have been tried or even identified, and he and the accused need not have known each other.[320] Since in both *Stakić* and *Brđanin* the prosecution failed to convince the Trial Chambers that genocide had occurred in the first place, each Chamber acquitted its respective accused of complicity in genocide.[321]

4.4.3 Mental elements: intentional action and awareness of crime

4.4.3.1 The accused acted intentionally, and was aware of the essential elements of the crime of genocide, including the perpetrator's mental state

The formulation of the *Semanza* Trial Judgement best encapsulates the mental elements of complicity in genocide-aiding and abetting: 'The accused must have acted intentionally and with the awareness that he was contributing to the crime of genocide, including all its material elements.'[322] Thus, the accused must have intentionally engaged in the conduct in question, but he need not have intended that genocide be committed;[323] he need merely have known that he contributed to the realisation of the crime of genocide. Moreover, the accused need not have possessed genocidal intent, but he must have been aware of the material elements of the crime of genocide and that the crime had been, was being, or would be committed with genocidal intent.[324]

---

[318] *Semanza* Trial Judgement, *supra* note 2, paras. 435–436, 553. The Appeals Chamber subsequently found that Semanza's participation in the Musha church and Mwulire Hill events was more appropriately characterised as 'ordering', reversed the Article 2(3)(e) conviction, and entered a conviction for genocide under Article 2(3)(a) via ordering in Article 6(1). *Semanza* Appeal Judgement, *supra* note 9, paras. 388–389, p. 125.

[319] *Blagojević and Jokić* Trial Judgement, *supra* note 7, para. 638; *Brđanin* Trial Judgement, *supra* note 2, para. 728; *Stakić* Trial Judgement, *supra* note 21, para. 534; *Musema* Trial Judgement, *supra* note 10, para. 173; *Akayesu* Trial Judgement, *supra* note 14, para. 529.

[320] *Stakić* Trial Judgement, *supra* note 21, para. 533; *Musema* Trial Judgement, *supra* note 10, para. 174; *Akayesu* Trial Judgement, *supra* note 14, para. 531.

[321] *Brđanin* Trial Judgement, *supra* note 2, paras. 989–991; *Stakić* Trial Judgement, *supra* note 21, paras. 559–561.

[322] *Semanza* Trial Judgement, *supra* note 2, para. 395.

[323] *Akayesu* Trial Judgement, *supra* note 14, para. 539.

[324] *Krstić* Appeal Judgement, *supra* note 9, paras. 140, 142; *Blagojević and Jokić* Trial Judgement, *supra* note 7, para. 782; *Brđanin* Trial Judgement, *supra* note 2, para. 730; *Bagilishema* Trial Judgement, *supra* note 29, para. 71; *Musema* Trial Judgement, *supra* note 10, paras. 180–181.

On the count of complicity in genocide charged against the accused Blagojević, the *Blagojević and Jokić* Trial Chamber was satisfied that the prosecution had proven all the requisite mental elements beyond a reasonable doubt. Blagojević had allowed the resources of his brigade of the VRS to be used in the knowledge that such use would contribute substantially to the killing of Bosnian Muslims, and he was aware of the physical perpetrators' intent to destroy, in whole or in part, the Bosnian Muslim group as such.[325] The Chamber inferred Blagojević's awareness of the perpetrators' genocidal intent from several factors, including his knowledge that the Bosnian Muslim population had been driven from Srebrenica to Potočari, that the Muslim men had been separated from the rest of the population, and that members of his brigade had assisted in the murder of Muslim men detained in Bratunac.[326]

4.5 Complicity and aiding and abetting in the International Criminal Court and internationalised tribunals

4.5.1 The International Criminal Court

Article 25 of the Rome Statute sets forth almost all the forms of individual criminal responsibility within the Court's jurisdiction.[327] Sub-paragraph 3(c) of this Article provides:

3. In accordance with this Statute, a person shall be criminally responsible and liable for punishment for a crime within the jurisdiction of the Court if that person:
   [. . .]
   (c) For the purpose of facilitating the commission of such a crime, aids, abets or otherwise assists in its commission or its attempted commission, including providing the means for its commission[.][328]

---

[325] *Blagojević and Jokić* Trial Judgement, *supra* note 7, paras. 785–786.   [326] *Ibid.*, para. 786.

[327] Article 28 of the Rome Statute deals with superior responsibility, which is the subject of Chapter 3 of this book. It is important to note, despite the structure of the Rome Statute and the terminology sometimes used in judgements and academic literature, that superior responsibility is not different from individual criminal responsibility. Rather, it is an integral part of the responsibility regime of international criminal law, which is premised on the penal liability of individuals for their own illegal conduct. The confusion may stem from the fact that forms of responsibility are often described as the methods of participation in a crime, whereas an accused held liable under superior responsibility need not have participated in the crime in any way, and may have had no connection to the criminal conduct save his failure to prevent, intervene to stop, or punish it. See generally Chapter 3. Nonetheless, recognition that a superior is held liable for his own conduct, and that superior responsibility is therefore part of individual criminal responsibility, is crucial to an understanding of the functioning of international criminal adjudication. See, e.g., 1996 Draft Code, *supra* note 166, Art. 2(3)(c) (providing, in the general article on individual criminal responsibility, that an individual 'shall be responsible for a crime if [he] fails to prevent or repress the commission of such a crime in the circumstances set out in article 6 [on superior responsibility]').

[328] Rome Statute, *supra* note 157, Art. 25(3)(c). See Kai Ambos, 'General Principles of Criminal Law in the Rome Statute', (1999) 10 *Criminal Law Forum* 11, ('The Rome Statute does not offer a solution for acts of complicity after the commission of the crime. The International Law Commission['s 1996 Draft Code] only included such acts within the concept of complicity if they were based on a commonly agreed plan[.]').

Unlike the *ad hoc* Statutes, the Rome Statute does not have a provision on complicity in genocide. Indeed, although the provision on genocide also takes its lead from the Genocide Convention, it does not include the text that has proved so troublesome for the *ad hoc* Tribunals.[329] Article 6, entitled simply 'Genocide', reproduces only Article II of the Genocide Convention, listing the underlying offences which may constitute genocide if committed with the requisite intent.[330]

As the relevant *travaux* demonstrate, the Rome Statute's drafters purposely took the decision to omit the text of Article III of the Convention, in the belief that – with the notable exception of direct and public incitement to genocide[331] – the modes of participation in the offences which may constitute the crime of genocide were adequately captured in the existing forms of responsibility set forth in Article 25.[332] This decision, and the more

---

[329] See *supra* Sections 4.1–4.2.

[330] See Rome Statute, *supra* note 147, Art. 6:

For the purpose of this Statute, 'genocide' means any of the following acts committed with intent to destroy, in whole or in part, a national, ethnical, racial or religious group, as such:

(a) Killing members of the group;

(b) Causing serious bodily or mental harm to members of the group;

(c) Deliberately inflicting on the group conditions of life calculated to bring about its physical destruction in whole or in part;

(d) Imposing measures intended to prevent births within the group;

(e) Forcibly transferring children of the group to another group.

[331] Direct and public incitement to genocide was given its own provision, in Article 25(3)(e) of the Rome Statute. See Per Saland, 'International Criminal Law Principles', in Roy S. Lee (ed.), *The International Criminal Court: The Making of the Rome Statute* (1999), p. 200 (noting that incitement, along with the qualifiers 'direct and public', was limited to genocide, as no agreement could be reached on its application to other crimes). Despite the placement of this provision in the Article devoted to forms of responsibility, the drafting history and commentary on Article 25(3)(e) make it clear that it is intended to be treated in the same manner as it is in the *ad hoc* Tribunals – that is, as an inchoate crime, not a true form of responsibility. See *ibid.* (noting that the plenipotentiaries in Rome relied on the Genocide Convention as the basis for the uncontroversial inclusion of incitement in the Statute); see also *supra* text accompanying notes 10–12 (*ad hoc* jurisprudence clarifying that incitement in the Genocide Convention is an inchoate crime); Ambos, *supra* note 328, p. 14:

[I]ncitement with regard to genocide does not require the commission or even attempted commission of the actual crime, in this case genocide ... A person, who directly and publicly incites the commission of genocide is punishable for the incitement even if the crime of genocide *per se* is never actually committed.

See also Andrea Sereni, 'Individual Criminal Responsibility' in Lattanzi and Schabas (eds.), (2004) 2 *Essays*, *supra* note 138, pp. 112–113 (correctly noting that 'the actual or attempted commission of the crime [of direct and public incitement to commit genocide] is irrelevant', but incorrectly labelling incitement to commit genocide a form of responsibility).

[332] See Report of the Preparatory Committee on the Establishment of an International Criminal Court, Draft Statute and Draft Final Act, UN Doc. A/CONF.183/2/Add. 1, 14 April 1998, p. 14 (noting, in a footnote to the proposed reproduction of complicity in genocide as a 'punishable act' of genocide, that 'the Working Group will return to the question of the placement of article III of the Genocide Convention once the Working Group on general principles of criminal law has considered this issue'); Committee of the Whole, Summary Record of the 3rd Meeting, held on 17 June 1998, UN Doc. A/CONF.183/C.1/SR.3, 20 November 1998 ('Summary Record'), para. 174 (noting that the proposed text of the article on genocide would be referred to the Drafting Committee without the text of Article III of the Genocide Convention, at least until further work had been done on the part of the Rome Statute dealing with individual criminal responsibility); Report of the Working Group on General Principles of Criminal Law, UN Doc. A/CONF.183/C.1/WGGP/L.4, 18 June 1998, p. 3 (recommending, in a

streamlined approach to the application of the forms of responsibility to genocide it heralded, are significant support for the arguments of certain scholars that the inclusion of Article III's text in the *ad hoc* Statutes was the result of inadvertent or inattentive drafting, and should not be given undue weight in chambers' determinations.[333]

As far as can be determined, there has been no actual practice at the ICC on the scope and application of Article 25(3)(c), or the application of this provision to the offences listed in Article 6. As discussed in an earlier chapter, the arrest warrants unsealed so far rely on sub-paragraphs (3)(a) and/or (3)(b) of Article 25 to ground the charges against the accused;[334] none to date alleges that the accused is responsible for aiding, abetting, or otherwise assisting in the commission or attempted commission of a crime, and none has yet charged an accused with genocide.[335] In addition, no chamber of the ICC has yet publicly opined on Article 25(3)(c) or the application of Article 25 to Article 6.

In light of the discussion above on the proper construction of Article 4/2 of the *ad hoc* Statutes,[336] it is worth noting that the Rome Statute has many more inchoate crimes than its *ad hoc* predecessors. In the same spare drafting style that led to the creation of a single default provision on the mental element for all crimes within the ICC's jurisdiction,[337] however, most of these additional inchoate crimes are invoked by a single sub-paragraph awkwardly placed in the larger

footnote to the provision on direct and public incitement in what would eventually become Article 25, that '[t]he second paragraph of the definition of the crime of genocide in article 5 [reproducing Article III of the Convention] which appears between square brackets should be deleted'); Report of the Drafting Committee to the Committee of the Whole, UN Doc. A/CONF.183/C.1/L.91, 16 July 1998, p. 2 (adopting this recommendation, and limiting the text of then Article 5 – now Article 6 – to reproducing Article II of the Convention). See also Herman von Hebel and Darryl Robinson, 'Crimes with the Jurisdiction of the Court', in Lee, *supra* note 331, p. 90 n. 38 (referring indirectly to this drafting history). See especially William A. Schabas, 'Genocide', in Otto Triffterer (ed.), *Commentary on the Rome Statute of the International Criminal Court* (1999), pp. 115–116 (arguing, *inter alia*, that to follow the *ad hoc* Statutes' approach to incorporation of the Genocide Convention 'would have introduced a degree of redundancy, in that other provisions of the [Rome] Statute also dealt with secondary participation and the inchoate offences of conspiracy, incitement and attempt' and noting that '[i]ndeed, the problem [of redundancy] exists in the *ad hoc* statutes').

[333] See *supra* notes 124–127, 332, and accompanying text.
[334] See Chapter 2, text accompanying note 734.
[335] This situation may change, however, if charges result from the referral to the Court by the Security Council of the conflict in Darfur, Sudan. See Report of the International Commission of Inquiry on Darfur to the United Nations Secretary-General pursuant to Security Council Resolution 1564 of 18 September 2004, 25 January 2005, available at www.un.org/News/dh/sudan/com_inq_darfur.pdf, p. 4 ('The Commission concluded that the Government of the Sudan has not pursued a policy of genocide ... [but] does recognise that in some instances individuals, including Government officials, may commit acts with genocidal intent. Whether this was the case in Darfur, however, is a determination that only a competent court can make on a case by case basis.'); Security Council Resolution 1593, UN Doc. S/RES/1593 (2005), 31 March 2005 (in which the Council, '[a]cting under Chapter VII of the Charter of the United Nations, ... [d]ecide[d] to refer the situation in Darfur since 1 July 2002 to the Prosecutor of the International Criminal Court').
[336] See *supra* text accompanying notes 2–57.   [337] See Rome Statute, *supra* note 157, Art. 30.

provision on individual criminal responsibility.[338] Article 25(3)(f) provides that a person shall be liable for a crime within the Court's jurisdiction if he,

[a]ttempts to commit such a crime by taking action that commences its execution by means of a substantial step, but the crime does not occur because of circumstances independent of the person's intentions. However, a person who abandons the effort to commit the crime or otherwise prevents the completion of the crime shall not be liable for punishment under this Statute for the attempt to commit that crime if that person completely and voluntarily gave up the criminal purpose.

In practical terms, the first sentence in the sub-paragraph doubles the number of punishable offences within the Court's jurisdiction: in addition to the commission of the offences within the categories of war crimes, crimes against humanity and genocide, the Statute provides jurisdiction for the imposition of liability for the unrenounced attempt to commit the crimes.[339] To attempted genocide,[340] which exists in the *ad hoc* Statutes, is therefore added attempted murder as a crime against humanity, attempted deportation as a grave breach, and so on. This doubling of crimes is made clear by the fact that almost all the provisions on forms of responsibility within Article 25 of the Rome Statute refer to two basic kinds of crimes – those that are committed, and those that are attempted.[341] As a result of the intense debates over the concept of conspiracy,[342] however, there is no provision in the Rome Statute on conspiracy to commit genocide, and the only other inchoate crime clearly recognised therein is direct and public incitement to genocide.

[338] In many ways, the inclusion of provisions on inchoate crimes (direct and public incitement, for genocide; and attempt, when applied to all crimes) within the article devoted to forms of responsibility risks recreating the intellectual and practical confusion that has marked the *ad hoc* Tribunals' attempts to deal with similarly poorly structured provisions on genocide. As there has been no practice to date, however, it is not yet possible to tell whether the ICC will avoid the potential pitfalls set up by the structure of Article 25.

[339] See Saland, *supra* note 331, p. 198 (noting that Article 25 covers 'the responsibility of principals and all other modes of participation (except command responsibility), and ... both completed crimes and attempted ones'.); Kai Ambos, 'Individual Criminal Responsibility', in Otto Triffterer (ed.), *Commentary on the Rome Statute of the International Criminal Court* (1999), p. 488 (observing that the Rome Statute follows one particular legislative approach to criminalising attempt, but does not limit it to any particular crime within the jurisdiction of the Court).

[340] That is, the attempt to commit genocide through any of the means or methods represented in the underlying offences listed in Article 4/2(2).

[341] See Article 25(3)(b), (c), and (d). Sub-paragraph (3)(a), as befits the provision on direct and indirect perpetration, refers only to commission. Sub-paragraph (3)(e) refers neither to commission nor attempted commission, because the conduct described therein is not a form of responsibility, but rather is itself an inchoate crime. See *supra* notes 10, 331, and accompanying text; see also Ambos, *supra* note 339, p. 487; Schabas, *supra* note 332, p. 115 (noting that Article III(c) of the Genocide Convention 'create[d] an *offence* of incitement that is distinct from incitement as a form of complicity [that is, a form of responsibility], in that "direct and public incitement" within the meaning of the Convention may be created even if nobody is in fact incited') (emphasis added).

[342] See, e.g., Schabas, *supra* note 332, pp. 115–116 (noting the different treatment of conspiracy in the common and civil law traditions, and the relatively inadequate compromise of the adoption of the terms of the provision on common-purpose liability, discussed above in Chapter 2).

4.5.2 The internationalised tribunals

4.5.2.1 Special Court for Sierra Leone (SCSL)

Article 6(1) of the SCSL Statute, essentially identical to Article 7/6(1) of the
ad hoc Statutes, provides:

A person who planned, instigated, ordered, committed or *otherwise aided and abetted
in the planning, preparation or execution of a crime* referred to in articles 2 to 4 of the
present Statute shall be individually responsible for the crime.[343]

The work of the SCSL is focused on five indictments,[344] and all five allege
that the accused charged therein are liable under all of the forms of responsibility explicitly or implicitly included in Article 6(1) of the SCSL Statute,[345]
including aiding and abetting, for all of the criminal conduct alleged in the
relevant indictment.[346] Although at least one pre-trial decision has stated that
the law may require the indictment to indicate clearly and disjunctively which
form of responsibility in Article 6(1) is charged with regard to each crime,[347] it

---

[343] Statute of the Special Court for Sierra Leone, 2178 UNTS 138, UN Doc. S/2002/246 (2002), Appendix II
('SCSL Statute'), Art. 6(1). It should be noted that, befitting the SCSL's status as a hybrid court, this
provision of the SCSL Statute apparently limits the direct application of the forms of responsibility
recognised in international criminal law to the international crimes listed in the Statute. By referring
specifically to Articles 2 to 4 of the Statute, Article 6 explicitly excludes the crimes under Sierra Leonean
law listed in Article 5. Pursuant to Article 6(5) of the Statute, '[i]ndividual criminal responsibility for
the[se] crimes . . . shall be determined in accordance with the respective laws of Sierra Leone'.

[344] These indictments are those against Charles Taylor; Brima, Kamara, and Kanu ('*AFRC* Case'); Sesay,
Kallon, and Gbao ('*RUF* Case'); Norman, Fofana, and Kondewa ('*CDF* Case'); and Johnny Paul
Koroma. The current total of five is the result of the consolidation of several indictments into the joint
indictments faced by the three groups of accused in the multi-defendant trials, as well as the withdrawal
of indictments against Foday Sankoh and Sam Bockarie after their deaths in 2003. See *Prosecutor* v.
Sankoh, Case No. SCSL-2003-02-PT, Withdrawal of Indictment, 8 December 2003 (Trial Chamber
endorsing Prosecutor's withdrawal of indictment); *Prosecutor* v. *Bockarie*, Case No. SCSL-2003-04-PT,
Withdrawal of Indictment, 8 December 2003 (same). Trials have concluded in two of the three multi-
defendant cases – judgements are expected in 2007 – and pre-trial proceedings against Taylor began after
his rendition in March 2006; Koroma is still at large.

[345] The form implicitly included in this Article is joint criminal enterprise. See Chapter 2, text accompanying
note 738.

[346] See *Prosecutor* v. *Brima, Kamara and Kanu*, Case No. SCSL-2004-16-PT, Further Amended Consolidated
Indictment, 18 February 2005 ('Current *AFRC* Indictment'), para. 35; *Prosecutor* v. *Sesay, Kallon and
Gbao*, Case No. SCSL-2004-15-T, Corrected Amended Consolidated Indictment, 2 August 2006 ('Current
RUF Indictment'), para. 38; *Prosecutor* v. *Norman, Fofana and Kondewa*, Case No. SCSL-2004-14-PT,
Indictment, 5 February 2004 ('*CDF* Indictment'), para. 20; *Prosecutor* v. *Koroma*, Case No. SCSL-2003-
03-I, Indictment, 7 March 2003 ('*Koroma* Indictment'), para. 26; *Prosecutor* v. *Taylor*, Case No. SCSL-03-
01-I, Amended Indictment, 16 March 2006 ('Amended *Taylor* Indictment'), p. 2 (alleging simply that 'the
Accused, pursuant to Article 6.1 and, or alternatively, Article 6.3 of the Statute, is individually criminally
responsible for the crimes alleged below'); *ibid.*, para. 33 (including language virtually identical to that used
in indictments in other cases).

[347] See *Prosecutor* v. *Sesay*, Case No. SCSL-2003-05-PT, Decision and Order on Defence Preliminary
Motion for Defects in the Form of the Indictment, 13 October 2003, para. 12; see also Chapter 3, text
accompanying notes 665–668 (discussion of this decision). But see *Prosecutor* v. *Kondewa*, Case No.
SCSL-2003-12-PT, Decision and Order on Defence Preliminary Motion for Defects in the Form of the
Indictment, 27 November 2003, para. 10 (holding that the Prosecution is not obliged to elect between the
different forms of responsibility under Article 6(1), and noting that the distinction between the various

does not appear that this ruling has affected the pleading practice of the Special Prosecutor. Instead, although four of the five indictments have been amended since the date of this decision,[348] all but one simply repeat the terms of Article 6(1), alleging that the accused,

by their acts or omissions are individually criminally responsible for the crimes referred to in Articles 2, 3 and 4 of the Statute as alleged in this Indictment, which crimes each of them planned, instigated, ordered, committed, or in whose planning, preparation or execution each Accused otherwise aided or abetted, or which crimes were within a common purpose, plan or design[.][349]

The sole exception is the case summary in the case against Charles Taylor. After the particular procedural history that led to the filing of two separate instruments setting out the charges in this case,[350] the Prosecutor has specifically alleged in the case summary all the elements of the forms of responsibility as they have been developed in the *ad hoc* jurisprudence. The allegations with regard to aiding and abetting are among the most detailed in this document, asserting:

Between about 30 November 1996 and about 18 January 2002, the Accused assisted in the commission of the alleged crimes by providing various forms of support. Such support included the provision of: military training, both in Liberia and Sierra Leone; facilities in Liberia; safe havens in Liberia; personnel drawn from the NPFL, other organized armed groups within Liberia and from the Liberian population in general; arms and associated materiel such as ammunition; communications equipment including satellite phones; and other supplies such as food, uniforms and petrol. To ensure the timely and safe delivery of this support to the RUF, AFRC, AFRC/RUF Junta or alliance and to the Liberian fighters in Sierra Leone, the Accused also provided Liberian escorts and vehicles.
    The essential support set out above provided practical assistance, encouragement and/or moral support to the RUF, AFRC, AFRC/RUF Junta or alliance and Liberian fighters in carrying out the crimes alleged in the Amended Indictment, and had a substantial effect on the commission of those crimes[.][351]

This reliance on the precedents of the *ad hoc* Tribunals is also evident in judicial pronouncements at the SCSL. In the decision on motions for judgement of acquittal issued at the midpoint of the case against Brima, Kamara and Kanu,

forms was 'pre-eminently an evidentiary matter'; if the Prosecution 'has chosen to plead all the different heads of responsibility, consistent with its discretion ... [it] will carry the burden of proving the existence of each at the trial').

[348] See Current *AFRC* Indictment, *supra* note 346; Current *RUF* Indictment, *supra* note 346; *Norman et al.*, Case No. SCSL-04-14-AR73, Decision on Amendment of the Consolidated Indictment, 16 May 2005 (resulting in the approval of the *CDF* Indictment, *supra* note 346); Amended *Taylor* Indictment, *supra* note 346. The single indictment yet to be amended is that against Koroma, the only SCSL accused who remains at large.
[349] *CDF* Indictment, *supra* note 346, para. 20; Current *AFRC* Indictment, *supra* note 346, para. 35; Current *RUF* Indictment, *supra* note 346, para. 38; see also *Koroma* Indictment, *supra* note 346, para. 27.
[350] See Chapter 2, notes 739–746 and accompanying text.
[351] *Taylor*, Case Summary Accompanying the Amended Indictment, 16 March 2006, paras. 40–41.

the Trial Chamber held that satisfaction of the physical elements for aiding and abetting requires an accused to give practical assistance, encouragement, or support, and that this assistance have a substantial effect on the perpetration of the crime.[352] With regard to the mental element, the chamber ruled that the accused must know that his acts would assist in the commission of the crime, or was aware of a substantial likelihood that his acts would assist the commission of a crime, but that the aider and abettor was not required to have knowledge of the precise crime.[353] The aider and abettor only had to be aware that one of a number of crimes would 'probably' be committed, including the one actually committed.[354] Although this decision was rendered in March 2006, the only authority cited for its definition of aiding and abetting was the *Blaškić* Appeal Judgement, and the *AFRC* Chamber failed to note certain finer details of the definition as developed by the *ad hoc* chambers, such as the clarification that the accused may also be liable for aiding and abetting the planning or preparation of a crime, and that the punishable conduct for aiding and abetting can occur before, during or after the crime of the physical perpetrator.[355] Most significantly, the chamber's very brief discussion of the mental elements of aiding and abetting glosses over the issue of whether the accused's awareness of the criminal conduct of the physical perpetrator must be specific or general; an issue which was ostensibly clarified by the very judgement the SCSL chamber cites, but which in reality is a question that remains unresolved in the *ad hoc* jurisprudence.[356]

The crime of genocide is not within the jurisdiction of the Special Court,[357] nor does its Statute mention complicity as a form of responsibility within its jurisdiction, so there is no provision of its governing law, nor any aspect of its jurisprudence, that raises the issue of complicity in genocide.

4.5.2.2 East Timor: Special Panels for Serious Crimes (SPSC)

The primary provision of the constitutive document for the Special Panels with regard to individual criminal responsibility, Section 14 of UNTAET Regulation No. 2000/15, mirrored Article 25 of the Rome Statute. As such, Section 14.3(c) was the operative provision for aiding and abetting, providing:

---

[352] *Brima et al.*, Case No. SCSL-04-16-T, Decision on Defence Motions for Judgement of Acquittal Pursuant to Rule 98, 31 March 2006, para. 301.
[353] *Ibid.*, para. 302.   [354] *Ibid.*   [355] See *supra* text accompanying notes 217–225.
[356] See *supra* text accompanying notes 274–279.
[357] See Report of the Secretary-General on the Establishment of a Special Court for Sierra Leone, UN Doc. S/2000/915, 4 October 2000, para. 13:

> In its resolution 1315 (2000), the Security Council recommended that the subject-matter jurisdiction of the Special Court should include crimes against humanity, war crimes and other serious violations of international humanitarian law. Because of the lack of any evidence that the massive, large-scale killing in Sierra Leone was at any time perpetrated against an identified national, ethnic, racial or religious group with an intent to annihilate the group as such, the Security Council did not include the crime of genocide in its recommendation, nor was it considered appropriate by the Secretary-General to include it in the list of international crimes falling within the jurisdiction of the Court.

14.3. In accordance with the present regulation, a person shall be criminally responsible and liable for punishment for a crime within the jurisdiction of the panels if that person:

[. . .]

(c) For the purpose of facilitating the commission of such a crime, aids, abets or otherwise assists in its commission or its attempted commission, including providing the means for its commission[.][358]

Genocide was within the jurisdiction of the Special Panels,[359] and the applicable provision again followed the ICC model, omitting any reference to 'punishable acts' of genocide, and reproducing only Article II of the Genocide Convention. Nonetheless, allegations of genocide were never the focus of the investigations or of the judicial panels, perhaps because the work of the bodies and organisations concerned was, in practice, temporally limited to the period immediately before, during and after the Popular Consultation in 1999, when there was no indication that the crimes in question were committed with genocidal intent.[360]

Like other aspects of the SPSC's practice,[361] however, pleadings and decisions both cited and relied upon precedents established by the *ad hoc* Tribunals when dealing with allegations of aiding and abetting.[362]

4.5.2.3 The Extraordinary Chambers in the Courts of Cambodia (ECCC)

As is the case with common-purpose liability[363] and superior responsibility,[364] the approach taken by the governing law of the hybrid Cambodia chambers to aiding and abetting largely adopts the wording of the *ad hoc* Statutes. In relevant part, Article 29 of the Law on the Establishment of the Extraordinary Chambers in the Courts of Cambodia for the Prosecution of Crimes Committed during the Period of Democratic Kampuchea provides:

---

[358] United Nations Transitional Administration in East Timor, Regulation No. 2000/15 on the Establishment of Panels with Exclusive Jurisdiction over Serious Criminal Offences, UN Doc. UNTAET/REG/2000/15, 6 June 2000 ('SPSC Regulation'), Section 14(c).

[359] See *Ibid.*, Section 4.4.

[360] See, e.g., Report of the International Commission of Inquiry on East Timor to the Secretary-General, UN Doc. A/54/726, S/2000/59, 31 January 2000, para. 123 (concluding that 'there were patterns of gross violations of human rights and breaches of humanitarian law which varied over time and took the form of systematic and widespread intimidation, humiliation and terror, destruction of property, violence against women and displacement of people', but no mention of genocide).

[361] See Chapter 2, text accompanying notes 762–766; Chapter 3, text accompanying notes 697–702.

[362] See, e.g., *Prosecutor* v. *Joni Marques, Manuel da Costa, João da Costa, Paulo da Costa, Amélio da Costa, Hilário da Silva, Gonsalo dos Santos, Alarico Fernandes, Mautersa Monis and Gilberto Fernandes*, Case No. 09/2000, Judgement, 11 December 2001, available at http://ist-socrates.berkeley.edu/~warcrime/ET-Docs/CE-SPSC%20Final%20Decisions/2000/09-2000%20part%201%20Joni%20et%20al%20Judgment.pdf, pp. 38–40 (recounting the arguments of the prosecution in that case, which cited several ICTY and ICTR judgements, albeit without specifying whether they were trial or appeal judgements).

[363] See *supra* Chapter 2, text accompanying notes 774–775.

[364] See *supra* Chapter 3, text accompanying notes 703–705.

Any Suspect who planned, instigated, ordered, *aided and abetted*, or committed the crimes referred to in article 3 new, 4, 5, 6, 7 and 8 of this law shall be individually responsible for the crime.[365]

In turn, Article 4 of the Law provides:

The Extraordinary Chambers shall have the power to bring to trial all Suspects who committed the crimes of genocide as defined in the Convention on the Prevention and Punishment of the Crime of Genocide of 1948, and which were committed during the period from 17 April 1975 to 6 January 1979.

The acts of genocide, which have no statute of limitations, mean any acts committed with the intent to destroy, in whole or in part, a national, ethnical, racial or religious group, such as:

- killing members of the group;
- causing serious bodily or mental harm to members of the group;
- deliberately inflicting on the group conditions of life calculated to bring about its physical destruction in whole or in part;
- imposing measures intended to prevent births within the group;
- forcibly transferring children from one group to another group.

The following acts shall be punishable under this Article:

- attempts to commit acts of genocide;
- conspiracy to commit acts of genocide;
- participation in acts of genocide.[366]

It is notable, however, that unlike the *ad hoc* Statutes, the governing law of the ECCC does not merely reproduce the text of Article III of the Genocide Convention, focusing instead on only certain of the 'punishable acts' which may constitute genocide. In particular, no mention is made of direct and public

---

[365] The Law on the Establishment of the Extraordinary Chambers in the Courts of Cambodia for the Prosecution of Crimes Committed during the Period of Democratic Kampuchea, as amended on 27 October 2004, Doc. No. NS/RKM/1004/006, unofficial translation by the Council of Jurists and the Secretariat of the Task Force, revised on 29 September 2005, available at http://www.cambodia.gov.kh/krt/english/law%20on%20establishment.htm, Art. 29 (emphasis added).

[366] *Ibid.*, Art. 4. Although the extensive massacres that characterised the Khmer Rouge regime are routinely referred to in news reports and other general literature as 'genocide', this popular view does not take account of the specific legal requirements for the establishment of this international crime, which excludes acts targeting groups that are only political or social in nature. In fact, the inclusion of genocide within the jurisdiction of the ECCC was actually in response to a much more limited range of the regime's activities. See Report of the Group of Experts for Cambodia established pursuant to General Assembly Resolution 52/135, annexed to UN Doc. A/53/850, S/1999/231, 16 March 1999, para. 63:

> In the view of the Group of Experts, the existing historical research justifies including genocide within the jurisdiction of a tribunal to prosecute Khmer Rouge leaders. In particular, evidence suggests the need for prosecutors to investigate the commission of genocide against the Cham, Vietnamese and other minority groups, and the Buddhist monkhood. The Khmer Rouge subjected these groups to an especially harsh and extensive measure of the acts enumerated in the Convention. The requisite intent has support in direct and indirect evidence, including Khmer Rouge statements, eyewitness accounts and the nature and number of victims in each group, both in absolute terms and in proportion to each group's total population. These groups qualify as protected groups under the Convention: the Muslim Cham as an ethnic and religious group; the Vietnamese communities as an ethnic and, perhaps, a racial group; and the Buddhist monkhood as a religious group.

incitement, and the reference to complicity in genocide appears to have been replaced by a potentially broader – and certainly vaguer – category labelled 'participation'. Since the very purpose of the forms of responsibility in international criminal law is to capture the different possible modes of participation in the commission of a crime, the precise scope and function of this particular provision of the Law is unclear.

To date, there is not much available material relating to the functioning of the Extraordinary Chambers, and little academic discussion. The available documentation on the cases in which preparations have begun is sparse. The prosecutors and judges of the Extraordinary Chambers, both Cambodian and international, were only appointed in May 2006,[367] and trials were not expected to begin before 2007.[368] For these reasons, it will not be possible to understand how this hybrid court will apply this and other forms of responsibility in international criminal law until pre-trial and trial proceedings get under way. At very least, it would seem that the ECCC's limited departure from the *ad hoc* model will not shield its future jurisprudence from the problems of confusion and redundancy that plague the interpretation and application of the forms of responsibility to the underlying offences and 'punishable acts' of genocide in those older international tribunals.

4.5.2.4 Supreme Iraqi Criminal Tribunal (SICT)

In contrast to its approach to common-purpose liability, where it adopted the ICC model and mirrored the text of Article 25 of the Rome Statute,[369] the relevant provision of the SICT Statute repeats the drafting error of the *ad hoc* Statutes and reproduces both Articles II and III of the Genocide Convention.[370] Its provision on aiding and abetting, however, returns to the ICC model and essentially copies Article 25(3)(c).[371]

The first proceeding against Saddam Hussein and his co-accused (the 'Dujail case') did not charge genocide; the second, which began in September 2006 and does charge this crime, seems marred with chaos and procedural confusion similar to that which marked most of the first trial, so it may be

---

[367] See AU Washington College of Law: War Crimes Research Office, Extraordinary Chambers in the Courts of Cambodia Status Updates, available at http://www.wcl.american.edu/warcrimes/krt_updates.cfm (noting that by Royal Decree NS/RKT/0506/214 on 7 May 2006, King Norodom Sihamoni of Cambodia appointed 17 national and 12 international judges and prosecutors to serve on the Extraordinary Chambers).

[368] Office of the Governor-General of New Zealand, Press Release, 'Cartwright appointed Cambodian War Crimes Tribunal trial judge', 9 May 2006, available at http://www.gov-gen. govt.nz/media/news.asp?type = current&ID = 164.

[369] See Chapter 2, text accompanying notes 783–785.

[370] See Law No. 10 (2005), Law of the Iraqi Higher Criminal Court, available at http://www.law.case.edu/saddamtrial/documents/IST_statute_official_english.pdf, Art. 11.

[371] *Ibid.*, Art. 15(4).

equally difficult to determine how the judges approach the application of the forms of responsibility to this crime.[372]

In the Dujail case, Saddam Hussein was not charged as an aider and abettor of the crimes alleged; rather, the focus of the case against him as framed by the trial chamber was his role as an author of the crimes or the superior of the physical perpetrators and intermediate commanders.[373] In apparent recognition of their leadership positions, the three other high-ranking accused in the case were similarly not charged with aiding and abetting.[374] The remaining accused in the case, all lower-ranking local officials, were charged with aiding and abetting the crimes alleged in the charging instruments, by virtue of, *inter alia*, their provision of identifying information about the victims, which led to their arrest, detention, torture and murder by state security forces.[375] Three of the four were convicted on this basis; and sentenced to fifteen years' imprisonment for their involvement in murder as a crime against humanity one was acquitted due to insufficient evidence.[376]

---

[372] See Chapter 2, text accompanying notes 787–788. Hussein was executed in December 2006, and is therefore no longer an accused in this second proceeding. See *infra*, note 376.

[373] In this first proceeding, Hussein was charged with the forms of responsibility set forth in subparagraphs (2)(a), (b), and (d) of Article 15, namely commission 'whether as an individual, jointly with another or through another person, regardless of whether that [other] person is criminally responsible'; ordering, soliciting, or inducing; and common-purpose liability. See *Saddam Hussein*, Case No. 1/1st Criminal/ 2005, Accusation Document, 15 May 2006, available at http://www.law.case.edu/saddamtrial/ documents/20060515_indictment_trans_saddam_hussein.pdf ('*Hussein* Charging Instrument'), pp. 3–4.

[374] See *Barzan Ibrahim Al-Hasan*, Case No. 1/1st Criminal/2005, Accusation Document, 15 May 2006, available at http://www.law.case.edu/saddamtrial/documents/20060515_indictment_trans_barzan_ibrahim.pdf, p. 3; *Taha Yasin Ramadan*, Case No. 1/1st Criminal/2005, Accusation Document, 15 May 2006, available at http://www.law.case.edu/saddamtrial/documents/20060515_indictment_trans_taha_yasin_ramadan.pdf, p. 3; *Awad al-Bandar*, Case No. 1/1st Criminal/2005, Accusation Document, 15 May 2006, available at http://www.law.case.edu/saddamtrial/documents/20060515_indictment_trans_awad_al-bandar.pdf, p. 3.

[375] See, e.g., *Ali Dayih Ali*, Case No. 1/1st Criminal/2005, Accusation Document, 15 May 2006, available at http://www.law.case.edu/saddamtrial/documents/20060515_indictment_trans_ali_dayih.pdf, pp. 1, 3. The charging instruments for the other three accused, Mizhar Abdullah Ruwayyid, Abdullah Kazim Ruwayyid, and Mohammed Azawi Ali, are available at http://www.law.case.edu/saddamtrial/ content.asp?id = 9.

[376] See Case No. 1/9 1st/2005, Judgement, 22 November 2006 ('Dujail Judgement') (English translation issued 4 December 2006), Part VI, pp. 21, 35–36, 47–48, 50–51 (convicting and sentencing all except Mohammed Azawi Ali). Three of the four high-ranking accused – Hussein; Barzan Ibrahim Al-Hassan, his half-brother and former head of the Intelligence Service (also known as Barzan Ibrahim al-Tikriti); and Awad Hamad Al-Bandar, former chief judge of the Iraqi Revolutionary Court – were sentenced to death by hanging as punishment for their roles in murder as a crime against humanity; the fourth, Taha Yasin Ramadan, was sentenced to life imprisonment. See *ibid.*, p. 51; see also *ibid.*, pp. 51–52 (pronouncing the lesser sentences also imposed for other crimes). The death sentences were carried out on 30 December 2006 and 15 January 2007. See BBC News, 'Saddam Hussein executed in Iraq', 30 December 2006, available at http://news.bbc.co.uk/2/hi/middle_east/6218485.stm; John F. Burns, 'Two Hussein Allies Are Hanged; One Is Decapitated', *New York Times*, 15 January 2007, available at http://www.nytimes. com/2007/01/15/world/middleeast/16iraqcnd.html?ex = 1169614800&en = 75fe7d64a9f1ada7&ei = 5070.

4.6 Conclusion

As a form of responsibility, aiding and abetting has been applied in a wide variety of factual circumstances and, importantly, to a diverse range of accused, including political[377] and military[378] superiors of varying seniority; detention-facility wardens;[379] miscellaneous participants in group criminality;[380] suppliers of weapons and equipment;[381] and enthusiastic onlookers.[382] This diversity of application is likely due not only to the fact that the mental elements required for aiding and abetting liability are more relaxed than those required for other forms of responsibility, but also that the requisite physical elements are also quite broad, encompassing a wide range of activities. As a result, aiding and abetting has been employed very frequently in the *ad hoc* Tribunals, and will probably continue to play an important role in international criminal adjudication, even as the cases brought involve accused increasingly senior in rank.[383] Complicity in genocide, by contrast, has been discussed in the *ad hoc*

---

[377] See, e.g., *Brđanin* Trial Judgement, *supra* note 2, paras. 396, 469, 473–476, 532 (finding former Bosnian Serb political leader in the Autonomous Region of Krajina guilty of aiding and abetting wilful killing as a grave breach of the Geneva Conventions, as part of a scheme to manipulate the balance of power between Bosnian Serbs and non-Serbs in Krajina); *Prosecutor* v. *Gacumbitsi*, Case No. ICTR-2001-64-T, Judgement, 14 June 2004, para. 288 (finding former *bourgmestre* of Rusomo commune of Rwanda guilty of aiding and abetting the killing of members of the Tutsi ethnic group, as part of a scheme to perpetrate genocide).

[378] See, e.g., *Krstić* Appeal Judgement, *supra* note 9, paras. 138–144 (finding former Commander of the Drina Corps of the Bosnian Serb Army guilty of aiding and abetting the genocide of Bosnian Muslims in Srebrenica); *Blagojević and Jokić* Trial Judgement, *supra* note 7, paras. 770, 772 (convicting former Chief of Engineering of the Zvornik Brigade of the Bosnian Serb Army of aiding and abetting murder as a violation of the laws or customs of war and as a crime against humanity through 'co-ordinating, sending and monitoring the deployment of Zvornik Brigade resources and equipment to the mass execution sites' around Srebrenica, with knowledge that these actions assisted the commission of murder); *Naletilić and Martinović* Trial Judgement, *supra* note 150, paras. 507, 511 (convicting Naletilić, the leader of the Bosnian Croat paramilitary group known as the Convicts' Battalion, of aiding and abetting murder as a violation of the laws or customs of war and as a crime against humanity).

[379] See, e.g., *Aleksovski* Trial Judgement, *supra* note 151, paras. 228–229 and p. 92 (finding former prison warden guilty of aiding and abetting outrages upon personal dignity for violence and degrading treatment perpetrated against Muslim detainees at his prison); *Krnojelac* Trial Judgement, *supra* note 153, para. 171 (finding former prison warden guilty of aiding and abetting inhumane acts as a crime against humanity and cruel treatment as a violation of the laws or customs of war for contributing to the perpetuation of non-Serb detainees' deplorable living conditions).

[380] See, e.g., *Vasiljević* Appeal Judgement, *supra* note 103, paras. 133–134, 143 (finding a member of a paramilitary group guilty of aiding and abetting murder as a violation of the laws or customs of war and as a crime against humanity, and of inhumane acts as a crime against humanity, for his assistance in the killing of seven Muslim men).

[381] See, e.g., *Rutaganda* Trial Judgement, *supra* note 10, paras. 385, 386 (finding the accused, a businessman, guilty of aiding and abetting genocide for personally distributing firearms and machetes to Interahamwe assailants that were then used in the killing of Tutsis).

[382] See, e.g., *Furundžija* Trial Judgement, *supra* note 139, paras. 270–275 (finding the accused guilty of aiding and abetting outrages upon personal dignity as a violation of the laws or customs of war for interrogating a victim while his associate raped her); *Niyitegeka* Trial Judgement, *supra* note 60, paras. 461–462 (finding the accused guilty of aiding and abetting inhumane acts as a crime against humanity for rejoicing while a prominent Tutsi was killed and further defiled after his death).

[383] But see *supra*, text accompanying notes 334, 373–376 (ICC and SICT not yet charging accused, or not charging the most senior accused with aiding and abetting).

jurisprudence on very few occasions.[384] Convictions entered pursuant to complicity in genocide have been much rarer, and they are likely to remain that way throughout the remainder of the life of the ICTY and ICTR. As discussed above, in the wake of the *Krstić* Appeals Chamber's holding that the forms of responsibility in Article 7/6(1) may be read into Article 4/2(3) – thus unequivocally permitting a conviction for aiding and abetting genocide[385] – the prosecution has amended at least two relevant indictments to remove charges of complicity in genocide, relying instead on charges of aiding and abetting genocide to capture the accused's criminality.[386] This approach seems eminently sensible, and promises to bring the *ad hoc* jurisprudence in line with that anticipated for the ICC.

The *Krstić* line of authority is based, in significant part, on the belief that all provisions in the Tribunal's Statutes must be given effect, and that it would have been inappropriate to declare that the wholesale inclusion of the text of Article III of the Genocide Convention in Article 4/2(3) was a drafting error. The drafters of the Rome Statute were able to avoid this interpretational morass by relying almost exclusively on the existing forms of responsibility and other provisions on inchoate offences to capture the 'punishable acts' of Article III. The ICC approach may have been a minor milestone in the developing sophistication of international criminal law, not only because it treats the crime of genocide in a manner that is more rationalised and more easily applied in real cases, but also because it recognises the limitations of using instruments, such as the Genocide Convention, that were never intended as criminal codes. It is unfortunate, therefore, that the two most recent attempts to codify crimes and forms of responsibility within the jurisdiction of a court or tribunal empowered to hear international criminal cases – the ECCC and the SICT – have repeated the error of the *ad hoc* Statutes, by including 'punishable acts' in their respective provisions on genocide, notwithstanding the adoption of the ICC model for all the other forms of responsibility. It may be hoped, however, that they will also follow the lead of the *ad hoc* Prosecutors, and opt for a solution grounded in practicality to the problem created by their governing legal instruments.

---

[384] See *supra* text accompanying notes 59–67.   [385] See *supra* text accompanying notes 71–73, 100–102.
[386] See *supra* note 129 and accompanying text.

5

Planning, instigating and ordering

CONTENTS

Article 7(1) of the ICTR Statute and Article 6(1) of the ICTR Statute ('Article 7/6(1)') provide for the imposition of liability on persons who plan, instigate, or order crimes within the jurisdiction of the Tribunals in the following terms:

A person who planned, instigated, ordered, committed or otherwise aided and abetted in the planning, preparation or execution of a crime referred to in ... the present Statute, shall be individually responsible for the crime.[1]

Planning, instigating and ordering, as defined in the jurisprudence of the *ad hoc* Tribunals, have very similar elements; indeed, their respective mental elements are identical.[2] Unlike joint criminal enterprise (JCE), superior responsibility, complicity in genocide, or even aiding and abetting, these forms of responsibility do not appear to have presented major interpretational or definitional difficulties to the chambers of the *ad hoc* Tribunals, and their elements have undergone relatively little alteration since they were solidified in the *Akayesu* and *Blaškić* Trial Judgements.

This chapter begins by discussing the evolution of the elements of planning, instigating and ordering from this early jurisprudence to the most recent judgements, with particular focus on the ICTY Appeals Chamber's affirmation that these forms of responsibility have two alternative mental elements: 'direct intent', or that the accused intended that the crime planned, instigated, or ordered be committed; and 'indirect intent', or that the accused was aware of the substantial likelihood that a crime would be committed as a consequence of his conduct.[3] Sections 5.2, 5.3 and 5.4 then analyse, respectively, the *ad hoc* Tribunals' definition and application of the elements of planning, instigating and ordering. As in the previous chapters of this book, Section 5.5 explores the treatment of these three forms of accomplice liability in other international criminal jurisdictions.

5.1 Evolution of the elements of planning, instigating and ordering in the jurisprudence of the *ad hoc* tribunals

The elements of planning, instigating and ordering have been defined and developed in a largely parallel fashion since the earliest judgements of the *ad hoc* Tribunals. *Tadić*, the first trial judgement of the ICTY, took on the task of ascertaining, in respect of an accused who does not physically perpetrate the crime in question, what conduct would 'sufficiently connect ... [him] to the crime such that he can be found criminally culpable pursuant to the Statute'.[4]

---

[1] Statute of the International Criminal Tribunal for the Prosecution of Persons Responsible for Serious Violations of International Humanitarian Law Committed in the Territory of the former Yugoslavia since 1991, (1993) 32 ILM 1159, as amended by Security Council Resolution 1660 of 28 February 2006, Art. 7(1); Statute of the International Criminal Tribunal for Rwanda, (1994) 33 ILM 1602, as amended by Security Council Resolution 1534 of 26 March 2004, Art. 6(1).

[2] See *infra* text accompanying notes 47–51.   [3] See *infra* text accompanying notes 21–60.

[4] *Prosecutor* v. *Tadić*, Case No. IT-94-1-T, Opinion and Judgement, 7 May 1997 ('*Tadić* Trial Judgement', para. 673.

Upon examining various international instruments[5] and post-Second World War judgements,[6] the Trial Chamber reached the following conclusion, apparently applicable to all forms of responsibility in Article 7(1) of the ICTY Statute except physical commission:

> While the [post-Second World War] judgments generally failed to discuss in detail the criteria upon which guilt was determined, a clear pattern does emerge upon an examination of the relevant cases. First, there is a requirement of intent, which involves awareness of the act of participation coupled with a conscious decision to participate by planning, instigating, ordering, committing or otherwise aiding and abetting in the commission of a crime. Second, the prosecution must prove that there was participation in that the conduct of the accused contributed to the commission of the illegal act.[7]

The Chamber did not give differentiated treatment to planning, instigating and ordering, and, indeed, turned its attention to aiding and abetting directly after performing its analysis of purported sources of customary international law.[8] The next two ICTY trial judgements to discuss the elements of planning, instigating and ordering – *Čelebići* in November 1998 and *Aleksovski* in July 1999 – endorsed the *Tadić* definition as reflective of custom.[9] Like *Tadić*, neither provided further elaboration on the elements of planning, instigating and ordering, and focused instead on aiding and abetting.[10]

The Trial Chamber in the first ICTR judgement – *Akayesu* in September 1998 – also acknowledged *Tadić*'s single set of elements for all non-commission forms of responsibility in Article 7/6(1).[11] It opted for a more nuanced

---

[5] See *ibid.*, paras. 663–664, 666 (citing Treaty of Versailles), opened for signature 28 June 1919, 11 *Martens Nouveau Recueil* 323, Art. 229; Charter of the International Military Tribunal for the Trial of the Major War Criminals, appended to Agreement for the Prosecution and Punishment of Major War Criminals of the European Axis, 8 August 1945, 59 Stat. 1544, as amended; Protocol to Agreement and Charter, 6 October 1945, Art. 6; Control Council Law No. 10, Art. II(2); Convention Against Torture and Other Cruel, Inhuman or Degrading Treatment or Punishment, opened for signature 4 February 1985, G. A. Res. 39/46 (1984), reprinted in 23 ILM 1027 (1984), as modified, 24 ILM 535 (1985), Art. 4(1); International Convention on the Suppression and Punishment of the Crime of Apartheid, opened for signature 30 November 1973, G. A. Res. 3068 (XXVIII) (1973), Art. III); *ibid.*, para. 688 (analysing the Draft Code of Crimes Against the Peace and Security of Mankind (1996), in Report of the International Law Commission on the Work of Its Forty-eighth Session, UN Doc. A/51/10 (1996), Arts. 2(3), 24).

[6] See *ibid.*, paras. 675–687. [7] *Ibid.*, para. 674. [8] *Ibid.*, paras. 689–692.

[9] See *Prosecutor* v. *Delalić, Mucić, Delić and Landžo*, Case No. IT-96-21-T, Judgement, 16 November 1998 ('*Čelebići* Trial Judgement'), paras. 325–326; *Prosecutor* v. *Aleksovski*, Case No. IT-95-14/1-T, Judgement, 25 June 1999 ('*Aleksovski* Trial Judgement'), paras. 60–61. Both Chambers drew on *Tadić*'s holding that an accused aider and abettor's contribution must have a 'direct and substantial effect on the commission of the illegal act', *Tadić* Trial Judgement, *supra* note 4, para. 689, and appear to have extended it to planning, instigating, and ordering. See *Čelebići* Trial Judgement, *supra*, para. 326; *Aleksovski* Trial Judgement, *supra*, para. 61.

[10] See *Čelebići* Trial Judgement, *supra* note 9, paras. 327–328; *Aleksovski* Trial Judgement, *supra* note 9, paras. 62–65. As mentioned in Chapter 2, *Čelebići* also made a prototypical reference – the first in the *ad hoc* jurisprudence – to the common-purpose doctrine. See *Čelebići* Trial Judgement, *supra* note 9, para. 328; see also Chapter 2, note 8.

[11] *Prosecutor* v. *Akayesu*, Case No. ICTR-96-4-T, Judgement, 2 September 1998 ('*Akayesu* Trial Judgement'), para. 477.

approach to the physical elements of planning, instigating and ordering, although it maintained a unitary mental element: '[T]he forms of participation referred to in Article 6(1) [of the ICTR Statute] cannot render their perpetrator criminally liable where he did not act knowingly, and even where he should have had such knowledge.'[12] The *Akayesu* Chamber defined planning as 'implying that one or several persons contemplate designing the commission of a crime at both the preparatory and execution phases'.[13] Instigation 'involves prompting another to commit an offence'.[14] The Chamber drew a distinction between instigation as a form of responsibility in Article 7/6(1) and 'direct and public incitement to commit genocide', an inchoate crime in Article 2(3)(c) of the ICTR Statute: instigation 'is punishable only where it leads to the actual commission of an offence desired by the instigator'.[15] The Chamber set forth two unique elements for ordering: first, '[o]rdering implies a superior-subordinate relationship between the person giving the order and the one executing it'; and second, 'the person in a position of authority uses it to convince another to commit an offence'.[16] With the exception of instigation, whose definition appears to have been gleaned from the dictionary,[17] no authority is cited as support for these precise physical elements. Nevertheless, with some relatively minor alterations,[18] *Akayesu's* physical elements have been consistently endorsed by the chambers of both *ad hoc* Tribunals[19] since their

---

[12] *Ibid.*, para. 479.   [13] *Ibid.*, para. 480.   [14] *Ibid.*, para. 482.

[15] *Ibid.* See Chapter 4, text accompanying notes 2–58, for a discussion of the inchoate genocide-related crimes in the *ad hoc* Statutes.

[16] *Akayesu* Trial Judgement, *supra* note 11, para. 483.   [17] See *ibid.*, para. 481 n. 82.

[18] See, e.g., *Prosecutor v. Strugar*, Case No. IT-01-42-T, Judgement, 31 January 2005 ('*Strugar* Trial Judgement'), para. 332 (holding that a 'causal link' must be shown 'between the act of ordering and the physical perpetration of a crime', but that the order need not be the but-for cause of the crime); *Prosecutor v. Ndindabahizi*, Case No. ICTR-2001-71-I, Judgement and Sentence, 15 July 2004 ('*Ndindabahizi* Trial Judgement'), para. 456 (clarifying that instigation may take place 'verbally or by other means of communication'); *Prosecutor v. Galić*, Case No. IT-98-29-T, Judgement and Opinion, 5 December 2003 ('*Galić* Trial Judgement'), para. 169 (holding that not only instigating, but also planning and ordering, may be effected by means of a culpable omission); *Prosecutor v. Stakić*, Case No. IT-97-24-T, Judgement, 31 July 2003 ('*Stakić* Trial Judgement'), para. 443 (holding that, while an accused who physically perpetrates a crime cannot also be convicted for planning it, his involvement in the planning can be considered as an aggravating factor in sentencing); *ibid.*, para. 445 (holding that an accused may not be held liable for ordering a crime and for physically perpetrating that same crime); *Prosecutor v. Bagilishema*, Case No. ICTR-95-1A-T, Judgement, 7 June 2001 ('*Bagilishema* Trial Judgement'), para. 30 (holding that an accused may incur liability not only if he formulates a criminal plan, but also if he 'endors[es] a plan proposed by another'); *Prosecutor v. Kordić and Čerkez*, Case No. IT-95-14/2-T, Judgement, 26 February 2001 ('*Kordić and Čerkez* Trial Judgement'), paras. 386–387 (holding that an accused may not be held liable for planning a crime and for physically perpetrating that same crime, and that an accused's instigation need not be the but-for cause of the instigated crime).

[19] See *Prosecutor v. Ntagerura, Bagambiki and Imanishimwe*, Case No. ICTR-99-46-A, Judgement, 7 July 2006 ('*Ntagerura et al.* Appeal Judgement'); para. 365 (ordering only); *Prosecutor v. Kamuhanda*, Case No. ICTR-99-54A-A, Judgement, 19 September 2005 ('*Kamuhanda* Appeal Judgement'); paras. 75–76 (ordering only); *Prosecutor v. Semanza*, Case No. ICTR-97-20 A, Judgement ('*Semanza* Appeal Judgement'), paras. 361, 363 (ordering only); *Prosecutor v. Kordić and Čerkez*, Case No. IT-95-14/2-A, Judgement, 17 December 2004 ('*Kordić and Čerkez* Appeal Judgement'), paras. 26–28; *Prosecutor v. Muvunyi*, Case No. ICTR-00-55A-T, Judgement and Sentence ('*Muvunyi* Trial Judgement'),

importation into ICTY jurisprudence in the March 2000 *Blaškić* Trial Judgement.[20]

Blaškić expounded a mental element common to planning, instigating and ordering different from that set forth in previous jurisprudence: '[P]roof is required that whoever planned, instigated or ordered the commission of a crime possessed the criminal intent, that is, that he directly or indirectly intended that the crime in question be committed.'[21] The Chamber provided no explanation of what it meant by 'direct or indirect intent' in this portion of the judgement, and instead scattered ostensible definitions of indirect intent throughout its factual findings. As noted by the Appeals Chamber, these formulations are often inconsistent with one another,[22] some defining what would appear to be a recklessness standard,[23] and at least one a negligence

paras. 464–468 (instigating and ordering only); *Prosecutor v. Mpambara*, Case No. ICTR-01-65-T, Judgement, 11 September 2006 ('*Mpambara* Trial Judgement'), paras. 18–20; *Prosecutor v. Orić*, Case No. IT-03-68-T, Judgement, 30 June 2006 ('*Orić* Trial Judgement'), paras. 270–273 (instigating only); *Prosecutor v. Limaj, Bala and Musliu*, Case No. IT-03-66-T, Judgement, 30 November 2005 ('*Limaj et al.* Trial Judgement'), paras. 513–515; *Strugar* Trial Judgement, *supra* note 18, paras. 331–332 (ordering only); *Ndindabahizi* Trial Judgement, *supra* note 18, para. 456 (instigation only); *Prosecutor v. Brđanin*, Case No. IT-99-36-T, Judgement, 1 September 2004 ('*Brđanin* Trial Judgement'), paras. 268–270; *Prosecutor v. Gacumbitsi*, Case No. ICTR-2001-64-T, Judgement, 17 June 2004 ('*Gacumbitsi* Trial Judgement'), para. 271 (planning); *ibid.*, para. 279 (instigating); *ibid.*, para. 281 (ordering); *Galić* Trial Judgement, *supra* note 18, para. 168; *Prosecutor v. Kajelijeli*, Case No. ICTR-98-44A-T, Judgement and Sentence, 1 December 2003 ('*Kajelijeli* Trial Judgement'), paras. 761–763; *Stakić* Trial Judgement, *supra* note 18, paras. 442–443 (planning and ordering only); *Prosecutor v. Semanza*, Case No. ICTR-97-20-T, Judgement and Sentence, 15 May 2003 ('*Semanza* Trial Judgement'), paras. 380–382; *Prosecutor v. Naletilić and Martinović*, Case No. IT-98-34-T, Judgement, 31 March 2003 ('*Naletilić and Martinović* Trial Judgement'), paras. 59–61; *Prosecutor v. Kamuhanda*, Case No. ICTR-99-54-T, Judgement and Sentence, 22 January 2003 ('*Kamuhanda* Trial Judgement'), paras. 592–594; *Prosecutor v. Kvočka, Kos, Radić, Žigić and Prcać*, Case No. IT-98-30/1-T, Judgement, 2 November 2001 ('*Kvočka et al.* Trial Judgement'), paras. 243, 250 (instigating only); *Prosecutor v. Krstić*, Case No. IT-98-33-T, Judgement, 2 August 2001 ('*Krstić* Trial Judgement'), para. 601; *Bagilishema* Trial Judgement, *supra* note 18, para. 30; *Kordić and Čerkez* Trial Judgement, *supra* note 18, paras. 386–388; *Prosecutor v. Musema*, Case No. ICTR-96-13-T, Judgement and Sentence, 27 January 2000 ('*Musema* Trial Judgement'), paras. 119–121; *Prosecutor v. Rutaganda*, Case No. ICTR-96-3-T, Judgement, 6 December 1999 ('*Rutaganda* Trial Judgement'), paras. 37–39; *Prosecutor v. Kayishema and Ruzindana*, Case No. ICTR-95-1-T, Judgement, 21 May 1999 ('*Kayishema and Ruzindana* Trial Judgement'), para. 199.

20 See *Prosecutor v. Blaškić*, Case No. IT-95-14-T, Judgement, 3 March 2000 ('*Blaškić* Trial Judgement'), paras. 279–281 (largely quoting the language of *Akayesu* setting forth the physical elements of planning, instigating and ordering). The Chamber also introduced several innovations into these elements. For instigating, the Chamber held that the physical element may be fulfilled through 'both acts and omissions', and that there must be a 'causal relationship between the instigation and the physical perpetration of the crime'. *Ibid.*, para. 280 (citing the *Concise Oxford Dictionary* (10th edn 1999), p. 734). For ordering, '[i]t is not necessary that an order be given in writing or in any particular form'; the order may be explicit or implicit; it need not have been given by the accused directly to the physical perpetrator; and the order's illegality need not have been 'apparent on its face'. *Ibid.*, paras. 281–282.
21 *Ibid.*, para. 278 (emphasis added) (citing no authority).
22 See *Prosecutor v. Blaškić*, Case No. IT-95-14-A, Judgement, 29 July 2004 ('*Blaškić* Appeal Judgement'), para. 40.
23 See, e.g., *Blaškić* Trial Judgement, *supra* note 20, para. 592 ('[B]y giving orders to the Military Police in April 1993, when he knew full well that there were criminals in its ranks, the accused intentionally took the risk that very violent crimes would result from their participation in the offensives.'); *ibid.*, para. 653 ('[E]ven though General Blaškić did not explicitly order the expulsion and killing of the civilian Muslim populations, he deliberately ran the risk of making them their property the primary targets of the "sealing off" and offensives launched on 18 April 1993.'); *ibid.*, para. 738 ('[B]y ordering the forced

348   *Forms of responsibility in international criminal law*

standard.[24] The *Blaškić* Appeals Chamber's analysis of the mental element of ordering is discussed below.[25]

The next ICTY trial chamber to consider planning, instigating and ordering – *Kordić and Čerkez* in February 2001 – endorsed *Blaškić*'s direct and indirect intent dichotomy, again without elaboration; strangely, however, in the next paragraph it held that instigating requires direct intent, apparently without realising the contradiction.[26] Subsequent chambers provided insight into what 'direct intent' and 'indirect intent' may entail, although their holdings were not uniform. The ICTR Trial Chamber in the June 2001 *Bagilishema* Judgement held that an accused charged with planning, instigating, or ordering must have 'possessed criminal intent, that is, that he or she intended that the crime be committed';[27] the Chamber did not allow for the possibility that liability might ensue where the accused merely knows that the crime will possibly or probably be committed as a result of his conduct. The ICTY Trial Chamber in the November 2001 *Kvočka* Judgement appears to have defined both direct and indirect intent in respect of instigation,[28] although it did not cite *Blaškić* or *Kordić and Čerkez* as authorities: 'The required *mens rea* is that the accused intended to provoke or induce the commission of the crime, or was aware of the substantial likelihood that the commission of a crime would be a probable consequence of his acts.'[29] The July 2003 *Stakić* Trial Judgement, citing

labour Blaškić knowingly took the risk that his solders might commit violent acts against vulnerable detainees[.]'); *ibid.*, para. 741 ('[A]lthough General Blaškić did not order that hostages be taken, it is inconceivable that as commander he did not order the defence of the town where his headquarters were located. Blaškić deliberately ran the risk that many detainees might be taken hostage for this purpose.').

[24] See, e.g., *ibid.*, para. 474 ('[A]ny person who, in ordering an act, knows that there is a risk of crimes being committed and accepts that risk, shows the degree of intention necessary (recklessness) so as to incur responsibility for having ordered, planned, or incited the commi[ssion] of the crimes.').

[25] See *infra* text accompanying notes 31–46.

[26] Compare *Kordić and Čerkez* Trial Judgement, *supra* note 18, para. 386 ('[A]n accused will only be held responsible for planning, instigating or ordering a crime if he directly or indirectly intended that the crime be committed.'), with *ibid.*, para. 387 ('[I]t must be provided that the accused directly intended to provoke the commission of the crime.').

[27] *Bagilishema* Trial Judgement, *supra* note 18, para. 31.

[28] One paragraph earlier, the Trial Chamber listed only the indirect-alternative as applicable to all 'forms of criminal participation under Article 7(1)' – that is, 'the accused acted in the awareness of the substantial likelihood that a criminal act or omission would occur as a consequence of his conduct.' *Kvočka et al.* Trial Judgement, *supra* note 19, para. 251. The Trial Chamber in the December 2003 *Galić* Judgement likewise listed only indirect intent, also holding that it applies to all Article 7/6(1) forms of responsibility. *Galić* Trial Judgement, *supra* note 18, para. 172.

[29] *Kvočka et al.* Trial Judgement, *supra* note 19, para. 252. The Trial Chamber cited *Akayesu* Trial Judgement, *supra* note 11, para. 482 as its only supporting authority for this proposition. Yet the cited paragraph of *Akayesu* contains no statement whatsoever concerning the requisite mental element of instigating or any other form of responsibility. *Kvočka*'s standard in respect of instigating was later endorsed in the March 2003 *Naletilić and Martinović* Trial Judgement, which set forth the physical elements of all three forms of responsibility but omitted to expound a mental element for planning and ordering. See *Naletilić and Martinović* Trial Judgement, *supra* note 19, paras. 59–61.

Blaškić, provided a similar definition of direct and indirect intent to order, although it propounded the two species of intent as cumulative, not alternative: 'The person "ordering" must have the required *mens rea* for the crime with which he is charged and must have been aware of the substantial likelihood that the crime committed would be the consequence when executing or otherwise furthering the implementation of the order.'[30]

In two judgements in 2004, the ICTY Appeals Chamber established the authoritative definitions of direct and indirect intent. The Appeals Chamber in *Blaškić* addressed the mental element of ordering, declining to consider the parties' arguments in relation to planning and instigating because the Trial Chamber had not convicted the accused pursuant to either of those two forms of responsibility.[31] The Chamber observed that it had not yet 'had the occasion to pronounce on' the mental element of ordering,[32] and turned to several national jurisdictions to determine 'whether a standard of *mens rea* that is lower than direct intent may apply in relation to ordering … and if so, how it should be defined'.[33] Upon examining the recklessness provision of the American Law Institute's Model Penal Code,[34] a single House of Lords opinion,[35] and one judgement of the Australian High Court,[36] the Appeals Chamber drew the general conclusion that, '[i]n common law systems, the *mens rea* of recklessness is sufficient to ground liability for serious crimes such as murder or manslaughter'.[37] The Chamber defined recklessness as,

incorporat[ing] the awareness of a risk that the result or consequence will occur or will probably occur, and the risk must be unjustifiable or unreasonable. The mere possibility of a risk that a crime or crimes will occur as a result of the actor's conduct generally does not suffice to ground criminal responsibility.[38]

---

[30] *Stakić* Trial Judgement, *supra* note 18, para. 445 (citing *Blaškić* Trial Judgement, *supra* note 20, para. 278). Although *Stakić* defined the physical elements of planning as well as ordering, it did not define a mental element for planning. See *ibid.*, para. 443. In spite of these developments at the ICTY, several ICTR trial judgements from 2003 and 2004 continued to set forth what was essentially a repetition of *Akayesu*'s unitary mental element applicable to planning, instigating, ordering, and aiding and abetting. See *Kamuhanda* Trial Judgement, *supra* note 19, para. 599 (holding that the accused must 'act[ ] with the knowledge that his or her act(s) assist in the commission of the crime by the actual perpetrator(s)'); *Kajelijeli* Trial Judgement, *supra* note 19, para. 768 (identical language to *Kamuhanda*); *Semanza* Trial Judgement, *supra* note 19, para. 388 ('[T]he *mens rea* requirement will be satisfied where an individual acts intentionally and with the awareness that he is influencing or assisting the principal perpetrator to commit the crime.').
[31] *Blaškić* Appeal Judgement, *supra* note 22, para. 32.   [32] *Ibid.*, para. 33.   [33] *Ibid.*, para. 32.
[34] American Law Institute, *Model Penal Code* (1962), Sec. 2.02(c).
[35] *R.* v. *G. and Another*, [2004] 1 A.C. 1034, 1057 (opinion of Lord Bingham).
[36] *R.* v. *Crabbe*, (1985) 58 ALR 417, 469.   [37] *Blaškić* Appeal Judgement, *supra* note 22, para. 34.
[38] *Ibid.*, para. 38.

The Chamber also invoked a treatise on French criminal law,[39] a commentary on the Italian Penal Code,[40] and a decision of the German Bundesgerichtshof[41] to ascertain that, '[i]n civil law systems, the concept of *dolus eventualis* may constitute the requisite *mens rea* for crimes'.[42] From the sources cited by the Chamber, civil-law *dolus eventualis* seems to amount to knowledge on the part of the accused of the mere possibility that a crime will occur because of his conduct, and is thus different from common-law recklessness requiring awareness that the crime will occur or will probably occur.[43]

It is questionable whether these particular sources – all of which relate to the required mental state in respect of the commission of crimes, not other forms of responsibility – constitute proper authority for divining the mental element of ordering in international criminal law. While it did not explicitly state that it was dispensing with civil-law *dolus eventualis* in favour of common-law recklessness, the Appeals Chamber's ultimate definition of indirect intent drew heavily on the latter to the exclusion of the former by emphasising the need for the accused to be aware of the 'substantial like-lihood' that the crime will occur:

[I]t appears that under the Trial Chamber's standard, any military commander who issues an order would be criminally responsible, because there is always a possibility that violations could occur. The Appeals Chamber considers that an awareness of a higher likelihood of risk and a volitional element must be incorporated in the legal standard[44] ... The Appeals Chamber therefore holds that a person who orders an act or omission with the awareness of the substantial likelihood that a crime will be committed in the execution of that order, has the requisite *mens rea* for establishing liability under Article 7(1) pursuant to ordering. Ordering with such awareness has to be regarded as accepting that crime.[45]

Remarkably, even though this definition of indirect intent is virtually identical to those of the *Kvočka* and *Stakić* Trial Chambers,[46] nowhere did the Appeals Chamber acknowledge these ICTY precedents.

Noting that, unlike *Blaškić*, the *Kordić and Čerkez* Trial Chamber had convicted Kordić not only for ordering crimes, but also for planning and

---

[39] Francis Le Gunehec, 'Elément moral de l'infraction', in Marie-Françoise Homassel (ed.), 1 *Juris-Classeur Pénal Code* (2002), fascicule 20 (15 July 2002), pp. 11–12.

[40] Alberto Crespi, Giuseppe Zuccalà, and Frederico Stella, *Commentario breve al Codice penale* (1986), p. 103.

[41] BGHSt 36, 1–20.   [42] *Blaškić* Appeal Judgement, *supra* note 22, para. 39.

[43] See also *ibid.*, para. 33 (drawing a distinction between ordering and the third category of JCE, as liability for the latter may attach to the accused 'even where he only knew that the perpetration of such a crime was merely a possible consequence, rather than substantially likely to occur'). See also Chapter 2, text accompanying notes 389–454 (discussing in detail the jurisprudence on this aspect of the mental element of the third category); *ibid.*, text accompanying note 433 (discussing this holding of the *Blaškić* Appeals Chamber).

[44] *Blaškić* Appeal Judgement, *supra* note 22, para. 41.   [45] *Ibid.*, para. 42.

[46] See *supra* text accompanying notes 29–30.

instigating them,[47] the Appeals Chamber in the December 2004 *Kordić and Čerkez* Judgement extended its definition of the mental element for ordering to planning and instigating. In a very brief discussion that did not attempt an analysis of past Tribunal jurisprudence or outside sources, the Chamber held that the mental element of any of these forms of responsibility may be established by proof that the accused 'acted with direct intent in relation to his own planning, instigating, or ordering',[48] or had the awareness of the substantial likelihood that a crime would be committed 'in the execution of the order',[49] 'in the execution of the plan',[50] or as a result of the instigation.[51]

The *Blaškić* and *Kordić and Čerkez* definitions of direct and indirect intent have been generally repeated in subsequent ICTY jurisprudence,[52] and in at least one ICTR trial judgement,[53] although the trial chambers have tended to

---

[47] *Kordić and Čerkez* Appeal Judgement, *supra* note 19, para. 25.

[48] *Ibid.*, para. 29.   [49] *Ibid.*, para. 30.   [50] *Ibid.*, para. 31.

[51] *Ibid.*, para. 32. The actual language of the Appeals Chamber was as follows: 'With respect to "instigating", a person who instigates another person to commit an act or omission with the awareness of the substantial likelihood that a crime will be committed *in the execution of that instigation*, has the requisite *mens rea* for establishing responsibility under Article 7(1) of the Statute pursuant to instigating.' *Ibid.* (emphasis added). The somewhat awkward phrase 'in the execution of that instigation' was repeated by the *Limaj* Trial Chamber. See *Limaj et al.* Trial Judgement, *supra* note 19, para. 514.

[52] See, e.g., *Prosecutor v. Galić*, Case No. IT-98-29-A, Judgement, 30 November 2006 ('*Galić* Appeal Judgement'), para. 152 (ordering); *Limaj et al.* Trial Judgement, *supra* note 19, para. 513 (planning); *ibid.*, para. 514 (instigating); *ibid.*, para. 515 (ordering); *Strugar* Trial Judgement, *supra* note 18, para. 333 (ordering); *Brđanin* Trial Judgement, *supra* note 19, para. 270 (ordering). The *Orić* Trial Chamber, dealing exclusively with instigating in its June 2006 judgement, did not strictly follow the *Kordić and Čerkez* Appeals Chamber's definition of the mental element, and instead embarked on a somewhat confusing examination of 'cognitive' and 'volitional' requirements out of a professed need to provide 'further clarification' than what had been provided in previous jurisprudence. See *Orić* Trial Judgement, *supra* note 19, paras. 277–279; see also *ibid.*, para. 279 (emphasis added, footnotes removed):

[F]irst, with regard to his own conduct, the instigator must be aware of his influencing effect on the principal perpetrator to commit the crime, as well as the instigator, even if neither aiming at nor wishing so, must at least accept that the crime be committed. Second, with regard to the principal perpetrator, the instigator must be both aware of, and agree to, the intentional completion of the principal crime. Third, with regard to the volitional element of intent, the instigator, when aware that the commission of the crime will *more likely than not* result from his conduct, may be regarded as accepting its occurrence.

This third element identified by the Trial Chamber may simply be an unfortunately worded attempt to adhere to the *Kordić and Čerkez* Appeals Chamber's 'awareness of the substantial likelihood' standard for instigating.

[53] See *Muvunyi* Trial Judgement, *supra* note 19, para. 465. The *Muvunyi* Chamber's formulation of the mental element for instigating is peculiar and self-contradictory, however, articulating a requirement of direct or indirect intent cumulatively with a requirement of intention to provoke or induce the crime, or awareness of the substantial likelihood of the crime's commission:

The *mens rea* required to establish a charge of instigating a statutory crime is proof that the [a]ccused directly or indirectly intended that the crime in question be committed and that he intended to provoke or induce the commission of the crime, or was aware of the substantial likelihood that the commission of the crime would be a probable consequence of his acts.

Ibid. But see *Ntagerura et al.* Appeal Judgement, *supra* note 19, para. 365 and n. 733 (setting forth, in respect of ordering, a rather confusing definition of direct intent – 'l'élément moral … requis est établi lorsque cette personne a agi avec l'intention direct de donner l'ordre' – and merely mentioning, instead of expressly endorsing, the *Blaškić* Appeals Chamber's definition of indirect intent for ordering).

formulate direct intent in terms clearer than those employed by the Appeals Chamber.[54] The *Brđanin* Trial Chamber held that an accused instigator must have 'intended to provoke or induce the commission of the crime',[55] and an accused orderer 'must have the required *mens rea* for the crime with which he is charged'.[56] The *Strugar* Trial Chamber, dealing only with ordering, stated that 'the accused in issuing the order [must have] intended to bring about the commission of the crime'.[57] For its part, the *Limaj* Trial Chamber held that an accused planner must have 'an intent that the crime be committed';[58] an accused instigator must have 'intended to provoke or induce the commission of the crime';[59] and an accused orderer must have 'intended to bring about the commission of the crime'.[60]

In light of these clarifications, perhaps the most straightforward formulation of the two alternatives would be the following: the accused intended that the crime planned, ordered or instigated be committed, or he was aware of the substantial likelihood that the crime would be committed as a result of his conduct. No chamber of either *ad hoc* Tribunal appears to have pronounced on how these alternatives function when the accused is charged with a specific-intent crime such as genocide or persecution as a crime against humanity. In the absence of any precedent expressly setting forth some different formulation, it can probably be safely assumed that an accused planner, orderer, or instigator will bear liability for a specific-intent crime if he possesses the requisite genocidal or discriminatory intent himself, or if he is aware of the substantial likelihood that the crime committed as a result of his conduct will be committed with genocidal or discriminatory intent.[61]

In a succinct discussion of planning, instigating and ordering,[62] the *Kordić and Čerkez* Appeals Chamber essentially endorsed the physical elements expounded by the *Kordić and Čerkez* Trial Chamber, articulating them as follows:

---

[54] Bizarrely, many judgements of both *ad hoc* Tribunals – even those rendered subsequent to the *Blaškić* and *Kordić and Čerkez* Appeal Judgement – have omitted to mention any mental element at all for planning, instigating, or ordering even though they discussed one or more of these forms' physical elements. See *Muvunyi* Trial Judgement, *supra* note 19, para. 468 (September 2006; no mental element for ordering despite articulation of physical elements); *Mpambara* Trial Judgement, *supra* note 19 (September 2006); *Ndindabahizi* Trial Judgement, *supra* note 18 (July 2004); *Gacumbitsi* Trial Judgement, *supra* note 19 (June 2004); *Krstić* Trial Judgement, *supra* note 19 (August 2001); *Musema* Trial Judgement, *supra* note 19 (January 2000); *Rutaganda* Trial Judgement, *supra* note 19 (December 1999). For a discussion of the persuasive effect of ICTY Appeals Chamber jurisprudence on ICTR trial chambers, see Chapter 2, note 94.

[55] *Brđanin* Trial Judgement, *supra* note 19, para. 269.   [56] *Ibid.*, para. 270.

[57] *Strugar* Trial Judgement, *supra* note 18, para. 333.

[58] *Limaj et al.* Trial Judgement, *supra* note 19, para. 513.   [59] *Ibid.*, para. 514.   [60] *Ibid.*, para. 515.

[61] For the treatment of specific-intent crimes in relation to the other forms of responsibility, see the chart 'Comparison of required mental states, with regard to intent, for imposition of liability under each form of responsibility' in the Annex of this book.

[62] See *Kordić and Čerkez* Trial Judgement, *supra* note 18, paras. 386–388. As mentioned above, the *Kordić and Čerkez* Trial Chamber's definition of the physical elements largely reproduces, with some innovations, the elements first set forth by the ICTR Trial Chamber in *Akayesu*. See *supra* notes 18–19 and accompanying text.

The *actus reus* of 'planning' requires that one or more persons design the criminal conduct constituting one or more statutory crimes that are later perpetrated. It is sufficient to demonstrate that the planning was a factor substantially contributing to such criminal conduct.[63]

The *actus reus* of 'instigating' means to prompt another person to commit an offence. While it is not necessary to prove that the crime would not have been perpetrated without the involvement of the accused, it is sufficient to demonstrate that the instigation was a factor substantially contributing to the conduct of another person committing the crime.[64]

The *actus reus* of 'ordering' means that a person in a position of authority instructs another person to commit an offence. A formal superior-subordinate relationship between the accused and the perpetrator is not required.[65]

Although these physical elements are formulated in terms of designing, prompting, or instructing the commission of a crime or an offence, the Appeals Chamber's respective definitions of the indirect-intent mental element created an alternative physical element whereby the accused need only design, prompt, or order 'an act or omission', provided he is aware of the substantial likelihood that the physical perpetrator will commit a crime in the realisation of that act or omission.[66] The findings of the *Strugar* Trial Chamber reflect this alternative: Pavle Strugar, a general in the Yugoslav Army, ordered his troops to engage in a lawful attack on Croatian defensive positions stationed on Mount Srđ, overlooking Dubrovnik. While the Trial Chamber declined to find Strugar guilty as an orderer because he was only aware of the 'possibility' that his forces would 'resort to deliberate and indiscriminate shelling' of Dubrovnik, it clearly implied that he would have been convicted on this basis had he been aware of the substantial likelihood that criminal shelling would occur, even though he did not specifically order any criminal activities.[67]

This chapter proceeds by examining, in turn, the elements of planning, instigating and ordering – including how they have been applied in the jurisprudence of the *ad hoc* Tribunals – in light of the *Kordić and Čerkez* Appeals

---

[63] *Kordić and Čerkez* Appeal Judgement, *supra* note 19, para. 26 (footnote removed) (citing *Kordić and Čerkez* Trial Judgement, *supra* note 18, para. 386).

[64] *Ibid.*, para. 27 (footnote removed) (citing *Kordić and Čerkez* Trial Judgement, *supra* note 18, para. 387).

[65] *Ibid.*, para. 28 (footnotes removed) (citing *Kordić and Čerkez* Trial Judgement, *supra* note 18, para. 388).

[66] See *ibid.*, para. 30 (holding that 'a person who orders *an act or omission* with the awareness of the substantial likelihood that a crime will be committed in the execution of that order[] has the requisite *mens rea*') (emphasis added); *ibid.*, para. 31 (holding that 'a person who plans an *act or omission* with the awareness of the substantial likelihood that a crime will be committed in the execution of that plan[] has the requisite *mens rea*') (emphasis added); *ibid.*, para. 32 (holding that 'a person who instigates another person to commit an *act or omission* with the awareness of the substantial likelihood that a crime will be committed in the execution of that instigation[] has the requisite *mens rea*').

[67] See *Strugar* Trial Judgement, *supra* note 18, paras. 346–347. See also *Galić* Appeal Judgement, *supra* note 52, para. 177 n. 507 (reiterating that, where the accused instructs another not to perform an act, liability for ordering may ensue as long as the accused is aware of the substantial likelihood that such omission will amount to the commission of a crime).

Chamber's creation of an alternative physical element to accompany the indirect-intent mental element. That is, liability may ensue where the accused designs, prompts or instructs the commission of a crime with the intent that the crime be committed. Alternatively, liability may ensue where the accused designs, prompts, or instructs certain conduct – or, in the words of the Appeals Chamber, an 'act or omission'[68] – with the awareness of the substantial likelihood that a crime will be committed in carrying out that conduct.

5.2 Elements of planning

5.2.1 Design of conduct with intent or awareness of substantial likelihood

The accused designed criminal conduct with the intent that a crime be committed; or he designed an act or omission, aware of the substantial likelihood that a crime would be committed in the realisation of that act or omission

An accused may incur liability for planning in two alternative scenarios: (1) where he designs criminal conduct[69] with the intent that a crime be committed in the execution of that design;[70] or (2) where he designs an act or omission aware of the substantial likelihood that a crime will be committed in the realisation of that act or omission.[71]

---

[68] *Kordić and Čerkez* Appeal Judgement, *supra* note 19, paras. 30–32 (repeating the term 'act or omission' for all three forms of responsibility).

[69] *Kordić and Čerkez* Appeal Judgement, *supra* note 19, para. 26 (holding that 'one or more persons [must] design criminal conduct constituting one or more statutory crimes'); *Mpambara* Trial Judgement, *supra* note 19, para. 20; *Limaj et al.* Trial Judgement, *supra* note 19, para. 513; *Brđanin* Trial Judgement, *supra* note 19, para. 268; *Kamuhanda* Trial Judgement, *supra* note 19, para. 592; *Galić* Trial Judgement, *supra* note 18, para. 168; *Kajelijeli* Trial Judgement, *supra* note 19, para. 761; *Stakić* Trial Judgement, *supra* note 18, para. 443; *Semanza* Trial Judgement, *supra* note 19, para. 380 (citing the definition of 'plan' in *Black's Law Dictionary* (6th edn 1990), p. 1150, and holding that '"planning" envisions one or more persons formulating a method of design or action, procedure, or arrangement for the accomplishment of a particular crime'.); *Naletilić and Martinović* Trial Judgement, *supra* note 19, para. 59; *Krstić* Trial Judgement, *supra* note 19, para. 601; *Kordić and Čerkez* Trial Judgement, *supra* note 18, para. 386; *Blaškić* Trial Judgement, *supra* note 20, para. 278; *Rutaganda* Trial Judgement, *supra* note 19, para. 37; *Akayesu* Trial Judgement, *supra* note 11, para. 480.

[70] See *Kordic and Cerkez* Appeal Judgement, *supra* note 47, para. 29 (holding that the accused must have 'acted with direct intent in relation to his own planning'); *Limaj et al.* Trial Judgement, *supra* note 19, para. 513 (holding that the accused may incur liability where he 'plans an act or omission with an intent that the crime be committed'). Accord *Brđanin* Trial Judgement, *supra* note 19, para. 268; *Bagilishema* Trial Judgement, *supra* note 18, para. 30 (holding that the accused must have 'intended that the [planned] crime be committed'); *Kordić and Čerkez* Trial Judgement, *supra* note 18, para. 386 (holding that an accused must have 'directly or indirectly intended that the crime be committed'); *Blaškić* Trial Judgement, *supra* note 20, para. 278 (same as *Kordić and Čerkez* Trial Judgement).

[71] *Kordić and Čerkez* Appeal Judgement, *supra* note 19, para. 31; *Limaj et al.* Trial Judgement, *supra* note 19, para. 513 (holding that the accused may incur liability where he 'plans an act or omission ... with an awareness of the substantial likelihood that a crime will be committed in the execution of that plan'). Accord *Brđanin* Trial Judgement, *supra* note 19, para. 268 ('[I]t needs to be established that the accused, directly or indirectly, intended that the crime in question be committed.'); *Galić* Trial Judgement, *supra* note 18, para. 172 ('The requisite *mens rea* for all forms of participation under Article 7(1) [of the ICTY Statute] is that the accused acted in the awareness of the substantial likelihood

Planning can be done by one person acting alone or by several persons working together.[72] For his role in drawing up, together with others, a plan to transfer the Muslim civilian population out of the Bosnian village of Sovići,[73] the *Naletilić and Martinović* Trial Chamber convicted Mladen Naletilić, a Bosnian Croat paramilitary commander, of planning the unlawful transfer of civilians as a grave breach of the Geneva Conventions.[74] The *Nahimana* Trial Chamber found Jean-Bosco Barayagwiza, one of the leaders of a radical Hutu political party,[75] guilty of planning extermination as a crime against humanity for his 'critical role' in a 'predefined and structured plan to kill Tutsi civilians' in the Rwandan town of Gisenyi.[76] Specifically, it was Barayagwiza who orchestrated the transport of assailants to Gisenyi from neighbouring areas,[77] and the delivery of weapons to be used by these assailants in the killing of Tutsis.[78] The Chamber found that at least thirty Tutsi civilians, including children and elderly persons, were ultimately killed with the weapons organised and delivered by the accused.[79]

Beginning with the June 2001 *Bagilishema* Trial Judgement, several ICTR judgements have held that liability for planning may ensue not only for those who formulate the plan themselves, but also for those who 'endors[e] a plan proposed by another'.[80] In upholding the Trial Chamber's conviction of Dario Kordić, a high-ranking Bosnian Croat politician, for approving a plan for crimes to be committed in the Kiseljak municipality of Bosnia, the *Kordić and Čerkez* Appeals Chamber evinced a certain degree of sympathy for the ICTR approach: 'The Appeals Chamber considers that Kordić[,] by approving the general criminal plan discussed on the 15 April 1993 meeting, acted with the

that a criminal act or omission would occur as a consequence of his conduct.') (quotation marks omitted); *Kordić and Čerkez* Trial Judgement, *supra* note 18, para. 386 (same as *Brđanin* Trial Judgement); *Blaškić* Trial Judgement, *supra* note 20, para. 278 (same as *Brđanin* Trial Judgement). See *supra*, text accompanying notes 21–60, for a discussion of the evolution of the direct- and indirect-intent alternatives in the jurisprudence of the *ad hoc* Tribunals, and the difference between these two types of intent.

[72] See *Rutaganda* Trial Judgement, *supra* note 19, para. 37 ('one or more persons contemplate designing the commission of a crime'); *Akayesu* Trial Judgement, *supra* note 11, para. 480 ('"[P]lanning, unlike complicity or plotting, can be an act committed by one person.'). Accord *Galić* Trial Judgement, *supra* note 18, para. 168 ('one or more persons'); *Kajelijeli* Trial Judgement, *supra* note 19, para. 761 ('one or more persons'); *Stakić* Trial Judgement, *supra* note 18, para. 443 ('one or several persons'); *Semanza* Trial Judgement, *supra* note 19, para. 380 ('one or more persons'); *Naletilić and Martinović* Trial Judgement, *supra* note 19, para. 59 ('one or several persons'); *Krstić* Trial Judgement, *supra* note 19, para. 601 ('one or more persons'); *Blaškić* Trial Judgement, *supra* note 20, para. 278 ('one or several persons').

[73] See *Naletilić and Martinović* Trial Judgement, *supra* note 19, paras. 529–531.

[74] See *ibid.*, paras. 512, 527, 531. The Appeals Chamber upheld this conviction. *Prosecutor* v. *Naletilić and Martinović*, Case No. IT-98-34-A, Judgement, 3 May 2006, para. 369.

[75] See *Prosecutor* v. *Nahimana, Barayagwiza and Ngeze*, Case No. ICTR-99-52-T, Judgement and Sentence, 3 December 2003 ('*Nahimana et al.* Trial Judgement'), paras. 6, 98, 697–699.

[76] *Ibid.*, paras. 954, 1067. [77] See *ibid.*, para. 730.

[78] See *ibid.*, para. 954. [79] See *ibid.*, paras. 720, 730.

[80] *Bagilishema* Trial Judgement, *supra* note 18, para. 30 ('The level of participation must be substantial, such as formulating a criminal plan or endorsing a plan proposed by another.'). Accord *Mpambara* Trial Judgement, *supra* note 19, para. 20; *Kamuhanda* Trial Judgement, *supra* note 19, para. 592; *Kajelijeli* Trial Judgement, *supra* note 19, para. 761; *Semanza* Trial Judgement, *supra* note 19, para. 380.

awareness that there was a substantial likelihood that the criminal conduct would be repeated in the following attacks by the [Croatian Defence Council] in the Lašva Valley.'[81]

While most judgements have mechanically replicated *Akayesu*'s formulation that planning 'impl[ies] that one or several persons *contemplate* designing the commission of a crime',[82] a handful of judgements, including the *Kordić and Čerkez* Appeal Judgement,[83] hold simply that the accused must 'plan' or 'design' the conduct in question.[84] Since, as discussed below, planning liability cannot ensue unless a crime is actually committed in execution of the plan,[85] it would appear that these latter judgements set forth the more appropriate standard: the plan must surely exist not only in the accused's mind, but also in words, writing, or some other transmittable form. Furthermore, although the *Kordić and Čerkez* Appeal Judgement is silent on the issue, ICTY and ICTR trial jurisprudence prior and subsequent to that judgement has held that the accused must design the plan 'at both the preparatory and execution phases'.[86] No chamber has explained what planning 'at both the preparatory and execution phases' entails; one possible meaning is that the planner must design all aspects of the criminal activity, including not only when and how the planned conduct will be carried out, but also the preliminary steps the physical perpetrator must take in order to carry through with the conduct at a later time.

---

[81] *Kordic and Cerkez* Appeal Judgement, *supra* note 47, para. 982.

[82] *Akayesu* Trial Judgement, *supra* note 11, para. 480 (emphasis added). Accord *Brđanin* Trial Judgement, *supra* note 19, para. 268; *Kamuhanda* Trial Judgement, *supra* note 19, para. 592; *Kajelijeli* Trial Judgement, *supra* note 19, para. 761; *Stakić* Trial Judgement, *supra* note 18, para. 443; *Naletilić and Martinović* Trial Judgement, *supra* note 19, para. 59; *Kordić and Čerkez* Trial Judgement, *supra* note 18, para. 386; *Blaškić* Trial Judgement, *supra* note 20, para. 279; *Rutaganda* Trial Judgement, *supra* note 19, para. 37. Curiously, two ICTR trial judgements set forth formulations whereby the accused need merely contemplate the commission of a crime, as opposed to contemplating *designing* the commission of a crime. See *Gacumbitsi* Trial Judgement, *supra* note 19, para. 271 ('Planning presupposes that one or more person[s] contemplate the commission of a crime at both its preparatory and execution phases'); *Musema* Trial Judgement, *supra* note 19, para. 119 (same as *Gacumbitsi* Trial Judgement).

[83] See *Kordić and Čerkez* Appeal Judgement, *supra* note 19, paras. 26, 31.

[84] See *Mpambara* Trial Judgement, *supra* note 19, para. 20 ('formulation of a design'); *Galić* Trial Judgement, *supra* note 18, para. 168 ('one or more persons designed the commission of a crime'); *Semanza* Trial Judgement, *supra* note 19, para. 380; *Krstić* Trial Judgement, *supra* note 19, para. 601 ('one or more persons design the commission of a crime').

[85] See *infra* text accompanying notes 91–92.

[86] *Akayesu* Trial Judgement, *supra* note 11, para. 479. Accord *Limaj et al.* Trial Judgement, *supra* note 19, para. 513; *Brđanin* Trial Judgement, *supra* note 19, para. 268; *Gacumbitsi* Trial Judgement, *supra* note 19, para. 271; *Kamuhanda* Trial Judgement, *supra* note 19, para. 592; *Galić* Trial Judgement, *supra* note 18, para. 168; *Kajelijeli* Trial Judgement, *supra* note 19, para. 761; *Stakić* Trial Judgement, *supra* note 18, para. 443; *Semanza* Trial Judgement, *supra* note 19, para. 380; *Naletilić and Martinović* Trial Judgement, *supra* note 19, para. 59; *Krstić* Trial Judgement, *supra* note 19, para. 601; *Kordić and Čerkez* Trial Judgement, *supra* note 18, para. 386; *Blaškić* Trial Judgement, *supra* note 20, para. 279; *Musema* Trial Judgement, *supra* note 19, para. 119; *Rutaganda* Trial Judgement, *supra* note 19, para. 37.

An accused may not be convicted for planning and physically committing the same crime,[87] but according to the *Brđanin* and *Stakić* Trial Chambers, the accused's involvement in the planning of a crime may be considered as an aggravating factor if he is convicted for physically committing that crime.[88] The *Stakić* Trial Chamber accordingly aggravated the sentence of the accused after determining that he had not only committed, but planned and ordered as well, deportation as a crime against humanity.[89] Moreover, although it made no explicit statement to this effect, the *Nahimana* Trial Chamber also appears to have treated the involvement of the three accused in the planning of the crimes they were convicted of committing as an aggravating factor.[90]

5.2.2 Substantial contribution

The accused's conduct substantially contributed to the perpetration of a crime
The ICTY Appeals Chamber and a number of trial chambers have held that liability for planning cannot be inchoate, and that a crime must actually be perpetrated in execution of the accused's plan.[91] It would seem, however, that

---

[87] *Brđanin* Trial Judgement, *supra* note 19, para. 268 ('Where an accused is found guilty of having committed a crime, he or she cannot at the same time be convicted of having planned the same crime.'); *Galić* Trial Judgement, *supra* note 18, para. 168 n. 280 ('If the person planning a crime also commits it, he or her [*sic*] is only punished for the commission of the crime and not for its planning[.]'); *Stakić* Trial Judgement, *supra* note 18, para. 443; *Naletilić and Martinović* Trial Judgement, *supra* note 19, para. 59; *Kordić and Čerkez* Trial Judgement, *supra* note 18, para. 386; *Blaškić* Trial Judgement, *supra* note 20, para. 268; *Akayesu* Trial Judgement, *supra* note 11, paras. 468, 532.

[88] *Brđanin* Trial Judgement, *supra* note 19, para. 268; *Stakić* Trial Judgement, *supra* note 18, para. 443.

[89] *Stakić* Trial Judgement, *supra* note 18, para. 914, affirmed in *Prosecutor v. Stakić*, Case No. IT-97-24-A, Judgement, 22 March 2006 ('*Stakić* Appeal Judgement'), para. 413 (noting that an accused's 'role in the planning and ordering of deportation is not an element required to prove the commission of deportation ... [but] may be taken into account as an aggravating factor because of the contribution that planning and ordering make to the commission of a crime[, and] may bear on the moral culpability of the perpetrator').

[90] See *Nahimana et al.* Trial Judgement, *supra* note 75, para. 1102 (emphasising, in the section of the judgement on aggravating and mitigating circumstances, that 'all three Accused were involved in the planning of these criminal activities and were disposed to acting in a manner contrary to the duty imposed upon them by their respective positions'); *ibid.*, paras. 1096, 1105–1108 (convicting the three accused of genocide, conspiracy to commit genocide, direct and public incitement to commit genocide, and persecution and extermination as crimes against humanity, and sentencing two of them to life imprisonment and one to thirty-five years).

[91] See *Kordić and Čerkez* Appeal Judgement, *supra* note 19, para. 26 ('The *actus reus* of "planning" requires that one or more persons design the criminal conduct constituting one or more statutory crimes *that are later perpetrated.*') (emphasis added); *Mpambara* Trial Judgement, *supra* note 19, para. 20 ('Planning is the formulation of a design by which individuals *will execute a crime.*') (emphasis added); *Limaj et al.* Trial Judgement, *supra* note 19, para. 513; *Brđanin* Trial Judgement, *supra* note 19, para. 267 ('[P]roof is required that the crime in question has actually been committed by the principal offender(s).'); *Kamuhanda* Trial Judgement, *supra* note 19, para. 589; *Galić* Trial Judgement, *supra* note 18, para. 168; *Kajelijeli* Trial Judgement, *supra* note 19, para. 758; *Semanza* Trial Judgement, *supra* note 19, para. 378 (holding that 'a crime within the Tribunal's jurisdiction must have been completed before an individual's participation in that crime will give rise to criminal responsibility' and that 'Article 6(1) [of the ICTR Statute] does not punish inchoate offences, which are punishable only for the crime of genocide pursuant to Article 2(3)(b), (c), and (d)'); *Musema* Trial Judgement, *supra* note 19, para. 115; *Rutaganda*

the prosecution need not prove that the crime would not have been committed absent the accused's contribution; in the words of the ICTY Appeals Chamber, '[i]t is sufficient to demonstrate that the planning was a factor substantially contributing to such criminal conduct'.[92]

5.3 Elements of instigating

5.3.1 *Prompting of conduct with intent or awareness of substantial likelihood*

The accused prompted criminal conduct with the intent that a crime be committed; or he prompted an act or omission, aware of the substantial likelihood that a crime would be committed in the realisation of that act or omission

An accused may incur liability for instigating in two alternative scenarios: (1) where he prompts criminal conduct[93] with the intent that a crime be committed as a result of that prompting;[94] or (2) where he prompts an act or

Trial Judgement, *supra* note 19, para. 34; *Kayishema and Ruzindana* Trial Judgement, *supra* note 19, para. 198; *Akayesu* Trial Judgement, *supra* note 11, para. 473. But see Antonio Cassese, *International Criminal Law* (2003), p. 193 ('[I]t would seem that the gravity of international crimes (or at least the most serious among them) may warrant the conclusion that planning the commission of one or more such crimes is punishable *per se* even if the crime is not actually perpetrated.').

92 *Kordić and Čerkez* Appeal Judgement, *supra* note 19, para. 26. Accord *Mpambara* Trial Judgement, *supra* note 19, para. 20; *Limaj et al.* Trial Judgement, *supra* note 19, para. 513; *Kamuhanda* Trial Judgement, *supra* note 19, paras. 590, 592; *Kajelijeli* Trial Judgement, *supra* note 19, para. 759; *Semanza* Trial Judgement, *supra* note 19, paras. 379, 380; *Bagilishema* Trial Judgement, *supra* note 18, para. 30 (holding that 'the [accused's] level of participation must be substantial'). See also *Kayishema and Ruzindana* Trial Judgement, *supra* note 19, para. 198 (holding that the accused's conduct must have 'contributed to, or . . . had an effect on, the commission of the crime').

93 *Kordić and Čerkez* Appeal Judgement, *supra* note 19, para. 27 ('The *actus reus* of "instigating" means to prompt another person to commit an offence.'); *Muvunyi* Trial Judgement, *supra* note 19, para. 464; *Mpambara* Trial Judgement, *supra* note 19, para. 18; *Orić* Trial Judgement, *supra* note 19, para. 270; *Limaj et al.* Trial Judgement, *supra* note 19, para. 514; *Brđanin* Trial Judgement, *supra* note 19, para. 269; *Ndindabahizi* Trial Judgement, *supra* note 18, para. 456; *Kamuhanda* Trial Judgement, *supra* note 19, para. 592; *Galić* Trial Judgement, *supra* note 18, para. 168; *Kajelijeli* Trial Judgement, *supra* note 19, para. 762; *Semanza* Trial Judgement, *supra* note 19, para. 381; *Naletilić and Martinović* Trial Judgement, *supra* note 19, para. 60; *Kvočka et al.* Trial Judgement, *supra* note 19, para. 243; *ibid.*, para. 252 ('The *actus reus* required for "instigating" a crime is any conduct by the accused prompting another person to act in a particular way.'); *Krstić* Trial Judgement, *supra* note 19, para. 601; *Bagilishema* Trial Judgement, *supra* note 18, para. 30; *Kordić and Čerkez* Trial Judgement, *supra* note 20, para. 280; *Musema* Trial Judgement, *supra* note 19, para. 120; *Rutaganda* Trial Judgement, *supra* note 19, para. 38; *Akayesu* Trial Judgement, *supra* note 11, para. 482.

94 *Kordić and Čerkez* Appeal Judgement, *supra* note 19, para. 29; *Muvunyi* Trial Judgement, *supra* note 19, para. 465; *Mpambara* Trial Judgement, *supra* note 19, para. 18; *Limaj et al.* Trial Judgement, *supra* note 19, para. 514; *Brđanin* Trial Judgement, *supra* note 19, para. 269; *Ndindabahizi* Trial Judgement, *supra* note 18, para. 456 ('Instigation is urging or encouraging . . . another person to commit a crime, with the intent that the crime will be committed.'); *Gacumbitsi* Trial Judgement, *supra* note 19, para. 279; *Naletilić and Martinović* Trial Judgement, *supra* note 19, para. 60; *Kvočka et al.* Trial Judgement, *supra* note 19, para. 252; *Bagilishema* Trial Judgement, *supra* note 18, para. 31; *Kordić and Čerkez* Trial Judgement, *supra* note 18, para. 387; *Blaškić* Trial Judgement, *supra* note 20, para. 278.

omission aware of the substantial likelihood that a crime will be committed in the realisation of that act or omission.[95]

The 'urging, encouraging, or prompting'[96] that constitutes instigation may take place verbally or by other means of communication,[97] but it would seem that verbal instigation is the usual method. The *Aleksovski* Trial Chamber found the accused, a prison warden, guilty of instigating outrages upon personal dignity as a violation of the laws or customs of war for verbally prompting guards at his prison to mistreat detainees.[98] Similarly, the Trial Chamber in *Akayesu* convicted the accused, a Rwandan *bourgmestre*, of instigating rape as a crime against humanity for his verbal encouragement to Interahamwe rapists with statements such as '[n]ever ask me again what a Tutsi woman tastes like'.[99] The *Orić* Trial Chamber drew a distinction between instigating and aiding and abetting: for instigating liability to arise, the accused's conduct 'has to be more than merely facilitating the commission of the principal offence', and if the physical perpetrator 'has definitively decided to commit the crime' independently of the accused's conduct, 'further encouragement or moral support may merely, though still, qualify as aiding and abetting'.[100]

Early ICTR trial chambers had some difficulty distinguishing between the form of responsibility 'instigation' under Article 7/6(1) and the inchoate crime of 'direct and public incitement to commit genocide' under Article 4(3)(c) of the ICTY Statute and Article 2(3)(c) of the ICTR Statute ('Article 4/2(3)(c)'). Remarking that, in the French text of the ICTR Statute, both species of

---

[95] *Kordić and Čerkez* Appeal Judgement, *supra* note 19, para. 30; *Muvunyi* Trial Judgement, *supra* note 19, para. 465; *Limaj et al.* Trial Judgement, *supra* note 19, para. 514; *Brdanin* Trial Judgement, *supra* note 19, para. 269; *Galić* Trial Judgement, *supra* note 18, para. 172; *Naletilić and Martinović* Trial Judgement, *supra* note 19, para. 60; *Kvočka et al.* Trial Judgement, *supra* note 19, para. 252 ('The required *mens rea* is that the accused intended to provoke or induce the commission of the crime, or was aware of the substantial likelihood that the commission of a crime would be a probable consequence of his acts.'); *Blaškić* Trial Judgement, *supra* note 20, para. 278 ('[P]roof is required that whoever ... instigated ... the commission of a crime possessed the criminal intent, that is, that he directly or indirectly intended that the crime in question be committed.'). But see *Orić* Trial Judgement, *supra* note 19, para. 279 (holding that the accused need merely be 'aware that the commission of the crime will *more likely than not* result from his conduct') (emphasis added). See *supra*, text accompanying notes 21–60, for a discussion of the evolution of the direct- and indirect-intent alternatives in the jurisprudence of the *ad hoc* Tribunals, and the difference between these two types of intent.

[96] *Semanza* Trial Judgement, *supra* note 19, para. 381. See also *Muvunyi* Trial Judgement, *supra* note 19, para. 464 ('encouraged, urged, or otherwise prompted'); *Mpambara* Trial Judgement, *supra* note 19, para. 18 ('urging or encouraging'); *Orić* Trial Judgement, *supra* note 19, para. 271 ('inciting, soliciting or otherwise inducing'); *Ndindabahizi* Trial Judgement, *supra* note 18, para. 456 ('urging or encouraging'); *Bagilishema* Trial Judgement, *supra* note 18, para. 30 ('urging or encouraging').

[97] *Mpambara* Trial Judgement, *supra* note 19, para. 18; *Ndindabahizi* Trial Judgement, *supra* note 18, para. 456.

[98] See *Aleksovski* Trial Judgement, *supra* note 9, para. 88, p. 92.

[99] See *Akayesu* Trial Judgement, *supra* note 11, paras. 422, 692.

[100] *Orić* Trial Judgement, *supra* note 19, para. 271. The Trial Chamber dubbed the physical perpetrator who has decided to commit the crime absent the accused's prompting the '*omnimodo facturus*'. *Ibid.*

conduct are referred to using the same word – *incitation* – the *Akayesu* Trial Chamber held that instigation, like incitement to commit genocide, must be both direct and public;[101] the *Rutaganda* and *Musema* Trial Chambers endorsed this view.[102] Upon reviewing this holding in June 2001, the ICTR Appeals Chamber overturned the Trial Chamber: unlike the provision on incitement to commit genocide in Article 4/2(3)(c),[103] the plain language of Article 7/6(1) in both English and French reveals that 'neither text contains any suggestion or recommendation that incitement [that is, "instigation"[104]] must be direct and public'.[105] The Appeals Chamber accordingly concluded that instigation 'need not be "direct and public" ',[106] and this holding has been followed in subsequent ICTR judgements.[107] Possibly, then, these chambers would allow a conviction to be entered for instigating where the accused's prompting was transmitted to the physical perpetrator through some non-public means (for example, in a letter or a telephone conversation), by means of an intermediary,[108] where the prompting occurred by means of a 'vague or indirect suggestion',[109] or where it was not 'aimed at causing a specific offence to be committed'.[110] The *Muvunyi* Trial Chamber observed in this vein that

---

[101] *Ibid.*, para. 481 (citing Virginia Morris and Michael P. Scharf, 1 *The International Criminal Tribunal for Rwanda* (1998), p. 239). Chapter 4, text accompanying notes 2–58, discusses the relationship of the inchoate genocide-related crimes in Article 4/2(3) to the forms of responsibility.

[102] See *Musema* Trial Judgement, *supra* note 19, para. 120 (January 2000); *Rutaganda* Trial Judgement, *supra* note 19, para. 38 (December 1999).

[103] *Prosecutor* v. *Akayesu*, Case No. ICTR-96-4-A, Judgement, 1 June 2001 ('*Akayesu* Appeal Judgement'), para. 480.

[104] Notwithstanding the *Akayesu* Appeals Chamber's criticism of the 'glaring disparity' caused by the use of two different terms in the English version of the ICTR Statute and the use of only one word (*incitation*) in the French version of the Statute, *ibid.*, para. 478, in the original French version of the judgement, the Chamber itself used the term *incitation* when referring to both 'instigation' in Article 6(1) and 'incitement to commit genocide' in Article 2(3)(c). In the subsequently released English version of the judgement, the translators appear unfortunately to have used the term 'incitement' on several occasions when referring not only to incitement to commit genocide in Article 2(3)(c), but also to instigation in Article 6(1). See *ibid.*, paras. 478, 483. The ironic result was the Appeals Chamber's perpetuation of the very confusion it criticised.

[105] *Ibid.*　　[106] *Ibid.*, para. 483.

[107] See *Muvunyi* Trial Judgement, *supra* note 19, para. 464; *Gacumbitsi* Trial Judgement, *supra* note 19, para. 279; *Kamuhanda* Trial Judgement, *supra* note 19, para. 593; *Kajelijeli* Trial Judgement, *supra* note 19, para. 762; *Semanza* Trial Judgement, *supra* note 19, para. 381. *Accord Orić* Trial Judgement, *supra* note 19, para. 273.

[108] See *Orić* Trial Judgement, *supra* note 19, para. 276 (holding that the accused's conduct 'need … not necessarily have direct effect, as prompting another to commit a crime can also be procured by means of an intermediary').

[109] See *Akayesu* Trial Judgement, *supra* note 11, para. 557 (holding that direct and public incitement to commit genocide under Article 2(3)(c) of the ICTR Statute must be 'more than mere vague or indirect suggestion').

[110] See *Kajelijeli* Trial Judgement, *supra* note 19, para. 852 (discussing the 'direct' element of direct and public incitement to genocide and remarking that, in civil law systems, the equivalent crime of 'provocation' 'is regarded as being direct where it is aimed at causing a specific offence to be committed'). While it is easy to see how the public or private nature of the accused's conduct could be a plausible and appropriate distinguishing factor between incitement and instigation, it is less clear why the 'directness' of the conduct – or of the link between that conduct and the crime that is urged – should be viewed as an acceptable distinction. No chamber has articulated an example of 'indirect instigation', beyond the odd

'private, implicit or subdued forms of instigation could ground liability under Article 6(1) if the Prosecution can prove the relevant causal nexus between the act of instigation and the commission of the crime'.[111]

An accused may not be convicted for instigating and physically committing the same crime.[112] Moreover, in contrast to ordering and superior responsibility, instigating does not require that the accused have any sort of authority over the physical perpetrator.[113] According to the *Orić* Trial Chamber, provided the accused has the requisite intent, his presence or absence of the accused from the scene of the crime, the size of his audience, and the existence of intermediaries between him and the physical perpetrator or perpetrators are all irrelevant.[114]

The *Blaškić* Trial Chamber hypothesised that the prompting that constitutes instigation may occur not only through positive action, but also through a culpable omission.[115] As an example of an omission amounting to instigation, the Chamber quoted from the Regulations Concerning the Application of

---

notion of instigation by intermediary. See *Orić* Trial Judgement, *supra* note 19, para. 274. Moreover, the very idea that instigation need not be direct is inconsistent with the causation requirement that has been repeatedly put forth as an element of this form of responsibility. See, e.g., *Rutaganda* Trial Judgement, *supra* note 19, para. 38 (instigating must lead to actual commission of crime); *Musema* Trial Judgement, *supra* note 19, para. 120 (unlike direct and public incitement to commit genocide, instigating must result in commission of a crime); *Blaškić* Trial Judgement, *supra* note 20, para. 278 ('In the case of instigating ... proof is required of a causal connection between the instigation and the fulfilment of the *actus reus* of the crime.'); *Kamuhanda* Trial Judgement, *supra* note 19, paras. 592–593 ('causal connection' required for instigating). Indeed, the causation requirement for instigation has been much more frequently and expressly articulated than an analogous requirement for planning and ordering, suggesting a greater preoccupation on the part of chambers that causation be shown for instigating than for planning and ordering. See *supra* note 91 (causation for planning); *infra* note 173 (causation for ordering). It would have been preferable, and more doctrinally defensible, if the *Akayesu* Appeals Chamber's attempt to distinguish incitement from instigation had been limited to two clear points: the latter need not be public, but does require that the crime actually be committed.

[111] *Muvunyi* Trial Judgement, *supra* note 19, para. 464.

[112] *Blaškić* Trial Judgement, *supra* note 20, para. 278; *Akayesu* Trial Judgement, *supra* note 11, paras. 468, 532. See also *Prosecutor v. Stakić*, Case No. IT-97-24, Decision on Rule 98 *bis* Motion for Judgement of Acquittal, 31 October 2002, para. 107 (holding that '[t]he Trial Chamber, already at this stage, considers that an accused can not be convicted as an instigator if he would be found guilty of having directly/physically perpetrated the same crime'); *ibid.*, para. 108 (holding, on the basis of the evidence produced by the prosecution during its case-in-chief that 'no reasonable trier of fact could sustain a conviction of the Accused for instigating the commission of the crimes' in question, and granting this portion of the relief sought by the accused in his motion for judgement of acquittal).

[113] *Orić* Trial Judgement, *supra* note 19, para. 272 ('[A]lthough the exertion of influence would hardly function without a certain capability to impress others, instigation, different from "ordering", which implies at least a factual superior-subordinate relationship, does not presuppose any kind of superiority.') (footnote removed); *Brđanin* Trial Judgement, *supra* note 19, para. 359; *Semanza* Trial Judgement, *supra* note 19, para. 257.

[114] *Orić* Trial Judgement, *supra* note 19, para. 273. See also *Brđanin* Trial Judgement, *supra* note 19, para. 359 (holding that 'it is immaterial whether ... other persons would necessarily have to be involved before the crime was actually committed').

[115] See *Blaškić* Trial Judgement, *supra* note 20, para. 339; *ibid.*, para. 280 (stating that '[t]he wording [of Article 7/6(1) is sufficiently broad to allow for the inference that both acts and omissions may constitute instigating and that this notion covers both express and implied conduct').

International Law to the Armed Forces of the Socialist Federal Republic of Yugoslavia:[116] 'A military commander is responsible as ... an instigator if, by not taking measures against subordinates who violate the law of war, he allows his subordinate units to continue to commit the acts.'[117] The Trial Chamber qualified this passage with the caveat that, under the ICTY Statute, liability for instigation in such a scenario could only ensue if the prosecution proves that 'the subordinates would not have committed the subsequent crimes if the commander had not failed to punish the earlier ones'.[118] Subsequent trial chambers of both *ad hoc* Tribunals have repeated the proposition that instigation may occur by omission, but it would appear that they have all done so without exploring in any detail the propriety of such a proposition,[119] when liability in such a situation may be more accurately and permissibly described as superior responsibility.[120]

5.3.2 *Substantial contribution*

The accused's conduct substantially contributed to the perpetration of a crime
    As with planning and ordering,[121] liability for instigating cannot be inchoate: a crime must actually be perpetrated as a result of the accused's

---

[116] *Ibid.*, para. 338.
[117] Socialist Federal Republic of Yugoslavia Federal Secretariat for National Defence, Regulations Concerning the Application of International Law to the Armed Forces of SFRY (1988), Art. 21, reprinted in M. Cherif Bassiouni (ed.), *The Law of the International Criminal Tribunal for the Former Yugoslavia* (1996), p. 661.
[118] *Blaškić* Trial Judgement, *supra* note 20, para. 339. This element of but-for causation for instigation by omission stands in contrast to instigation by positive action, which does not require but-for causation. See *infra* text accompanying note 124.
[119] See *Muvunyi* Trial Judgement, *supra* note 19, para. 464 ('[I]nstigation may arise from a positive act or a culpable omission.'); *Orić* Trial Judgement, *supra* note 19, para. 273 (holding that instigation liability may arise on the basis of an omission 'provided ... the instigator is under a duty to prevent the crime from being brought about'); *Limaj et al.* Trial Judgement, *supra* note 19, para. 514 ('Both acts and omissions may constitute instigating, which covers express and implied conduct.'); *Brđanin* Trial Judgement, *supra* note 19, para. 269 (same as *Limaj et al.* Trial Judgement); *Kamuhanda* Trial Judgement, *supra* note 19, para. 593; *Galić* Trial Judgement, *supra* note 18, para. 168 ('It has been held in relation to "instigating" that omissions amount to instigation in circumstances where a commander has created an environment permissive of criminal behaviour by subordinates.'); *Kajelijeli* Trial Judgement, *supra* note 19, para. 762; *Naletilić and Martinović* Trial Judgement, *supra* note 19, para. 60; *Kordić and Čerkez* Trial Judgement, *supra* note 18, para. 387. Moreover, while the *Galić* Appeals Chamber held unequivocally that liability for ordering cannot ensue on the basis of an omission, it left open the possibility that the physical elements of other Article 7/6(1) forms of responsibility may be fulfilled by omission where a superior-subordinate relationship exists between the accused and the physical perpetrator. See *Galić* Appeal Judgement, *supra* note 52, para. 176 ('The failure to act of a person in a position of authority, who is in a superior-subordinate relationship with the physical perpetrator, may give rise to another mode of responsibility under Article 7(1) of the [ICTY] Statute or superior responsibility under Article 7(3)[.]'); see also *infra* text accompanying notes 148–150 (discussing *Galić*'s holding that 'ordering by omission' does not exist).
[120] See generally Chapter 3 (on superior responsibility). See also Chapter 4, text accompanying notes 210–211 (making the same observation with respect to 'aiding and abetting by omission').
[121] See *supra* note 91 and accompanying text; *infra* note 172 and accompanying text.

prompting.[122] Although some causal connection must be shown between the conduct of the accused and that of the physical perpetrator,[123] the chambers have consistently held that the prosecution need not prove that the crime would not have been committed absent the accused's contribution.[124] The *Blaškić* Trial Chamber carved out an exception to this rule: an accused's failure to punish the crimes of his subordinates can only be regarded as instigating them to commit further crimes where it is proven that these later crimes would not have occurred but for the earlier failure to punish.[125] Although many subsequent judgements have repeated *Blaškić*'s holding that instigation may occur by omission,[126] no chamber has expressly endorsed the proposition that instigation by omission requires but-for causation. Moreover, no chamber – including *Blaškić* – seems to have made factual findings on whether the accused before it is responsible for instigation by omission. This failure to actually make factual findings on instigation by omission could be explained by the apparent applicability of superior responsibility to the very scenario described by the *Blaškić* Trial Chamber; it may be that the chambers faced with this factual scenario in practice have implicitly opted to examine the accused's liability under the rubric of superior responsibility to the exclusion of instigation by omission.[127]

---

[122] See *Kordić and Čerkez* Appeal Judgement, *supra* note 19, para. 27 (holding the accused's prompting must have been 'a factor substantially contributing to the conduct of another person *committing the crime*') (emphasis added); *Mpambara* Trial Judgement, *supra* note 19, para. 18 ('Unlike the crime of direct and public incitement [to commit genocide], instigation does not give rise to liability unless the crime is ultimately committed.'); *Orić* Trial Judgement, *supra* note 19, para. 269 n. 732; *Brđanin* Trial Judgement, *supra* note 19, para. 267; *Ndindabahizi* Trial Judgement, *supra* note 18, para. 456 (same as *Mpambara* Trial Judgement); *Galić* Trial Judgement, *supra* note 18, para. 168 ('"Instigating" means prompting another to commit an offence, which is actually committed.'); *Kajelijeli* Trial Judgement, *supra* note 19, para. 758; *Semanza* Trial Judgement, *supra* note 19, para. 378; *Musema* Trial Judgement, *supra* note 19, paras. 115–116, 120; *Rutaganda* Trial Judgement, *supra* note 19, paras. 34, 38; *Akayesu* Trial Judgement, *supra* note 11, paras. 473, 481 (holding that, unlike the inchoate crime of direct and public incitement to commit genocide under Article 4/2(3)(c), instigation 'is punishable only where it leads to the actual commission of an offence desired by the instigator').

[123] See *Muvunyi* Trial Judgement, *supra* note 19, para. 464; *Limaj et al.* Trial Judgement, *supra* note 19, para. 514; *Brđanin* Trial Judgement, *supra* note 19, para. 269; *Gacumbitsi* Trial Judgement, *supra* note 19, para. 279; *Kamuhanda* Trial Judgement, *supra* note 19, para. 593; *Kajelijeli* Trial Judgement, *supra* note 19, para. 762; *Semanza* Trial Judgement, *supra* note 19, para. 381; *Bagilishema* Trial Judgement, *supra* note 18, para. 30 ('Proof is required of a causal connection between the instigation and the *actus reus* of the crime.'); *Kordić and Čerkez* Trial Judgement, *supra* note 18, para. 387 (holding that 'the contribution of the accused [must have] in fact had an effect on the commission of the crime'); *Blaškić* Trial Judgement, *supra* note 20, paras. 278, 280. See also *infra* note 128 and accompanying text.

[124] See *Kordić and Čerkez* Appeal Judgement, *supra* note 19, para. 27; Accord *Prosecutor v. Gacumbitsi*, Case No. ICTR-2001-64-A, Judgement, 7 July 2006 ('*Gacumbitsi* Appeal Judgement'), para. 129; *Orić* Trial Judgement, *supra* note 19, para. 274; *Limaj et al.* Trial Judgement, *supra* note 19, para. 514 ('A nexus between the instigation and the perpetration must be demonstrated[,] but it need not be shown that the crime would not have occurred without the accused's involvement.') (footnote removed); *Brđanin* Trial Judgement, *supra* note 19, para. 269; *Galić* Trial Judgement, *supra* note 18, para. 168; *Naletilić and Martinović* Trial Judgement, *supra* note 19, para. 60; *Kvočka et al.* Trial Judgement, *supra* note 19, para. 252; *Kordić and Čerkez* Trial Judgement, *supra* note 18, para. 387.

[125] *Blaškić* Trial Judgement, *supra* note 20, para. 339.

[126] See *supra* note 119 and accompanying text. [127] See *supra* text accompanying notes 115–120.

As established by the ICTY Appeals Chamber in *Kordić and Čerkez* and endorsed by the ICTR Appeals Chamber in *Gacumbitsi*, the accused's prompting must have been 'a factor substantially contributing to the conduct of another person in committing the crime'.[128] The *Ndindabahizi* Trial Chamber found the accused, the Minister of Finance of the Interim Government of Rwanda, guilty of instigating genocide for his words of encouragement to the attackers who killed thousands of Tutsi at Gitwa Hill on 26 April 1994:[129] 'When the Accused arrived, the attackers gathered around; when he spoke, they listened. His position as a Minister of Government lent his words considerable authority.'[130] Through his words and deeds, Emmanuel Ndindabahizi 'directly and substantially contributed to the mass killing of Tutsi' at Gitwa Hill.[131]

5.4 Elements of ordering

5.4.1 Instruction to engage in conduct with intent or awareness of substantial likelihood

The accused instructed another to engage in criminal conduct with the intent that a crime be committed; or he instructed another to engage in an act or omission aware of the substantial likelihood that a crime would be committed in the realisation of that act or omission

An accused may incur liability for ordering in two alternative scenarios: (1) where he instructs another to engage in criminal conduct[132] with the intent

---

[128] *Kordić and Čerkez* Appeal Judgement, *supra* note 19, para. 27. Accord *Gacumbitsi* Appeal Judgement, *supra* note 124, para. 129 (quoting *Kordić and Čerkez* Appeal Judgement); *ibid.*, para. 130 (finding that the Trial Chamber had correctly determined that the accused had not substantially contributed through his conduct to certain rapes, and that the Trial Chamber accordingly did not err when in acquitting him of instigating these rapes); *Muvunyi* Trial Judgement, *supra* note 19, paras. 464, 466; *Orić* Trial Judgement, *supra* note 19, para. 274; *Limaj et al.* Trial Judgement, *supra* note 19, para. 514; *Kamuhanda* Trial Judgement, *supra* note 19, para. 590; *Kajelijeli* Trial Judgement, *supra* note 19, para. 759; *Semanza* Trial Judgement, *supra* note 19, para. 379; *Bagilishema* Trial Judgement, *supra* note 18, para. 30. The level of contribution required of the accused has been articulated in somewhat different terms by several other trial chambers. See *Mpambara* Trial Judgement, *supra* note 19, para. 18 (holding that 'instigation does not arise unless it has directly and substantially contributed to the perpetration of the crime by another person'); *Brđanin* Trial Judgement, *supra* note 19, para. 269 (holding that 'the instigation [must have been] a factor clearly contributing to the conduct of other persons committing the crime in question'); *Ndindabahizi* Trial Judgement, *supra* note 18, para. 456 (same as *Mpambara* Trial Judgement); *Kvočka et al.* Trial Judgement, *supra* note 19, para. 252 (same as *Brđanin* Trial Judgement); *Galić* Trial Judgement, *supra* note 18, para. 168 (same as *Brđanin* Trial Judgement); *Naletilić and Martinović* Trial Judgement, *supra* note 19, para. 60 (same as *Brđanin* Trial Judgement). See also *infra* note 123 and accompanying text.
[129] See *Ndindabahizi* Trial Judgement, *supra* note 18, para. 464.   [130] *Ibid.*, para. 463.   [131] *Ibid.*
[132] *Galić* Appeal Judgement, *supra* note 52, para. 176; *Semanza* Appeal Judgement, *supra* note 19, para. 361; *Kordić and Čerkez* Appeal Judgement, *supra* note 19, para. 28; *Muvunyi* Trial Judgement, *supra* note 19, para. 467; *Mpambara* Trial Judgement, *supra* note 19, para. 19; *Limaj et al.* Trial Judgement, *supra* note 19, para. 515; *Brđanin* Trial Judgement, *supra* note 19, para. 270; *Gacumbitsi* Trial Judgement, *supra* note 19, para. 281; *Kamuhanda* Trial Judgement, *supra* note 19, para. 594; *Galić* Trial Judgement,

that a crime be committed in the execution of that instruction;[133] or (2) where he instructs another to engage in an act or omission aware of the substantial likelihood that a crime will be committed in the realisation of that act or omission.[134]

The accused need not give the order directly to the physical perpetrator.[135] Moreover, although some trial jurisprudence states that the accused must use his position of authority to 'convince',[136] 'persuade',[137] 'impel',[138] or 'compel'[139] the person ordered to engage in criminal conduct, several other judgements – including the *Ntagerura* Appeal Judgement – hold simply that the accused must use his position of authority in issuing the order or in instructing the person ordered.[140] It would appear that these latter judgements regard the requisite compulsion or persuasion to be implied in the accused's position of authority over the other person.

supra note 18, para. 168; *Kajelijeli* Trial Judgement, *supra* note 19, para. 763; *Stakić* Trial Judgement, *supra* note 18, para. 445; *Semanza* Trial Judgement, *supra* note 19, para. 382; *Krstić* Trial Judgement, *supra* note 19, para. 601; *Bagilishema* Trial Judgement, *supra* note 18, para. 30; *Blaškić* Trial Judgement, *supra* note 20, para. 281; *Musema* Trial Judgement, *supra* note 19, para. 121; *Rutaganda* Trial Judgement, *supra* note 19, para. 39; *Akayesu* Trial Judgement, *supra* note 11, para. 483.

[133] *Ntagerura et al.* Appeal Judgement, *supra* note 19, para. 365; Kordić and Cerkez Appeal Judgement, *supra* note 19, para. 29; *Limaj et al.* Trial Judgement, *supra* note 19, para. 515; *Strugar* Trial Judgement, *supra* note 18, para. 333; *Brđanin* Trial Judgement, *supra* note 19, para. 270; *Stakić* Trial Judgement, *supra* note 18, para. 445; *Bagilishema* Trial Judgement, *supra* note 18, para. 30; *Kordić and Čerkez* Trial Judgement, *supra* note 18, para. 386; *Blaškić* Trial Judgement, *supra* note 20, para. 278.

[134] *Galić* Appeal Judgement, *supra* note 52, para. 152; *Kordić and Čerkez* Appeal Judgement, *supra* note 19, para. 30; *Blaškić* Appeal Judgement, *supra* note 22, para. 42; *Limaj et al.* Trial Judgement, *supra* note 19, para. 515; *Strugar* Trial Judgement, *supra* note 18, para. 333; *Brđanin* Trial Judgement, *supra* note 19, para. 270; *Galić* Trial Judgement, *supra* note 18, para. 172; *Stakić* Trial Judgement, *supra* note 18, para. 445; *Kordić and Čerkez* Trial Judgement, *supra* note 18, para. 386; *Blaškić* Trial Judgement, *supra* note 20, para. 278. See *supra*, text accompanying notes 21–60, for a discussion of the evolution of the direct- and indirect-intent alternatives in the jurisprudence of the *ad hoc* Tribunals, and the difference between these two types of intent.

[135] *Strugar* Trial Judgement, *supra* note 18, para. 331; *Brđanin* Trial Judgement, *supra* note 19, para. 270; *Naletilić and Martinović* Trial Judgement, *supra* note 19, para. 61; *Kordić and Čerkez* Trial Judgement, *supra* note 18, para. 388; *Blaškić* Trial Judgement, *supra* note 20, para. 282.

[136] See *Stakić* Trial Judgement, *supra* note 18, para. 445; *Krstić* Trial Judgement, *supra* note 19, para. 601; *Blaškić* Trial Judgement, *supra* note 20, para. 281; *Akayesu* Trial Judgement, *supra* note 11, para. 483.

[137] *Musema* Trial Judgement, *supra* note 19, para. 121; *Rutaganda* Trial Judgement, *supra* note 19, para. 39.

[138] *Kamuhanda* Trial Judgement, *supra* note 19, para. 594; *Kajelijeli* Trial Judgement, *supra* note 19, para. 763.

[139] *Muvunyi* Trial Judgement, *supra* note 19, para. 467; *Gacumbitsi* Trial Judgement, *supra* note 19, para. 281; *Semanza* Trial Judgement, *supra* note 19, para. 382; *Bagilishema* Trial Judgement, *supra* note 18, para. 30 (holding that '[t]he principle of criminal responsibility applies also to an individual . . . who uses his or her authority to order, and thus compel a person subject to that authority, to commit a crime'.).

[140] See *Ntagerura et al.* Appeal Judgement, *supra* note 19, para. 365 (holding that the physical element of ordering is fulfilled when the accused, '*usant de sa position d'autorité*, donne l'ordre') (emphasis added); *Mpambara* Trial Judgement, *supra* note 19, para. 19; *Brđanin* Trial Judgement, *supra* note 19, para. 270 ('Responsibility for ordering requires proof that a person in a position of authority uses that authority to instruct another to commit an offence.'); *Galić* Trial Judgement, *supra* note 18, para. 168. Cf. *Kordić and Čerkez* Appeal Judgement, *supra* note 19, para. 28 (holding merely that 'a person in a position of authority instructs another person to commit an offence' without stating that the former must use that authority in instructing the latter).

The order need not be in writing or take any particular form;[141] it can be express or implied;[142] and the existence of an order may be proven through direct or circumstantial evidence.[143] The Trial Chamber in *Galić* gave a number of examples of circumstantial evidence permitting an inference that a crime was ordered:

'[O]rdering' . . . may be inferred from a variety of factors, such as the number of illegal acts, the number, identity and type of troops involved, the effective command and control exerted over these troops, the logistics involved, the widespread occurrence of the illegal acts, the tactical tempo of operations, the *modus operandi* of similar acts, the officers and staff involved, the location of the superior at the time and the knowledge of that officer of criminal acts committed under his command.[144]

The *Kamuhanda* Trial Chamber added that '[t]he position of authority of the person who gave an order may be inferred from the fact that the order was obeyed'.[145] As with planning and instigating,[146] an accused may not be convicted for ordering and physically committing the same crime.[147]

While it left open the possibility that the physical elements of other forms of responsibility may be fulfilled through an omission on the part of the accused,[148] the *Galić* Appeals Chamber in its November 2006 Judgement held that liability for ordering cannot ensue on the basis of an omission. Observing that it could not 'conceive of a situation in which an order would be given by an omission, in the absence of a prior positive act', the Appeals Chamber concluded that 'the omission of an act cannot equate to the mode of liability of ordering under Article 7(1) of the [ICTY] Statute'.[149] The Chamber

---

[141]   *Kamuhanda* Appeal Judgement, *supra* note 19, para. 76; *Limaj et al.* Trial Judgement, *supra* note 19, para. 515; *Strugar* Trial Judgement, *supra* note 18, para. 331; *Brđanin* Trial Judgement, *supra* note 19, para. 270; *Galić* Trial Judgement, *supra* note 18, para. 168; *Naletilić and Martinović* Trial Judgement, *supra* note 19, para. 61; *Kordić and Čerkez* Trial Judgement, *supra* note 18, para. 388; *Blaškić* Trial Judgement, *supra* note 20, para. 281.

[142]   *Naletilić and Martinović* Trial Judgement, *supra* note 19, para. 61; *Blaškić* Trial Judgement, *supra* note 20, para. 281.

[143]   *Galić* Appeal Judgement, *supra* note 52, para. 178 ('The Appeals Chamber . . . concludes that the mode of liability of ordering can be proven, like any other mode of liability, by circumstantial or direct evidence[.]'); *Kamuhanda* Appeal Judgement, *supra* note 19, para. 76; *Muvunyi* Trial Judgement, *supra* note 19, para. 468; *Limaj et al.* Trial Judgement, *supra* note 19, para. 515; *Strugar* Trial Judgement, *supra* note 18, para. 331; *Galić* Trial Judgement, *supra* note 18, para. 171; *Kordić and Čerkez* Trial Judgement, *supra* note 18, para. 388; *Blaškić* Trial Judgement, *supra* note 20, para. 281.

[144]   *Galić* Trial Judgement, *supra* note 18, para. 171.

[145]   *Kamuhanda* Trial Judgement, *supra* note 19, para. 594.

[146]   See *supra* text accompanying notes 87, 112.

[147]   *Stakić* Trial Judgement, *supra* note 18, para. 445; *Blaškić* Trial Judgement, *supra* note 20, para 278; *Akayesu* Trial Judgement, *supra* note 11, paras. 468, 532.

[148]   *Galić* Appeal Judgement, *supra* note 52, para. 176 ('The failure to act of a person in a position of authority, who is in a superior-subordinate relationship with the physical perpetrator, may give rise to another mode of responsibility under Article 7(1) of the [ICTY] Statute or superior responsibility under Article 7(3)[.]').

[149]   *Ibid.*, para. 176. The Appeals Chamber added in a footnote that '[i]t would thus be erroneous to speak of "ordering by omission"'. *Ibid.*, para. 177 n. 508.

distinguished the situation in which the accused orders another not to perform an act, where the accused is aware of the substantial likelihood that such omission will amount to or result in the commission of a crime.[150]

5.4.2 Authority of accused

The accused enjoyed authority – formal or informal – over the person to whom the order was given

Prior to the respective ICTY and ICTR Appeal Judgements in *Kordić and Čerkez* and *Semanza*, the jurisprudence of the *ad hoc* Tribunals was inconsistent regarding the required relationship between the accused and the person ordered. The ICTR Trial Chamber in *Akayesu* opined that '[o]rdering implies a superior-subordinate relationship between the person giving the order and the one executing it',[151] and this formulation was subsequently repeated by the *Blaškić* Trial Chamber of the ICTY and a number of ICTR trial chambers.[152] The Trial Chamber in *Kordić and Čerkez*, interpreting *Akayesu* as requiring a formal relationship between the accused and the person ordered, held that 'no formal superior-subordinate relationship is required' provided 'the accused possessed the authority to order';[153] the Trial Chamber remarked that it 'disagree[d] with the *Blaškić* and *Akayesu* Trial Chambers in this respect'.[154]

Several subsequent judgements of both *ad hoc* Tribunals followed the *Kordić and Čerkez* approach to the apparent exclusion of that of *Akayesu*,[155] although the ICTR Trial Chamber in *Semanza* opted for the *Akayesu* formulation.[156] After discussing Laurent Semanza's influence among the Interahamwe militiamen who physically perpetrated the massacre at Musha church,[157] the Chamber chose not to convict him of ordering genocide and extermination as a crime against humanity for this incident, and instead convicted him of complicity in genocide and aiding and abetting extermination.[158] The

[150] *Ibid.*, para. 177 n. 507. [151] *Ibid.*, para. 483.

[152] *Semanza* Trial Judgement, *supra* note 19, para. 382; *Blaškić* Trial Judgement, *supra* note 20, para. 281 (quoting *Akayesu*); *Musema* Trial Judgement, *supra* note 19, para. 121; *Rutaganda* Trial Judgement, *supra* note 19, para. 39.

[153] *Kordić and Čerkez* Trial Judgement, *supra* note 18, para. 388. [154] *Ibid.*, para. 388 n. 533.

[155] See *Gacumbitsi* Trial Judgement, *supra* note 19, para. 282; *ibid.*, para. 281 (observing that, on this issue, 'the two *ad hoc* Tribunals have ruled differently'); *infra* text accompanying notes 167–168 (discussing this aspect of the *Gacumbitsi* Trial Judgement); *Kamuhanda* Trial Judgement, *supra* note 19, para. 594; *Kajelijeli* Trial Judgement, *supra* note 19, para. 763. Cf. *Naletilić and Martinović* Trial Judgement, *supra* note 19, para. 61 (quoting *Akayesu* and then appearing to follow *Kordić and Čerkez* – '[a] formal superior-subordinate relationship is not required' – without acknowledging that these two standards may be inconsistent with one another).

[156] *Semanza* Trial Judgement, *supra* note 19, para. 382.

[157] See *ibid.*, paras. 178, 196, 425–429, 446–449.

[158] See *ibid.*, paras. 430, 435–435, 465, 553. *See* Chapter 4, text accompanying notes 51–55, for a more detailed discussion of Semanza's conviction for complicity in genocide.

prosecution argued on appeal that the Trial Chamber had erroneously imposed a requirement that there be a formal relationship between Semanza and the physical perpetrators.[159] Endorsing the position established by the ICTY Appeals Chamber five months previously in the December 2004 *Kordić and Čerkez* Judgement,[160] the ICTR Appeals Chamber held that '[n]o formal superior-subordinate relationship between the accused and the perpetrator is required. It is sufficient that there is some position of authority on the part of the accused that would compel another to commit a crime in following the accused's order'.[161] The Chamber added that 'authority creating the kind of superior-subordinate relationship envisaged under Article 6(1) of the [ICTR] Statute for ordering may be informal or of a purely temporary nature', and '[w]hether such authority exists is a question of fact'.[162]

On the facts before it, the Appeals Chamber determined that the Trial Chamber had erred in finding that Semanza did not possess the requisite level of authority over the physical perpetrators:

In the present case, the evidence is that the Appellant directed attackers, including soldiers and Interahamwe, to kill Tutsi refugees who had been separated from the Hutu refugees at Musha church. According to the Trial Chamber, the refugees 'were then executed on the directions' of the Appellant. On these facts, no reasonable trier of fact could hold otherwise than that the attackers to whom the Appellant gave directions regarded him as speaking with authority. That authority created a superior-subordinate relationship which was real, however informal or temporary, and sufficient to find the Appellant responsible for ordering under Article 6(1) of the Statute.[163]

The Appeals Chamber accordingly overturned the Trial Chamber's convictions for complicity in genocide and aiding and abetting extermination, and substituted convictions for ordering genocide and ordering extermination 'in relation to the massacre at Musha church'.[164] Subsequent trial and appellate jurisprudence of both Tribunals has consistently followed *Kordić and Čerkez* and *Semanza* in holding that the authority of the accused may be informal,[165]

---

[159] *Semanza* Appeal Judgement, *supra* note 19, paras. 349–351.
[160] *Kordić and Čerkez* Appeal Judgement, *supra* note 19, para. 28 ('A formal superior-subordinate relationship between the accused and the perpetrator is not required.').
[161] *Semanza* Appeal Judgement, *supra* note 19, para. 361.
[162] *Ibid.*, para. 363.   [163] *Ibid.* (footnote removed).
[164] *Ibid.*, para. 364. Accord, *ibid.*, para. 389, pp. 125–126 (increasing Semanza's sentence from twenty-four-and-a-half years to thirty-four-and-a-half years). Chapter 6, text accompanying notes 123–176, discusses how the form of responsibility pursuant to which an accused is convicted relates to the sentence imposed on him.
[165] See *Galić* Appeal Judgement, *supra* note 52, para. 176; *Kamuhanda* Appeal Judgement, *supra* note 19, para. 75 (endorsing the *Semanza* Appeals Chamber's holding and observing that, in contrast to superior responsibility under Article 6(3) of the ICTR Statute, ordering does not require the accused to have 'effective control' over the person ordered, but merely that he have 'authority'); *Muvunyi* Trial Judgement, *supra* note 19, para. 467; *Mpambara* Trial Judgement, *supra* note 19, para. 19; *Limaj et al.* Trial Judgement, *supra* note 19, para. 515 ('[I]t is sufficient that the orderer possesses the authority, either

although the *Muvunyi* Trial Chamber observed that proof of a formal superior-subordinate relationship 'may be evidentially relevant' to show that the accused had authority over the person ordered.[166]

The ICTR Trial Chamber in *Gacumbitsi*, which rendered its judgement in June 2004 – well before the *Semanza* Appeal Judgement – followed the *Kordić and Čerkez* Trial Judgement in holding that a formal superior-subordinate relationship is not required.[167] The Chamber provided some insight into how one goes about determining whether a given accused had sufficient authority, in the circumstances, to engage his liability as an orderer:

> The authority of an influential person can derive from his social, economic, political or administrative standing, or from his abiding moral principles ... When people are confronted with an emergency or danger, they can naturally turn to such [an] influential person, expecting him to provide a solution, assistance or take measures to deal with the crisis. When he speaks, everyone listens to him with keen interest; his advice commands overriding respect over all others and the people could easily see his actions as an encouragement ... In certain circumstances, the authority of an influential person is enhanced by a lawful or unlawful element of coercion, such as declaring a state of emergency, the *de facto* exercise of an administrative function, or even the use of threat or unlawful force. The presence of a coercive element is such that it can determine the way the words of the influential person are perceived. Thus, mere words of exhortation or encouragement would be perceived as orders within the meaning of Article 6(1) [of the ICTR Statute]. Such a situation does not, *ipso facto*, lead to the conclusion that a formal superior-subordinate relationship exists between the person giving the order and the person executing it. As a matter of fact, instructions given outside a purely informal context by a superior to his subordinate within a formal administrative hierarchy, be they *de jure* or *de facto*, would also be considered as an 'order' within the meaning of Article 6(1) of the Statute.[168]

This clarification that an accused orderer need merely possess informal and temporary authority over the person ordered is one of the major factors

---

de jure or *de facto*, to order the commission of an offence, and that his authority can be reasonably implied.'); *Strugar* Trial Judgement, *supra* note 18, para. 331; *Brđanin* Trial Judgement, *supra* note 19, para. 270. But see *Strugar* Trial Judgement, *supra* note 18, para. 331 (holding that 'ordering requires that at the time of the offence, an accused possessed the authority to issue *binding* orders to the alleged perpetrator') (emphasis added). The *Strugar* Trial Chamber did not clarify what it meant by 'binding' orders, but the thrust of the pre-*Strugar* case law and *Strugar*'s own affirmation that no formal relationship is required suggest that the order need not be binding in a legal sense. Perhaps the Chamber was merely referring to orders that are impossible for the other person to ignore in practice (for example, due to psychological, moral, or social influences). The only 'ordering' scenario that *Strugar* itself discusses took place in a formal military hierarchy in which Strugar's orders were in fact legally binding on his military subordinates. See *ibid.*, paras. 334–347. Cf. *Muvunyi* Trial Judgement, *supra* note 19, para. 467 (holding that the accused must use his position of authority 'to issue a binding instruction to or otherwise compel another to commit a crime').

[166] *Ibid.*   [167] *Gacumbitsi* Trial Judgement, *supra* note 19, para. 282.   [168] *Ibid.*

370 Forms of responsibility in international criminal law

distinguishing ordering from superior responsibility under Article 7(3) of the ICTY Statute and Article 6(3) of the ICTR Statute. In the latter form of responsibility, while the superior-subordinate relationship between the accused and his subordinate may be *de jure* or *de facto*, the accused must always possess 'effective control' over the subordinate – that is, the material ability to prevent or punish the subordinate's criminal conduct.[169] By contrast, ordering has no requirement of effective control.[170]

5.4.3 Direct and substantial contribution

The accused's conduct had a direct and substantial effect on perpetration of a crime

As with planning and instigating,[171] liability for ordering cannot be inchoate: a crime must actually be perpetrated in the execution of the accused's order.[172] Although some causal connection must be shown between the conduct of the accused and that of the physical perpetrator,[173] the prosecution need not prove that the crime would not have been committed absent the accused's contribution.[174] While the ICTY Appeals Chamber in *Kordić and Čerkez* established for both planning and instigating that the accused's conduct must have been 'a factor substantially contributing to the conduct of another person in committing the crime',[175] it was curiously silent on how strong the causal connection between the conduct of an accused orderer and that of the physical perpetrator must be. The ICTR Appeals Chamber in *Kamuhanda*, dealing exclusively with ordering, subsequently set forth what

---

[169] See *Gacumbitsi* Appeal Judgement, *supra* note 124, para. 143; *Kordić and Čerkez* Appeal Judgement, *supra* note 19, para. 840. See also Chapter 3, text accompanying notes 210–219.

[170] *Kamuhanda* Appeal Judgement, *supra* note 19, para. 75:

Superior responsibility under Article 6(3) of the [ICTR] Statute requires that the accused exercise 'effective control' over his subordinates to the extent that he can prevent them from committing crimes or punish them after they have committed the crimes. To be held responsible under Article 6(1) of the Statute for ordering a crime, on the contrary, it is sufficient that the accused have authority over the perpetrator of the crime[.]

[171] See *supra* notes 91, 122, and accompanying text.

[172] *Brđanin* Trial Judgement, *supra* note 19, para. 267; *Kajelijeli* Trial Judgement, *supra* note 19, para. 758; *Semanza* Trial Judgement, *supra* note 19, para. 378; *Musema* Trial Judgement, *supra* note 19, paras. 115–116; *Rutaganda* Trial Judgement, *supra* note 19, paras. 34, 38; *Akayesu* Trial Judgement, *supra* note 11, para. 473.

[173] *Strugar* Trial Judgement, *supra* note 18, para. 332 ('[A] causal link between the act of ordering and the physical perpetration of a crime, analogous to that which is required for "instigating", also needs to be demonstrated as part of the *actus reus* of ordering.') (footnote removed).

[174] *Ibid.*

[175] *Kordić and Čerkez* Appeal Judgement, *supra* note 19, para. 27 (instigating). Accord, *ibid.*, para. 26 ('It is sufficient to demonstrate that the planning was a factor substantially contributing to such criminal conduct.').

may actually be a more stringent standard: the accused's order must have 'a direct and substantial effect on the commission of the illegal act'.[176]

5.5 Planning, instigating and ordering in the International Criminal Court and internationalised criminal tribunals

5.5.1 The International Criminal Court

Article 25 of the Rome Statute sets forth almost all the forms of individual criminal responsibility within the jurisdiction of the International Criminal Court (ICC).[177] Sub-paragraph 3(b) of this Article provides:

3. In accordance with this Statute, a person shall be criminally responsible and liable for punishment for a crime within the jurisdiction of the Court if that person:
   [...]
   (b) Orders, solicits or induces the commission of such a crime which in fact occurs or is attempted[.][178]

Unlike the *ad hoc* Statutes, the Rome Statute does not specifically refer to liability for planning crimes, but it is likely that almost all the conduct that is characterised as 'planning' by the *ad hoc* Tribunals would be covered by the relatively broad categories of responsibility expressed in subparagraphs (3)(c) and (3)(d) of Article 25.[179] Similarly, although the Rome Statute contains no explicit reference to the form of responsibility termed 'instigation' by the *ad hoc* Statutes, contemporaneous commentary suggests that the terms 'solicits' and 'induces' cover similar substantive ground.[180]

---

[176] *Kamuhanda* Appeal Judgement, *supra* note 19, para. 75. Cf. *Kamuhanda* Trial Judgement, *supra* note 19, para. 590 (holding that the accused's conduct must have 'substantially contributed to, or ha[ve] had a substantial effect on, the completion of a crime'); *Galić* Trial Judgement, *supra* note 18, para. 169 (holding that the accused's conduct must have had 'a positive effect in bringing about the commission of crimes'); *Kajelijeli* Trial Judgement, *supra* note 19, para. 759 (same as *Kamuhanda* Trial Judgement); *Semanza* Trial Judgement, *supra* note 19, para. 379 (same as *Kamuhanda* Trial Judgement).

[177] Article 28 of the Rome Statute deals with superior responsibility, which is the subject of Chapter 3 of this book. See also Chapter 4, note 327 (despite superior responsibility's inclusion in a different provision of the Rome Statute, it is very much a part of individual criminal responsibility).

[178] Rome Statute of the International Criminal Court, entered into force 1 July 2002, UN Doc. A/CONF. 183/9 (1998) ('Rome Statute'), Art. 25(3)(b).

[179] *Ibid.*, Art. 25(3)(c) ('For the purpose of facilitating the commission of such a crime, aids, abets or *otherwise assists in its commission or its attempted commission*') (emphasis added); *ibid.*, Art. 25(3)(d) ('*In any other way* contributes to the commission or attempted commission of such a crime by a group of persons acting with a common purpose') (emphasis added). Although the second provision is limited by its terms to criminal activity by a group of persons, presumably excluding liability for the sole planner of a crime committed by a single perpetrator, the first provision would seem broad enough to ground a finding of responsibility for such an accused.

[180] See, e.g., Kai Ambos, 'Individual Criminal Responsibility', in Otto Triffterer (ed.), *Commentary on the Rome Statute of the International Criminal Court* (1999), p. 480:

The cases begun to date at the ICC have focused on allegations of commission, as set forth in sub-paragraph (3)(a) of the Statute,[181] and the forms of responsibility in sub-paragraph (3)(b) to ground the charges against the accused, instead of other forms of responsibility.[182] Given the manner in which the relevant court documents describe the position of the accused with regard to the alleged physical perpetrators, these cases are likely to involve consideration of similar facts – and the application of similar legal standards – as those encountered and employed by the *ad hoc* Tribunals under the rubrics of planning, instigating, and ordering.[183] It remains to be seen whether, in application of its provision on ordering, the ICC will follow the lead of the *ad hoc* Tribunals, and determine that neither a formal superior-subordinate relationship nor 'effective control', as that term is employed in the context of

> Inducing is a kind of umbrella term covering soliciting which in turn, has a stronger and more specific meaning than inducing. Inducing is broad enough to cover any conduct which causes or leads another person to commit a crime, including soliciting that person ... In sum, both forms of complicity are applicable to cases in which a person is influenced by another to commit a crime. Unlike the case of 'ordering' a superior-subordinate relationship is not necessary.

Although such observations would indicate that all the types of conduct listed in sub-paragraph 3(b) are forms of responsibility, it should be noted that solicitation is treated as an inchoate crime in certain domestic jurisdictions. See, e.g., Tex. Penal Code Ann. §15.03 (Vernon 1994), which lists 'criminal solicitation' under 'Title 4: Inchoate Offences' along with conspiracy and attempt, and provides as follows:

> A person commits an offense if, with intent that a capital felony or felony of the first degree be committed, he requests, commands, or attempts to induce another to engage in specific conduct that, under the circumstances surrounding his conduct as the actor believes them to be, would constitute the felony or make the other a party to its commission.

Since other inchoate crimes – incitement and attempt – are also discussed in Article 25, one cannot completely dismiss the possibility that solicitation may also be treated as an inchoate crime before the ICC. See Chapter 4, text accompanying notes 336–342.

[181] Rome Statute, *supra* note 178, Art. 25(3)(a) (referring to a person who '[c]ommits ... a crime, whether as an individual, jointly with another or through another person, regardless of whether that other person is criminally responsible'). See Chapter 2, text accompanying notes 722–734.

[182] See Chapter 2, text accompanying note 734; Chapter 3, text accompanying note 621; Chapter 4, text accompanying note 334.

[183] See, e.g., *Situation in Uganda*, Case No. ICC-02/04-01/05, Warrant of Arrest for Joseph Kony issued on 8 July 2005 as amended on 27 September 2005, 27 September 2005, paras. 9–10 (emphasis added):

> Considering the specific allegations that ... senior LRA commanders are the key members of 'Control Altar', the section representing the core LRA leadership responsible for *devising and implementing LRA strategy*, including standing orders to attack and brutalise civilian populations;
> Having examined the Prosecutor's submission that, in his capacity as overall leader and Commander-in-Chief of the LRA, individually or together with other persons whose arrests are sought by the Prosecutor, Joseph Kony committed, *ordered or induced the commission* of several crimes within the jurisdiction of the Court during the period from 1 July 2002 to REDACTED 2004 ...

Interestingly, the arrest warrant against the only ICC accused in custody thus far charges him with responsibility only under Article 25(3)(a) for commission, notwithstanding the evidence apparently presented of his superior position and references to the hierarchical organisation of the Lord's Resistance Army. See *Situation in the Democratic Republic of the Congo in the Case of Prosecutor v. Thomas Lubanga Dyilo*, Case No. ICC-01/04-01/06, Warrant of Arrest, 10 February 2006, pp. 3–4. Presumably, then, the prosecution's case will rest on the theory that Lubanga committed these crimes through others, namely his subordinates. See Chapter 2, text accompanying notes 723–725.

superior responsibility, is required for the imposition of liability on an accused orderer.[184]

5.5.2 *The internationalised tribunals*

5.5.2.1 *Special Court for Sierra Leone (SCSL)*

Article 6(1) of the SCSL Statute, essentially identical to Article 7/6(1) of the *ad hoc* Statutes, provides:

A person who *planned, instigated, ordered*, committed or otherwise aided and abetted in the planning, preparation or execution of a crime referred to in articles 2 to 4 of the present Statute shall be individually responsible for the crime.[185]

The work of the SCSL is focused on five indictments,[186] and all five allege that the accused charged therein are liable under all of the forms of responsibility explicitly or implicitly included in Article 6(1) of the SCSL Statute[187] – including planning, instigating and ordering – for all criminal conduct alleged in the relevant indictment.[188] Although at least one pre-trial decision has stated that the law may require the indictment to indicate clearly and disjunctively which form of responsibility in Article 6(1) is charged with regard to each

---

[184] See *supra* text accompanying notes 165–170.

[185] Statute of the Special Court for Sierra Leone, 2178 UNTS 138, UN Doc. S/2002/246 (2002), Appendix II ('SCSL Statute'), Art. 6(1) (emphasis added). It should be noted that, befitting the SCSL's status as a hybrid court, this provision of the SCSL Statute apparently limits the direct application of the forms of responsibility recognised in international criminal law to the international crimes listed in the Statute. By referring specifically to Articles 2 to 4 of the Statute, Article 6 explicitly excludes the crimes under Sierra Leonean law listed in Article 5. Pursuant to Article 6(5) of the Statute, '[i]ndividual criminal responsibility for the[se] crimes ... shall be determined in accordance with the respective laws of Sierra Leone'.

[186] These indictments are those against Charles Taylor; Brima, Kamara and Kanu ('*AFRC* Case'); Sesay, Kallon and Gbao ('*RUF* Case'); Norman, Fofana and Kondewa ('*CDF* Case'); and Johnny Paul Koroma. The current total of five is the result of the consolidation of several indictments into the joint indictments faced by the three groups of accused in the multi-defendant trials, as well as the withdrawal of indictments against Foday Sankoh and Sam Bockarie after their deaths in 2003. See *Prosecutor* v. *Sankoh*, Case No. SCSL-2003-02-PT, Withdrawal of Indictment, 8 December 2003 (Trial Chamber endorsing Prosecutor's withdrawal of indictment); *Prosecutor* v. *Bockarie*, Case No. SCSL-2003-04-PT, Withdrawal of Indictment, 8 December 2003 (same). Trials have concluded in two of the three multi-defendant cases – judgements are expected in 2007 – and pre-trial proceedings against Taylor began after his rendition in March 2006; Koroma is still at large.

[187] The form implicitly included in this Article is joint criminal enterprise. See *supra* Chapter 2, text accompanying note 738.

[188] See *Prosecutor* v. *Brima, Kamara and Kanu*, Case No. SCSL-2004-16-PT, Further Amended Consolidated Indictment, 18 February 2005 ('Current *AFRC* Indictment'), para. 35; *Prosecutor* v. *Sesay, Kallon and Gbao*, Case No. SCSL-2004-15-T, Corrected Amended Consolidated Indictment, 2 August 2006 ('Current *RUF* Indictment'), para. 38; *Prosecutor* v. *Norman, Fofana and Kondewa*, Case No. SCSL-2004-14-PT, Indictment, 5 February 2004 ('*CDF* Indictment'), para. 20; *Prosecutor* v. *Koroma*, Case No. SCSL-2003-03-I, Indictment, 7 March 2003 ('*Koroma* Indictment'), para. 26; *Prosecutor* v. *Taylor*, Case No. SCSL-03-01-I, Amended Indictment, 16 March 2006 ('Amended *Taylor* Indictment'), p. 2 (alleging simply that 'the Accused, pursuant to Article 6.1 and, or alternatively, Article 6.3 of the Statute, is individually criminally responsible for the crimes alleged below'); *ibid.*, para. 33 (including language virtually identical to that used in indictments in other cases).

crime,[189] it does not appear that this ruling has affected the pleading practice of the Special Prosecutor. Instead, although four of the five indictments have been amended since the date of this decision,[190] all but one simply repeat the terms of Article 6(1), alleging that the accused,

by their acts or omissions are individually criminally responsible for the crimes referred to in Articles 2, 3 and 4 of the Statute as alleged in this Indictment, which crimes each of them planned, instigated, ordered, committed, or in whose planning, preparation or execution each Accused otherwise aided or abetted, or which crimes were within a common purpose, plan or design[.][191]

The sole exception is the case summary in the case against Charles Taylor. After the particular procedural history that led to the filing of two separate instruments setting out the charges in this case,[192] the Prosecutor has specifically alleged in the case summary the material facts relating to the forms of responsibility, following closely the terms in which their elements have been expressed in the *ad hoc* jurisprudence. The allegations with regard to planning, instigating and ordering are among the most detailed in this document, asserting as follows:

Planning
[Taylor], individually, or participating with his direct subordinates and/or high level leaders of the RUF, AFRC and AFRC/RUF Junta or alliance, planned armed operations in Sierra Leone which were themselves crimes or involved the commission of crimes alleged in the Amended Indictment.

Instigating
Throughout the armed conflict, [Taylor] encouraged the actions of the RUF, AFRC and AFRC/RUF Junta or alliance, and Liberian fighters, thereby prompting the perpetrators to commit the crimes alleged in the Amended Indictment.

---

[189] See *Prosecutor* v. *Sesay*, Case No. SCSL-2003-05-PT, Decision and Order on Defence Preliminary Motion for Defects in the Form of the Indictment, 13 October 2003, para. 12; see also Chapter 3, text accompanying notes 665–668 (discussion of this decision). But see *Prosecutor* v. *Kondewa*, Case No. SCSL-2003-12-PT, Decision and Order on Defence Preliminary Motion for Defects in the Form of the Indictment, 27 November 2003, para. 10 (holding that the Prosecution is not obliged to elect between the different forms of responsibility under Article 6(1), and noting that the distinction between the various forms was 'pre-eminently an evidentiary matter'; if the Prosecution 'has chosen to plead all the different heads of responsibility, consistent with its discretion . . . [it] will carry the burden of proving the existence of each at the trial'). See generally Chapter 6.

[190] See Current *AFRC* Indictment, *supra* note 188; *Sesay et al.*, Current *RUF* Indictment, *supra* note 188; *Norman et al.*, Case No. SCSL-04-14-AR73, Decision on Amendment of the Consolidated Indictment, 16 May 2005 (resulting in the approval of the *CDF* Indictment, *supra* note 188); Amended *Taylor* Indictment, *supra* note 188. The single indictment yet to be amended is that against Koroma, the only SCSL accused who remains at large.

[191] *CDF* Indictment, *supra* note 188, para. 20; Current *AFRC* Indictment, *supra* note 188, para. 35; Current *RUF* Indictment, *supra* note 188, para. 38; see also *Koroma* Indictment, *supra* note 188, para. 27.

[192] See Chapter 2, notes 739–746 and accompanying text.

Ordering

Through his positions ... and his close associations with ... senior leaders of RUF and AFRC, AFRC/RUF Junta or alliance [*sic*], [Taylor], individually, or in concert with those senior leaders, exercised *de jure* or *de facto* control over the perpetrators of the crimes alleged in the Amended Indictment ...

[Taylor] provided instruction, direction and guidance involving the commission of crimes alleged in the Amended Indictment directly to, and through, senior and/or intermediate level commanders within the RUF, AFRC, AFRC/RUF Junta or alliance, and directly to, or through intermediate level superiors of Liberian fighters.[193]

It is worth noting, perhaps, that the case summary does not specifically and clearly allege that Taylor gave direct orders for the commission of crimes, although the indictment itself plainly charges ordering in its litany of forms of responsibility implicated by the accused's alleged conduct.[194]

More marked reliance on the precedents of the *ad hoc* Tribunals is evident in judicial pronouncements at the SCSL. In the decision on motions for judgement of acquittal issued at the midpoint of the case against Brima, Kamara and Kanu, the Trial Chamber held that the requirements for each form of responsibility were as follows:

'Planning' implies that one or several persons contemplate designing the commission of a crime at both the preparatory and execution phases. The *actus reus* requires that the accused, alone or together with others, designed the criminal conduct constituting the crimes charged. It is sufficient to demonstrate that the planning was a factor substantially contributing to such criminal conduct. The *mens rea* requires that the accused acted with direct intent in relation to his own planning or with the awareness of the substantial likelihood that a crime would be committed in the execution of that plan. Planning with such awareness has to be regarded as accepting that crime.[195]
[...]
'Instigating' means prompting another to commit an offence. Both acts and omissions may constitute instigating, which covers express as well as implied conduct. A nexus between the instigation and the perpetration must be proved, but it is not necessary to demonstrate that the crime would not have been perpetrated without the involvement of the accused. The *actus reus* requires that the accused prompted another person to commit the offence and that the instigation was a factor substantially contributing to the conduct of the other person(s) committing the crime. The *mens rea* requires that

---

[193] *Taylor*, Case Summary Accompanying the Amended Indictment, 16 March 2006, paras. 34–37.

[194] Amended *Taylor* Indictment, *supra* note 188, para. 33.

[195] *Brima et al.*, Case No. SCSL-04-16-T, Decision on Defence Motions for Judgement of Acquittal Pursuant to Rule 98, 31 March 2006, para. 284 (citing, but not attributing the almost verbatim language to, the *Brđanin, Stakić* and *Krstić* Trial Judgements, and the *Kordić and Čerkez* Appeal Judgement). See also *ibid.*, para. 285 ('Where an accused is found guilty of having committed a crime, he or she cannot at the same time be convicted of having planned the same crime.') (citing *Kordić and Čerkez* Trial Judgement, *supra* note 13, para. 386).

the accused acted with direct intent or with the awareness that a crime would be committed in the execution of that instigation.[196]

[...]

Responsibility for ordering requires proof that a person in a position of authority uses that authority to instruct another to commit an offence. A formal superior/subordinate relationship between the accused and the perpetrator is not required. It is sufficient that the accused possessed the authority to order the commission of an offence and that such authority can be reasonably implied. There is no requirement that the order be given in writing or in any particular form, and the existence of the order may be proven through circumstantial evidence. It is not necessary for the order to be given by the superior directly to the person(s) who perform(s) the *actus reus* of the offence. What is important is the [accused] commander's *mens rea*, not that of the subordinate executing the order ... The *mens rea* requires that the accused acted with direct intent in relation to his own ordering or with the awareness of the substantial likelihood that a crime would be committed in the execution of that order.[197]

Unfortunately, this heavy reliance on the elements developed by the *ad hoc* chambers also appears unquestioning, and is not balanced by an independent examination of the basis (in logic, if not in law) for some of the holdings in question. Most notably, like most *ad hoc* trial benches after the *Blaškić* Trial Judgement, the *AFRC* Chamber simply repeated the statement that an accused could instigate by omission without considering whether other forms of responsibility would be more appropriate for the hypothetical factual situations originally offered in support of the theory.[198] Although the jurisprudence of the ICTY and ICTR is justifiably given significant weight in respect of the legal definitions of the crimes and forms of responsibility in international law, it is to be hoped that other successor courts will take a more critical view of their decisions and judgements.

5.5.2.2 East Timor: Special Panels for Serious Crimes (SPSC)

The primary provision of the constitutive document for the Special Panels with regard to individual criminal responsibility, Section 14 of UNTAET Regulation No. 2000/15, mirrored Article 25 of the Rome Statute. As such, Section 14.3(b) was the operative provision for ordering, soliciting, or inducing, providing:

14.3. In accordance with the present regulation, a person shall be criminally responsible and liable for punishment for a crime within the jurisdiction of the panels if that person:
    [...]

---

[196] *Ibid.*, para. 293 (similarly citing, but not attributing the almost verbatim language to, the *Akayesu* and *Brđanin* Trial Judgements and the *Kordić and Čerkez* Appeal Judgement).

[197] *Ibid.*, paras. 295–296 (similarly citing, but not attributing the almost verbatim language to, the *Krstić*, *Brđanin*, *Kordić and Čerkez*, *Akayesu* and *Blaškić* Trial Judgements and the *Kordić and Čerkez* Appeal Judgement).

[198] See *supra* text accompanying notes 119–120.

(b) orders, solicits or induces the commission of such a crime which in fact occurs or is attempted[.][199]

The practice of the SPSC had relatively little to add to the range of inter-national judicial experience with these forms of responsibility. First, many of the cases heard by the panels involved low-level perpetrators, charged with physical commission of one or a few crimes. Moreover, because of the mixed subject-matter jurisdiction of the panels, such cases might not even have involved crimes under international law.[200] In other cases involving more senior accused, it is often difficult to discern the legal basis for the court's conclusion of guilt or innocence with regard to the crimes charged.[201] In general, if the panel was satisfied that the accused were deeply involved and participated in the crimes charged – by their presence or encouragement, command of others, or actual physical commission – a guilty verdict was reached, with little attention paid to the elements of the forms of responsibility, and very little explanation offered.[202]

5.5.2.3 *The Extraordinary Chambers in the Courts of Cambodia (ECCC)*

As is the case with common-purpose liability,[203] superior responsibility,[204] and aiding and abetting,[205] the approach taken by the governing law of the hybrid Cambodia chambers to planning, instigating and ordering largely adopts the wording of the *ad hoc* Statutes. In relevant part, Article 29 of the Law on the

[199] United Nations Transitional Administration in East Timor, Regulation No. 2000/15 on the Establishment of Panels with Exclusive Jurisdiction over Serious Criminal Offences, UN Doc. UNTAET/REG/2000/15, 6 June 2000 ('SPSC Regulation'), Section 14.3(b).
[200] See, e.g., *Prosecutor* v. *João Fernandes*, Case No. 01/00. C.G.2000, Sentencing Judgement, 25 January 2000 (accused pleaded guilty to single count of murder as a domestic crime, not as a crime against humanity; sentenced to twelve years' imprisonment); *Prosecutor* v. *Julio Fernandez*, Case No. 02/00. C.G.2000, Judgement, 27 February 2001 (accused found guilty of single count of murder as a domestic crime, not as a crime against humanity; sentenced to seven years' imprisonment with credit for time served).
[201] See Chapter 2, text accompanying notes 767–769.
[202] See, e.g., *Prosecutor* v. *Joni Marques, Manuel da Costa, João da Costa, Paulo da Costa, Amélio da Costa, Hilário da Silva, Gonsalo dos Santos, Alarico Fernandes, Mautersa Monis and Gilberto Fernandes*, Case No.09/2000, Judgement, 11 December 2001, available at http://ist-socrates.berkeley.edu/~warcrime/ET-Docs/CE-SPSC%20Final%20Decisions/2000/09-2000%20part%201%20Joni%20Marques%20et%20al%20Judgement.pdf, pp. 357–364, 371–381, 384–391. See especially *ibid.*, pp. 359–360, paras. 710, 716–717 (emphasis in original):

The order to kill [the victim] came either from Joni Marques or Rahmad – just after they came out of the room where they were holding a meeting. Anyhow, the Court is of the opinion that the order to kill was the outcome of what had been discussed by both of them, given the close ties between Team Alfa and Indonesian military officers ...

[Joni Marques] was one of the persons in charge. A palpable assumption of that belief is that Joni Marques, as soon as the victim died, *ordered* the burial.

His *mens rea* arises from the evidence that, by participating in the decision-making for ordering the killing of the victim, he really knew that it would occur by other expeditious means. For him, the death was an expected result.
[203] See Chapter 2, text accompanying notes 774–775.
[204] See Chapter 3, text accompanying notes 703–705.
[205] See Chapter 4, text accompanying notes 363–366.

Establishment of the Extraordinary Chambers in the Courts of Cambodia for the Prosecution of Crimes Committed during the Period of Democratic Kampuchea provides:

Any Suspect who *planned, instigated, ordered,* aided and abetted, or committed the crimes referred to in article 3 new, 4, 5, 6, 7 and 8 of this law shall be individually responsible for the crime.[206]

To date, there is not much available material relating to the functioning of the Extraordinary Chambers, and little academic discussion. The available documentation on the cases in which preparations have begun is sparse. The prosecutors and judges of the Extraordinary Chambers, both Cambodian and international, were only appointed in May 2006,[207] and trials were not expected to begin before 2007.[208] For these reasons, it will not be possible to understand how this hybrid court will apply this and other forms of responsibility in international criminal law until pre-trial and trial proceedings get under way.

5.5.2.4 *Supreme Iraqi Criminal Tribunal (SICT)*

As in its approach to common-purpose liability, where it adopted the ICC model and mirrored the text of Article 25 of the Rome Statute,[209] the relevant provision of the SICT Statute essentially copies Article 25(3)(b), providing for jurisdiction over the imposition of criminal responsibility on a person who 'orders, solicits or induces the commission of such a crime [within the jurisdiction of the SICT], which in fact occurs or is attempted'.[210]

In the first proceeding against Saddam Hussein and his co-accused (the 'Dujail case'), both the lead accused and three other defendants were charged with ordering the crimes at issue.[211] As a result of the imperfect unofficial

---

[206] The Law on the Establishment of the Extraordinary Chambers in the Courts of Cambodia for the Prosecution of Crimes Committed during the Period of Democratic Kampuchea, as amended on 27 October 2004, Doc. No. NS/RKM/1004/006, unofficial translation by the Council of Jurists and the Secretariat of the Task Force, revised on 29 September 2005, available at http://www.cambodia.-gov.kh/krt/english/law%20on%20establishment.htm, Art. 29 (emphasis added).

[207] See AU Washington College of Law: War Crimes Research Office, Extraordinary Chambers in the Courts of Cambodia Status Updates, available at http://www.wcl.american.edu/warcrimes/krt_updates.cfm (noting that by Royal Decree NS/RKT/0506/214 on 7 May 2006, King Norodom Sihamoni of Cambodia appointed seventeen national and twelve international judges and prosecutors to serve on the Extraordinary Chambers).

[208] Office of the Governor-General of New Zealand, Press Release, 'Cartwright appointed Cambodian War Crimes Tribunal trial judge', 9 May 2006, available at http://www.gov-gen.govt.nz/media/news.asp?type=current&ID=164.

[209] See Chapter 2, text accompanying notes 783–785.

[210] Statute of the Iraqi special Tribunal, Art. 15(4) available at http://www.iraq-ist.org/en/about/sec4.htm.

[211] See *Saddam Hussein*, Case No. 1/1st Criminal/2005, Accusation Document, 15 May 2006, available at http://www.law.case.edu/saddamtrial/documents/20060515_indictment_trans_saddam_hussein.pdf ('*Hussein* Charging Instrument'), pp. 3–4; *Barzan Ibrahim Al-Hasan*, Case No. 1/1st Criminal/2005, Accusation Document, 15 May 2006, available at http://www.law.case.edu/saddamtrial/documents/

translations of the charging instruments that are publicly available, it is unclear whether these accused were also charged with soliciting or inducing the crimes.[212] In the written judgement finally issued in November 2006, all four accused were convicted of ordering some or all of the crimes for which they were held responsible. The court's conclusions with regard to ordering were set out in brief, descriptive passages, which either repeated facts already found elsewhere in the judgement, or merely communicated the judges' conclusions that the evidence demonstrated that the accused had ordered the crimes.[213] Three of the convicted men – Hussein; Barzan Ibrahim Al-Hassan, his half-brother and former head of the Intelligence Service;[214] and Awad Hamad Al-Bandar, former chief judge of the Iraqi Revolutionary Court – were sentenced to death by hanging as punishment for their roles in murder as a crime against humanity; the fourth, Taha Yasin Ramadan, was sentenced to life imprisonment for his involvement in the same crime.[215] The death sentences were carried out on 30 December 2006 and 15 January 2007.[216]

The charging instruments in the second trial ('Anfal case'), begun in September 2006, were not yet public by the time this book was concluded. Those proceedings seem marred with chaos and procedural confusion similar to that which marked most of the first trial, so it may be equally difficult to determine how the judges approach the application of these forms of responsibility to the crimes charged in respect of that case.[217]

5.6 Conclusion

Unlike JCE, superior responsibility, complicity in genocide, and even aiding and abetting, the forms of responsibility of planning, instigating and ordering

20060515_indictment_trans_barzan_ibrahim.pdf, p. 3; *Taha Yasin Ramadan*, Case No. 1/1st Criminal/ 2005, Accusation Document, 15 May 2006, available at http://www.law.case.edu/saddamtrial/ documents/20060515_indictment_trans_taha_yasin_ramadan.pdf, p. 3; *Awad al-Bandar*, Case No. 1/ 1st Criminal/2005, Accusation Document, 15 May 2006, available at http://www.law.case.edu/ saddamtrial/documents/20060515_indictment_trans_awad_al-bandar.pdf, p. 3.

[212] See, e.g., Hussein Charging Instrument, *supra* note 211, p. 3 ('The person is considered responsible according to the stipulations of this code and to the stipulations of the penal code if he commits the following: ... Ordering the committing of a crime that was in fact committed, initiated, or urged and perpetrated to be committed.').

[213] See, e.g., Case No. 1/9 1st/2005, Judgement, 22 November 2006 ('Dujail Judgement') (English translation issued 4 December 2006), Part III, pp. 21–22, 34, 40, 45–46 (tribunal's conclusions with regard to ordering charges against Saddam Hussein).

[214] Also known as Barzan Ibrahim al-Tikriti.

[215] Dujail Judgement, *supra* note 213, Part VI p. 51; see also *ibid.*, pp. 51–52 (pronouncing the lesser sentences also imposed for other crimes).

[216] See BBC News, 'Saddam Hussein executed in Iraq', 30 December 2006, available at http://news. bbc.co.uk/2/hi/middle_east/6218485.stm; John F. Burns, 'Two Hussein Allies Are Hanged; One Is Decapitated', *New York Times*, 15 January 2007, available at http://www.nytimes.com/2007/01/15/ world/middleeast/16iraqcnd.html?ex = 1169614800&en = 75fe7d64a9f1ada7&ei = 5070.

[217] See Chapter 2, text accompanying notes 787–788. Since Hussein was executed in December 2006, he is no longer an accused in this second proceeding.

have been the subject of very little debate or controversy in the *ad hoc* jurisprudence, and indeed, on only seven occasions have the Tribunals' Appeals Chambers had occasion to deal with their elements in any detail.[218] While the resulting jurisprudential consistency and predictability is to be welcomed, it may be unfortunate that the chambers have not seen fit to subject the origins of these elements to any greater scrutiny. This observation holds particularly true for the physical elements, which were created by the *Akayesu* Trial Chamber citing no authority but the dictionary,[219] and have simply been perpetuated in the subsequent jurisprudence with very little alteration or commentary. Nevertheless, it is certain that planning, instigating and ordering have proven to be important and suitable mechanisms for describing the criminal conduct of a number of accused in civilian and military leadership positions.[220]

---

[218] See *Ntagerura et al.* Appeal Judgement, *supra* note 19, paras. 363–366; *Gacumbitsi* Appeal Judgement, *supra* note 124, paras. 113–117, 127–138; *Kamuhanda* Appeal Judgement, *supra* note 19, paras. 58–66, 73–76; *Semanza* Appeal Judgement, *supra* note 19, paras. 349–364; *Kordić and Čerkez* Appeal Judgement, *supra* note 19, paras. 28–32; *Blaškić* Appeal Judgement, *supra* note 22, paras. 27–42; *Akayesu* Appeal Judgement, *supra* note 103, paras. 474–483.

[219] See *supra* text accompanying notes 11–20.

[220] See, e.g., *Galić* Trial Judgement, *supra* note 18, paras. 747–752 (finding Galić, the commander of the Sarajevo Romanija Corps of the Bosnian Serb Army, guilty of ordering acts of violence calculated to spread terror among the civilian population as a violation of the laws or customs of war, and murder and inhumane acts as crimes against humanity, for his role in the shelling and sniping of civilians during the siege of Sarajevo); *Kordić and Čerkez* Trial Judgement, *supra* note 18, paras. 607–610, 626, 630–631, 642 (finding the accused Kordić, a high-level Bosnian Croat politician, guilty of planning and instigating various crimes perpetrated by units of the Croatian Defence Council (HVO) against Muslim civilians in the village of Ahmići); *ibid.*, paras. 577–586, 829 (finding Kordić guilty of planning, instigating and ordering crimes perpetrated by the HVO in the village of Busovača); *Rutaganda* Trial Judgement, *supra* note 19, paras. 229, 230, 244, 406, 416–418 (finding Rutaganda, the second vice-president of the National Committee of the Interahamwe, guilty of ordering extermination as a crime against humanity for, among other conduct, his role in instructing Interahamwe assailants to kill ten Tutsi detainees with machetes). See also *supra* text accompanying notes 73–74 (discussing planning findings for Mladen Naletilić, a Bosnian Croat paramilitary leader); 75–79 (discussing planning findings for Jean-Bosco Barayagwiza, a Hutu politician); 98 (discussing instigating findings for Zlatko Aleksovski, a Bosnian Croat prison warden); 99 (discussing instigating findings for Jean-Paul Akayesu, a Rwandan *bourgmestre*); 129–131 (discussing instigating findings for Emmanuel Ndindabahizi, a Rwandan government minister); 157–164 (discussing ordering findings for Laurent Semanza, a Rwandan *bourgmestre*).

6

Concurrent convictions and sentencing

This chapter deals with a number of practical questions concerning forms of responsibility that trial chambers must address when drafting a judgement. As the preceding chapters have demonstrated, the jurisprudence of the *ad hoc* Tribunals has identified various forms of responsibility enshrined in Article 7(1) of the ICTY Statute and Article 6(1) of the ICTR Statute ('Article 7/6(1)'), on the one hand, and Article 7(3) of the ICTY Statute and Article 6(3) of the ICTY Statute ('Article 7/6(3)'), on the other: planning, instigating, ordering, committing (including participating in a joint criminal enterprise, or JCE), aiding and abetting, and superior responsibility through the failure to prevent or the failure to punish subordinate criminal conduct.[1] The chambers have consistently permitted the *ad hoc* Prosecutors to charge several – or indeed all – of these forms of responsibility simultaneously under the same count of the indictment and in respect of the same crime.[2] Section 6.1 of this chapter sets forth the Tribunals' law and practice on how a chamber goes about choosing, from

---

[1] As discussed in Chapter 4, the authors take the view that 'complicity in genocide' in Article 4(3)(e) of the ICTY Statute and Article 2(3)(e) of the ICTR Statute is not a single form of responsibility, but rather a package that combines a form or forms of responsibility ('complicity') with the category of offences that constitute genocide. In the recent practice of the *ad hoc* Tribunals, complicity in genocide has been avoided by the Tribunals' respective Prosecutors and by chambers, who have preferred to characterise the accused's liability in the relevant circumstances as aiding and abetting genocide – that is, aiding and abetting in Article 7/6(1) 'read into' genocide under Article 4(3)(a) of the ICTY Statute and Article 2(3)(a) of the ICTY Statute. See Chapter 4, text accompanying notes 56–57, 128–138.

[2] See *infra* text accompanying notes 4–12.

among simultaneously charged forms of responsibility, that which best encapsulates the accused's contribution to the crime. The section also explores the extent to which the chamber must examine the accused's liability pursuant to those forms of responsibility it does not ultimately select to describe his conduct, and whether it may convict an accused concurrently for the same crime under two or more different forms of responsibility. Section 6.2 of the chapter then discusses how the form or forms of responsibility through which an accused is or could be found guilty affect the severity of his sentence. This chapter does not include a comparative survey of the practice of the other international or hybrid courts and tribunals, as they have either not included significant discussions of these issues in their jurisprudence, or not yet issued relevant decisions and judgements.

6.1 Choosing among forms of responsibility

The chambers of the *ad hoc* Tribunals have identified a number of pleading principles relating to the forms of responsibility to which the prosecution must adhere in the indictment.[3] Since it is not always possible for the

---

[3] See, e.g., *Prosecutor* v. *Simić*, Case No. IT-95-9-A, Judgement, 28 November 2006 ('*Simić* Appeal Judgement'), para. 22 (JCE pleading principles); *Prosecutor* v. *Kvočka, Radić, Žigić and Prcać*, Case No. IT-98-30/1-A, Judgement, 28 February 2005 ('*Kvočka et al.* Appeal Judgement'), para. 41 (when the prosecution charges the accused with ordering a crime, it must plead the 'material facts which allege[ ] that [the] [a]ccused ordered the commission' of the crime); *ibid.*, para. 65 (with respect to higher-level accused, the material facts that must be pleaded are those establishing the accused's responsibility, and 'less precision is required' in pleading the physical perpetrators' conduct); *Prosecutor* v. *Blaškić*, Case No. IT-95-14-A, Judgement, 29 July 2004 ('*Blaškić* Appeal Judgement'), para. 218 (listing the material facts that must be pleaded when an accused is charged with superior responsibility); *ibid.*, para. 226 (when the prosecution charges the accused with instigating a crime, it must describe precisely 'the instigating acts, and the instigated persons or groups of persons'); *Prosecutor* v. *Krnojelac*, Case No. IT-97-25-A, Judgement, 17 September 2003 ('*Krnojelac* Appeal Judgement'), para. 138 ('[T]he Prosecution must identify precisely the form or forms of liability alleged for each count as soon as possible and, in any event, before the start of trial.'); *Prosecutor* v. *Popović, Beara, Nikolić, Borovčanin, Tolimir, Miletić, Gvero, Pandurević and Trbić*, Case No. IT-05-88-PT, Decision on Motions Challenging the Indictment pursuant to Rule 72 of the Rules, 31 May 2006 ('*Popović et al.* Pre-Trial Indictment Decision'), paras. 4–5 (pleading principles for Articles 7/6(1) and 7/6(3)); *ibid.*, para. 25 ('[I]f the accused is charged with the "commission" of a crime, it should be made clear in the indictment whether he is charged with physical commission or participation in a JCE, or both.'); *ibid.*, para. 40 (where the prosecution charges conduct other than physical commission, 'the identity of the physical perpetrators may be indicated by "category" or "group"'); *Prosecutor* v. *Pavković, Lazarević, Đorđević and Lukić*, Case No. IT-03-70-PT, Decision on Vladimir Lazarević's Preliminary Motion on Form of Indictment, 8 July 2005, para. 7 (listing the material facts that must be pleaded when an accused is charged with JCE responsibility); *ibid.*, para. 10 (listing the material facts that must be pleaded when an accused is charged with superior responsibility); *ibid.*, para. 25 (the prosecution must identify JCE participants 'so far as their identity is known'); *Prosecutor* v. *Čermak and Markač*, Case No. IT-03-73-PT, Decision on Ivan Čermak and Mladen Markač's Motions on Form of Indictment, 8 March 2005, para. 10 (superior responsibility pleading principles); *Prosecutor* v. *Mrkšić, Radić and Šljivančanin*, Case No. IT-95-13/1-PT, Decision on Form of Consolidated Amended Indictment and on Prosecution Application to Amend, 23 January 2004, paras. 21–34 (JCE pleading principles); *ibid.*, paras. 35–44 (superior responsibility pleading principles); *Prosecutor* v. *Mrkšić*, Case No. IT-95-13/1-PT, Decision on Form of the Indictment, 19 June 2003 ('*Mrkšić* June 2003 Pre-Trial Indictment Decision'), paras. 9–10 (pleading principles for Articles 7/6(1) and 7/6(3)); *ibid.*, para. 65 (superior responsibility pleading principles); *Prosecutor* v. *Krnojelac*, Case No. IT-97-25-PT, Decision on the Defence Preliminary

prosecution to know ahead of trial which form of responsibility it will be able to prove on the basis of the available evidence, the chambers have allowed it to charge an accused with liability for the same crime simultaneously under more than one form of responsibility.[4] At the same time, however, they have encouraged the prosecution to be as specific as possible in the indictment with respect to which of the charged forms of responsibility relate to which crime,[5] warning that an indictment lacking sufficient specificity might later be deemed defective because it is too vague or fails in

Motion on the Form of the Indictment, 24 February 1999 ('*Krnojelac* February 1999 Pre-Trial Indictment Decision'), para. 13 (the prosecution must identify 'the particular acts of the accused himself or the particular course of conduct on his part which are alleged to constitute that responsibility'); *ibid.*, para. 19 (superior responsibility pleading principles); *Prosecutor* v. *Blaškić*, Case No. IT-95-14-PT, Decision on the Defence Motion to Dismiss the Indictment based upon Defects in the Form Thereof (Vagueness/Lack of Adequate Notice of Charges), 4 April 1997 ('*Blaškić* Pre-Trial Indictment Decision'), paras. 30–32 (general pleading principles for Articles 7/6(1) and 7/6(3)).

4 See *Blaškić* Appeal Judgement, *supra* note 3, para. 226 ('The Prosecution [i]s not required to choose between different forms of participation under Article 7(1); it [i]s entitled to plead all of them.'); *Popović et al.* Pre-Trial Indictment Decision, *supra* note 3, para. 25 (same); *Mrkšić* June 2003 Pre-Trial Indictment Decision, *supra* note 3, para. 56 (the prosecution may plead the first and third categories of JCE concurrently for the same crime); *ibid.* para. 62 ('[T]he Prosecution is not required to choose between different heads of responsibility. In this case it has chosen to plead all the different heads of responsibility, as is its right. It will be required to prove the existence of each of these at trial.'); *Krnojelac* February 1999 Pre-Trial Indictment Decision, *supra* note 3, para. 3; *Blaškić* Pre-Trial Indictment Decision, *supra* note 3, para. 32. See also *Prosecutor* v. *Kondewa*, Case No. SCSL-2003-12-PT, Decision and Order on Defence Preliminary Motion for Defects in the Form of the Indictment, 27 November 2003, para. 10 (holding that the Prosecution is not obliged to elect between the different forms of responsibility under Article 6(1), and noting that the distinction between the various forms was 'pre-eminently an evidentiary matter'; if the Prosecution 'has chosen to plead all the different heads of responsibility, consistent with its discretion ... [it] will carry the burden of proving the existence of each at the trial'); Chapter 4, text accompanying notes 347–349 (discussing the Special Court for Sierra Leone Prosecutor's practice of pleading forms of responsibility by simply repeating the terms of the Statute's analogue to Article 7/6(1)).

5 See *Prosecutor* v. *Aleksovski*, Case No. IT-95-14/1-A, Judgement, 24 March 2000 ('*Aleksovski* Appeal Judgement'), para. 171 n. 319 ('The practice by the Prosecution of merely quoting the provisions of Article 7(1) in the indictment is likely to cause ambiguity, and it is preferable that the Prosecution indicate in relation to each individual count precisely and expressly the particular nature of the responsibility alleged[.]'). Accord *Simić* Appeal Judgement, *supra* note 3, para. 21; *Prosecutor* v. *Semanza*, Case No. ICTR-97-20-A, Judgement, 20 May 2005 ('*Semanza* Appeal Judgement'), para. 357; *Prosecutor* v. *Kordić and Čerkez*, Case No. IT-95-14/2-A, Judgement, 17 December 2004 ('*Kordić and Čerkez* Appeal Judgement'), para. 129; *Prosecutor* v. *Ntakirutimana and Ntakirutimana*, Case Nos. ICTR-96-10-A and ICTR-96-17-A, Judgement, 13 December 2004 ('*Ntakirutimana and Ntakirutimana* Appeal Judgement'), para. 473 ('While ... it has been the practice of the Prosecution to merely quote the provisions of Article 6(1) [of the ICTR Statute], and in the ICTY Article 7(1), the Prosecution has also long been advised by the Appeals Chamber that it is preferable for it not to do so.'); *Blaškić* Appeal Judgement, *supra* note 3, para. 226; *Prosecutor* v. *Delalić, Mucić, Delić and Landžo*, Case No. IT-96-21-A, Judgement, 20 February 2001 ('*Čelebići* Appeal Judgement'), para. 350; *Popović et al.* Pre-Trial Indictment Decision, *supra* note 3, para. 25; *Mrkšić* June 2003 Pre-Trial Indictment Decision, *supra* note 3, para. 9 ('Depending on the circumstances of the case, it may be required that with respect to an Article 7(1) case against an accused, the Prosecution [must] indicate in relation to each individual count precisely and expressly the particular nature of the responsibility alleged[.]') (internal quotation marks removed); *Prosecutor* v. *Krnojelac*, Case No. IT-97-25-PT, Decision on Preliminary Motion on Form of Amended Indictment, 11 February 2000 ('*Krnojelac* February 2000 Pre-Trial Indictment Decision'), para. 60 ('It would be preferable in future cases that an indictment indicate in relation to each individual count precisely *and expressly* the particular nature of the responsibility alleged.'); *Blaškić* Pre-Trial Indictment Decision, *supra* note 3, para. 32.

some other respect to put the accused on adequate notice of the scope of the charges against him.[6]

In spite of this frequently repeated admonition, the usual practice of the *ad hoc* Prosecutors has been simply to list all the forms of responsibility under which they intend to charge an accused as applicable to every crime that appears in the indictment, often by means of a general paragraph in the introductory portion of the indictment preceding the section that lists the counts and the facts underlying them.[7] One of the three indictments in the *Milošević* case, for example, contained the following two introductory paragraphs on the accused's individual criminal responsibility:

Slobodan Milošević is individually criminally responsible for the crimes referred to in Articles 2, 3, and 5 of the Statute of the Tribunal and described in this indictment, which he planned, instigated, ordered, committed, or in whose planning, preparation, or execution he otherwise aided and abetted. By using the word committed in this indictment the Prosecutor does not intend to suggest that the accused physically committed any of the crimes charged personally. Committing in this indictment refers to participation in a joint criminal enterprise[.][8]

Slobodan Milošević, while holding positions of superior authority, is also individually criminally responsible for the acts or omissions of his subordinates, pursuant to Article 7(3) of the Statute of the Tribunal ... [9]

The indictment went on largely to repeat the language of Article 7(1) of the ICTY Statute in the first paragraph under each count, as in the following under Count 1, which charged persecution as a crime against humanity:

From on or about 1 August 1991 until June 1992, Slobodan Milošević, acting alone or in concert with other known and unknown members of a joint criminal enterprise, planned, instigated, ordered, committed, or otherwise aided and abetted the planning, preparation, or execution of the persecutions of the Croat and other non-Serb civilian

---

[6] See *Semanza* Appeal Judgement, *supra* note 5, paras. 356–357; *Kordić and Čerkez* Appeal Judgement, *supra* note 5, para. 129; *Čelebići* Appeal Judgement, *supra* note 5, para. 351 ('[F]ailure to identify expressly the exact mode of participation is not necessarily fatal to an indictment if it nevertheless makes clear to the accused the nature and cause of the charge against him.') (internal quotation marks removed); *Mrkšić* June 2003 Pre-Trial Indictment Decision, *supra* note 3, para. 9; *Prosecutor* v. *Brđanin and Talić*, Case No. IT-99-36-PT, Decision on Objections by Momir Talić to the Form of the Amended Indictment, 20 February 2001, para. 10; *Krnojelac* February 2000 Pre-Trial Indictment Decision, *supra* note 5, para. 60 ('It must be firmly stated that such a form of pleading is likely to cause ambiguity, as the present case has demonstrated.'); *Krnojelac* February 1999 Pre-Trial Indictment Decision, *supra* note 3, para. 7.

[7] See *Krnojelac* February 1999 Pre-Trial Indictment Decision, *supra* note 3, para. 3 (noting that the indictment's general introductory paragraphs asserting the accused's responsibility both under Article 7(1) and Article 7(3) of the ICTY Statute were 'clearly intended to be read distributively as applying to all the counts in the indictment', and holding that while '[t]his indictment may not be the most stylish of pleadings ... this particular complaint as to form is rejected').

[8] *Prosecutor* v. *Milošević*, Case No. IT-02-54-T, Second Amended Indictment, 23 October 2002, para. 5.

[9] *Ibid.*, para. 29.

population in the territories of the SAO SBWS, the SAO Western Slavonia, the SAO Krajina, and the Dubrovnik Republic.[10]

Then, in the paragraph actually setting forth Count 1, the Prosecutor merely made reference to Article 7(1) and Article 7(3):

By these acts and omissions, Slobodan Milošević committed: *Count 1*: Persecutions on political, racial, and religious grounds, a crime against humanity, punishable under Articles 5(h), and 7(1) and 7(3) of the Statute of the Tribunal.[11]

Although the Trial Chamber never had the opportunity to pronounce on this issue, these quoted passages apparently alleged Milošević's liability for persecution under Count 1 through every form of responsibility in Article 7(1) and Article 7(3) except physical commission – that is, he was charged with planning, instigating, ordering, and aiding and abetting persecution; participating in a JCE whose object or natural and foreseeable consequence was persecution; and failing to prevent and punish persecution carried out by his subordinates. Many other indictments in current and past cases in the *ad hoc* Tribunals follow the same pattern as the *Milošević* indictment in their lack of specificity in pleading forms of responsibility.[12]

This state of affairs leaves trial chambers with something of a dilemma when the time comes to determine the guilt or innocence of the accused for each of the crimes charged. A trial chamber at the judgement stage is unlikely to refuse to make findings on a given form of responsibility because its pleading in the indictment was defective, although some chambers have refused to make findings on inadequately pleaded forms.[13] The consensus among the chambers seems to be that a trial chamber faced with an indictment structured in a

---

[10] *Ibid.*, para. 34.   [11] *Ibid.*, para. 37.

[12] Indeed, the similarly structured indictment in *Krnojelac* drew rebukes from the Pre-Trial Chamber that the Prosecutor's pleading style was 'clumsy' and 'not ... the most stylish'. *Krnojelac* February 1999 Pre-Trial Indictment Decision, *supra* note 3, paras. 3, 7.

[13] See, e.g., *Prosecutor v. Gacumbitsi*, Case No. ICTR-2001-64-T, Judgement, 14 June 2004 ('*Gacumbitsi* Trial Judgement'), para. 289 (declining to make findings on whether the accused's JCE liability had been established 'because it was not pleaded clearly enough to allow the Accused to defend himself adequately.'); *Prosecutor v. Gacumbitsi*, Case No. ICTR-2001-64-A, Judgement, 7 July 2006 ('*Gacumbitsi* Appeal Judgement'), paras 164–179 (upholding Trial Chamber); *Prosecutor v. Ntagerura, Bagambiki and Imanishimwe*, Case No. ICTR-99-46-T, Judgement and Sentence, 25 February 2004 ('*Ntagerura et al.* Trial Judgement'), para. 34 (finding that, because the prosecution had not adequately pleaded JCE, the Trial Chamber would 'not consider the Prosecution's arguments ... to hold the accused criminally responsible based on th[e] theory' of JCE); *Prosecutor v. Ntagerura, Bagambiki and Imanishimwe*, Case No. ICTR-99-46-A, Judgement, 7 July 2006 ('*Ntagerura et al.* Appeal Judgement'), paras. 33–45, 362 (upholding Trial Chamber); *Prosecutor v. Ntakirutimana and Ntakirutimana*, Case Nos. ICTR-96-10 and ICTR-96-17-T, Judgement and Sentence, 21 February 2003 (making no mention of JCE); *Ntakirutimana and Ntakirutimana* Appeal Judgement, *supra* note 5, paras. 479–484 (finding that, by merely making general allegations of responsibility pursuant to Article 6(1) of the ICTR Statute and not specifically charging participation in a JCE or a common purpose, the indictment did not obviously allege JCE liability, and upholding the Trial Chamber's implicit refusal to consider that form of responsibility). See also Chapter 2, text accompanying notes 125–134, discussing these cases in greater detail.

manner similar to that in *Milošević* has the discretion to choose under which of the charged forms of responsibility, if any, to convict an accused for a given crime. Although most chambers appear simply to choose the appropriate form or forms without expounding an explicit rule, a number of others, beginning with the December 1998 *Furundžija* Trial Judgement, have stated expressly that this choosing process falls within the discretion of the trial chamber.[14]

While the jurisprudence on choosing among forms of responsibility is relatively sparse, it has identified two major limitations on the chamber's discretion to choose. First, although a chamber is not obliged to make exhaustive factual findings on those forms of responsibility that have been charged in respect of a given crime but under which it decides not to analyse the accused's liability, it would appear that the chamber must at least endeavour to give some justification as to why it has selected a certain form or forms and discarded the others. The *Brđanin* Trial Judgement is perhaps the most complete in this regard. There, the Trial Chamber provided an exhaustive thirty-eight-paragraph rationalisation of its decision to analyse Radoslav Brđanin's liability pursuant to JCE, instigating, ordering, and aiding and abetting, but not planning and superior responsibility, which had also been charged.[15] Near the other end of the spectrum are judgements such as that in *Kunarac*, in which a single paragraph explains the Trial Chamber's choice of physical commission and aiding and abetting over the other charged forms of responsibility:

Because the Prosecution failed to identify the precise basis on which it wanted the Trial Chamber to convict the accused, the Trial Chamber has proceeded to make findings upon those parts of Article 7(1) which it considers to be relevant. The Trial Chamber has not discussed the law with regard to common purpose because it is not necessary do so in this case. Where it has found an accused not guilty of a particular charge, it has done so either because the witnesses could not recall the incident described in the Indictment or because it was not satisfied beyond a reasonable doubt that the accused had been reliably identified with respect to a specific incident.[16] Having reviewed the evidence, the Trial Chamber is of the view that the following heads of responsibility

---

[14] See *Prosecutor v. Furundžija*, Case No. IT-95-17/1-T, Judgement, 10 December 1998, para. 189:

[A]s the Prosecution has relied on Article 7(1) without specification and left the Trial Chamber the discretion to allocate criminal responsibility, it is empowered and obliged, if satisfied beyond reasonable doubt that the accused has committed the crimes alleged against him, to convict the accused under the appropriate head of criminal responsibility within the limits of the Amended Indictment.

Accord *Prosecutor v. Semanza*, Case No. ICTR-97-20-T, Judgement and Sentence, 15 May 2003 ('*Semanza* Trial Judgement'), para. 397; *Prosecutor v. Kunarac, Kovač and Vuković*, Case Nos. IT-96-23-T and IT-96-23/1-T, Judgement, 22 February 2001 ('*Kunarac et al.* Trial Judgement'), para. 388; *Prosecutor v. Krstić*, Case No. IT-98-33-T, Judgement, 2 August 2001 ('*Krstić* Trial Judgement'), para. 602; *Prosecutor v. Kupreškić, Kupreškić, Kupreškić, Josipović, Papić and Šantić*, Case No. IT-95-16-T, Judgement, 14 January 2000, para. 746.

[15] See *Prosecutor v. Brđanin*, Case No. IT-99-36-T, Judgement, 1 September 2004 ('*Brđanin* Trial Judgement'), paras. 339–377.

[16] *Kunarac et al.* Trial Judgement, *supra* note 14, para. 388 (footnote omitted).

could apply to the acts charged in the Indictment: 'committing' as a form of perpetration and 'aiding and abetting'. Those heads of responsibility will be reviewed in turn.[17]

The *Krajišnik* and *Simba* Trial Chambers lie even beyond *Kunarac*: after deciding to analyse the responsibility of their respective accused exclusively pursuant to JCE, each of these chambers summarily dismissed all other charged forms of responsibility without much further discussion.[18] Of these different approaches, that taken by the *Brđanin* Chamber would certainly seem to be the safest, as it is most likely to withstand appellate scrutiny.[19]

Second, a chamber must have regard to the law on what has been termed 'concurrent convictions',[20] or the conviction of an accused pursuant to more

---

[17] *Ibid.*, para. 389. See also *Krstić* Trial Judgement, *supra* note 14, paras. 602–610 (holding that, since the prosecution did not charge Krstić under any specific Article 7(1) form of responsibility, it was within the Trial Chamber's discretion to choose the appropriate form 'within the limits of the indictment and fair notice of the charged and insofar as the evidence permits', and ultimately deciding that Krstić's involvement in the alleged crimes charged would most appropriately be evaluated under the rubric of JCE) (quotation at para. 602).

[18] See *Prosecutor v. Krajišnik*, Case No. IT-00-39-T, Judgement, 27 September 2006, para. 877 ('On the facts of this case ... the Chamber finds JCE to be the most appropriate mode of liability. Therefore, other forms of liability charged in the indictment will not be further considered in this judgement.'). The 'other forms of responsibility' charged in the *Krajišnik* indictment were planning, instigating, ordering, aiding and abetting, and superior responsibility; all were alleged in respect of every crime charged in the indictment. See *Prosecutor v. Krajišnik and Plavšić*, Case Nos. IT-00-39-PT and IT-00-40-PT, Amended Consolidated Indictment, 7 March 2002, paras. 3–10, pp. 7, 10–11. See also *Prosecutor v. Simba*, Case No. ICTR-2001-76-I, Amended Indictment, 10 May 2004, pp. 2, 11–12 (charging Simba with planning, instigating, ordering, and aiding and abetting genocide, complicity in genocide, extermination as a crime against humanity, and murder as a crime against humanity; and with superior responsibility for failing to prevent or punish genocide and extermination as a crime against humanity). The Prosecutor withdrew its pleading of complicity in genocide and superior responsibility before the end of trial. *Prosecutor v. Simba*, Case No. ICTR-01-76-T, Judgement and Sentence, 13 December 2005, paras. 4, 13; *ibid.*, para. 385 (ignoring all charged forms of responsibility except JCE).

[19] See, e.g., *Gacumbitsi* Appeal Judgement, *supra* note 13, para. 123. The Appeal Judgement in *Brđanin* has not yet been issued. In *Gacumbitsi*, however, the ICTR Appeals Chamber found that the Trial Chamber had erred in examining Sylvestre Gacumbitsi's liability for the murders of two Tutsi women only under the rubric of ordering, even though aiding and abetting had also been pleaded sufficiently 'to put the Appellant on notice that he was charged with aiding and abetting the murders'. The Appeals Chamber determined, from an examination of the Trial Chamber's factual findings on Gacumbitsi's involvement in the murders, that he should bear liability for them as an aider and abettor, and entered a new conviction on this basis. *Ibid.*, para. 124. See also *ibid.*, paras. 206–207 (increasing Gacumbitsi's sentence from thirty years to life imprisonment as a result of this and another new conviction, and because 'the Trial Chamber erred in failing to give proper weight to the gravity of the crimes committed by the Appellant and to his central role in those crimes') (quotation at para. 206). See also *infra* text accompanying notes 123–176 (discussing the forms of responsibility and sentencing).

[20] See *Prosecutor v. Jokić*, Case No. IT-01-42/1, Judgement, 30 August 2005 ('*Jokić* Judgement on Sentence Appeal'), *para. 24; Prosecutor v. Kajelijeli*, Case No. ICTR-98-44A, Judgement, 23 May 2005 ('*Kajelijeli* Appeal Judgement'), para. 81; *Kordić and Čerkez* Appeal Judgement, *supra* note 5, para. 35; *Blaškić* Appeal Judgement, *supra* note 3, para. 89; *Prosecutor v. Galić*, Case No. IT-98-29, Judgement, 5 December 2003 ('*Galić* Trial Judgement'), para. 177; *Prosecutor v. Naletilić and Martinović*, Case No. IT-98-34, Judgement, 31 March 2003 ('*Naletilić and Martinović* Trial Judgement'), para. 80; *Prosecutor v. Blaškić*, Case No. IT-95-14, Judgement, 3 March 2000 ('*Blaškić* Trial Judgement'), para. 338. But see *Kamuhanda v. Prosecutor*, Case No. ICTR-99-54A-A, Judgement, 19 September 2005 ('*Kamuhanda* Appeal Judgement'), Separate Opinion of Judge Wolfgang Schomburg, para. 387; *Brđanin* Trial Judgement, *supra* note 15, para. 339; *Gacumbitsi* Trial Judgement, *supra* note 13, para. 266 (all referring to 'cumulative' charging of forms of responsibility).

than one form of responsibility in respect of the same crime. Concurrent convictions should be distinguished from 'cumulative convictions', or convictions for more than one crime on the basis of the same conduct. The case law has consistently held that cumulative convictions are only permissible where each of the crimes in question contains a materially distinct element that the other does not; if two crimes charged in respect of the same conduct do not contain at least one mutually distinct element, a chamber may only convict the accused of the crime with the more specific element or elements.[21] As concerns the different notion of concurrent convictions, two categories of have been recognised in the jurisprudence: (1) concurrent convictions pursuant to more than one Article 7/6(1) form of responsibility – that is, planning, instigating, ordering, committing (including JCE), and aiding and abetting – and (2) concurrent convictions pursuant to a form of Article 7/6(1) responsibility on the one hand, and superior responsibility under Article 7/6(3) on the other. Each of these categories will be discussed in turn.

6.1.1 Concurrent convictions pursuant to more than one Article 7/6(1) form of responsibility

There would appear to be no general rule against simultaneously convicting an accused for more than one Article 7/6(1) form of responsibility in respect of the same crime,[22] and a number of chambers have entered concurrent convictions on this basis.[23] To verify the absence of a blanket prohibition on

---

[21] See *Ntagerura et al.* Appeal Judgement, *supra* note 13, para. 425; *Prosecutor* v. *Stakić*, Case No. IT-97-24-A, Judgement, 22 March 2006 ('*Stakić* Appeal Judgement'), para. 355; *Semanza* Appeal Judgement, *supra* note 5, para. 315; *Kordić and Čerkez* Appeal Judgement, *supra* note 5, paras. 1032–1033; *Prosecutor* v. *Krstić*, Case No. IT-98-33-A, Judgement, 19 April 2004 ('*Krstić* Appeal Judgement'), paras. 216, 227; *Čelebići* Appeal Judgement, *supra* note 5, para. 413; *Prosecutor* v. *Strugar*, Case No. IT-01-42-T, Judgement, 31 January 2005 ('*Strugar* Trial Judgement'), para. 447; *Prosecutor* v. *Blagojević and Jokić*, Case No. IT-02-60-T, Judgement, 17 January 2005, ('*Blagojević and Jokić* Trial Judgement'), para. 799.

[22] But see *infra* text accompanying notes 41–47 (setting forth trial chamber jurisprudence holding that an accused cannot be convicted of a form of accomplice liability in respect of a given crime if he is also convicted of committing that same crime).

[23] See, e.g., *Kajelijeli* Trial Judgement, *supra* note 20, paras. 842, 845 (finding Kajelijeli responsible for instigating, ordering, and aiding and abetting genocide perpetrated against Tutsis in the Mukingo, Nkuli and Kigombe *communes* of Rwanda); *Prosecutor* v. *Kordić and Čerkez*, Case No. IT-95-14/2-T, Judgement, 26 February 2001 ('*Kordić and Čerkez* Trial Judgement'), para. 834, pp. 305–306 (finding that Kordić had planned, instigated, and ordered a number of crimes against humanity and violations of the laws or customs of war, and entering a single conviction pursuant to these forms under the relevant count); *Prosecutor* v. *Kayishema and Ruzindana*, Case No. ICTR 95-1-T, Judgement, 21 May 1999 ('*Kayishema and Ruzindana* Trial Judgement'), para. 571, p. 235 (convicting Ruzindana of genocide after finding that he 'instigated, ordered, committed and otherwise aided and abetted in the preparation and execution of the massacre that resulted in thousands of murders with the intent to destroy the Tutsi ethnic group'.) (quotation at para. 571); *Prosecutor* v. *Akayesu*, Case No. ICTR-96-4-T, Judgement, 2 September 1998 ('*Akayesu* Trial Judgement'), paras. 692, 695 (finding that Akayesu 'by his own words, specifically ordered, instigated, aided and abetted' a number of acts of sexual violence, and convicting him of rape as a crime against humanity) (quotation at para. 692).

Article 7/6(1) concurrent convictions, one must examine the views of the judges of the ICTR Appeals Chamber set forth in a series of separate opinions appended to the September 2005 *Kamuhanda* Judgement. The Trial Chamber convicted Jean Kamuhanda, a Rwandan government minister, of instigating, ordering, and aiding and abetting genocide and extermination as a crime against humanity for his participation in the massacre of Tutsis at the Gikomero Parish compound.[24] The Appeals Chamber found that the evidence did not support the Trial Chamber's finding that Kamuhanda had instigated these crimes,[25] and stated as follows with respect to ordering and aiding and abetting:

> The factual findings of the Trial Chamber support the Appellant's conviction for aiding and abetting as well as for ordering the crimes. Both modes of participation form distinct categories of responsibility. In this case, however, both modes of responsibility are based on essentially the same set of facts: the Appellant 'led' the attackers in the attack and he ordered the attackers to start the killings. On the facts of this case, with the Appeals Chamber disregarding the finding that the Appellant distributed weapons for the purposes of determining whether the Appellant aided and abetted the commission of the crimes, the Appeals Chamber does not find the remaining facts sufficiently compelling to maintain the conviction for aiding and abetting. In this case the mode of responsibility of ordering fully encapsulates the Appellant's criminal conduct at the Gikomero Parish Compound.[26]

The Chamber concluded that, 'although the finding ... for aiding and abetting ... is supported by the Trial Chamber's factual findings, the Appeals Chamber, Judge Shahabuddeen dissenting, deems it appropriate to confirm only the finding of the Appellant's individual criminal responsibility for ordering the crimes'.[27]

In a separate opinion, Judge Schomburg opined that the Appeals Chamber dismissed the aiding and abetting charges in this instance because convicting Kamuhanda for ordering and aiding and abetting the same crimes 'would be impermissibly cumulative'.[28] Explaining his reasoning in a somewhat cryptic manner, Judge Schomburg does not appear to have opposed all Article 7/6(1) concurrent convictions, but only those that give the impression that the accused is being punished twice for the same conduct:

> [T]his outcome has nothing to do with the fact that there is only one conviction for multiple modes of liability under Article 6(1) of the Statute. On the one hand, a conviction for several modes of liability has to reflect the entirety of the criminal

---

[24] *Prosecutor* v. *Kamuhanda*, Case No. ICTR-99-54A-T, Judgement and Sentence, 22 January 2003 ('*Kamuhanda* Trial Judgement'), para. 648.
[25] *Kamuhanda* Appeal Judgement, *supra* note 20, paras. 66, 88.   [26] *Ibid.*, para. 77.   [27] *Ibid.*, para. 88.
[28] *Ibid.*, Separate Opinion of Judge Wolfgang Schomburg, para. 387.

conduct. On the other hand, a conviction must not give even the impression of punishing an accused twice for the same conduct under two heads of liability. Thus, it would be both a violation of this latter fundamental principle of criminal law and a violation of the principle of logic to punish a person for having ordered *and* aided and abetted at the same time and in relation to the same offence, if ordering and aiding and abetting are based on the same criminal conduct.[29]

In Judge Schomburg's ostensible view, concurrent convictions for ordering and aiding and abetting – at least in this particular instance – give the impression of double punishment and must for that reason be avoided.

Three of the other four judges on the bench seised of *Kamuhanda* – Judges Shahabuddeen, Meron and Weinberg de Roca – expressed the contrary view that concurrent convictions under more than one Article 7/6(1) form of responsibility are *per se* permissible,[30] as '[t]here is no reason why a single crime cannot be perpetrated by multiple methods'.[31] The fifth judge, Judge Mumba, did not append a separate opinion to the judgement, so it is not possible to discern whether she, like Judge Schomburg, interpreted the main opinion's statement as recognising or establishing a ban on at least some types of Article 7/6(1) concurrent convictions. Even if she did agree with Judge Schomburg, however, those two judges would form only a 2–3 minority. Contrary to the interpretation of Judge Schomburg, as well as that of the *Orić* Trial Chamber, which cited *Kamuhanda* for the proposition that 'the ... various modes of individual criminal responsibility are to be understood as separate alternatives',[32] the evident conclusion is that the *Kamuhanda* Appeal Judgement did not create any sort of prohibition on Article 7/6(1) concurrent convictions. The Chamber's dismissal of aiding and abetting liability in respect of the Gikomero Parish massacre should therefore be understood as restricted to the facts of that case.[33]

---

[29] *Ibid.*, para. 389 (emphasis in original).

[30] See *ibid.*, Separate and Partially Dissenting Opinion of Judge Mohamed Shahabuddeen, para. 402; *ibid.*, Separate Opinion of Presiding Judge Theodor Meron, para. 366 ('[I]t is not my view that paragraph 77 in anyway [*sic*] extends the reach of *Čelebići* [which held that cumulative convictions under more than one crime are impermissible]. In that respect, I agree with Judge Shahabuddeen that there is no reason why a single crime cannot be perpetrated by multiple methods.') (internal quotation marks removed); *ibid.*, Separate Opinion of Judge Inés Mónica Weinberg de Roca on Paragraph 77 of the Judgement, para. 417 ('I agree with Judge Shahabuddeen that a conviction based on more than one of the modes of responsibility enumerated at Article 6(1) of the Statute is not impermissibly cumulative.').

[31] *Ibid.*, Separate and Partially Dissenting Opinion of Judge Mohamed Shahabuddeen, para. 402. Accord *ibid.*, Separate Opinion of Presiding Judge Theodor Meron, para. 366; *ibid.*, Separate Opinion of Judge Inés Mónica Weinberg de Roca on Paragraph 77 of the Judgement, para. 417.

[32] *Prosecutor v. Orić*, Case No. IT-03-68-T, Judgement, 30 June 2006 ('*Orić* Trial Judgement'), para. 269 (citing *Kamuhanda* Appeal Judgement, *supra* note 20, para. 77 and Judge Shahabuddeen's separate opinion).

[33] See especially *Kamuhanda* Appeal Judgement, *supra* note 20, para. 77 (the Chamber's repeated use of the words '[i]n this case' and '[o]n the facts of this case').

Of the three judges in apparent disagreement with Judge Schomburg, only Judge Shahabuddeen provided an extensive explanation of his position. He opined that the Appeals Chamber was not in this instance dealing with a question to be analysed under the law on cumulative convictions; as discussed above,[34] this body of law allows the conviction of an accused for two separate crimes based on the same conduct only where each crime contains at least one element that the other lacks. Since 'ordering and aiding and abetting (like the other acts mentioned in [Article 6(1) of the ICTR Statute] are merely ... methods of engaging individual responsibility for a crime referred to in [A]rticles 2 to 4 of the Statute',[35] the rationale for the prohibition on cumulative convictions is absent from a scenario involving concurrent convictions under Article 7/6(1): 'The fact that more than one method is employed [in realising a crime] does not mean that there is more than one conviction for the crime,'[36] although the accused's involvement in a crime through multiple methods may have the effect of aggravating his sentence.[37] Judge Shahabuddeen also distinguished the rule against concurrent convictions under an Article 7/6(1) form of responsibility, on the one hand, and Article 7/6(3), on the other (a rule discussed in detail below):[38] while it would be illogical to hold an accused liable both for his active advancement of a crime through a form of responsibility such as ordering, and for his passive failure to prevent or punish that crime, 'there is no illogicality arising from contradictory assumptions of fact in holding that the accused can both aid and abet another to commit a crime and can order that other to commit that crime'.[39] According to Judge Shahabuddeen, a trial chamber should accordingly be free to find the accused liable based on several of the forms of responsibility in Article 7/6(1) at once: '[w]ere it otherwise, there would be a failure to define the true measure of the criminal conduct of the accused'.[40]

---

[34] See *supra* text accompanying note 21.

[35] *Kamuhanda* Appeal Judgement, *supra* note 20, Separate and Partially Dissenting Opinion of Judge Mohamed Shahabuddeen, para. 405.

[36] *Ibid.*, para. 408. *Accord, ibid.*, para. 413 ('[A] finding that multiple methods had been used by the accused does not signify that he has been subjected to separate convictions for multiple crimes.'); para. 414 ('[T]here being only one conviction, there is no basis on which to apply the law relating to the subsuming of a conviction for one crime by a conviction for another crime which rests on a more specific provision.'). See also *Kordić and Čerkez* Appeal Judgement, *supra* note 5, para. 1033 (holding that '[t]he cumulative convictions test serves twin aims: ensuring that the accused is convicted only for distinct offences, and at the same time, ensuring that the convictions entered fully reflect his criminality').

[37] *Kamuhanda* Appeal Judgement, *supra* note 20, Separate and Partially Dissenting Opinion of Judge Mohamed Shahabuddeen, paras. 406, 408. See also *infra* text accompanying notes 123–176 (discussing the forms of responsibility and sentencing).

[38] See *infra* text accompanying notes 49–111.

[39] *Kamuhanda* Appeal Judgement, *supra* note 20, Separate and Partially Dissenting Opinion of Judge Mohamed Shahabuddeen, para. 411.

[40] *Ibid.*, para. 413.

Notwithstanding the apparent conclusion from *Kamuhanda* that there is no general rule prohibiting Article 7/6(1) concurrent convictions, a few trial chambers predating the *Kamuhanda* Appeal Judgement held that an accused cannot bear liability for committing a crime and also for having been an accomplice to that crime through, for example, planning, instigating, or ordering.[41] These chambers expressed a clear preference for a conviction under the former – including, presumably, 'commission' by means of participation in a JCE[42] – instead of the latter. In respect of planning, the *Brđanin* Trial Chamber held that, '[w]here an accused is found guilty of having committed a crime, he or she cannot at the same time be convicted of having planned the same crime'.[43] In the same vein for instigating and ordering, the *Stakić* Trial Chamber held that an 'accused can not be convicted as an instigator if he would be found guilty of having directly/physically perpetrated the same crime',[44] and that 'an additional conviction for ordering a particular

---

[41] See *Blaškić* Trial Judgement, *supra* note 20, para. 278 ('[I]n general, a person other than the person who planned, instigated or ordered is the one who perpetrated the *actus reus* of the offence.'). Accord *Akayesu* Trial Judgement, *supra* note 23, para. 468 ('[T]he Chamber finds that it is not justifiable to convict an accused of two offences in relation to the same set of facts where ... one offence charges accomplice liability and the other offence charges liability as a principal, e.g. genocide and complicity in genocide.'). See also *Semanza* Trial Judgement, *supra* note 14, para. 397 ('Where a count seemingly charges both direct and accomplice liability under Article 6(1) and another count specifically alleges complicity for the identical criminal acts, the Chamber will narrow the scope of the broader count so as to eliminate any overlap.').

[42] For example, the *Stakić* Trial Chamber found that the accused had fulfilled the elements of deportation as a crime against humanity not only as an orderer and planner, but also through a form of 'commission' responsibility it deemed 'co-perpetratorship'. See *Prosecutor v. Stakić*, Case No. IT-97-24-T, Judgement, 29 October 2003 ('*Stakić* Trial Judgement'), paras. 468, 712. Yet the Chamber ultimately convicted Stakić only as a 'committer' of this crime, considering his planning and ordering as factors aggravating his sentence; the sentence imposed on Stakić was life imprisonment. *Ibid.* para. 914, p. 253. The Appeals Chamber subsequently held that co-perpetratorship is not a form of responsibility within the jurisdiction of the ICTY, and substituted a conviction pursuant to JCE for this crime. *Stakić* Appeal Judgement, *supra* note 20, paras. 62–63, 104. See Chapter 2 notes 46, 147 (setting forth the jurisprudence holding that JCE is a means of 'committing' a crime, implicitly included under that term in Article 7/6(1)); text accompanying notes 596–622, 647–658 (describing this aspect of the *Stakić* Trial and Appeal Judgements).

[43] *Brđanin* Trial Judgement, *supra* note 15, para. 268. Accord *Galić* Trial Judgement, *supra* note 20, para. 168 n. 280 ('If the person planning a crime also commits it, he or her [*sic*] is only punished for the commission of the crime and not for its planning[.]'); *Stakić* Trial Judgement, *supra* note 42, para. 443; *Naletilić and Martinović* Trial Judgement, *supra* note 20, para. 59; *Kordić and Čerkez* Trial Judgement, *supra* note 23, para. 386. See also *Prosecutor v. Brima, Kamara and Kanu*, Case No. SCSL-04-16-T, Decision on Defence Motions for Judgement of Acquittal Pursuant to Rule 98, 31 March 2006, para. 285 ('Where an accused is found guilty of having committed a crime, he or she cannot at the same time be convicted of having planned the same crime.').

[44] *Prosecutor v. Stakić*, Case No. IT-97-24, Decision on Rule 98 *bis* Motion for Judgement of Acquittal, 31 October 2002, para. 107. See also *ibid.*, para. 108 (holding, on the basis of the evidence produced by the prosecution during its case-in-chief that 'no reasonable trier of fact could sustain a conviction of the Accused for instigating the commission of the crimes' in question, and granting this portion of the relief sought by the accused in his motion for judgement of acquittal). Cf. *Akayesu* Trial Judgement, *supra* note 23, para. 532 ('[A]n individual cannot ... be both the principal perpetrator of a particular act and the accomplice thereto.'); *Prosecutor v. Karemera, Ngirumpatse and Nzirorera*, Case No. ICTR-98-44-T, Decision on Defence Motions Challenging the Pleading of a Joint Criminal Enterprise in a Count of Complicity in Genocide in the Amended Indictment, 18 May 2006, para. 9 (same).

crime is not appropriate where the accused is found to have committed the same crime'.[45] The *Brđanin* and *Stakić* Chambers added that the accused's involvement in the planning of a crime may be considered as an aggravating factor if he is convicted of committing that crime.[46] The *Stakić* Trial Chamber aggravated the accused's sentence for 'committing' deportation as a crime against humanity because he had also planned and ordered that crime.[47] Although the *Stakić* Appeals Chamber upheld this sentence of aggravation against an appeal from the accused, it did not clarify whether the Trial Chamber's exposition and application of a putative rule preventing concurrent convictions was correct.[48] Indeed, the Appeals Chamber has never approved such a rule, which would appear fundamentally inconsistent with the principle set forth by the majority in *Kamuhanda*.

6.1.2 Concurrent convictions pursuant to Article 7/6(1) and Article 7/6(3)

As suggested by Judge Shahabuddeen in his *Kamuhanda* separate opinion,[49] in contrast to concurrent convictions for two different forms of Article 7/6(1) responsibility, an absolute rule has existed since early in the *ad hoc* jurisprudence prohibiting concurrent convictions pursuant to a form of Article 7/6(1) responsibility on the one hand, and superior responsibility under Article 7/6(3) on the other. This rule has its foundations in the March 2000 *Blaškić* Trial Judgement, in which the Trial Chamber observed at paragraph 337 that '[i]t would be illogical to hold a commander criminally responsible for planning, instigating or ordering the commission of crimes and, at the same time, reproach him for not preventing or punishing them'.[50] The Chamber did not elaborate on this position or establish any hierarchy between the Article 7/6(1)

---

[45] *Stakić* Trial Judgement, *supra* note 42, para. 445.

[46] *Brđanin* Trial Judgement, *supra* note 15, para. 268; *Stakić* Trial Judgement, *supra* note 42, para. 443. See also *infra*, text accompanying notes 123–176 (discussing the forms of responsibility and sentencing).

[47] See *supra* note 42. See also *Prosecutor* v. *Nahimana, Barayagwiza and Ngeze*, Case No. ICTR-99-52-T, Judgement and Sentence, 3 December 2003, para. 1102 (emphasising, in the section of the judgement on aggravating and mitigating circumstances, that 'all three Accused were involved in the planning of these criminal activities and were disposed to acting in a manner contrary to the duty imposed upon them by their respective positions'); *ibid.*, paras. 1096, 1105–1108 (convicting the three accused of genocide, conspiracy to commit genocide, direct and public incitement to commit genocide, and persecution and extermination as crimes against humanity, and sentencing two of them to life imprisonment and one to thirty-five years).

[48] *Stakić* Appeal Judgement, *supra* note 20, para. 413 (holding that Stakić's 'role in the planning and ordering of deportation . . . may be taken into account as an aggravating factor because of the contribution that planning and ordering make to the commission of a crime').

[49] See *supra* text accompanying notes 38–39.

[50] *Blaškić* Trial Judgement, *supra* note 20, para. 337. While *Blaškić* is generally considered to be the first judgement to set forth a rule against concurrent convictions under Articles 7/6(1) and 7/6(3), the notion that such convictions may be inappropriate appears to have surfaced even earlier in the ICTR, in the following passage of the May 1999 *Kayishema and Ruzindana* Trial Judgement: '[I]f the Chamber is

forms of responsibility and superior responsibility, but instead proceeded to hypothesise on how an accused superior might engage in 'aiding and abetting by omission' and 'instigating by omission'.[51] It then went on to contradict its own holding, however, apparently convicting Tihomir Blaškić for both committing and failing to prevent and punish nearly every crime (18 out of 21) for which he was charged with responsibility.[52]

While at least two ICTY trial chambers prior to *Blaškić* entered concurrent convictions under Article 7(1) and Article 7(3), which were upheld on appeal,[53] subsequent trial chambers uniformly followed the principle set forth in that judgement.[54] Yet the majority of these later chambers did not cite *Blaškić* as precedent.[55] For example, the Trial Chamber in the March 2002 *Krnojelac* Judgement, citing no authority at all, seems to have arrived independently at the same conclusion as *Blaškić*, although it worded the prohibition somewhat more clearly: '[T]he Trial Chamber is of the view that it is inappropriate to

satisfied beyond reasonable doubt that the accused ordered the alleged atrocities then it becomes unnecessary to consider whether he tried to prevent; and irrelevant whether he tried to punish.' *Kayishema and Ruzindana* Trial Judgement, *supra* note 23, para. 223.

[51] *Blaškić* Trial Judgement, *supra* note 20, paras. 337–339. See Chapter 4, text accompanying notes 192–216, and Chapter 5, text accompanying notes 115–120, 125–127, for a discussion of whether aiding and abetting by omission and instigating by omission are properly regarded as having a sound basis in international criminal law.

[52] *Blaškić* Trial Judgement, *supra* note 20, pp. 267–269 (including grave breaches, violations of the laws or customs of war, and crimes against humanity under 18 separate counts). See also *ibid.*, p. 267 (finding Blaškić guilty of ordering various forms of persecution as a crime against humanity).

[53] See, e.g., *Aleksovski* Appeal Judgement, *supra* note 5, paras. 77, 192 (upholding *Aleksovski* Trial Judgement, *supra* note 5, para. 228, which convicted the accused for outrages upon personal dignity as a violation of the laws or customs of war pursuant to both Articles 7(1) and 7(3) of the ICTY Statute); *Čelebići* Appeal Judgement, *supra* note 5, paras. 745–746. The Appeals Chamber upheld the Trial Chamber's conviction of the accused Mucić for two crimes: wilfully causing great suffering or serious injury to body or health as a grave breach of the Geneva Conventions, and cruel treatment as a violation of the laws or customs of war. The Trial Chamber had entered these two convictions concurrently pursuant to Article 7(1) – apparently finding that Mucić had physically committed these crimes – and Article 7(3), based on Mucić's failure both to prevent and punish the crimes. *Prosecutor* v. *Delalić, Mucić, Delić and Landžo*, Case No. IT-96-21-T, Judgement, 16 November 1998, para. 1123. The Appeals Chamber added that, where an accused is convicted concurrently under Articles 7(1) and 7(3) in respect of the same crime, 'the Trial Chamber must take into account the fact that both types of responsibility were proved in its consideration of sentence').

[54] See *Gacumbitsi* Trial Judgement, *supra* note 13, para. 266; *Ntagerura et al.* Trial Judgement, *supra* note 13, para. 623; *Galić* Trial Judgement, *supra* note 20, para. 177; *Stakić* Trial Judgement, *supra* note 42, para. 464 (citing paragraph 337 of the *Blaškić* Trial Judgement); *Naletilić and Martinović* Trial Judgement, *supra* note 20, paras. 79–81 (citing paragraph 337 of the *Blaškić* Trial Judgement); *Prosecutor* v. *Krnojelac*, Case No. IT-97-25-T, Judgement, 15 March 2002 ('*Krnojelac* Trial Judgement'), para. 173; *Krstić* Trial Judgement, *supra* note 14, para. 605 (citing paragraph 337 of the *Blaškić* Trial Judgement); *ibid.*, para. 652 (declining to enter a conviction for failing to prevent or punish genocide, despite the fact that all the elements for Article 7(3) liability had been fulfilled in respect of Krstić, because his liability would be sufficiently expressed in a finding of guilt pursuant to Article 7(1)); *Kordić and Čerkez* Trial Judgement, *supra* note 23, para. 371. See also the trial judgements cited in note 67, *infra*.

[55] See, e.g., *Gacumbitsi* Trial Judgement, *supra* note 13, para. 266 (citing no authority); *Ntagerura et al.* Trial Judgement, *supra* note 13, para. 623 (citing the *Naletilić and Martinović* and *Krnojelac* Trial Judgements); *Galić* Trial Judgement, *supra* note 20, para. 177 (citing the *Krnojelac* and *Krstić* Trial Judgements); *Krnojelac* Trial Judgement, *supra* note 54, para. 173; *Kordić and Čerkez* Trial Judgement, *supra* note 23, para. 371 (citing *Prosecutor* v. *Mladić and Karadžić*, Case Nos. IT-95-5-R61 and IT-95-18-R61, Review of the Indictments Pursuant to Rule 61 of the Rules of Procedure and Evidence, 11 July 1996, para. 83.

convict under both [Article 7(1) and Article 7(3) of the ICTY Statute] for the same count based on the same acts.'[56] Regrettably, few of these chambers, including that in *Krnojelac*, articulated any reasoning justifying the prohibition,[57] although the *Kordić and Čerkez* Trial Chamber provided some elaboration of the distinct nature of liability under Article 7/6(1) and Article 7/6(3) that may help shed light on why concurrent convictions under those two provisions could be considered illogical:

> Article 7(1) is concerned with persons directly responsible for planning, instigating, ordering, committing, or aiding and abetting in the planning, preparation or execution of a crime. Thus, both the individual who himself carries out the unlawful conduct and his superior who is involved in the conduct not by physical participation, but for example by ordering or instigating it, are covered by Article 7(1). For instance, a superior who orders the killing of a civilian may be held responsible under Article 7(1), as might a political leader who plans that certain civilians or groups of civilians should be executed, and passes these instructions on to a military commander. The criminal responsibility of such superiors, either military or civilian, in these circumstances is personal or direct, as a result of their direct link to the physical commission of the crime[58] ... [By contrast,] [t]he type of responsibility provided for in Article 7(3) may be described as 'indirect' as it does not stem from a 'direct' involvement by the superior in the commission of a crime but rather from his omission to prevent or punish such offence, i.e. of his failure to act in spite of knowledge. This responsibility arises only where the superior is under a legal obligation to act ... Liability under Article 7(3) is based on an omission as opposed to positive conduct.[59]

Although it followed previous jurisprudence in holding that liability for instigating and committing under Article 7/6(1) may ensue not only through positive action, but also through culpable omission,[60] the *Kordić and Čerkez* Trial Chamber did not acknowledge that these forms effected through omission would more appropriately be categorised alongside superior responsibility as

---

[56] *Krnojelac* Trial Judgement, *supra* note 54, para. 173.

[57] See *Gacumbitsi* Trial Judgement, *supra* note 13, para. 266; *Ntagerura et al.* Trial Judgement, *supra* note 13, para. 623; *Galić* Trial Judgement, *supra* note 20, para. 177; *Naletilić and Martinović* Trial Judgement, *supra* note 20, paras. 79–81; *Krnojelac* Trial Judgement, *supra* note 54, paras. 172–173; *Krstić* Trial Judgement, *supra* note 14, para. 605.

[58] *Kordić and Čerkez* Trial Judgement, *supra* note 23, para. 367.

[59] *Ibid.*, para. 369. See also *Stakić* Trial Judgement, *supra* note 42, para. 465 (providing a one-sentence rationale: 'Article 7(3) serves primarily as an omnibus clause in cases where the primary basis of responsibility can not be applied.'); *Prosecutor v. Naletilić and Martinović*, Case No. IT-98-34-A, Judgement, 3 May 2006 ('*Naletilić and Martinović* Appeal Judgement'), para. 613 ('[A] Trial Chamber has the discretion to find that *direct responsibility*, under Article 7(1) of the Statute, is aggravated by a perpetrator's position of authority.'); *Blaškić* Pre-Trial Indictment Decision, *supra* note 3, para. 31 ('A reading of the provisions of the Statute reveals the existence of two distinct types of responsibility: the one referred to in Article 7(1), which will be called direct command responsibility[,] and the one referred to in Article 7(3)[,] which will be called indirect responsibility.').

[60] *Kordić and Čerkez* Trial Judgement, *supra* note 23, para. 376 (committing liability may ensue through a culpable omission); *ibid.*, para. 387 (holding that '[b]oth positive acts and omissions may constitute instigation').

species of 'indirect' responsibility. It would appear that this 'direct/indirect' dichotomy between Article 7/6(1) and Article 7/6(3) is not as clear-cut as the *Blaškić* and *Kordić and Čerkez* Trial Chambers – and indeed most chambers of the *ad hoc* Tribunals – have assumed.[61]

Expressing its concern at the Trial Chamber's blanket concurrent convictions of Blaškić in spite of that Chamber's own holding in paragraph 337,[62] the *Blaškić* Appeals Chamber adopted the position that concurrent convictions under Article 7/6(1) and Article 7/6(3) are impermissible. In addition to its apparent espousal of the reasoning put forth by the Trial Chamber that such convictions would be 'illogical',[63] the Appeals Chamber added the following: '[T]he provisions of Article 7(1) and 7(3) connote distinct categories of criminal responsibility. However, the Appeals Chamber considers that, in relation to a particular count, it is not appropriate to convict under both Article 7(1) and Article 7(3) of the Statute.'[64] It concluded that the Trial Chamber had erred in convicting Blaškić concurrently 'in relation to the same counts based on the same facts',[65] and stated that it would only consider the propriety of the Trial Chamber's convictions of Blaškić pursuant to Article 7(3) where the Trial Chamber had made discrete factual findings relating to superior responsibility.[66] Subsequent chambers of both *ad hoc* Tribunals have uniformly followed the *Blaškić* Appeal Judgement, often by simply quoting *Blaškić*, and generally without elaborating on or expanding that judgment's sparse reasoning.[67]

---

[61] See *infra* text accompanying notes 96–111 (elaborating on this proposition).

[62] See *Blaškić* Appeal Judgement, *supra* note 3, para. 89.

[63] See *ibid.*, para. 90 n. 182 (Appeals Chamber stating that its rationale is '[i]n line with paragraph 337 of the Trial Judgement'). See also *Kamuhanda* Appeal Judgement, *supra* note 20, Separate and Partially Dissenting Opinion of Judge Mohamed Shahabuddeen, para. 410 (underlining removed):

> The Blaškić rule is based on the illogicality of holding, under [A]rticle 7(1) of the ICTY Statute, that the crime committed by a subordinate was in the first instance ordered by the accused himself, and of at the same time holding, under [A]rticle 7(3), that the accused, as the superior, failed to prevent the commission of the crime by the subordinate or failed to punish the subordinate for committing it.

> Judge Shahabuddeen was here referring specifically to the rule created by the *Blaškić* Appeals Chamber, and not that of the Trial Chamber, as the context of the discussion and his citations reveal. It should be noted that he was one of the three judges in the *Blaškić* Trial Chamber, and that he did not sit on the appeals bench in *Blaškić*.

[64] *Blaškić* Appeal Judgement, *supra* note 3, para. 91.   [65] *Ibid.*, para. 92.

[66] *Ibid.*, para. 93. Based on this and other errors committed by the Trial Chamber, the Appeals Chamber acquitted Blaškić of a remarkable number of the crimes for which the Trial Chamber had convicted him, and reduced his sentence from forty-five to nine years' imprisonment. *Ibid.*, pp. 257–258.

[67] See *Gacumbitsi* Appeal Judgement, *supra* note 13, para. 142; *Naletilić and Martinović* Appeal Judgement, *supra* note 59, para. 368; *Jokić* Judgement on Sentence Appeal, *supra* note 20, paras. 24, 27 (endorsing the *Blaškić* rationale as 'applicable in the present case'); *ibid.*, para. 27 (overturning the Trial Chamber's convictions under Article 7(3) because they had been impermissibly entered concurrently with Article 7(1)); *Kajelijeli* Appeal Judgement, *supra* note 20, para. 81 (ICTR Appeals Chamber authoritatively endorsing the *Blaškić* holding for that Tribunal, and vacating the accused's Article 6(3) conviction for genocide after determining that the Trial Chamber had erroneously convicted him under both Articles 6(1) and 6(3) on the same facts); *Kvočka et al.* Appeal Judgement, *supra* note 3, para. 104; *Kordić and Čerkez* Appeal Judgement, *supra* note 5, paras. 34–35 (restating the quoted passage from *Blaškić* almost verbatim,

In holding that concurrent convictions under Article 7/6(1) and Article 7/6(3) are impermissible, the *Blaškić* Trial Judgement did not address which provision should be used in this circumstance, and trial judgements rendered in the interim between the March 2000 *Blaškić* Trial Judgement and the July 2004 *Blaškić* Appeal Judgement were inconsistent on this question. The Trial Chambers in the February 2001 *Kordić and Čerkez* Judgement and the August 2001 *Krstić* Judgement expressed a preference for Article 7/6(1) over Article 7/6(3);[68] in the words of the *Krstić* Trial Chamber,

where a commander participates in the commission of a crime through his subordinates, by 'planning', 'instigating' or 'ordering' the commission of the crime, any responsibility under Article 7(3) is *subsumed* under Article 7(1). The same applies to the commander who incurs criminal responsibility under the joint criminal enterprise doctrine through the physical acts of his subordinates.[69]

Conversely, the *Krnojelac* Trial Chamber in its March 2002 Judgement held that a chamber has the discretion to choose between Article 7/6(1) and Article 7/6(3):

Where the Prosecutor alleges both heads of responsibility within the one count, and the facts support a finding of responsibility under both heads of responsibility, the Trial Chamber *has a discretion to choose* which is the most appropriate head of responsibility under which to attach criminal responsibility to the [a]ccused.[70]

The Chamber went on to find that, although Milorad Krnojelac had through his conduct fulfilled the elements both of aiding and abetting and superior

---

and also overturning a conviction under Article 7(3) entered by the Trial Chamber concurrently with Article 7(1)); *Orić* Trial Judgement, *supra* note 32, para. 343; *Prosecutor v. Rajić*, Case No. IT-95-12-S, Sentencing Judgement, 8 May 2006 ('*Rajić* Sentencing Judgement'), para. 106; *Prosecutor v. Rajić*, Case No. IT-95-12-S, Clarifications on Convictions Entered, 16 November 2005 ('*Rajić* Clarifications on Convictions Entered'), p. 4; *Brđanin* Trial Judgement, *supra* note 15, para. 285. But see *Prosecutor v. Marculino Soares*, Case No. 02/2002-B, Julgamento, 1 December 2004, p. 30 (panel of the East Timor Special Panels for Serious Crimes convicting the accused, a militia leader, of murder and inhumane acts as crimes against humanity concurrently pursuant to Section 14(a) and Section 16 of UNTAET Regulation 2000/15, respectively for co-perpetrating these crimes ('*em co-autoria com outros*') and for failing to prevent and punish them as a superior; but not acknowledging *Blaškić* or indeed any other judicial precedent) (judgement in Portuguese); see also United Nations Transitional Administration in East Timor, Regulation No. 2000/15 on the Establishment of Panels with Exclusive Jurisdiction over Serious Criminal Offences, UN Doc. UNTAET/REG/2000/15, 6 June 2000, Sections 14(a), 16.

68 *Krstić* Trial Judgement, *supra* note 14, para. 605; *Kordić and Čerkez* Trial Judgement, *supra* note 23, para. 371('[W]here the evidence presented demonstrates that a superior would not only have been informed of subordinates' crimes committed under his authority, but also exercised his powers to plan, instigate or otherwise aid and abet ... these crimes, the type of criminal responsibility incurred may be better characterised by Article 7(1).'). See also *Kayishema and Ruzindana* Trial Judgement, *supra* note 23, para. 223.

69 *Krstić* Trial Judgement, *supra* note 14, para. 605 (emphasis added). Thus, despite the fact that all the elements for superior responsibility had been fulfilled in respect of Krstić, the Trial Chamber declined to enter a conviction for genocide under Article 7(3) of the ICTY Statute because Krstić's liability was sufficiently expressed in a finding of guilt for 'committing' under Article 7(1), on the basis of his participation in a JCE. *Ibid.*, paras. 644–645, 652.

70 *Krnojelac* Trial Judgement, *supra* note 54, para. 173 (emphasis added).

responsibility in respect of inhumane acts perpetrated against detainees at his prison, '[i]n the circumstances before it, the Trial Chamber considers that the criminality of the Accused is better characterised as that of an aider and abettor'.[71] Most subsequent chambers prior to the *Blaškić* Appeal Judgement – that is, those in *Naletilić and Martinović* (March 2003),[72] *Galić* (December 2003),[73] *Ntagerura* (February 2004)[74] and *Gacumbitsi* (June 2004)[75] – followed the *Krnojelac* approach, although *Gacumbitsi* did not explicitly acknowledge the *Krnojelac* precedent. By contrast one Trial Chamber – *Stakić* in July 2003 – erroneously professed to endorse *Krnojelac* but actually followed *Krstić*.[76]

The *Blaškić* Appeal Judgement rectified this disharmony by effectively endorsing the *Krstić* approach obliging a chamber to give preference to Article 7/6(1):

Where both Article 7(1) and Article 7(3) responsibility are alleged under the same count, and where the legal requirements pertaining to both of these heads of responsibility are met, a Trial Chamber should enter a conviction on the basis of Article 7(1) only, and consider the accused's superior position as an aggravating factor in sentencing.[77]

In May 2005, the ICTR Appeals Chamber in *Kajelijeli* adopted this rule (the '*Blaškić* rule') as authoritative for the chambers of the ICTR.[78]

The *Orić* Chamber provided a helpful clarification to the *Blaškić* rule. Naser Orić, a Bosnian Muslim army commander, was alleged to be responsible for wanton destruction of cities, towns or villages not justified by military necessity, a violation of the laws or customs of war under Article 3(b) of the ICTY Statute. This crime was charged in both Count 3 and Count 5 of the indictment for what was largely the same conduct – that is, attacks perpetrated by Orić's forces against Serb villages in eastern Bosnia. Count 3 averred that the accused had failed to prevent and punish wanton destruction on the basis of a long list of

---

[71] *Ibid.* The crimes at issue were inhumane acts as a crime against humanity and cruel treatment as a violation of the laws or customs of war. See *ibid.*, paras. 171–174.

[72] *Naletilić and Martinović* Trial Judgement, *supra* note 20, para. 81.

[73] *Galić* Trial Judgement, *supra* note 20, para. 177.

[74] *Ntagerura et al.* Trial Judgement, *supra* note 13, para. 623 ('If an accused may be held criminally responsible for a crime under either Article 6(1) or Article 6(3), the Chamber will enter a conviction on the form of responsibility that best characterises the accused's role in the crime.').

[75] *Gacumbitsi* Trial Judgement, *supra* note 13, para. 266 (citing no authority).

[76] *Stakić* Trial Judgement, *supra* note 42, para. 466:

In cases where the evidence leads a Trial Chamber to the conclusion that specific acts satisfy the requirements of Article 7(1) and that the accused acted as a superior, this Trial Chamber shares the view of the *Krnojelac* Trial Chamber that a conviction should be entered under Article 7(1) only and the accused's position as a superior taken into account as an aggravating factor.

[77] *Blaškić* Appeal Judgement, *supra* note 3, para. 91.

[78] *Kajelijeli* Appeal Judgement, *supra* note 20, para. 81.

attacks; Count 5 alleged his liability for instigating and aiding and abetting based on a shorter list consisting entirely of attacks also included under Count 3.[79] The Trial Chamber observed that the precedent of *Blaškić* – which speaks of the impermissibility of concurrently convicting an accused under Article 7(1) and 7(3) where both 'are alleged under the same *count*'[80] – did not address the scenario where an accused is charged pursuant to these two provisions in respect of the same crime but under different counts.[81] The Chamber considered that this 'formal splitting in two counts' was not 'so decisive that principally different results would be feasible',[82] and concluded that,

if the accused's conduct fulfils the elements both of commission or of participation according to Article 7(1) of the Statute and of superior criminal responsibility according to Article 7(3) of the Statute with regard to the same principal crime on basically the same facts, regardless of whether indicted in the same or in different counts, the accused will be convicted only under the heading of Article 7(1) of the Statute in terms of the more comprehensive wrongdoing.[83]

The Trial Chamber ultimately found that Orić's contribution to the incidents described in Counts 3 and 5 did not satisfy the elements of aiding and abetting,[84] instigating,[85] or superior responsibility,[86] and it consequently never reached the point at which it had to choose among these forms. Nonetheless, the Chamber must be correct in holding that the operation of the *Blaškić* rule cannot depend upon how the prosecution organised the crimes and forms of responsibility in its charging instrument. Instead, a chamber must examine the indictment as a whole to determine whether a form of Article 7/6(1) responsibility and superior responsibility are in fact concurrently alleged in respect of the same crime based on the same underlying criminal conduct.[87]

The paucity of the *Blaškić* Appeals Chamber's reasoning in support of the hierarchy it established – along with that of later trial and appeals chambers of both Tribunals, which have consistently followed the *Blaškić* rule[88] – is

[79] *Prosecutor v. Orić*, Case No. IT-03-68-PT, Third Amended Indictment, 30 June 2005, paras. 27–37.
[80] *Blaškić* Appeal Judgement, *supra* note 3, para. 91 (emphasis added).
[81] *Orić* Trial Judgement, *supra* note 32, para. 342.   [82] *Ibid.*   [83] *Ibid.*, para. 343.
[84] *Ibid.*, paras. 686–688.   [85] *Ibid.*, para. 688.   [86] *Ibid.*, paras. 708, 716.
[87] Cf. *Prosecutor v. Haradinaj, Balaj and Brahimaj*, Case No. IT-04-84-PT, Decision on Motion to Amend the Indictment and on Challenges to the Form of the Amended Indictment, 25 October 2006, para. 13 ('[I]t is each charge that holds the potential of exposing the accused to individual criminal liability. The counts in an indictment, by contrast, merely reflect the way in which the Prosecution chose to organise the charges in relation to the crimes allegedly committed.'); *Prosecutor v. Popović, Beara, Nikolić, Borovčanin, Tolimir, Miletić, Gvero and Pandurević*, Case No. IT-05-88-PT, Decision on Further Amendments and Challenges to the Indictment, 13 July 2006, para. 11 n. 26 (same).
[88] See *Prosecutor v. Galić*, Case No. IT-98-29-A, Judgement, 30 November 2006 ('*Galić* Appeal Judgement'), para. 186; *Naletilić and Martinović* Appeal Judgement, *supra* note 59, paras. 368–369

remarkable. The *Blaškić* Appeals Chamber itself did not provide any explanation of why, if concurrent convictions under Article 7/6(1) and Article 7/6(3) are impermissible because the two provisions 'connote distinct categories of criminal responsibility',[89] a chamber is obliged to select the former over the latter. In his separate opinion in *Kamuhanda*, Judge Shahabuddeen suggested that Article 7/6(1) is to be preferred, at least where ordering is the form of responsibility at issue, because 'the assumption of the ordering situation ... is that the accused actively advanced the commission of the crime[,] [whereas] the assumption of the command responsibility situation under [A]rticle 7(3) is that he did not'.[90] This rationale resonates with the *Kordić and Čerkez* Trial Chamber's distinction, described above,[91] between the forms of 'direct' responsibility in Article 7/6(1), and 'indirect' responsibility as enshrined by Article 7/6(3);[92] it is also in line with the *Stakić* Trial Chamber's characterisation of Article 7/6(3) as 'an omnibus clause' to be relied upon 'in cases where the primary basis of responsibility can not be applied'.[93] The *Orić* Trial Chamber, in contrast to virtually all other chambers subsequent to the *Blaškić* Appeal Judgement, set forth a rather extensive explanation for the hierarchy in terms very much in line with the views of Judge Shahabuddeen and the *Stakić* Trial Chamber:

In giving particular significance to the crime base to which the individual criminal responsibility is attached, and to the peculiar content of wrongfulness by which each of the two types of responsibilities in Articles 7(1) and 7(3) of the Statute are characterised, the Trial Chamber finds that active involvement by way of participating in the principal crime carries greater weight than failure by omission. Further, the Trial Chamber finds that participation in the crime means to have made a causal contribution to the impairment of the protected interest, whereas the failure as a superior need not necessarily contribute to the injury as such, but may merely involve the omission of his duty, as is particularly evident in the case of failure to punish.[94]

(quoting *Blaškić* and upholding the Trial Chamber's decision to convict Naletilić as a planner under Article 7(1), even though the elements of superior responsibility had also been established for the crime in question); *Jokić* Judgement on Sentence Appeal, *supra* note 20, para. 27; *Kvočka et al.* Appeal Judgement, *supra* note 3, para. 104; *Kordić and Čerkez* Appeal Judgement, *supra* note 5, paras. 33–34 (reproducing *Blaškić*'s concurrent-convictions discussion almost verbatim); *ibid.*, para. 35 (holding that the Trial Chamber's concurrent convictions constituted legal error 'invalidating the Trial Judgement in this regard'); *Orić* Trial Judgement, *supra* note 32, para. 343; *Rajić* Sentencing Judgement, *supra* note 67, para. 106 (quoting *Blaškić*); *Rajić* Clarifications on Convictions Entered, *supra* note 67, pp. 4–5 (citing *Blaškić*); *Brđanin* Trial Judgement, *supra* note 15, para. 285.

[89] *Blaškić* Appeal Judgement, *supra* note 3, para. 91.

[90] *Kamuhanda* Appeal Judgement, *supra* note 20, Separate and Partially Dissenting Opinion of Judge Mohamed Shahabuddeen, para. 410.

[91] See *supra* text accompanying notes 59–60.

[92] *Kordić and Čerkez* Trial Judgement, *supra* note 23, paras. 367, 369.

[93] *Stakić* Trial Judgement, *supra* note 42, para. 465.

[94] *Orić* Trial Judgement, *supra* note 32, para. 342 (footnote omitted).

The *Orić* Chamber concluded that '[t]hese differences in the substance and degree of wrongfulness of active participation and passive non-preventing or non-punishing crimes of subordinates warrant[ed]' the Chamber's endorsement of the *Blaškić* rule.[95]

Whatever the justification offered for the *Blaškić* rule, however, it seems inconsistent with the deference traditionally accorded to trial chambers' findings to require that a conviction under Article 7/6(1) always be entered instead of one under Article 7/6(3). The apparent attraction of 'logical' approaches to concurrent convictions aside, the determination of which form of responsibility best fits with the factual findings made on the evidence presented over the course of the entire proceedings is one best left to the trier of fact, unrestricted by the straitjacket of a rule that is indifferent to the infinite variety of factual circumstances that arise in these cases. In other words, the *Blaškić* rule should have been a guideline instead, so as to allow trial chambers to reconcile the principle it seeks to protect with their own analysis and conclusions.

Even if the *Blaškić* rule were suitable in some circumstances, what the chambers following the rule have persistently failed to take into account is the propriety of the Appeals Chamber's absolute dichotomy when the physical element of the Article 7/6(1) form of responsibility in question is fulfilled by means of an omission. Although, as discussed in Chapters 4 and 5 of this book, the authors maintain serious doubts about whether aiding and abetting by omission and instigating by omission are properly founded in international criminal law,[96] it remains the case that that their existence has been recognised by a number of chambers – including many of those who have expounded the *Blaškić* rule, both before and after the *Blaškić* Appeal Judgement, albeit without a great deal of legal reasoning or attempts to apply these forms to the facts before them.[97] The hypothetical scenario often invoked is that of an

---

[95] *Ibid.*, para. 343.

[96] See Chapter 4, text accompanying notes 192–216; Chapter 5, text accompanying notes 115–120, 125–127.

[97] For aiding and abetting by omission, see the following: *Blaškić* Appeal Judgement, *supra* note 3, para. 47 ('The Appeals Chamber leaves open the possibility that in the circumstances of a given case, an omission may constitute the *actus reus* of aiding and abetting.'); *Prosecutor* v. *Muvunyi*, Case No. ICTR-00-55A-T, Judgement, 11 September 2006 ('*Muvunyi* Trial Judgement'), para. 470; *Prosecutor* v. *Mpambara*, Case No. ICTR-01-65-T, Judgement, 11 September 2006 ('*Mpambara* Trial Judgement'), para. 22; *Orić* Trial Judgement, *supra* note 32, para. 283; *Strugar* Trial Judgement, *supra* note 21, para. 349; *Blagojević and Jokić* Trial Judgement, *supra* note 21, para. 726; *Brđanin* Trial Judgement, *supra* note 15, para. 271; *Galić* Trial Judgement, *supra* note 20, para. 168; *Kajelijeli* Trial Judgement, *supra* note 20, para. 766; *Prosecutor* v. *Simić, Tadić and Zarić*, Case No. IT-95-9-T, Judgement, 17 October 2003, para. 162; *Naletilić and Martinović* Trial Judgement, *supra* note 67, para. 63; *Prosecutor* v. *Vasiljević*, Case No. IT-98-32-T, Judgement, 29 November 2002 ('*Vasiljević* Trial Judgement'), para. 70; *Krnojelac* Trial Judgement, *supra* note 54, para. 88; *Kunarac et al.* Trial Judgement, *supra* note 14, para. 391; *Blaškić* Trial Judgement, *supra* note 20, para. 284; *Aleksovski* Trial Judgement, *supra* note 5, para. 129. For instigating by omission, see the following: *Muvunyi* Trial Judgement, *supra*, para. 464; *Orić* Trial Judgement, *supra* note 32, para. 273; *Prosecutor* v. *Limaj, Bala and Musliu*, Case No. IT-03-66-T, Judgement, 30 November 2005 ('*Limaj et al.*

accused superior who, by not punishing his subordinates for past crimes or not intervening to stop ongoing crimes, provides encouragement to those subordinates to continue committing crimes or to commit them again in the future; in this way, according to these chambers, the accused may instigate or aid and abet the commission of the crimes.[98] This scenario of inaction on the part of an accused superior should certainly be classified alongside superior responsibility as a form of 'indirect', and not 'direct', responsibility, as those two terms have been defined by the *Kordić and Čerkez* Trial Chamber.

By the strict operation of the *Blaškić* rule, however, an accused found to be potentially liable through aiding and abetting by omission or instigating by omission, and also as a superior under Article 7/6(3), could only be convicted pursuant to one or both of the former to the exclusion of the latter merely because they happen to appear in the Statute under Article 7/6(1). The *Blaškić* Appeals Chamber cannot possibly have intended such an outcome. The more likely explanation is that this eventuality never occurred to the Appeals Chamber, nor to any of the other chambers that have adopted the *Blaškić* rule. Had any of them actually envisioned this possibility, they may have opted to place aiding and abetting by omission and instigating by omission on par with superior responsibility, thereby leaving it within the discretion of the chamber to choose which of these forms of omission liability best describes the contribution of the accused to the crime on the facts before it.

The *Strugar* Trial Judgement provides perhaps the only example in the jurisprudence of a chamber's attempt to avoid being forced, by operation of the *Blaškić* rule, to convict the accused pursuant to aiding and abetting by omission instead of superior responsibility. Ironically, although the Chamber's preoccupation with *Blaškić* is evident upon reading the relevant part of the judgment,[99] the Chamber never explicitly restated the *Blaškić* rule, perhaps because it did not ultimately find that the accused fulfilled the elements of any of the charged Article 7(1) forms of responsibility, and so the question of choosing never arose.[100] Pavle Strugar was a general in the Yugoslav People's Army charged, *inter alia*, with aiding and abetting a number of violations of the

Trial Judgement'), para. 514; *Brđanin* Trial Judgement, *supra* note 15, para. 269; *Kamuhanda* Trial Judgement, *supra* note 24, para. 593; *Galić* Trial Judgement, *supra* note 20, para. 168; *Kajelijeli* Trial Judgement, *supra* note 20, para. 762; *Naletilić and Martinović* Trial Judgement, *supra* note 67, para. 60; *Kordić and Čerkez* Trial Judgement, *supra* note 23, para. 387. Cf. *Galić* Appeal Judgement, *supra* note 88, paras. 176–177 (holding that 'ordering by omission' does not exist).

[98] See, e.g., *Mpambara* Trial Judgement, *supra* note 97, para. 23; *Galić* Trial Judgement, *supra* note 20, para. 169; *Kordić and Čerkez* Trial Judgement, *supra* note 23, para. 371; *Blaškić* Trial Judgement, *supra* note 20, paras. 337–339.

[99] See *Strugar* Trial Judgement, *supra* note 21, paras. 349–356, 446.

[100] Cf. *Orić* Trial Judgement, *supra* note 32, paras. 342–343 (restating and discussing the *Blaškić* rule even though it never ultimately had to choose between Articles 7(1) and 7(3) of the ICTY Statute in respect of the same crime). See also *supra* text accompanying notes 79–87 (discussing this aspect of *Orić*).

laws or customs of war, as well as failing to prevent and punish these crimes, in respect of his forces' unlawful shelling of the Old Town of Dubrovnik on the morning of 6 December 1991.[101] The prosecution argued in its final trial brief that, even though Strugar had not been physically present to witness the shelling, his failure to intervene to stop the shelling exposed him to liability not only as a superior under Article 7(3) of the ICTY Statute, but also as an aider and abettor.[102] While Strugar had issued a ceasefire order, he only did so three hours after he discovered that his troops might be engaging in unlawful shelling, and he took no steps afterward to undertake an adequate investigation into the events.[103]

The Trial Chamber acknowledged that the *Blaškić* Appeal Judgement left open the possibility 'that in the circumstances of a given case an omission may constitute the *actus reus* of aiding and abetting',[104] and that several trial chambers had hypothesised that such liability might arise where a military commander fails in a duty to prevent his subordinates' crimes.[105] The Chamber concluded, however, that Strugar could not bear aiding and abetting liability:[106] he had made an effort to stop the shelling, and his failure to carry out an investigation occurred so long after the commission of the offences that it could not have had the 'direct and substantial effect' required of aiding and abetting by omission.[107] '[I]n the absence of more settled jurisprudence as to whether, and if so in what circumstances, an omission may constitute the *actus reus* of aiding and abetting,' the Chamber determined that Strugar's failure to take more effective measures was more properly regarded in the context of superior responsibility under Article 7(3).[108] It ultimately convicted him pursuant to this provision of the ICTY Statute for failing to prevent and punish two violations of the laws or customs or war in relation to the 6 December 1991 shelling.[109]

As the authors have argued in Chapter 4,[110] this course of action on the part of the *Strugar* Trial Chamber reveals the inappropriateness of imposing aiding and abetting liability on a superior for failing to intervene to stop his subordinates' criminal conduct and, by logical analogy, for failing to punish those responsible for such conduct. Superior responsibility under Article 7/6(3) is

---

[101] See *Prosecutor v. Strugar*, Case No. IT-01-42-PT, Third Amended Indictment, paras. 1, 11–25 (especially para. 15).
[102] *Strugar* Trial Judgement, *supra* note 21, para. 352.
[103] See *ibid.*, 352–355.   [104] *Blaškić* Appeal Judgement, *supra* note 3, para. 47.
[105] *Strugar* Trial Judgement, para. 349.
[106] *Ibid.*, para. 356.   [107] *Ibid.*, para. 355.   [108] *Ibid.*
[109] *Ibid.*, paras. 446, 478. These crimes were attacks on civilians, and destruction of wilful damage done to institutions dedicated to religion, charity, and education, the arts and sciences, historic monuments and works of art and science.
[110] See Chapter 4, text accompanying note 206 *et seq.*

tailor-made for circumstances such as those in *Strugar*.[111] The universal and frequent endorsement of the *Blaškić* rule by the trial and appeals chambers of both *ad hoc* Tribunals leaves little hope that the Appeals Chamber will, before the end of the Tribunals' respective mandates, change course and restore the complete freedom of trial chambers to select from among the charged forms of responsibility the most appropriate to describe the accused's contribution to the crime on the facts before it, even where this selection may result in a finding of guilt pursuant to Article 7/6(3) to the exclusion of Article 7/6(1).[112] It is to be hoped, however, that future benches of the Appeals Chamber will take note of the nonsensical result when the *Blaškić* rule operates to compel a chamber to choose aiding and abetting by omission or instigating by omission over superior responsibility, and at least vary the rule in that regard.

The case law has long held that an accused's superior position may be taken into account as a factor militating in favour of an aggravation of his sentence where he is convicted pursuant to some form of responsibility other than superior responsibility.[113] The *Blaškić* Appeals Chamber relied on this jurisprudence in support of its holding that a chamber choosing Article 7/6(1) over Article 7/6(3) *'should ...* consider the accused's superior position as an aggravating factor in sentencing',[114] and the subsequent *Jokić* Appeals Chamber clarified that taking the accused's superior position into account as an

[111] Accord Silva Hinek, 'The Judgment of the International Criminal Tribunal for the Former Yugoslavia in *Prosecutor* v. *Pavle Strugar*', (2006) 19 *Leiden Journal of International Law* 477, 486:

There is no doubt that the trial chamber was correct when it held that the accused's failure to take more effective measures to stop the shelling was more properly regarded in the context of command responsibility under Article 7(3). After all, the accused's circumstances reflect what is the paradigm Article 7(3) case, that of a military commander issuing orders and failing to prevent and/or punish crimes committed by his subordinates.

[112] Indeed, as recently as November 2006, the ICTY Appeals Chamber was presented with a clear opportunity to reconsider the *Blaškić* rule, and opted to reaffirm it. As mentioned above, the *Galić* Trial Chamber endorsed the *Krnojelac* Trial Chamber's position that a chamber has the discretion to choose between Article 7(1) and Article 7(3) of the ICTY Statute where the facts satisfy the elements of a form of responsibility from each provision for the same crime. The Appeals Chamber held that the Trial Chamber's conclusion was in error, and reiterated that Article 7(1) must prevail over Article 7(3) in such a circumstance. It did not, however, overturn any of the Trial Chamber's convictions, as in the relevant instances the Trial Chamber had chosen Article 7(1) over Article 7(3). See *Galić* Appeal Judgement, *supra* note 88, para. 186; see also *supra* note 73 and accompanying text (discussing the *Galić* Trial Chamber's endorsement of *Krnojelac*).

[113] See *Prosecutor* v. *Kupreškić, Kupreškić, Kupreškić, Josipović and Šantić*, Case No. IT-95-16-A, Appeal Judgement, 23 October 2001, para. 451; *Čelebići* Appeal Judgement, *supra* note 5, para. 745; *Aleksovski* Appeal Judgement, *supra* note 5, para. 183. Cf. *Naletilić and Martinović* Appeal Judgement, *supra* note 59, paras. 613, 626 (holding that a chamber may not use the accused's position of superior authority as a factor aggravating his sentence where he is convicted pursuant to Article 7(3) of the ICTY Statute, as opposed to Article 7(1)).

[114] *Blaškić* Appeal Judgement, *supra* note 3, para. 91 (emphasis added). Accord *Naletilić and Martinović* Appeal Judgement, *supra* note 59, paras. 368–369, 613, 626; *Jokić* Judgement on Sentence Appeal, *supra* note 20, para. 28; *Kajelijeli* Appeal Judgement, *supra* note 20, para. 82; *Kvočka et al.* Appeal Judgement, *supra* note 3, para. 104; *Kordić and Čerkez* Appeal Judgement, *supra* note 5, para. 34; *Orić* Trial Judgement, *supra* note 32, para. 343 (explaining that such aggravation is necessary because 'the final sentence should reflect the totality of the culpable conduct'); *Rajić* Sentencing Judgement, *supra* note 67, para. 106; *Rajić* Clarifications on Convictions Entered, *supra* note 67, p. 5; *Brđanin* Trial Judgement,

aggravating factor in this circumstance is indeed obligatory.[115] In upholding the Trial Chamber's aggravation of Stakić's sentence pursuant to Article 7(1) because of his superior position, the *Stakić* Appeals Chamber explained that it is not the accused's superior position alone, but his abuse of that position, that calls for a more serious sentence.[116] In accordance with this principle, the *Kajelijeli* Appeals Chamber vacated Juvénal Kajelijeli's conviction for failing to prevent and punish genocide after determining that the Trial Chamber had erroneously convicted him pursuant to both Article 6(1) of the ICTR Statute (for instigating, ordering, and aiding and abetting genocide) and Article 6(3) based on the same facts.[117] Nevertheless, the Appeals Chamber considered that it was 'still necessary to determine, for purposes of sentencing, whether the Trial Chamber was correct in its finding that the Appellant held a *de facto* superior position as a civilian over the Interahamwe'.[118] After finding that the evidence established that Kajelijeli did indeed hold such a position, the Chamber concluded that the sentence imposed by the Trial Chamber in relation to the count of genocide had already taken adequate account of his superior position.[119] In a similar manner, after upholding the Trial Chamber's convictions of Miodrag Jokić for aiding and abetting a number of crimes,[120] the Appeals Chamber vacated the Trial Chamber's concurrent convictions of the accused for failing to prevent and punish these same crimes;[121] the Appeals Chamber left the Trial Chamber's sentence intact,

---

supra note 15, para. 285; *Ntagerura et al.* Trial Judgement, *supra* note 13, para. 623; *Stakić* Trial Judgement, *supra* note 42, paras. 465, 912; *Naletilić and Martinović* Trial Judgement, *supra* note 20, para. 81; *Krnojelac* Trial Judgement, *supra* note 54, para. 496 (considering it 'more appropriate to enter a conviction under Article 7(1) [for aiding and abetting]' and 'tak[ing] into account the Accused's position as a superior as a factor aggravating his criminal responsibility under Article 7(1)').

[115] *Jokić* Judgement on Sentence Appeal, *supra* note 20, para. 28 (relying on the imperative language in *Čelebići* Appeal Judgement, *supra* note 5, para. 745 and holding that 'the Trial Chamber was required to take the Appellant's superior position into account as an aggravating factor in sentencing'[.]). Accord *Kajelijeli* Appeal Judgement, *supra* note 20, para. 82; *Naletilić and Martinović* Trial Judgement, *supra* note 20, para. 81 (holding that 'the form of responsibility ... which was not chosen ... must be considered as an aggravating circumstance, because the final sentence should reflect the totality of the culpable conduct').

[116] *Stakić* Appeal Judgement, *supra* note 20, para. 411. Accord *Simić* Appeal Judgement, *supra* note 3, para. 268. The *Stakić* Appeals Chamber accordingly dismissed an argument of the accused relying on the position taken by Judge Nieto-Navia in his separate opinion appended to the *Galić* Trial Judgement: 'I respectfully submit that considering his position as a military commander as an aggravating circumstance is analogous to concluding that being a husband is an aggravating circumstance with respect to the crime of uxoricide.' *Galić* Trial Judgement, *supra* note 20, Separate and Partially Dissenting Opinion of Judge Nieto-Navia, para. 121. See also *infra* note 123 (discussing the *Galić* Appeals Chamber's approval of the Trial Chamber's aggravation of Galić's sentence in respect of ordering based on his abuse of his position of authority).

[117] *Kajelijeli* Appeal Judgement, *supra* note 20, para. 81 (overturning *Kajelijeli* Trial Judgement, *supra* note 20, paras. 842–843, 905–906).

[118] *Kajelijeli* Appeal Judgement, *supra* note 20, para. 82 (italics on 'Interahamwe' removed).

[119] *Ibid.*, paras. 318–319.

[120] See *Prosecutor v. Jokić*, Case No. IT-01-42/1-S, Sentencing Judgement, 18 March 2004, paras. 9, 57–58.

[121] *Jokić* Judgement on Sentence Appeal, *supra* note 20, para. 27.

however, finding that it adequately reflected the aggravating effect of Jokić's superior position.[122]

6.2 Forms of responsibility and sentencing

Much like the jurisprudence on choosing among forms of responsibility, the jurisprudence on the relationship between forms of responsibility and the severity of an accused's sentence – with the possible exception of that concerning the principles on aggravation discussed in Section 6.1 of this chapter[123] – is sparse and rather disjointed. Moreover, even where a chamber has overtly discussed, in the sentencing section of the judgement, its findings on the forms of responsibility under which the accused is or could have been found liable, it is often difficult to tell precisely how much weight the chamber gave those findings relative to other factors in determining the ultimate sentence.[124] With these caveats in mind, this section provides a broad sketch of several principles on the forms of responsibility and sentencing that have been discussed in the case law.

The trial and appeals chambers of both *ad hoc* Tribunals have made numerous statements and findings of fact evincing the view that an accused's aiding and abetting of a crime should be accorded less weight in sentencing than had he participated in the crime though one of the other forms of responsibility in Article 7/6(1). This proposition has been repeated most often with respect to JCE, often in the course of duplicating the *Tadić* Appeals Chamber's examination of the differences between JCE and aiding and abetting.[125] The ICTY

---

[122] *Ibid.*, paras. 30–31.

[123] See *supra* notes 46–48, 113–122. In respect of the form of responsibility 'ordering', the *Galić* Appeals Chamber held that the fact that the accused had a position of authority may not be considered as an aggravating factor in sentencing, because the possession of authority is one of the elements of that form of responsibility. See *Galić* Appeal Judgement, *supra* note 88, para. 412; see also Chapter 5, text accompanying notes 151–170 (discussing this element of ordering). Nevertheless, according to the Appeals Chamber, the accused's *level* of authority may be considered in sentencing. The Chamber accordingly upheld the Trial Chamber's aggravation of Galić's sentence based on findings that he 'breached his public duty from [his] very senior position, thereby abusing his position of authority'. *Galić* Appeal Judgement, *supra*, para. 412 (affirming *Galić* Trial Judgement, *supra* note 20, para. 765).

[124] See, e.g., *Krstić* Appeal Judgement, *supra* note 21, paras. 268, 272–273, 275 (decreasing Krstić's sentence from forty-six to thirty-five years after setting aside aiding and abetting convictions for genocide and murder as a violation of the laws or customs of war, but also discussing other mitigating factors unrelated to this change in form of responsibility that contributed to the reduction in sentence); *Krnojelac* Appeal Judgement, *supra* note 3, para. 264 (increasing Krnojelac's sentence from seven-and-a-half to fifteen years after overturning several aiding and abetting convictions and substituting convictions pursuant to JCE, but also altering the accused's verdict in several other aggravating ways so that it is impossible to tell how much relative weight the Appeals Chamber gave to the change in the form of responsibility); *Stakić* Trial Judgement, *supra* note 42, paras. 911–919 (convicting Stakić of 'committing' deportation as a crime against humanity; considering his ordering and planning of that crime as aggravating his sentence along with several other aggravating factors without specifying the relative weight of each factor; and sentencing the accused to life imprisonment).

[125] See *Prosecutor* v. *Tadić*, Case No. IT-94-1-A, Judgement, 15 July 1999, para. 229.

Appeals Chamber has held repeatedly that aiding and abetting is 'generally' or 'usually' considered to incur a lesser degree of culpability than participation in a JCE.[126] A few trial chambers have also made statements to this effect, justifying the distinction by reference to the absence of an element of shared intent in aiding and abetting. For example, the *Krnojelac* Trial Chamber opined that,

[t]he seriousness of what is done by a participant in a joint criminal enterprise who was not the principal offender is significantly greater than what is done by one who merely aids and abets the principal offender. That is because a person who merely aids and abets the principal offender need only be aware of the intent with which the crime was committed by the principal offender, whereas the participant in a joint criminal enterprise with the principal offender must share that intent.[127]

On appeal, the Appeals Chamber determined that the prosecution had not shown this holding to be erroneous.[128] It ultimately overturned the Trial Chamber's convictions of Milorad Krnojelac for aiding and abetting persecution as a crime against humanity[129] and cruel treatment as a violation of the laws or customs of war, and entered convictions for these crimes pursuant to the second category of JCE instead.[130] The Appeals Chamber increased Krnojelac's sentence from seven-and-half to fifteen years' imprisonment, although it is not possible to tell how much weight the Chamber gave the substitution of JCE for aiding and abetting in relation to the various other aggravating revisions it made to the Trial Chamber's conclusions on Krnojelac's guilt.[131]

In the same vein as *Krnojelac*, the *Vasiljević* Trial Chamber held that '[t]he fact that the aider and abettor does not share the intent of the principal

---

[126] See *Simić* Appeal Judgement, *supra* note 3, para. 265 (holding that 'aiding and abetting is a form of responsibility which generally warrants a lower sentence than is appropriate to responsibility as a participant in a joint criminal enterprise'); *Kvočka et al.* Appeal Judgement, *supra* note 3, para. 92 (same); *Krstić* Appeal Judgement, *supra* note 21, para. 268 (same); *Prosecutor* v. *Vasiljević*, Case No. IT-98-32-A, Judgement, 25 February 2004 ('*Vasiljević* Appeal Judgement'), para. 102 (holding that aiding and abetting 'is usually considered to incur a lesser degree of individual criminal responsibility than committing a crime'); *ibid.*, para. 182 (holding that 'aiding and abetting ... generally warrants a lower sentence than is appropriate to responsibility as a co-perpetrator' in a JCE); *Krnojelac* Appeal Judgement, *supra* note 3, para. 75.

[127] *Krnojelac* Trial Judgement, *supra* note 54, para. 75.

[128] *Krnojelac* Appeal Judgement, *supra* note 3, para. 75. In a footnote, the subsequent *Kvočka* Appeals Chamber cited the *Krnojelac* Appeals Chamber's paraphrasing of the Trial Chamber's holding –'[t]he acts of a participant in a joint criminal enterprise are more serious than those of an aider and abettor ... since a participant in a joint criminal enterprise shares the intent of the principal offender whereas an aider and abettor need only be aware of that intent' – apparently assuming that this particular rationale had been endorsed by the *Krnojelac* Appeals Chamber. See *Kvočka et al.* Appeal Judgement, *supra* note 3, para. 92 n. 204 (quoting *Krnojelac* Appeal Judgement, *supra* note 3, para. 75 in a parenthetical to that judgement's citation).

[129] Through the forms of imprisonment and inhumane acts.

[130] *Ibid.*, pp. 113–114 (overturning *Krnojelac* Trial Judgement, *supra* note 54, para. 536).

[131] See *ibid.*, para. 264 and pp. 113–115.

offender generally lessens his criminal culpability from that of an accused acting pursuant to a joint criminal enterprise who does share the intent of the principal offender';[132] the subsequent *Brđanin* Trial Chamber endorsed this language and reproduced it almost verbatim.[133] Also expressing agreement with this principle,[134] the *Vasiljević* Appeals Chamber reduced Mitar Vasiljević's sentence from twenty to fifteen years after overturning his convictions for several crimes perpetrated against a group of Muslim men pursuant to the first category of JCE, and convicting him instead for aiding and abetting these crimes.[135] The Appeals Chamber substituted the aiding and abetting convictions because it found that the evidence did not establish beyond a reasonable doubt that Vasiljević shared the intent of the physical perpetrators of the crimes, and that he could not consequently bear liability under the first category;[136] the evidence did, however, show that the accused knew his conduct would assist the physical perpetrators, and he thus fulfilled the mental elements of aiding and abetting.[137] In this instance, the Appeals Chamber stated explicitly that its modification of the Trial Chamber's sentence was 'due to the Appeals Chamber's finding that the Appellant was responsible as an aider and abettor' of the crimes in question.[138]

Similarly, the *Krstić* Appeals Chamber set aside Radislav Krstić's conviction for participating in a JCE to commit genocide and murder as a violation of the laws or customs of war in relation to the killing of thousands of Muslim males from Srebrenica during the period 13 to 19 July 1995;[139] it substituted convictions for aiding and abetting genocide and murder, and added new convictions for aiding and abetting extermination and persecution as crimes against humanity.[140] With regard to genocide, the Appeals Chamber found that '[t]here was a demonstrable failure by the Trial Chamber to supply adequate proof that ... Krstić possessed the genocidal intent' required to be convicted pursuant to the first category of JCE;[141] Krstić was aware, however, that his actions made a substantial contribution to the realisation of genocide

---

[132] *Vasiljević* Trial Judgement, *supra* note 97, para. 71.
[133] *Brđanin* Trial Judgement, *supra* note 15, para. 274.
[134] See *Vasiljević* Appeal Judgement, *supra* note 126, paras. 102, 182.
[135] *Ibid.*, paras. 181–82. The crimes at issue were murder as a violation of the laws or customs of war, murder as a crime against humanity, and inhumane acts as a crime against humanity. *Ibid.*, para. 135.
[136] See *ibid.*, paras. 131–132.   [137] See *ibid.*, paras. 134–135.   [138] See *ibid.*, para. 181.
[139] See *Krstić* Trial Judgement, *supra* note 14, paras. 644–646, 727.
[140] See *Krstić* Appeal Judgement, *supra* note 21, paras. 138, 143–144, 227, 237, p. 87. The forms of persecution in question were murder, inhumane acts, terrorising the civilian population, forcible transfer and destruction of civilian property. *Krstić* Trial Judgement, *supra* note 14, para. 727. The Trial Chamber had found that Krstić could bear liability for extermination and persecution perpetrated from 13 to 19 July 1995, but that convictions for these crimes would be impermissibly cumulative with the conviction for genocide. *Ibid.*, paras. 646, 687. The Appeals Chamber determined this holding to be erroneous. *Krstić* Appeal Judgement, *supra* note 21, paras. 227, 229.
[141] *Krstić* Appeal Judgement, *supra* note 21, para. 134.

by others,[142] and that these others possessed genocidal intent.[143] Such awareness, combined with his physical participation in allowing the resources of his
army corps to be used in support of the genocidal plan, exposed him to liability
for aiding and abetting genocide.[144] In discussing the reasons behind its
reduction of Krstić's sentence from forty-six to thirty-five years, the Appeals
Chamber endorsed the holding of the *Vasiljević* Appeals Chamber that 'aiding
and abetting ... generally warrants lower sentences than responsibility' for
participation in a JCE;[145] it found that the accused's lack of genocidal intent
'significantly diminishes his responsibility', and that '[t]he same analysis
applies to the reduction of Krstić's responsibility for the murders as a violation
of the laws or customs of war committed between 13 and 19 July 1995'.[146] As
with the *Krnojelac* Appeal Judgement, however, it is not possible to discern
precisely how significantly the replacement of JCE with aiding and abetting
contributed to the eleven-year reduction, as the Appeals Chamber also took
into account several unrelated mitigating factors that had not been considered
by the Trial Chamber.[147]

These chambers appear to regard JCE as being of greater gravity than aiding
and abetting at least in part because the latter does not require that the accused
have the intent to commit the crime with which he is charged.[148] It would seem
that none of the chambers adhering to this hierarchy between JCE and aiding
and abetting have had in mind that, like aiding and abetting, certain categories
of JCE do not demand that the accused himself possess the intent required of
the crime. *Vasiljević* and *Krstić* concerned accused convicted as participants in
the first category of JCE, and *Krnojelac* concerned an accused convicted as a
participant in a second-category JCE for persecution as a crime against
humanity. As discussed in Chapter 2, the first category of JCE requires shared

---

[142] See *ibid.*, para. 136. [143] *Ibid.*, para. 143. [144] See *ibid.*, paras. 137, 144.
[145] *Ibid.*, para. 268. [146] *Ibid.*
[147] See *ibid.*, paras. 272–273. Although, as discussed, the Appeals Chamber also added new convictions for
aiding and abetting extermination and persecution as crimes against humanity, it stated expressly that
these new convictions were not taken into account as factors aggravating Krstić's sentence because 'the
Prosecution did not seek an increase in sentence on the basis of these convictions'. *Ibid.*, para. 269. See
also *Simić* Appeal Judgement, *supra* note 3, para. 300, p. 115 (reducing Simić's sentence from seventeen
to fifteen years after overturning his convictions as a participant in a JCE to commit several forms of
persecution as a crime against humanity; re-qualifying his participation in all but one of them –
inhumane treatment – as aiding and abetting; acquitting him of the charges of inhumane treatment;
and considering a number of other aggravating and mitigating factors); *ibid.*, Partially Dissenting
Opinion of Judge Liu, paras. 3, 5–6 (comparing the *Vasiljević* and *Krstić* Appeals Chambers' downward
adjustment of the sentences of their respective accused, and opining that Simić should have received
more than a two-year reduction).
[148] See *Blaškić* Appeal Judgement, *supra* note 3, para. 49; *Krstić* Appeal Judgement, *supra* note 21, para.
140; *Vasiljević* Appeal Judgement, *supra* note 126, paras. 102, 142; *Prosecutor v. Kayishema and
Ruzindana*, Case No. ICTR-95-1-A, Judgement (Reasons), 1 June 2001, para. 186. See also Chapter 4,
text accompanying notes 247–249, 283–300.

intent between the accused and the physical perpetrator,[149] and the second category requires that the accused possess specific intent if charged with a specific-intent crime such as genocide or persecution.[150] Yet a conviction for a purely general-intent crime pursuant to the second category of JCE requires merely that the accused know of the criminal nature of the system of ill-treatment and intend to further it – and not that he possess the intent to commit the crime with which he is charged.[151] Under the rationale put forth by the *Krnojelac* and *Vasiljević* Trial Chambers, and ostensibly endorsed by the Appeals Chamber, such a conviction should not receive a harsher sentence than a conviction for aiding and abetting. Likewise, because any conviction pursuant to the third category requires only that the accused have intended to participate in the JCE and to further its common purpose, with the awareness that the charged crime was possible,[152] such a conviction also would not warrant a more severe sentence than one for aiding and abetting the same crime.

Some chambers have suggested or made findings evincing the view that the other forms of responsibility in Article 7/6(1) – that is, planning, instigating, ordering, and physical commission – also entail a greater degree of culpability than aiding and abetting. Recalling the language of Article 7(1) of the ICTY Statute, which speaks in terms of 'planning, instigating, ordering, committing, *or otherwise* aiding and abetting',[153] the *Orić* Trial Chamber observed that aiding and abetting 'appears wide enough to serve as a residual category for all forms of participation listed in Article 7(1)',[154] and that 'mere aiding and abetting is commonly considered as a less grave mode of participation'.[155] The Chamber justified this differentiation by contrasting the physical elements of aiding and abetting, which requires only that the accused render assistance, encouragement or moral support to the physical perpetrator, with those of

---

[149] See *Stakić* Appeal Judgement, *supra* note 20, para. 65; *Kvočka et al.* Appeal Judgement, para. 110; *Ntakirutimana and Ntakirutimana* Appeal Judgement, *supra* note 5, para. 467. See also Chapter 2, text accompanying notes 268–283. For a comparative perspective of the respective intent requirements for all of the forms of responsibility, see the chart 'Comparison of required mental states, with regard to intent, for imposition of liability under each form of responsibility' in the Annex of this book.

[150] See *Kvočka et al.* Appeal Judgement, *supra* note 3, para. 110; *Krnojelac* Appeal Judgement, *supra* note 3, para. 111. See also Chapter 2, text accompanying notes 365–372.

[151] *Kvočka et al.* Appeal Judgement, *supra* note 3, para. 243; *Vasiljević* Appeal Judgement, *supra* note 126, para. 101. See also Chapter 2, text accompanying notes 309–350.

[152] *Stakić* Appeal Judgement, *supra* note 20, para. 87; *Kvočka et al.* Appeal Judgement, *supra* note 3, para. 83; *Blaškić* Appeal Judgement, *supra* note 3, para. 33. See also Chapter 2, text accompanying notes 382–388.

[153] Statute of the International Criminal Tribunal for the Prosecution of Persons Responsible for Serious Violations of International Humanitarian Law Committed in the Territory of the former Yugoslavia since 1991, (1993) 32 ILM 1159, as amended by Security Council Resolution 1660 of 28 February 2006, Art. 7(1) (emphasis added).

[154] *Orić* Trial Judgement, *supra* note 32, para. 280.   [155] See *ibid.*, para. 281

physical commission and instigation, which are more difficult for the accused to fulfil as they generally require more active involvement.[156]

The clearest and most authoritative exposition of the position that ordering justifies a more severe penalty than aiding and abetting was made by the ICTR Appeals Chamber in *Semanza*. Upon assessing the evidence relating to Laurent Semanza's participation in the massacre of Tutsis by Interahamwe militiamen at the Musha church, the Trial Chamber chose not to convict him of ordering genocide and extermination as a crime against humanity in relation to this incident, and instead convicted him of complicity in genocide and aiding and abetting extermination as a crime against humanity.[157] In a welcome departure from the usual practice, the Trial Chamber specified the precise proportion of Semanza's total sentence comprised by each of his several convictions;[158] these two convictions warranted concurrently running sentences of fifteen years each,[159] out of a total sentence of twenty-four years and six months.[160] The Appeals Chamber determined that the Trial Chamber had erred in finding that Semanza did not possess the requisite level of authority over the physical perpetrators to expose him to liability for ordering.[161] It accordingly set aside the convictions for complicity in genocide and aiding and abetting extermination, and substituted convictions for ordering genocide and ordering extermination 'in relation to the massacre at Musha church'.[162]

In assessing the appropriate sentence to impose upon Semanza, the Appeals Chamber observed as follows:

Despite the Trial Chamber's conscientious treatment of the Appellant's sentence, the Appeals Chamber is not satisfied that the fifteen-year sentences for complicity in genocide and aiding and abetting extermination that the Trial Chamber imposed are commensurate with the gravity of the Appellant's offences, as determined by the Appeals Chamber. The Appeals Chamber has concluded above that the Appellant's actions at Musha church amounted to perpetration in the form of ordering rather than mere complicity in genocide and aiding and abetting extermination. This form of direct perpetration entails a higher level of culpability than complicity in genocide and

---

[156] See *ibid.*

[157] See *Semanza* Trial Judgement, *supra* note 14, paras. 430, 435–436, 465, 553. See Chapter 4, text accompanying notes 51–55, for a more detailed discussion of Semanza's conviction for complicity in genocide.

[158] *Semanza* Trial Judgement, *supra* note 14, paras. 585–589.

[159] *Ibid.*, para. 585 ('Since these crimes are based on identical sets of facts ... the sentences for these two counts will run concurrently.').

[160] *Ibid.*, para. 590. The Trial Chamber's total sentence of twenty-five years was subject to a six-month reduction for certain violations of Semanza's pre-trial rights, resulting in a 'final sentence [of] twenty-four years and six months imprisonment.' See also, *ibid.*, paras. 579–580 (discussing the violations).

[161] *Semanza* Appeal Judgement, *supra* note 5, para. 363. See Chapter 5, text accompanying notes 156–164, for a more detailed discussion of this finding and its implications for the law on ordering.

[162] *Semanza* Appeal Judgement, *supra* note 5, para. 364.

aiding and abetting extermination convictions entered by the Trial Chamber. The Appeals Chamber recently held in *Krstić* that 'aiding and abetting is a form of responsibility which generally warrants lower sentences than responsibility as a co-perpetrator.' The Appeals Chamber endorses this reasoning to the extent that a higher sentence is likely to be imposed on a principal perpetrator vis-à-vis an accomplice in genocide and on one who orders rather than merely aids and abets exterminations.[163]

The Chamber concluded that 'the Trial Chamber's fifteen-year sentences (for aiding and abetting) are therefore inadequate in light of the Appellant's level of culpability', and that a single twenty-five-year sentence was appropriate in light of the new convictions for ordering genocide and extermination.[164] Upon finding no further error in the Trial Chamber's sentence,[165] the Appeals Chamber left the remaining nine-and-a-half years of the Trial Chamber's sentence intact, resulting in a final sentence of thirty-four-and-a-half years.[166] As planning and instigating have elements that are very similar to those of ordering – including virtually identical mental elements – under the *Semanza* approach they can probably also be regarded as warranting a higher sentence than aiding and abetting.[167]

As concerns superior responsibility, the *Hadžihasanović and Kubura* Trial Chamber held as follows:

The concept of command responsibility . . . is exceptional in law in that it allows for a superior to be found guilty of a crime even if he had no part whatsoever in its commission (absence of an *actus reus*), and even if he never intended to commit the crime (absence of *mens rea*). Accordingly, the Chamber finds that the *sui generis* nature of command responsibility under Article 7(3) of the Statute may justify the fact that the sentencing scale applied to those Accused convicted solely on the basis of Article 7(1) of the Statute, or cumulatively under Articles 7(1) and 7(3), is not applied to those convicted solely under Article 7(3), in cases where nothing would allow that responsibility to be assimilated or linked to individual responsibility under Article 7(1).[168]

This position was endorsed by the Trial Chamber in *Orić*, which added that 'the *sui generis* nature of superior responsibility pursuant to Article 7(3) of the [ICTY] statute allow[s] for an even greater flexibility in the determination of

---

[163] *Ibid.*, para. 388. (footnote removed) (quoting *Krstić* Appeal Judgement, *supra* note 21, para. 268).
[164] *Ibid.*, para. 389.   [165] See *ibid.*, paras. 380, 395, 398–399.
[166] *Ibid.*, p. 126 (entering 'a sentence of thirty-five years' imprisonment, subject to credit being given . . . for the period already spent in detention, and subject to a further six-month reduction as ordered by the Trial Chamber for violations of fundamental pre-trial rights'). See also *supra* note 160 (describing the Trial Chamber's six-month reduction of Semanza's sentence due to violations of his pre-trial rights).
[167] See generally Chapter 5, notes 4–68.
[168] *Prosecutor* v. *Hadžihasanović and Kubura*, Case No. IT-01-47-T, Judgement, 15 March 2006 ('*Hadžihasanović and Kubura* Trial Judgement'), para. 2076.

sentence'.[169] Taking into account this and a variety of other factors,[170] both Trial Chambers proceeded to impose very low sentences on their respective accused: Hadžihasanović received a sentence of five years;[171] Kubura received a sentence of two-and-a-half years;[172] and Orić received a sentence of two years.[173]

From the jurisprudence discussed in this section it would appear that, in general, the chambers of the *ad hoc* Tribunals have regarded participation in a given crime through planning, instigating, ordering or committing (including JCE) as more grave – and thus deserving of a harsher sentence – than participation through aiding and abetting, or the failure to prevent or punish the crime's commission as a superior. Perhaps because the chambers' findings are justifiably tailored to the facts and circumstances of the particular case before them, however, the rather disjointed jurisprudence on forms of responsibility and sentencing provides few additional indications. The keenest insight on this subject may have come from the *Krnojelac* Trial Chamber. Notwithstanding its articulation of the seemingly absolute rule that '[t]he seriousness of what is done by a participant in a joint criminal enterprise ... is significantly greater than what is done by one who merely aids and abets',[174] the Chamber also warned against relying too heavily on artificial categorisations of offenders based on the form of responsibility under which they are or may be held liable:

There are ... circumstances in which a participant in a joint criminal enterprise will deserve greater punishment than the principal offender deserves. The participant who plans a mass destruction of life, and who orders others to carry out that plan, could well receive a greater sentence than the many functionaries who between them carry out the actual killing. Categorising offenders may be of some assistance, but the particular category selected cannot affect the maximum sentence which may be imposed and it does not compel the length of sentences which will be appropriate in the particular case.[175]

This case-by-case approach to individual criminal responsibility and sentencing is certainly the most prudent and appropriate. Factors such as the accused's position of authority or influence, the gravity and scale of the crime, the actual importance of his contribution to the commission of the crime, and the zeal with which the accused participated in it should surely weigh heaviest in the ultimate determination of his sentence, whatever the form of

---

[169] *Orić* Trial Judgement, *supra* note 32, para. 724.
[170] See *Hadžihasanović and Kubura* Trial Judgement, *supra* note 168, paras. 2078–2084, 2088–2092; *Orić* Trial Judgement, *supra* note 32, 725–781.
[171] *Hadžihasanović and Kubura* Trial Judgement, *supra* note 168, para. 2085, p. 625.
[172] *Ibid.*, para. 2093, p. 627. [173] *Orić* Trial Judgement, *supra* note 32, para. 783.
[174] *Krnojelac* Trial Judgement, *supra* note 54, para. 75. [175] *Ibid.*, para. 77.

responsibility through which he is convicted.[176] Indeed, an accused superior found guilty pursuant to Article 7/6(3) may well deserve a harsher punishment than the foot soldiers who physically perpetrated the crimes in question in spite of his contribution only through the failure to act, and his lack of intent to commit those crimes.

[176] See *Galić* Appeal Judgement, *supra* note 88, para. 412 (holding that the accused's high level of authority or abuse of that authority may be considered aggravating factors if he is convicted of ordering a crime); *Prosecutor* v. *Musema*, Case No. ICTR-96-13-A, Judgement, 16 November 2001, para. 383 ('[T]he most senior members of a command structure, that is, the leaders and planners of a particular conflict, should bear heavier criminal responsibility than those lower down the scale, such as the foot soldiers carrying out the orders.'); *Hadžihasanović and Kubura* Trial Judgement, *supra* note 168, para. 2073 ('When a person is found responsible solely on the basis of Article 7(1) of the [ICTY] Statute, or cumulatively in conjunction with Article 7(3), the gravity of the offence is evaluated in view of two elements: the inherent gravity of the acts committed and the form and degree of the Accused's participation in the crimes in question.'); *Blagojević and Jokić* Trial Judgement, *supra* note 21, para. 702 n. 2160 (holding that the relative significance of the accused's role in a JCE will be reflected in the sentence that a chamber imposes on him if it finds him guilty); *Prosecutor* v. *Ndindabahizi*, Case No. ICTR-2001-71-I, Judgement and Sentence, 15 July 2004, para. 500 ('The Chamber has ... considered the principle of gradation in sentencing, according to which the highest penalties are to be imposed upon those who planned or ordered atrocities, or those who committed crimes with particular zeal or sadism.'); *Prosecutor* v. *Serugendo*, Case No. ICTR-2005-84-I, Judgement and Sentence, 12 June 2006, para. 83 (same); *Prosecutor* v. *Ntakirutimana and Ntakirutimana*, Case Nos. ICTR-96-10 and ICTR-96-17-T, Judgement and Sentence, 21 February 2003, para. 884 (same).

7

Conclusion

CONTENTS

As the preceding chapters have shown, the forms of responsibility play an extremely important role in international criminal adjudication, and a significant part of the jurisprudence of the *ad hoc* Tribunals has been devoted to their identification, elaboration and application. The extent of that effort, and the degree of controversy surrounding certain of the forms of responsibility, may seem surprising to the domestic practitioner, accustomed to the relatively settled law of a specific jurisdiction on these issues. Three particular characteristics of international criminal law explain the emphasis on and significance of the forms of responsibility.

First, the principal preoccupation of international criminal law is the ascription of personal penal liability to a wide range of individuals, with regard to criminal conduct that frequently extends over a broad geographic area and an extended period of time. The involvement of each individual may vary significantly, and it is the task of decision-makers in this area to ensure that the law is robust enough to capture all the participants in international crimes, yet precise enough to comply with the fundamental principle that an individual may only be punished for his own criminal conduct, which must bear a sufficiently significant relationship to the crimes charged.

Second, while international criminal law draws on the substantive and procedural law of several domestic jurisdictions, it remains a relatively new system of law, which must nonetheless deal with the complicated factual circumstances of the cases, and the unique demands of public international legal rules developed to regulate the conduct of hostilities and the treatment of civilians and civilian property in times of war and peace. Viewed as such, the debates about the content or scope of a particular form of responsibility are not surprising, but rather to be expected, because a definitive answer is rarely to be found in precedent or reliance on a domestic analogue. What *is* surprising is the extent to which international courts forget that they are still engaged in the process of refining the law, and sometimes rely too heavily on the hastily reached or poorly supported conclusions of others.[1]

Third, and most importantly, the forms of responsibility are intended, by design and application, to be a relatively separate part of substantive international criminal law. They are given their own provisions in the basic instruments of the courts and tribunals, and have judicially developed elements that – despite a few decisions to the contrary[2] – are independent of both the nature of the conflict and the crimes that are alleged in the indictment. It is important to keep in mind, therefore, that a given form of responsibility must be capable of application to very different facts, while remaining logically consistent with the simultaneous application of the legal requirements for different international crimes. In light of those demands, and in keeping with the separateness of the design, it is understandable that increasing attention has been paid to the forms of responsibility.

7.1 Innovations in the law on forms of responsibility in the *ad hoc* Tribunals

In a relatively short time, the *ad hoc* Tribunals have developed profoundly the meaning and scope of forms of responsibility in international criminal law. In doing so, they have fleshed out the more 'traditional' or easily identifiable ones. They have also expanded and redefined forms of responsibility, often to encapsulate the criminal conduct of high-level accused whose interaction with the actual commission of crimes is more remote and takes place through multiple layers of other individuals or organisations. The appropriateness of this activity has really depended upon the particular form of responsibility in question, the extent to which its sources in international law have been credibly identified, and the degree of expansion involved.

An example of an apparently measured and logical approach concerns superior responsibility. There are indications, in the *Boškoski and Tarčulovski*

---

[1] See, e.g., Chapter 4, text accompanying notes 142, 194–216 (discussion of aiding and abetting by omission); Chapter 5, text accompanying notes 115–20 (discussion of instigation by omission); *infra*, text accompanying notes 19–23 (discussion of JCE).

[2] See Chapter 2, text accompanying notes 667–8 (*Gacumbitsi* Appeal Judgement apparently holding that a new form of 'commission' is only applicable to genocide); Chapter 3, text accompanying note 180 (describing the *Hadžihasanović* interlocutory appeal decision, which could be read as holding that superior responsibility in internal armed conflicts is only available for violations of the laws or customs of war).

and *Orić* cases, that chambers consider it appropriate to hold an accused responsible for a failure to prevent or punish his subordinate's ordering, planning, instigating, physical commission (including by omission), or aiding and abetting of a crime, or his participation in a joint criminal enterprise ('JCE').[3] Therefore, notwithstanding the fact that Article 7(3) of the ICTY Statute and Article 6(3) of the ICTR Statute ('Article 7/6(3)') refer to an accused superior's responsibility for *acts* which are *committed* by a subordinate, liability extends beyond mere commission, a position clearly consistent with the logic and principle of a superior's responsibility under international criminal law.

The *ad hoc* Tribunals also appear to be sympathetic to the imposition of guilt on an accused who participates in a JCE in which the crime that is the object of the enterprise (or a natural and foreseeable consequence of it) is committed by someone outside the enterprise, with whom one of the participants has a relationship via another form of responsibility. This expansion in the definition of forms of responsibility, discussed further below, was envisaged in pre-trial decisions in the *Milutinović* and *Popović* cases, and actually applied in the *Krajišnik* Trial Judgement.[4] Although in contradiction to the position set forth in the *Brđanin* Trial Judgement,[5] there appears to be a building inevitability that the Appeals Chambers (themselves preoccupied with the broad applicability of JCE liability) will extend this form of responsibility further.

Interestingly, while chambers of the *ad hoc* Tribunals appear to be generally willing to recognise combinations and extensions of the recognised forms of responsibility – including through an expansive attitude to what has been described as the 'contours' of a particular form of responsibility[6] – they have been generally hostile to introducing 'new' forms of responsibility. This hostility can be seen in the rejection by two different chambers of the *Stakić* Trial Chamber's 'indirect co-perpetratorship',[7] and in the *Krstić* Appeals Chamber's refusal, despite its acknowledgement that complicity in genocide included conduct 'striking broader' than aiding and abetting, to elaborate

---

[3] See Chapter 3, text accompanying notes 543–620.
[4] See Chapter 2, text accompanying notes 549–589.   [5] See *ibid.*, text accompanying notes 466–480.
[6] See *Prosecutor* v. *Milutinović, Šainović, Ojdanić, Pavković, Lazarević, Đorđević and Lukić*, Case No. IT-05-87-PT, Decision on Ojdanić's Motion Challenging Jurisdiction: Indirect Co-Perpetration, 22 March 2006 ('*Milutinović et al.* ICP Pre-Trial Decision'), para. 23 (holding that whether the physical perpetrator must be a participant in the JCE 'does not raise the issue of the Tribunal's jurisdiction over the activities of a JCE, but instead relates to the contours of JCE responsibility').
[7] See Chapter 2, text accompanying notes 635–646 (*Milutinović* Pre-Trial Chamber's rejecting indirect co-perpetratorship as defined by the *Stakić* Trial Chamber); *ibid.*, notes 647–658 (*Stakić* Appeals Chamber also rejecting indirect co-perpetratorship).

further as to what such broader conduct might entail.[8] The *Milutinović* Pre-Trial Chamber took a similar position when considering possible forms of co-perpetration and indirect perpetration:

> The Trial Chamber acknowledges the possibility that some species of co-perpetration and indirect perpetration can be found in various legal systems throughout the world. Nevertheless, as mandated by the Appeals Chamber, the task before the Trial Chamber is not to determine whether co-perpetration or indirect perpetration are general principles of law, but instead to determine whether the form of responsibility alleged in ... the Proposed Amended Joinder Indictment existed in customary international law at the relevant time.[9]

This jurisprudence reveals a perceptible contradiction with respect to the interpretation and evolution of forms of responsibility by the *ad hoc* Tribunals. This phenomenon may be explained by what Theodor Meron describes as a 'conservative and traditional approach' to the identification, interpretation and application of customary international law by the Tribunals.[10] Yet this view is challenged by at least three particular facts in relation to the forms of responsibility. First, in reality the effect of expanding the 'contours' of forms of responsibility (JCE, superior responsibility, or others) signifies a widening net of responsibility in international criminal law. Second, the ICTY Appeals Chamber in *Tadić* was willing, in the first place, to find that the notion of 'commission' enshrined in the Statute implicitly included participation in a JCE as ostensibly recognised in customary international law – a proposition that is itself highly questionable and certainly radically expansive. Third, the ICTR Appeals Chamber, beyond endorsing JCE as applicable in that Tribunal,[11] has recently expanded the scope of commission liability even further – at least in respect of genocide – to encompass acts beyond physical commission or participation in a JCE; these include, apparently, being present at the crime scene, supervising and directing the commission of the crime, and participating in it by separating victims so that they may be killed.[12] However such expansive legal activity is achieved, it has a material impact on the law and must be properly supported and explained, something that is unfortunately not done often enough in the *ad hoc* Tribunals.

---

[8] *Prosecutor v. Krstić*, Case No. IT-98-33-A, Judgement, 19 April 2004 ('*Krstić* Appeal Judgement'), para. 139. See also Chapter 4, text accompanying notes 93–111. A possible consequence of identifying complicity in genocide as being a potentially broader form of responsibility than aiding and abetting, while declining to explain further, is that the proposition is rendered both meaningless and confusing.

[9] *Milutinović et al.* ICP Pre-Trial Decision, *supra* note 6, para. 39.

[10] Theodor Meron, 'Editorial Comment: Revival of Customary Humanitarian Law', (2005) 99 *American Journal of International Law* 817, 821. See also Theodor Meron, *Human Rights and Humanitarian Norms as Customary International Law* (1989), pp. 96–97.

[11] See Chapter 2, text accompanying notes 107–113.   [12] See *ibid.*, text accompanying notes 662–702.

7.2 The *ad hoc* Tribunals' emphasis on 'commission' liability

One of the few subjects of academic debate on the forms of responsibility in recent years has been the rapid and largely unrestrained expansion of JCE in the *ad hoc* Tribunals. Commentators have criticised the ICTY Appeals Chamber not only for the unconventional methodology it employed in *Tadić* to ascertain the existence of the doctrine in customary international law – complete with its three discrete and rather detailed categories[13] – but also for the potentially negative effect the doctrine's application may have on the development of international criminal law, particularly through its perceived watering-down of the principle of culpability.[14] In relation to the first criticism, it is indeed curious that the Appeals Chambers have, since *Tadić*,[15] taken the view that they need not reconsider the customary basis for JCE liability, even though the typical JCE accused is now far more distant from the perpetration of the crimes than was Duško Tadić when he accompanied a small band of assailants as they marauded through Jaskići murdering Muslim civilians.[16] The ICTY Appeals Chamber made this position clear in the May 2003 *Milutinović* decision on interlocutory appeal:

---

[13] See, e.g., Chapter 2, note 52 and sources cited therein.

[14] See, e.g., Mark Osiel, 'The Banality of Good: Aligning Incentives against Mass Atrocity', (2005) 105 *Columbia Law Review* 1751, 1771 (JCE 'lures international law to a point where liability threatens to exceed the scope of moral culpability'); George P. Fletcher and Jens David Ohlin, 'Reclaiming Fundamental Principles of Criminal Law in the Darfur Case', (2005) 3 *Journal of International Criminal Justice* 539, 550 (JCE's imposition of equal responsibility to all participants, regardless of individual role, 'clearly violates the basic principle that individuals should only be punished for personal culpability'); William A. Schabas, '*Mens Rea* and the International Criminal Tribunal for the Former Yugoslavia', (2003) 37 *New England Law Review* 1015, 1034 (although JCE 'facilitate[s] the conviction of individual villains who have apparently participated in serious violations of human rights', it also 'result[s] in discounted convictions that inevitably diminish the didactic significance of the Tribunal's judgements and that compromise its historical legacy'); Shane Darcy, 'An Effective Measure of Bringing Justice?: The Joint Criminal Enterprise Doctrine of the International Criminal Tribunal for the Former Yugoslavia', (2004) 20 *American University International Law Review* 153, 188 (the third category of JCE 'does not meet the requirements of the established *nulla poena sine culpa* principle'); Allison Marston Danner and Jenny S. Martinez, 'Guilty Associations: Joint Criminal Enterprise, Command Responsibility, and the Development of International Criminal Law', (2005) 93 *California Law Review* 75, 149–154 (giving suggestions on how the JCE doctrine may be reformed to 'ensure that [it] adheres more closely to the criminal law culpability principle') (quotation at p. 150); Allison Marston Danner, 'Joint Criminal Enterprise and Contemporary International Law', (2004) *Proceedings of the Ninety-Eighth Annual Meeting of the American Society of International Law* 186, 188 (JCE 'has in practice strayed far from the focus of individual culpability that distinguishes the criminal law paradigm', and 'approaches dangerously close to guilt by association').

[15] With the possible exception of the ICTR Appeals Chamber in *Rwamakuba*, which examined purported sources of custom, including post-Second World War judgements, to ascertain whether customary international law recognised JCE liability for genocide at the time of the events in Rwanda. See Chapter 2, text accompanying notes 101–105 (discussion of the October 2004 *Rwamakuba* decision on interlocutory appeal).

[16] See *Prosecutor v. Tadić*, Case No. IT-94-1-A, Judgement, 15 July 1999, paras. 230–234 (describing the activities of Tadić's JCE). See also *Milutinović et al.* ICP Pre-Trial Decision, *supra* note 6, Separate Opinion of Judge Iain Bonomy, para. 7 (remarking that the JCE scenario alleged in the *Milutinović*

The Appeals Chamber was satisfied [in *Tadić*], and is still satisfied now, that the Statute provides, albeit not explicitly, for joint criminal enterprise as a form of criminal liability and that its elements are based on customary law[17] ... The Appeals Chamber does not propose to revisit its finding in *Tadić* concerning the customary status of this form of liability.[18]

In sharp contrast to *Tadić*, the *Milutinović* case, along with others in respect of which judgement has been rendered and JCE liability imposed – including *Stakić* in the Appeals Chamber and *Krajišnik* in the Trial Chamber – involve accused who occupied high leadership positions in the political or military hierarchy of the former Yugoslavia. Serious questions remain as to whether, even if there is a basis in custom for the type of JCE found to exist in *Tadić*, customary international law supports the imposition of JCE liability on these high-ranking persons. This question has not yet been answered satisfactorily in the *ad hoc* jurisprudence, and it is quite possible that it will not be addressed to any meaningful extent before the end of the Tribunals' respective mandates.

As discussed in Chapter 2, the *ad hoc* Prosecutors, and especially the Prosecutor of the ICTY, have come to place heavy reliance on JCE as the key theory of liability linking the persons they have accused to crimes committed by other, often far-removed, persons,[19] in spite of the simultaneous practice of pleading all the forms of responsibility in respect of every crime charged in the indictment.[20] This reliance on and confidence in JCE as the 'magic bullet'[21] connecting the accused to the crime has no doubt been fuelled by the posture of chambers such as that in *Krajišnik*. In opting to convict Krajišnik for a

---

indictment is 'far removed from the circumstances in *Tadić*' and that '[t]here was no reason for the [*Tadić* Appeals] Chamber to address the broader and more complex factual situations that arise in this Indictment').

[17] *Prosecutor* v. *Milutinović, Šainović and Ojdanić*, Case No. IT-99-37-AR72, Decision on Dragoljub Ojdanić's Motion Challenging Jurisdiction – Joint Criminal Enterprise, 21 May 2003, para. 21.

[18] *Ibid.*, para. 29. Accord *Prosecutor* v. *Karemera, Ngirumpatse and Nzirorera*, Case Nos. ICTR-98-44-AR72.5, ICTR-98-44-AR72.6, Decision on Jurisdictional Appeals: Joint Criminal Enterprise, 12 April 2006, para. 16 (ICTR Appeals Chamber reaffirming that 'it is clear that there is a basis in customary international law for ... JCE liability').

[19] See Chapter 2, notes 796–798 and accompanying text (remarking that 15 of the remaining 21 cases before the ICTY charge JCE as one of the bases, if not the primary basis, for the accused's liability, and listing the cases on the respective dockets of the ICTY and ICTR alleging JCE). See also William A. Schabas, *The UN International Criminal Tribunals: The Former Yugoslavia, Rwanda and Sierra Leone* (2006), p. 311 (asserting that *Tadić*'s recognition of JCE 'prompted a dramatic alteration in the approach of the Prosecutor'); Darcy, *supra* note 14, pp. 168–169, 181; Kelly D. Askin, 'Reflections on Some of the Most Significant Achievements of the ICTY', (2003) 37 *New England Law Review* 903, 911 (remarking that '[p]articipating in a joint criminal enterprise has become the principal charging preference in ICTY indictments'); Mark J. Osiel, 'Modes of Participation in Mass Atrocity', (2005) 38 *Cornell Journal of International Law* 793, 797 (opining that JCE's appeal is due to its ability to 'reach conduct by those outside any formal chain of military command' including 'paramilitaries or civilian leaders, or officers in staff rather than line positions').

[20] See Chapter 6, text accompanying note 7 (describing this practice).

[21] Schabas, *supra* note 14, p. 1032. See also Osiel, *supra* note 19, para. 794 (arguing that the upsurge in JCE allegations has been prompted by the ICTY Prosecutor's 'self-interest ... in maximizing convictions of multiple defendants on the most grievous charges').

considerable number of crimes exclusively on the basis of JCE without exploring his potential liability under any of the other charged forms of responsibility, or considering it necessary to examine whether the physical perpetrators adhered to the common criminal purpose,[22] the Trial Chamber demonstrated substantial confidence that the Appeals Chamber would sanction its extremely broad application of the doctrine, and that the Appeals Chamber would not uphold the *Brđanin* Trial Chamber's requirement of participation by the physical perpetrator in the enterprise.[23] Whether or not *Brđanin* was correct in expounding this particular limitation, it should be applauded for its preoccupation – all too rare in the case law – with preventing the doctrine from expanding so far that the link between the accused and the crime becomes too tenuous to withstand scrutiny under the principle of culpability.

The increasing willingness of chambers to convict the accused before them pursuant to JCE, rather than through another of the charged forms of responsibility, could perhaps be partially explained by a visceral desire to label the accused a 'committer' of the crime in question, as if that label carried with it a special stigma that the other forms of responsibility lack. This way of thinking is perceptible in Judge Bonomy's separate opinion to the March 2006 *Milutinović* decision on indirect co-perpetration, where he posited the following hypothetical scenario:

A colonel and a general ... agree to wipe out a village ... It is left to the general to decide on the precise means, whether they be his own personnel, a group of paramilitaries, shelling by him personally, or one massive bombing that he and another plant and set ... The general decides to order men under his command to attack the village, and the inhabitants who remain are murdered. Those who assist the general believe they are acting in the course of an ongoing combat and that the village is a terrorist stronghold. Only the general and the colonel have it in mind that this will be a good way to terrorise the local population into leaving the country. The colonel cannot 'order' the general. If it was the general's idea, the colonel cannot have instigated or planned it. He may be an aider or abettor, but does that adequately reflect the level of his responsibility? Common sense might suggest that the general and colonel committed the atrocity in concert with one another, and that their responsibility for 'committing' the crime could be established without a determination being made about the criminal responsibility of those acting under their command.[24]

Judge Bonomy's suggestion that liability for 'committing' a crime is somehow more opprobrious than aiding and abetting is understandable, given the usual hierarchy between these two methods of participation in national criminal law,

---

[22] See Chapter 2, text accompanying notes 574–588.
[23] See *ibid.*, text accompanying notes 466–480 (discussion of this holding in *Brđanin*).
[24] *Milutinović et al.* ICP Pre-Trial Decision, *supra* note 16, Separate Opinion of Judge Iain Bonomy, para. 4. See also Chapter 2, text accompanying notes 555–564 (discussing Judge Bonomy's separate opinion in greater detail).

as well as the ICTY Appeals Chamber's repeated pronouncements, discussed in Chapter 6, that aiding and abetting warrants a lower sentence than participation in a JCE.[25]

The *Gacumbitsi* Appeals Chamber seems to have adopted a similar attitude in divining a new method of incurring liability for commission. Out of an apparent concern that it would be unjust to convict Gacumbitsi as a 'mere' orderer and instigator of genocide for his contribution to the massacre of Tutsis at Nyarabuye Parish, the Chamber made the following finding:

[I]n the circumstances of this case, the modes of liability used by the Trial Chamber to categorize this conduct – 'ordering' and 'instigating' – do not, taken alone, fully capture the Appellant's criminal responsibility. The Appellant did not simply 'order' or 'plan' genocide from a distance and leave it to others to ensure that his orders and plans were carried out; nor did he merely 'instigate' the killings. Rather, he was present at the crime scene to supervise and direct the massacre, and participated in it actively by separating the Tutsi refugees so that they could be killed. The Appeals Chamber finds ... that this constitutes 'committing' genocide.[26]

The view that commission liability occupies the highest position in a hierarchy of forms of responsibility is also evident in the holdings of a number of trial chambers that, where the accused's conduct fulfils the elements of both 'commission' and a form of accomplice liability, the chamber must convict the accused of commission only.[27]

Although the assumption that accomplice liability is by definition less grave than commission may be appropriate in domestic criminal law, it cannot hold true in international criminal law. The contribution of an accomplice to the realisation of an international crime is frequently more substantial than that of the physical perpetrator because, for instance, the accused's position of influence or authority has a legitimising effect on the actions of the physical perpetrator, or the accused makes available the means necessary for a multitude of physical perpetrators to bring to fruition a massive crime. Consider, for instance, the role of Radislav Krstić in the Srebrenica massacre: the Appeals Chamber downgraded his role from participation in a first-category JCE to aiding and abetting because, according to the Chamber, the evidence failed to establish his genocidal intent.[28] Yet Krstić's conduct in placing the personnel and other resources of the

---

[25] See Chapter 6, text accompanying notes 126–147.

[26] *Prosecutor* v. *Gacumbitsi*, Case No. ICTR-2001-64-A, Judgement, 7 July 2006, para. 61. See also Chapter 2, text accompanying notes 662–702 (discussion of this portion of *Gacumbitsi*).

[27] See Chapter 6, text accompanying notes 41–48 (discussion of this trial jurisprudence). Much of this jurisprudence, in using the term 'accomplice', either states explicitly or assumes that JCE is not a form of accomplice liability. The analysis in this section of this chapter, in setting forth this aspect of the jurisprudence, adopts the terminology used therein. See Chapter 1, note 9.

[28] *Krstić* Appeal Judgement, *supra* note 8, para. 134.

Drina Corps of the Bosnian Muslim Army at the disposal of the genocide's planners was certainly more opprobrious than that of most of the individual killers, and indeed was found by the Appeals Chamber to be significant enough to warrant a relatively severe sentence of thirty-five years.[29] Imagine, moreover, that Krstić had possessed genocidal intent but at least one of the elements of JCE had not been proven; if he had killed one or even several of the Srebrenica victims by his own hand in addition to aiding and abetting the massacre through the provision of Drina Corps resources, would the extent of his culpable conduct be best reflected in a conviction for 'committing' genocide against a few victims, as opposed to aiding and abetting the genocide of thousands? A similar question can be asked with respect to Gacumbitsi: even though, as the ICTR Appeals Chamber acknowledged, he did physically kill at least one of the Nyarabuye Parish victims, was his overall role in the massacre not better described as an orderer and instigator of genocide, and does this role not carry more stigma than being one of the scores of 'committers'?

7.3 Limitations on trial chamber discretion in choosing forms of responsibility

Another issue that emerges from any analysis of jurisprudential development in the *ad hoc* Tribunals is the extent to which the Appeals Chambers have a tendency to interfere with the exercise of discretion by trial chambers, often without articulating clearly the legal principle underlying such intervention. A regrettable example of this is the *Blaškić* Appeals Chamber's ruling that where criminal responsibility is charged for the same conduct under Article 7(1) of the ICTY Statute and Article 6(1) of the ICTR Statute on the one hand, and Article 7/6(3) on the other, a chamber is obliged to enter a conviction under the former (the '*Blaškić* rule').[30] Up until the imposition of this regime, trial chambers varied in their treatment of concurrent convictions under Article 7/6(1) and Article 7/6(3)[31] – a point which itself suggests the appropriateness of leaving the trial chamber to determine the appropriate form of responsibility in contemplation of all the evidence led. Such a limitation on the manner in which trial chambers are to determine responsibility is counterintuitive because, barring an obvious error of law or abuse of discretion, the Appeals Chamber cannot be in the best position to reach such a conclusion and a trial chamber should left to analyse and determine the responsibility of an accused before it. Characterising criminal responsibility in the complex factual and legal

---

[29] See *ibid.*, para. 275.
[30] See *Prosecutor* v. *Blaškić*, Case No. IT-95-14-A, Judgement, 29 July 2004, para. 91. See also Chapter 6, text accompanying notes 76–112 (discussion of the *Blaškić* rule).
[31] See Chapter 6, text accompanying notes 50–61.

environment of international criminal law is never as simple as placing superior responsibility at the far end of the spectrum.[32] As discussed in Chapter 6, the jurisprudence has recognised forms of omission liability potentially entailing less direct involvement on the part of the accused than superior responsibility, but based on the Appeals Chamber's reasoning, a trial chamber would have to impose those forms in preference to superior responsibility.[33] Furthermore, there are a myriad of intangibles that emerge from contemplation of all the evidence that tend to suggest the nature of an accused's involvement in the commission of crimes.

This position is even more egregious because, as mentioned, prosecutors in international criminal tribunals tend to plead all forms of responsibility in the alternative, leaving it to the trial chamber to assess and consider how – if at all – an accused's criminal responsibility is to be attributed.[34] Were the chamber in the case of a high-level accused such as Slobodan Milošević to determine that guilt as a superior was the most appropriate way to characterise his criminal responsibility, it would still be required to analyse all other forms of responsibility – presumably element by element – to eliminate their applicability. This could lead to at least two infelicitous outcomes: the requirement that the chamber undertake unnecessarily an enormous analytical exercise, and the possible fulfilment of the elements of a form of responsibility less appropriately characteristic of the accused's involvement in the crimes, which would nevertheless have to be imposed under the *Blaškić* rule.

The authors consider that the *Blaškić* rule has had and will continue to have undesirable consequences. It is hoped that the International Criminal Court and other international criminal tribunals will not follow this precedent. As for the trial chambers of the ICTY and ICTR, which are meanwhile bound to apply the *Blaškić* rule, it is hoped that the rule will be interpreted broadly as meaning that the most direct form of conduct will attract responsibility, placing the possible forms of omission liability (with respect to aiding and abetting and instigation) either on par with or behind superior responsibility. In this way, some measure of damage control may at least be achieved.

7.4 The future development of the law on forms of responsibility

For all of its flaws, it is clear that the jurisprudence of the *ad hoc* Tribunals has made an invaluable contribution to the practical application of some of the

[32] Cf. Osiel, *supra* note 19, pp. 793–794 ('I think the [ICTY] is making it too hard to find people liable under command responsibility, but too easy to hold them liable as participants in a joint criminal enterprise.'); accord Osiel, *supra* note 14, p. 1861 ('At the international level, superior responsibility is today used too little, enterprise participation too much.').
[33] See Chapter 6, text accompanying notes 96–112.   [34] See *ibid.*, text accompanying note 7.

most fundamental norms in international law. At times, that contribution has gone beyond the four corners of international criminal law, and added to the discourse on broader questions of public international law.[35] In general, however, the impact of the Tribunals' work is most evident where one might expect it: the results of their criminal proceedings are reported by the media, debated in regional politics, examined by scholars and taught in schools. Most importantly, the case law is invoked by the growing body of international criminal practitioners and repeatedly employed by other international and hybrid courts and domestic courts applying international criminal law. An important part of the legacy and qualified success of the Tribunals is therefore the crucial role that they have played in the development of a sophisticated system of criminal law for the international community.

With regard to the forms of responsibility, the influence of the *ad hoc* jurisprudence has already been felt in the hybrid or internationalised courts, which frequently turn to decisions and judgements of the ICTY and the ICTR in interpreting or applying their own statutes, despite differences in terminology and apparent scope of the respective provisions. Since the practice of the ICC has been limited to date, it remains to be seen whether – and to what extent – it will similarly rely on the pronouncements of its provisional predecessors. While there are key differences between the respective models of individual criminal responsibility represented in the Rome Statute and the *ad hoc* Statutes,[36] it is certain that the work of the ICTY and the ICTR on the forms of responsibility will form a significant corpus of reference material for any current or future practitioner or judge of the ICC. The decisions and judgements of these two UN tribunals remain the most extensive body of law to apply the sometimes esoteric rules of public international law to actual events and persons, and it is the forms of responsibility which ensure that individuals are held responsible for the conduct which violates those rules. It is equally certain, however, that the differences between the ICC and *ad hoc* Statutes – particularly the forms of responsibility that explicitly appear only in the former – will lead to both an expansion of the current law on individual criminal responsibility and further refinement of the existing forms.

---

[35] See, e.g., *Prosecutor* v. *Tadić*, Case No. IT-94-1-A, Judgement, 15 July 1999, paras. 84, 120, 125–131, 137–138 (devising a test for the attribution of state responsibility that is less restrictive than those previously used by the International Court of Justice); *Prosecutor* v. *Mrkšić, Radić, Šljivančanin and Dokmanović*, Case No. IT-95-13a-PT, Decision on the Motion for Release by the Accused Slavko Dokmanović, 22 October 1997, paras. 74–75, 77–78, 88 (determining that luring an accused across an international border to enable his arrest does not violate international law).

[36] These distinctions are discussed in detail in the respective sections of Chapters 2 to 5.

Annex: Elements of forms of responsibility in international criminal law

Joint criminal enterprise (JCE)

a. *Physical elements (common to all three categories, unless specified)*
   i. The JCE consisted of two or more persons.
   ii. A common plan, design, or purpose existed which amounted to or involved the commission of a crime provided for in the Statute.
      i. *First and third categories*: The accused and at least one other person came to an express or implied agreement that a particular crime would be committed.
      ii. *Second category*: The JCE co-participants need not have reached any agreement; the system of ill-treatment itself is the common purpose.
   iii. The accused participated in the common plan, design, or purpose.
b. *Mental elements of the first category (JCE I)*
   i. The accused's participation in the common plan, design, or purpose was voluntary.
   ii. The accused and the physical perpetrator shared the intent to commit the crime that is the object of the JCE.
   iii. For specific-intent crimes, the accused possessed the specific intent required of the crime.
c. *Mental elements of the second category (JCE II)*
   i. The accused had personal knowledge of the criminal nature of the system of ill-treatment.
   ii. The accused intended to further the criminal purpose of the system of ill-treatment.
   iii. For specific-intent crimes, the accused possessed the specific intent required of the crime.
d. *Mental elements of the third category (JCE III)*
   i. The accused intended to participate in the JCE.
   ii. The accused intended to further the criminal purpose of the JCE.
   iii. The crime with which the accused is charged was a natural and foreseeable consequence of the execution of the JCE.
   iv. The accused was aware that the commission of the crime with which he is charged was possible.

Superior responsibility

a. A superior-subordinate relationship existed between the accused and the person or persons for whose criminal conduct he is alleged to be responsible.
b. The accused knew or had reason to know that the criminal conduct in question was about to be, was being, or had been realised by one or more subordinates.
   i. *Alternative mental element #1*: Actual knowledge: The accused knew that the criminal conduct in question was about to be, was being, or had been realised by one or more subordinates.
   ii. *Alternative mental element #2*: Reason to know: The accused had reason to know that the criminal conduct in question was about to be, was being, or had been realised by one or more subordinates.
c. The accused failed to take the necessary and reasonable measures to prevent or punish the subordinate criminal conduct in question.
   i. *Common sub-element for 'failure to prevent' and 'failure to punish'*: the accused failed to take measures that were necessary and reasonable.
   ii. *First form of superior responsibility*: Failure to prevent: The accused failed to take all measures within his material ability to prevent the subordinate or subordinates from engaging in the criminal conduct in question.
   iii. *Second form of superior responsibility*: Failure to punish: The accused failed to take all measures within his material ability to ensure that punishment was dispensed upon the subordinate or subordinates for engaging in the criminal conduct in question.

'Plain English' *translations of differing mental state standards in superior responsibility*

When the legal standard says …	It really means …
Actual knowledge (or simply 'knowledge')	The accused 'knew' of subordinate criminal conduct
Inferred actual knowledge	The accused 'must have known' or 'could not have *not* known' of subordinate criminal conduct
Negligence [not applied in modern international criminal law]	The accused 'should have known' of subordinate criminal conduct
Constructive knowledge or 'had reason to know'	The accused had enough signs, clues, suspicion, or other information to take steps to prevent or halt subordinate criminal conduct, or to trigger an investigation into subordinate conduct.[1]

---

[1] Some judgements have applied a variant of this test that amounts to 'the accused *would have known if* …'. See Chapter 3, text accompanying notes 414–420 (*Strugar* Trial Judgement), 421–434 (*Orić* Trial Judgement). If this test is divorced from the possession of admonitory information (the signs, clues and similar information mentioned above), it comes impermissibly close to a surreptitious application of the negligence standard. That is, it risks imposing an additional duty upon a superior – that of actively seeking out information – which has been rejected by the *ad hoc* Tribunals.

Aiding and Abetting[2]

a. *Physical elements*
    i. The accused lent practical assistance, encouragement, or moral support to the physical perpetrator in committing a crime.
    ii. The practical assistance, encouragement, or moral support had a substantial effect on the commission of the crime by the physical perpetrator.
b. *Mental elements*
    i. The accused acted intentionally with knowledge or awareness that his act would lend assistance, encouragement, or moral support to the physical perpetrator.
    ii. The accused was aware of the essential elements of the physical perpetrator's crime, including the perpetrator's mental state.

Planning

a. The accused designed criminal conduct with the intent that a crime be committed; or he designed an act or omission, aware of the substantial likelihood that a crime would be committed in the realisation of that act or omission.
b. The accused's conduct substantially contributed to the perpetration of a crime.

Instigating

a. The accused prompted criminal conduct with the intent that a crime be committed; or he prompted an act or omission, aware of the substantial likelihood that a crime would be committed in the realisation of that act or omission.
b. The accused's conduct substantially contributed to the perpetration of a crime.

Ordering

a. The accused instructed another to engage in criminal conduct with the intent that a crime be committed; or he instructed another to engage in an act or omission aware of the substantial likelihood that a crime would be committed in the realisation of that act or omission.
b. The accused enjoyed authority – formal or informal – over the person to whom the order was given.
c. The accused's conduct had a direct and substantial effect on perpetration of a crime.

---

[2] As explained in Chapter 4, the only instances where the elements of complicity in genocide have been set forth by the *ad hoc* Tribunals have been where the kind of complicity in question was functionally indistinguishable from aiding and abetting. See Chapter 4, text accompanying notes 303–308. Consequently, no separate listing of those elements is provided here.

Comparison of required mental states, with regard to intent, for imposition of liability under each form of responsibility

	JCE I	JCE II	JCE III	Superior Responsibility	Aiding and Abetting	Planning	Instigating	Ordering
Requires general intent to commit crime?	YES[3]	NO[4]	NO[5]	NO[6]	NO[7]	YES, for 1 of 2 alternatives[8]	YES, for 1 of 2 alternatives[9]	YES, for 1 of 2 alternatives[10]
Requires specific intent if specific-intent crime charged?	YES[11]	YES[12]	NO[13]	NO[14]	NO[15]	YES, for 1 of 2 alternatives[16]	YES, for 1 of 2 alternatives[17]	YES, for 1 of 2 alternatives[18]

As discussed in Chapter 5, the mental element for planning, instigating and ordering may also be satisifed by proof of the accused's awareness of the substantial likelihood that the crime will be committed as a result of his conduct. This alternative mental state does not require that the accused have either general or specific intent.[19]

---

[3] See Chapter 2, text accompanying notes 268–283.
[4] See *ibid.*, text accompanying notes 309–350.   [5] See *ibid.*, text accompanying notes 382–384.
[6] See Chapter 3, text accompanying notes 354–356.
[7] See Chapter 4, text accompanying notes 248–250.
[8] See Chapter 5, text accompanying notes 48–51, 70.
[9] See *ibid.*, text accompanying notes 48–51, 94.
[10] See *ibid.*, text accompanying notes 45, 48–51, 133.
[11] See Chapter 2, text accompanying notes 284–293.
[12] See *ibid.*, text accompanying notes 365–372.   [13] See *ibid.*, text accompanying notes 384–388.
[14] See Chapter 3, text accompanying notes 357–361.
[15] See Chapter 4, text accompanying notes 283–300.
[16] See Chapter 5, text accompanying note 61.   [17] See *ibid.*   [18] See *ibid.*
[19] See *ibid.*, text accompanying notes 48–61, 71, 95, 134.

Index

References in brackets following page numbers are to footnotes.